Environmental Economics and Sustainability

Environmental Economics and Sustainability

Edited by Brian Chi-ang Lin and Siqi Zheng

WILEY Blackwell

This edition first published 2017
Chapters © 2017 The Authors
Book compilation © 2017 John Wiley & Sons Ltd
Originally published as a special issue of the *Journal of Economic Surveys* (Volume 30, Issue 3)

Blackwell Publishing was acquired by John Wiley & Sons in February 2007. Blackwell's publishing program has been merged with Wiley's global Scientific, Technical, and Medical business to form Wiley-Blackwell.

Registered Office
John Wiley & Sons Ltd, The Atrium, Southern Gate, Chichester, West Sussex, PO19 8SQ, United Kingdom

Editorial Offices
350 Main Street, Malden, MA 02148-5020, USA
9600 Garsington Road, Oxford, OX4 2DQ, UK
The Atrium, Southern Gate, Chichester, West Sussex, PO19 8SQ, UK

For details of our global editorial offices, for customer services, and for information about how to apply for permission to reuse the copyright material in this book please see our website at www.wiley.com/wiley-blackwell.

The rights of Brian Chi-ang Lin and Siqi Zheng to be identified as the authors of the editorial material in this work have been asserted in accordance with the UK Copyright, Designs and Patents Act 1988.

Wiley also publishes its books in a variety of electronic formats. Some content that appears in print may not be available in electronic books.

Designations used by companies to distinguish their products are often claimed as trademarks. All brand names and product names used in this book are trade names, service marks, trademarks or registered trademarks of their respective owners. The publisher is not associated with any product or vendor mentioned in this book. This publication is designed to provide accurate and authoritative information in regard to the subject matter covered. It is sold on the understanding that the publisher is not engaged in rendering professional services. If professional advice or other expert assistance is required, the services of a competent professional should be sought.

Library of Congress Cataloging-in-Publication Data applied for.

9781119328209

Front Cover image © Chien-Ju Weng

A catalogue record for this book is available from the British Library.

This book is published in the following electronic formats: ePDFs (9781119328087); Wiley Online Library (9781119328223); ePub (9781119328193)

Set in 10/12pt Times by Aptara Inc., New Delhi, India

1   2017

CONTENTS

1

A NEW DIRECTION IN ENVIRONMENTAL ECONOMICS

Brian Chi-ang Lin

National Chengchi University

Siqi Zheng

Massachusetts Institute of Technology and Tsinghua University

1. Introduction

The global economy has evolved into a borderless age of climate change. Numerous studies such as those of Stern (2007) and Jones *et al.* (2013) have pointed out that the nature of climate change is an international and intergenerational externality problem. This human-induced change in the rising global mean temperature is mainly due to the enormous emission of carbon dioxide arising from the combustion of fossil fuels. To date, more than 100 countries have adopted a global warming limit of 2 °C or below (relative to preindustrial times) as a general guideline (IPCC, 2007). That is, the concentration of carbon dioxide should be maintained at a range of 400–450 parts per million (ppm). The United States and China, the two largest national economies in the world, have recently unveiled a negotiated deal to reduce their greenhouse gas (GHG) output, with China agreeing to cap its emissions by 2030 or earlier and the United States pledging to cut its emissions to 26–28% below the 2005 levels by 2025.

The issues of climate change include not only the key investigation of global warming but also the concerns about rising sea levels, melting glaciers, changes in precipitation and storminess, and so on. Thus, climate change has become a complicated problem of uncertainty to a greater extent than any other environmental externality. Over the past two decades, academics and researchers have employed various methods to provide estimates of the economic effects of climate change. An early study conducted by Nordhaus (1994) indicates that the effect of 3 °C global warming is equivalent to a 1.3% decline in GDP. Later studies have estimated net gains and losses associated with climate change for various regions at different times (see, for example, Mendelsohn *et al.*, 2000; Tol, 2002; and Hope, 2006). According to Dell *et al.* (2014), estimates across labor productivity, industrial output, and economic growth approximately converge to a 1–2% decline per 1 °C in poor countries.

Environmental Economics and Sustainability, First Edition. Edited by Brian Chi-ang Lin and Siqi Zheng.
Chapters © 2017 The Authors. Book compilation © 2017 John Wiley & Sons, Ltd. Published 2017 by John Wiley & Sons, Ltd.

Not surprisingly, sustainability has emerged as one of the most pressing issues in the 21st century since it was recognized that everyone has a stake in Our Common Future. Reacting to this phenomenon, governments all over the world have begun to implement energy preservation and carbon emission reduction policies, as well as spearheading other related initiatives. These governments have recognized that, to address such hazards, economic planning is necessary. Governments are obligated to initiate various cooperative and institutional mechanisms to internalize individual choices. They also have to coordinate various needs and interests, and to ensure an equal chance of participation for people at all levels of society.

2. Overview of Scholarly Findings

2.1 *Econometric Modeling of Climate Change*

This special issue seeks to offer a timely collection of papers that critically address the aforementioned challenges. Climate change, via a change in Mother Nature, may trigger unexpected consequences of economic evolution in the long run. The lead paper in this special issue by Pretis, Schneider, Smerdon, and Hendry presents an econometric methodology for detecting breaks at any point in time-series regression models, particularly applied to modeling climate change. Econometric modeling in this paper is statistically formulated without prior knowledge about stochastic breaks of climate time series and their occurrence or magnitude. The detection of structural breaks is focused on breaks in the mean through the general-to-specific approach of step-indicator saturation (SIS) and impulse-indicator saturation (IIS). The results indicate that 74% of all larger Northern Hemisphere volcanic eruptions over 20 Tg can be detected on average within an interval of ± 1 year in the model temperature series spanning from years 850–2005. The break detection procedure demonstrated in this paper, according to the authors, is also instrumental for detecting previously unknown events as well as forecasting economic recessions.

2.2 *Air Pollutants and CO_2 emissions*

The second paper by Giovanis and Ozdamar provides a new way to qualify people's marginal willingness-to-pay (MWTP) for reducing air pollutants. Air pollution generates significant negative impact on well-being, as observed in health, mood, and life satisfaction. It is crucial to have reliable estimates of the public willingness-to-pay for air pollution reduction, and they will be the key parameters in the benefit-cost analysis of public investment with the purpose of mitigating pollution. The merit of their data set is that the detailed micro-level data (from the Swiss Household Panel survey) with respondents' zip municipality codes allow the authors to map air pollution to individuals far more accurately. The authors also limit their sample to nonmovers, so as to address the possible endogeneity problem from the sorting of individuals across places with different pollution levels. A unique methodology contribution of this paper is estimating the panel structural equation model (SEM), along with a simple fixed effects regression analysis, in order to examine the causal effects of permanent income on life satisfaction, and then to calculate the MWTP values. Overall, the results show that the MWTPs are relatively low for NO_2, CO, and PM_{10}, while the highest values are observed for O_3 and SO_2. Additionally, it is also found that there is evidence of a substantial trade-off between income and air quality.The third paper by Auffhammer, Sun, Wu, and Zheng is a city-level analysis. They first provide the estimates of city-level industrial CO_2 emissions and their growth rates for all 287 Chinese prefecture-level cities during the years of 1998–2009. Then, they decompose the CO_2 emission changes into scale, composition, and technique effects. An interesting finding is that the three effects differ significantly across the three tiers of cities. The scale effect contributes to rising CO_2 emissions, while the technique effect leads to declining CO_2 emissions in all cities. The composition effect leads to increasing CO_2 emissions in the third-tier cities, while it reduces CO_2 emissions in the first- and second-tier cities, perhaps due to the relocation of energy-intensive industries from the latter to the former type of city. Based on the decomposition results, they also find that the inflow of foreign direct investment (FDI) pulls down energy intensity and thus CO_2 emissions by generating a significant technique effect (with the other two effects found to be insignificant), while the environmental regulations help cities to reduce their industrial CO_2 emissions through all three channels.

2.3 *Environmental Sustainability, Waste Management and Recycling*

To date, more and more countries in the world have taken measures to promote environmental sustainability. For instance, the Netherlands Organisation for Applied Scientific Research (TNO) published a report in 2013 (TNO, 2013) analyzing the opportunities and challenges facing the Netherlands as the country moves toward a more circular economy. It focuses on recycling in the metal and electrical sectors and the use of waste streams from biomass. The study reports that, by 2013, the Netherlands was already recycling 78% of its waste, incinerating 19% and dumping only 3%. The fourth paper by Chen, Lin, and Anderson elaborates the notion of environmental sustainability and proposes that the government can initiate a spending scheme for the green public good provision. This paper focuses on the expenditure side of the budget and argues that implementation of green spending has the potential to not only give rise to benefits of the so-called double dividend but also generate additional benefits. Specifically, the environmental sustainability condition can be met as long as the total usage of environmentally polluted resources generated by households does not exceed the equivalent absorptive capacity provided via the provision of green public goods. In other words, the provision of green public goods contributes to the attainment of the macro-environmental equilibrium. This paper also presents a greened Samuelson rule, that is, a modified Samuelson rule associated with the environmental sustainability condition.

Clearly, household waste management and recycling raise a variety of questions and also require proper cooperation among local communities. In this regard, the fifth paper by Briguglio provides a review of the relevant literature and synthesizes it around two themes: initial conditions conductive to household cooperation and intervention that may stimulate cooperation. According to the author, household cooperation in waste management is primarily stimulated by the members' desire to satisfy their moral preferences. As long as such favorable preferences exist, higher cooperation among households can be expected. However, households have limited space and time constraints for cooperation. Policy makers could further check the demographic data on poverty, dwelling size, and household size, and do their best to help communities relieve their constraints. Generally speaking, waste management intervention for household cooperation involves three attributes, namely, convenience, charges, and communication. A review in the literature also confirms that intervention may incur unintended consequences. To advocate environmental intervention, further research on the design of incentives is essential.

In general, recycling behavior is not only an individual behavior but also a social behavior. To encourage recycling behavior, it is important to analyze other social factors that may affect individual recycling. The sixth paper by Kirakozian initially reviews three major types of economic incentive instruments, namely, taxes, subsidies, and the deposit refund system for encouraging household waste recycling. Overall, people are not motivated solely by monetary compensation and these instruments appear to be complementary. The economic incentive instruments will be effective if they are coupled with other forms of state intervention. Also, sufficient provision of information to consumers is important for them to make a change in recycling behaviors. As for the impact of social factors on recycling, social norms or social pressure arising from self-image could lead individuals to adopt behaviors consistent with the public interest. To encourage more household recycling, the paper suggests a combination of economic incentive mechanisms and behavioral instruments that change the preferences of individuals toward more environmentally friendly behaviors.

2.4 *Cultural Evolution, Globalization, and Environmental Innovation*

In documented Chinese history, climate changes and geographic conditions are constraints of the economic evolution in ecologically fragile regions. Ecologically fragile regions in China are almost all located in western China, which cover 6.87 million km^2, accounting for 71.54% of China's total area. The seventh paper by Deng, Wang, and Zhao reviews the research records of several key factors closely associated with economic evolution in the history of ecologically fragile regions in China, including climate change, cultural transition, economic base, resource endowment, and transportation accessibility. This study focuses on five representative geographic units selected from ecologically fragile regions of western China, and examines the paths of economic evolution mixed with adaptive cultures response to climate change in each region. From the record counts in the most recent 200 years on Google Scholar, the authors search the combinations of key words to examine economic evolution in each selected part of ecologically fragile regions. The authors find that the economic evolution with regional climate changes interactively experience three stages of culture-hindered, culture-mixed, and culture-impelled adaptation diversely. Regions that have higher economic performance with less innovative records are highly likely to have a relatively large number of indigenous knowledge unpublished throughout cultural evolution.

The eighth paper by Bu, Lin, and Zhang asks an important question "Whether globalization is good or bad for the environment?" In the literature, nearly all related studies use trade or FDI to measure globalization, and dimensions of globalization other than economic globalization have largely been ignored (Frankel, 2003). In fact, pollution issues cannot be assessed from a single perspective. Globalization has been associated with a remarkable growth in the level of popular concerns for political, economic, and sociocultural issues – including pollution – on a global basis due to accelerated economic growth, intimate regional cooperation, and widespread cultural broadcasting. This paper takes advantage of the Konjunkturforschungsstelle (KOF) globalization index (overall index and sub-indices for economic, social, and political globalization) to examine the effects of the whole globalization and its three sub-dimensions on a country's pollution (the three pollution indicators are as follows: GHG, CO_2, and CO_2 from the manufacturing and construction sector), with a panel data sample of 166 countries from 1990 to 2009. They also use the instrumental variable method to address the potential endogeneity problem. On average, increased carbon emissions move in tandem with higher levels of economic, social, and political globalization. Such effects are larger and more significant for non-OECD countries than OECD-countries. To understand the underlying mechanisms, the authors further examine such effects in the CO_2 from the manufacturing and construction sector. The results support that pollution haven effects do exist for this energy-intensive sector, and all globalization indices lead to a cleaner environment in OECD countries and to almost continuous environmental degradation in non-OECD countries. This also means that not only economic globalization, but also political and social globalization will enable OECD countries to shift those high-carbon industries to developing countries.

The achievement of strong decoupling between economic growth and environmental degradation crucially depends on technological improvements that reduce environmental pressure from production and consumption. Therefore, environmental technological innovation may potentially lead to win-win situations in which improvements in environmental quality and economic growth coexist. The ninth paper by Barbieri, Ghisetti, Gilli, Marin, and Nicolli reviews the literature on environmental innovation (EI) using the main path analysis tool. They summarize that this literature revolves around the following four topics: determinants of EI; economic effects of EI; environmental effects of EI; and policy inducement in EI. The main path analysis results show that the "determinants of EI" and "inducement mechanism" subfields have a long tradition in academic research, while the "environmental effects" field is still in the early stages of development, and the literature on "economic effects" can be expanded in numerous ways. The authors highlight the directions of potential future research.

2.5 International Environmental Agreements

There is little doubt that international cooperation across countries is instrumental for resolving environmental issues such as climate change in the global community. To further environmental cooperation in the global community, international environmental agreements (IEAs) have gradually become an important instrument and have drawn considerable attention in the literature (see, for example, McGinty, 2007; Ferrara *et al.*, 2009; Pavlova and de Zeeuw, 2013). The 10th paper by Íriş develops a dynamic game in which countries attempt to maintain cooperation on agreed-upon emission policies with the presence of a free-riding public goods problem. The paper assumes that IEAs are self-enforcing since there is no supranational authority to enforce cooperative mechanisms. Building on the work of Mendez and Trelles (2000) and taking the countries' economic target into account, this paper has derived some results consistent with those of Mendez and Trelles (2000). The first proposition in the paper states that if a country is more concerned with its economic target, then it is more difficult for this country to sustain cooperation at the agreed emission. Concurrently, it is easier for other countries to sustain cooperation. The second proposition states that if all countries have stronger economic target concerns, then it is easier for some sufficiently developed countries to sustain an agreed-upon cooperative emission level. The final paper by Rogna claims to offer some solution concepts in cooperative game theory for analyzing IEAs. The author emphasizes the Chander and Tulkens (1995) solution and proposes two alternative concepts: the Rawlsian Nucleolus and a 'revisited' Nash Bargaining solution. Based upon a numerical comparison of the aforementioned solution concepts, the author concludes that the Rawlsian Nucleolus is the core solution with the highest redistributive properties. That is, the Rawlsian Nucleolus is the most beneficial solution for poor countries that are suffering from climate change.

3. Final Remark

Overall, the aforementioned papers provide theoretical analyses, empirical advances, methodological discussions, or further reflections on environmental economics with endeavors for enhancing sustainability. Six out of the 11 papers collected in this special issue were originally presented at a conference held in Taipei on August 24, 25, and 26, 2015. The conference took place at National Chengchi University (NCCU) and was jointly organized by the authors of the present introduction on behalf of their respective affiliated institutions, the Department of Public Finance at National Chengchi University and the Department of Construction Management at Tsinghua University. The conference was entitled "The Economics of Climate Change" and gathered presentations of 12 papers together with two keynote addresses by Professors Leslie T. Oxley and Alexey A. Voinov. In the first day of the conference, Professor Yuan-Tseh Lee, 1986 Nobel Prize laureate in Chemistry, delivered a distinguished guest lecture entitled "Climate Change and Survival of Humanity on Earth" following a welcome address delivered by the NCCU President, Professor Edward H. Chow.

References

Chander, P. and Tulkens, H. (1995) A core-theoretic solution for the design of cooperative agreements on transfrontier pollution. *International Tax and Public Finance* 2: 279–293.

Dell, M., Jones, B.F. and Olken, B.A. (2014) What do we learn from the weather? The new climate-economy literature. *Journal of Economic Literature* 52: 740–798.

Ferrara, I., Missios, P. and Yildiz, H.M. (2009) Trading rules and the environment: Does equal treatment lead to a cleaner world? *Journal of Environmental Economics and Management* 58: 206–225.

Frankel, J.A. (2003) *The Environment and Globalization.* Working Paper No. 10090. Cambridge, MA: National Bureau of Economic Research.

Hope, C.W. (2006) The marginal impact of CO_2 from PAGE2002: An integrated assessment model incorporating the IPCC's five reasons for concern. *The Integrated Assessment Journal* 6: 19–56.

IPCC (2007) *Climate Change 2007: Synthesis Report.* Cambridge, UK.

Jones, B., Keen, M. and Strand, J. (2013) Fiscal implications of climate change. *International Tax and Public Finance* 20: 29–70.

McGinty, M. (2007) International environmental agreements among asymmetric nations. *Oxford Economic Papers* 59: 45–62.

Mendelsohn, R., Morrison, W., Schlesinger, M. and Andronova, N.G. (2000) Country-specific market impacts of climate change. *Climate Change* 45: 553–569.

Mendez, L. and Trelles, R. (2000) The abatement market a proposal for environmental cooperation among asymmetric countries. *Environmental and Resource Economics* 16: 15–30.

Nordhaus, W.D. (1994) *Managing the Global Commons: The Economics of Climate Change.* Cambridge, MA: MIT Press.

Pavlova, Y. and de Zeeuw, A. (2013) Asymmetries in international environmental agreements. *Environment and Development Economics* 18: 51–68.

Stern, N. (2007) *The Economics of Climate Change: The Stern Review.* New York: Cambridge University Press.

TNO (2013) Opportunities for a circular economy in the Netherlands. TNO 2013 R10864, Delft.

Tol, R.S.J. (2002) Estimates of the damage costs of climate change: Part II. Dynamic estimates. *Environmental and Resource Economics* 21: 135–160.

2

DETECTING VOLCANIC ERUPTIONS IN TEMPERATURE RECONSTRUCTIONS BY DESIGNED BREAK-INDICATOR SATURATION

Felix Pretis

University of Oxford

Lea Schneider

Johannes Gutenberg University

Jason E. Smerdon

Lamont-Doherty Earth Observatory, Columbia University

David F. Hendry

University of Oxford

1. Introduction

Breaks in time series come in many shapes and may occur at any point in time – distorting inference in-sample and leading to forecast failure out-of-sample if not appropriately modelled. Often an approximate shape of a break can be postulated *a priori*, either from previous observations or theory. For example, smooth transitions are common in economic time series following recessions or policy interventions, while sudden drops followed by smooth reversions to the mean are typical in climate time series such as temperature records after a large volcanic eruption (e.g. Kelly and Sear, 1984). While the approximate form of a break may be known, the timings and magnitudes of breaks are often unknown. Here, we propose an econometric approach for detecting breaks of any specified shape in regression models using an indicator saturation procedure. Our approach is based on recent developments in variable selection within regression models that involve more variables than observations (Castle *et al.*,

Environmental Economics and Sustainability, First Edition. Edited by Brian Chi-ang Lin and Siqi Zheng.

2011). By selecting over a complete set of designed break indicators, our approach produces estimates of the break magnitude and timing without imposing limits on the number of breaks that may occur, even at the start or end of a sample.

A structural break is defined as a time-dependent change in a model parameter resulting from a change in the underlying data generating process (DGP). For example, a volcanic eruption leading to a rapid climatic cooling corresponds to a temporary shift in the mean of the surface temperature process. The detection of structural breaks in time series has received significant attention in the recent literature – with a growing interest in econometric models of climate change (e.g. Estrada *et al.*, 2013; Pretis *et al.*, 2015a). The focus has primarily remained on breaks in the mean through the form of step functions (Step-Indicator Saturation – SIS, Castle *et al.*, 2015b; Pretis, 2015b), smooth transition functions (González and Teräsvirta, 2008), breaks in regression coefficients (see, e.g. Bai and Perron, 1998, 2003; Perron and Zhu, 2005; Perron and Yabu, 2009), or individual outliers or groups of outliers that can be indicative of different forms of breaks (Impulse-Indicator Saturation – IIS, see Hendry *et al.*, 2008).

Broadly grouped into 'specific-to-general' and 'general-to-specific', there exist a plethora of approaches for the detection of structural breaks. Perron (2006) provides a broad overview of specific-to-general methods, some of which are subject to an upper limit on the number of breaks, a minimum break length, co-breaking restrictions, as well as ruling out breaks at the beginning or end of the sample, though Strikholm (2006) proposes a specific-to-general algorithm that allows for breaks at the start or end of a sample and relaxes the break length assumption.

Indicator saturation (IIS, SIS) provides an alternative approach using an extended general-to-specific methodology based on model selection. By starting with a full set of step indicators in SIS and removing all but significant ones, structural breaks can be detected without having to specify a minimum break length, maximum break number or imposed co-breaking. Crucially this also allows model selection to be conducted jointly with break detection as non-linearities, dynamics, theory-motivated variables and break functions are selected over simultaneously.

Step functions and impulses are nevertheless only the simplest of many potential break specifications and may not provide the closest approximation to the underlying break. Ericsson (2012) proposes a wide range of extensions to impulse and step shifts. Here, we show that the principle of SIS can be generalized to any form of deterministic break function. An advantage over existing methods is an expected higher frequency of detection when a break function approximates the true break,[1] high flexibility as multiple types of break functions can be selected over and improvements in forecasting where designed functions act as continuous intercept corrections. Moreover, by being a structured search, the retention of irrelevant effects can be controlled.

The method is illustrated using an econometric model of climate variation – detecting volcanic eruptions in a time series of Northern Hemisphere (NH) mean temperature spanning roughly 1200 years, derived from a fully coupled global climate model simulation. Our technique demonstrates that eruptions can be statistically detected without prior knowledge of their occurrence or magnitude– and hence may prove useful for estimating the past impacts of volcanic events using proxy reconstructions of hemispheric or global mean temperatures. Specifically, this can lead to an improved understanding of the effect of stratospheric aerosols on temperatures (with relevance to geo-engineering and pollution control), and more generally, the break detection procedure can be applied to evaluate policy interventions (e.g. the Montreal Protocol: see Estrada *et al.*, 2013; and Pretis and Allen, 2013), correct for measurement changes by detecting and subsequently removing shifts, and function as a robust forecasting device.

Section 2 introduces the methodology and investigates the properties of break detection in the presence of breaks and under the null of no breaks. Section 3 applies the method to detect volcanic eruptions in simulated climate data, and considers designed indicator functions as a robust forecasting device. The conclusions of our work are discussed in Section 4.

2. Break Detection Using Designed Indicator Functions

Breaks are intrinsically stochastic without prior knowledge of their timings and magnitudes. Using a full set of break functions allows us to model the responses deterministically. The detection of structural breaks in regression models can be formulated as a model selection problem where we select over a full set of break functions, a subset of which accurately describes the underlying 'true' break. Consider a simple model as

$$\mathbf{y} = \mathbf{Z}\boldsymbol{\beta} + \boldsymbol{\epsilon} \tag{1}$$

where $\mathbf{y}$ and $\boldsymbol{\epsilon}$ are $(T \times 1)$ vectors, $\boldsymbol{\beta}$ is a $(k \times 1)$ vector and $\mathbf{Z}$ is a $(T \times k)$ matrix $\mathbf{Z} = (\mathbf{z}_1, \ldots, \mathbf{z}_k)$ of rank k. We investigate the presence of structural breaks in any of the $\boldsymbol{\beta}$ where $\mathbf{z}$ may be a constant, trend or random variable. For each break type at any point in time for each variable whose coefficient is allowed to break, we augment the above model by a $(T \times T)$ break function matrix $\mathbf{D}$:[2]

$$\mathbf{y} = \mathbf{Z}\boldsymbol{\beta} + \mathbf{D}\boldsymbol{\gamma} + \boldsymbol{\epsilon} \tag{2}$$

where $\boldsymbol{\gamma}$ is a $(T \times 1)$ vector. The specification of $\mathbf{D}$ is such that the first column $\mathbf{d}_1$ $(T \times 1)$ is set to denote some specified break function $d(t)$ of length L, where $d_{1,t} = d(t)$ for $t \le L$ and 0 otherwise, $d_{1,t} = 0$ for $t > L$. All further columns $\mathbf{d}_j$ (for $j = 2, \ldots, T$) in $\mathbf{D}$ are set such that $d_{j,t} = d_{j-1,t-1}$ for $t \ge j$ and 0 otherwise. The break matrix $\mathbf{D}$ is then defined as $\mathbf{D} = (\mathbf{d}_1, \mathbf{d}_2, \ldots, \mathbf{d}_T)$, where $\mathbf{d}_j$ denotes a vector with break at time $t = j$:

$$\mathbf{D} = (\mathbf{d}_1, \mathbf{d}_2, \ldots, \mathbf{d}_T)$$
$$\mathbf{d}_1 = (d_1, d_2, \ldots, d_{L-1}, d_L, 0, \ldots, 0)'$$
$$\mathbf{d}_2 = (0, d_1, d_2, \ldots, d_{L-1}, d_L, 0, \ldots, 0)'$$
$$\mathbf{d}_3 = (0, 0, d_1, d_2, \ldots, d_{L-1}, d_L, 0, \ldots, 0)'$$
$$\vdots \tag{3}$$

This specification provides a general framework within which multiple break types can be analysed – Table 1 provides a non-exhaustive overview.[3]

The form of the break function $d(t)$ has to be designed *a priori*, but this is implicitly done in most structural break detection methods. For example, outlier detection through finding impulses (IIS, in Hendry *et al.*, 2008) sets the break vector in $\mathbf{d}_1$ such that $d(t) = 1$ and $L = 1$, while a search for step shifts (SIS) sets $d(t) = 1$ and the length to $T - t + 1$, that is, the break function continues until the end of the sample. Breaks in linear trends (see, e.g. Perron and Zhu, 2005; Perron and Yabu, 2009; Estrada *et al.*, 2013) can be constructed by setting $d(t) = t$ and the length to $T - t + 1$. Pretis *et al.* (2015a) apply indicator saturation using broken trends and step shifts to evaluate climate models. Breaks in coefficients on random variables z_t (see, e.g. Bai and Perron, 2003; Ericsson, 2012; Kitov and Tabor, 2015) can be constructed by interacting

Table 1. Break Function Specifications.

	Break Value: $d(t)$	Length:
Deterministic Breaks		
General Case	$d(t)$	L
Impulses (IIS)	1	1
Step Shifts (SIS)	1	$T - t + 1$
Broken Trends	t	$T - t + 1$
Volcanic Functions	see equation (31)	3
Random Variables		
Coeff. on z_t (MIS)	$z_t \cdot d_{t,SIS}$	$T - t + 1$

$$D = \begin{pmatrix} d_1 & 0 & \cdots & \cdots & \cdots & 0 \\ d_2 & d_1 & 0 & \cdots & \cdots & \vdots \\ \vdots & d_2 & d_1 & 0 & \cdots & \vdots \\ d_L & \vdots & d_2 & d_1 & 0 & \vdots \\ \vdots & d_L & \vdots & d_2 & d_1 & 0 \\ 0 & 0 & d_L & d_3 & d_2 & d_1 \end{pmatrix}$$

z_t with a full set of step shifts. Sudden declines followed by a smooth recovery to the mean in hemispheric temperature responses are introduced here as volcanic functions and considered in Sections 2.1 and 3. Linear combinations of multiple break functions can allow for varying lengths of breaks without pre-specification.

Searching for breaks in k variables implies that the complete break matrix across all k variables $\mathbf{D}$ is of dimension $(T \times kT)$. The inclusion of kT additional variables leads to the total number of variables N exceeding the number of observations, $N > T$, even for $k = 1$. Thus, a methodology allowing for more variables than observations is required.

Selection of models with more variables than observations has primarily relied on either shrinkage-based penalized likelihood methods (Tibshirani, 1996; Zou and Hastie, 2005; Tibshirani, 2011) or general-to-specific methodology in the econometrics literature (see, e.g. Castle *et al.*, 2011). Kock and Teräsvirta (2015) compare the general-to-specific model selection algorithms *Autometrics*, to *QuickNet* – an artificial neural-network method proposed by White (2006), and to a shrinkage-based bridge estimator from Huang *et al.* (2008) in the context of forecasting.

Here we rely on general-to-specific model selection due to methods based on forward stepwise searches not performing as well in break detection contexts (see Section 2.1.2 for a simple comparison, or Epprecht *et al.* (2013), and Hendry and Doornik (2014) for comparisons on general variable selection). Cox and Snell (1974) discuss some of the challenges of the general variable selection problem and Hoover and Perez (1999) show the feasibility of general-to-specific model selection for $N \ll T$. When facing more variables than observations, the general-to-specific approach is closely linked to robust statistics. Saturating a model with a full set of $0/1$ indicator functions from which selections are made is equivalent to a robust one-step M-estimator using Huber's skip function (see Johansen and Nielsen, 2009, 2013 for the iterated case, and Johansen and Nielsen, 2016 for an overview). Here, we generalize this allowing for any form of designed break function in place of impulses, and formulate break detection as a model selection problem.

To estimate model (2) saturated with a full set of break functions $\mathbf{D}$ (so $N > T$), we rely on a block-partitioning estimation procedure (Doornik, 2010; Hendry and Johansen, 2015). For this, we partition $\mathbf{D}$ into b blocks of n_i variables such that $n_i \ll T$ and $\sum_{i=1}^{b} n_i = N$. In the simplest case of testing for a break in a single variable (e.g. the intercept), a split-half approach (see Figure 1 and *Algorithm 1* in the supplementary material) is feasible: initially, we include the first half of $\mathbf{D}_1 = (\mathbf{d}_1, \dots, \mathbf{d}_{T/2})$ and retain only significant break indicators. We repeat the

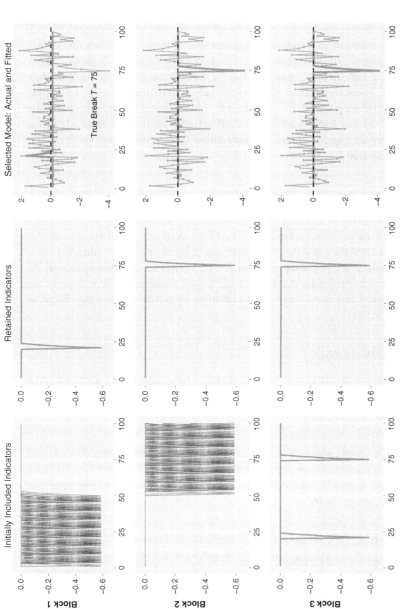

Figure 1. Split-Half Approach for a Single Unknown Break of the Shape of a Volcanic Function at $T = 75$.

Note: Left column shows included indicators in each step, middle column shows the retained indicators and right column graphs the selected model with actual and fitted data. Block 1 (top panel) includes the first half of break functions and retains a single one as the mean is lowered in the second half due to the presence of a break at $t = 75$. Block 2 (middle panel) then includes the second half retaining the correct break function. Block 3 uses the union of retained indicators from blocks 1 and 2 in which now the first indicator is rendered insignificant by the mean being correctly estimated due to the second indicator capturing the break. Using a saturating set of break functions at 1% the break at $T = 75$ is detected without prior knowledge and is the only break function retained.

step for the second half of break functions d_j (for $j = T/2 + 1, \dots T$) and finally combine the retained sets and only keep significant indicators. This split-half approach is considered here for analytical tractability in Section 2.1.2.

In practice, however, we rely on a multi-split and multi-path search to lower the variance of the estimators, allow for any number of variables for a given set of observations and to avoid a breakdown of the procedure if the breaks cannot be adequately modelled through split-half indicators.[4] This can be implemented through the general-to-specific model selection algorithm *Autometrics* (*Algorithm 2* in the supplementary material), described in Doornik, 2009a, or the *gets* package in the statistical software environment *R* (Pretis *et al.*, 2016). The algorithm (referred to as multi-path throughout the paper) avoids path dependence through a tree-structure and uses a parallel stepwise backwards search, while testing for encompassing and congruence (Hendry, 1995). See Hendry and Pretis (2013) for an application of the algorithm to econometric modelling of climate change. A simulation-based comparison to shrinkage methods is provided in Section 2.1.2.

2.1 Properties of Designed Break Functions in the Presence of Breaks

To assess the theoretical power of the proposed methodology, we first investigate the properties in the benchmark case of a single break matched by a correctly timed break indicator in Section 2.1.1. Section 2.1.2 then assesses the properties of break-indicator saturation when the break date and magnitude are unknown. Section 2.1.3 investigates uncertainty around the break date and 2.2 describes the properties in the presence of no breaks. Theory results are derived for general designed functions, simulation examples are based on a volcanic break as characterized by equation (31).

2.1.1 Power for Known Break Date

We investigate the theoretical power of detecting a break in a time series given a known break date. Consider a DGP coinciding with the model for a single known break in an intercept:

$$y_t = \mu + \lambda d_t + \epsilon_t \tag{4}$$

where $\epsilon_t \sim \text{IN}(0, \sigma_\epsilon^2)$. The break shifts μ to $\mu + \lambda d_t$ where d_t is a break function of length L beginning at time $t = T_1$ where $(T_1 + L) \leq T$ such that $d_t \neq 0$ for $T_1 \leq t < (T_1 + L)$ and 0 otherwise. The estimators $\hat{\mu}$ and $\hat{\gamma}$ (where $\hat{\gamma}$ is the estimator for λ) in a correctly specified model for a known break are given by

$$\begin{pmatrix} \hat{\mu} - \mu \\ \hat{\gamma} - \lambda \end{pmatrix} = \begin{pmatrix} T_d^{-1} \left(\sum_{t=T_1}^{T_1+L-1} d_t^2 \sum_{t=1}^{T} \epsilon_t - \sum_{t=T_1}^{T_1+L-1} d_t \sum_{t=T_1}^{T_1+L-1} d_t \epsilon_t \right) \\ T_d^{-1} \left(\sum_{t=T1}^{T_1+L-1} d_t \epsilon_t - \sum_{t=T_1}^{T_1+L-1} d_t \sum_{t=1}^{T} \epsilon_t \right) \end{pmatrix} \tag{5}$$

where $T_d = T[\sum_{t=T_1}^{T_1+L-1} d_t^2 - \frac{1}{T}(\sum_{t=T_1}^{T_1+L-1} d_t)^2]$. The estimators are unbiased for the break and intercept: $E[\hat{\mu} - \mu] = 0$ and $E[\hat{\gamma} - \lambda] = 0$. The variance of the estimators is given by

$$V \begin{pmatrix} \hat{\mu} - \mu \\ \hat{\gamma} - \lambda \end{pmatrix} = \sigma_\epsilon^2 T_d^{-1} \begin{pmatrix} \sum_{t=T_1}^{T_1+L-1} d_t^2 & -\sum_{t=T_1}^{T_1+L-1} d_t \\ -\sum_{t=T_1}^{T_1+L-1} d_t & T \end{pmatrix} \tag{6}$$

The distribution of the break estimator is then:

$$(\hat{\gamma} - \lambda) \sim N\left(0, \sigma_\epsilon^2 \left[\sum_{t=T_1}^{T_1+L-1} d_t^2 - \sum_{t=T_1}^{T_1+L-1} d_t \bar{d}\right]^{-1}\right) \tag{7}$$

where $\bar{d} = 1/T \sum_{t=1}^{T} d_t$. For the special case when step-indicators are chosen as the functional form of d_t and the single break lasts from $t = 0$ to $t = T_1 < T$, equation (5) simplifies to $\hat{\mu} - \mu = \bar{\epsilon}_2$ and $\hat{\gamma} - \lambda = \bar{\epsilon}_1 - \bar{\epsilon}_2$, where $\bar{\epsilon}_1 = 1/T_1 \sum_{t=1}^{T_1} \epsilon_t$ and $\bar{\epsilon}_2 = 1/(T - T_1) \sum_{t=T_1+1}^{T} \epsilon_t$.[5]

2.1.2 Potency for an Unknown Break Date

When the break date is unknown, we propose to saturate the regression model using a full set of specified break indicators and select significant breaks through an extended general-to-specific algorithm (Castle *et al.*, 2011). We assess the methodology in the selection context using two main concepts: the null retention frequency of indicators is called the gauge, comparable to the size of a test denoting its (false) null rejection frequency, but taking into account that indicators that are insignificant on a pre-assigned criterion may nevertheless be retained to offset what would otherwise be a significant misspecification test (see Johansen and Nielsen, 2016, for distributional results on the gauge). The non-null retention frequency when selecting indicators is called its potency, comparable to a similar test's power for rejecting a false null hypothesis.

Here we investigate the feasibility of the proposed method by deriving the analytical properties of the split-half approach for an unknown break. Figure 1 illustrates the split-half method for a single unknown break. In practice, we rely on a multi-path, multi-block search algorithm (such as *Autometrics*, see *Algorithm 2* in the supplementary material) to reduce the variance of the estimators.

Consider a single break falling into the first half of the sample beginning at time T_1 for L periods such that $0 < T_1 < T_1 + L < T/2$. In matrix form, the DGP is given as

$$\mathbf{y} = \lambda \mathbf{d}_{T_1} + \epsilon \tag{8}$$

where $\epsilon \sim N(\mathbf{0}, \sigma^2 \mathbf{I})$ for simplicity and the $(T \times 1)$ vector $\mathbf{d}_{T_1}$ denotes a break at $t = T_1$ for L periods. Using a split-half approach, we assess the properties of detecting the single break when the break date is unknown. The split-half model for the first half of break functions is

$$\mathbf{y} = \mathbf{D}_1 \boldsymbol{\gamma}_{(1)} + \mathbf{v} \tag{9}$$

where $\boldsymbol{\gamma}_{(1)} = (\gamma_1, \gamma_2, \cdots \gamma_{T/2})'$ and $\mathbf{D}_1 = (\mathbf{d}_1, \ldots, \mathbf{d}_{T/2})$. The estimator $\hat{\boldsymbol{\gamma}}_{(1)}$ equals:[6]

$$\hat{\boldsymbol{\gamma}}_{(1)} = \left(\mathbf{D}_1' \mathbf{D}_1\right)^{-1} \mathbf{D}_1' \mathbf{y} = \lambda \left(\mathbf{D}_1' \mathbf{D}_1\right)^{-1} \mathbf{D}_1' \mathbf{d}_{T_1} + \left(\mathbf{D}_1' \mathbf{D}_1\right)^{-1} \mathbf{D}_1' \epsilon \tag{10}$$

$$= \lambda \mathbf{r} + \left(\mathbf{D}_1' \mathbf{D}_1\right)^{-1} \mathbf{D}_1' \epsilon$$

where the $(T/2 \times 1)$ vector $\mathbf{r}$ is equal to one at $t = T_1$ and zero otherwise, $r_t = 1_{\{t=T_1\}}$. It follows that $E[\hat{\boldsymbol{\gamma}}_{(1)}] = \lambda \mathbf{r}$ and $V[\hat{\boldsymbol{\gamma}}_{(1)}] = \sigma_\epsilon^2 (\mathbf{D}_1' \mathbf{D}_1)^{-1}$. We find for the first half, for normal error terms:

$$\left(\hat{\boldsymbol{\gamma}}_{(1)} - \lambda \mathbf{r}\right) \sim N\left(\mathbf{0}, \sigma_\epsilon^2 \left(\mathbf{D}_1' \mathbf{D}_1\right)^{-1}\right) \tag{11}$$

Therefore conventional t-tests can be used to assess the significance of individual indicators. The estimator $\widehat{\boldsymbol{\gamma}}_{(2)}$ on the second half of indicators, $\mathbf{D}_2 = (\mathbf{d}_{T/2+1}, \dots, \mathbf{d}_T)$, will miss the break in the DGP in the first half described by $\mathbf{d}_{T_1}$ and equals

$$\widehat{\boldsymbol{\gamma}}_{(2)} = \lambda \left(\mathbf{D}_2'\mathbf{D}_2\right)^{-1} \mathbf{D}_2'\mathbf{d}_{T_1} + \left(\mathbf{D}_2'\mathbf{D}_2\right)^{-1} \mathbf{D}_2'\boldsymbol{\epsilon} \tag{12}$$

For step shifts, Castle *et al.* (2015b) show that the indicator in $\mathbf{D}_2$ closest to the sample split will be retained in the second set of indicators. For the general form of break functions, retention in $\mathbf{D}_2$, when there is a break in the first half, will depend on the specific functional form. However, conditional on the break indicator being correctly retained in the first set $\mathbf{D}_1$, retention of irrelevant indicators in $\mathbf{D}_2$ does not affect the correct identification of the break overall: let $\mathbf{D}_{1*}$ and $\mathbf{D}_{2*}$ denote the set of retained break functions in the first and second set, respectively, where retention is based on a retention rule such as $\mathbf{d}_j$ is retained if $|t_{\widehat{\gamma}_j}| \geq c_\alpha$. The final step in the split-half procedure is then to combine the retained indicators using $\mathbf{D}_U = [\mathbf{D}_{1*}\mathbf{D}_{2*}]$ and estimate the model:

$$\mathbf{y} = \mathbf{D}_U\boldsymbol{\gamma}_{(U)} + \mathbf{v} \tag{13}$$

This yields the estimator $\widehat{\boldsymbol{\gamma}}_{(U)}$ unbiased for the true break:[7]

$$\widehat{\boldsymbol{\gamma}}_{(U)} = \lambda\mathbf{r} + \left(\mathbf{D}_U'\mathbf{D}_U\right)^{-1} \mathbf{D}_U'\boldsymbol{\epsilon} \tag{14}$$

The carried-forward break function in $\mathbf{D}_{1*}$ correctly identifies the true break, and coefficients on all other break functions will thus be zero in expectation. The proof is identical to that given for the first half of indicators in the supplementary material. This shows that, conditional on retaining the correct break indicator in $\mathbf{D}_1$, the retention of indicators in $\mathbf{D}_2$ does not affect the correct identification of the break, when the first and second set are combined and reselected over. The distribution of the final split-half estimator is then given by

$$\left(\widehat{\boldsymbol{\gamma}}_{(U)} - \lambda\mathbf{r}\right) \sim N\left(\mathbf{0}, \sigma_\epsilon^2 \left(\mathbf{D}_U'\mathbf{D}_U\right)^{-1}\right) \tag{15}$$

Reselection then results in only the true break indicator being retained in expectation.[8]

This result generalizes the specific case of step indicators presented in Castle *et al.* (2015b). Even though the break date and magnitude are unknown, the use of a fully saturated set of break indicators allows us to obtain an unbiased estimate of the break magnitude and timing. The estimator then follows a normal distribution subject to correct specification of the break function. Thus the estimated coefficient at the break time, $\widehat{\gamma}_{T_1}$, is in expectation equal to the break magnitude, while all other estimated coefficients are mean-zero in expectation. This result generalizes to multiple breaks falling in a single split. As in the case of the known break timing, the variance of the estimator depends on the specified break function. Let $\delta_{k,j}$ denote the (k,j) element of the matrix $(\mathbf{D}_1'\mathbf{D}_1)^{-1}$. The variance of the coefficient at the breakpoint in the first half is therefore:

$$V[\widehat{\gamma}_{T_1}] = \sigma_\epsilon^2 \delta_{T_1,T_1} \tag{16}$$

For iid error terms ϵ, and $\mathbf{D}$ specified as a full set of step functions, the split-half model (without selection) yields $\delta_{j,j} = 2$, so the break coefficient has twice the error variance. For the proposed volcanic function (derived and assessed in detail in Section 3) modelling a single drop followed by a reversion to the mean, we find that $\delta_{j,j} = 3.7$, thus $V[\widehat{\gamma}_{T_1}] = 3.7\sigma_\epsilon^2$. This can be compared to the known-break/single-indicator case where the variance is given by equation (6) and for the volcanic function equals $2.3\sigma_\epsilon^2$ (for $T = 100$). Due to collinearity of break functions, the variance of the estimator is higher in a fully saturated model. In the more general case, δ_{T_1,T_1} depends on the specification of the break function but can be computed *a priori*. The t-statistic is then given as

$$t_{\widehat{\gamma}_{T_1}} = \frac{\widehat{\gamma}_{T_1}}{\widehat{\sigma}_\epsilon \sqrt{\delta_{T_1,T_1}}} \approx \frac{\left(\widehat{\gamma}_{T_1} - \lambda\right)}{\sigma_\epsilon \sqrt{\delta_{T_1,T_1}}} + \frac{\lambda}{\sigma_\epsilon \sqrt{\delta_{T_1,T_1}}} \sim N\left(\frac{\lambda}{\sigma_\epsilon \sqrt{\delta_{T_1,T_1}}}, 1\right) \qquad (17)$$

In practice, we use sequential elimination of the break indicators or a multi-path search to eliminate insignificant indicators reducing the variance of the estimators from a saturated model (16) closer to the single break (6) and increasing the power of detection.

For dynamic time-series models, the above approach can be extended by including time-dependent covariates. Valid conditioning (e.g. through the inclusion of auto-regressive terms in the case of non-iid errors) can be ensured by always including the covariates in each block estimation step and only selecting over the break functions. Johansen and Nielsen (2009) provide the asymptotics under the null of no break for the special case of impulses for stationary and unit-root non-stationary autoregressive processes (see Johansen and Nielsen, 2013, for the iterated version). The case for general break functions is discussed in Section 2.2, and the supplementary material provides simulation results for an AR(1) model and DGP.[9]

Simulation Performance based on Volcanic Break Functions. Table 2 reports simulation results ($T = 100$) for a DGP with a single unknown volcanic break at $t = T_1 = 25$ of magnitude λ followed by a smooth reversion to the mean.[10] Equation (31) provides the exact functional form. Simulations are assessed by the retention/detection frequency (potency) for a single break and average retention of spurious breaks (gauge).[11]

The trade-off between potency and level of significance of selection α is shown in Figure 2 for a single volcanic break. A multi-path search generally increases the power of detection relative to the split-half approach. Figure 3 shows the results for split-half (dashed) and multi-path (solid) selection when using volcanic functions for a break of $\lambda = 6$. Consistent with derived theory (16), the estimator has 3.7 times the variance of the error term when using split-half estimation for the given function. Using a multi-path search reduces the variance drastically. Any selection bias of the multi-path search estimates can be controlled through bias correction after selection (see Castle *et al.*, 2011 and Pretis, 2015b). The supplementary material provides simulation results for a simple autoregressive DGP and model.

Table 2. Potency of Detecting an Unknown Break When Using Split-Half and Multi-Path Searches.

	Split-Half		Multi-Path	
	Potency	Gauge $\mathbf{D}_1$	Potency	Gauge
$\lambda = 6$, trough = 3.48	0.69	0.013	0.88	0.015
$\lambda = 4$, trough = 2.23	0.30	0.013	0.50	0.014
$\lambda = 2$, trough = 1.16	0.06	0.013	0.11	0.015

Notes: Statistics were generated from 1000 simulations and detection significance was set to $\alpha = 0.01$, with a length of $L = 3$. Break magnitude λ corresponds to the full response in standard deviations of the error term ($\sigma_\epsilon = 1$) over the entire break, the trough is 0.58λ.

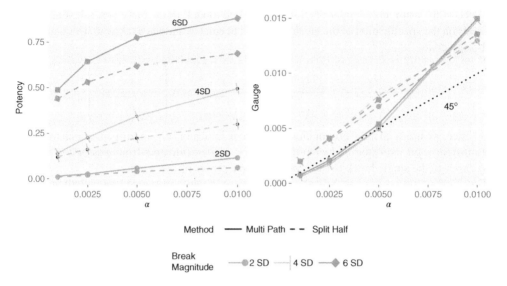

Figure 2. (Left) Potency of Detecting a Volcanic Break of Magnitude λ for Level of Significance α Using Split-Half and Multi-Path Selection and (Right) Proportion of Spuriously Retained Break Indicators (Gauge).

Note: Break magnitude λ corresponds to the full response in standard deviations of the error term ($\sigma_\varepsilon = 1$) over the entire break, the trough is 0.58λ, 6 standard deviations (SD) therefore refers to a trough of 3.48SD.

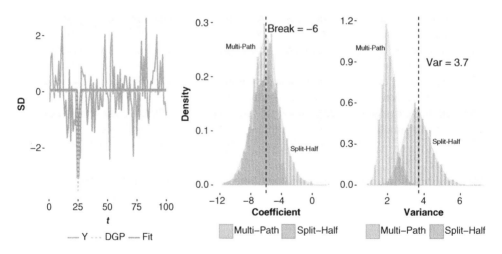

Figure 3. Estimated Break Indicator and Variance for Unknown Break Using Split-Half (purple/shaded dark, on right) and Multi-Path (orange/shaded light, on left) Selection.

Notes: The left panel shows a simulated time series with the true break shown as dotted and the fit as solid. The middle panel shows the distribution of the estimated coefficient, the right panel shows the variance of the coefficient. Vertical dashed lines show the true break magnitude and analytical variance of the split-half coefficient.

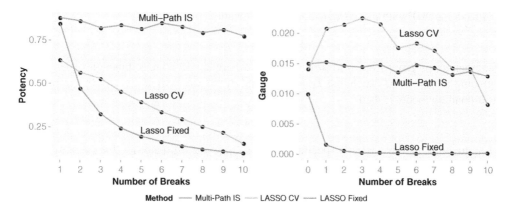

Figure 4. (Left) Average Potency of Detecting Increasing Numbers of Volcanic Breaks Using Multi-Path Indicator Saturation at $\alpha = 0.01$ (IS), Cross-Validated Lasso (CV) and Lasso with Fixed Penalty (Fixed) Where the Penalty is Set Such That the False-Positive Rate Approximates that of the Indicator Saturation Procedure under the Null of No Break; and (Right) Corresponding False-Positive Rate (Gauge).

Note: M = 1000 replications.

Comparison to Shrinkage-based Methods. Shrinkage-based methods using penalized likelihood estimation (Zou and Hastie, 2005; Tibshirani, 2011) provide an alternative to the general-to-specific algorithm used here in selecting models with more variables than observations. Figure 4 shows the simulation outcomes comparing multi-path indicator saturation (for $\alpha = 0.01$), the Lasso (Tibshirani, 1996, estimated using LARS, see Efron *et al.*, 2004) where cross-validation is used to determine the penalty and the Lasso where the penalty is set such to approximate the false-positive rate of the IS procedure under the null of no breaks (≈ 0.01). The simulation uses a total break magnitude of six standard deviations (implying a trough of $3.48\sigma_e$) for an increasing number of evenly spaced breaks from 0 up to 10 in a sample of $T = 100$. The general-to-specific multi-path algorithm exhibits stable power exceeding that of the penalized likelihood methods across any number of breaks. The false-positive rate remains stable and close to the theory level of 0.01. The shrinkage-based procedures, due to their similarity to forward-selection, show decreasing potency as the number of breaks increases, and the false-positive rate is difficult to control.

2.1.3 Uncertainty on the Break Date

An estimated uncertainty on the break magnitude and coefficient path (the time-varying intercept in the regression) can be computed given the distribution of the break estimator (see Pretis, 2015b). While of considerable interest, it is non-trivial, however, to quantify the uncertainty around the timing of the break (see Elliott and Müller, 2007). This is particularly true for the literature focusing on break detection using general-to-specific methodology. Here we investigate the uncertainty around the timing of estimated break points when using break-indicator saturation by computing the analytical power of a single break indicator when the break function is correctly specified but the break time is not. This is a simplification as it only considers a single mistimed indicator, while the indicator saturation approach includes a saturating set.

Consider a DGP with just a single break in the mean:

$$y_t = \lambda d_{T_1,t} + \epsilon_t \tag{18}$$

The break shifts $E[y_t]$ from 0 to λd_{T_1} at $t = T_1$ where d_{T_1} is a break function of length L beginning at time $t = T_1$ such that $T_1 + L < T$ and $d_{T_1} = (0, \dots, d_1, d_2, \dots, d_L, 0, \dots, 0)$. The corresponding model is then

$$y_t = \gamma d_{j,t} + v_t \tag{19}$$

When the break date is correctly specified, $d_{j,t} = d_{T_1,t}$, so the estimator for λ is given by

$$\hat{\gamma}_{t=T_1} - \lambda = \left(\sum_{t=T_1}^{T_1+L} d_{T_1,t}^2 \right)^{-1} \left(\sum_{t=T_1}^{T_1+L} d_{T_1,t} \epsilon_t \right) \tag{20}$$

Similarly for a test of the hypothesis: $\lambda = 0$, the t-statistic has a non-centrality of $E[t_{\hat{\gamma},t=T_1}] =$

$$\psi = \frac{\lambda \sqrt{\left(\sum_{t=T_1}^{T_1+L} d_{T_1,t}^2 \right)}}{\sigma_\epsilon} \text{ and the normal distribution}$$

$$t_{\hat{\gamma},t=T_1} \approx \frac{\hat{\gamma}_{t=T_1} \sqrt{\left(\sum_{t=T_1}^{T_1+L} d_{T_1,t}^2 \right)}}{\sigma_\epsilon} \sim N(\psi, 1) \tag{21}$$

The non-centrality ψ increases in the break magnitude λ, varies with the break length L, and will depend on the underlying break function given by d_t.

Now consider the model being incorrectly specified for the break date, such that $d_{j,t} \neq d_{T_1,t}$ but is shifted by K periods $d_{j,t} = d_{T_1 \pm K,t}$. The estimator for λ is then

$$\hat{\gamma}_{t=T_1 \pm K} - \lambda = \lambda \left[\left(\sum_{t=T_1}^{T_1+L} d_{j,t}^2 \right)^{-1} \left(\sum_{t=T_1}^{T_1+L} d_{j,t} d_{T_1,t} \right) - 1 \right] + \left(\sum_{t=T_1}^{T_1+L} d_{j,t}^2 \right)^{-1} \left(\sum_{t=T_1}^{T_1+L} d_{j,t} \epsilon_t \right) \tag{22}$$

For a fixed length L and a forced mistiming, it follows that $\hat{\gamma}_{t \neq T_1}$ is not an unbiased estimator for λ. Note that if d_j is functionally specified correctly such that the only difference to the true break function is through K lags, $\mathbf{d}_j = \mathbf{d}_{T_1 \pm K}$, then it holds that $(\sum_{t=T_1}^{T_1+L} d_{j,t}^2) = (\sum_{t=T_1}^{T_1+L} d_{T_1,t}^2)$. Equally $(\sum_{t=T_1}^{T_1+L} d_{j,t} d_{T_1,t}) = (\sum_{t=T_1}^{T_1+L} d_{T_1 \pm K,t} d_{T_1,t})$ for $K \leq L$ and 0 for $K > L$. Using this, we derive an expression for the approximate t-statistic associated with the estimator given a break function time misspecified by K lags:

$$E \left[t_{\hat{\gamma},t=T_1 \pm K} \right] \approx \frac{E \left[\hat{\gamma}_{t=T_1 \pm K} \right]}{\sigma_\epsilon \left(\sum_{t=T_1}^{T_1+L} d_{T_1}^2 \right)^{-1/2}} = \frac{\lambda \left(\sum_{t=T_1}^{T_1+L} d_{T_1 \pm K} d_{T_1} \right)}{\sigma_\epsilon \left(\sum_{t=T_1}^{T_1+L} d_{T_1}^2 \right)^{1/2}} \tag{23}$$

This is equal to the non-centrality of the correct break date ψ scaled by a factor less than one, decreasing with the distance K from the correct date

$$E \left[t_{\hat{\gamma},t=T_1 \pm K} \right] \approx \psi \left(\frac{\sum_{t=T_1}^{T_1+L} d_{T_1 \pm K,t} d_{T_1,t}}{\sum_{t=T_1}^{T_1+L} d_{T_1,t}^2} \right) \leq \psi \tag{24}$$

For a given break specification d_t and break length L, the corresponding power function can be computed to provide an approximate measure of power for detection of a break at $t = T_1$ in the neighbourhood of T_1. Note that $E[t_{\hat{\gamma}, t=T_1 \pm K}]$ is zero outside a neighbourhood of L. The associated t-statistic of a break indicator further away from the true break date T_1 than the break length L is zero in expectation, since $(\sum_{t=T_1}^{T_1+L} d_{j,t} d_{T_1,t}) = 0$ for $K > L$. Intuitively, longer breaks increase the likelihood that a break indicator that is not perfectly coincident with the break date will appear significant, and we can expect the retention to be equal to the nominal significance level outside a $t = T_1 \pm L$ interval.

As before we consider the special case of volcanic functions and also provide results from step shifts for comparison. Figure 5 shows the analytical as well as simulated non-centrality and power around a true break date at $t = 26$ of length $L = 3$ for $\alpha = 0.05$. The Monte Carlo simulations match the theoretical powers and non-centralities closely.

For no break, the analytical power is uniform and equal to the nominal significance level. When there is a break outside of the interval $T_1 \pm L$, the expected retention of the break indicator equals the nominal significance level. For a step shift of a forced length, given (24), the non-centrality decreases linearly as the numerator falls by $1/L$ per shifted period relative to the correct break date. For longer breaks this implies that the power around the true break date is close to uniform. In the case of volcanic functions, due to the particular functional form, the power and retention probability drop more rapidly and peak clearly around the true break date. The special case presented here only considers the properties of a single time-misspecified indicator of a fixed length in the model. However, model selection in the indicator saturation approach alleviates many of these concerns in practice. When selecting from a full set of break functions (see Section 2.1.2) it is less likely that a break function at $T_1 + -K$ appears significant because the correct T_1 indicator is included in the same model, a mistimed indicator in a fully saturated model would likely appear significant only if a chance draw of the error offsets the shift.

2.2 Properties under the Null of No Break

Under the null hypothesis when there are no breaks in the DGP, there are two primary concerns regarding the inclusion of a full set of break functions in the statistical model. First, when including a full set of break functions, break indicators may be retained spuriously, and secondly, there may be concerns about the effect on the distributions of coefficients on variables that are known to be relevant – in other words, does saturating a model with irrelevant variables affect relevant ones?

First, we consider the spurious retention of break indicators. Under the null of no breaks, $\lambda = 0$, the DGP from (8) is given by

$$\mathbf{y} = \boldsymbol{\epsilon} \tag{25}$$

Based on the above results, when using a split-half approach with a full set of break indicators, the expectation of the estimated coefficients in the first half is given by

$$E[\hat{\gamma}_{(1)}] = E\left[\left(\mathbf{D}_1' \mathbf{D}_1\right)^{-1} \mathbf{D}_1' \boldsymbol{\epsilon}\right] = \mathbf{0} \tag{26}$$

The same result generalizes to the union of retained indicators $\mathbf{D}_U$. Thus, the t-statistics of the included break functions will be centred around zero in expectation when there is no break.

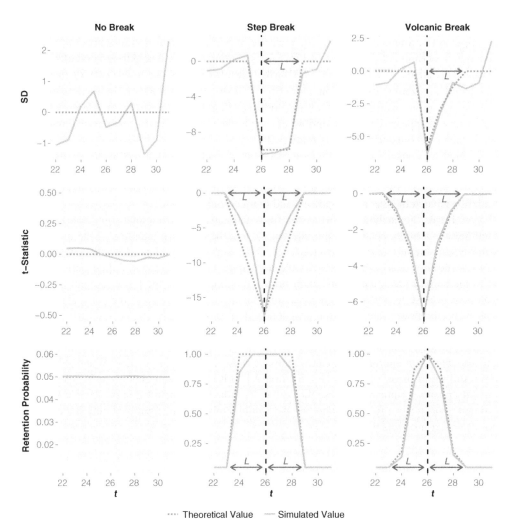

Figure 5. Power and Retention Frequency around the Break Date Where the Timing of the Break Functions is Imposed without Selection.

Notes: Simulated data with and without shifts (top), associated non-centrality and simulated t-statistics (middle), analytical and simulated power (bottom) around break $\lambda = -10$ at $T_1 = 26$ of length $L = 3$ and interval $T_1 \pm K$ for $\alpha = 0.05$. Left shows no break, middle a step-break and right panel a volcanic function break. Analytical non-centralities and powers are shown as dotted, simulated t-statistics and retention are shown as solid. Dashed lines mark the break occurrence. Outside of an interval $T_1 = 26 \pm L$ the retention probability and analytical power are equal to the nominal significance level of $\alpha = 0.05$.

Using the selection rule that retains the break function $\mathbf{d}_j$ if $|t_{d_j}| > c_\alpha$, then $\alpha T/2$ indicators will be retained on average in each half. Combining the retained indicators in the final set, αT indicators are retained in expectation. The proportion of spurious indicators can thus be controlled through the nominal significance level of selection. The properties under the null are confirmed below using Monte-Carlo simulations.

Table 3. Retention of Spurious Volcanic Break Functions When There is No Break.

Significance Level	Split-Half One-Cut		Multi-Path Search
	Gauge $\mathbf{D}_1$	Gauge $\mathbf{D}_2$	Gauge $\mathbf{D}$
$\alpha = 0.05$	0.056	0.054	0.30
$\alpha = 0.01$	0.013	0.012	0.015
$\alpha = 0.005$	0.007	0.007	0.005
$\alpha = 0.0025$	0.004	0.004	0.002
$\alpha = 0.001$	0.002	0.002	0.001

Table 3 and Figure 6 report the simulation results when there are no breaks in the DGP but a full set of break functions (of the form of volcanic functions) is included. When using a split-half approach with a one-cut variable selection decision based on the absolute t-statistic, the proportion of irrelevant retained indicators is close to the nominal significance level. In practice, when using a multi-path, multi-split procedure (here implemented through *Autometrics*) the gauge is close to the nominal significance level for low levels of α. A conservative approach (low $\alpha \leq 1\%$) is recommended in practice.[12] When compared to results in Castle *et al.* (2015b), there is little notable difference between different specifications of break functions, consistent with the analytical properties of irrelevant indicators.

We now assess the second consideration, which is the effect of including a full set of break indicators when theory variables $\mathbf{X}$ are included in the model but are not selected over ('forced'). These could include contemporaneous covariates or autoregressive dynamic variables. For the specific case when the elements of $\mathbf{D}$ are specified to be impulse indicators, Johansen and Nielsen (2009) derive the asymptotic distribution of β in the full split-half approach in stationary and unit-root non-stationary regressions using the equivalence of IIS and one step Huber-skip M-estimators. For an iterated procedure (e.g. resembling the multi-block approach in *Autometrics*) the distributional results under the null for IIS are derived in Johansen and Nielsen (2013). For the general form of designed indicator functions, we follow theory for the substeps of split-half estimation where $N \ll T$ in each step, and appeal to simulation results for the overall algorithm. Consider a simple DGP:

$$\mathbf{y} = \mathbf{X}\boldsymbol{\beta} + \boldsymbol{\epsilon} \tag{27}$$

where $\boldsymbol{\epsilon} \sim \text{iid}(0, \sigma_\epsilon^2 \mathbf{I})$ and the elements of $\mathbf{X}$ (dynamic or static) are assumed to be relevant and not selected over. The model relying on the split-half approach saturated with the first half of the break functions is then

$$\mathbf{y} = \mathbf{X}\boldsymbol{\beta} + \mathbf{D}_1\boldsymbol{\gamma}_{(1)} + \mathbf{v} \tag{28}$$

where the true $\boldsymbol{\gamma}_{(1)} = \mathbf{0}$. Following Hendry and Johansen (2015), given that there is no break in the DGP, the inclusion of a full set of irrelevant additional variables $\mathbf{D}_1$ need not affect the distribution of the included relevant parameters $\boldsymbol{\beta}$. Orthogonalizing $\mathbf{X}$ and $\mathbf{D}_1$ by regressing each column of $\mathbf{D}_1$ on $\mathbf{X}$ yields the estimator $\widehat{\boldsymbol{\beta}}^*$ with asymptotic distribution:[13]

$$\sqrt{T}\begin{pmatrix} \widehat{\boldsymbol{\beta}}^* - \boldsymbol{\beta} \\ \widehat{\boldsymbol{\gamma}}_{(1)} - \mathbf{0} \end{pmatrix} \overset{D}{\to} N\left[\begin{pmatrix} \mathbf{0} \\ \mathbf{0} \end{pmatrix}, \sigma_\epsilon^2 \begin{pmatrix} \boldsymbol{\Sigma}_{\mathbf{XX}}^{-1} & \mathbf{0} \\ \mathbf{0} & \boldsymbol{\Sigma}_{\mathbf{D}_1\mathbf{D}_1|\mathbf{X}}^{-1} \end{pmatrix}\right] \tag{29}$$

PRETIS *ET AL.*

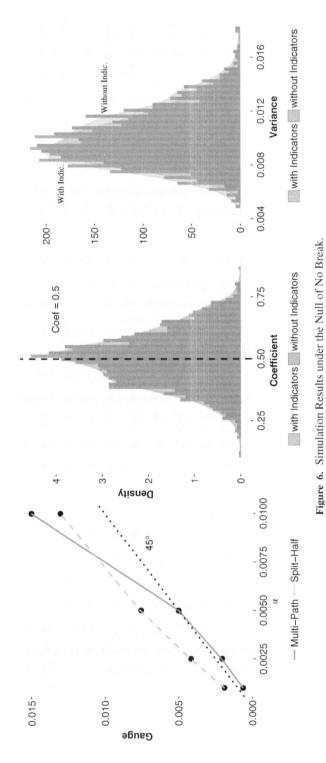

Figure 6. Simulation Results under the Null of No Break.

Notes: (Left) Proportion of irrelevant retained break functions (gauge) using split-half and multi-path selection for varying α when there is no break. (Middle and Right) Simulated distributions and densities of coefficient $\hat{\beta}$ (true $\beta = 0.5$) on forced parameter x_t; with (orange/shaded light) – anc without (purple/shaded dark) – a full set of break functions.

The distribution of the parameters $\widehat{\beta^*}$ on the correct variables $\mathbf{X}$ is unaffected by the inclusion of the orthogonalized break indicators $\mathbf{D}_1$ when there is no break. The equivalent result holds when the second half of break indicators $\mathbf{D}_2$ is included and the resulting union of retained indicators from $\mathbf{D}_1$ and $\mathbf{D}_2$ given that $N < T$. Orthogonalization relative to shifts, however, is not necessary for estimation in practice. Figure 6 shows the simulated distribution of $\widehat{\beta}$ for a single x_t when a full set of break functions is included and selected at $\alpha = 0.005$ (orange/shaded light) and when break functions are not included (purple/shaded dark). The distribution of $\widehat{\beta}$ is unaffected by the saturation of a full set of break functions. In practice, the main risk is the spurious retention of break indicators, but this can be controlled through a conservative selection mechanism (low α).

3. Empirical Illustration for Climate Time Series: Detection of Volcanic Eruptions from Simulated Model Surface Air Temperature Data

Large volcanic eruptions that inject significant amounts of sulphate aerosols into the stratosphere cause short-lived (multi-year) radiative imbalances that induce surface cooling. Over the course of the last several millennia there have been numerous eruptions that have had impacts on global mean temperatures. Identifying their climatic fingerprint is an important scientific endeavour that relies critically on the robust characterization of the timing and magnitude of past volcanism. An accurate understanding of the impact of past eruptions can lead to more accurate estimates of the effect of stratospheric aerosols – to guide policy from geoengineering to pollution controls. Records of climatically relevant events primarily rely on sulphur deposits in ice cores (see, e.g. Gao *et al.*, 2008; Crowley and Unterman, 2012). However, there remains uncertainty in the precise timing, magnitude and climatic impact of past volcanic activity (Schmidt *et al.*, 2011; Anchukaitis *et al.*, 2012; Brohan *et al.*, 2012; Mann *et al.*, 2012; Baillie and McAneney, 2015). Statistical methods such as the break detection methodology presented herein can therefore augment previous volcanic reconstruction estimates by providing additional characterizations of the timing and magnitude of temperature responses to volcanic eruptions when coupled with large-scale proxy estimates of past temperature variability, for example, from tree-rings. As a synthetic evaluation of the performance of the break-indicator saturation method, we search for volcanic eruptions in surface air temperature output from model simulations. While there is some disagreement on the timing, magnitude and climatic impact of real eruptions over the past several millennia, the present simulation is forced with deterministic (known, imposed) eruptions. It therefore can function as a useful tool for assessing the detection efficacy of the proposed statistical methodology in real-world scenarios when the timing and exact DGP of volcanic eruptions are uncertain.

For our empirical illustration, we use the NH mean surface air temperature from the historical simulation of the National Center for Atmospheric Research (NCAR) Community Climate System Model 4 (CCSM4) and the Last Millennium (LM) simulation (Landrum *et al.*, 2013). These simulations were made available as part of the Coupled and Paleoclimate Model Intercomparison Projects Phases 5 and 3 (CMIP5/PMIP3), respectively (Taylor *et al.*, 2012). Collectively, the two simulations span the period 850–2005 C.E. To imitate potential proxy reconstructions (e.g. tree-ring based), temperatures for extratropical land areas (30°–90° N) were extracted from the model and only summer months (June–August) were used to build annual averages. This time period is expected to show the strongest cooling in response to an eruption (e.g. Zanchettin *et al.*, 2013 argue for a winter-warming effect) and is associated with the seasonal sampling window of many proxies such as dendroclimatic records. Temperatures

are reported as anomalies relative to the 1850–1999 mean. The model is forced with the volcanic reconstruction by Gao *et al.* (2008) that reports volcanic activity as stratospheric sulphate loadings in teragrams (Tg). While the model is forced with multiple radiative forcing
conditions (e.g. solar irradiance, greenhouse gases, volcanoes, land cover changes and anthropogenic aerosol changes), for the present experiments we treat these as unknown and work with
the univariate NH mean temperature series, although multivariate models with more forcing
variables could improve the detection algorithm. For a real-world scenario, however, estimates
of climate-forcing and -sensitivity are uncertain (IPCC, 2013) and may prove to be of limited
use in explaining non-volcanic temperature variation in proxy reconstructions, particularly in
the presence of changes in measurement (see, e.g. Pretis and Hendry, 2013).

3.1 *Simulation Setup*

We design a break function to capture the temperature response to a large-scale volcanic eruption using a simple zero-dimensional energy balance model (EBM) that equates incoming to
outgoing energy derived from simple physics-based models of climate (see, e.g. section 1 in
Rypdal, 2012, section 1 in Schwartz, 2012 or Pretis, 2015a for linking system EBMs to econometric system models)

$$C\frac{dT'}{dt} = F - \theta T' \tag{30}$$

where θ is the climate feedback, C is the heat capacity, T' the temperature deviation from
steady state (similar to the measured temperature anomaly as a departure from a long-term
average) and F denotes radiative forcing (the variable that in our system describes the volcanic
shock). The feedback response time of the model is given by $\tau = \frac{C}{\theta}$. Assuming a volcanic
forcing effect of an impulse injection of stratospheric aerosols of F decaying exponentially
at rate $-1/\gamma$ yields the following functional form of a volcanic function for the associated
temperature response:[14]

$$T'_t = d_t = \begin{cases} \frac{1}{C}e^{\frac{-\theta}{C}t}F\left(\frac{\theta}{C} - \frac{1}{\gamma}\right)^{-1}\left[e^{t\left(\frac{\theta}{C} - \frac{1}{\gamma}\right)} - 1\right] & t \leq L \\ 0 & t < T_1, t > L \end{cases} \tag{31}$$

Intuitively, equation (31) states that a volcanic eruption through F leads to a sudden drop
in temperatures, followed by a smooth reversion back to the original equilibrium. Different
parameter calibrations are explored in the simulation section below. The main results are reported for a normalized temperature response where the feedback response time is set to 1,
and the length of the volcanic impact is set to $L = 3$ to approximate the theory. The decay
of stratospheric aerosols is modelled as $\gamma = 0.5$ (function *a*) and $\gamma = 3$ (function *b*) to capture
one-period and two-period cooling, respectively. On visual inspection (see Figure 7) these calibrations closely match the average-model response based on a superposed epoch analysis of
all large-scale volcanic eruptions in the climate model (Mass and Portman, 1989). The average model response in temperature is a drop by approximately 1–1.5 °C, followed by a smooth
reversion to the previous mean over a 3–4 year period. While Gao *et al.* (2008) estimate the
retention time for sulphate aerosols to be 2–3 years, a climatic perturbation of 4 years is in
line with findings by Landrum *et al.* (2013). It is important to emphasize that the in-sample
response to a volcanic eruption is not used to design the break function – the method is not
trained and evaluated on the same set of observations.

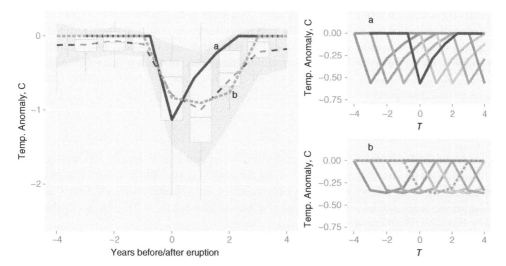

Figure 7. Superposed Epoch Analysis of the Model Temperature Response to Simulated Volcanic Eruptions and Sets of Volcanic Functions.

Notes: (Left) Superposed epoch analysis (Mass and Portman, 1989) of NH mean model temperature response to volcanoes with sulphate emissions >20 Tg (42 events, dashed) with 1 sample standard deviation bands (shaded) and distribution over volcanoes (box-plots). Approximate temperature response using a zero-dimensional energy balance model (EBM) used as volcanic function (a) is given as solid and function (b) in as dotted. (Right) Sets of EBM-based volcanic break functions for the two different specifications (a) (top) and (b) (bottom) to approximate the temperature response in years T relative to an eruption at $t = 0$.

In a more theoretical approach, which avoids particular shape parameters, a single peak (impulse) could be followed by autoregressive reversion to the mean where we search over a full set of impulses and full set of breaking autoregressive coefficients.

The DGP for the response variable NH temperature (T_t) is

$$T_t = f(X_t, V_t) + \epsilon_t \tag{32}$$

To simulate sampling uncertainty of a proxy-based reconstruction, we generate 100 replications of the outcome by adding $\epsilon_t \sim IN(0, \sigma_\epsilon^2)$ to the NH mean temperature. The main results here are presented for simulations setting $\sigma_\epsilon = 0.2$ which is half the sample standard deviation of the NH time series of 0.4: the effect of the magnitude of noise is explored in Figure 9. The function $f(X_t, V_t)$ mapping volcanic, V_t, and other forcing, X_t, on to temperature is unknown and the observed forcing variables V_t and X_t are equally treated as unknown. As a proof of concept, we consider two models (intercept-only, and AR(1) with intercept)[15] to detect eruptions:

$$y_t = \mu + \gamma' \mathbf{d}_t + v_t \tag{33}$$

$$y_t = \rho y_{t-1} + \mu + \gamma' \mathbf{d}_t + v_t \tag{34}$$

where $\mathbf{d}_t$ is a full set of volcanic break functions (31) to be selected over.[16] To reduce computational requirements due to the varying simulation setup, the full-sample is split into 10 subsamples of $T = 115$ observations each.[17] There is little difference between full-sample and subsampling performance aside from computational speed (the supplementary material provides the results for a full-sample simulation). Selection is conducted at $\alpha = 0.01$ implying an expected gauge of 1% (approximately one break function spuriously retained per sub-sample). Higher retention of break functions can be an indicator of model misspecification. Simulations are evaluated based on the retention frequency of known individual volcanic events (potency), the average potency over all volcanoes and the proportion of spurious eruptions detected (gauge).

3.2 *Illustration Results*

Figure 8 and Tables 4 and 5 show the results of detected volcanic events in 100 replications of the modelled NH mean temperature[18] using the model (a) volcanic function. The retained volcanic breaks coincide predominantly with the simulated volcanic eruptions. Few spurious volcanoes are detected, and those that are spurious exhibit retention frequencies drastically lower than those of volcanoes used to force the model.

Most large-scale simulated volcanic eruptions are detected consistently: 74% of all larger (>20 Tg) NH eruptions are detected on average within an interval of ±1 year (57% of all global eruptions, many of which appear to have had little impact on NH temperatures). Consistent with the basic analytical results presented in the previous section, the intervals of selection around the correct break dates are small. While increasing the band from 0 to 1 generally yields an increase in potency, outside of ±1 year there is little difference (see Table 4). An uncertainty in break dates of ±1 year can be the result of a monthly dated volcanic forcing record coupled with an annually dated temperature record, for example, a December eruption will mainly affect the following year. The season of sulphur injection – before or after summer – can cause offsets in the timing of the temperature response. Equally there may be regional sampling biases based on the construction of the NH mean surface air temperature.

Augmenting the designed break functions (a) by an autoregressive model results in nearly similar potency and gauge relative to the baseline model using just a constant (see Table 4 and Figure 9).

The retention frequency of volcanic functions increases with the magnitude of sulphate emissions of the volcanic eruption (Figure 9). While the overall potency for all volcanoes in the NH within a 1-year interval is 33%, this increases to 74% when larger volcanic eruptions over 20 Tg are considered. Given that potency covers all of the volcanic forcing, much of which is small in magnitude, the result is unsurprising. In particular, the lower potency for small eruptions is not driven by an inconsistency in selection of the same volcano over multiple experiments, but rather in the variation in temperature response between volcanoes. Eruptions in 1641 (Parker) and 1600 (Huaynaputina) are detected 100% of the time while the eruption of 1783 (Laki) is not detected in any of the outcomes. In contrast to most of the other volcanoes, Laki is a high-latitude volcano. Because the CCSM4 model uses spatially resolved sulphate estimates, this eruption only affects the northernmost areas and causes only a minor hemispheric cooling of $-0.15°$, which is much lower in magnitude than that of any of the other major volcanic events (see Figure 7).[19]

Equally, the potency is affected by the chosen standard deviation of the noise process added to the model mean. The main results here are reported for added noise with a standard deviation of half the sample standard deviation. Figure 9 shows the potency for varying levels of noise.

The proportion of spuriously detected volcanoes (gauge) at around 0.02 is close to the nominal significance level ($1/T \approx 0.01$). The fact that it is slightly higher is likely due to the misspecification of the model, which is only run on a constant (including an autoregressive term

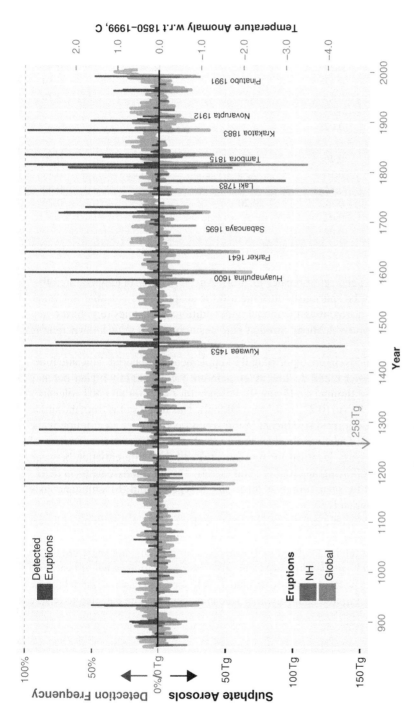

Figure 8. Detected Model Volcanic Eruptions from 850 to 2005.

Notes: Detected (top) volcanic eruptions in the model temperature series from 850 to 2005 using function (a) modelling a single-period drop followed by a reversion to the mean together with an intercept. Bar height indicates detection frequency [0, 100%] across 100 simulations. Stacked sulphur deposition record (bottom) used to force model temperatures are shown for Northern Hemisphere (blue/shaded dark) and global measurements (orange/shaded light) in Tg. Simulated model mean temperature anomalies used to detect the above volcanic eruptions are shown in grey. Mean NH surface temperature data are taken from the Last Millenium and historical simulation of the NCAR CCSM4 model as part of the CMIP5/PMIP3 data archive.

Table 4. Potency and Gauge for Volcanic Functions (a).

Function (a)	T	$t = T \pm 1$	$t = T \pm 2$	$t = T \pm 3$
Potency NH Tg > 20	0.45	0.74	0.74	0.74
Potency NH Tg > 0	0.17	0.33	0.34	0.35
Potency Global Tg > 20	0.32	0.57	0.59	0.59
Potency Global Tg > 0	0.11	0.22	0.25	0.26
Gauge NH	0.02			
Gauge Global	0.02			
Function (a) + AR(1)				
Potency NH Tg > 20	0.46	0.70	0.70	0.70
Potency NH Tg > 0	0.16	0.30	0.31	0.31
Potency Global Tg > 20	0.31	0.52	0.54	0.54
Potency Global Tg > 0	0.11	0.20	0.22	0.23
Gauge NH	0.02			
Gauge Global	0.02			

in the alternate specification) and set of break functions. Any variability in temperature other than volcanic eruptions may be spuriously attributed to the shape of the volcanic functions. This could be controlled by augmenting the model with additional dynamics (e.g. further autoregressive terms, long-term fluctuations through sine-cosine processes) or known forcing series.

Results for volcanic functions (b) are reported in the supplementary material. Volcanic functions (b) that capture the slower initial decline in temperature yield a slightly higher potency when measured at the precise timing (see Figure 9). Potency for $t = T_i$ for all i NH volcanoes using (b) is 0.32 versus 0.17 for (a) (0.23 vs. 0.11 for Global). This result stems from the single drop in function (a) often being most significant in the second period after an eruption if the cooling lasts for two periods. Once we consider the interval of $T_i \pm 1$ years or volcanoes of larger scale the results are nearly identical for functions (a) and (b). Differentiation between one or two-period cooling following an eruption, and thereby further improvements in detection, could be implemented by searching over functions of type (a) and (b) simultaneously controlling the gauge appropriately.

In summary, large-scale volcanic eruptions can consistently be detected within a ± 1 year interval. Even though the model is likely misspecified when using only a constant, few spurious volcanic eruptions are retained. The signal-to-noise ratio remains, however, crucial in detection. When the method is applied to real-world proxy reconstructions where lower temperature spikes and higher noise levels can be expected, a well-specified baseline model for the temperature process will be required against which volcanic events can be detected to ensure a high power of detection.

3.2.1 *Forecasting during Breaks*

While breaks (such as volcanic eruptions) are by their nature stochastic, using a deterministic approach through a full set of break functions allows us to account for the underlying breaks and model the responses deterministically. This can improve forecasts during breaks if the break function is well specified. Once the break is observed (in this case a volcanic eruption),

Table 5. Potency of Detection of Volcanic Eruptions >20 Tg using Volcanic Functions (a) for Intervals $t = T \pm 1, 2, 3$.

NH Volcano	Tg	Potency $t = T$	$t = T \pm 1$	$t = T \pm 2$	$t = T \pm 3$
939	31.83	0	0.02	0.02	0.03
1167	29.535	0	0	0	0
1176	45.761	0.06	1	1	1
1227	58.644	0.01	0.02	0.06	0.06
1258	145.8	1	1	1	1
1284	23.053	0.14	0.97	0.97	0.97
1452	44.6	0.3	1	1	1
1459	21.925	0.26	0.98	0.98	0.98
1584	24.228	0.11	0.77	0.8	0.8
1600	46.077	1	1	1	1
1641	33.805	1	1	1	1
1719	31.483	0.75	1	1	1
1783	92.964	0.02	0.02	0.03	0.05
1809	27.558	0.67	0.99	0.99	0.99
1815	58.694	0.91	1	1	1
1835	26.356	1	1	1	1

Global Volcano	Tg	Potency $t = T$	$t = T \pm 1$	$t = T \pm 2$	$t = T \pm 3$
854	21.387	0	0.02	0.03	0.03
870	22.276	0	0.25	0.25	0.25
901	21.283	0	0.34	0.5	0.54
939	33.128	0	0.02	0.02	0.03
1001	21.011	0	0.4	0.4	0.4
1167	52.114	0	0	0	0
1176	45.761	0.06	1	1	1
1227	67.522	0.01	0.02	0.06	0.06
1258	257.91	1	1	1	1
1275	63.723	0	0.06	0.08	0.08
1284	54.698	0.14	0.97	0.97	0.97
1341	31.136	0	0	0	0.01
1452	137.5	0.3	1	1	1
1459	21.925	0.26	0.98	0.98	0.98
1584	24.228	0.11	0.77	0.8	0.8
1600	56.591	1	1	1	1
1641	51.594	1	1	1	1
1693	27.098	0	0	0.03	0.07
1719	31.483	0.75	1	1	1
1783	92.964	0.02	0.02	0.03	0.05
1809	53.74	0.67	0.99	0.99	0.99
1815	109.72	0.91	1	1	1
1835	40.16	1	1	1	1
1883	21.864	0	0.98	0.98	0.98
1963	20.87	0	0.43	0.63	0.63
1991	30.094	0	0.48	0.48	0.48

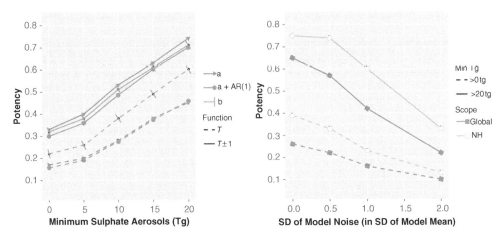

Figure 9. (Left) Detection Potency of NH Eruptions for Given Minimum Sulphate Emissions and Timing for Functions (a), (a) + AR(1) and (b) at the Precise Timing T (Dashed) and in the Interval of $T \pm 1$ (Solid); and (Right) Detection for Varying Levels of Noise Added in the Simulation for Function (a) for All Eruptions (Dashed) and Large Eruptions over 20 Tg (Solid).

a forecasting model can be augmented with a break indicator where the magnitude is determined through estimation in the first break period. This indicator then acts as a continuous intercept correction, thereby improving the forecast performance during the break. To illustrate this concept, Figure 10 shows a 1-step forecast for NH model mean temperatures following the simulated 1641 eruption, together with the root-mean-squared (RMSE) forecast errors for all NH (>20 Tg) model eruptions based on volcanic function (a). Using volcanic indicators to forecast through the breaks yields on average a lower forecast RMSE (RMSE = 0.51) when compared to a simple AR(1) model (RMSE = 0.71) or even a robust forecasting device (RMSE = 0.66) (Clements and Hendry, 1999).[20] Crucially, this depends on the correct specification of the break function – for volcanic eruptions further improvements could be achieved by switching to volcanic function (b) if the initial cooling lasts for two periods. Detection of breaks based on theory-informed break functions can therefore act as a robust forecasting device through a continuous intercept correction from climate to economic time series.

4. Conclusion

Saturating a regression model with a full set of designed break functions, and removing all but significant ones through a general-to-specific algorithm yields unbiased estimates of the break magnitude and time. By initializing the model with a full set of break functions many of the shortcomings associated with a forward selection or specific-to-general approach in break detection can be avoided. Analytical properties and non-centralities can be derived for any deterministic break function and can be extended to breaks in random variables when interacted with the deterministic break specifications. The break detection procedure exhibits desirable properties both in the presence of breaks (stable potency across multiple breaks) and under the null hypothesis of no breaks where the spurious retention of break functions can be controlled through a chosen significance level of selection. The multi-path algorithm (*Autometrics*) outperforms shrinkage-based estimators, especially when facing multiple breaks. We provide

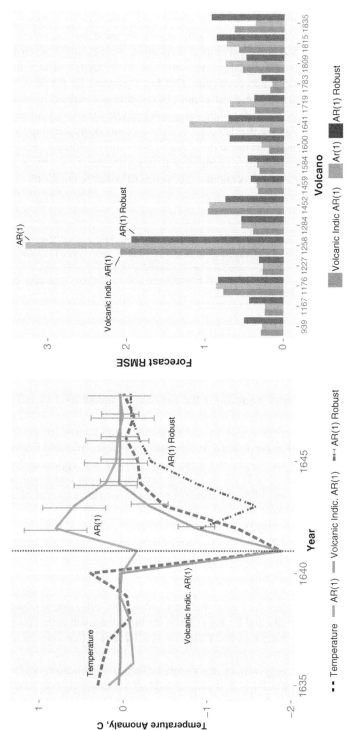

Figure 10. One-Step Forecasts through Volcanic Eruptions using Break Indicators.

Notes: (Left) Forecast performance across different methods: model mean temperature during the simulated 1641 eruption (dashed), one-step forecasts from 1641 onwards are shown for using an AR(1) model with volcanic indicator (purple/shaded dark), an AR(1) model without a volcanic indicator (orange/shaded light) and a robust AR(1) forecast (green/dot-dashed) (Clements and Hendry, 1999). Models are estimated from 1605 until 1641. (Right) one-step forecast root-mean-squared-error (RMSE) over all NH model volcanic eruptions (>20 Tg) for an AR(1) model with volcanic indicator (purple/left), without (orange/middle) and robust AR(1) forecast (green/right). Using volcanic indicators, on average, improves the forecast performance during the break period. However, when no break occurs (little to no temperature response), using a break indicator can result in higher RMSE as seen, for example, for the 1783 model Laki eruption.

some initial insight into uncertainty on the break date by assessing the retention probability of mistimed break estimators. Break-indicator saturation appears to be effective for detecting large-scale temperature responses to volcanic eruptions. This was shown using surface air temperature output from a combined LM and historical climate simulation. Statistically searching over a set of break functions consistently detects large eruptions from the simulated surface air temperatures without prior knowledge of their occurrence. This holds promise for future volcanic detection efforts using real-world proxy reconstructions of temperature variability over the last several millennia. More broadly, break detection using designed functions and indicator saturation provide a framework to analyse the detection of breaks of any designed shape at any point in time, with applications ranging from the detection of previously unknown events (such as shifts in time series due to measurement changes or policy impacts), to acting as a robust forecasting device during breaks – from economic recessions to volcanic eruptions.

Acknowledgements

We thank Vanessa Berenguer-Rico, Guillaume Chevillon, Niels Haldrup, Eric Hillebrand, Søren Johansen, Katarina Juselius, Oleg Kitov, John Muellbauer, Bent Nielsen, Max Roser, Timo Teräsvirta, and anonymous referees for helpful comments and suggestions. Financial support from the Open Society Foundations, the Oxford Martin School, the Robertson Foundation, and the British Academy, is gratefully acknowledged. LDEO contribution number 7983.

Notes

1. For example, SIS exhibits higher power in detecting step shifts than using impulses alone – see Castle *et al.* (2015b).
2. For k breaking variables, this implies augmenting the full-sample model by k $(T \times T)$ matrices.
3. While the framework presented here provides an encompassing specification for many break types, the construction of $\mathbf{D}$ is not limited to this particular case. Additional sets of specifications for step shifts are considered in Castle *et al.* (2015b). The appeal of the specification here is that the definition of $\mathbf{D}$ allows for a general framework under which properties can be analysed where many of the previously proposed cases are a special case of $\mathbf{D}$.
4. In a simple split-half analysis, there may be an identification problem if the sample-split coincides perfectly with a structural break. This is overcome by varying the block partitioning as is done in the software implementations of the algorithm.
5. See the supplementary material for proof.
6. Proof given in the supplementary material.
7. In practice, selection bias can be controlled using bias correction after orthogonalization of the selected regressors – see Hendry and Krolzig (2005) for the orthogonal case, Pretis (2015b) for bias correction of step functions and Castle *et al.* (2015a) for bias correction with correlated variables.
8. The split-half approach is not the only way of analysing the theory of indicator saturation: rather than splitting the functions into a first and second half, alternatively one could consider including every other break function in two sets such that $\mathbf{D}_1$ covers breaks at $t = 1, 3, 5 \ldots$ and $\mathbf{D}_2$ covers breaks at $t = 2, 4, 6 \ldots$. Retention frequencies in this setup can be derived using the results in Section 2.1.3.

9. While our analysis concentrates on small-sample properties, the asymptotic rates of convergence will generally depend on the specification of the break function – varying scaling to obtain non-degenerate limit distributions may therefore be required. In the case of step functions $(d_t = 1, L = T)$ and the simple no-intercept case, pre-multiplying the estimator by $\sqrt{T}$ yields asymptotic normality for the break estimator when $T^{-1} \sum_{t=T_1}^{T_1+L-1} d_t^2 = T^{-1}L \to \tau$ as $T \to \infty$. In other words, the ratio of break length to the sample size remains constant as the sample size increases – this can be interpreted as obtaining more information on the break period or sampling at higher frequencies as $T \to \infty$. A similar analysis can be applied to the volcanic functions considered here, where either the break length scales with the sample size, or alternatively the magnitude increases similar to the asymptotic analysis for a single impulse in Doornik *et al.* (1998).

10. For a volcanic break, λ denotes the entire temperature response over the specified length L, thus the trough will be less than λ. For the present specification of $L = 3$, the initial trough of the function equals 0.58λ.

11. All simulations and applications using the multi-path search *Autometrics* are coded using the *Ox* programming language (Doornik, 2009b). Simulations using the Lasso are coded using the package `glmnet` (Friedman *et al.*, 2010) in *R*.

12. Results of high gauge for high significance levels (e.g. $\alpha \geq 0.05$) are consistent with previous results found by Bergamelli and Urga (2013) for step functions. Once a large number of spurious breaks is retained, it becomes more likely to keep additional spurious breaks. The results for the gauge in Table 3 are consistent with the distributional theory for the gauge in Johansen and Nielsen (2016).

13. Where $T^{-1}\mathbf{X}'\mathbf{X} \overset{P}{\to} \Sigma_{XX}$ for stochastic $\mathbf{X}$, and $\mathbf{D}_1$ is scaled such that either the break length scales with the sample size, or alternatively the break magnitude increases such that $T^{-1}\mathbf{D}_1'\mathbf{D}_1 \to \Sigma_{\mathbf{D}_1}$ is constant, and for stochastic $\mathbf{X}$ it holds that $T^{-1}(\hat{\mathbf{u}}'\hat{\mathbf{u}}) \overset{P}{\to} \Sigma_{\mathbf{D}_1\mathbf{D}_1|X}$ where $\hat{\mathbf{u}} = \mathbf{D}_1 - \mathbf{X}\hat{\Gamma}$ from orthogonalization regressions. See the supplementary material for a proof based on Hendry and Johansen (2015).

14. See the supplementary material for a derivation. For break detection, the function is normalized to sum to 1 over L.

15. Unless otherwise stated, results refer to the intercept-only case. The intercept term and the autoregressive terms are not selected over.

16. Given the specification of the volcanic break function and if σ_ϵ was the only noise added to the DGP, then the approximate expected non-centrality for a single unknown break using (17) is $\lambda(0.2\sqrt{3.7}))^{-1} \approx 0.4^{-1}\lambda$ where λ is the full temperature response following a volcanic eruption. Since the specified volcanic function has an approximate trough of $0.58\ \lambda$, a temperature drop of $1°$ after a volcanic eruption implies that overall $\lambda \approx 1.7$. Thus in absence of additional noise and for a single volcanic break with an immediate temperature response of $1°$, the expected t-statistic is approximately ≈ 4.3. The analytical probability of detecting this eruption is roughly: $P(|t| > c_\alpha) \approx 0.96$ for $\alpha = 0.01$. Large eruptions should be consistently detected if the break function is correctly specified and if σ_ϵ was the only source of noise.

17. The total sample size is $T = 1155$, resulting in nine subsamples of $T = 115$ observations and one subsample of $T = 120$ observations. Significance levels are scaled accordingly. Using a 3 GHz processor, the subsample approach requires ≈ 5 seconds to cover the entire sample for one replication (across 10 subsamples), compared to ≈ 5 minutes for one replication using a full-sample approach.

18. Retained volcanic functions with positive coefficients are dropped since these likely constitute positive outliers. The focus here lies on the detection of volcanic events which have a negative temperature response.

19. There is considerable uncertainty on the impact of the Laki eruption, for example, Schmidt *et al.* (2012) find the observed NH peak temperature response to Laki to be around $-1°$, suggesting that the LM simulation used here may not reflect the entire impact of the eruption, while D'Arrigo *et al.* (2011) argue that Winter impacts were likely independent of the Laki eruption. Notably, the eruption's noxious fumes at the time were discussed in White's (1789) treatment of phenology.

20. The robust forecasting device is based on first differences using the forecasting model for $T + 1|T$ given by: $y_{T+1|T} = y_T + \hat{\rho}\Delta y_T$ where ρ is estimated using an AR(1) model. No error bars are shown on the robust forecast in Figure 10 (dot-dashed) due to the non-standard distribution of the forecast.

References

Anchukaitis, K.J., Breitenmoser, P., Briffa, K.R., Buchwal, A., Büntgen, U., Cook, E.R., D'Arrigo, R.D., Esper, J., Evans, M.N., Frank, D., Grudd, H., Gunnarson, B.E., Hughes, M.K., Kirdyanov, A.V., Körner, C., Krusic, P.J., Luckman, B., Melvin, T.M., Salzer, M.W., Shashkin, A.V., Timmreck, C., Vaganov, E.A. and Wilson, R.J.S. (2012) Tree rings and volcanic cooling. *Nature Geoscience* 5(12): 836–837.

Bai, J. and Perron, P. (1998) Estimating and testing linear models with multiple structural changes. *Econometrica* 66: 47–78.

Bai, J. and Perron, P. (2003) Computation and analysis of multiple structural change models. *Journal of Applied Econometrics* 18: 1–22.

Baillie, M. and McAneney, J. (2015) Tree ring effects and ice core acidities clarify the volcanic record of the first millennium. *Climate of the Past* 11(1): 105–114.

Bergamelli, M. and Urga, G. (2013) Detecting multiple structural breaks: a Monte Carlo study and application to the Fisher equation for US. Discussion Paper, Cass Business School, London.

Brohan, P., Allan, R., Freeman, E., Wheeler, D., Wilkinson, C. and Williamson, F. (2012) Constraining the temperature history of the past millennium using early instrumental observations. *Climate of the Past Discussions* 8(3): 1653–1685.

Castle, J.L. and Shephard, N. (2009) *The Methodology and Practice of Econometrics*. Oxford: Oxford University Press.

Castle, J.L., Doornik, J.A. and Hendry, D.F. (2011) Evaluating automatic model selection. *Journal of Time Series Econometrics* 3(1). doi:10.2202/1941-1928.1097.

Castle, J.L., Doornik, J.A. and Hendry, D.F. (2015a) Bias correction after selection with correlated variables. University of Oxford Economics Discussion Paper.

Castle, J.L., Doornik, J.A., Hendry, D.F. and Pretis, F. (2015b) Detecting location shifts by step-indicator saturation during model selection. *Econometrics* 3: 240–264.

Clements, M.P. and Hendry, D.F. (1999) *Forecasting Non-Stationary Economic Time Series*. Cambridge, MA: MIT Press.

Cox, D.R. and Snell, E.J. (1974) The choice of variables in observational studies. *Applied Statistics* 23(1): 51–59.

Crowley, T.J. and Unterman, M.B. (2012) Technical details concerning development of a 1200-yr proxy index for global volcanism. *Earth System Science Data Discussions* 5(1): 1–28.

D'Arrigo, R., Seager, R., Smerdon, J.E., LeGrande, A.N., and Cook, E.R. (2011) The anomalous winter of 1783–1784: Was the Laki eruption or an analog of the 2009–2010 winter to blame? *Geophysical Research Letters*, 38. L05706, doi:10.1029/2011GL046696.

Doornik, J.A. (2009a) *Autometrics*. In J.L. Castle and N. Shephard (eds.), (pp. 88–121). Oxford: Oxford University Press.

Doornik, J.A. (2009b) *An Object-Oriented Matrix Programming Language Ox 6*. London: Timberlake Consultants Press.

Doornik, J.A. (2010) Econometric model selection with more variables than observations. Working paper, Economics Department, University of Oxford.

Doornik, J.A., Hendry, D.F. and Nielsen, B. (1998) Inference in cointegrated models: UK M1 revisited. *Journal of Economic Surveys* 12: 533–572.

Efron, B., Hastie, T., Johnstone, I., Tibshirani, R. (2004) Least angle regression. *Annals of Statistics* 32(2): 407–499.

Elliott, G. and Müller, U.K. (2007) Confidence sets for the date of a single break in linear time series regressions. *Journal of Econometrics* 141(2): 1196–1218.

Epprecht, C., Guegan, D. and Veiga, Á. (2013) Comparing variable selection techniques for linear regression: Lasso and autometrics. Documents de travail du Centre d'Economie de la Sorbonne 2013.80.

Ericsson, N.R. (2012) Detecting crises, jumps, and changes in regime. Working Paper, Board of Governors of the Federal Reserve System, Washington, DC.

Estrada, F., Perron, P. and Martínez-López, B. (2013) Statistically derived contributions of diverse human influences to twentieth-century temperature changes. *Nature Geoscience* 6: 1050–1055.

Friedman, J., Hastie, T. and Tibshirani, R. (2010) Regularization paths for generalized linear models via coordinate descent. *Journal of Statistical Software* 33(1): 1–22. Retrieved from http://www.jstatsoft.org/v33/i01/

Gao, C., Robock, A. and Ammann, C. (2008) Volcanic forcing of climate over the past 1500 years: an improved ice core-based index for climate models. *Journal of Geophysical Research: Atmospheres* 113(D23).

González, A. and Teräsvirta, T. (2008) Modelling autoregressive processes with a shifting mean. *Studies in Nonlinear Dynamics & Econometrics* 12(1): 1–24.

Hendry, D.F. (1995) *Dynamic Econometrics*. Oxford: Oxford University Press.

Hendry, D.F. and Doornik, J.A. (2014) *Empirical Model Discovery and Theory Evaluation*. Cambridge MA: MIT Press.

Hendry, D.F. and Johansen, S. (2015) Model discovery and Trygve Haavelmo's legacy. *Econometric Theory* 31: 93–114.

Hendry, D.F. and Krolzig, H.M. (2005) The properties of automatic Gets modelling. *Economic Journal* 115: C32–C61.

Hendry, D.F. and Pretis, F. (2013) Anthropogenic influences on atmospheric CO_2. In R. Fouquet (ed.), *Handbook on Energy and Climate Change* (pp. 287–326). Cheltenham: Edward Elgar.

Hendry, D.F., Johansen, S. and Santos, C. (2008) Automatic selection of indicators in a fully saturated regression. *Computational Statistics* 23: 337–339.

Hoover, K.D. and Perez, S.J. (1999) Data mining reconsidered: encompassing and the general-to-specific approach to specification search. *Econometrics Journal* 2: 167–191.

Huang, J., Horowitz, J.L. and Ma, S. (2008) Asymptotic properties of bridge estimators in sparse high-dimensional regression models. *Annals of Statistics* 36(2): 587–613.

IPCC (2013) *Fifth Assessment Report: Climate Change 2013: Working Group I Report: The Physical Science Basis*. Geneva: IPCC. Retrieved from https://www.ipcc.ch/report/ar5/wg1/. (accessed on February 2015).

Johansen, S. and Nielsen, B. (2009) *An analysis of the indicator saturation estimator as a robust regression estimator*. In J.L. Castle and N. Shephard (eds.) (pp. 1–36). Oxford: Oxford University Press.

Johansen, S. and Nielsen, B. (2013) Outlier detection in regression using an iterated one-step approximation to the Huber-skip estimator. *Econometrics* 1(1): 53–70.

Johansen, S. and Nielsen, B. (2016) Asymptotic theory of outlier detection algorithms for linear time series regression models (with discussion). *Scandinavian Journal of Statistics* 43(2): 321–348.

Kelly, P.M. and Sear, C.B. (1984) Climatic impact of explosive volcanic eruptions. *Nature* 311(5988): 740–743.

Kitov, O. and Tabor, M.N. (2015) Detecting structural breaks in linear models: a variable selection approach using multiplicative indicator saturation. *University of Oxford Economics Discussion Paper*.

Kock, A.B. and Teräsvirta, T. (2015) Forecasting macroeconomic variables using neural network models and three automated model selection techniques. *Econometric Reviews, Forthcoming*. doi:10.1080/07474938.2015.1035163.

Landrum, L., Otto-Bliesner, B.L., Wahl, E.R., Conley, A., Lawrence, P.J., Rosenbloom, N. and Teng, H. (2013) Last millennium climate and its variability in CCSM4. *Journal of Climate* 26(4): 1085–1111.

Mann, M.E., Fuentes, J.D. and Rutherford, S. (2012) Underestimation of volcanic cooling in tree-ring-based reconstructions of hemispheric temperatures. *Nature Geoscience* 5: 202–205.

Mass, C.F. and Portman, D.A. (1989) Major volcanic eruptions and climate: a critical evaluation. *Journal of Climate* 2(6): 566–593.

Perron, P. (2006) Dealing with structural breaks. In *Palgrave Handbook of Econometrics* (Vol. 1, pp. 278–352). London: MacMillan.

Perron, P. and Yabu, T. (2009) Testing for shifts in trend with an integrated or stationary noise component. *Journal of Business & Economic Statistics* 27(3): 369–396.

Perron, P. and Zhu, X. (2005) Structural breaks with deterministic and stochastic trends. *Journal of Econometrics* 129(1): 65–119.

Pretis, F. (2015a) Econometric models of climate systems: the equivalence of two-component energy balance models and cointegrated VARs. *University of Oxford Economics Discussion Paper 750*.

Pretis, F. (2015b) Testing for time-varying predictive accuracy using bias-corrected indicator saturation. *University of Oxford Economics Discussion Paper*.

Pretis, F. and Allen, M. (2013) Climate science: breaks in trends. *Nature Geoscience* 6: 992–993.

Pretis, F. and Hendry, D. (2013) Some hazards in econometric modelling of climate change. *Earth System Dynamics* 4(2): 375–384.

Pretis, F., Mann, M.L. and Kaufmann, R.K. (2015a) Testing competing models of the temperature hiatus: assessing the effects of conditioning variables and temporal uncertainties through sample-wide break detection. *Climatic Change* 131(4): 705–718.

Pretis, F., Sucarrat, G. and Reade, J. (2016) General-to-specific modelling and indicator saturation with the R package gets. University of Oxford Economics Discussion Paper 794.

Rypdal, K. (2012) Global temperature response to radiative forcing: solar cycle versus volcanic eruptions. *Journal of Geophysical Research: Atmospheres* 117(D6).

Schmidt, G.A., Jungclaus, J.H., Ammann, C.M., Bard, E., Braconnot, P., Crowley, T., Delaygue, G., Joos, F., Krivova, N.A., Muscheler, R., Otto-Bliesner, B.L., Pongratz, J., Shindell, D.T., Solanki, S.K., Steinhilber, F., and Vieira, L.E.A. (2011) Climate forcing reconstructions for use in PMIP simulations of the last millennium (v1.0). *Geoscientific Model Development* 4(1).

Schmidt, A., Thordarson, T., Oman, L.D., Robock, A. and Self, S. (2012) Climatic impact of the long-lasting 1783 Lakieruption: inapplicability of mass-independent sulfur isotopic composition measurements. *Journal of Geophysical Research: Atmospheres* 117: D23(16), doi:10.1029/2012JD018414.

Schwartz, S.E. (2012) Determination of Earth's transient and equilibrium climate sensitivities from observations over the twentieth century: strong dependence on assumed forcing. *Surveys in Geophysics* 33(3-4): 745–777.

Strikholm, B. (2006) Determining the number of breaks in a piecewise linear regression model (Tech. Rep.). SSE/EFI Working Paper Series in Economics and Finance.

Taylor, K.E., Stouffer, R.J. and Meehl, G.A. (2012) An overview of CMIP5 and the experiment design. *Bulletin of the American Meteorological Society* 93(4): 485–498.

Tibshirani, R. (1996) Regression shrinkage and selection via the Lasso. *Journal of the Royal Statistical Society Series B (Methodological)* 58(1): 267–288.

Tibshirani, R. (2011) Regression shrinkage and selection via the Lasso: a retrospective. *Journal of the Royal Statistical Society Series B (Statistical Methodology)* 73(3): 273–282.

White, G. (1789) *The Natural History of Selborne.* Oxford: Reprint by Anne Secord, Oxford University Press, 2013.

White, H. (2006) Approximate nonlinear forecasting methods. In G. Elliot, C.W.J. Granger and A. Timmermann (eds.), *Handbook of Economic Forecasting* (pp. 459–512). Amsterdam: Elsevier.

Zanchettin, D., Timmreck, C., Bothe, O., Lorenz, S.J., Hegerl, G., Graf, H.-F., Luterbacher, J., Jungclaus, J.H. (2013) Delayed winter warming: a robust decadal response to strong tropical volcanic eruptions? *Geophysical Research Letters* 40(1): 204–209.

Zou, H. and Hastie, T. (2005) Regularization and variable selection via the elastic net. *Journal of the Royal Statistical Society Series B (Statistical Methodology)* 67(2): 301–320.

Supporting Information

Additional Supporting information may be found in the online version of this article at the publisher's website:

Supplementary Material

3

STRUCTURAL EQUATION MODELLING AND THE CAUSAL EFFECT OF PERMANENT INCOME ON LIFE SATISFACTION: THE CASE OF AIR POLLUTION VALUATION IN SWITZERLAND

Eleftherios Giovanis

Verona University

Oznur Ozdamar

Adnan Menderes University and Bologna University

1. Introduction

Air pollution has harmful effects on human health and ecosystems. Thus, it can also impact the Earth's climate. It is well known that pollutants released into the atmosphere not only cause local air pollution, but they also cause regional air pollution, such as acid rain and huge plumes of smoke covering large areas. The high levels of pollutants are more harmful in causing global environmental problems, as ozone depletion and climate change. Especially, O_3 and SO_2 contribute to global warming which is linked to climate change.

Air pollution also has significant negative impact on well-being, such as life satisfaction and health status. It is, therefore, crucial to have reliable estimates of the public willingness-to-pay for air pollution reduction. Overall, there are mainly three popular methods for the environmental valuation that are revealed preference, stated preference and the life satisfaction approach.

Revealed preference relies on hedonic price analysis, that is, uses variations in house price to elucidate the price attached to a cleaner environment. This approach has some limitations, such as it requires the market of interest (typically the housing market) to be in equilibrium at even small geographical level (Frey *et al.*, 2010), the cost of migration is not considered (Bayer *et al.*, 2009) in the approach and the consumption of the public good examined is detectable (Rabin, 1998), which is the air pollution in our case.

Environmental Economics and Sustainability, First Edition. Edited by Brian Chi-ang Lin and Siqi Zheng.

Chapters © 2017 The Authors. Book compilation © 2017 John Wiley & Sons, Ltd. Published 2017 by John Wiley & Sons, Ltd.

The second approach is the stated preference, which is based on contingent valuation from surveys, and attempts to directly elucidate the environmental value from questions presented to the respondents (Carson *et al.*, 2003). The drawbacks of this approach include the superficial and misleading answers by the respondents due to the hypothetical nature of the surveys or the lack of financial implications (Kahneman *et al.*, 1999).

The third approach is the life satisfaction approach (LSA). One of the main advantages of this method is that it does not rely on how the people directly evaluate the environmental conditions, as in the case of the stated preference approach, neither it requires the housing market to be on equilibrium, as it is the main assumption of the revealed preference approach. Instead individuals are asked to evaluate their general life satisfaction controlling for pollution, income and other socio-economic and weather factors. In the LSA the perception of causal relationships is not required, as it is assumed that air quality leads to life satisfaction changes. Previous research studies examined the relationship between life satisfaction, income and air pollution (Luechinger, 2009; Levinson, 2012).

Nevertheless one important disadvantage of the LSA is the plausible reverse causality between income and life satisfaction, as happier people can be more productive and earn more (Powdthavee, 2010). Overall, Stutzer and Frey (2012) suggest that instrumental variable approaches are hardly convincing. This is because almost every factor can determine the life satisfaction. In line with the previous issue, another common limitation of the LSA is the small estimated income coefficients. This is explained by the fact that individuals compare their current income with their past income, as well as, with their peers' income, indicating that both relative and absolute income can be important (Ferreira and Moro, 2010; Levinson, 2012). Tsui (2014) examined the effects of income on happiness in Taiwan. The results support that people are happier not only with changes in absolute income, but also with changes related to the expected and relative income.

Although there are disadvantages of LSA approach as stated preferences and revealed preferences also have, due to its comparative advantages, it is the most appropriate approach to analyse the link between life satisfaction, income and air pollution. It is the reason we use it in our study as previous studies also did that focus on analysing a similar relationship.

However, there are significant contributions of this study compared to many others. First, the relevant analysis relies on detailed micro-level data, using SHP's respondents' zip municipality codes, which allows for mapping the air pollution to individuals more accurately, than previous studies did, where the geographical level was larger (Welsch, 2002, 2006; Luechinger, 2009, 2010; Ferreira and Moro, 2010; Levinson, 2012; Ferreira *et al.*, 2013). Secondly the sample is split to the non-movers and the movers. This can allow to reduce the endogeneity coming from the residential sorting, where the respondents choose where to reside. Thus, those who are more averted to air pollution they will choose locations with cleaner air, resulting to biased air coefficients downwards. Similarly, Luechinger (2009), explored the non-movers and the individuals who are moving across the boundaries of the counties were excluded. In this way, the individual specific fixed effects absorb the county specific effects. Additionally, the air pollution is taken based on daily values, making it more exogenous and avoiding the above-mentioned sorting problem. However, one important issue of the study by Luechinger (2009) and our study is that the sorting process is not observed, as those who are more averted to air pollution have decided to choose locations with clean air and those who are less averted have moved to more polluted areas before the surveys take place. Therefore, as it is pointed out by Luechinger (2009), individuals might become accustomed to the air pollution if they are less sensitive to it, or they might sort into polluted areas at the first place if they are less concerned about air quality. Therefore, for this reason the estimates will take place for both non-movers and movers. On the other hand, people might sort into polluted areas not because are less concerned, but because there might be more opportunities make them happier such as labour market choices. Usually cities are more polluted because of the traffic; nevertheless, cities and urban areas offer opportunities of proximity, a variety of labour and health services choices, which are mainly centralised.

The aim of the paper is to examine the determinants of life satisfaction and to propose a theoretical model where permanent income is considered as one of the important determinants of life satisfaction which cannot be measured directly. However, the impossibility or difficulty to measure abstract variables, such as the permanent income and life satisfaction can be overcome using SEM since it treats them as latent variables, controlling for confounding effects as measurement error. Furthermore, SEM enables a researcher to test a set of regression equations simultaneously. Thus, the main advantage of SEM is to construct a model that combines the determinants of life satisfaction with the permanent income. The concept of permanent income was proposed by Friedman (1957) and is one of the most important developments in empirical social sciences. The model is based on the hypothesis that permanent income might be more important factor on life satisfaction and common proxies for permanent income which most closely capture the concept are examined. In addition, SEM is suggested as it is a more flexible statistical model which allows for measurement error in the income. For the robustness check and to examine the causal effects of permanent income on life satisfaction, and then to calculate the MWTP values, a simple fixed effects regression will also be analysed along with a panel structural equation model (SEM). In order to do that, a model that relates the components of socioeconomic factors and permanent income to life satisfaction is formulated. The results from fixed effects regression analysis show that the MWTP values expressed in 2013 US dollar prices are $8,900, $11,995, $6,580, $1,940, $2,320 for one standard deviation reduction in ozone (O_3), sulphur dioxide (SO_2), nitrogen dioxides (NO_2), carbon monoxide (CO) and particulate matter less than 10 microns (PM_{10}), respectively. On the other hand, employing the SEM the respective values of MWTP values are lower and equal at $6,710, $9,876, $5,390, $1,930 and $2,135. The structure of the paper has as follows: In the next section a brief literature review on the previous environmental valuation approaches is discussed. In Section 3, the methodology and data are presented, while in Section 4 the empirical results are reported. Finally, the concluding remarks are discussed in the last section.

2. Literature Review

Initially, previous researches on revealed preference methods are presented. Under the assumption of perfectly competitive housing market, a change in any environmental characteristics is reflected by a change in market price, and reflects the buyers' marginal willingness-to-pay (MWTP) for this characteristic; see Rosen (1974) for details on hedonic pricing. One of the first studies that employed the hedonic pricing method is by Ridker and Henning (1967), who estimated that a one standard deviation change in sulphate leads to a 2.8% change in the values of residential properties. Numerous studied followed the same methodology and are reviewed in Smith and Huang's (1995) meta-analysis. However, this method is subject to a number of criticism, such as the study by Bayer *et al.* (2009), who show that when moving is costly, estimates relying on hedonic valuation of the housing market are biased downwards. The form can be another issue as Kuminoff *et al.* (2010) point out where a framework incorporating quasi-experimental identification and spatial fixed effects can be more flexible than the standard linear specifications.

In the literature three main sorting and hedonic pricing models have additionally been developed in order to improve the estimates; the Pure Characteristics (PC) sorting, the Random Utility (RU) sorting and the Calibrated Sorting (CS) models. The differences in these models include: the set of choices faced by each household; the shape of the preference function specification and the development of instruments to control for endogenous amenities (Bayer and Timmins, 2005, 2007; Kuminoff *et al.*, 2013).

Regarding preferences in the PC specification, every household is required to have for every amenity the same relative preferences, while the specification in the CS allows the households to differ in their relative preferences relaxing in this way the illustration of preference heterogeneity. In the PC model, the vertically differentiated case dominates where the households agree on the community ranking by the provision of a public good or amenity and on the spatial substitution opportunities. On the other hand, in the CS and RU models the horizontal differentiation condition applies, where a broader diversity in the substitution possibilities is allowed. However, there is a bias/variance trade-off in the vertical/horizontal modelling. The PC estimator is biased by the vertically differentiated condition leading to biased conclusions on welfare measures. On the contrary, the restriction that creates bias is removed by the horizontal differentiation, but untested distributional assumptions are created due the dimensions of preferences which are added in the modelling which drive the estimates (Kuminoff *et al.*, 2013). In the case of the instrumental variable approach and the CS model, the assumption about the relative importance of unobserved amenities is not required as it has been illustrated by Ferreyra (2007) and Calabrese *et al.* (2007). The instruments employed in the PC model are constructed using the ranking of the community income functions, while in the RU sorting model the instruments are developed by the functions of the exogenous attributes of substitute locations (Kuminoff *et al.*, 2013). Nevertheless, there are still drawbacks as the instrumental variable approaches employed in the PC and RU model will be consistent as long as the instruments are valid, that is, exogenous and not weak, while a specific form of the amenity's production function is required in CS model (Kuminoff *et al.*, 2013).

Furthermore, the previous research studies using stated preference methods are discussed. Contingent evaluation studies are difficult to compare because each study is unique and it depends on the description of the good to be evaluated; the payment method to be made; and the eliciting values method (Croper and Oates, 1992, 710). The study by Loehman and De (1982) shows that the yearly MWTP values range between US $7 and $46 for a one-day per year reduction in severe cough, severe shortness of breath, and minor eye irritation. Hall *et al.* (1992) found that the MWTP value per day for a one-day-per-year reduction in minor restricted-activity is equal at US $23 deflated at 1990 prices. Hammitt and Zhou (2006) using the contingent valuation method, explored the indoor pollution and specifically the PM_{10} and SO_2. The authors found that the statistical cost of a cold, chronic bronchitis and the value per statistical life range, respectively, between $3 and $6, $500 and $1,000 and $4,200 and $16,900 based on 2000 prices. The stated preference approach has been subject of criticism on two main points. Firstly, the individuals have not always adequate understanding of the good they are asked to evaluate. Second, a major disadvantage is the strategic behaviour or the limited incentives given to respondents, resulting to disclosure of their true demand. The consequence is that the estimates will be biased since the respondents give misleading answers (Luechinger, 2009; MacKerron and Mourato, 2009; Frey *et al.*, 2010).

However, other studies used the approaches of the choice modelling (CM) or choice experiments (CEs) suggesting that these can be more proper than the contingent valuation in order to calculate the MWTP (Hanley *et al.*, 2001a; Campbell, 2007; Campbell *et al.*, 2008). These type of experiments are based on survey methodology to model the preferences for goods, which are described regarding their attributes and levels. Furthermore, the alternative series of preferences are provided to the respondents, which differ in levels and terms and then they are asked to choose the most preferred one or to rank the pool of alternatives. In the next step, the price or cost is concluded as one of the goods' attributes which allows to recover indirectly the respondent's choices or rankings (Hanley *et al.*, 2001a; Campbell *et al.*, 2011). In addition, it is suggested that CE approach can be more enlightening than the studies, using the discrete CV approach, since the respondents can choose or express their preference for a specific good given a range of payment amounts. Finally, CE approach relies on the respondents'ranking ratings among a series of alternative packages that the MWTP can be indirectly calculated, avoiding or minimising the strategic behaviour commonly presented in the CV approach (Hanley *et al.*, 2001a; Campbell *et al.*, 2011).

Nevertheless, CEs have also weakness. One drawback is the statistical problems derived from the repeated answers for each respondent, as well as, the correlation among the responses should be considered (Adamowicz *et al.*, 1998). In addition, the study design in CE modelling can be sensitive, as the estimates depend on the way that the choice of the levels to represent them are selected and the way that the respondents receive them are neutral or not. This implies that there might be an impact on the marginal utilities values (Hanley *et al.*, 2001a, 2001b) found that the respondents are affected from the way that the choices are given to them. Changing the number of choice tasks has a significant impact on the respondent's preferences.

To alleviate the dependence on the housing market and to evaluate the willingness-to-pay, researchers have also used life satisfaction. Welsch (2002) explored 54 countries in 1990 and 1995, using cross sectional data, where the dependent variable is the country average happiness. MWTP is found to be \$126 for a 1 $\mu g/m^3$ decrease in nitrogen dioxide (NO_2). In another study, Welsch (2006) employed a series of the Eurobarometer cross-sectional survey during the period 1990–1997 for 10 European countries. The MWTP was found equal at \$184 and \$519 for 1 $\mu g/m^3$ decrease, respectively, in lead (Pb) and NO_2. However, these studies are likely to be biased by measurement error due to the aggregation of pollution to national level. To reduce this aggregation problem, Ferreira and Moro (2010) used a micro-level data the Irish National Survey on Quality of Life which took place in 2001. The authors found that the MWTP to pay for a reduction of 1 $\mu g/m^3$ of PM_{10} is €945. Rehdanz and Maddison (2008) found that the air pollution levels in Germany have negative relationship with life satisfaction. The estimates in previous studies, such as those by Ferreira and Moro (2010) and MacKerron and Mourato (2009) are based on cross-sectional data and do not account for the endogeneity of pollution. For instance, areas with high pollution levels are likely to also have some other amenities that negatively affect life satisfaction. The most relevant paper to our study is by Luechinger (2009) who also uses an individual level panel data (the German Socio-Economic Panel (GSOEP). Luechinger (2009) used as an instrumental variable for SO_2 the mandated installation of scrubbers at power plants and he found that the MWTP is \$313, while it becomes smaller (\$183) when no instrument is considered.

SEM has been previously applied on life satisfaction studies. Powdthavee and Wooden (2015) used SEM in order to examine the effects of sexual identity on life satisfaction through seven channels: income, employment, health, partner, relationships, children, friendship networks and education in Australia and the United Kingdom. Generally, the SEM has not been applied on the valuation of air pollution using the LSA. This study contributes to the previous literature by three ways. First, by mapping air pollution concentrations on municipality zip code level and conventional fixed effects estimates for five air pollutants. Second, SEM approach is expanded including additionally the air pollutants. Third, permanent income is incorporated in the analysis. Overall, SEM enables a researcher to test a set of regression equations simultaneously. Thus, the main advantage of SEM is to construct a model that combines the determinants of life satisfaction with income. Thus, using SEM both the direct and indirect effects of variables such as age or marital status among others can be simultaneously considered. For example, in the analysis of life satisfaction it is important to separate the direct effect of some variables, that is, education from their indirect effect, for example, via its effect on income. In addition, it is impossible to disentangle these factors in a single equation model in which the reduced form parameters include both the direct and indirect effects. SEM approach can entail this.

3. Methodology

3.1 Fixed Effects

The panel data model estimated is

$$LS_{i,j,t} = \beta_0 + \beta_1 \log(y)_{i,j,t} + \varphi' e_{j,t} + \gamma' Z_{i,j,t} + \delta' W_{j,t} + \mu_i + M_j + \theta_t + M_j T + \varepsilon_{i,j,t} \quad (1)$$

where LS denotes the life satisfaction for individual i in location (zip code) j and in time t, $\log(y)$ is the logarithm of the equivalent household income deflated in 2012 prices and e is the air pollution measured-in that case five air pollutants. Vector Z includes personal and household characteristics, while W includes the weather conditions. Set μ_i is the individual fixed effects, M_j is the location fixed effects and set θ_t is a time-specific vector of indicators for the day of the week, month and the year of the survey. In addition, the regressions control for $M_j T$ which is a set of area-specific time trends. Standard errors are clustered at the area-specific time trends. For cross-sectional data or panel data random effects analysis the ordered Probit and Logit models can be applied. However, these models do not allow fixed effects estimation analysis. In this case the approach developed by van Praag and Ferrer-i-Carbonell (2004) is applied, the 'Probit-adapted' method, where the dependent variable is transformed to a standardised continuous variable, which is normally-distributed. For a marginal change of air pollutant e, the MWTP can be derived by differentiating (1) and setting $dLS = 0$. That is the income drop that would lead to the same reduction in life satisfaction than an increase in pollution. Thus, the MWTP can be calculated as

$$MWTP = -\frac{\partial LS}{\partial e} \bigg/ \frac{\partial LS}{\partial \log(y)} \quad (2)$$

Then the MWTP (2) is multiplied by the average household income in order to get the MWTP values. The within-person estimations achieved with the panel data fixed effects are useful when it is difficult to measure unobserved confounders including determinants of location selection. These are most appropriate for exposure (air pollution) and outcome (life satisfaction) relationships with short lag times as is the case of the current study. Cross-sectional studies exploring the relationship between well-being and air pollution are particularly liable to residential self-selection bias resulted from unmeasured area selection factors. Nevertheless, fixed effects even if they will greatly reduce the potential bias coming from omitted variables, this bias is not completely eliminated, since there might still be unobservable factors driving air pollution and which are correlated with the life satisfaction. Regarding the sample selection, usually residential relocation is triggered by events such as employment changes and marriage which may influence life satisfaction and thus restricting the sample to the movers may induce selection bias (Hernan *et al.*, 2004). Using panel data, the area fixed effects for the non-movers will be eliminated, while in the case of the movers the error term will contain the difference in the area fixed effects of the two residences which is likely to be correlated with the difference of the air pollution levels across the two locations.

However, as it has been mentioned in the introduction section the limitation of the sample to the non-movers may reduce the endogeneity from the residential sorting but it does not account for issues coming from the sorting process. In particular, individuals who are averted to air pollution have already lived or moved to locations with cleaner air before the implementation of the surveys. Thus, similarly to the study by Luechinger (2009) the sorting process is not observed and this might have an effect on the estimated coefficients. Thus, restricting the sample only to the non-movers the above selection bias is generated. For this reason the Heckman selection model is suggested (see for more technical details Heckman, 1979) in order to account for the selection bias. The study by Ioannides and Zabel (2008) follows this approach in order to explore the neighbourhood effects on housing demand. Therefore, this approach is adjusted in the case of the air pollution and its effects on moving location.

3.2 *Panel Structural Equation Modelling (SEM)*

Structural equation models (SEMs) with latent variables provide a very general framework for modelling of relationships in multivariate data (Bollen, 1989). A SEM is applied in order to examine whether the proposed causal relationship is consistent with the patterns found among variables in the empirical data. SEM uses a two-step process: the measurement model and the structural equation model. More specifically, the measurement model specifies how the latent (unobserved) variables or hypothetical constructs are measured in terms of the observed variables. The observed variables and unobserved constructs are linked by one of two factor equations for observations $i = 1, \ldots, N$:

$$x_i = u_x + \Lambda_x \xi_i + \delta_i^x \tag{3}$$

$$y_i = u_y + \Lambda_y \eta_i + \delta_i^y \tag{4}$$

Model (3) relates xs or $x_i = (x_{i1}, \ldots \ldots, x_{iq})'$ to an n-vector of latent variables $\xi_i = (\xi_{i1}, \ldots \ldots, \xi_{in})'$, $n \leq q$, through the $q \times n$ factor loadings matrix Λ_x. Similarly, model (4) relates the vector of indicators $y_i = (y_{i1}, \ldots \ldots, y_{ip})'$ to an m-vector of latent variables $\eta_i = (\eta_{i1}, \ldots \ldots, \eta_{im})'$, $m \leq p$, through the $p \times m$ factor loadings matrix Λ_y. The vectors δ_i^x and δ_i^y are the measurement error terms, while vectors u_x and u_y are the intercept terms of the measurement models.

The next step is to examine and determine the lack of the fit. The model fit evaluation is based on three goodness-of-fit indices; comparative fit index (CFI) developed by Bentler (1990) Tucker–Lewis index (TLI) proposed by Tucker and Lewis (1973) and the root mean square error of approximation (RMSEA). The CFI and TLI indices ranges between 0 and 1 and the larger they are the better the fit is. According to Bentler (1990) and Hu and Bentler (1999), a CFI and TLI value of greater than 0.90 can be expected for a good fit to the data, while values higher than 0.95 indicate very good fit. RMSEA measures the degree of model adequacy based on population discrepancy in relation to degrees of freedom. As a rule of thumb, if the value of RMSEA is lower than 0.05 indicates a good fit, values between 0.05 and 0.08 suggest accept-able fit, while values higher than 0.10 imply poor model fit (Hancock and Mueller, 2006). The last index is the root mean square residual (RMSR), which is a measure of the mean absolute value of the covariance residuals. In general, values less than 0.1 indicate favourable estimates. The SEM examined in this case is incorporated into a panel framework and it is

$$y_{it}^m = a_{y_i}^m + \beta_m \eta_{it}^m + e_{it}^m \tag{5}$$

$$\eta_{it}^s = \alpha_{\eta_i}^s + \Gamma \pi_{it}^s + u_{it}^s \tag{6}$$

$$H_{it}^p = \alpha_{H_{it}}^p + \Phi h_{it}^p + v_{it}^p \tag{7}$$

$$LS_{it} = a_{LSi} + \beta \eta_{it} + \gamma_m \sum_{m-1}^{3} X_{mit} + \delta_s \sum_{s-1}^{4} \Gamma_{sit} + \phi_p \sum_{s-1}^{6} \Phi_{pit} + \theta' Z_{it} + \varepsilon_{it} \tag{8}$$

The term y_{it} in (5) represents the effect indicators of income (η), which are assumed to be gen-erated by the latent income variable with $m = 1, 2, \ldots, M$, denoting the number of indicators, for individual i in time t and with error e_{it}^m. In the measurement Equation (6) the income is the latent dependent variable, Γ is the vector of coefficients for the exogenous variables included in π_{it}^s, and u_{it} is the disturbance error with $E(u_{it}) = 0$, $COV(u_{it}, \pi_{it}^s) = 0$ and $COV(u_{it}, e_{it}) = 0$. In the measurement Equation (7), H_{it} represents the indicators of the latent variable health status, Φ is the vector of coefficients included in h_{it}^p, and v_{it} is the disturbance error with $E(v_{it}) = 0$.

Equation (8) is the final estimated equation, with β representing the permanent income's estimated coefficient, γ_m, δ_s and φ_p are the estimated coefficients of the *effects* and *causal* indicators from (5) to (7) for $m = 1,..,5$, $s = 1,..,3$ and $p = 1,....,6$ denoting the number of indicators described below; θ' indicates the estimated coefficients of the control variables (Z) and ε_{it} is the disturbance term with $E(\varepsilon_{it}) = 0$, $COV(\varepsilon_{it}, X_{mit}) = 0$, $COV(\varepsilon_{it}, \Gamma_{sit}) = 0$, $COV(\varepsilon_{it}, \Phi_{mit}) = 0$. In the case that health status and permanent income are not latent variables the fit of this model to the data will be statistically insignificant and poor. The parameters α_{yi}^m, α_{yi}^s, α_{Hi}^p and α_{LSi} represent the unobserved individual-specific effects, allowing us to estimate a fixed effects SEM. The indirect effects of income through X_{mit} for each m are given by $\beta_m \times \gamma_m$. The indicators of income are distinguished in two categories; the *causal* indicators which are the determinants of household income and variables that are affected by income and are called *effect* indicators. The *causal* indicators are nationality, job status, education and the place of location-municipality in this case, while the *effects* indicators are the house expenses, house tenure and household size. Job status and education can be clearly important factors of permanent income. Previous studies used them as proxies. Houthakker (1957) and Mayer (1963) analysing the relationship between income and consumption, they treated job status as a proxy for permanent income. In addition, Hauser and Warren (1997) argue that job status proxies permanent income because it is more stable over time than income is. Similarly, edu-cation is treated an additional proxy since it is more stable than income and it is a significant factor of the latter. The third *causal* indicator is the location of residence, which municipality is used in this study. This can be meaningful as controlling at the same time for municipal-ity, various economic factors are considered, as regional wealth, unemployment and industrial characteristics among others. Thus, the location can be an important factor of permanent in-come. Nationality is taken as an additional factor, because the Swiss citizens might consider

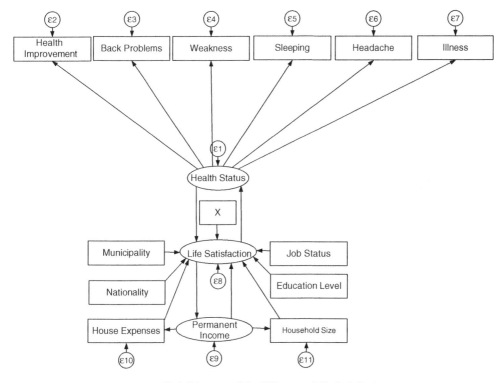

Figure 1. Path Diagram of the Effects on Life Satisfaction.

a more permanent life in Switzerland than the non-Swiss citizens, formulating in this way the permanent income. Finally, life satisfaction is considered as the last factor. This is based on the hypothesis that permanent income can be caused by life satisfaction, as people can earn more in the long term if they are more satisfied, examining in this way the possible reverse causality between them. Regarding the *effects* indicators, the household size, house tenure (owned a house or not) and the house expenses can be considered as logical effects of permanent income. Finally, the indicators for health status are the improvements on health, whether the respondent had an illness or accident, whether he/she had back problems, weaknesses problems, headache and sleeping problems in the last 12 months. In Figure 1, the path diagram of the effects of the permanent income and the other control variables on the life satisfaction is presented. Moreover, the reverse causality between life satisfaction and health status, as well as between life satisfaction and permanent income is examined.

4. Data

The SHP started in 1999 with slightly more than 5000 households and it includes questions about the household composition and socioeconomic demographics. This study uses the SHP waves 2–15, that is, years 2000–2013.[1] Based on the happiness literature (Clark and Oswald, 1994, 1996; Ferreira and Moro, 2010; Ferreira *et al.*, 2013) the demographic and household variables of interest are household income, gender, age, household size, health status, job status, house tenure, marital status, education level, municipalities and community typology, such

Table 1. Summary Statistics.

Air pollutant	Mean	Standard deviation	Min	Max
Life satisfaction	8.027	1.467	0	10
Equivalent household income	56,670.47	57,456.89	0	5,541.319
O_3	56.6671	27.232	1.19	215.22
SO_2	2.531	1.992	0.12	60.14
NO_2	31.325	24.755	0.03	103.97
CO	381.761	343.385	0.0	1988.74
PM_{10}	20.903	12.005	0.70	195.14

Note: Air pollutants are measured in micrograms per cubic meter ($\mu g/m^3$).

as whether the area is urban, sub-urban among others. In addition, the regressions consider the day of the week, the month of the year, the wave of the survey and area specific trends. The weather conditions are additionally considered, as they can influence life satisfaction and these are: the average temperature, the difference between the maximum and minimum temperature – which proxies for clear skies and humidity – (Levison, 2012), the precipitation and the wind speed. The dependent variable is the life satisfaction which is an ordered variable measured in a Likert scale from 0 (not satisfied at all) to 10 (completely satisfied).

In order to map and convert the point data from the monitoring stations into data up to zip code level we used the inverse distance weighting (IDW); a GIS-based interpolation method with a radius of 20 km including the 90% of the SHP sample. There are 2551 municipalities and the SHP is based on 2198 municipalities. Based on Table 1, the air pollutants present a significant deviation among them. For this reason the standardised coefficients are obtained.

In Table 2, the correlation coefficients between the various pollutants and the life satisfaction are reported. These correlations are based on the average pollution levels at the nearest monitoring station at the day before the interview. The correlation between all air pollutants

Table 2. Correlation between Air Pollutants and Life Satisfaction.

	Life satisfaction	O_3	SO_2	NO_2	CO	PM_{10}
O_3	− 0.0109***					
	(0.000)					
SO_2	− 0.0113***	− 0.1353***				
	(0.000)	(0.000)				
NO_2	− 0.0098***	− 0.5078***	0.3078***			
	(0.000)	(0.000)	(0.000)			
CO	− 0.0057***	− 0.2620***	0.0788***	0.4680***		
	(0.0000)	(0.0000)	(0.000)	(0.000)		
PM_{10}	− 0.0078***	− 0.4094***	0.2860***	0.7173***	0.3160***	
	(0.0000)	(0.0000)	(0.000)	(0.000)	(0.0002)	
Household income	0.0904***	− 0.0217***	− 0.0173***	− 0.0102***	− 0.0079**	− 0.0084**
	(0.0000)	(0.000)	(0.000)	(0.000)	(0.0138)	(0.0204)

Note: p-Values are in brackets, *** and ** indicate significance at 1% and 5% level.

is positive with the exception of the ground-level ozone. The negative correlation between O_3 and the other pollutants is induced by seasonal variations in the occurrence of these pollutants. More specifically, O_3 formed in high temperature and solar radiation levels, especially during summer (Bauer and Langmann, 2002; Toro *et al.*, 2006). The remained pollutants are coming caused mainly from cars, trucks and buses, power plants, industry, landfills and not from weather; however their impact depends on the latter. More specifically, the main pollutants from diesel fuel vehicles include CO and NO_2 from which the secondary pollutant O_3 is formed (Charron and Harrison, 2003; Toro *et al.*, 2006). The positive correlation between CO and NO_2 is explained by the fact that the effect of CO is that it slowly burns nitrogen monoxide (NO) to NO_2 (Vingarzan, 2004). Nitrogen oxides are mainly originated from anthropogenic sources and the increased production of O_3 in the lower layer which the latter is associated with volatile organic compounds (VOCs), besides temperature and solar radiation (Wennberg *et al.*, 1998; Bauer and Langmann, 2002; Toro *et al.*, 2006). In other studies a positive correlation between CO, NO_2 and SO_2 has been found (Wang *et al.*, 2002).

Based on the correlation matrix in Table 2, the association between household income and the air pollutants examined. Since the correlation does not give enough information for the relationship between income and air pollution the Environmental Kuznets Curve (EKC) hypothesis is examined and the results are presented in Figures 2–6 for linear and quadratic predicted values of the air pollutants. The EKC hypothesis has been inspired by Kuznets (1955) who predicted that the relationship between income inequality and per-capita income is characterised by an inverted U-shaped curve. This suggests that as the income is increased the

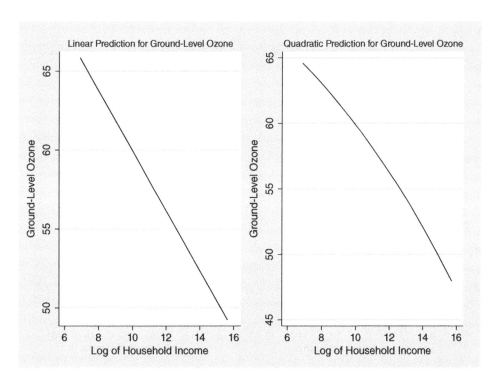

Figure 2. Linear and Quadratic Prediction Plots between Ground Level Ozone and Household Income.

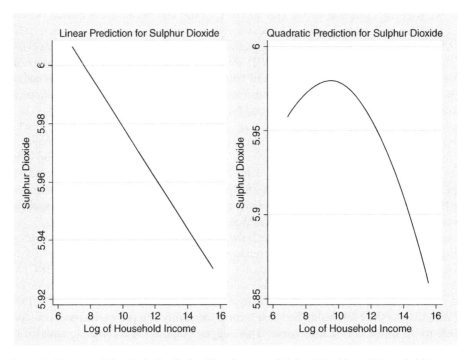

Figure 3. Linear and Quadratic Prediction Plots between Sulphur Dioxide and Household Income.

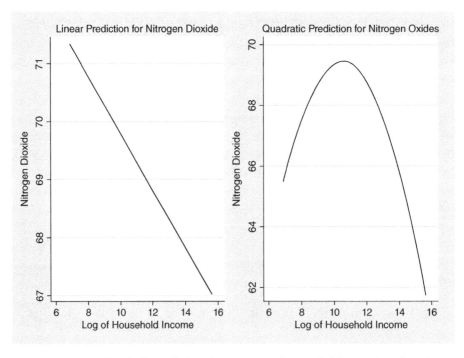

Figure 4. Linear and Quadratic Prediction Plots between Nitrogen Oxides and Household Income.

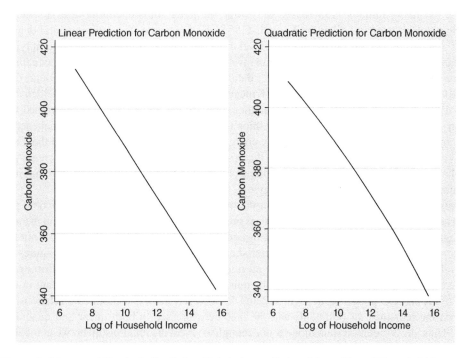

Figure 5. Linear and Quadratic Prediction Plots between Carbon Monoxide and Household Income.

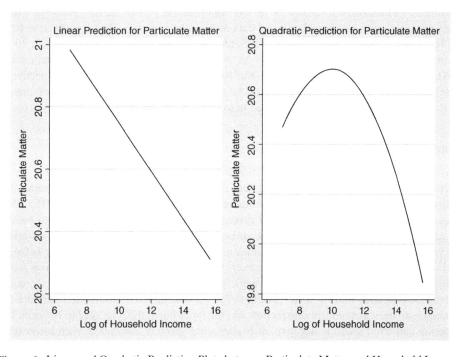

Figure 6. Linear and Quadratic Prediction Plots between Particulate Matter and Household Income.

income inequality initially is increased too, while the latter starts declining after a specific turning point of income. Following Kuznets (1955), EKC assumes the environmental degradation or pressure increases up to a certain level of income and after that it decreases implying that the environmental impact indicator is an inverted U-shaped function of income per capita. The majority of the studies exploited panel data based on country level and they found that the EKC hypothesis holds (Grossman and Krueger, 1993, 1995; Panayotou, 1997; Selden and Song, 1994; Vollebergh et $al.$, 2009). In another study, Bölük and Mert (2014) examined the carbon dioxide emissions in 16 European Union (EU) countries by separating the final energy consumption into fossil fuel and renewable energy consumption. The authors found the EKC hypothesis does not hold and they suggest that a shift in renewable energy might decrease the greenhouse gas emission, because it contributes by around 50% less per unit energy that it is consumed by the conventional fossil energy use.

In Figures 2–6 the relationship between the air pollutants and the household income per capita considering linear and quadratic terms is presented. In all cases the cubic term on income is insignificant, as well as the EKC hypothesis and the shape holds either controlling or not for additional individual and household characteristics. According to the left side of the Figures 2–6 the relationship between income and the air pollutants is linear and negative, confirming so far the correlation in Table 2. Regarding the quadratic term on income is insignificant in the cases of O_3 and CO presented in Figures 2 and 5. However, there is a significant relationship between the remained air pollutants and the income expressed in both linear and quadratic terms. Thus, the correlation standalone is not enough to reveal the relationship between income and pollution, where for SO_2, NO_2 and PM_{10} there is a quadratic relationship according to the figures on the right side suggesting that an inverted U-shaped curve exists for these pollutants and the EKC hypothesis holds. Previous studies suggest that the EKC hypothesis may be varied depending on various factors, such as the period examined, the type of the data analysis, which can be time-series, cross-sectional or panel data or it can be a matter of the specification from of the function estimated (Panayotou, 1997; Selden and Song, 1994; Vollebergh et $al.$, 2009; Giovanis, 2012). Nevertheless, these issues are not the main interest of the study and overall the EKC hypothesis holds for SO_2, PM_{10} and NO_2 and the turning points are, respectively, $22,500 and $26,300 and $32,200. It should be noticed that the relationships do not change when the income expressed in levels instead in logarithms is considered.

5. Empirical Results

The results are reported in Table 3, while the findings for the socio-economic and personal characteristics are not explicitly discussed here as it is out of the study's scope. Overall, the findings are generally consistent with other studies (Luechinger, 2009; Levinson, 2012). Married are more satisfied than singles, while divorced and widowed are more likely to be less satisfied with their lives than singles are. Regarding job status, unemployed report lower levels of life satisfaction than those who are full time employed, while there is no difference between retired and part time employed. The home owners report higher levels of life satisfaction, while it seems that household size is associated negatively with life satisfaction. Finally, increases on average temperature and the difference between maximum and minimum temperature are associated with increases on life satisfaction. On the other hand, the relationship between life satisfaction and wind speed is negative, as higher wind speed is associated, with lower temperature. Even though wind speed can clean the air from pollutants the lower temperatures associated with it can have stronger effect on life satisfaction.

Table 3. Life Satisfaction Estimates for Nonmovers.

Variables	Adapted Probit FE	SEM
Log of equivalent household income	0.0774***	0.1015***
	(0.0138)	(0.0083)
O_3	− 0.0023***	− 0.0022***
	(0.0007)	(0.0002)
SO_2	− 0.0031***	− 0.0033***
	(0.0006)	(0.0007)
NO_2	− 0.0017***	− 0.0018***
	(0.0005)	(0.0004)
CO	− 0.0005**	− 0.0006**
	(0.0003)	(0.0003)
PM_{10}	− 0.0006**	− 0.0007***
	(0.00033)	(0.0003)
Average temperature	0.0008***	0.0006***
	(0.0002)	(0.0003)
Maximum–minimum temperature	0.0003***	0.0004***
	(0.00013)	(0.0002)
Wind speed	− 0.0009***	− 0.0007***
	(0.0002)	(0.0002)
Precipitation	0.0003	0.0004
	(0.0002)	(0.0003)
Age	− 0.1709***	− 0.1425***
	(0.0066)	(0.0430)
Age square	0.0019***	0.0024***
	(0.0003)	(0.0008)
Age cubic	− 1.11e-0.5***	− 1.21e-0.5***
	(2.13e-06)	(4.76e-06)
Household size	− 0.0081*	− 0.0126***
	(0.0042)	(0.0040)
Job status (ref = full-time)		
Job status (part-time)	− 0.0113	− 0.0114
	(0.0202)	(0.0213)
Job status (unemployed)	− 0.3786***	− 0.3189***
	(0.0670)	(0.1163)
Job status (retired)	− 0.0326	− 0.0320
	(0.0369)	(0.0409)
Marital status (ref = single)		
Marital status (married)	0.1321***	0.1624***
	(0.0353)	(0.0235)
Marital status (widowed)	− 0.2934***	− 0.3046**
	(0.1050)	(0.1346)
Marital status (divorced)	− 0.2916*	− 0.2640*
	(0.1685)	(0.1710)
Tenure (ref = tenant)		
Tenure house (owner/co-owner)	0.0491**	0.0450***
	(0.0241)	(0.0091)

(*continued*)

Table 3. (*Continued*)

Variables	Adapted Probit FE	SEM
Education (ref = incomplete compulsory school)		
Education level (compulsory elementary school)	-0.0703^{***}	-0.0595^{**}
	(0.0196)	(0.0275)
Education level (technical or vocational school)	0.0399	0.0344
	(0.0556)	(0.0498)
Education level (university)	-0.0598^{*}	-0.0823^{***}
	(0.0320)	(0.0282)

Variables	Adapted Probit FE	SEM	t-Statistic for the difference of MWTP between FE and SEM ($\text{MWTP}_{\text{FE}} - \text{MWTP}_{\text{SEM}}$)
No. of obs.	71,084	71,084	
R^2	0.3218		
AIC statistic	89,896.56	81,992.01	
BIC statistic	90,863.73	82,341.65	
χ^2/df	0.164		
Root mean square error of approximation (RMSEA)		0.0025	
CFI		0.945	
TLI		0.924	
RMS		0.010	
MWTP for a drop of one standard deviation in O_3 per year	\$8,900	\$6,710	167.365 [0.000]
MWTP for a drop of one standard deviation in SO_2 per year	\$11,995	\$9,876	165.482 [0.000]
MWTP for a drop of one standard deviation in NO_2 per year	\$6,580	\$5,390	163.638 [0.000]
MWTP for a drop of one standard deviation in CO per year	\$1,940	\$1,680	114.571 [0.000]
MWTP for a drop of one standard deviation in PM_{10} per year	\$2,320	\$2,135	101.041 0.000

Note: Standard errors are in brackets ***, ** and * indicate significance at 1%, 5% and 10% level. *p*-values are in square brackets.

The first remarkable finding is the cubic relationship between age and life satisfaction. While previous studies found that life satisfaction is rather flat throughout the life cycle (Myers, 2000) or there is an inverted U-shaped association (Easterlin, 2006), the findings in this study shows that after some point of the life cycle life satisfaction is reduced. The second remarkable finding is that there is a negative relationship between education level and life satisfaction, while a positive relationship is usually found (Easterlin, 2001, 2006; Bruni and Porta, 2005; Ferreira *et al.*, 2013; Giovanis, 2014). On the other hand, these estimates are consistent with other studies which found a negative relationship especially in the developed nations (see e.g. Veenhoven, 1996; Dockery, 2003, 2010). This brings a great interest to further understand the relationship between education and subjective wellbeing. From previous research it is well established from both human capital theory and empirical evidence that higher educational attainment can enhance a person's future outcomes, including better career and employment opportunities increasing income and wealth and thus health outcomes (Sweetland, 1996). One possible explanation can be the fact that people who do well in education are those who tend to be happy and mentally resilient in the first place and that attaining educational qualifications per se makes little difference. Thus, education may have a negative impact, for example through raising aspirations and expectations that are not met and by leading to occupations that carry high levels of stress. More specifically, studies from Britain and the USA found a negative correlation between education and job satisfaction, indicating dissatisfaction among individuals with higher levels of education (Clark and Oswald, 1996; Ross and van Willigen, 1997; Stutzer, 2004; Verhaest and Omey, 2009). This dissatisfaction may be due to the lack of jobs at higher levels and the expectation of high educated individuals, the stress related to jobs at higher positions, and to mismatches between aspiration and expectations with employment possibilities for high educated people. Therefore, education can be significantly related to job satisfaction and as the latter is an important component of the life satisfaction, including income, health and other factors, leading to the negative relationship between higher educated people and their life satisfaction. Previous studies employing the Swiss Household Panel survey found the same concluding remarks (Stutzer, 2004; Krause, 2010). However, this needs further in-depth investigation as the relationship may vary depending on gender, age and health among other factors.

Regarding SEM, it is a useful tool which allows us to explore the direct and indirect effects. More specifically, as it has been shown in Figure 1 and the methodological framework, education has direct effects on life satisfaction and indirect effects through permanent income. Thus, the results show that while the indirect effects of education on life satisfaction through income are positive, the direct effects are negative. However, the total effects presented in Table 3 are negative as the direct effects exceed the indirect effects. These results can be explained as follows. Higher and better education provides individuals with better labour and market opportunities leading to increase on income, wealth and health outcome. This further leads to life satisfaction increase because income and wealth are tools which allow people to achieve specific goals and targets. On the other hand, education may present this direct negative association with life satisfaction, since individual have accomplished many goals regarding the educational attainment and achievement leaving them with less room for increases in life satisfaction relatively to people who still try to study, educate themselves and accomplish additional goals in their lives.

Based on Table 3 and the adapted Probit FE estimates, increasing O_3, SO_2, NO_2, CO and PM_{10} by one standard deviation reduces life satisfaction by 0.0023, 0.0031, 0.0017, 0.0005 and 0.0006, respectively. The respective MWTP values expressed in 2013 US dollar prices are $8900, $11,995, $6580, $1940 and $2320. More specifically, based on the relation (2), the MWTP is the ratio of the partial derivative of life satisfaction with respect to air pollutant explored over the partial derivative of life satisfaction with respect to the logarithm of the household income. Then this ratio is multiplied by the average household income in order to calculate the MWTP in monetary values (Welsch, 2002, 2006; Luechinger, 2009; Levinson, 2012). The estimate air pollutant coefficients are small; however the results are consistent with the findings of previous studies. For instance Levinson (2012) found the estimated coefficients of the standardised PM_{10} and O_3 equal at 0.0014 and 0.00021. The low estimated air pollutant coefficients may be due the air quality improvement during the period examined.

Moreover, it might be the case that the public goods or the public bads in our case, play a lower or less significant role on overall well-being and life satisfaction than the personal and household characteristics do, such as income, employment status, marital status and others. In addition, when no controls are included into the regressions the air pollutant coefficients are larger, but controlling for additional individual and household characteristics their effect is reduced as expected, confirming the importance of other factors on life satisfaction. In addition, these controls may be correlated with air pollutants, like marital status, education and employment.

The results in Table 3 refer to MWTP for changes in standard deviation. More specifically, the MWTP for one standard deviation change in O_3, which is equal at 27 and the average value of O_3, which amounts to 56, constitutes a 48% change in O_3. The percentage changes in the remained pollutants for one standard deviation change are: 78%, 76%, 90% and 60% for SO_2, NO_2, CO and PM_{10}, respectively.

Regarding the SEM the results are reported in the second column of Table 3. In this case it is observed that the income effect on life satisfaction is higher than the respective one derived from the adapted Probit FE and it is equal at 0.1015. This has as a consequence that the MWTP will be lower and the values are: $6710, $9876, $5390, $1930 and $2135, respectively, for O_3, SO_2, NO_2, CO and PM_{10}. Thus, the MWTP derived by SEM are less by 15–25% for O_3, SO_2 and NO_2, while the respective reduction for CO and PM_{10} ranges between 5% and 8%. In Table 3, the t-statistic and the respective p values for the comparison of the mean MWTP between adapted Probit FE and SEM are reported. In all cases it is concluded that the MWTP values are statistically different. The same concluding remarks are derived with the bootstrap t-statistics. The chi-square goodness-of-fit test and the root mean square error of approximation (RMSEA) descriptive model fit statistic are reported. The chi-square test of model fit is not significant and the RMSEA value 0.0025 is much lower than the value of 0.05 proposed by Hu and Bentler (1999) as an upper boundary. Moreover, the CFI and TLI are very close to unit and equal at 0.95 and 0.92, respectively, while RMSR 0.010, much lower than the proposed value of 0.1. Thus, based on these statistics it is concluded that the proposed model fits the data well.

In Table 4, the estimates of life satisfaction regressions for the movers sample are reported. While the household income is significant not all the air pollutants are. This can be explained by the fact the movers sample is endogenous and not stable across location and time. More specifically, there are individuals that have moved more than once across the period examined to areas with varying air pollution levels and types creating this bias in the estimates. In addition, it has been found that SO_2 and O_3 have strongest effect for non-movers than movers, as well as more persistent effects than the rest of the air pollutants. This can have various explanations. First, O_3 has slightly been increased, while the other pollutants presented a significant declining and especially CO. Second, even if O_3 and SO_2 are invisible, they are mainly responsible for the formation of the winter smog (SO_2) and for summer smog (O_3), thus they can be observed and felt by people (Ponka, 1990; Medina-Ramon et al., 2006) Moreover, there is evidence that O_3 produces short-term effects on mortality and respiratory morbidity, even at the low concentration levels (Ponka, 1990) while the effects of SO_2 are direct, especially on health, and its effects are felt very quickly, where most people would feel the worst symptoms in 10–15 minutes after breathing. Furthermore, air pollutants have different effects on health and thus on peoples' life satisfaction, since it is the most important component of the life satisfaction as it can be confirmed by the estimates in Table 3. For instance, a study in Helsinki, found that in a model containing temperature, NO, NO_2, CO, SO_2, O_3 and PM_{10}, simultaneously, NO, O_3

Table 4. Life Satisfaction Estimates for Movers.

Variables	Adapted Probit FE	SEM
Log of equivalent household income	0.1201[**]	0.1344[**]
	(0.0526)	(0.0572)
O_3	− 0.0038	− 0.0045
	(0.0073)	(0.0051)
SO_2	− 0.0054	− 0.0057
	(0.0065)	(0.0041)
NO_2	− 0.0025[**]	− 0.0032[*]
	(0.0012)	(0.0017)
CO	− 0.0011	− 0.0014
	(0.0023)	(0.0012)
PM_{10}	− 0.0014[*]	− 0.0018
	(0.0008)	(0.0014)
No. of obs.	3,517	3,517
R^2	0.4321	
Root mean square error of approximation (RMSEA)		0.0683
CFI		0.883
TLI		0.845
RMS		0.084
MWTP for a drop of one standard deviation in O_3 per year		
MWTP for a drop of one standard deviation in SO_2 per year		
MWTP for a drop of one standard deviation in NO_2 per year	$6,169	$4,480
MWTP for a drop of one standard deviation in CO per year		
MWTP for a drop of one standard deviation in PM_{10} per year	$3,454	

Note: Standard errors are in brackets, [**] and [*] indicate significance at 5% and 10% level.

and CO alone were significant predictors of respiratory hospital admissions (Ponka, 1990). On the other hand, SO_2 and PM_{10} have been found to have more significant adverse effects on cardiovascular diseases than O_3 (Ponka, 1990; Medina *et al.*, 2006; Brauer *et al.*, 2012). Schwartz (1991) analysed the relationship between air pollution and daily mortality in Detroit, during the period 1973–1982 and he found a positive relationship between mortality and particulate matters, but no significant relationship between mortality, O_3 and SO_2. Schwartz *et al.* (1991) explored the variation of the daily hospital admissions and the daily visits to paediatricians for obstructive bronchitis in children in five German towns in the mid-1980s and they found that in regression models where only one pollutant was included – SO_2, NO_2 and total suspended particles (TSP) – were all significant, where TSP is an archaic measure of PM which has been replaced afterwards. However, in the two pollutant models NO_2 and SO_2 were both insignificant, while TSP remained significant in the regression with SO_2. A study exploring the long term effects of air pollution in a Dutch cohort, black smoke (BS) and nitrogen dioxide (NO_2) were found to be positively associated with respiratory mortality but not significant estimates were found for SO_2 and $PM_{2.5}$ (Beelen *et al.*, 2008) Therefore, the studies are mixed finding negative effects of every pollutant depending on the area and period examined. Moreover, the results of this study cannot be fully compared with previous studies, since it examines the five most important pollutants, while the previous studies explored a less number of air pollutants (Levinsion, 2012; Welsch, 2002, 2006).

Table 5. Life Satisfaction Robustness checks for Nonmovers.

Variables	OLS fixed effects	GMM system	BUC
Life satisfaction one lag		0.1334^{***}	
		(0.0078)	
Log of equivalent household income	0.0687^{***}	0.0954^{***}	0.2143^{***}
	(0.0315)	(0.0071)	(0.0713)
O_3	-0.0025^{***}	-0.0024^{***}	-0.0081^{**}
	(0.0008)	(0.0005)	(0.0038)
SO_2	-0.0033^{***}	-0.0030^{***}	-0.0108^{**}
	(0.0007)	(0.0004)	(0.0053)
NO_2	-0.0016^{**}	-0.0018^{***}	-0.0058^{*}
	(0.0007)	(0.0001)	(0.0023)
CO	-0.0005^{*}	-0.0007^{**}	-0.0017^{**}
	(0.0003)	(0.0003)	(0.0018)
PM_{10}	-0.0007^{*}	-0.0008^{**}	-0.0020^{*}
	(0.00038)	(0.0004)	(0.0025)
No. of obs.	71,084	55,892	58,419
R^2	0.3476		
Wald chi-square		8913.30	9711.1
		$[0.000]$	$[0.000]$
Arellano-Bond test for AR(2) in first differences		1.65	
		$[0.208]$	
Exogeneity test		0.40	
LR chi-square		$[0.818]$	
MWTP for a drop of one standard deviation in O_3 per year	$9,206	$8,180	$8,535
MWTP for a drop of one standard deviation in SO_2 per year	$12,935	$11,175	$11,320
MWTP for a drop of one standard deviation in NO_2 per year	$6,725	$5,685	$6,270
MWTP for a drop of one standard deviation in CO per year	$2,135	$1,905	$1,935
MWTP for a drop of one standard deviation in PM_{10} per year	$2,510	$2,150	$2,300

Note: Standard errors are in brackets, ***, ** and * indicate significance at 1%, 5% and 10% level. *p*-values are in square brackets.

In Table 5, the robustness checks for the life satisfaction regressions and the non-movers sample are presented. More specifically, three alternative methods are applied, the OLS with fixed effects, the 'BlowUp and Cluster' (BUC) estimator (see Baetschmann *et al.*, 2015 for technical details), and the GMM system (Blundell and Bond, 1998). The results are similar and the MWTP are close to those found with the Probit adapted fixed effects, with the exception of the GMM, whose MWTP are closer to those derived by the SEM relatively to the other methods. It should be noted that the estimated coefficients of BUC are higher than the coefficients obtained from the other methods, since BUC uses the binary conditional logit model and the coefficients are always higher than OLS regressions. Moreover, the number of observations is much less in BUC, which is common in the cases where variables are constant. More precisely, if an individual reports the same level of life satisfaction, that is, takes value 1 during the whole period examined, then it will be dropped from the sample. This can be one disadvantage of the BUC estimator, as also the estimates with fixed effects do not suffer when the well-being variable is measured in a wide scale from 0 to 10. On the other hand, the main issue is the possible degree of reverse causality between income and life satisfaction.

Overall, all the studies examine the mean change and not standard deviation, with the exception the study by Levinson (2012). However, he examined the PM_{10} in the USA and the MWTP was found equal at \$15,000 in 2012 prices, which is close to our findings, regarding SO_2 and the fixed effects model. However, this study examines additional air pollutants, relies on more precise geographical and spatial area for the air mapping and uses actual income levels rather than mid-points of income scales as it is employed in the study by Levinson (2012).

However, one issue is that the air pollution depends on the location that respondents are moving to, which can be heterogeneous and since the air pollutants are significantly correlated as it has been seen in Table 2, the MWTP of one pollutant may partially represent the MWTP of another. For instance, the MWTP for O_3 may partly represent the MWTP value for NO_2. In order to explore the individual MWTP separate regressions for each pollutant are taken place for both mover and non-movers. In this case it could be argued that the omitted variable bias can be an issue since air pollutants are correlated, but it does not imply that are also confounders. The results are presented in Table 6, where only the coefficients of main interest are reported which are the air pollutants and the income. Based on the results the estimated coefficients for CO and O_3 are insignificant in the movers sample, while the effects of PM_{10} and NO_2 are found to be higher than the respective effects found in Table 3 and 4. Moreover, as it has been discussed in the methodology section, limiting the sample to non-movers may reduce the endogeneity issue coming from residential mobility; however it creates another selection bias due the fact that some of the respondents have already moved to cleaner or dirtier areas before the survey implementation. More specifically, this study proposes a Heckman Selection model into a Structural Equation Modelling framework. This is acceptable since the Heckman model is a two-step model. In particular, in the first step a binary Probit model is estimated exploring the determinants of the selection variable, where in the case examined is the moving status, and then the Inverse Mills ratio is calculated. In the second step the observation function is estimated, which is the life satisfaction, including the same factors as previously, where the Inverse Mills ratio is included as an additional regressor. In the case that Mill ratio is insignificant, it can be claimed that there is no selection bias. Furthermore, it should be noticed, that since panel data are employed, the first step includes a Logit rather than a Probit model, because the former allows for fixed effects. Therefore, the Heckman selection model is applied and the results are presented in Table 7. Finally, the annual averages of the air pollutants and the annual household income with one lag are considered. The reason for this specification is that we find to be more reasonable to explore the probability of the respondents having moved to another location given the pollution and household income one year before, since the survey is conducted annually.

Based on the results of Table 7 the probability of moving is the highest in the case of SO_2 followed by O_3 and PM_{10}, while the respective probabilities are significantly lower in the cases of NO_2 and CO. The MWTP for the air pollutants differ from the respective values found in Table 3 and are closer to SEM. However, the MWTP for PM_{10} and NO_2 are higher and for O_3 become lower. This might indicate that in Table 3 the estimates provide partially the MWTP for each pollutant, while in Table 4 and the movers sample most of the air pollutants are even insignificant. There is no clear explanation for these findings. One reason can be the fact that O_3 is correlated with these two air pollutants, as well as, its formation depends on NO_2 levels, besides the temperature and solar radiation. The small number of moving cases as the location

Table 6. Life Satisfaction SEM Estimates for Air Pollutants.

Variables	Panel A: Nonmovers				
Log of equivalent household income	0.1015^{***}	0.1080^{***}	0.1004^{***}	0.1079^{***}	0.1021^{***}
	(0.0179)	(0.0198)	(0.0176)	(0.0198)	(0.0187)
O_3	-0.0022^{***}				
	(0.0009)				
SO_2		-0.0036^{***}			
		(0.0011)			
NO_2			-0.0019^{**}		
			(0.0008)		
CO				-0.0009^{**}	
				(0.0004)	
PM_{10}					-0.0017^{**}
					(0.0008)
No. of obs.	71,172	71,128	71,225	71,112	71,121
MWTP for a drop of one standard deviation in air pollutant	$6,200	$10,100	$5,500	$2,500	$5,100

	Panel B: Movers				
Equivalent household income	0.1358^{**}	0.1353^{**}	0.1351^{*}	0.1338^{**}	0.1325^{**}
	(0.0618)	(0.0625)	(0.0622)	(0.0782)	(0.0582)
O_3	-0.0020				
	(0.0014)				
SO_2		-0.0031^{*}			
		(0.0014)			
NO_2			-0.0029^{*}		
			(0.0015)		
CO				-0.0010	
				(0.0013)	
PM_{10}					-0.0019^{*}
					(0.0007)
No. of obs.	3,526	3,522	3,532	3,525	3,523
MWTP for a drop of one standard deviation in air pollutant	$4,700	$8,300	$4,300	$2,200	$5,000

Note: Standard errors are in brackets***, ** and * indicate significance at 1%, 5% and 10% level.

they moved may be another cause. Another possible explanation is that conditioning on one or more variables the causal path is blocked-off. For instance, the effect of O_3 on life satisfaction, when the regression is conditioning or controlling for PM_{10}, might be blocked-off, for example, $O_3 \rightarrow PM_{10} \rightarrow LS$ and there is no indirect effect from O_3 to life satisfaction (Spirtes *et al.*, 2000; Pearl, 2000, 2009). Moreover, the inverse Mills ratio is insignificant in all cases indicating that there is no evidence that the selection bias is quantitatively important. Overall, the procedures in Tables 6 and 7 suggest that in order to consider in the analysis latent variables, accounting for measurement error and selection bias and to properly estimate the MWTP individually for each air pollutant the Heckman selection model into a Structural Equation Model framework can be an alternative valuable option.

Table 7. SEM and Heckman Selection Model Fixed Effects.

Variables	Observation equation DV: life satisfaction				
Log of equivalent household income	0.1029^{***}	0.1040^{***}	0.1016^{***}	0.1050^{***}	0.1006^{***}
	(0.0291)	(0.0272)	(0.0275)	(0.0281)	(0.0274)
O_3	-0.0021^{**}				
	(0.0009)				
SO_2		-0.0035^{**}			
		(0.0016)			
NO_2			-0.0018^{*}		
			(0.0010)		
CO				-0.0009^{*}	
				(0.0005)	
PM_{10}					-0.0017^{**}
					(0.0006)

	Selection equation DV: moving status				
Equivalent household income	-0.0411^{**}	-0.0402^{**}	-0.0397^{**}	-0.0394^{**}	-0.0396^{**}
	(0.0182)	(0.0183)	(0.0182)	(0.0182)	(0.0182)
O_3	0.0052^{***}				
	(0.0006)				
SO_2		0.0096^{**}			
		(0.0045)			
NO_2			0.0016^{*}		
			(0.0009)		
CO				0.0001^{***}	
				(0.00004)	
PM_{10}					0.0038^{***}
					(0.0011)
Inverse Mills ratio	-0.2197	-0.5306	-0.3827	-1.3975	-0.7667
	(1.102)	(1.396)	(1.168)	(1.317)	(1.282)
No. of obs.	55,054	54,717	55,223	53,984	53,494
Wald chi-square	1804.45	1768.01	1793.46	1434.71	1659.83
	[0.000]	[0.000]	[0.000]	[0.000]	[0.000]
Rho	-0.2442	-0.5337	-0.4064	-0.9127	-0.6869
	[0.842]	[0.704]	[0.743]	[0.289]	[0.650]
MWTP for a drop of one standard deviation in air pollutant	$6,100	$10,000	$5,400	$2,600	$5,100

Note: Standard errors are in brackets, *p*-values within square brackets ***, ** and * indicate significance at 1%, 5% and 10% level.

The SEM estimates differ from the fixed effects from various aspects. First, it allows to treat health status and permanent income as latent variables accounting for measurement error. Even if the argument that income and expenditures can be a good measure of standard of living and well-being, they might be measured with error. Second, SEM allows a simultaneity regression approach accounting also for possible reciprocal effects between income and life satisfaction and between life satisfaction and health status. A simultaneous approach can be applied for example with seemingly unrelated regressions (SURE), but they do not treat the variables of interest as latent. Third, depending on the theoretical model examined it is possible to derive the direct and indirect effects of the explanatory variables. For instance, education has an indirect effect on life satisfaction as it acts as a causal indicator of permanent income and at the same time has a direct effect on life satisfaction. Similarly, the reciprocal effects between life satisfaction and health status can be explored as well as the indirect effects of health status on permanent income through life satisfaction. For instance based on Figure 1, job status has a direct effect on life satisfaction as well as an indirect effect through permanent income. The direct effect for an unemployed is –0.2505, while the indirect effect through income is –0.0684 resulting to a total effect of –0.3189. Additional relationships can be derived from Figure 1. Continuing with the unemployed, as the job status is a causal indicator of income, it has a direct effect on income equal at –0.1034 as it is expected since unemployed reduces the income. Additionally, there is an indirect effect through life satisfaction, since the model allows for reciprocal effect, and the effect is negative and equal at –0.0342 resulting to a total effect of –0.1376. Thus, unemployment can have a direct effect on income but also a moderating effect through life satisfaction, since less happy or satisfied people are more likely to earn less. Finally, the results support that there is a reverse causality as the people who report higher life satisfaction levels are associated with increases on income by 137.00 (SE: 10.480) Swiss franc on average, while the health is improved by 0.103 (SE: 0.0439). The estimated coefficients are not reported, but are significant at 1% and 5%, respectively. Similarly, other effects can be derived.

It should be noticed that SEM could include additional factors for the measurement equation of life satisfaction. More precisely, these are the emotion variables and their frequency, such as joy, worry, anger and sadness measured in the same scale as life satisfaction, from no frequency (taking value 0) to very frequent (taking value 10). The results are not presented here as the concluding remarks are the same and the coefficients sign is the same (i.e. positive effect of income and negative effect of air pollution on life satisfaction); however, are not the same. Regarding the emotion variables, a negative relationship between the frequency of anger, worry and sadness with life satisfaction is presented, while a positive association between joy and life satisfaction is reported. Moreover, the big five personality traits have been included into SHP in 2009 (wave 11) until 2011 (wave 13) which can be included in a similar fashion with the emotion variables. In this case the life satisfaction can be treated as a latent and unobserved variable and the SEM application could valuable since there might be measurement error in life satisfaction. However, this will restrict the sample of the analysis to 6 waves (and three waves for the personality traits) instead of 14 waves that have been used in this study. This is important because it is desirable, using panel data, to follow the same individual and examine the effects of air pollution across a long time of period. Nevertheless, this is proposed for further research including these factors as additional variables into the measurement equation of life satisfaction, as it has been described in the methodology part, as well as additional covariates in the life satisfaction regressions. Furthermore, using SEM framework, many effects through various paths can be additionally explored. More precisely the theoretical model in this study assumes a direct effect of air pollution on life satisfaction. However, it is likely that indirect effects through health status or job status might be evident, as air pollution affects the health which is a major element of the human capital and development and the impact on job status can be associated with productivity effect from air quality.

Overall, the findings suggest that the MWTP for the air pollutants examined, with the exception of SO_2 and O_3 are relatively low, since are measured in terms of standard deviation, reflecting probably the reduction followed in these air pollutants since 1990s (European

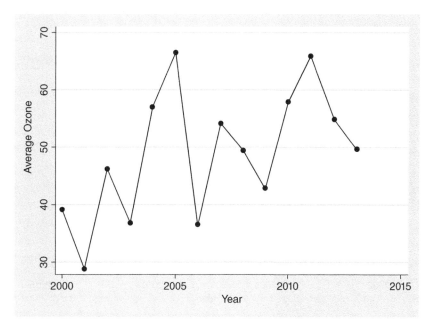

Figure 7. Annual Ozone Averages by Municipality.

Environmental Agency, 2013). It is suggested that the air quality has been improved in Switzerland and in 2010 the emissions overall were significantly lower than in 2000. However, in some (urban) areas, the combination of reduced NO_x and an increasing contribution of hemispheric background ozone is leading to increasing ozone levels in cities and increased population exposures to ground-level ozone (European Environmental Agency, 2013). Moreover, ozone depends mainly on solar radiation and temperature and thus the peak levels are higher reach during the summer. Therefore, while there has been an improvement on air quality regarding the remained air pollutants examined in this study, O_3 still has persistent effects owned also to climate change and increase on temperature. Regarding the high MWTP values for SO_2 and O_3 can also be explained that are observed by the people, as the former is responsible for the formation of winter smogs, while the latter is mainly responsible for the summer smogs. Since people are educated about the cause and effects of air pollutants, it is reasonable that the MWTP to be higher for these two air pollutants (Notholt *et al.*, 2005). In Figures 7–11, the annual averages based on municipality level for the air pollutants during the period examined are reported. It becomes clear that there is a reduction for all pollutants, especially for CO. The only exception is O_3 which presents a small increase. This can explain also the high MWTP for this pollutant.

6. Conclusions

The findings show that income effects are underestimated when the reverse causality is not considered leading to higher monetary values. In addition, the importance of this study comes from the fact that the analysis relies on detailed micro-level data, using highly spatially disaggregated data based on municipality zip codes, capturing more precise the air pollution effects,

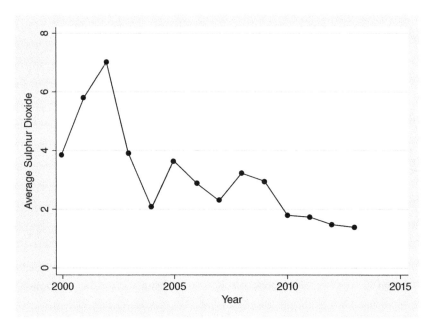

Figure 8. Annual Sulphur Dioxide Averages by Municipality.

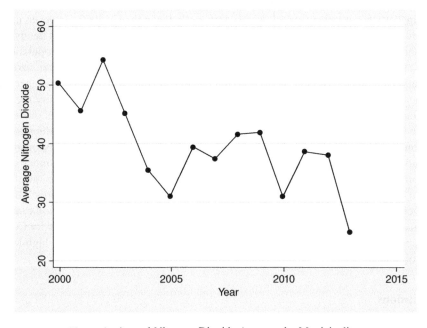

Figure 9. Annual Nitrogen Dioxide Averages by Municipality.

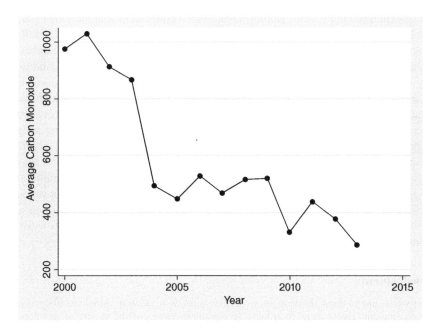

Figure 10. Annual Carbon Monoxide Averages by Municipality.

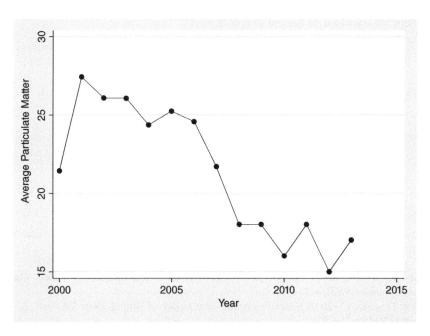

Figure 11. Annual Particulate Matter less than 10 Microns Averages by Municipality.

which are not captured in previous studies. Overall the results show that the MWTP are relatively low for NO_2, CO and PM_{10}, while the highest values are observed for O_3 and SO_2.

One important point revealed by this study, consistent with the previous researches is the negative and significant direct effects of air pollution on individuals' well being. Additionally, this study showed that there is evidence of a substantial trade-off between income and air quality. Larger scale researches, using more than one country and based on high spatially disaggregated data is suggested in order to clarify the potentially complex links between well-being, income and individuals' exposure to air pollution. This could offer further insights to policy makers in order to achieve happier, cleaner and more sustainable cities. In addition, the life satisfaction approach as well as the SEM framework proposed can be useful for policy makers on environmental regulation decision making. Moreover, future structural modelling applications including additional robustness checks for gender, age groups, urban versus rural areas among others, is suggested. Furthermore, the application and test of SEM in other surveys and datasets, and the quest for the causal effects of income and public goods on life satisfaction can be continued.

Acknowledgements

The authors would like to thank the anonymous reviewers for their valuable comments, suggestions and constructive comments that greatly contributed to the improvement of the quality of this paper. Any remaining errors or omissions remain the responsibility of the authors.

The authors would also like to thank Denise Bloch at FORS, Bureau 5614 Quartier UNIL-Mouline Bâtiment Géopolis 1015 Lausanne for providing the access to the Swiss Household Panel Survey Data. In addition, they are grateful to Dr. Rudolf Weber at Eidg. Departement für Umwelt, Verkehr, Energie und Kommunikation UVEK Bundesamt für Umwelt BAFU Abteilung Luftreinhaltung und Chemikalien CH-3003 Bern, who provided the relevant air pollution data.

Note

1. The first wave is not considered as the life satisfaction question is not included.

References

Adamowicz, W., Louviere, J. and Swait, J. (1998) Introduction to attribute-based stated choice methods. Final Report to National Oceanic and Atmospheric Administration (NOAA), US.

Baetschmann, G., Staub, K.E. and Winkelmann, R. (2015) Consistent estimation of the fixed effects ordered Logit model. *Journal of the Royal Statistical Society: Series A (Statistics in Society* 178(3): 685–703.

Bauer, S.E. and Langmann, B. (2002) Analysis of a summer smog episode in the Berlin-Brandenburg region with a nested atmosphere—chemistry model. *Atmospheric Chemistry and Physics* 2(4): 259–270.

Bayer, P. and Timmins, C. (2005) On the equilibrium properties of locational sorting models. *Journal of Urban Economics* 57(3): 462–477.

Bayer, P. and Timmins, C. (2007) Estimating equilibrium models of sorting across locations. *Economic Journal* 117(518): 353–374.

Bayer, P., Keohane, N.O. and Timmins, C. (2009) Migration and hedonic valuation: The case of air quality. *Journal of Environmental Economics and Management* 58: 1–14.

Beelen, R., Hoek, G., van den Brandt, P.A., Goldbohm, R.A. Fischer, P., Schouten, L.J., Jerrett, M., Hughes, E., Armstrong, B. and Brunekreef, B. (2008) Long-term effects of traffic-related air pollution on mortality in a Dutch cohort (NLCS-AIR Study). *Environmental Health Perspectives* 116(2): 196–202.

Bentler, P.M. (1990) Comparative Fit Indexes in Structural Models. *Psychological Bulletin* 107(2): 238–246.

Blundell, R. and Bond, S. (1998) Initial conditions and moment restrictions in dynamic panel data models. *Journal of Econometrics* 87: 115–143.

Bollen, K.A. (1989) *Structural Equations with Latent Variables.* 1st edition, John Wiley & Sons, New York.

Bölük, G. and Mert, M. (2014) Fossil and renewable energy consumption, GHGs (greenhouse gases) and economic growth: Evidence from a panel of EU (European Union) countries. *Energy* 74(1): 439–446.

Brauer, M., Amann, M., Burnett, R.T., Cohen, A., Dentener, F., Ezzati, M., Henderson, S.B., Krzyzanowski, M., Martin, R.V., Van Dingenen, R., van Donkelaar, A. and Thurston, G. (2012) Exposure assessment for estimation of the global burden of disease attributable to outdoor air pollution. *Environmental Science and Technology* 46: 652–660.

Bruni, L. and Porta, P. (2005) *Economics and Happiness: Framing the Analysis.* New York: Oxford University Press.

Calabrese, S., Epple, S. and Romano, R. (2007) On the political economy of zoning. *Journal of Public Economics* 91(1–2): 25–49.

Campbell, D. (2007) Willingness to pay for rural landscape improvements: Combining mixed Logit and random-effects models. *Journal of Agricultural Economics* 58(3): 467–483.

Campbell, D., Hutchinson, G. and Scarpa, R. (2008) Incorporating discontinuous preferences into the analysis of discrete choice experiments. *Environmental and Resource Economics* 41: 401–417.

Campbell, D., Hensher, D.A. and Scarpa, R. (2011) Nonattendance to attributes in environmental choice analysis: A latent class specification. *Journal of Environmental Planning and Management* 54(8): 1061–1076.

Carson, R.T., Mitchell, R.C., Hanemann, W.M., Kopp, R.J., Presser, S. and Ruud, P.A. (2003) Contingent valuation and lost passive use: Damages from the Exxon Valdez oil spill. *Environmental and Resource Economics* 25: 257–286.

Charron, A. and Harrison, R.M. (2003) Primary particle formation from vehicle emissions during exhaust dilution in the roadside atmosphere. *Atmospheric Environment* 37(29): 4109–4119.

Clark, A.E. and Oswald, A.J. (1994) Unhappiness and unemployment. *The Economic Journal* 104: 648–659.

Clark, A.E. and Oswald, A.J. (1996) Satisfaction and comparison income. *Journal of Public Economics* 61: 359–381.

Croper, M.L. and Oates, W.E. (1992) Environmental economics: A survey. *Journal of Economic Literature* 302: 675–740.

Dockery, A.M. (2003) Happiness, life satisfaction and the role of work: Evidence from two Australian surveys. HILDA Working Paper No.3/10.

Dockery, A.M. (2010) 'Education and happiness in the school-to-work transition', National Centre for Vocational Education Research (NCVER), Adelaide.

Easterlin, R. (2001) Income and happiness: Towards a unified theory. *Economic Journal* 111: 465–484.

Easterlin, R.A. (2006) Life cycle happiness and its sources: Intersections of psychology, economics, and demography. *Journal of Economic Psychology* 27: 463–482.

European Environmental Agency. (2013) *Air Pollution Fact Sheet 2013 Switzerland.* Copenhagen, Denmark: European Environment Agency.

Ferreira, S. and Moro, M. (2010) On the use of subjective well-being data for environmental valuation. *Environmental and Resource Economics* 46(3): 249–273.

Ferreira, S., Akay, A., Brereton, F., Cuñado, J., Martinsson, P., Moro, M. and Ningal, T.F. (2013) Life satisfaction and air quality in Europe. *Ecological Economics* 8: 1–10.

Ferreyra, M.M. (2007) Estimating the effects of private school vouchers in multidistrict economies. *American Economic Review* 97(3): 789–817.

Frey, B., Luechinger, S. and Stutzer, A. (2010) The life satisfaction approach to environmental valuation. *Annual Review of Resource Economics* 2: 139–160.

Friedman, M. (1957) *A theory of the consumption function*. Princeton, New Jersey, USA: Princeton University Press.

Giovanis, E. (2012) Environmental Kuznets curve: Evidence from the British household panel survey. *Journal of Economic Modelling* 30: 602–611.

Giovanis, E. (2014) relationship between well-being and recycling rates: Evidence from life satisfaction approach in Britain. *Journal of Environmental Economics and Policy* 3(2): 201–214.

Grossman, G.M. and Krueger, A.B. (1993) Pollution and growth: What do we know? In I. Goldin and L. Winters (eds.), *The Economics of Sustainable Development*. Cambridge, MA: MIT Press.

Grossman, G.M. and Krueger, A.B. (1995) Economic growth and the environment. *Quarterly Journal of Economics* 110(2): 353–377.

Hall, J.V., Winer, A.M., Kleinman, M.T., Lurmann, F.W., Brajer, V. and Colome, S.D. (1992) Valuing the health benefits of cleaner air. *Science* 255: 812–817.

Hammitt, J.K. and Zhou, Y. (2006) The economic value of air-pollution-related health risks in China: A contingent valuation study. *Environmental and Resource Economics* 33: 399–423.

Hancock, G. R. and Mueller, R. O. (2006) *Structural equation modeling: A second course*. Information Age Publishing, Inc. Greenwich, Charlotte, North Carolina, USA.

Hanley, N., Koop, G., Wright, R. and Alvarez-Farizo, B. (2001a) Go climb a mountain: An application of recreational demand models to rock climbing. *Journal of Agricultural Economics* 52(1): 36–51.

Hanley, N., Mourato, S. and Wright, R.E. (2001b) Choice modelling approaches: A superior alternative for environmental valuation? *Journal of Economic Surveys* 15(3): 435–462.

Hauser, R.M. and Warren, J.R. (1997) Socioeconomic indexes for occupations: A review, update, and critique. In A.E. Raftery (ed.), *Sociological Methodology* (pp. 177–298). Cambridge: Blackwell.

Heckman, J. (1979) Sample selection bias as a specification error. *Econometrica* 47(1): 153–161.

Hernan, M.A., Hernandez-Diaz, S. and Robins, J.M. (2004) A structural approach to selection bias. *Epidemiology* 15: 615–625.

Houthakker, H.S. (1957) The permanent income hypothesis: A review article. *American Economic Review* 47(2): 396–404.

Hu, L. and Bentler, P.M. (1999) Cutoff criteria in fix indexes in covariance structure analysis: Conventional criteria versus new alternatives. *Structural Equation Modeling* 6(1): 1–55.

Ioannides, Y.M. and Zabel, J.E. (2008) Interactions, neighbourhood selection and housing demand. *Journal of Urban Economics* 63: 229–252.

Kahneman, D., Ritov, I. and Schkade, D. (1999) Economic preferences or attitude expressions? An analysis of dollar responses to public issues. *Journal of Risk and Uncertainty* 19: 220–242.

Krause, A. (2010) The effect of unemployment on life and satisfaction an analysis for Switzerland in its cultural diversity. Working Paper, Lausanne. Available at: http://www.iza.org/conference_files/ReDisWeBe2010/krause_a5647.pdf (Retrieved on 15 August 2015)

Kuminoff, N.V., Parmeter, C.F. and Pope, J.C. (2010) Which hedonic models can we trust to recover the marginal willingness to pay for environmental amenities? *Journal of Environmental Economics and Management* 63: 145–160.

Kuminoff, N.V., Smith, V.K. and Timmins, C. (2013) The new economics of equilibrium sorting and policy evaluation using housing markets. *Journal of Economic Literature* 51(4): 1007–1062.

Kuznets, S. (1955) Economic growth and income inequality. *American Economic Review* 45: 1–28.

Levinson, A. (2012) Valuing public goods using happiness data: The case of air quality. *Journal of Public Economics* 96 (9–10): 869–880.

Loehman, E. and De, V. (1982) Application of stochastic choice modeling to policy analysis of public goods: A case study of air quality improvements. *The Review of Economics and Statistics* 64: 474–480.

Luechinger, S. (2009) Valuing air quality using the life satisfaction approach. *Economic Journal* 119(536): 482–515.

Luechinger, S. (2010) Life satisfaction and transboundary air pollution. *Economics Letters* 1071: 4–6.

MacKerron, G. and Mourato, S. (2009) Life satisfaction and air quality in London. *Ecological Economics* 685: 1441–1453.

Mayer, T. (1963) The permanent income theory and occupational groups. *Review of Economics and Statistics* 45(1): 16–22.

Medina-Ramon, M., Zanobetti, A. and Schwartz, J. (2006) The effect of ozone and PM10 on hospital admissions for pneumonia and chronic obstructive pulmonary disease: A National Multicity Study. *American Journal of Epidemiology* 163(6): 579–588.

Muthen, B. and Asparouhov, T. (2012) Bayesian structural equation modeling: A more flexible representation of substantive theory. *Psychological Methods* 17(3): 313–335.

Myers, D.G. (2000) The funds, friends, and faith of happy people. *American Psychologist* 55 (1): 56–67.

Notholt, J., Luo, B.P., Fueglistaler, S., Weisenstein, D., Rex, M., Lawrence, M.G., Bingemer, H., Wohltmann, I., Corti, T., Warneke, T., von Kuhlmann, R. and Peter, T. (2005) Influence of tropospheric SO2 emissions on particle formation and the stratospheric humidity. *Geophysical Research Letters* 32: L07810, doi:10.1029/2004GL022159.

Panayotou, T. (1997) Environmental Kuznets curve. *Environment and Development Economics* 2: 465–484.

Pearl, J. (2000) *Causality. Models, Reasoning, and Inference*. Cambridge: Cambridge University Press.

Pearl, J. (2009) Causal inference in statistics: An overview. *Statistical Surveys* 3: 96–146.

Ponka, A. (1990) Absenteeism and respiratory disease among children and adults in Helsinki in relation to low level air pollution in Helsinki. *Environmental Research* 52: 34–46.

Powdthavee, N. (2010) How much does money really matter? Estimating the causal effects of income on happiness. *Empirical Economics* 39: 77–92.

Powdthavee, N. and Wooden, M. (2015) Life satisfaction and sexual minorities: Evidence from Australia and the United Kingdom. *Journal of Economic Behavior and Organization* 116: 107–126.

Rabin, M. (1998) Psychology and economics. *Journal of Economic Literature* 361: 11–46.

Rehdanz, K. and Maddison, D. (2008) Local environmental quality and life-satisfaction in Germany. *Ecological Economics* 64: 787–797.

Ridker, R.G. and Henning, J.A. (1967) The determinants of residential property values with special reference to air pollution. *The Review of Economics and Statistics* 492: 246–257.

Rosen, S. (1974). Hedonic prices and implicit markets: Product differentiation in pure competition. *Journal of Political Economy* 82: 34–55.

Ross, C.E. and Van Willigen, M. (1997) Education and the subjective quality of life. *Journal of Health and Social Behavior* 38(3): 275–297.

Scheines, R., Hoijtink, H. and Boomsma, A. (1999) Bayesian estimation and testing of structural equation models. *Psychometrika* 64: 37–52.

Schwartz, J. (1991) Particulate air pollution and daily mortality in Detroit. *Environmental Research* 56: 204–213.

Schwartz, J., Spix, C., Wichmann, H.E. and Malin, E. (1991) Air pollution and acute respiratory illness in five German communities. *Environmental Research* 56: 1–14.

Selden, T. and Song, D. (1994) Environmental quality and development: Is there a Kuznets curve for air pollution emissions? *Journal of Environmental Economics and Management* 27: 147–162.

Smith, V.K. and Huang, J.C. (1995) Can markets value air quality? A meta-analysis of hedonic property value models. *Journal of Political Economy* 1031: 209–227.

Spirtes, P., Glymour, C. and Scheines, R. (2000) *Causation, Prediction, and Search* (2nd edn). Cambridge, MA: MIT Press.

Stutzer, A. (2004) The role of income aspirations in individual happiness. *Journal of Economic Behaviour and Organisation* 54: 89–109.

Stutzer, A. and Frey, B. (2012) Recent developments in the economics of happiness: A selective overview, Discussion Paper No 7978, The Institute for the Study of Labour (IZA), Bonn.

Sweetland, S.R. (1996) Human capital theory: Foundations of a field of inquiry. *Review of Educational Research* 66(3): 341–359.

Toro, M.V., Cremades, L.V. and Calbo, J. (2006) Relationship between VOC and NOx emissions and chemical production of tropospheric ozone in the Aburra Valley (Colombia). *Chemosphere* 65(5): 881–888.

Tsui, H.C. (2014) What affects happiness: Absolute income, relative income or expected income. *Journal of Policy Modeling* 36(6): 994–1007.

Tucker, L.R. and Lewis, C. (1973) A reliability coefficient for maximum likelihood factor analysis. *Psychometrica* 38(1): 1–10.

Van Praag, B.M.S. and Ferrer-i-Carbonell, A. (2004) *Happiness Quantified: A Satisfaction Calculus Approach*. Oxford: Oxford University Press.

Veenhoven, R. (1996) Developments in satisfaction research. *Social Indicators Research* 37: 1–46.

Verhaest, D. and Omey, E. (2009) Objective over-education and worker well-being: A shadow price approach. *Journal of Economic Psychology* 30: 469–481.

Vingarzan, R. (2004) A review of surface ozone background levels and trends. *Atmospheric Environment* 38(21): 3431–3442.

Vollebergh, R.J.H., Melenberg, B. and Dijkgraaf, E. (2009) Identifying reduced-form relations with panel data: The case of pollution and income. *Journal of Environmental Economics and Management* 58(1): 27–42.

Wang, T., Cheung, T.F. and Li, Y.S. (2002) Emission characteristics of CO, NOx, SO2 and indications of biomass burning observed at a rural site in eastern China. *Journal of Geophysical Research* 107(D12): 4157, doi:10.1029/2001JD000724.

Welsch, H. (2002) Preferences over prosperity and pollution: Environmental valuation based on happiness surveys. *Kyklos* 55(4): 473–494.

Welsch, H. (2006) Environment and happiness: Valuation of air pollution using life satisfaction data. *Ecological Economic* 58: 801–813.

Wennberg, P.O., Hanisco, T.F., Jaegle, L., Jacob, D.J., Hintsa, E.J., Lanzendorf, E.J., Anderson, J.G., Gao, R.-S. Keim, E.R., Donnelly, S.G., Del Negro, L.A., Fahey, D.W., McKeen, S.A., Salawitch, R.J., Webster, C.R., May, R.D., Herman, R.L., Proffitt, M.H., Margitan, J.J., Atlas, E.L., Schauffler, S.M., Flocke, F., McElroy, C.T. and Bui, T.P. (1998) Hydrogen radicals, nitrogen radicals, and the production of O3 in the upper troposphere. *Science* 279(5347): 49–53.

4

THE DECOMPOSITION AND DYNAMICS OF INDUSTRIAL CARBON DIOXIDE EMISSIONS FOR 287 CHINESE CITIES IN 1998–2009

Maximilian Auffhammer

UC Berkeley & National Bureau of Economic Research

Weizeng Sun

Jinan University & Tsinghua University

Jianfeng Wu

Fudan University

Siqi Zheng

Department of Urban Studies and Planning, Massachusetts Institute of Technology & Hang Lung Center for Real Estate, Tsinghua University

1. Introduction

Urban energy use significantly contributes to climate change. According to the Fifth Assessment Report of the Intergovernmental Panel on Climate Change (IPCC), urban areas account for between 67% and 76% of global energy consumption and generate about three quarters of global carbon emissions (Creutzig *et al.*, 2013). This share is even larger in China where 85% of carbon emissions are attributed to urban economic activities, and this share will likely increase as China's urban population is projected to grow by 240 million over the next 35 years (Liu, 2015).

Industrialization and urbanization have gone hand in hand during China's rapid economic development. In the past three decades China has been the 'The World's Factory' (e.g. 40% of the world's clothes are 'Made in China'[1]), largely driven by the fast growth of export-oriented, labor- and energy-intensive industries in cities. In urban areas the industrial sector emits much more carbon dioxide than the residential sector. In 2011, China's industrial sector consumed about 71% of the country's total energy, while in the USA, the manufacturing sector's share reached a peak of 41% in 1951, and declined to 32% in 2013.[2,3]

Environmental Economics and Sustainability, First Edition. Edited by Brian Chi-ang Lin and Siqi Zheng.
Chapters © 2017 The Authors. Book compilation © 2017 John Wiley & Sons, Ltd. Published 2017 by John Wiley & Sons, Ltd.

While cities play an important role in shaping China's CO_2 emissions, the patterns and dynamics of city-level CO_2 emissions in China remain largely unexplored due to data unavailability. Some studies examine the provincial level CO_2 emissions across China, but they do not perform disaggregate analysis at the city level (Wang *et al.*, 2014; Xu and Lin, 2015). A city-level study by Zheng *et al.* (2010) estimates household carbon emissions across 74 Chinese cities, and ranks those cities with respect to a standardized household's carbon emissions. They find that based on this criterion, even in the dirtiest city (Daqing), a standardized household produces only one-fifth the emissions compared to those in America's greenest city (San Diego). However, such patterns may flip if we look at the industrial carbon emissions in those cities. A recent report by the PBL Netherlands Environmental Assessment Agency estimates that the emitted CO_2 per GDP (corrected for purchasing power parity) in China reached 650 kg CO_2/1000 USD, which is almost twice as much as that of the USA (330 kg CO_2/ 1,000 USD).[4]

The first purpose of our paper is to conduct an accounting style decomposition of city-level industrial carbon dioxide emissions growth into three separate effects: the scale, composition and technique effects. In line with Copeland and Taylor (2004), these three effects work together to determine the total energy consumption, and thus CO_2 emissions, for a city's industrial sector. Scale refers to the output located in a city while composition refers to a city's industry mix and the vintage of its capital stock. Technique represents energy consumption per unit of economic activity. We do such decomposition work for Chinese prefecture-level and above cities during the period of 1998–2009. China has 287 prefecture-level and above cities, which vary significantly in population size and productivity level. Following the city classification method in OECD (2005), we group them into three tiers based on city size and economic development stage: 4 first-tier cities (Beijing, Shanghai, Guangzhou and Shenzhen), 31 second-tier cities including capital cities across all provinces in China and 252 third-tier cities (all the other prefecture-level cities). This decomposition exercise helps us better understand how cities behave differently according to the dynamics of their industrial carbon dioxide emissions.

The second goal of our paper is to gain a better understanding of the environmental consequences of the influx of FDI and environmental regulations. We do this by examining their impacts on the scale, composition and technique effects for the industrial CO_2 emission growth path. The relationship between FDI and a city's (local and global) pollution is ambiguous, depending on two competing forces (Copeland and Taylor, 2004). The first is the raw scale of capital investment such as heavy machines and construction equipment in factories. This should lead to a positive effect of FDI on CO_2 emissions ('pollution haven' hypothesis). On the other hand, FDI may help a city to upgrade the quality of its capital stock and such technique effect may translate into lower energy consumption and CO_2 emissions. The optimistic case would be more likely if new capital is significantly cleaner than older durable capital. Therefore the decomposition analysis will help us determine whether the scale or the technique effect dominates the impact of FDI inflow on the industrial CO_2 emissions trend in urban China.

Where firms locate is both a function of the natural advantages of different geographic areas and of the regulatory policies and incentives offered by different local governments. Local governments who are aware of this strategic dynamic must decide whether to enforce regulations and pay the price of losing some mobile dirty jobs or to enjoy the environmental gains of deindustrializing. A strand of the literature on environmental regulation has documented that differential enforcement of pollution regulation encourages industrial migration to areas featuring laxer regulation (Kahn, 1997; Becker and Henderson, 2000; Greenstone, 2002; Kahn and Mansur, 2013). In the richer first-tier and some of the second-tier cities, Chinese local governments are starting to enforce stricter environmental regulations (Zheng and Kahn, 2013). Based on our decomposition results, we are able to explore how typical environmental regulations affect a city's industrial pollution via these three channels – losing dirty firms (both scale and composition effects) or encouraging incumbent firms to improve their technology (technique effect).

The remainder of this paper is organized as follows: Section 3.2.1.2 surveys the relevant literature. Section 3.2.1.3 presents the decomposition analysis of CO_2 emissions across cities in China. Section 4 investigates the impacts of FDI and environmental regulations on the changes in CO_2 emissions and its decomposed parts. Section 5 concludes.

2. Survey of Related Literature

2.1 Scale, Composition, Technique Effects and the Decomposition Methodology

A change in energy consumption, pollution and carbon dioxide emissions can be decomposed into three channels: the scale effect, the composition effect and the technique effect (see Copeland and Taylor, 1994, 2003; Grossman and Krueger, 1995; Antweiler et al., 2001; Managi et al., 2009). The scale effect measures the effect on pollution of an increase in the economy size that results from income-driven growth in production. Other things being equal, a positive scale effect means that rising industrial output will drive up CO_2 emissions. Managi et al. (2009) find a positive effect of trade openness on CO_2 emissions for non-OECD countries, providing suggestive evidence of the scale effect from trade-driven increases in industrial production. The second is the composition effect, which measures the impacts of a change in industrial composition. This effect could be positive or negative, depending on the abundance of resources and the strength of environmental policy of the economy. For instance, a shift in an economy from relatively clean service industries towards relatively dirty ones such as steel and cement production is considered a composition effect and will lead to an increase in energy consumption and CO_2 emissions. Moreover, the composition effect may also be positive if more stringent environmental regulations increase costs and drive out polluting firms. A recent study by Zheng and Kahn (2013) shows that the rising costs and tighter environmental standards – especially for carbon dioxide and sulfur dioxide emissions – in the large Chinese cities have pushed those heavily polluting manufacturers to shut down their factories or to relocate them to other places with laxer environmental regulations.

The third one is the technique effect, which relates to the change in the production technique of a given industry. All else being equal, if the manufacturers in an industry adopt more efficient environmentally friendly production methods and improve management quality, it will induce a negative technique effect, thus reducing energy consumption and CO_2 emissions per unit of economic activity within this industry. Shapiro and Walker (2015) find that the observed decrease in nitrogen oxide emissions (NO_x) in the USA during the period of 1990–2008 is more attributable to falling pollution per unit of output within industries at a more disaggregated level, suggesting the existence of a technique effect in those industries. A study focusing on China by Zhang (2012) finds that the changes in input mix, sector energy intensity, fuel mix and carbon intensity of fuels can offset the increasing trade-induced carbon emissions in twenty-six sectors including agriculture, mining, manufacturing and service industries. His analysis provides some evidence that the technique effect contributes to mitigating pollution emissions arising from the energy consumption by trade-oriented sectors.

The decomposition of energy consumption, pollution and CO_2 emission changes into scale, composition and technique effects can be found in several studies. Some of them rely on the Divisia index method (Lin and Chang, 1996; Viguier, 1999). Another avenue makes use of structural decomposition analysis (SDA) based on input-output tables. This line of decomposition methods is based on regression analysis performed on aggregate data, and is often referred to as a 'top-down' approach. Twenty years ago, Grossman and Krueger (1995) introduced scale, composition and technique effects into the trade and the environment literature by developing a bottom-up approach, which relies on disaggregated emission and economic activity data.

Many studies have applied this 'bottom-up' approach to investigate the air-pollution dynamics using both cross-country and within-country data. For example, using data of sulfur dioxide concentrations across 293 cities in 44 countries from the Global Environment Monitoring Project over the period 1971–1996, Antweiler *et al.* (2001) decompose the pollution impacts of free trade into scale (GDP), composition (capital-labor endowment ratios), and technique effects. They regress pollution concentrations on representative variables of the above three effects. They attempt to distinguish between the pollution impacts of income changes brought on by international trade from those created by factor accumulation. Their empirical results show a positive scale effect, a negative technique effect and a negative composition effect. The composition effect caused by trade is found to vary across countries depending on relative income and factor endowments. Dean (2002) applies this decomposition framework to estimate the effect of trade openness on water pollution at the provincial level in China from 1987 to 1995. She estimates a two-equation model in which trade has both a direct effect on environmental quality through a composition effect and an indirect effect through an induced technique effect. She finds that the inflow of pollution-intensive industries aggravates environmental damage in China, but openness tends to reduce the environmental costs through stronger regulation as trade-induced income increases. Shapiro and Walker (2015) recently explained the decline of air pollution in the USA between 1990 and 2008 by utilizing this bottom-up decomposition approach. Following this decomposition methodology, this paper examines the change in CO_2 emissions in the context of China for a large number of cities and with more disaggregated sub-sectors in Section 3.2.1.3.

2.2 *The Impact of FDI and Environmental Regulation on Industrial CO_2 Emissions*

The decomposition framework allows scholars to better understand the dynamics and the underlying mechanisms of industrial CO_2 emissions at a geographic level (national, state/provincial, or city). In this paper we focus on two underlying forces, FDI and environmental regulation, and examine how they affect the three decomposition effects, thus shaping CO_2 emissions dynamics. Existing studies show mixed empirical findings on their effects since they examine different samples in different study periods. Moreover, current studies lack of a clean identification strategy to separate the different channels. Our analysis attempts to improve upon the literature by explicitly looking at their impacts on all three decomposition effects. We first survey the related literature.

2.2.1 *FDI*

Previous studies have highlighted the role played by the influx of FDI on local environmental quality in China. Ex ante, there are two different possible channels associated with urban

FDI inflows. One possibility is that cities experiencing increased FDI inflows become dirtier as the scale of industrial production increases and the composition of industries tilts towards dirtier heavy manufacturing. In a system of cities where foreign investors can choose between many cities within a developing country, they may seek out cities with laxer environmental regulation. This is a pollution haven effect (Copeland and Taylor, 2004). The empirical analyses by He (2006, 2009) show that pollution (which should be positively correlated with CO_2 emissions) and FDI are positively correlated in China as FDI increases industrial output and pushes up carbon emissions.

The other possibility is that FDI reduces energy consumption and thus CO_2 emissions in a city because such new capital from western countries helps to modernize the capital stock, leading to a technique effect. Zheng *et al.* (2010) use data across 35 major Chinese cities for the years 2003–2006 and report a negative correlation between a city's FDI influx and its ambient air pollution levels. Wang and Jin (2007) find that foreign firms exhibit better environmental performance than state-owned and privately owned firms as they adopt cleaner techniques in production.

Therefore we predict that the impact of the inflow of FDI on pollution varies across cities depending on whether the technique effect can outpace its scale effect, and the direction of its composition effect. We will use our decomposition results to explicitly test this hypothesis in Section 4.

2.2.2 *Environmental Regulations*

The current literature argues that local officials' incentives and efforts to regulate pollution vary across different regions and cities in China. Van Rooij and Lo (2010) show that the more developed cities in coastal China have more stringent environmental regulations. Zheng *et al.* (2014) also find that people in richer cities in China are willing to pay more for the clean environment and this incentivizes their local leaders to pursue more stringent environmental regulations. In China, as in the rest of the world, regulators rely on two types of environmental regulation: one is a standards-driven administrative intervention such as stipulation of scrubber installment (Xu *et al.*, 2009); the second relies on economic incentives including pollution levy (Wang and Wheeler, 2005; Lin, 2013) and more recently local cap and trade markets (Auffhammer and Gong, 2015).

Stringent environmental regulations will cause regulated firms to bear compliance costs, and this will push them to either improve their production technology (technique effect), or locate to regions with laxer regulations, known as the pollution haven hypothesis (scale and composition effects). The empirical studies of US manufacturing provide evidence that manufacturing firms tend to move to less regulated areas (Henderson, 1996; Berman and Bui, 2001a, 2001b; Greenstone, 2002). In China, mayors of big coastal cities face incentives leading them to drive dirty firms out of their cities, whereas the city mayors in under-developed areas welcome them because of the investment, job opportunities and fiscal revenue brought by those energy-intensive manufacturers. The recent literature shows that the city mayors in inland China face incentives to accept large firms' heavy pollution in return for the generation of local tax revenue, jobs and economic growth (see Yu *et al.*, 2013; Jiang *et al.*, 2014). Moreover, relocation of dirty firms due to tight pollution regulation has been found to take place both across regions and within regions in China. For instance, Guangdong province is subsidizing polluting firms in the Pearl River Delta to relocate to the northern part of the province and Jiangsu province drives those firms to the north-Jiangsu (*Subei*) area. These moves reflect the provincial governments' strategy to green the big city by moving dirty industrial activities further from the major population centers and to narrow income gaps across cities by spreading wealth to the poor underperforming areas (Zheng and Kahn, 2013; Cai *et al.*, 2016). Again, our decomposition results will help us look into the above channels, which may be different across different tiers of cities.

3 Decomposition of Carbon Dioxide Emissions in Chinese Cities

3.1 *Decomposition Framework*

Following the recent literature (e.g. Shapiro and Walker, 2015), we decompose the change in a city's industrial CO_2 emissions into scale, composition and technique effects. Let x_{kit} be the output measure (we use value-added in this paper) for industry i in city k in year t, e_{kit} be the CO_2 emission intensity per unit of output. Then, CO_2 emissions for city k in year t, P_{kt}, is given by

$$P_{kt} = \sum_i x_{kit} \cdot e_{kit} \tag{1}$$

Let X_{kt} be the total output for all industries in city k in year t and θ_{kit} the output share of industry i in city k in year t. Then Equation (1) can be rewritten as follows:

$$P_{kt} = X_{kt} \cdot \sum_i \theta_{kit} \cdot e_{kit} \tag{2}$$

or in vector notation:

$$P = X\theta' e \tag{3}$$

where θ and **e** are $M \times 1$ vectors that include the each industrial activity's output share and its pollution intensity, respectively, and M *is* the number of industries in a given city.

By total differentiation of Equation (3), the change in CO_2 emissions can be decomposed into the following expression:

$$\Delta P_{kt} = \Delta X_{kt} \cdot \sum_i \theta_{kit} \cdot e_{kit} + X_{k,t-1} \cdot \sum_i \Delta\theta_{kit} \cdot e_{kit} + X_{k,t-1} \cdot \sum_i \theta_{ki,t-1} \cdot \Delta e_{kit} \tag{4}$$

In Equation (4), the first term of RHS is the scale effect, measuring the impact of the increased size of total output on CO_2 emissions, holding industrial composition and emission intensities of all industries constant. The second term is the composition effect, measuring how the change in the industrial composition affects CO_2 emissions, holding the scale and emission intensities constant. The last term is the technique effect, capturing the effect of the changes in emission intensities on CO_2 emissions, holding the scale and composition effects constant.

3.2 *Data Issues*

To conduct the decomposition analysis, we need to econometrically estimate three key parameters in Equation (4): $X_{kt}, \theta_{kit}, e_{kit}$. In this paper, we consider 44 sub-sectors (See Appendix A) across 287 prefecture-level-and-above cities in China during the time period of 1998–2009.[5] The finer level of industrial disaggregation can help us to better understand the changes in industrial composition and how such changes matter for our decomposition results (Sinton and Levine, 1994; Fisher-Vanden *et al.*, 2004). The terms X_{kt} and θ_{kit} can be estimated by using the industrial production data from the database of Annual Survey of Industrial Firms (ASIFs) (for the manufacturing sector)[6] and from the China's Urban Statistical Yearbooks (for construction and service sectors).

3.2.1 Data Sources

We now list the data sources we use to construct our database of CO_2 emissions by city and industry for the 1998–2009 period in China. This emissions database is combined with production and energy data to carry out our decomposition exercise.

3.2.1.1 Output data. In this analysis, we measure carbon dioxide emission intensity by CO_2 emissions per unit of value added instead of gross output. The reason is that double counting problem inherent in the gross output measure may lead to inconsistent aggregation at the sector level (Ma and Stern, 2008). The value added at the sub-sectoral levels in the manufacturing sector is calculated by aggregating the firm-level value added data. The firm-level data are collected from the Annual Survey of Industrial Firms (ASIFs) dataset released by National Bureau of Statistics (NBS) from 1998 to 2009. All the value added data are converted to constant 1998 prices. The value added for the construction and service industries and their related sub-sectors are collected from China's Urban Statistical Yearbooks in the corresponding years.

3.2.1.2 Energy consumption data. Energy consumption data come from the provincial energy balance tables published by NBS in the corresponding years, which provides us with the quantities of various types of energy consumptions at the provincial level for six relatively aggregated sectors.[7] Those tables report each sector-province's energy consumption information for 20 types of energy, including 17 kinds of fossil fuels, 2 secondary energy types (heating power and electricity), and 1 other energy category.[8] In this analysis, we only consider the CO_2 emissions generated from end-use energy consumption. For example, we count the CO_2 emissions from the consumption of goods and services which are produced using electricity but we will not count the CO_2 emissions from the generation of electricity itself.

3.2.1.3 CO_2 emission factors. CO_2 emission factors for different types of energy are collected from the 2006 IPCC Guidelines for National Greenhouse Gas Inventories. Following most of the literature, we use these factors to convert energy consumption data into CO_2 emissions figures.

3.2.2 Calculating the Scale and Composition Effects

The value-added of the whole industrial sector in city k in year t (X_{kt}) is calculated by aggregating the value-added of all industries in city k in year t, $X_{kt} = \sum_i x_{kit}$. The share of sub-sector i in city k in year t (θ_{kit}) is calculated as $\theta_{kit} = \frac{x_{kit}}{X_{kt}}$.

3.2.3 Calculating the Technique Effect

The key task in this decomposition exercise is the estimation of the CO_2 emission intensity (e_{kit}) at the more disaggregated sector level (44 sub-sectors) across 287 cities. First, we calculate total CO_2 emissions for the six more aggregated sectors at the provincial level by summing up the products of each fossil fuel type's consumption quantity and its corresponding CO_2 emission factor across all types of fossil fuels.[9] Then, we obtain CO_2 emission intensities at the provincial level for these six relatively aggregated sectors by dividing a sector's CO_2 emissions in a province by the corresponding value added number. Finally, we infer the city- and sub-sector-specific CO_2 emission intensity by multiplying the provincial- and sector-specific emission intensity with a 'conversion factor'.

We construct our conversion factor based on the underlying assumption that TFP is negatively related to energy use and thus emission intensity at the firm level. A broad set of studies support our assumption. Based on the model of Melitz (2003), Kreickemeier and Richter (2014) illustrate that firm heterogeneity can affect environmental performance. As pollution is incorporated as a joint output of production, more efficient input use turns out to have lower emission intensity, so the firm heterogeneity argument implies that firm productivity is negatively related to emissions intensity. Bloom *et al.* (2010) empirically show that more productive firms associated with higher management quality are likely to increase the efficiency of input uses, thus leading to lower greenhouse gas emissions. Another line of studies in the trade and productivity literature argues that the correlation between TFP and energy use and emissions involves technology adoption. Bustos (2011) studies new technology adoption by heterogeneous firms and refines the Melitz model. According to her model, decreasing trade costs allow high productivity firms to upgrade technology since they benefit more from lower variable costs. Cui *et al.* (2012) consider environmental pollution and technology choice into a trade model with heterogeneous firms. Their model predicts that only the productive firm has the profitable incentive to adopt emission saving technology and to export. Based on the above studies, to keep it simple but without loss of generality, we construct the conversion factor which is the inverse ratio of city- and sub-sector-specific TFP over the provincial-sector-specific TFP. Martin (2011) and Shapiro and Walker (2015) also build their empirical analysis on a similar assumption. The apparent advantage here is that we have all the TFP measures needed for calculating those conversion factors coming from ASIFs dataset and China's Urban Statistical Yearbooks.[10]

3.3 Decomposition Patterns

Based on the estimates of X_{kt}, θ_{kit}, e_{kit}, we employ Equation (4) to conduct the decomposition. We are able to calculate the CO_2 emission numbers (in levels), and its growth rates (in differences), as well as the three decomposed effects within the differences, by sub-sector by city by year. We are also able to aggregate those numbers to provincial and national levels.

Figure 1(a) illustrates the average annual industrial CO_2 emissions in 287 cities during this 12-year period. We can see significant spatial variation. Large cities, especially the four first-tier cities, emit the most CO_2. Figure 1(b) shows the average annual CO_2 emissions per value added (in Yuan). This CO_2 emission intensity also varies a lot across different cities. However, Figure 2 clearly shows that this intensity has a clear declining trend over time in most cities, attributed to both composition and technique effects. According to our calculation, two first-tier cities, Shanghai and Beijing, rank at the very top places in terms of total CO_2 emissions because of the size of their economies; Urumqi and Xining are among the highest CO_2 emission intensity cities due to the large share of heavy industries in their economies. The annual industrial CO_2 emissions per capita for all cities during the sample period is 2.5 tons, which is 3.4 times as many as the annual residential CO_2 emissions per capita (Zheng *et al.*, 2010). The industrial sector dominates the urban CO_2 emissions in China.

Figure 2 depicts the positions of the 287 cities in terms of their annual growth rates in both total industrial CO_2 emissions (X axis) and CO_2 emission intensities (Y axis). The annual

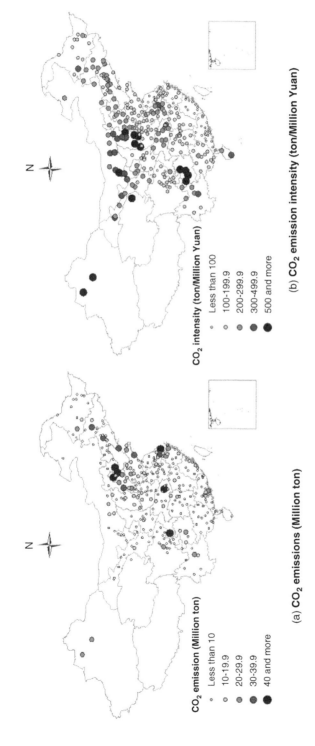

(a) CO$_2$ emissions (Million ton)

(b) CO$_2$ emission intensity (ton/Million Yuan)

Figure 1. Average Annual CO$_2$ Emissions and Emission Intensity in 287 Cities during 1998 and 2009.

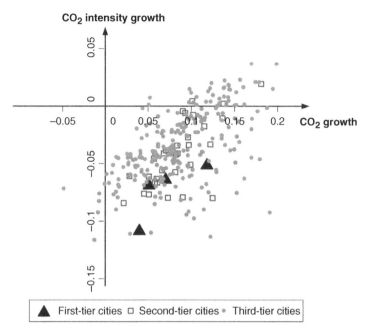

Figure 2. Annual Industrial CO_2 Emissions Growth and CO_2 Emission Intensity Growth in 287 Cities.

growth rate of industrial CO_2 emissions during this 12-year period is 9.3% for all cities, and 7.4%, 8.9% and 9.4% for the first-tier, second-tier and third-tier cities, respectively. These figures are lower than a recent all sector forecasting exercise by Auffhammer and Carson (2008) based on population projections, which did not account for recent policy intervention and other potential local determinants. Our estimates at the disaggregated city level show that, a large portion of cities locate in the fourth quadrant, enjoying a decline in CO_2 emission intensity (composition and technique effects) but experiencing rising industrial CO_2 emissions due to the sizable scale effect. The first-tier cities are all in the fourth quadrant, and they are among the cities with the fastest declining CO_2 emission intensity. Most of the second-tier cities are also in the fourth quadrant, and they locate at the upper right of first-tier cities, which indicates a relatively higher CO_2 emission growth rate but a slower CO_2 emission intensity decline compared to the first-tier cities. A large share of the third-tier cities are also in the fourth quadrant, while a small number of cities locate in the first quadrant with growth in both CO_2 emission and its intensity. Shizuishan and Yinchuan (both in Ningxia Province) are the top two cities in terms of total CO_2 emission growth and CO_2 emission intensity growth because of their large share of energy-intensive industries; Beijing ranks at the top in terms of total CO_2 emissions decline, thanks to its successful and ongoing transformation to service industries and the vast technical innovations.

Now we turn to our decomposition results. We first look at the national level numbers. Figure 3(a) illustrates the decomposition results for total industrial CO_2 emissions at the national level. We first look at the changes between the initial and end years. Arrow ① shows that, if we had held the composition of industries and the production technology constant ($\Delta\theta = 0$, $\Delta e = 0$) during this 12-year period, what the size of the total industrial CO_2 emissions would be (the column length between C and F). This scale effect equals to a 221% increase (37 billion tons).

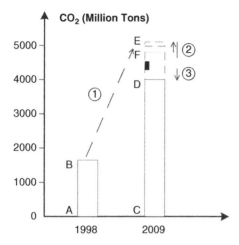

① B→F: Scale effect ② F→E: Composition effect

③ E→D: Technique effect

(a)

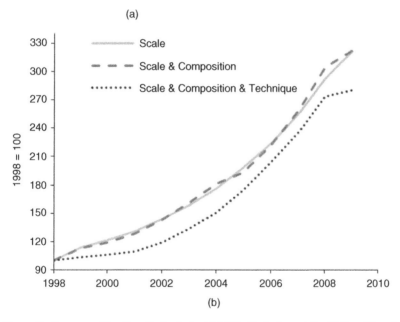

(b)

Figure 3. Decomposition Results for Industrial CO_2 Emissions at the National Level.

Arrow ② measures the composition effect. It is positive, but the size is small (1.3%, 22 million tons in total and 3.03 tons per value-added million Yuan) due to the mix of negative composition effects in some cities but positive effects in other cities. The column length between C and E is what the CO_2 emissions would be if every industrial activity still used the production techniques from 1998, which combines the scale and composition effects. Arrow ③ indicates the technique effect, which reduces CO_2 emissions. Its size is much larger than that of the composition effect, with contributing to a 41% decrease (690 million tons in total and 97.5 tons per value-added million Yuan) in CO_2 emissions from China's urban industrial sector.

Figure 3(b) plots these three effects at the national level in each of the 12 years. The solid line depicts the pure scale effect (the would-be CO_2 emissions in each year if all industries keep the same shares and the same production technology as those in 1998). The middle dashed line plots what CO_2 emissions would be in each year if every industrial activity used the original production technique in 1998 (the combination of both scale and composition effects). The gap between the middle dashed and the solid lines shows that the composition effect has led to a smaller change in CO_2 emissions between 1998 and 2007 with somewhat rising CO_2 emissions in the last two years. The bottom dashed line depicts CO_2 emissions when considering all three decomposed effects, so this measures the real CO_2 emissions in every year. The gap between this line and the middle dashed line reveals that the technique effect always works to reduce carbon dioxide emissions over time.

For the purposes of this paper we are more interested in the city-level industrial CO_2 emissions dynamics. Figure 4(a) shows some interesting patterns in these dynamics. We find the three effects play different roles at the three tiers of cities. The scale effect contributes to the rise of CO_2 emissions in all three tiers of cities. The absolute value of this effect is the largest for the first-tier cities and the smallest for the third-tier cities. The technique effect universally leads to the reduction of CO_2 emissions for all three tiers, indicating that all cities have enjoyed the improvements in both production technology and management quality. At the same time, the composition effect on CO_2 emissions is mild. We find that the composition effect contributes to the rising CO_2 emissions in the third-tier cities, while it reduces CO_2 emissions in the first-tier and second-tier cities. Figure 4(b) shows the dynamic change in CO_2 emission per capita across different tiers of cities between 1998 and 2009. We find that second-tier cities have higher levels of CO_2 emissions per capita than the other two. The decomposition patterns using CO_2 emissions per capita across these three groups of cities are quite similar to those using total CO_2 emission illustrated in Figure 4(a). Our decomposition results suggest that there may be a relocation of those energy-intensive industries from the first-tier and second-tier cities to those third-tier medium- and small-sized cities. In this sense, larger cities enjoy less CO_2 emissions at the expense of the increasing emissions in medium- and small-sized cities, so the domestic 'pollution haven' does exist. Yet this effect appears to be small.

We further examine CO_2 emissions changes over time across these three tiers of cities, respectively (See Appendix B). The results show that the increased CO_2 emissions in the first-tier cities over the past decade is more attributable to the scale effect, but the composition change towards cleaner industries and the technique improvement helps to offset the otherwise much higher CO_2 emissions. The second-tier cities have experienced similar patterns of these three decomposed effects on the change in CO_2 emissions but the contribution of composition effect on emission reduction is smaller than in the first-tier cities. In the third-tier cities only the technique effect works to reduce CO_2 emissions, but both the scale and composition effects work to increases emissions.

4. The Impacts of FDI and Environmental Regulations on Scale, Composition and Technique Effects

Using the results from Section 3.2.1.3, we are able to examine the impacts of FDI and environmental regulations on these three decomposed effects, and thus gain a better understanding of the underlying mechanisms why such impacts are heterogeneous across cities.

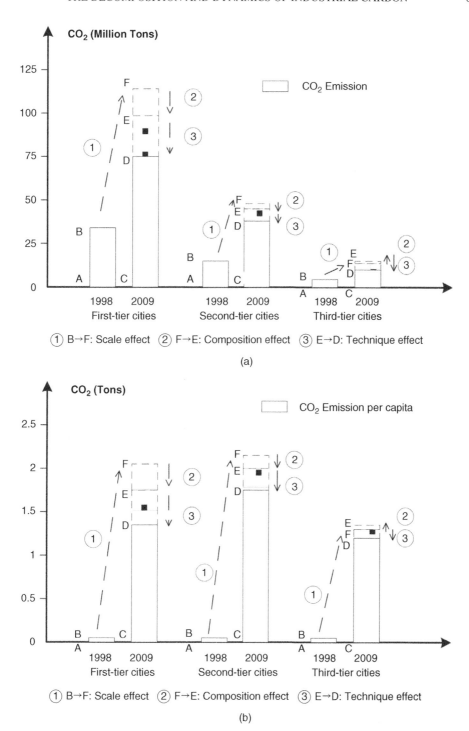

Figure 4. The Decomposition Results of CO_2 Emission across Three Tiers of Cities: 1998 versus 2009.

Table 1. Cross-City Variations in FDI, Industrial Electricity Price and Waste Water Treatment Fee.

	(1)	(2)	(3)	(4)
	The ratio of FDI to GDP	Industrial electricity price (RMB/KWH)	Industrial waste water treatment fee (RMB/ton)	Environmental Regulation Index (ERI) (1998–2009)
First-tier cities	0.85%	0.46	1.14	0.37
Second-tier cities	0.58%	0.34	0.83	0.31
Third-tier cities	0.29%	0.35	0.52	0.26

4.1 FDI Measures and Proxies for Environmental Regulation Intensity

4.1.1 FDI and Its Instrumental Variable

We use the ratio of annual foreign direct investment (FDI) in a city's total GDP as the proxy for a city's participation in global trade, which of course is a strong assumption. The city-level data sets on FDI and GDP are from the China's Urban Statistical Yearbooks in the corresponding years. Column (2) in Table 1 illustrates the average ratios of FDI in total GDP for three tiers of cities, respectively. The first-tier cities have received much more FDI compared to the other two tiers of cities.

When examining the impact of FDI on energy and environmental indicators, a typical challenge a researcher faces is the endogeneity arising from possible reverse causality. If those Chinese cities with more energy-intensive industries impose more regulations and if FDI flows to less regulated areas, then FDI will be pushed to less energy-intensive cities and the OLS estimate will be biased toward finding that FDI lowers CO_2 emissions. Conversely, if some cities are clean as they impose more regulation, the OLS estimate will be biased toward finding that FDI increases CO_2 emissions (Keller and Arik, 2002). Therefore, we use an IV strategy to overcome this endogeneity issue. Following Zheng *et al.* (2010), we take advantage of the regional favoritism exhibited by China's government to construct the instrumental variables. Cities on the coast, especially those close to major ports, receive favorable 'open-door' development policies from the central government and this encourages greater FDI to flow to these cities. Therefore, we use a city's distance to the closest major port as IV for our FDI measure. This variable is time-invariant so we can only use this to explain the spatial variation in FDI inflows.

4.1.2 Proxies for Environmental Regulations

To measure local officials' effort in regulating pollution associated with CO_2 emissions, we develop an Environmental Regulation Index (*ERI*) by combining two observable regulation tools at the city level. One is related to the differentiated industrial electricity pricing across cities. In China, as a legacy of communism, the central government has used its power to control energy prices (Tan and Frank, 2009). However, recently the central government is increasingly willing to allow energy prices to fluctuate and decentralize the energy pricing power to the local level, which enables local governments to use energy prices as a policy tool to attract or regulate energy- and pollution-intensive industries. We collect the price of electricity for industrial usage across provinces from China's Price Yearbooks in the corresponding years.[11] As shown in Column (3) of Table 1, there is big variation in the electricity price across the three tiers of cities. The other is the industrial sewage treatment fee that firms have to pay. Lan *et al.* (2011) use this measure to proxy for the stringency of local governments' pollution regulation. The data on industrial sewage investment is collected from China's Urban Statistical Yearbooks in the corresponding years. Column (4) in Table 1 illustrates the industrial sewage treatment fees in the unit of RMB/ton. The data reveals that first-tier cities in China are likely to put more investment on industrial sewage treatment than the other two groups of cities.

Calculating *ERI* begins with transforming two city-level environmental regulation indicators, electricity price changes (*EPC*) and industrial waste water treatment fee (*IWWTF*), to two standardized and comparable performance scores ranging from 0 to 1 ($SCORE_{EPC}$ and $SCORE_{IWWTF}$), respectively. *ERI* for city k is then calculated by averaging the two standardized scores of these two indicators in city k:

$$ERI_k = (SCORE_{EPC,k} + SCORE_{IWWTF,k})/2 \qquad (5)$$

In Equation (5), $SCORE_k = (Z_k - L)/(H - L)$, in which H is the highest level of the indicator, L is the lowest level of the indicator and Z_k is the value of the indicator for city k.

Column (5) in Table 1 presents the *ERI* across cities. It is found that first-tier cities have higher *ERI* values than that of the other two groups of cities, which is consistent with the statistics of the two individual indicators in Column (3) and (4).

4.2 Estimation Results

We examine the effects of these local factors on the change in carbon dioxide emissions and its three decomposed components using China's city-level data between 1998 and 2009 via a reduced form approach. Equation (6) is in the form of first-difference because the three decomposed effects are with respect to the changes in CO_2 emissions. The first-difference specification also enables us to drop out city-level time-invariant unobservables. We also include regional fixed effects to control for region-specific trend in CO_2 emissions changes.

$$\Delta Y_k = \alpha_0 + \alpha_1 \cdot \Delta \ln(FDI_k) + \alpha_2 \cdot ERI_k + \mathbf{X} \cdot \beta + r_k + \varepsilon_k \qquad (6)$$

We have four versions of the dependent variable ΔY_k, including the total changes in CO_2 emissions from 1998 to 2009, as well as three decomposed components in city k; ΔFDI_k is the change in the share of total GDP for city k between 1998 and 2009; ERI_k is city k's environmental regulation index; $\mathbf{X}$ is vector of control variables including the changes in GDP, share of secondary industry in GDP and share of tertiary industry in GDP; r_k is regional fixed effects[12] and ε_k is the error term.

Table 2 reports the OLS estimation results and Table 3 provides those with FDI being instrumented with the distance to the closest port. Firstly, we look at the estimated coefficients of the change in our FDI measure (FDI to GDP ratio) using OLS. The coefficient is negative and significant at the 1% level, suggesting that the inflow of FDI pulls down energy intensity and thus CO_2 emissions. Specifically, a 10% increase in the FDI to GDP ratio contributes to a 1.74 percentage point decrease in CO_2 emissions. As for the three decomposed effects, the estimated coefficient of the change in the FDI measure the technique effect is significantly negative, while the estimates on the other two effects are insignificant. These suggest that the inflow of FDI works on pollution emission more through the technique effect than the

Table 2. Effects of FDI and Environmental Regulations on CO_2 Emissions and the Three Decomposed Effects (OLS).

	(1) ΔCO_2 emissions	(2) Scale effect	(3) Composition effect	(4) Technique effect
ΔLog(*FDI*)	−0.174***	−0.009	−0.005	−0.053**
	(0.045)	(0.036)	(0.011)	(0.022)
ERI	−1.981***	−1.191***	−0.262**	−0.527**
	(0.473)	(0.338)	(0.114)	(0.205)
ΔLog(*GDP*)	1.698***	2.278***	−0.117**	−0.422***
	(0.210)	(0.143)	(0.0513)	(0.093)
Δ*Secondary Industry GDP Share*	0.055***	0.032***	0.030***	−0.011
	(0.010)	(0.008)	(0.00251)	(0.016)
Δ*Tertiary Industry GDP Share*	0.002	0.0158*	0.005	−0.019***
	(0.013)	(0.009)	(0.00318)	(0.006)
Constant	−0.217	−0.725***	0.023	0.442***
	(0.299)	(0.212)	(0.0714)	(0.128)
Region fixed effects	Yes	Yes	Yes	Yes
Observations	186	186	186	186
R^2	0.603	0.721	0.641	0.329

Note: Standard errors are reported in parentheses, which are clustered by province. *$p < 0.10$, **$p < 0.05$, ***$p < 0.01$.

Table 3. Effects of FDI and Environmental Regulations on CO_2 Emissions and the Three Decomposed Effects (Using IV for FDI).

	(1) ΔCO_2 emissions	(2) Scale effect	(3) Composition effect	(4) Technique effect
ΔLog(*FDI*)	−0.689***	−0.076	0.024	−0.431*
	(0.241)	(0.435)	(0.045)	(0.231)
ERI	−1.729***	−0.899**	−0.269**	−0.435
	(0.623)	(0.405)	(0.113)	(0.332)
ΔLog(*GDP*)	1.533***	2.298***	−0.109**	−0.502***
	(0.281)	(0.243)	(0.053)	(0.155)
Δ*Secondary Industry GDP Share*	0.057***	0.055***	0.030***	0.001
	(0.014)	(0.020)	(0.002)	(0.010)
Δ*Tertiary Industry GDP Share*	−0.010	0.019	0.005	−0.019**
	(0.018)	(0.016)	(0.003)	(0.009)
Constant	0.018	−0.425	−0.063	0.669**
	(0.495)	(0.482)	(0.091)	(0.300)
Region fixed effects	Yes	Yes	Yes	Yes
Observations	186	186	186	186
R^2	0.591	0.738	0.627	0.420

Note: Standard errors are reported in parentheses, which are clustered by province. *$p < 0.10$, **$p < 0.05$, ***$p < 0.01$.

scale effect. This justifies why we find the optimistic result that FDI helps a city to reduce CO_2 emissions (and corresponding energy consumption). The underlying reasons may be that FDI brings in cleaner capital, technology and better management skills. As the IV estimation results suggest (see Table 3), the inflow of FDI reduces CO_2 emissions, but with larger magnitudes in terms of its impact on the total CO_2 emission change and the change of the technique component compared with OLS estimates. A 10% increase in the FDI to GDP ratio leads to a 6.89 percentage point decrease in total CO_2 emissions and a 4.31 percentage point decrease in CO_2 emissions due to the technique effect. This finding is consistent with our statistical analysis in Table 1 that the cities with more FDI also impose more regulation on the environment.

In Table 3, as expected, the Environmental Regulation Index has a negative impact on industrial carbon emissions. If we look into the three decomposed effects, we can see that stringent environmental regulation works through all three channels – the scale of production drops, the industrial composition shifts towards cleaner industries, and the production technology and management quality also increase (a significant negative technique effect). The magnitudes of the three coefficients suggest that the scale effect dominates this process. The observed composition effect due to the enforcement of environmental regulations is consistent with those in previous studies in the USA such as Berman and Bui (2001a, 2001b) and Henderson (1996). As the instrumental variable strategy here is less than perfect due to the lack of time series variation in the instrument, these results should be taken as suggestive.

The estimated coefficients on the other control variables are also consistent with our expectations. Cities with higher GDP growth experience a larger increase in CO_2 emission mainly due to the increases in economic scale, which dominates the changes from cleaner industry composition and more efficient production technology. The growth in the share of secondary industry is found to increase the cities' CO_2 emission through scale and composition effect, while the growth of tertiary industry helps to decrease CO_2 emission by improving production technology.

We are also interested in whether the effect of FDI and environment regulation on CO_2 emissions varies across these three tiers of cities. We estimate Equation (6) separately for the first, second-tier cities and third-tier cities, and the regression results are provided in Table 4. It shows that the change in FDI had insignificant effect on CO_2 emissions in the first and second-tier cities, while it tends to decrease CO_2 emissions in the third tier cities mainly through the technique effect. A possible explanation is that the first- and second-tier cities already have advanced technologies (in our study period) so the marginal effect of FDI is weak; while its marginal effect is much larger in the third tier cities where production technologies stand at a lower level. Stringent environmental regulation is found to contribute to the declining CO_2 emission in all three groups of cities. This mitigation effect is mostly attributed to the technique effect in the first- and second-tier cities, while to the scale and composition effects in the third-tier cities. Our results indicate that the environmental regulation in the first- and second-tier cities helps to promote the adoption of greener production technology, but it constrains the scale expansion and the receipt of dirty industries (relocating from the first and- second-tier cities) in the third-tier cities.

5. Conclusions

In 2007, China became the largest greenhouse gas emitter in the world. 85% of China's GHG emissions are attributed to urban economic activities, and this share will continue to increase

Table 4. Effects of FDI and Environmental Regulations on CO_2 Emissions in Different Cities (Using IV for FDI).

	(1) ΔCO_2 emissions	(2) Scale effect	(3) Composition effect	(4) Technique effect
First- and second-tier cities				
$\Delta Log(FDI)$	−1.173	−1.174	−0.090	0.140
	(0.940)	(0.815)	(0.121)	(0.192)
ERI	−3.453[*]	−1.394	0.116	−1.473[***]
	(2.090)	(1.768)	(0.270)	(0.503)
Third-tier cities				
$\Delta Log(FDI)$	−0.656[**]	−0.082	−0.024	−0.567[**]
	(0.265)	(0.349)	(0.049)	(0.226)
ERI	−1.425[**]	−1.050[***]	−0.291[**]	−0.145
	(0.643)	(0.338)	(0.115)	(0.474)

Note: Standard errors are reported in parentheses, which are clustered by province. Other specifications are same with those of Table 3. [*]$p < 0.10$, [**]$p < 0.05$, [***]$p < 0.01$.

with China's rapid urbanization process. This paper enriches our understanding of city-level industrial CO_2 emissions in China and its dynamics by decomposing CO_2 emission changes into scale, composition and technique effects over the past decade (all 287 prefecture-level-cities in 1998–2009).

The paper first reviews the literature on the decomposition analysis and several local determinants that shape such dynamics. We then use city-level data in China to decompose the changes in industrial CO_2 emissions into the scale, composition and technique effects. Our estimates show that the industrial CO_2 emissions per capita are about 3.4 times larger than the residential CO_2 emissions per capita in China's urban sector and the industrial CO_2 emissions have been increasing by 9.3% annually during this 12-year period. The decomposition analysis shows that the three effects play different roles in the three tiers of cities. The scale effect contributes to the rise of CO_2 emissions in all cities. On the other hand, the technique effect universally leads to the reduction of CO_2 emissions in all three tiers of cities, indicating that all cities have enjoyed the improvements in both production technology and management quality towards energy efficiency. The composition effect on CO_2 emissions is mild – it contributes to the rising CO_2 emissions in the third-tier cities, while it reduces CO_2 emissions in the first-tier and second-tier cities. These patterns suggest that there may be a relocation of those energy-insensitive industries from the first-tier and second-tier cities to those third-tier medium- and small-sized cities. In this sense, larger cities enjoy less CO_2 emissions at the expense of the increasing emissions in medium- and small-sized cities.

Our decomposition results facilitate us to provide some suggestive evidence as to how FDI inflow and environmental regulations drive the change in CO_2 emissions and its decomposed three effects. It is found that the inflow of FDI pulls down energy intensity and thus CO_2 emissions by generating significant technique effect (and the other two effects are insignificant), so it brings in cleaner production technology and better management quality. The environmental regulations help cities to reduce their industrial CO_2 emissions through all three channels –the economy scale shrinks, the industrial composition shifts towards cleaner industries and the energy-efficient technologies and management skills also improve.

Our empirical results clearly indicate that shifting towards less-energy-intensive industries (composition effect), exploiting 'clean' fuel inputs and fostering technology transfers (technique effect), matter for China in curbing carbon dioxide emissions during its ongoing urbanization and industrial progress. The Chinese government has pledged to wean its economy away from reliance on fossil fuels as it grows. In November 2014, China and the US unveiled new pledges on greenhouse gas emissions. The deal commits China to reducing greenhouse gas emissions after a peak in 2030 (and ideally sooner). China also aims to have non-fossil fuels make up 20% of its primary energy consumption by 2030. It is the first time China, the world's largest emitter by far in absolute terms (roughly 28% of the world's CO_2 emissions in 2014), has agreed to set a ceiling, albeit an undefined one, on overall emissions. To achieve this goal, the central government in China will come up with ways of incentivizing local officials to go green, and city mayors will make their own trade-off between their economic growth (scale), and environmental goals (economic restructure and technology improvements). The decomposition framework in our paper can help policy makers and scholars to observe such trade-offs and the underlying rationales.

Acknowledgements

We deeply appreciate anonymous referees for their insightful comments. Weizeng Sun and Siqi Zheng thank the National Natural Science Foundation of China (No. 71273154, No. 71322307, No. 71533004) and the Key Project of National Social Science Foundation of China (No. 13AZD082), and Volvo Group in a research project of Tsinghua University's Research Center for Green Economy and Sustainable Development for research support. Jianfeng Wu thanks the School of Economics at Fudan University for granting us access to key data. He thanks the MOE Project of the Key Research Institute of the Humanities and Social Sciences at the China Center for Economic Studies (CCES), and the Research Institute of Chinese Economy (RICE) at Fudan University. He also thanks the National Natural Science Foundation of China (No. 71573054).

Notes

1. Source: China Textile Industry Development Report 2010–2011. Published by China Textile & Apparel Press, 2011.
2. 'Consumption of Energy by Sector (2011)', National Bureau of Statistic of China, accessed October 14, 2014, http://www.stats.gov.cn/tjsj/ndsj/2013/indexeh.htm
3. 'Consumption & Efficiency', U.S. Energy Information Administration, accessed October 14, 2014, http://www.eia.gov/consumption/
4. See 'Trends in Global CO_2 Emissions 2014 Report', available on http://edgar.jrc.ec. europa.eu/news_docs/jrc-2014-trends-in-global-co2-emissions-2014-report-93171.pdf
5. We refer to the aggregation in two levels, industries and sector. In China, the whole economy is often divided into three industries, the primary, secondary and service industries. The secondary industry includes three sectors, Mining, Manufacturing, Electric Power-Gas-and-Water (EGW), and Construction Sector. The service industry includes three sectors, Transportation, Storage, Post and Telecommunication Services Sector (TSPTS), Wholesale, Retail, and Accommodation, Catering Sector (WRTCS), and Others Service Sector. The sectors of Mining, Manufacturing, and EGW are further disaggregated into 6, 30 and 3 sub-sectors, respectively.
6. See Brandt *et al.* (2012).
7. See footnote 5 for details.

8. Other energy includes those such as wind and solar energy that does not generate pollution emissions.

9. We convert the two secondary energy types, electricity and heating power, into the corresponding fossil fuels that generate them on the basis of the provincial energy balance tables.

10. The calculation of TFP for manufacturing firms is done according to the method in Brandt *et al.* (2012). For non-manufacturing firms we consider labor productivity as an alternative of TFP due to data limitations.

11. China's Price Yearbooks provide annual the price of electricity at the provincial level for different kinds of usage such as industrial use and residential use.

12. Cities are divided into seven regions: North China, Northeast China, East China, Central China, South China, Southwest China and Northwest China.

References

Antweiler, W., Copeland, B. and Taylor, M. (2001) Is free trade good for the environment? *American Economic Review* 91: 877–908.

Auffhammer, M. and Carson, R.T. (2008) Forecasting the path of China's CO_2 emissions using province level information. *Journal of Environmental Economics and Management* 55(3): 229–247.

Auffhammer, M. and Gong, Y. (2015) China's Carbon Emissions from fossil fuels and market based opportunities for control. *Annual Review of Resource Economics* 7: 11–34.

Becker, R. and Henderson, J.V. (2000) Effects of air quality regulations on polluting industries. *Journal of Political Economy* 108(2): 729–758.

Berman, E. and Bui, L.T.M. (2001a) Environmental regulation and labor demand: Evidence from the South Coast Air Basin. *Journal of Public Economics* 79(2): 265–295.

Berman, E. and Bui, L.T.M. (2001b) Environmental regulation and productivity: Evidence from oil refineries. *Review of Economics and Statistics* 83(3): 498–510.

Bloom, N., Genakos, R., Martin, R. and Sadun, R. (2010) Modern accounting: Good for the environment or just hot air? *Economic Journal* 120: 551–572.

Brandt, L., Biesebroeck, J. V. and Zhang, Y. (2012) Creative accounting or creative destruction? Firm-level productivity growth in Chinese manufacturing. *Journal of Development Economics* 97(2): 339–351.

Bustos, P. (2011) Trade liberalization, exports and technology upgrading: Evidence on the impact of MERCOSUR on Argentinean firms. *American Economic Review* 101(1): 304–340.

Cai, F., Chen, Y. and Qing, G. (2016) Polluting thy neighbor: The case of river pollution in China. *Journal of Environmental Economics and Management* 76: 86–104.

Copeland, B.R. and Taylor, M.S. (1994) North-south trade and the environment. *Quarterly Journal of Economics* 109(3): 755–787.

Copeland, B.R. and Taylor, M.S. (2003) *Trade and the Environment: Theory and Evidence*. Princeton: Princeton University Press.

Copeland, B.R. and Taylor, M.S. (2004) Trade, growth, and the environment. *Journal of Economic Literature* 42(1): 7–71.

Creutzig, F., Baiocchi, G., Bierkandt, R., Oichler, P.-P. and Seto, K.C. (2013) Global typology of urban energy use and potentials for an urbanization mitigation wedge. *Proceedings of the National Academy of Science of the United States of America* 112(20): 6283–6288.

Cui, H., Lapan, H. and Moschini, G. (2012) Are exporters more environmentally friendly than non-exporters? Theory and evidence. Working paper No.12022, Department of Economics, Iowa State University.

Dean, J.M. (2002) Does trade liberalization harm the environment? A new test. *Canadian Journal of Economics* 35(4): 819–842.

Fisher-Vanden, K., Jefferson, G.H., Liu, H. and Tao, Q. (2004) What is driving China's decline in energy intensity? *Resource and Energy Economics* 26: 77–97.

Greenstone, M. (2002) The impacts of environmental regulations on industrial activity: Evidence from the 1970 and 1977 Clean Air Act Amendments and the Census of manufacturers. *Journal of Political Economy* 110(6): 1175–1219.

Grossman, G.M. and Krueger, A.B. (1995) Economic growth and the environment. *Quarterly Journal of Economics* 110(2): 353–377.

He, J. (2006) Pollution Haven Hypothesis and environmental impacts of Foreign Direct Investment: The case of industrial emission of sulfur dioxide (SO_2) in Chinese provinces. *Ecological Economics* 60(1): 228–245.

He, J. (2009) China industrial SO_2 emissions and its economic determinants of EKC's reduced vs. structural model and the role of international trade. *Environmental and Development Economics* 14(2): 227–262.

Henderson, J.V. (1996) Effects of air quality regulation. *American Economic Review* 86(4): 789–813.

Kahn, M.E. (1997) Particulate pollution trends in the United States. *Regional Science and Urban Economics* 27(1): 87–107.

Kahn, M.E. and Mansur, E.T. (2013) Do local energy prices and regulation affect the geographic concentration of employment? *Journal of Public Economics* 101: 105–114.

Keller, W. and Arik, L. (2002) Pollution abatement costs and foreign direct investment inflows to US states. *Review of Economics and Statistics* 84(4): 691–703.

Kreickemeier, U. and Richter, P.M. (2014) Trade and the environment: The role of firm heterogeneity. *Review of International Economics* 22(2): 209–225.

Jiang, L., Lin, C. and Lin, P. (2014) The determinants of pollution levels: Firm-level evidence from Chinese manufacturing. *Journal of Comparative Economics* 42(1): 118–142.

Lan, H., Livermore, M.A. and Wenner, C.A. (2011) Water pollution and regulatory cooperation in China. *Cornell International Law Journal* 44(2): 349–383.

Lin, L. (2013) Enforcement of pollution levies in China. *Journal of Public Economics* 96: 32–43.

Lin, S.J. and Chang, T.C. (1996) Decomposition of SO_2, NO_X and CO_2 emissions from energy use of major economic sectors in Taiwan. *Energy Journal* 17(1): 1–17.

Liu, Z. (2015) China's Carbon Emission Report 2015. Belfer center for science and international affairs, Harvard Kennedy School.

Ma, C. and Stern, D.I. (2008) China's changing energy intensity trend: A decomposition analysis. *Energy Economics* 30: 1037–1053.

Martin, L.A. (2011) Energy efficiency gains from trade: Greenhouse gas emissions and India's manufacturing sector. Mimeography, Berkeley ARE.

Managi, S., Hibiki, A. and Tsurumi, T. (2009) Does trade openness improve environmental quality? *Journal of Environmental Economics and Management* 58: 346–363.

Melitz, M.J. (2003) The impact of trade on intra-industry reallocations and aggregate industry productivity. *Econometrica* 71(6):1695–1725.

OECD (2015) Urban Policy Review: China 2015. Available at http://www.oecd.org/china/oecd-urban-policy-reviews-china-2015-9789264230040-en.htm. (accessed on April 18, 2015).

Sinton, J.E., and Levine, M.D. (1994) Changing energy intensity in Chinese industry: The relative importance of structural shift and intensity change. *Energy Policy* 22: 239–255.

Shapiro, J.S. and Walker, R. (2015) Why is pollution from U.S. manufacturing declining? The roles of trade, regulation, productivity, and preferences. NBER Working Paper No. 20879.

Tan, X. and Frank, W. (2009) Does China underprice its oil consumption? Working Paper. Department of Economics, Stanford University.

Van Rooij, B. and Lo, C.W. (2010) Fragile convergence: Understanding variation in the enforcement of China's industrial pollution law. *Law and Policy* 32(1): 14–37.

Viguier, L. (1999) Emissions of SO_2, NO_X and CO_2 in transition economies: Emissions inventories and Divisia index analysis. *Energy Journal* 20(2): 59–87.

Wang, H. and Wheeler, D. (2005) Financial incentives and endogenous enforcement in China's pollution levy system. *Journal of Environmental Economics and Management* 49: 174–196.

Wang, S., Fang, C., Guan, X., Pang, B. and Ma, H. (2014) Urbanization, energy consumption, and carbon dioxide emissions in China: A panel data analysis of China's provinces. *Applied Energy* 136: 738–749.

Wang, H. and Jin, Y. (2007) Industrial ownership and environmental performance: Evidence from China. *Environmental and Resource Economics* 36(3): 255–273.

Xu, B. and Lin, B. (2015) How industrialization and urbanization process impacts on CO2 emissions in China: Evidence from nonparametric additive regressions models. *Energy Economics* 48: 188–202.

Xu, Y., Williams, R.H. and Socolow, R.H. (2009) China's rapid development of SO_2 scrubbers. *Energy and Environmental Science* 2(5): 459–465.

Yu, J., Zhou, L. and Zhu, G. (2013) Strategic interaction in political competition: Evidence from spatial effects across Chinese cities. *Working paper.*

Zhang, Y. (2012) Scale, technique and composition effects in trade-related carbon emissions in China. *Environment and Resource Economics* 51: 371–389.

Zheng, S. and Kahn, M. E. (2013) Understanding China's urban pollution dynamics. *Journal of Economic Literature* 51(3): 731–772.

Zheng, S., Kahn, M.E. and Liu, H. (2010) Towards a system of open cities in China: Home prices, FDI flows, and air quality in 35 major cities. *Regional Science and Urban Economics* 40(1): 1–10.

Zheng S., Kahn, M.E., Sun, W. and Luo, D. (2014) Incentivizing China's urban mayors to mitigate pollution externalities: The role of the central government and the public environmentalism. *Regional Science and Urban Economics* 47: 61–71.

Appendix A

List of 44 Sectors/Subsectors

No.	Name of industry sector	No.	Name of industry sector
1	Agriculture, forestry, animal husbandry and fishery, water conservation	15	Timber processing, bamboo, cane palm fiber and straw production
2	Coal mining and dressing	16	Furniture manufacturing
3	Petroleum and natural gas mining	17	Papermaking and paper production
4	Ferrous metals mining and dressing	18	Printing and record medium reproduction
5	Nonferrous metals mining and dressing	19	Cultural and educational, arts and crafts, sports and entertainment
6	Nonmetal minerals mining and dressing		
7	Others mining and quarrying	20	Petroleum processing, coking and nuclear fuel processing
8	Agricultural and sideline products processing	21	Raw chemical materials and chemical production
9	Food manufacturing		
10	Soft drinks manufacturing	22	Medical and pharmaceutical production
11	Tobacco processing	23	Chemical fiber
12	Textile industry	24	Rubber production
13	Garments and apparel industry	25	Rubber production
14	Leather, furs, down and related production, shoes manufacturing	26	Nonmetal mineral production
		27	Smelting and pressing of ferrous metals

No.	Name of industry sector	No.	Name of industry sector
28	Smelting and pressing of nonferrous metals	37	Waste resources and materials recovering
29	Metal production	38	Production and supply of electricity and heating power
30	Equipment in common use		
31	Special purpose equipment	39	Production and supply of gas
32	Transport equipment	40	Production and supply of water
33	Electric equipment and machinery	41	Construction sector
34	Telecommunications, computer and other electronic equipment	42	Transportation, storage and postal services sector
35	Instruments, meters, cultural and clerical machinery	43	Wholesale, retail and accommodation, catering sector
36	Handicraft article and other manufacturing	44	Other service sectors

Note: #1 sector belongs to the primary industry, #2–7 are mining sectors, #8–37 are manufacturing sectors, #38–40 are electric power-gas-and-water sectors, #42–44 sectors belong to service industries.

Appendix B

Decomposition Effects of CO_2 Emissions for Three-Tier Cities from 1998 to 2009

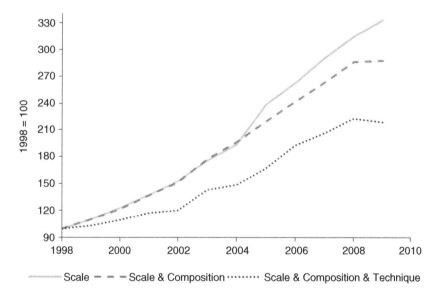

Figure A1. Decomposition Effects of CO_2 Emission for First-Tier Cities from 1998 to 2009.

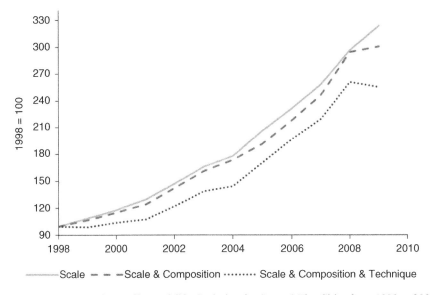

Figure A2. Decomposition Effects of CO_2 Emission for Second-Tier Cities from 1998 to 2009.

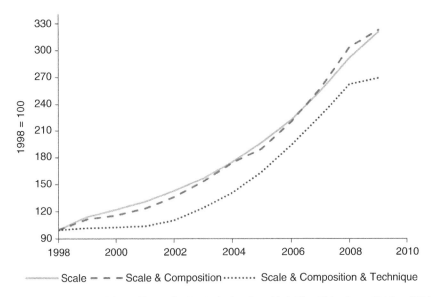

Figure A3. Decomposition Effects of CO_2 Emission for Third-Tier Cities from 1998 to 2009.

5

ENVIRONMENTAL SUSTAINABILITY AND THE GREENED SAMUELSON RULE

Yunmin Chen

Academia Sinica
Taiwan

Brian Chi-ang Lin

Department of Public Finance
National Chengchi University
Taiwan

John E. Anderson

Department of Economics
University of Nebraska-Lincoln
USA

1. Introduction

Environmental issues have drawn more and more attention and the analysis of market-based policy instruments such as taxes and charges for reducing environmental externalities has been well documented in the literature. Although a wide range of environmental externalities such as various types of pollution have been examined, the practical experiences have shown that the role of environmental taxes and charges is very limited. Clearly, higher tax rates create a political obstacle to the promotion of the environmental tax base and system. To help resolve the critical issues of environmental deterioration, this paper proposes that the government can initiate a spending scheme for the green public good provision.

To demonstrate that government green spending can be an affective measure for not only lowering tax rates but also improving environmental quality, we extend the model examined in the literature of optimal taxation by incorporating the condition of environmental sustainability. To the best of our knowledge, we are the first to discuss the problem of environmental sustainability in the optimal taxation literature. Our approach can also be seen as part of a

Environmental Economics and Sustainability, First Edition. Edited by Brian Chi-ang Lin and Siqi Zheng.
Chapters © 2017 The Authors. Book compilation © 2017 John Wiley & Sons, Ltd. Published 2017 by John Wiley & Sons, Ltd.

literature that integrates environmental sustainable development with optimal taxation.[1] In terms of the appropriate benefit measure for additional output of green public goods and the appropriate quantity that the government should provide, we are following the well-established path of Atkinson and Stern (1974) who build on Diamond and Mirrlees (1971) and Stiglitz and Dasgupta (1971).

It is also well recognized that asymmetric information problems are prevalent in this society. Various characteristics, for instance, productivity and taste, are publicly unobservable. It is of interest to ask: how the tax policy is tailored to a private information environment. To address this issue, there already exists an array of papers in optimal taxation literature considering that the social planner designs efficient mechanism so as to let agents reveal hidden information.[2] To proceed, this paper answers what features optimal taxation should possess in a normative perspective, while encompassing two critical elements: hidden information as well as environmental sustainability.

This paper is closely related to Pirttilä and Tuomala (1997) who employ a self-selection approach in tax analysis that is characterized by an economy with two types of households (i.e. two types of households with different earning abilities) to analyze the impact of environmental externalities on proportional commodity taxation and non-linear income taxation. They show that the existence of pollution will lead to higher marginal tax rates to amend negative externalities and also affect the optimal provision of public goods.

The present paper differs from Pirttilä and Tuomala (1997) in that the government has perfect foresight with the goal of achieving environmental sustainability. In this regard, the government provides not only traditional public goods (such as military weapons which are detrimental for the environment) but also green public goods that promote environmental sustainability. The provision of green public goods includes, for example, toxic clean-up and pollution prevention, biodiversity conservation, wetland conservation and management, supply of renewable energy sources or/and technologies, fuel-efficient public transportation, research and development for reducing greenhouse gas emissions, strict enforcement of environmental laws for improving environmental quality, and spending measures to help the environment self-renew sustainably, and so on. The key distinguishing characteristic of such public goods is that they provide positive environmental externalities.

The notion of greening government has, so far, been focused on the revenue side of the budget. The double dividend literature is the primary place where this issue has been considered with environmental taxes having generally been regarded as a method for reducing environmental deterioration and improving efficiency by replacing distortionary tax revenues in a revenue neutral way. According to this approach, new environmental taxes not only benefit the environment but also have the potential to reduce the distortions of the existing tax system if used to replace highly distorting taxes, resulting in two benefits or a douxble dividend. Goulder (1994) and Bovenberg and Goulder (2002) explain the attractiveness of this policy option in two parts. Interest in the second dividend is due to the political attractiveness of 'no regrets' policies. That is, if the second dividend is realized, then environmental improvement is produced at no cost to the economy. Interest is also driven by the desire to justify reforms despite substantial uncertainty regarding the magnitude of the first (environmental) dividend. Bovenberg and Goulder demonstrate, however, that while the double dividend is theoretically possible, it is, 'unlikely to arise except under fairly unusual circumstances'. They use a general equilibrium model to diagnose the effects of a revenue-neutral environmental tax reform and find that the tax reform results in a reduction in employment which reduces the tax base. Hence, by harming employment pollution taxes narrow the tax base rather than widen it. As a result, the non-environmental component of the tax reform has a negative effect on welfare and the double dividend fails. They caution, however, that overall welfare may still rise if the pollution taxes are not too large. If the pollution taxes are small they create small employment reductions which may be overcome by larger initial incremental improvements in the benefits from pollution reduction. They conclude that even in the case of the failure of the double dividend claim it does not necessarily mean that green tax reform is inefficient. Rather, it means that environmental improvement has its cost.

Parry and Bento (2000) provide a review of double dividend studies. They note that the early literature on this topic found little reason to expect that the double dividend would be realized with implementation of environmental taxes. Parry and Bento consider the issue more carefully, however, by extending the existing models to include important tax-advantaged consumption goods. In particular, they include housing and medical care sectors in their model. With those sectors included, the efficiency gains associated with implementing environmental taxes are larger. The reason, of course, is due to the pre-existing distortions in both product and factor markets caused by the income tax preferences for housing and medical care. Parry and Bento found that with this modification in the model a double dividend is more likely to occur.

Parry (1998) advises on the circumstances under which a double dividend is more (or less) likely to occur. If the existing tax system is fully efficient in the Ramsey sense, the likelihood of environmental taxes producing a double dividend is eliminated. But, if the more likely case of an inefficient initial tax system obtains, then the prospect of a double dividend arises. He makes the case, however, that it is more economically appropriate to reform the tax system to reduce its inefficiencies than to attack the problem indirectly by way of adopting new environmental taxes. Beyond that, Parry cautions that it is highly unlikely that the new revenue generated by environmental taxes will all (or even mostly) be used to replace revenue generated by existing inefficient taxes. If that is the case, the prospects for realizing double dividends are reduced substantially.

Hanson and Sandalow (2006) have produced suggestions for greening the tax code by implementing environmental taxes and fees as replacements for traditional revenue sources. Their tax suggestions include both elimination of existing tax preferences in the tax code and adoption of new pollution taxes. Potential measures to limit or eliminate environmentally damaging tax expenditures include: repeal of expensing for the extractive industry's exploration and development costs, restrictions on 'qualified parking' to carpools and parking at public transportation stations, repeal of enhanced oil recovery cost tax credits and expensing of tertiary injectants, capitalization costs of producing timber, repeal of 'percentage depletion allowance' for extractive industries, and elimination of the SUV tax deduction. Their suggestions for new pollution taxes to consider include: water pollution taxes, nitrogen fertilizer taxes, and carbon taxes.

While a number of policy analyses and studies have examined the issue of greening the tax system, as suggested above, there is little research on the expenditure side of the government's budget. Reflecting on the United Nations Environment Progamme (UNEP) proposal for a Global Green New Deal which called on G20 countries to allocate 1% of GDP to expenditures on green initiatives, Barbier (2010) comments that, 'Only a handful of economies devoted a significant chunk of their total fiscal stimulus to green projects. Most were cautious about making low-carbon and other environmental investments during a recession, and some did not implement any green stimulus measures at all . . . Supported by the right policies, green spending can be very effective'. For example, Houser *et al.* (2009) have estimated that a one billion dollar investment in energy efficiency and clean energy in the USA can generate eventual energy savings of $450 million per year as well as reduce annual greenhouse gas emissions by more than half a million tons by 2020 and create 30,000 job-years. In comparison with traditional fiscal stimulus in the form of income tax reductions or road building, their estimated employment effects are about 20% greater.

The present paper places the focus on the expenditure side of the budget and argues that implementation of green spending has the potential to not only give rise to benefits of the so-called double dividend but also generate additional benefits. The provision of green public goods contributes to the attainment of the macro-environmental equilibrium. Also, the provision of green public goods could lead to a reduction in the individual marginal effective tax rate. The rest of the paper is organized as follows. Section 2 extends the model developed by Pirttilä and Tuomala (1997), which determines the optimal combination of non-linear income tax and linear commodity taxes in the presence of negative externalities, by introducing a government environmental sustainability condition. After deriving the first-order conditions for the government's optimization problem, Section 3 presents a modified *greened* version of the Samuelson rule, that is, the optimal provision of the public good in connection with environmental sustainability. Section 4 analyses the optimal tax structure, including individual effective marginal tax rates and commodity taxes. Section 5 provides some discussions for policy implication and concludes.

2. The Model

2.1 *The Consumer's Optimization Problem*

We consider an economy consisting of two types of households with identical preferences, similar to the approach used in Pirttilä and Tuomala (1997). Type-2 households have higher productivity and receive a higher wage rate: $w^2 > w^1$. Households supply labour and earn income $Y^h = w^h L^h$, where Y^h denotes income and L^h denotes the labour supply of household h. Assume that each household has a utility function such that

$$u^h = u\left(X^h, l^h, G, E\right), h = 1, 2 \tag{1}$$

where X^h is the quantity consumed of the private good by household h ($h = 1, 2$ indicating a household's type) and $X^h = (X_i), i = c, d$. Good c is environmentally clean.[3] Good d, however, is environmentally polluted or harmful, and creates negative externalities. Leisure is given by $l^h = 1 - L^h$ after we normalize the time endowment. We further assume that the government provides not only traditional public goods (such as national defence weapons which are detrimental for the environment), G, but also green public goods, E, for promoting environmental sustainability. The fact that the green public good, E, appears in the household's utility function indicates that consumers are increasingly aware of the importance of environmental sustainability and enjoy the provision of green public goods.[4]

To analyze the government's optimization problem, we follow Christiansen (1984) and Edwards *et al.* (1994) and break the consumer's optimization into two stages. With given labour supply, a fixed amount of after-tax income, B^h, is optimally allocated over the consumption goods at the first stage. We denote the vector of consumer prices by $Q = (q_i) = (p_i + t_i)$, where p_i and t_i stand for constant producer price and commodity tax rate of good i. The consumer's first-stage optimization gives conditional indirect utility,

$$V^h\left(Q, B^h, Y^h, G, E, w^h\right) = \max_X \left\{ u\left(X^h, \frac{Y^h}{w^h}, G, E\right) \middle| \sum_i q_i X_i^h = B^h \right\} \tag{2}$$

Solving (2) and using Roy's Identity gives conditional demand functions

$$X_i^h \left(Q, B^h, Y^h, G, E, w^h\right) = -\frac{V_i^h}{V_B^h} \tag{3}$$

where $V_i^h = \partial V^h / \partial q_i$.

At the second stage, given the budget constraint $B^h = Y^h - T(Y^h)$, the optimal working hours will be determined to maximize the conditional utility function, where T is the income tax function. The second stage optimization gives the following condition

$$V_B^h(1 - T') + V_Y^h = 0 \tag{4}$$

where T' is the marginal income tax rate.

2.2 The Government's Optimization Embedded with a Vision of Environmental Sustainability

Since the dawn of the twenty-first century, environmental degradation has rapidly emerged as one of the most formidable challenges for pursuing the goal of sustainable development (e.g. Dietz *et al.*, 2003; Diamond, 2005; Meadows *et al.*, 2005; Broecker, 2007). So far, the exploration of sustainability has led to several alternative definitions such as *weak sustainability*, *strong sustainability*, and others. In this paper, environmental sustainability refers to a sustainable state that satisfies the following condition: the total employment of environmentally harmful resources generated in an economy can be equally offset by the provision of government green public goods. This concept is partially inspired by Daly's exposition of a sustainable economy, a steady-state economy (SSE). According to Daly (1973, 1977, 2005), the SSE refers to an economy whose scale remains at a constant level. This level neither depletes the materials from the environment beyond its regenerative capacity nor pollutes the environment beyond its absorptive capacity. Of course, a fixed scale is just one possible case. This concept of sustainability also permits real economic growth over time, provided that the harmful effects are offset by beneficial effects. In this way, we are suggesting a net zero impact policy approach.

To help promote the notion of sustainability into practice, we argue that the government can play a leading role in initiating various schemes for promoting environmental sustainability. Among various plausible measures, we suggest that implementation of government green spending can be an effective instrument for enhancing both environmental sustainability and economic efficiency.

To manage a macro-environmental sustainable economy, the environmental sustainability constraint is given by

$$\eta(E) = \sum_h X_d^h \left(Q, B^h, Y^h, G, E, w^h\right) \tag{5}$$

In Equation (5), $\eta(E)$ can be regarded as environmental quality or the supply of environmental resources, and the provision of green public goods is instrumental for elevating environmental quality (i.e. $\eta_E > 0$). The right-hand side of (5) can be regarded as the summation of environmentally harmful or polluted goods produced in an economy or the demand for environmental resources. Take the emission or waste from polluted and toxic goods for example. The environmental sustainability condition will be satisfied as long as the amount in implementing toxic clean-up and pollution prevention in the government sector is equal to the total emission or waste from polluted and toxic goods generated by all households.

Given the environmental sustainability condition, the government's budget constraint is given by

$$\sum_h \left(Y^h - \sum_i p_i X_i^h \left(Q, B^h, Y^h, G, E \right) \right) = \left[\Omega\phi \left(\sum_h X_d^h \right) + (1 - \Omega)\varphi(G) \right] E + G \qquad (6)$$

where the left-hand side has been rewritten using the consumer's budget constraints. The right-hand side of (6) is the total expenditure of the green public good and the traditional public good. The price of the public good is normalized to one and the price of the green public good is denoted by $\Omega\phi(\sum_h X_d^h) + (1 - \Omega)\varphi(G)$,[5] where $\phi' > 0$, $\varphi' \gtrless 0, 0 < \Omega < 1$, $\phi(0) = 1$, and $\varphi(0) = 1$. The symbol Ω measures the level of the polluting effect on the price of the green public good. Consider the scenario: when the pollution level increases, it'll become more difficult and costly for the government to improve the environment by providing the green public good.[6] Thus, it is straightforward to assume that the price of the green public good increases in the total consumption of dirty goods. The relationship between public goods and green public goods is captured by $\varphi(G)$. If the public good and the green public good are complements, that is, $\varphi' < 0$, a government finds it is less costly, for example, to preserve biodiversity if people receive adequate environmental education.[7]

We distinguish a green public good from traditional public good in order to accentuate the essential role of the former, especially in the presence of growing consciousness of environmental protection issues among consumers. Armed with the manipulation of Equation (6), we can inspect the effect of interaction between the traditional public good, the green public good, and the pollution level upon optimal fiscal policy.

The procedures to address our problem are outlined as follows. First, we solve a set of allocation $\{Q, B^h, Y^h, G, E\}$ where $h = 1, 2$ that optimizes the planning problem. Second, we pin down marginal tax rates, or more precisely the tax wedge, by comparing optimality conditions derived from planner's and individuals' problem. As such, given the tax schedule $\{q_i, T^h\}$, where $i = c, d$ and the levels of traditional and green public goods $\{G, E\}$, households would implement the constrained efficient allocations $\{B^h, Y^h\}$ in market equilibrium.

Introducing the Lagrange multipliers θ, λ, γ and μ, the appropriate Lagrangean function of the government's optimization problem is

$$\Gamma = V^1 \left(Q, B^1, Y^1, G, E \right) + \theta \left[V^2 \left(Q, B^2, Y^2, G, E \right) - \bar{V}^2 \right]$$
$$+ \lambda \left[V^2 \left(Q, B^2, Y^2, G, E \right) - \hat{V}^2 \left(Q, B^1, Y^1, G, E \right) \right]$$
$$+ \gamma \left\{ \sum_h \left(Y^h - \sum_i p_i X_i^h \left(Q, B^h, Y^h, G, E \right) \right) - \left[\Omega\phi \left(\sum_h X_d^h \right) + (1 - \Omega)\varphi(G) \right] E - G \right\}$$
$$+ \mu \left[\sum_h X_d^h \left(Q, B^h, Y^h, G, E, w^h \right) - \eta(E) \right], \qquad (7)$$

where $\hat{V}^2$ refers to the type-2 person mimicking the low-ability person. In (7), the government chooses to maximize V^1 subject to achieving a given utility level $\bar{V}^2$ for type-2 person. In addition, the government faces three further constraints. The second constraint is the binding self-selection constraint. The third constraint is the government budget constraint and the fourth constraint is the macro-environmental sustainability constraint. The first-order conditions are

$$V_Y^1 - \lambda \hat{V}_Y^2 + \gamma \left(1 - \sum_i p_i \frac{\partial X_i^1}{\partial Y^1}\right) - \gamma \Omega \phi' E \frac{\partial X_d^1}{\partial Y^1} + \mu \frac{\partial X_d^1}{\partial Y^1} = 0 \tag{8}$$

$$V_B^1 - \lambda \hat{V}_B^2 - \gamma \sum_i p_i \frac{\partial X_i^2}{\partial B^1} - \gamma \Omega \phi' E \frac{\partial X_d^1}{\partial B^1} + \mu \frac{\partial X_d^1}{\partial B^1} = 0 \tag{9}$$

$$(\theta + \lambda) V_Y^2 + \gamma \left(1 - \sum_i p_i \frac{\partial X_i^2}{\partial Y^2}\right) - \gamma \Omega \phi' E \frac{\partial X_d^2}{\partial Y^2} + \mu \frac{\partial X_d^2}{\partial Y^2} = 0 \tag{10}$$

$$(\theta + \lambda) V_B^2 - \gamma \sum_i p_i \frac{\partial X_i^2}{\partial B^2} - \gamma \Omega \phi' E \frac{\partial X_d^2}{\partial B^2} + \mu \frac{\partial X_d^2}{\partial B^2} = 0 \tag{11}$$

$$-V_B^1 X_j^1 - (\theta + \lambda) V_B^2 X_j^2 + \lambda \hat{V}_B^2 \hat{X}_j^2 - \gamma \sum_h \sum_i p_i \frac{\partial X_i^h}{\partial q_j}$$
$$- \gamma \Omega \phi' E \sum_h \frac{\partial X_d^h}{\partial q_j} + \mu \sum_h \frac{\partial X_d^h}{\partial q_j} = 0 \tag{12}$$

$$V_G^1 + (\theta + \lambda) V_G^2 - \lambda \hat{V}_G^2 - \gamma \sum_h \sum_i p_i \frac{\partial X_i^h}{\partial G}$$
$$- \gamma \left[\left[\Omega \phi' \sum_h \frac{\partial X_d^h}{\partial G} + (1 - \Omega) \varphi'\right] E + 1\right] + \mu \sum_h \frac{\partial X_d^h}{\partial G} = 0 \tag{13}$$

and

$$V_E^1 + (\theta + \lambda) V_E^2 - \lambda \hat{V}_E^2 - \gamma \sum_h \sum_i p_i \frac{\partial X_i^h}{\partial E} - \gamma [\Omega \phi + (1 - \Omega) \varphi]$$
$$- \gamma \Omega \phi' E \sum_h \frac{\partial X_d^h}{\partial E} + \mu \left(\sum_h \frac{\partial X_d^h}{\partial E} - \eta_E\right) = 0 \tag{14}$$

3. The Samuelson Rule for Optimal Provision with the Green Public Good (The Greened Samuelson Rule)

With the first-order conditions for the government's optimization problem derived, we turn to the natural question of the optimal provision of the green public good, following the approach of Samuelson (1954). In this way, we can further discuss the optimal provision of green public goods and public goods associated with the environmental sustainability constraint. It is important to do this because we know that the collective consumption involved with public goods violates the basic assumption of private goods in the canonical Arrow-Debreu model of a competitive economy. The presence of public goods results in failure of the competitive equilibrium, or what Samuelson referred to as the, 'impossibility of decentralized spontaneous solution'. He showed that there is no decentralized pricing mechanism that can determine the optimal levels of public goods. Inefficiency results, and thereby suggests a potential role for government to play in the provision of public goods in order to remedy the market failure. Lindahl (1919) suggested that if individuals could be charged personalized prices for public goods Pareto-efficiency could be restored. His approach effectively generalizes the Arrow–Debreu economy in which each commodity has a single price. Foley (1970) provides the modern analysis of Lindahl prices.

We begin this analysis by adding and subtracting $\lambda \hat{V}_B^2 (V_E^1/V_B^1)$ in (14) which gives

$$
\begin{aligned}
&\left(V_B^1 - \lambda \hat{V}_B^2\right) \frac{V_E^1}{V_B^1} + (\theta + \lambda) V_B^2 \frac{V_E^2}{V_B^2} - \lambda \hat{V}_B^2 \left(\frac{\hat{V}_E^2}{\hat{V}_B^2} - \frac{V_E^1}{V_B^1}\right) \\
&- \gamma \sum_h \sum_i p_i \frac{\partial X_i^h}{\partial E} - \gamma [\Omega \phi + (1 - \Omega)\varphi] - \gamma \Omega \phi' E \sum_h \frac{\partial X_d^h}{\partial E} + \mu \left(\sum_h \frac{\partial X_d^h}{\partial E} - \eta_E\right) = 0
\end{aligned}
\tag{15}
$$

Now, let MWP_{EB}^h denote the marginal willingness to pay for the green public good, or the marginal rate of substitution between the green public good and after-tax income (V_E^h/V_B^h). Substitution of (9) and (11) into (15) yields

$$
\begin{aligned}
&MWP_{EB}^1 \left(\gamma \sum_i p_i \frac{\partial X_i^1}{\partial B^1} + \gamma \Omega \phi' E \frac{\partial X_d^1}{\partial B^1} - \mu \frac{\partial X_d^1}{\partial B^1}\right) \\
&+ MWP_{EB}^2 \left(\gamma \sum_i p_i \frac{\partial X_i^2}{\partial B^2} + \gamma \Omega \phi' E \frac{\partial X_d^2}{\partial B^2} - \mu \frac{\partial X_d^2}{\partial B^2}\right) - \lambda \hat{V}_B^2 \left(M\hat{W}P_{EB}^2 - MWP_{EB}^1\right) \\
&- \gamma \sum_h \sum_i p_i \frac{\partial X_i^h}{\partial E} - \gamma [\Omega \phi + (1 - \Omega)\varphi] - \gamma \Omega \phi' E \sum_h \frac{\partial X_d^h}{\partial E} + \mu \left(\sum_h \frac{\partial X_d^h}{\partial E} - \eta_E\right) = 0
\end{aligned}
\tag{16}
$$

Use $\lambda^* (> 0)$ as a notation for $\lambda \hat{V}_B^2/\gamma$ and introduce the conditional demand function,

$$
\tilde{X}_i^h \left(Q, Y^h, \tilde{u}, G, E, w^h\right) = \arg\min_x \left\{ \sum_i q_i X_i^h \, \middle| \, u\left(X^h, \frac{Y^h}{w^h}, G, E\right) \geq \tilde{u} \right\}
\tag{17}
$$

Using the Slutsky equation, we can show that $\dfrac{\partial X_i^h}{\partial E} = \dfrac{\partial \tilde{X}_i^h}{\partial E} + MWP_{EB}^h \dfrac{\partial X_i^h}{\partial B^h}$ and $\sum_i p_i \dfrac{\partial \tilde{X}_i^h}{\partial E} = -MWP_{EB}^h - \sum_i t_i \dfrac{\partial \tilde{X}_i^h}{\partial E}$ (see Appendix A.1 and A.2). Using the aforementioned properties and results, (16) can be rearranged as

$$
\begin{aligned}
&\sum_h MWP_{EB}^h - \sum_h \sum_i t_i \frac{\partial \tilde{X}_i^h}{\partial E} - \lambda^* \left(M\hat{W}P_{EB}^2 - MWP_{EB}^1\right) - [\Omega \phi + (1 - \Omega)\varphi] \\
&- \Omega \phi' E \sum_h \frac{\partial \tilde{X}_d^h}{\partial E} - \frac{\mu}{\gamma} \left(\eta_E - \sum_h \frac{\partial \tilde{X}_d^h}{\partial E}\right) = 0
\end{aligned}
\tag{18}
$$

To evaluate the impact of the green public good on environmental sustainability, we define the feedback parameter $\sigma \equiv \dfrac{1}{\eta_E - \sum_h \frac{\partial \tilde{X}_d^h}{\partial E}}$. The value of σ will become smaller if the emergence of the green public good leads to lower consumption of the environmentally polluted goods.[8] Substitution of σ in (18) yields the following proposition.

Proposition 1. *In Pareto-efficient mixed taxation, the increased environmental quality via the provision of the green public good (or the shadow benefit of the green public good), measured in terms of government's revenue, $\frac{\mu}{\gamma}$, is given by*

$$
\frac{\mu}{\gamma} = \sigma \left\{ \sum_h MWP_{EB}^h + \sum_h \sum_i \frac{\partial \left(t_i X_i^h\right)}{\partial E} - \lambda^* \left(M\hat{W}P_{EB}^2 - MWP_{EB}^1\right) - [\Omega \phi + (1 - \Omega)\varphi] \right\}
$$
$$
+ \Omega \phi' E (1 - \eta_E \sigma)
\tag{19}
$$

Proposition 1 shows that the valuation of the green public good consists of six different impacts: (i) the feedback parameter, σ; (ii) the consumer's willingness to pay for the
green public good, $\sum_h MWP^h_{EB}$; (iii) a commodity tax revenue effect, $\sum_h \sum_i \frac{\partial(t_i X^h_i)}{\partial E}$; (iv) the
self-selection impact, $(M\hat{W}P^2_{EB} - MWP^1_{EB})$; (v) the price effect of the green public good,
$\Omega\phi + (1 - \Omega)\varphi$ and (vi) the polluting effect, $\Omega\phi' E$.

To highlight the implications of (19), we isolate and discuss each effect. Recall that if the
private information problem is absent, that is, there is observable productivity, we simply set
$\lambda = 0$, indicating that the incentive-compatibility constraint plays no role and the effect of
self-selection is mute.

To evaluate the sign of the shadow benefit of the green public good, we first consider the
feedback parameter. If improvement of the environment leads to a lower demand for dirty
goods, the value of σ falls. There are two opposing effects resulting from a decrease in σ. We
focus on the following effect: a reduction in σ will raise the value of $\frac{\mu}{\gamma}$ as long as ϕ' and η_E are
positive. The intuition is straightforward: the greater impact of green public goods generates
on environmental sustainability, the more benefits of green public goods will create.

The first term inside the brackets measures the sum of the marginal willingness to pay for
the green public good. The benefit is bigger if the consumers have stronger preferences for
environmental quality. The next term takes the impact of the green public good on the commodity tax revenues into account. If an increase in the green public good provision leads to a
higher collected tax revenue, the value of $\frac{\mu}{\gamma}$ rises, which in turn affects the green public good
provision.

The sign of the self-selection effect is determined by the magnitude of the green public
good's relative valuation by the type-1 person and by the type-2 person mimicking the type-1
choice. If the green public good and leisure are complements ($\frac{\partial MWP^h_{EB}}{\partial l^h} > 0$), the type-2 person
can work fewer hours than the type-1 person to earn a given level of income. In this case,
$M\hat{W}P^2_{EB} > MWP^1_{EB}$ and the influence of the self-selection term on the shadow benefit of the
green public good is negative. On the contrary, if $M\hat{W}P^2_{EB}$ is smaller than MWP^1_{EB}, that is, the
weakened self-selection constraint, then the self-selection effect will raise the value of $\frac{\mu}{\gamma}$. If
the price of the green public good increases, the expenditures on the green public good will
increase and the value of $\frac{\mu}{\gamma}$ will also fall. Finally, under the condition that $1 - \eta_E\sigma$ is positive,
a higher polluting effect will increase the benefit of the green public good. Overall, the sign
of the shadow benefit of the green public good is ambiguous. To help discuss the design of
government policy, we mostly assume that it is positive in the subsequent analysis.

To proceed, we further derive the Samuelson rule for optimal provision with the green public good. Maximizing the Lagrangean function given in (7) with respect to G and using MRS^h_{GB}
to denote the marginal rate of substitution of type h between the public good and private consumption (V^h_G/V^h_B) gives the following proposition.

Proposition 2. (Greened Samuelson Rule). *Pareto-improvement in the level of the public*
good provision and in income taxation, when the government has taken the environmental
sustainability condition into account, requires that

$$\sum_h MRS^h_{GB} = 1 + \lambda^* \left(M\hat{R}S^2_{GB} - MRS^1_{GB}\right) - \sum_h \sum_i t_i \frac{\partial X^h_i}{\partial G}$$
$$- \left(\frac{\mu}{\gamma} - \Omega\phi' E\right) \sum_h \frac{\partial X^h_d}{\partial G} + (1 - \Omega)\varphi' E \tag{20}$$

The expression in (20) represents the Samuelson rule for optimal provision with the public good or, in a simple term, the greened Samuelson rule.

Notice that if we abstract private information and environmental considerations from the model, (20) reduces to the original Samuelson rule, $\sum_h MRS^h_{GB} = 1$, where the left-hand side term is the benefit from an increase in public good provided, and the right-hand side term is the cost of the increased public good provision. Hence the reductions in terms in RHS of (20) can bring about a Pareto-improvement.

The greened Samuelson rule differs from the condition for Pareto-efficient provision of the public good presented in Proposition 4 of Pirttilä and Tuomala (1997) in several ways. The first three terms, as usual, measure the price of the public good, the self-selection impact, and the tax revenue impact. Provided that $\frac{\partial X^h_d}{\partial G} > 0$ is positive, the fourth term indicates that a Pareto-improving reform will take place if $\frac{\mu}{\gamma}$ rises or ϕ' falls. The fifth term shows that a decrease in φ' will lead to a Pareto-improvement.

These results lead to several policy implications. First, suppose the provision of a traditional public good stimulates the consumption of dirty goods. If resorting to policies that repress ϕ' is feasible, the government can rely on providing more green public goods rather than traditional public goods in order to improve social welfare. Second, if the provision of traditional public goods reduces the cost of producing green public goods, society can benefit from consuming both public goods. That suggests providing some traditional public goods may be preferable to providing others; for example, education may dominate national defence hardware in this regard.

4. The Optimal Tax Structure

4.1 *Individual Effective Marginal Tax Rates*

After examining the modification to the Samuelson rule, this section considers the decision of tax policy in the presence of externalities and green public goods. The government employs the measures of non-linear income taxation and linear commodity taxation to finance the expenditures of public goods and green public goods. The total taxes paid by individuals h are[9]

$$\tau\left(Y^h\right) = T\left(Y^h\right) + \sum_i t_i X^h_i \left(Q, Y^h - T\left(Y^h\right), Y^h, G, E, w^h\right) \tag{21}$$

Differentiating (21) with respect to Y gives the marginal effective tax rate (see Appendix A.3)

$$\tau'\left(Y^h\right) = \left(1 - \sum_i p_i \frac{\partial X^h_i}{\partial Y^h}\right) + \left(\frac{V_Y}{V_B}\right) \sum_i p_i \frac{\partial X^h_i}{\partial B^h} \tag{22}$$

To investigate the alternative marginal effective tax rates faced by the two types of households, (10) can be divided by (11) and rearranging terms as

$$\frac{V^2_Y}{V^2_B} \sum_i p_i \frac{\partial X^2_i}{\partial B^2} = -\left(1 - \sum_i p_i \frac{\partial X^2_i}{\partial Y^2}\right) + \left(\Omega\phi'E - \frac{\mu}{\gamma}\right)\left(\frac{\partial X^2_d}{\partial Y^2} - \frac{V^2_Y}{V^2_B} \cdot \frac{\partial X^2_d}{\partial B^2}\right) \tag{23}$$

By combining (22) and (23), the marginal tax rate faced by the high-ability household is given by

$$\tau'\left(Y^2\right) = \left(\Omega\phi'E - \frac{\mu}{\gamma}\right)\left(\frac{\partial X_d^2}{\partial Y^2} - \frac{V_Y^2}{V_B^2}\cdot\frac{\partial X_d^2}{\partial B^2}\right) \tag{24}$$

Provided that $\frac{\mu}{\gamma} > 0$ and $\frac{\partial X_d^2}{\partial Y^2} - \frac{V_Y^2}{V_B^2}\cdot\frac{\partial X_d^2}{\partial B^2} > 0,$[10] the marginal effective tax rate faced by the high-ability person will be determined by $\Omega\phi'E$ and $\frac{\mu}{\gamma}$. On the one hand, the marginal effective tax rate of the high income person increases if there is a rise in the relative weight of polluting impact, in the price of the green public good caused by increasing pollution, or in government green spending. On the other hand, the marginal effective tax rate of the high income person decreases if the green public good provision leads to an improvement in environmental quality (i.e. a rise in the value of $\frac{\mu}{\gamma}$).

Similarly, (8) can be divided by (9) and rearranging terms as

$$\frac{V_Y^1}{V_B^1}\sum_i p_i\frac{\partial X_i^1}{\partial B^1} = -\left(1 - \sum_i p_i\frac{\partial X_i^1}{\partial Y^1}\right) + \frac{\lambda\hat{V}_B^2}{\gamma}\left(\frac{\hat{V}_Y^2}{\hat{V}_B^2} - \frac{V_Y^1}{V_B^1}\right)$$
$$+ \left(\Omega\phi'E - \frac{\mu}{\gamma}\right)\left(\frac{\partial X_d^1}{\partial Y^1} - \frac{V_Y^1}{V_B^1}\cdot\frac{\partial X_d^1}{\partial B^1}\right) \tag{25}$$

By substituting (25) into (22), the marginal effective tax rate faced by the low-ability household is given by

$$\tau'\left(Y^1\right) = \lambda^*\left(\frac{\hat{V}_Y^2}{\hat{V}_B^2} - \frac{V_Y^1}{V_B^1}\right) + \left(\Omega\phi'E - \frac{\mu}{\gamma}\right)\left(\frac{\partial X_d^1}{\partial Y^1} - \frac{V_Y^1}{V_B^1}\cdot\frac{\partial X_d^1}{\partial B^1}\right) \tag{26}$$

The first term on the right-hand side is the marginal tax rate without externalities. The second term is a similar kind of externality-included term that discussed in the case of type-2 tax rule.

Proposition 3. *In a Pareto-efficient mixed taxation framework with the presence of externalities and green public goods, the marginal effective tax rates faced by both ability types of households will be determined by the following factors: (i) the relative weight of polluting impact, (ii) the price of the green public good caused by increasing pollution, (iii) government green spending and (iv) the value of $\frac{\mu}{\gamma}$.*

A rise in any of the first three factors will increase the marginal effective tax rate, whereas a rise in the value of $\frac{\mu}{\gamma}$ will decrease the marginal effective tax rate. On the one hand, when factors associated with more harmful pollution increase, consumers will encounter a higher marginal effective tax rate which is served as a mechanism to encourage consumers to cut the expenditure on dirty goods. On the other hand, if the government can implement a proper economic plan to fully exert the impact of green public goods on the environment, the marginal tax rate will decrease. This result also shows that there is a linkage between expenditure side and revenue side in government's budget constraint, through the mechanism that the mitigation of negative externality by providing green public goods causes less needs to rely on distortive tax instruments.

4.2 Optimal Commodity Taxation

Next we analyze the commodity taxes on the clean good and the polluted good in a Pareto-efficient mixed taxation framework. Rearranging (12) gives

$$-\sum_h \sum_i p_i \frac{\partial X_i^h}{\partial q_j} = \frac{1}{\gamma}\left[V_B^1 X_j^1 + (\theta + \lambda)V_B^2 X_j^2 - \lambda \hat{V}_B^2 \hat{X}_j^2\right] + \sum_h \frac{\partial X_d^h}{\partial q_j}\left(\Omega\phi'E - \frac{\mu}{\gamma}\right) \quad (27)$$

The consumer's budget constraint can be written as

$$\sum_h \sum_i t_i \frac{\partial X_i^h}{\partial q_j} = -\sum_h X_j^h - \sum_h \sum_i p_i \frac{\partial X_i^h}{\partial q_j} \quad (28)$$

(see Appendix A.4)

For convenience, we can define $\xi_j = \frac{1}{\gamma}[V_B^1 X_j^1 + (\theta + \lambda)V_B^2 X_j^2 - \lambda \hat{V}_B^2 \hat{X}_j^2] - \sum_h X_j^h$

Combining (27) and (28) and substituting ξ_j in the matrix form, we obtain

$$\begin{pmatrix} \sum_h \frac{\partial X_c^h}{\partial q_c} & \sum_h \frac{\partial X_d^h}{\partial q_c} \\ \sum_h \frac{\partial X_c^h}{\partial q_d} & \sum_h \frac{\partial X_d^h}{\partial q_d} \end{pmatrix} \cdot \begin{pmatrix} t_c \\ t_d \end{pmatrix} = \begin{pmatrix} \xi_c + \sum_h \frac{\partial X_d^h}{\partial q_j}\left(\Omega\phi'E - \frac{\mu}{\gamma}\right) \\ \xi_d + \sum_h \frac{\partial X_d^h}{\partial q_j}\left(\Omega\phi'E - \frac{\mu}{\gamma}\right) \end{pmatrix} \quad (29)$$

The coefficient matrix on the left is the transpose of the Hessian matrix and its determinant can be denoted as J. By using the Cramer's rule, we can state the following proposition.

Proposition 4. *In a Pareto-efficient mixed taxation framework, the commodity tax on the clean good, t_c, and the commodity tax on the polluted good, t_d, are given by*

$$t_c = \frac{1}{J}\sum_h \left(\xi_c \frac{\partial X_d^h}{\partial q_d} - \xi_d \frac{\partial X_d^h}{\partial q_c}\right) \quad (30)$$

and

$$t_d = \frac{1}{J}\sum_h \left(\xi_d \frac{\partial X_c^h}{\partial q_c} - \xi_c \frac{\partial X_c^h}{\partial q_d}\right) + \left(\Omega\phi'E - \frac{\mu}{\gamma}\right) \quad (31)$$

Proposition 4 indicates that the term $(\Omega\phi'E - \frac{\mu}{\gamma})$ disappears from the tax rule for the environmentally clean good since it doesn't contribute to any negative externality. The magnitude of $(\Omega\phi'E - \frac{\mu}{\gamma})$ depends on (i) the relative weight of polluting impact, (ii) the price of the green public good caused by increasing pollution, (iii) government green spending and (iv) the value of $\frac{\mu}{\gamma}$. A rise in any of the first three factors will increase the commodity tax rate, whereas a rise in the value of $\frac{\mu}{\gamma}$ will decrease the commodity tax rate. According to our argument, the essence of Pigouvian taxation for correcting negative externality is maintained here as well; any element pertaining to more (less) serious pollution impact induces a higher (lower) tax rate, and vice versa.

Propositions 3 and 4 state the results that suggest optimal taxation scheme so as to implement constrained efficient allocations. Despite the complicated form, it is believed that understanding these optimal properties well might facilitate the tax design in practice and the evaluation of the existing tax schedule.

5. Discussion and Conclusion

From the perspective of sustainable development, every human generation has a big stake in government provision of green public goods. To be considered *green* a public good cannot create an environmentally harmful or polluting impact (such as excessive use of non-renewable resources, fostering of waste and pollution, or discouragement of conservation) whether in the consumption process or employed as an input in a production process. Furthermore, green public goods possess the property that the present generation's consumption will not reduce the consumption of the future generation. This characteristic of intergenerational joint-consumption contrasts significantly with that of traditional public goods, which once consumed or utilized as an input in a region or a country can no longer be of further service to a future generation.

Analysis of optimal tax structures has been a primary concern for tax policy economists. Although the optimal tax literature has devoted considerable attention to the topic of correcting for environmental externalities, the concept of environmental sustainability has not yet been taken into account. To further discuss optimal tax structure and macro-environmental issues, this paper explicitly introduces the environmental sustainability constraint into the government's optimization problem. Specifically, the environmental sustainability condition can be met as long as the total usage of environmentally polluted resources generated by households does not exceed the equivalent absorptive capacity provided via the provision of green public goods.

Utilizing a standard model with two types of households from the optimal taxation literature, our results indicate that the overall effect of green spending, measured in terms of government's revenue, is subject to several factors such as the influence of green spending on environmental sustainability, the cost of green spending, the polluting effect, and so on. We also derive a greened Samuelson rule — a modified Samuelson rule associated with the environmental sustainability condition. We show that a Pareto-improving reform can take place if the shadow benefit of the green public good rises.

Acknowledgements

The second author is grateful to the Taiwan National Science Council (NSC) for financial support under Grant No. NSC 96-2415-H-004-016-MY3. Earlier versions of this paper benefited from comments received at the 80th Southern Economic Association Annual Conference in Atlanta, Georgia, USA, November 20–22, 2010, the International Conference on Public Finance Issues in China, Tsinghua University, Beijing, China, June 26–28, 2011, and the Association for Public Economic Theory 13th Annual Conference, Taipei, Taiwan, June 12–14, 2012. We especially would like to thank two anonymous reviewers and Joel Slemrod for their helpful comments.

Notes

1. For a recent review of the optimal tax literature and its policy implementations see Mankiw, Weinzierl, and Yagan (2009).
2. For example, see Atkinson and Stiglitz (1976), Stiglitz (1982), Boadway and Keen (1993) and Saez (2002, 2004).
3. The property of altruism or warm-glow that consumers possess to buy environmentally-friendly or green commodities is not considered in the model, since we now focus on investigating the main mechanism of pollution and traditional as well as green public goods to have impacts on optimal taxation in a situation where agents are simply

self-concerning. We thank one of the referees for pointing out that moral values, such as altruism and warm-glow concepts, possessed by the government but lacked by households, could be somehow revealed via sustainability constraint.

4. For simplicity, we assume that consumers benefit from green public goods and ignore the extent of pollution. To justify it, consider consumers in practice are less conscious of intangible pollution, whereas they are sufficed by green public goods which are more easily observable and 'promoted' by public authority.

5. For simplicity, we set the price of green public good in a relatively ad hoc way. However, in principle, this assumption insofar can still capture the idea concerning the relationship of pollution, traditional public goods and the difficulty in the provision of green public goods.

6. For example, a government which aims to preserve biodiversity in a damaged habitat must incur higher costs to accomplish the task.

7. In this case, 'education' is complementary to biodiversity, a type of green public good.

8. It is reasonable to assume that the green public good provision leads to a lower demand for the polluted goods, that is, $\frac{\partial \widetilde{X}_d^h}{\partial E} < 0$. Thus, the value of σ is positive.

9. We follow the procedures used in Pirttilä and Tuomala (1997) and employ effective tax rate to shed light on the contour of overall optimal taxation.

10. The sign of $\frac{V_Y^h}{V_B^h}$ is negative. We assume that the polluting good is a normal good, so the derivatives of X_d^h with respect to B and Y are positive.

References

Atkinson, A.B. and Stern, N.H. (1974) Pigou, taxation and public goods. *The Review of Economic Studies* 41(1): 119–128.

Atkinson, A.B. and Stiglitz, J.E. (1976) The design of tax structure: direct versus indirect taxation. *Journal of Public Economics* 6: 55–75.

Barbier, E. (2010) How is the global green new deal going? *Nature* 464: 832–833.

Boadway, R. and Keen, M. (1993) Public goods, self-selection, and optimal income taxation. *International Economic Review* 34(3): 463–478.

Bovenberg, A.L. and Goulder, L.H. (2002) Environmental taxation and regulation. In A.J. Auerbach and M. Feldstein (eds.), *Handbook of Public Economics*, Vol. 3 (pp. 1471–1545). Amsterdam: Elsevier.

Broecker, W.S. (2007) CO_2 arithmetic. *Science* 315(5817): 1371.

Christiansen, V. (1984) Which commodity taxes should supplement the income tax? *Journal of Public Economics* 24(2): 195–220.

Daly, H.E. (1973) The steady-state economy: toward a political economy of biophysical equilibrium and moral growth. In H.E. Daly (ed.), *Toward a Steady-State Economy* (pp. 149–174). San Francisco: W. H. Freeman and Company.

Daly, H.E. (1977) *Steady-State Economics: The Economics of Biophysical Equilibrium and Moral Growth*. San Francisco: W. H. Freeman and Company.

Daly, H.E. (2005) Economics in a full world. *Scientific American* 293(Special Issue): 100–107.

Diamond, J.M. (2005) *Collapse: How Societies Choose to Fail or Succeed*. New York: Viking.

Diamond, P.A. and Mirrlees, J.A. (1971) Optimal taxation and public production. *American Economic Review* 61(1): 8–27.

Dietz, T., Ostrom, E. and Stern, P.C. (2003) The struggle to govern the commons. *Science* 302(5652): 1907–1912.

Edwards, J., Keen, M. and Tuomala, M. (1994) Income tax, commodity taxes and public good provision: A brief guide. *Finanz Archiv* 51(4): 472–487.

Foley, D.K. (1970) Lindahl's solution and the core of an economy with public goods. *Econometrica* 38(1): 66–72.

Goulder, L.H. (1994) Environmental taxation and the "double dividend": A reader's guide. NBER Working Paper 4896.

Hanson, C. and Sandalow, D. (2006) *Greening the Tax Code*. Washington, DC: The Brookings Institution and the World Resources Institute. Retrieved from http://www.wri.org/publication/greening-tax-code (Last accessed 23 July 2015).

Houser, T., Mohan, S. and Heilmayr, R.A. (2009) A green global recovery? Assessing US economic stimulus and the prospects for internatioal coordination. policy brief number PB09-3, Washington, DC: Peterson Institute for International Economics and World Resources Institute.

Lindahl, E. (1919) Positive losum, di gerechtigkeit der besteurung, Lund, reprinted as just taxation—a positive solution. In R.A. Musgrave and A.T. Peacock (eds.), *Classics in the Theory of Public Finance, 1958*. London: Macmillan.

Mankiw, N.G., Weinzierl, M.C. and Yagan, D.F. (2009) Optimal taxation in theory and practice. *Journal of Economic Perspectives* 23(4): 147–174.

Meadows, D.H., Randers, J. and Meadows, D.L. (2005) *Limits to Growth: The 30-Year Update*. London: Earthscan.

Parry, I.W.H. (1998) The double dividend: When you get it and when you don't. *National Tax Association Proceedings of the Ninety-First Annual Conference*, pp. 46–51.

Parry, I.W.H. and Bento, A.M. (2000) Tax deductions, environmental policy, and the 'double dividend' hypothesis. *Journal of Environmental Economics and Management* 39(1): 67–96.

Pirttilä, J. and Tuomala, M. (1997) Income tax, commodity tax and environmental policy. *International Tax and Public Finance* 4(3): 379–393.

Saez, E. (2002) The desirability of commodity taxation under non-linear income taxation and heterogeneous tastes. *Journal of Public Economics* 83(2): 217–230.

Saez, E. (2004) Direct or indirect tax instruments for redistribution: short-run versus long-run. *Journal of Public Economics* 88(3–4): 503–518.

Samuelson, P.A. (1954) The pure theory of public expenditure. *Review of Economics and Statistics* 36(4): 387–389.

Stiglitz, J.E. (1982) Self-selection and Pareto efficient taxation. *Journal of Public Economics* 17(2): 213–240.

Stiglitz, J.E. and Dasgupta, P. (1971) Differential taxation, public goods, and economic efficiency. *The Review of Economic Studies* 38(2): 151–174.

Appendix

A.1 Since consumers are assumed to be rationally behaved, we can manipulate the dual properties to derive following equations:

$$X_i^h \left(Q, Y^h, I^h, G, E \right) = \tilde{X}_i^h(Q, u, G, E) \tag{A1.1}$$

$$I^h \left(Q, Y^h, u, G, E \right) = B^h \tag{A1.2}$$

Differentiating both (A1.1) and (A1.2) yields

$$\frac{\partial X_i^h}{\partial E} + \frac{\partial X_i^h}{\partial I^h} \cdot \frac{\partial I^h}{\partial E} = \frac{\partial \tilde{X}_i^h}{\partial E} \tag{A1.3}$$

$$\frac{\partial I}{\partial E} = -\frac{V_E^h}{V_B^h} \tag{A1.4}$$

Combing (A1.3) and (A1.4) and substituting the notation of MWP_{EB}^h, we obtain

$$\frac{\partial X_i^h}{\partial E} = \frac{\partial \tilde{X}_i^h}{\partial E} + MWP_{EB}^h \frac{\partial X_i^h}{\partial B^h} \tag{A1.5}$$

A.2 Using (A1.2), (A1.4) and $\sum_i p_i \tilde{X}_i^h = I^h - \sum_i t_i \tilde{X}_i^h$, we obtain

$$\sum_i p_i \frac{\partial \tilde{X}_i^h}{\partial E} = \frac{\partial I^h}{\partial E} + \sum_i t_i \frac{\partial \tilde{X}_i^h}{\partial E} = -MWP_{EB}^h + \sum_i t_i \frac{\partial \tilde{X}_i^h}{\partial E} \tag{A2.1}$$

A.3 Differentiating $\tau(Y^h)$ gives

$$\tau'\left(Y^h\right) = T'\left(Y^h\right) + \sum_i t_i \left[\frac{\partial X_i^h}{\partial B^h}(1 - T') + \frac{\partial X_i^h}{\partial Y^h} \right] \tag{A3.1}$$

where $B^h = Y^h - T(Y^h)$. Replacing the marginal income tax rate $T'(Y^h)$ by $1 + \frac{V_Y^h}{V_B^h}$ and rearranging (A3.1), we obtain

$$\tau'\left(Y^h\right) = 1 + \sum_i t_i \frac{\partial X_i^h}{\partial Y^h} + \frac{V_Y^h}{V_B^h}\left(1 - \sum_i t_i \frac{\partial X_i^h}{\partial B^h}\right) \tag{A3.2}$$

Due to $p_i = q_i - t_i$ and $\sum_i q_i X_i^h = B^h$, the following two properties can be derived:

$$\sum_i p_i \frac{\partial X_i^h}{\partial B^h} = 1 - \sum_i t_i \frac{\partial X_i^h}{\partial B^h} \tag{A3.3}$$

$$\sum_i p_i \frac{\partial X_i^h}{\partial Y^h} = -\sum_i t_i \frac{\partial X_i^h}{\partial Y^h} \tag{A3.4}$$

Equation (22) could be obtained after we substitute (A3.3) and (A3.4) into (A3.2).

A.4 Differentiating individual budget constraint and using $p_i = q_i - t_i$, we obtain

$$\sum_i p_i \frac{\partial X_i^h}{\partial q_j} = -X_j^h - \sum_i t_i \frac{\partial X_i^h}{\partial q_j} \tag{A4.1}$$

Equation (28) is simply the summation of (A4.1) over h.

6

HOUSEHOLD COOPERATION IN WASTE MANAGEMENT: INITIAL CONDITIONS AND INTERVENTION

Marie Briguglio

University of Malta

1. Introduction

Few environmental problems exemplify market-failure better than the problem of solid waste does. Its generation, a direct by-product of economic production and consumption, is intimately linked to economic activity and likely to remain so for the next few generations (Kinnaman, 2009; Ferrara and Missios, 2012). This comes at considerable economic cost: besides the costs of collection and transportation (and associated risks), as well as land acquisition, and infrastructural operating and closure costs (Adhikari *et al.*, 2010), waste generates well-documented environmental externalities (Kinnaman, 2006).

In several countries around the world, landfills are still the main solution for this waste stream (OECD, 2008). Associated external effects may include dust, odour, noise, pests, accident risk, air and climatic emissions (notably methane) and various discharges to soil, to ground/surface water bodies and to the marine environment. This can lead to their contamination, to negative health effects and to harmful effects on biodiversity and economic activity (Hoornweg and Bhada-Tata, 2012; European Environmental Agency, 2013). Other end-of-pipe solutions, such as incineration, are also associated with air and climatic pollution (Linderhof *et al.*, 2001; Edgerton *et al.*, 2009). Illegal storage or disposal of waste imposes even greater risks (Kuo and Perrings, 2010). While infrastructure in developed countries is increasingly built to mitigate environmental damage, this reduction in external costs comes at the expense of higher *explicit* costs. Policy-makers face a tough job in weighing the environmental and consequent socio-economic costs of poorly-managed waste against the (capital and running) costs of infrastructure, the (administrative, implementation and enforcement) cost of policy-design, and the possible losses in utility and productivity resulting from intervention.

Household waste is considered to be a particularly problematic source of waste (European Environmental Agency, 2009, 2013), and constitutes the bulk of Municipal Solid Waste (MSW) worldwide. World Bank projections suggest that, globally, MSW has increased from

Environmental Economics and Sustainability, First Edition. Edited by Brian Chi-ang Lin and Siqi Zheng.
Chapters © 2017 The Authors. Book compilation © 2017 John Wiley & Sons, Ltd. Published 2017 by John Wiley & Sons, Ltd.

0.7 billion tonnes per year in 2002, to 1.3 billion tonnes in 2012. It is forecast to rise to approx-imately 2.2 billion tonnes per year by 2025 (Hoornweg and Bhada-Tata, 2012). This increase is driven both by larger numbers of urban residents (estimated to rise from 2.9 billion in 2002 to 4.3 billion in 2025) and by higher per capital disposal rates (forecast to increase from 0.64 per person per day in 2002, to 1.42 per person per day in 2025). These, in turn, are asso-ciated with higher incomes, more intensive use of packaging materials and more disposable goods.

An oft adopted policy solution to reduce household waste going to landfill, is to encour-age its separation at source into recyclable or compostable components. Even if the cost of household time, storage, transportation, infrastructure, and management systems may not al-ways be significantly outweighed by the non-market social benefits of reducing environmental externalities, the goal of increasing household participation in waste separation is one that is vigorously pursued in several countries and regions (Kinnaman, 2006). Sometimes this policy stems from mandatory supra-national goals, as is the case in European Union countries (Kin-naman, 2006; European Environmental Agency, 2009, 2013). Certainly, the net benefits are larger when one considers the potential of reducing virgin material use (Dijkgraaf and Gradus, 2004; Ferrara and Missios, 2005), although rates of recovery vary between material types, and the reconversion process itself may use considerable amounts of energy (Hoornweg and Bhada-Tata, 2012). Whether separation/recycling activities are substitutive of waste reduction efforts by households constitutes still another complication, though studies generally find both outcomes to work in tandem (e.g. Van Houtven and Morris, 1999; Dijkgraaf and Gradus, 2004; Dahlén and Lagerkvist, 2010; Bucciol *et al.*, 2015).

The extent of policy intervention in the domain of household waste separation and recy-cling participation is mirrored by the voluminous economic research on the determinants of household cooperation in such activities. Spanning at least four decades, this literature is rich and nuanced, and includes a well-developed theoretical backbone that started with models of waste production (Wertz, 1976), and was later extended to consider recycling and illegal dis-posal (Fullerton and Kinnaman, 1996). Building on economic theories of altruism in the field of public goods (Andreoni, 1990), and upon insights on altruistic, moral and environmental behaviour from the field of social psychology (Schwartz, 1970; Schwartz, 1977; Stern, 2000), recent theoretical work has turned its attention to household motives, and the way in which these may interact with recycling intervention (Brekke *et al.*, 2003; Bruvoll and Nyborg, 2004; Brekke *et al.*, 2010).

The main muscle of this literature lies, however, in the range of applied studies which seek to ascertain the determinants of household waste generation and cooperation under different intervention regimes and in different contexts. Applied work in this field typically proceeds by deriving and estimating a reduced-form equation, or system of equations, and employing data drawn from one or more municipalities, or across an entire country. Much work on the economics of recycling is, in fact, based on aggregated cross-sectional, or panel data (e.g. Wertz, 1976; Callan and Thomas, 1997, 2006; Kinnaman and Fullerton, 2000; Berglund and Matti, 2006; Beatty *et al.*, 2007; Hage and Söderholm, 2008; Sidique *et al.*, 2010). This said, household-level survey-based data has become increasingly popular in economic analysis of recycling behaviour (e.g. Thøgersen, 1994; Van Houtven and Morris, 1999; Jenkins *et al.*, 2003; Berglund, 2006; Saphores *et al.*, 2006; Hage *et al.*, 2009; Sidique *et al.*, 2010). The use of experimental or quasi-experimental techniques characterizes some of the more recent efforts to understand the determinants of cooperation in the field (e.g. Bernstad, 2014; Czajkowski *et al.*, 2014).

In examining the extent of household cooperation in waste management, economic papers have mainly focused on waste separation rates, that is, recycling waste as a fraction of total waste generation (see for instance Callan and Thomas, 1997; Ando and Gosselin, 2005; Hage and Söderholm, 2009; Dahlén and Lagerkvist, 2010; Kuo and Perrings, 2010; Abbott *et al.*, 2011; Bel and Gradus, 2014; Lange *et al.*, 2014). In some instances authors focus on rates of recycling in single streams of waste (e.g. bottles in Viscusi *et al.*, 2011), while in others, the analysis extends to multiple streams (e.g. Ferrara and Missios, 2005). In some studies, recycling weight per capita was considered as the key dependent variable (e.g. Bartelings and Sterner, 1999; Yau, 2010; Briguglio *et al.*, 2015). This figure naturally captures not only changes in separation effort but also in waste generation itself (Yau, 2010), a concern which is also the case when cooperation is captured by recycling waste volumes (e.g. Nestor and Podolsky, 1998; Dijkgraaf and Gradus, 2004; Dahlén and Lagerkvist, 2010).

Some work has sought to capture the extent of household cooperation by quantifying the effort or the time spent on recycling (e.g. Reschovsky and Stone, 1994; Jenkins *et al.*, 2003; Meneses and Palacio, 2005; Meneses, 2010; Sidique *et al.*, 2010), including, for instance, recycling frequency (Barr, 2003), the number of waste fractions sorted (Ferrara and Missios, 2005; Czajkowski *et al.*, 2014), and the time dedicated to rinsing/separating waste (Berglund, 2006). The broader literature in psychology also considers intent to recycle and attitudes towards waste management as variables of interest (Hornik, 1995). This is the case in a handful of the papers reviewed here, some of which focus on attitudes (e.g. Valle *et al.*, 2005; Berglund, 2006), others on intent (Taylor and Todd, 1995; Barr 2004; Knussen and Yule, 2008; Bezzina and Dimech, 2011; Lange *et al.*, 2014). A small number of recent papers assess willingness to pay for recycling providing a monetary value of the net marginal cost of cooperation to households (Bruvoll *et al.*, 2002; Berglund, 2006).

Turning to the determinants of cooperation, while the early focus of applied work lay on demographic characteristics which could predict participation (e.g. Callan and Thomas, 1997; Hong and Adams, 1999), more recent work on recycling economics has also focused on the moral underpinnings of cooperation by household members (Brekke *et al.*, 2010; Viscusi *et al.*, 2011; Abbott *et al.*, 2013). In assessing the role of intervention, by far the strongest emphasis in economic studies on household waste has been on the responsiveness of households to convenience-based attributes and to monetary incentives, both of which change the cost-benefit trade-off faced by households (Reschovsky and Stone, 1994; Van Houtven and Morris, 1999; Jenkins *et al.*, 2003; Kinnaman, 2009; Kinnaman and Takeuchi, 2014). The role of communication as part of the intervention toolkit has received far less attention, not just in recycling, but in environmental economics more generally (Glaeser, 2014). Nonetheless, useful insights can be drawn from economic research on public goods and social dilemmas (e.g. Ledyard, 1995; Ahn *et al.*, 2010) as well as from work in the field of economic psychology on framing and priming to stimulate cooperation in environmental decisions (e.g. Ölander and Thøgersen, 2014).

A handful of studies have assessed participation in *mandatory* recycling schemes, where fines operate in the case of non-compliance. A review of the impacts of this more heavy-handed style of intervention falls outside the remit of the present survey where household cooperation is considered to be *voluntary*, even if stimulated by convenience, charges or communication intervention. Nonetheless, it is worth noting an early assessment in the literature, which finds that, though fines may work in tandem with convenience, making recycling mandatory without providing convenient infrastructure is likely to be both unpopular and ineffective (Reschovsky and Stone, 1994). Neither Kinnaman and Fullerton (2000) nor Jenkins *et al.* (2003) find any significant positive effect on recycling in scenarios where recycling is mandated (Kinnaman and Fullerton, 2000; Jenkins *et al.*, 2003). A more recent study suggests that mandatory recycling can harm personal motivation for recycling (Ferrara and Missios, 2012). Whether recycling is mandatory or not can be a moot point - if it is neither enforced by fines, nor perceived as such by households (Bruvoll *et al.*, 2002). The relationship between a fine and participation may also be diluted by low probabilities of detection and punishment (Akers, 1990).

The sections that follow review the literature on the determinants of household cooperation in waste management activities, detailing both the kind of initial household conditions that may lead to household participation in waste management activities, as well as the role that the design of scheme intervention plays in stimulating such cooperation. Section 2 examines the motives and the constraints that households may face in managing their waste, as well as the kind of demographics that tend to characterize participative households. This paves the way for Section 3, which examines how variations in policy design may alter the initial cost/benefit trade-offs with a view to enhancing cooperation. Three key attributes of intervention are reviewed, namely enhancing convenience, charging for waste disposal and communication campaigns. Section 4 summarizes the key policy cues and provides suggestions for further research.

2. Initial Conditions

Much of the work in economics which examines household waste management behaviour, utilizes a constrained utility maximization model as a starting point. In such a model, household members are conceptualized as wanting to enhance the utility they can achieve given their limited resources. Participation in a waste management scheme implies using limited resources, and incurs an opportunity cost (of time and of household space, for instance). But the effort may provide household members with marginal benefits, for instance the fulfilment of moral preferences. While costs may be expected to exert a negative influence on cooperation, benefits may stimulate cooperation. Furthermore, the diverse demographics that characterize households may act as proxies for these preferences and constraints, and may provide further insights on the initial conditions that can explain the willingness (or otherwise) of households to cooperate in a waste management scheme. Findings on the relationship between household motives and constraints and cooperation in waste management schemes are reviewed in Sections 2.1 and 2.2 respectively, while those between household demographics and cooperation are reviewed in Section 2.3.

2.1 *Moral Motivation*

There is a general consensus in the literature that household cooperation in sorting, storing and transporting recyclable waste is a behaviour driven by morality (Thøgersen, 1996). Responses to the introduction of separated waste collection schemes in the absence of any financial incentive, can be considered a manifestation of such motives (Abbott *et al.*, 2013). Indeed moral preferences may be strong enough for individuals to express a positive willingness-to-pay to recycle (Czajkowski *et al.*, 2014) and to recycle even in the presence of financial disincentives (Briguglio *et al.*, 2015).

Early commentators had practically dismissed the role of voluntary cooperation in public good scenarios (Hardin, 1968), expecting cooperation to be short-lived (Andreoni, 1995), made in error (Palfrey and Prisbrey, 1997), possibly as a recreational activity (Bruvoll *et al.*,

2002). But the possibility that households may be induced to cooperate without incentive in the provision of public goods, has recently emerged as an important phenomenon (Meier, 2007). By this token, several exponents have argued that exclusive reliance on standard economic models (based on the assumption of narrow self-interest), to model waste management cooperation, falls short of offering satisfactory insights to explain observed levels of sustained cooperation by households, and therefore to adequately inform policy (Thøgersen, 1996; Berglund, 2006; Kinnaman, 2006; Hage *et al.*, 2009; Viscusi *et al.*, 2011; Abbott *et al.*, 2013; Czajkowski *et al.*, 2014).

Much as theories of altruism (Schwartz, 1977; Stern, 2000) have provided the conceptual background to studies in recycling studies in the field of psychology (e.g. Ölander and Thøgersen, 2006), so has the theory of "warm-glow giving" (Andreoni, 1990, p. 464) served as a key theoretical workhorse, capable of explaining contributions to public goods, including recycling, in the field of economics (e.g. Abbott *et al.*, 2013). Contrary to notions of pure altruism, where the individual wants simply to benefit others by giving to a public good, the basic premise here is that the individual gets something back for cooperating: feeling good. This is an "impure" form of altruism (Andreoni, 1990, p. 464), which can encompass pure altruism as a very special case. Because this theory envisages individuals as receiving a private benefit from giving, it is capable of explaining why people cooperate in environmental domains, even when there are no legal, financial or social pressures to do so (Nyborg *et al.*, 2006). Once integrated within a utilitarian framework, the theory sees individuals trading off this "warm-glow" (Andreoni, 1990, p. 464) against other sources of well-being, with the aim of maximizing utility, subject to household constraints.

2.1.1 *Pro-Environmental Preferences*

Although Andreoni's theory attributes public good contributions to warm-glow, it does not examine the mechanisms behind this, nor their application to recycling specifically. Many studies that assess recycling behaviour describe the benefit that individuals receive from cooperating as being that of adhering to one's personal pro-environmental values (Bruvoll and Nyborg, 2004; Valle *et al.*, 2005; Berglund, 2006; Halvorsen, 2008; Hage *et al.*, 2009; Brekke *et al.*, 2010; Bezzina and Dimech, 2011). Some have described household members as being driven both by a desire to feel good, and by a desire to avoid the guilt of not giving enough (Brekke *et al.*, 2003). This notion of duty-orientation, in turn, echoes research in psychology which suggests that for personal moral norms to be activated, individuals must not only be aware of the problem and of the actions that can relieve it, but they must also perceive *themselves* as able to help and feel a sense of responsibility to be involved (Schwartz, 1970, 1977; Biel and Thøgersen, 2007).

Generally, and albeit using different measures of environmental concern and efficacy belief, studies on household waste management tend to confirm a relationship with such variables (Bruvoll *et al.*, 2002; Thøgersen, 2003; Valle *et al.*, 2005; Halvorsen, 2008; Bezzina and Dimech, 2011). One recent study on waste composting finds the relationship to be insignificant (Edgerton *et al.*, 2009), suggesting that this particular type of waste may not respond to environmental motives as much as other materials separated for recycling. As in other environmental domains, the gap between environmental values and action can been attributed to the existence of other determinants (Thøgersen, 2000; Kollmuss and Agyeman, 2002). Indeed environmental attitudes and behaviour seem to be most strongly correlated when structural conditions make this possible (Guagnano *et al.*, 1995; Ölander and Thøgersen, 2006).

Such conditions include favourable initial conditions (such as household demographics), and favourable interventions. The rest of this review examines both sets of conditions. Evidence of their relevance to waste management behaviour helps to explain why the environmental values of household members are insufficient to predict cooperation.

2.1.2 Conformity Preferences

The other main source of warm-glow which has received considerable attention in the environmental literature is that derived from adherence to social norms (Schwartz, 1977; Cialdini et al., 1991; Stern, 2000; Thøgersen, 2006; Biel and Thøgersen, 2007; Schultz et al., 2007). These are distinguishable from personal norms, by virtue of the fact that they are enforced by social sanction rather than pride or guilt (Frey and Stutzer, 2006). Social psychology also highlights differences between injunctive norms (what one thinks others should do) and the more influential, descriptive norms (what others actually do) (Cialdini et al., 1991; Schultz et al., 2007). This distinction is also reflected in economic models of environmental behaviour, some of which consider that it is *what others do* that informs the self-image benefits to be had from pro-environmental behaviour (Nyborg et al., 2006). The concept of adhering to some *socially optimal recycling contribution* which individuals hold themselves up against, is also one that has featured in economic models of recycling cooperation (Brekke et al., 2003; Halvorsen, 2008).

Earlier findings in psychology suggest that conformity increases in novel and ambiguous situations (Muzafer, 1935), a concept that is also entertained in economic models of conformity (Bernheim, 1994). Economic research on how people behave in public-good scenarios also suggests that conformity is higher in situations where the behaviour of others is visible (Fehr and Gachter, 2000; Fischbacher et al., 2001; Nyborg et al., 2006). This is confirmed in recycling research which suggests that both novelty and visibility hold relevance for understanding household cooperation, particularly at the early stages of an intervention (novelty) and wherever recycling facilities or collection are visible to the public (Vining and Ebreo, 1990; Taylor and Todd, 1995; Barr, 2003).

Work in psychology based on social identity and self-categorization theories, also finds that norm effects are moderated by the extent to which individuals actually identify with the context/group from which they stem (Goldstein et al., 2008; Nigbur et al., 2010). This too is found in experimental economics research, which documents higher contributions to public goods among homogenous groups (Gachter and Thoni, 2005), or where relationships are durable (Ostrom, 1998). Similarly, in the recycling field, there is evidence which suggests that the degree to which individuals feel a sense of community makes a positive difference (Owen and Videras, 2006). Indeed, in cross-sectional studies, small, close-knit, rural communities with permanent residents (rather than those high in tourism, migrants or rental residents) tend to find stronger participation (Callan and Thomas, 1997; Hong and Adams, 1999; Jenkins et al., 2003; Dijkgraaf and Gradus, 2004; Ferrara and Missios, 2005; Hage and Söderholm, 2008; Halvorsen, 2008).

Although convergent behaviour is notoriously hard to identify (Manski, 2000; Frey and Stutzer, 2006), some studies in the economics of recycling have documented situations in which the perceived social norm of recycling exerts a positive influence on cooperation. This is especially so in cases where the cooperative behaviour takes place at visible drop-off sites (e.g. Sidique et al., 2010). One difficulty with assessing the role of social norms is that these can be absorbed into personal norms (Schwartz, 1977), such that the distinction between personal and social norms is merely one of degree to which they are internalized (Thøgersen, 2006). To circumvent this problem, some studies employ constructs that combine the presence of both (e.g. Bezzina and Dimech, 2011). Some authors measure both personal and social norms separately and nonetheless find a positive relationship between perceptions of others' recycling efforts and the households' own efforts (e.g. Hage *et al.*, 2009). Others have distinguished both a direct effect of social norms as well as an indirect effect when interacted with personal norms (Valle *et al.*, 2005). The findings are not entirely unequivocal: in Viscusi *et al.* (2011) the effect of the social norm was not significant (Viscusi *et al.*, 2011). One reason for this may have been the manner in which norm was measured (by asking respondents whether they believed their neighbours would be upset with someone who did not recycle), and the fact that many respondents did not perceive there to be such a norm in the first place.

2.1.3 *Political Preferences*

While the recycling literature has paid considerable attention to environmental preferences and conformity as drivers of cooperation, elsewhere in the environmental economics literature, political preferences have started to emerge as promising predictors of household participation in public-good schemes (Kahn, 2007; Torgler and García-Valiñas, 2007; Dupont and Bateman, 2012; Costa and Kahn, 2013). Political interest, for instance, tends to be associated with higher environmental concern (Wakefield *et al.*, 2006; Torgler *et al.*, 2007) and right-wing ideology tends to be associated with lower willingness-to-pay for environmental goods, for environmental taxes and for environmental causes (see Dupont and Bateman, 2012 for a succinct review). A similar question has recently emerged in political science, investigating whether political preferences spill from voting to real-world behaviours (Gerber and Huber, 2010), including contributions to public goods (Bolsen *et al.*, 2014) and recycling specifically. Political preferences were found to interact with the way that recycling was presented to create diverse levels of recycling intent (McBeth *et al.*, 2013). Democrats and Liberals were also found to have higher actual recycling rates in the United States (Coffey and Joseph 2013).

Furthermore, in some economic studies on the determinants of recycling cooperation, political preferences have been considered as important control variables. Participation has been found to be higher among political activists in the Netherlands (Dijkgraaf and Gradus, 2004), among Green Party supporters in Sweden (Hage and Söderholm, 2008), and in some instances even among non-voters in Norway, whose higher recycling rates were attributed to protesting waste disposal fees (Halvorsen, 2008). In Brekke *et al.*'s 2010 study where political party affiliation was found to be insignificant as a determinant, the authors nonetheless argued that ignoring its effect could lead to exaggerated predictions of other moral motives (Brekke *et al.*, 2010). A recent study from Malta finds that voluntary recycling uptake was much higher in regions characterized by pro-government sentiment (Briguglio *et al.*, 2015). The role of political preferences as a determinant of household cooperation in waste management schemes appears to be an area that is ripe for further investigation.

2.2. *Constraints Inhibiting Cooperation*

Household members may have strong motivations to cooperate in a waste management scheme, but may still not cooperate if the marginal cost of doing so outweighs the marginal benefit. The economics literature on household waste has paid due attention to the opportunity costs that households may incur, whenever participation implies the use of some scarce household resource, such as time or space. Such constraints create negative pressures on co-operation regardless of the attributes of the intervention (be they incentives, convenience or communication-based) but they help policy-makers and scheme-operators identify the kind of households that may be resistant to cooperate. Moreover, the presence of such initial constraints helps inform the design of the intervention in order tip households in favour of participation.

2.2.1 *Time and Space*

One important finding that, in fact, emerges strongly, across the majority of studies, is that household constraints do tend to suppress cooperation in waste management. Theoretically the availability of household time and of household space, or more precisely, the lack thereof, is often modelled in economics as imposing a shadow-cost on household cooperation in recycling (Brekke *et al.*, 2003; Bruvoll and Nyborg, 2004; Brekke *et al.*, 2010). Although not everyone perceives the process of waste management as a burden in itself (Bruvoll *et al.*, 2002; Meneses, 2010), separating waste for recycling usually requires some household space and household members' time (Bartelings and Sterner, 1999; Halvorsen, 2008). These are limited resources, constrained by the availability of non-working time and by dwelling size, both of which are capable of yielding utility when used in ways other than sorting/storing waste.

In fact, empirical studies have been fairly consistent in finding that factors like limited stor-age space – especially outdoor space, like yards and porches – suppress uptake of recycling (Jenkins *et al.*, 2003; Ando and Gosselin, 2005). Limited time, similarly acts as a constraint on participation (Berglund, 2006; Suwa and Usui, 2007; Hage and Söderholm, 2008). Smells and the risk of attracting rats and other pests create further constraints towards particular types of waste, like biodegradable waste separation (Ölander and Thøgersen, 2006). The relevance of these kinds of constraints is further confirmed by consistent findings on the role of convenience attributes in intervention design (reviewed in Section 3).

2.2.2 *Habit*

While constraints can be considered as part of the cost-benefit trade-off which household mem-bers could actively consider, a further force which may constrain household behaviour, albeit in a less cognitive manner, is that of habit. In psychology, habit is known to act as a standard operating procedure, rendering actions routine, such that, after a certain time, no decision-making is actually entertained at all (Stern, 2000). In empirical assessment of household waste management behaviour, an oft used proxy for habit is the duration of a waste management programme itself. This is typically found to be a positive and significant determinant of par-ticipation (Bartelings and Sterner, 1999; Sidique *et al.*, 2010; Bucciol *et al.*, 2015; Briguglio *et al.*, 2015). But even apart from past behaviour, habitual behaviour measured as *frequency* has also been found to be an important determinant of uptake and intent in at least one study that examined the role of habit in more detail (Knussen and Yule, 2008).

2.3 *Demographic Characteristics and Cooperation*

Practically all studies that examine what determines recycling, feature a fairly standard set of demographic variables like education, age, income, gender, dwelling/household size and community characteristics. These are typically employed as proxies for the preferences and constraints described above, or as additional controls to reduce unobserved heterogeneity in a model. The findings are diverse and generally weak (Hornik, 1995), which is not entirely surprising, considering that they are only weakly linked to theoretical underpinnings. Diverse methodological approaches, and the diverse waste stream and schemes make it harder for household demographics to systematically predict household cooperation (van den Bergh, 2008).

2.3.1 *Education and Income*

The educational level of respondents (expressed, for instance, as years spent in education or degrees earned) is sometimes used to proxy environmental knowledge and awareness levels. As such it is normally hypothesized (and found) to exert a positive influence on cooperative effort (Hong and Adams, 1999; Jenkins *et al.*, 2003; Ando and Gosselin, 2005; Saphores *et al.*, 2006). The relationship may also be non-linear (Callan and Thomas, 2006) or occur only below certain levels (Ferrara and Missios, 2012). Similar findings emerge in environmental willingness-to-pay studies, where higher education is linked to higher offers for environmental services (Czajkowski *et al.*, 2014).

Some authors (e.g. Meneses and Palacio, 2005; Nixon and Saphores, 2009; Bezzina and Dimech, 2011) find no significant explanatory power on the education variable. One oft-considered reason for this lack of signal, is that the positive pressures of higher education may be off-set by the negative pressures of a higher opportunity cost of time which higher education households may incur (given that higher education is linked to higher income). In one Sweden-based study on household recycling, the relationship was not only found to be non-positive but actually negative, and statistically significant at the 5% level. The authors, in fact, suggest that this may be due to the high correlation between education, income and employment rates (Hage and Söderholm, 2008).

Income itself captures other theoretical priors such as financial flexibility (to purchase recyclables) and higher waste-generation levels (from which to separate recyclable waste) (Saltzman *et al.*, 1993; Callan and Thomas, 2006). Both priors, theoretically, exert positive pressures for recycling levels. On the other hand, higher income also comes with a higher opportunity cost of time, which could exert *negative* pressures on cooperative effort (Bruvoll *et al.*, 2002; Halvorsen, 2008). Indeed, in a good number of studies, the income variable is positive but not statistically significant (Kinnaman and Fullerton, 2000; Callan and Thomas, 2006; Hage and Söderholm, 2008; Hage *et al.*, 2009). In such studies, authors argue that the positive and negative effects of income seem to work against each other, resulting in an insignificant co-efficient on the income variable or proxy. The collinearity of socio-economic variables, like education and income also serves to reduce the explanatory power of each of them. This said, the relationship between income and recycling has been found to be significantly positive in a large number of studies (Jenkins, 1993; Callan and Thomas, 1997; Nestor and Podolsky, 1998; Suwa and Usui, 2007; Viscusi *et al.*, 2011). Relationships are particularly strong and positive for some recycling streams (like paper) given that certain products (like newspaper) are more likely to be purchased by higher income households (Jenkins *et al.*, 2003; Ferrara and Missios, 2005).

2.3.2 *Age and Gender*

Many recycling studies include an age-related variable as a determinant of cooperation, stipulated as household mean age, children by age group, or fraction of household members above or below a certain age (Vining and Ebreo, 1990; Bruvoll and Nyborg, 2004; Saphores *et al.*, 2006; Sidique *et al.*, 2010). While people beyond retirement age may have lower opportunity costs of time, as well as stronger levels of adherence to social norms (Bruvoll and Nyborg, 2004; Hage *et al.*, 2009; Bucciol *et al.*, 2015), this positive pressure on recycling may theoretically be off-set by the lower consumption levels that may also be at play. In some contexts (e.g. Jenkins, 1993), it is some other age group of the community which is found to recycle more (for instance, in Jenkins, 1993, the proportion aged 18–49). In general, however, elderly residents are found to recycle more (Vining and Ebreo, 1990; Meneses and Palacio, 2005; Saphores *et al.*, 2006; Sidique *et al.*, 2010).

Having young children in the household may provide a stronger (bequest) motive for pro-environmental behaviour (generally) and increased exposure to awareness-raising in schools (Dupont, 2004). But these positive pressures do not always outweigh the higher opportunity costs of time in families with children in waste management domains (Edgerton *et al.*, 2009). In fact, in one cross-country study, children under the age of five were found to suppress almost any stream of waste recycling (Ferrara and Missios, 2012).

In household-level studies, gender is sometimes included as a control variable, on the general expectation (drawn from the broader environmental literature) that females exhibit more pro-social behaviour (Zelezny *et al.*, 2000). Females do tend to report higher recycling participation rates (Ando and Gosselin, 2005; Meneses and Palacio, 2005; Oates and McDonald, 2006; Saphores *et al.*, 2006), and to bear a greater share of recycling chores (Meneses and Palacio, 2005), including recycling electronic waste at drop-off centres (Saphores *et al.*, 2006). This said, not all studies that control for gender find this to be a significant distinction (Hage and Söderholm, 2008; Hage *et al.*, 2009; Sidique *et al.*, 2010), suggesting that once other factors are accounted for (e.g. time, education, age), gender *per se* does not offer additional explanatory power.

2.3.3 *Dwelling Size and Community Characteristics*

Dwelling characteristics often emerge as significant indicators of household space constraints. Houses are associated with higher recycling rates than multi-family dwellings, like apartments (Ando and Gosselin, 2005; Hage and Söderholm, 2008; Hage *et al.*, 2009; Abbott *et al.*, 2013). For similar reasons, population density (associated with smaller dwellings) is sometimes hypothesized (and found) to exert negative pressures on cooperation (Berglund, 2006; Callan and Thomas, 2006; Suwa and Usui, 2007). Household size, in terms of its members, is sometimes used to proxy time constraints: larger households offer a bigger pool of leisure time from which recycling time may be drawn (Barr, 2003, 2004; Jenkins *et al.*, 2003; Ando and Gosselin, 2005; Valle *et al.*, 2005; Suwa and Usui, 2007; Nixon and Saphores, 2009), perhaps at a decreasing rate as size increases (Callan and Thomas, 2006).

Studies using aggregate data often include community characteristics as proxies for moral motives. Small communities and retirement areas tend to have higher recycling rates in comparison with large, highly urbanized centres, possibly capturing structural differences, as well as elements like higher identification with the locality and stronger norms (Callan and Thomas, 1997; Hage and Söderholm, 2008; Halvorsen, 2008). Recycling also tends to be higher among home-owners, who are theorized to have stronger attachment levels to their community (Jenkins *et al.*, 2003; Ferrara and Missios, 2005; Hage and Söderholm, 2008) in contrast with newly-arrived immigrants, foreigners and rental dwellers (Hong and Adams, 1999; Dijkgraaf and Gradus, 2004; Hage and Söderholm, 2008).

2.4 *Synthesis*

The literature reviewed thus far suggests that household cooperation in waste management is stimulated by members' desire to fulfil their moral preferences, and suppressed by the constraints of limited space and time. Habit also plays a role in determining household waste management behaviour. The literature further suggests that demographic characteristics can act as proxies for such preferences and constraints, in turn providing useful clues as to which households are more likely to participate in recycling schemes. Higher educated persons, females as well as residents in close-knit communities are associated with stronger coopera-tion, while smaller dwellings and households face higher constraints and demonstrate lower cooperation. Income and age cohorts, on the other hand, are harder to associate with cooper-ation as they can proxy several motives and constraints. These initial conditions offer various entry points for policy-makers or service-providers aiming to stimulate cooperation in waste management.

3. Intervention

Theoretically, the environmental benefits of waste management accrue collectively to all mem-bers of society: like other public goods, such benefits are characterized by non-rivalry and non-excludability (Baumol and Oates, 1988). If households are made up of rational, self-interested individuals, then it follows, by traditional economic assumptions, that they will tend to free-ride on the efforts of others. Individuals consider their private costs and benefits, to the exclusion of consideration of external (or social) costs, thereby over-producing environmen-tally harmful waste (Wertz, 1976; Fullerton and Kinnaman, 1996). Although the emergence of moral motives as drivers of cooperation suggests that households may glean some private benefits in waste management cooperation, there remains a theoretical justification for gov-ernment intervention to reduce waste externalities to optimal levels.

In theory then, government intervention can change waste management outcomes by altering the cost-benefit trade-offs that households face. Charges can make it more expensive for households to not cooperate or more financially rewarding for them to make the effort; convenience based attributes can relieve costs of cooperation by making fewer demands on time and space; communication can address information imperfections by promoting the convenient scheme attributes and the presence of charges. Moreover, if individuals derive private moral benefits from cooperation, then there is further scope for communication as moral suasion as an avenue to boost the perceived benefits of cooperation (Briguglio *et al.*, 2015).

In practice, intervention aimed at stimulating household cooperation in public goods typically does include not only the provision of infrastructure but also other elements like incentives and public communication (Gsottbauer and van den Bergh, 2011). A key question facing policy-makers is how best to combine elements of such intervention to achieve desirable outcomes (Fullerton *et al.*, 2010). This requires consideration not only of reliability, cost-effectiveness and economic efficiency, but also of concerns like distributional equity and political feasibility (Gsottbauer and van den Bergh, 2011). The next sections organize the findings from the literature around these three key components of waste management intervention targeting household cooperation, namely convenience, charges and communica-tion. Each section reviews the theoretical underpinnings, the evidence, and some of the key concerns.

3.1 *Convenience*

On the ground, the main point of entry for intervention by policy-makers and service-providers has generally been to design waste infrastructure and management schemes aimed at improving convenience and lowering costs and thereby boosting cooperation by households. Two meta-studies (Hornik, 1995; Ferrara and Missios, 2012) confirm that convenient scheme attributes do, in fact, constitute key precursor to cooperation. In their cross-country analysis, Ferrara and Missios conclude that having *any* type of service results in more recycling, but that kerb-side facilities tend to have the greatest positive impacts (Ferrara and Missios, 2012). Kerb-side collection services increase recycling (Jenkins *et al.*, 2003), even diverting recyclable waste from other (cheaper to administer but less convenient) disposal options (Beatty *et al.*, 2007).

Recycling also increases with more accessible collection (Ando and Gosselin, 2005; Saphores *et al.*, 2006) and with the possibility of combining recyclables (Judge and Becker, 1993; Wright *et al.*, 2014). Higher frequency of collection also increases uptake (Ferrara and Missios, 2005; Kuo and Perrings, 2010), a factor that can also be attributed to stimulating habit (Knussen and Yule, 2008; Viscusi *et al.*, 2011). Recent papers have examined whether it is possible to make the indoor aspects of recycling more convenient: providing convenient storage and collection system is found to help in recycling of biodegradable materials (Ölander and Thøgersen, 2006). Moreover, installing equipment for convenient segregation considerably increases separation of food waste, both in the short and long term (Bernstad *et al.*, 2013).

Convenience matters whether the scheme includes price incentives or not. The majority of studies consider the role of convenient attributes when these operate in synergy with incentives, and set out to parse out the effects of convenience versus incentives. Several studies consider regimes that include both enhanced convenience and *charges* for waste (for instance, Judge and Becker, 1993; Nestor and Podolsky, 1998; Bartelings and Sterner, 1999; Linderhof *et al.*, 2001; Jenkins *et al.*, 2003; Dijkgraaf and Gradus, 2004; Ferrara and Missios, 2005; Saphores *et al.*, 2006; Beatty *et al.*, 2007; Dahlén and Lagerkvist, 2010, 2012). In some such studies, the synergistic effects of convenience-based attributes and charges have been examined. The findings indicate that ease of separation of certain materials (like plastic) (Hage and Söderholm, 2008) and enhanced infrastructure/convenience create stronger responses to a charge (Callan and Thomas, 1997, 2006; Bartelings and Sterner, 1999). Other studies consider whether convenience matters when recycling waste disposal is subsidized (e.g. Reschovsky and Stone, 1994; Callan and Thomas, 1997; Viscusi *et al.*, 2011).

A good number of studies also consider the role of convenience in waste separation regimes devoid of any form of charges (e.g. Barr, 2004; Ando and Gosselin, 2005; Berglund, 2006; Halvorsen, 2008; Hage *et al.*, 2009; Bezzina and Dimech, 2011; Bernstad *et al.*, 2013; Czajkowski Kądziela and Hanley, 2014), while a recent study presents an interesting scenario in which residents recycled in the presence of (low) financial disincentives (Briguglio *et al.*, 2015). The findings strongly indicate that *ceteris paribus*, with or without the presence of price incentives, convenience-based attributes generate a positive effect on cooperation.

3.1.1 *Concerns with Enhancing Convenience*

It is safe to say that the key concern with making recycling schemes more convenient to households, is the cost of doing so (Kinnaman, 2006). Concerns that the cost of recycling programmes may outweigh their benefits have long been expressed, particularly if these unnecessarily offer state-of-the art infrastructure and service (Judge and Becker, 1993). As discussed earlier in this review, the social benefits of reducing environmental externalities do not always justify the cost of household time, storage, transportation, infrastructure, and management systems (Kinnaman, 2006), at least not for materials with low recover potential or involving high energy use for recovery (Hoornweg and Bhada-Tata, 2012).

A finding that also merits caution is that just as making recycling more convenient helps increase recycling, making *mixed* waste disposal convenient hinders recycling cooperation: the closer (Berglund, 2006) and the easier (Kuo and Perrings, 2010) it is to bin mixed (unseparated) waste, the lower recycling participation seems to be. While establishing collection and disposal methods for waste is still a challenge in many developing countries, several developed countries also offer highly convenient (and expensive) kerb-side waste collection mechanisms, alongside that of recycling.

An emergent concern is the prospect that, in the process of making recycling more convenient, the moral benefits of contributing may somehow be suppressed (Brekke *et al.*, 2003), though there is no evidence in practise that this is sufficiently large to overwhelm the positive effects of convenience on cooperation.

3.2 *Charges*

Since the earliest papers on the economics of household waste (Jenkins, 1993; Fullerton and Kinnaman, 1996; Hong and Adams, 1999), right up to the most recent work (Watkins *et al.*, 2012; Bel and Gradus, 2014, Bucciol *et al.*, 2015) contributions on the economics of household waste, have mainly focused their attention on the role of price in intervention. The main question asked has been whether paying more per unit for mixed waste disposal (relative to recycled waste), enhances the degree to which households cooperate in waste management schemes.

Indeed, monetary incentives constitute the canonical economic remedy to any environmental market-failure to incentivize households through price-based intervention (Hahn, 1989). Similarly, in the literature on the economics of waste, monetary incentives have also occupied centre-stage (Fullerton and Kinnaman, 1996; Kinnaman and Takeuchi, 2014). Theoretically, a "Pigouvian Tax" equal to the externality cost of waste, is capable of reducing waste up to the point where the marginal benefits of internalization equal the marginal costs of abatement (Pigou, 1960). This type of tax encourages lower-cost households to undertake the greatest level of effort, thereby minimizing damage to society both statically and dynamically (Baumol and Oates, 1988). And, as a double-dividend, such taxes raise revenue which can be used to reduce the (distorting) burden of the overall tax system, or ear-marked for waste management (Goulder and Parry, 2008), albeit the more successful the tax is in raising revenue, the less successful it is in changing behaviour (Fullerton and Kinnaman, 1996; Fullerton *et al.*, 2010). From the perspective of a utility-maximizing households with income constraints, the higher the marginal price of waste disposal, the less waste they will want to produce, considering that households derive benefits from using this income in ways other than paying for waste *(ceteris paribus)*.

On the ground, a practical example of a Pigouvian tax for waste is the oft-called Pay As You Throw tax, levied on garbage weight. Volume-based (rather than weight-based) schemes can come close to this theoretical ideal, and are easier to administer, but may lead to distortion through compaction. In practice, within the European Union alone, the majority of states employ volume-based schemes, although several do use weight-based schemes or a combination of systems including frequency-based schemes (Watkins *et al.*, 2012). While differentiated charging of mixed/recycled waste has occupied centre-stage in both theory and practise, the design of alternative incentives (like deposit-refund schemes) has also received some attention (see for instance, Ashenmiller, 2011). An insightful overview of the distinctions between advance disposal fees, recycling subsidies and deposit-refund schemes (in a producer context) is provided in Palmer *et al.* (1997), who find evidence for the latter as the least-cost option (Palmer *et al.*, 1997). Fullerton *et al.* (2010) also argue that alternative systems such as advance disposal fees for certain products or deposit-refund schemes may reduce certain risks (for instance the risk of illegal dumping), though they caution that these can also be more costly to operate (Fullerton, Leicester and Smith, 2010).

The majority of studies that set out to assess the role of price-based incentives confirm that they do indeed stimulate household cooperation in waste separation/recycling activity (Jenkins, 1993; Nestor and Podolsky, 1998; Bartelings and Sterner, 1999; Linderhof *et al.*, 2001; Dijkgraaf and Gradus, 2004; Ferrara and Missios, 2005; Callan and Thomas, 2006; Hage and Söderholm, 2008; Sidique *et al.*, 2010; Bucciol *et al.*, 2015). Some authors also report significant waste reduction effects (Van Houtven and Morris, 1999; Dahlén and Lagerkvist, 2010). This price effect appears to be vivid from the earliest studies (Jenkins 1993), to meta-reviews of such studies (e.g. Ferrara and Missios, 2012; Bel and Gradus, 2014), and across a wide range of waste materials (Ferrara and Missios, 2005).

There is, however, a small number of studies that fail to find a significant effect and the reasons for this merit consideration. Authors of such studies have argued that a reason for a low price effect may be that residents were already recycling prior to the introduction of a fee; that they may have reacted by compacting waste or indeed by dumping it illegally instead of recycling more of it (Fullerton and Kinnaman, 1996); that the price was too low for the high-income households upon which it was levied or that it sent a discontinuous signal, being subscription-based (Jenkins *et al.*, 2003). Reschovsky and Stone (1994) find price effects to only be significant in the presence of kerbside recycling collection, echoing findings presented earlier on the positive synergies between charges and convenience-based attributes (Reschovsky and Stone, 1994).

In general, reviews reveal a relatively low elasticity of response to price (Van Houtven and Morris, 1999; OECD, 2008; Watkins *et al.*, 2012) and considerable variation in its level: elasticity is estimated to lie between –0.12 and –0.39 (Kinnaman, 2009). Some studies detect larger long-run elasticities, as households find ways to react to the price (Dahlén and Lagerkvist, 2010). Others find that, in the long run, the effect of tax actually wears off (Suwa and Usui, 2007). Some leading exponents in the field have questioned whether the elasticity of response (albeit in the right direction) is sufficient to justify tariffs, particularly when considering other possible consequences (Kinnaman, 2006). In a recent meta-regression analysis (using a sample of 65 price elasticities from economic studies), Bel and Gradus (2014) find that elasticities tend to be higher in weight-based systems (Bel and Gradus, 2014).

Parsing out the net effect of price is somewhat confounded by the fact that per unit fees are generally accompanied by expanded door-to-door collection systems (Kinnaman, 2006) and/or intense promotion and education programmes (Thøgersen, 2003). Further obscuring the measurement of impact are, firstly, the lack of uniform, comparable waste collection in cross-sectional studies (Dahlén and Lagerkvist, 2010); secondly, the increased rigour in measurement of waste that typically accompanies the introduction of fees; and, thirdly, the unaccounted-for diversions of waste into compaction illegal disposal (Fullerton and Kinnaman, 1996).

3.2.1 *Concerns with Charges*

Although certainly popular in the field, waste disposal taxes are not universally adopted (Gsottbauer and van den Bergh, 2011). Their administrative and political costs, as well as environmental costs given the possibility of illegal-disposal of waste (Watkins *et al.*, 2012; Kinnaman and Takeuchi, 2014), and, to some degree, emerging concern with psychological reactions to the presence of a fee, are among the key issues that stack up as concerns with their use. Such concerns, have led some leading exponents to question whether the elasticity of response is sufficient to justify the presence of waste charges (Kinnaman, 2006).

One of the earliest concerns with per unit waste fees, already hinted at above, is that in suppressing one type of environmental problem (that of waste disposal), they may actually stimulate another, worse environmental problem: illegal disposal. A number of studies have flagged the prospect of burning, hiding, compacting or transporting waste elsewhere (Fullerton and Kinnaman, 1996; Bartelings and Sterner, 1999; Hong and Adams, 1999; Van Houtven and Morris, 1999; Linderhof *et al.*, 2001). While such options may not be considered in the absence of fees, setting a price on garbage disposal renders them more attractive on the margin (Fullerton and Kinnaman, 1996).

The introduction of financial incentives may also stimulate self-interested, cost-benefit thinking, leading to such options being entertained when they previously may not have been considered (Thøgersen, 1994; Bowles, 2008). A recent review suggests that illegal disposal may indeed be a realistic concern (Fullerton *et al.*, 2010), to the extent that avoiding marginal fees altogether and subsidizing garbage collection may be justified, as theorized in earlier literature (Fullerton and Kinnaman, 1996). But, even here, this finding is not uncontested (Watkins *et al.*, 2012; Bucciol *et al.*, 2015): contextual, demographic and moral considerations can be expected to make a difference; but, given the difficulty of finding data, they are far less scrutinized in research. Unsurprisingly, the shortage of waste treatment facilities is one factor that increases the frequency of illegal dumping (Ichinose and Yamamoto, 2011).

More recently, attention has shifted to another type of behavioural response to monetary incentives, namely that these suppress the benefits that household members get from cooperating of their own accord. In the broader environmental literature, the presence of a fee may be interpreted as controlling (Frey, 1999); as the matter of the problem having been take-over (Nyborg *et al.*, 2006); or indeed as a change from a community-based norm to one of exchange (Heyman and Ariely, 2004). Fees may suppress social sanctions, and this can also inhibit contribution (Fuster and Meier, 2010). If initial moral motives are high, then these crowding-out effects could reduce the benefits of the price incentive to such an extent that the net effect of a tax over what voluntary contribution would have produced may be nil or negative, as documented in some contexts (Frey and Jegen, 2001; Bowles, 2008). Very few studies have examined this phenomenon for waste disposal fees and those that have find no evidence that a tax erodes intrinsic motivation (Thøgersen, 2003; Halvorsen, 2008; Ferrara and Missios, 2012). One example of crowding-out effects in a waste context was that of irreversible reduction in willingness to accept a nuclear waste treatment plant once monetary compensation was offered (Frey and Oberholzer-Gee, 1997).

The interaction between moral motives and price incentives is more complex when considering that, contrary to crowding-out of moral benefits, monetary incentives can actually crowd them in. Price can be interpreted as acknowledging of effort (Frey, 1999), and higher fees have, in fact, been found to be associated with higher self-efficacy beliefs, possibly also due to their signalling a norm or inducing trial, and hence stimulating efficacy-belief (Thøgersen,

2003). This suggests that for household members, the benefit of avoiding waste disposal taxes is complementary to (and not substitutive of) the moral benefits they derive from recycling (Berglund and Matti, 2006). Distinctly different signals may be sent by the presence of a fee which can be understood as either acknowledging the good effort of households or allowing households to substitute effort by paying (Frey, 1997, 1999; Brekke *et al.*, 2010), depending on how it is communicated and perceived. In their discussion on payments to host communities for landfill siting in the US, for instance, Jenkins *et al.* (2004) present several cases where payment secures cooperation and successfully defrays opposition to landfills (Jenkins *et al.*, 2004).

Practitioners in the field will be particularly well aware of the fact that charging for waste can involve policy-makers in practical considerations beyond economic efficiency and environmental costs (Kallbekken and Sælen, 2011). The first hurdle lies in the actual design and implementation of a Pigouvian tax itself: in a world where information is costly, and administrators imperfect, setting an environmental tax itself runs into considerable institutional limitations (Fleischer, 2014). Other policy considerations which inhibit enthusiasm for such taxes include their (regressive) distributional impacts and their impact on a country's competitiveness - concerns which can be particularly vivid to finance ministers (Clinch *et al.*, 2006). These concerns hold true also of waste disposal taxes (Brown and Johnstone, 2014). Privatization of services poses another practical constraint specifically related to setting waste taxes in some countries (Davies and O'Callaghan-Platt, 2008).

Finally, it is worth considering the political considerations that may inhibit the greater use of waste fees (Thaler and Sunstein, 2008; Brown and Johnstone, 2014). This concern appears to be particularly relevant to marginal (Pay As You Throw) waste taxes in contexts where political competition is rife, given that they are considered to be a particularly salient kind of tax (Bracco *et al.*, 2013). Researchers in this field find evidence that preferences towards waste taxes are capable of significant changes not only following experience with them (Brown and Johnstone, 2014), but also with communication in the run up to their introduction (Convery *et al.*, 2007). In other public good domains, enhanced trust towards government also increases acceptance of taxes (Clinch *et al.*, 2006), suggesting interaction effects between political preferences and fees. The question remains open as to whether this is the case with waste fees.

3.3 *Communication*

Although mainstream economic theory considers information to be an important *pre-requisite* for individuals to make rational decisions, in public-good scenarios, communication as intervention has traditionally been considered as an element which is hard to manipulate to obtain the necessary pay-offs (Baumol and Oates, 1988; Tietenberg, 1998). As such, it has received much less scholarly attention; and experience with measuring the effect of communication campaigns on any environmental behaviour is limited, not only in economics, but across scholarly work in social sciences more generally (Collins *et al.*, 2003; Daugbjerg *et al.*, 2014; Glaeser, 2014). Yet, on the ground, the introduction of public-good schemes is very often accompanied by some kind of communication campaign, and often accorded hefty budgets (Graber and Smith, 2005; John, 2013). This appears to also be the case in the domain of waste management, where communication aspects can range from mass media to door-stepping techniques (Bruvoll and Nyborg, 2004; Bernstad *et al.*, 2013; Dupré, 2014).

The obvious starting point for communication intervention in the realm of waste management is to focus on promoting the attributes of the specific waste scheme in operation, for instance, the frequency of collection, the types of waste to be collected, the fees charged and the desired household behaviour, such as separating, rinsing and transporting waste for recycling (Dupré, 2014). In theory, given that cooperation is expected to be higher when constraints like time, effort and space are lower, then providing information on scheme attributes which relieve time, effort and space requirements should increase uptake, *ceteris paribus*.

Knowledge of scheme attributes, in fact, emerges as one of the best predictors in an early literature review in psychology (Hornik, 1995). In recycling studies which actually control for the effect of this, information campaigns connected to infrastructure or scheme attributes are found to be positively linked to participation (Vining and Ebreo, 1990; Gamba and Oskamp, 1994; Hornik, 1995; Barr, 2004; Sidique *et al.*, 2010; Bernstad *et al.*, 2013). Similarly *perceptions* of convenience or constraints (Ando and Gosselin, 2005; Sidique *et al.*, 2010; Bezzina and Dimech, 2011; Takahashi *et al.*, 2013), including perceived distance to recycling facilities (Lange *et al.*, 2014) are found to matter to observed cooperation. In fact, overall, knowledge of the recycling programme itself appears to predict uptake more than environmental awareness does (Dupré, 2014).

One set of attributes the communication of which has not, to date, received sufficient attention in recycling literature is that of incentives themselves. The question of how to communicate a fee/charge/tax is one that has recently started to be examined elsewhere in the literature, where authors have asked whether a simple fee label (its name) changes its outcomes (Chetty *et al.*, 2009; Congdon *et al.*, 2009; McCaffery and Baron, 2006). Theoretically, a label can act as a frame to direct attention to certain attributes, and, as in other framing effects, it is this re-focusing of attention that influences outcomes. There is some evidence to suggest that the word "tax" itself is one that can generate aversion (McCaffery and Baron, 2006) (and therefore stronger elasticities), particularly given certain political preferences (Clinch *et al.*, 2006; Sussman and Olivola, 2011). Studies on environmental behaviour generally find that with the right framing, and some social influence, even a temporary tax, set lower than the marginal social benefit, can bring about substantial changes in pro-environmental behaviour (Nyborg *et al.*, 2006). Findings like these lend further insights as to why empirical reactions to taxes are more diverse than standard environmental economics would predict. They also offer considerable scope for assessing interaction effects between communication and incentives in waste management.

But beyond the promotion of scheme attributes, communication intervention can also be aimed at stimulating moral motives. With the increased recognition that cooperation in waste management is driven by moral preferences (Hornik, 1995; Thøgersen, 1996; Kinnaman, 2006; Miafodzyeva and Brandt, 2012), which are themselves capable of influence (Thøgersen, 2003), the need to examine the role of moral suasion as intervention is one that is increasingly receiving attention in environmental economics, if not to stimulate moral motives, then at least to avoid inadvertently suppressing them, a prospect whose plausibility has been highlighted in other public-good domains (Frey, 1997; Nyborg and Rege, 2003; Bowles, 2008; Croson and Treich, 2014).

Only a small number of the studies on recycling control for the impact of such communication campaigns, and fewer still set out to explicitly examine their role or content (e.g. Bruvoll and Nyborg, 2004; Nixon and Saphores, 2009). The thin findings indicate that communication effort (defined as grant money) is positively associated with uptake (Callan and Thomas, 2006; Sidique *et al.*, 2010), although there are likely to be considerable lags between granting an award and its expenditure. In Valle *et al.* (2005), communication, defined as recycling-related promotional messages taken in by consumers (and including television, billboards, eco-spots, radio, and national newspapers), surprisingly creates no positive impact on planned behavioural control. The authors argue that the message may have been too aggressive, or even offensive, leading recipients to ignore it and call for more in-depth analysis of the impact of communication strategies (Valle *et al.*, 2005).

While it is clear that stronger moral motives are associated with stronger cooperation levels, there remains considerable scope to investigate the payback of communication campaigns intended to stimulate such moral motives by stimulating awareness of environmental impacts, and efficacy beliefs; or by promoting the sense of responsibility, as has been investigated in other environmental domains (Ajzen, 1992; Thøgersen, 2005; Nyborg *et al.*, 2006; Steg and Vlek, 2009). The potential of longer term investments in community education to enhance social values also remains to be investigated – not only for waste but for public goods more generally (Moore and Loewenstein, 2004).

One aspect of moral suasion which has received considerable attention in promoting pro-environmental behaviour is the potential of stimulating social norms. The role of perceived norms and community influences has been reviewed in Section 2 but its specific potential as an angle for communication intervention has received limited attention in waste management economics. Modelled theoretically, informing beliefs about norms has been shown to be capable of permanent increases in instances of pro-environmental behaviour (Nyborg *et al.*, 2006). In experimental tests of the type of content of communication that stimulates cooperation, the cooperative effort of others and acknowledgement of success are found to be particularly important (Cárdenas and Ostrom, 2004). Moreover, learning about the behaviour of non-cooperating others may inhibit cooperation, not least because it undermines efficacy belief (Ledyard, 1995; Gachter and Thoni, 2005). In social psychology too, normative information, especially the actual behaviour of (relevant) others, emerges as a core stimulant of cooperation (Cialdini *et al.*, 1991; Cialdini, 2003; Schultz *et al.*, 2007; Goldstein *et al.*, 2008).

Beyond content (be it promotion of scheme attributes, moral suasion or normative communication), the source of information itself presents an interesting question and one that has been examined in persuasion science (Jensen, 2013), in political communication and in policy promotion (Graber and Smith, 2005). Key attributes known to make a source successful include authority, similarity and likeability (Dolan *et al.*, 2012). In environmental policy too, the source of information emerges as one of the more consistent determinants of impact, often acting as a heuristic by which to assess complex scientific opinion (Bator and Cialdini, 2000; Nisbet, 2009; Ahn *et al.*, 2010). Only a handful of studies in the domain of waste management have explicitly examined how the channel of communication can influence cooperation. The findings indicate that the source of information does make a difference – trusted, close, sources are more likely to increase participation (Nixon and Saphores, 2009), including sources that are trusted politically (McBeth *et al.*, 2013; Briguglio *et al.*, 2015).

Findings in waste management also indicate that face-to-face communication matters (Nixon and Saphores, 2009), as does personal feedback (Nomura *et al.*, 2011; Bernstad *et al.*, 2013), suggesting that just as in other fields, the *channel* employed to communicate is relevant to stimulating household cooperation. In social-dilemma research conducted across numerous countries, communication in small group participative approaches is known to be effective to achieve cooperation (Ahn *et al.*, 2010), and face-to-face communication emerges as being particularly effective (Ledyard, 1995; Ostrom, 2000; Frey and Stutzer, 2006). The mechanisms underlying this result include the reduction of uncertainty, the ability to coordinate, the ability to gauge the extent to which others will cooperate the enhancement of group identity (Orbell *et al.*, 1990), as well as that of norms (Biel and Thøgersen, 2007).

That content, source and channel matter for communication effectiveness, are hardly novel insights for anyone involved in communication or marketing: these insights date back to Aristotle's elements (speaker, message, audience, occasion, effect) of communication (Jensen, 2013), they are echoed in Laswell's well-known maxim for mass communication *"who says what, in which channel, to whom, and, with what effect"* (Lasswell, 1948, p. 216) and they find resonance in social marketing approaches (McKenzie-Mohr *et al.*, 2011). They also feature in recent policy guidance based on behavioural economics (Dolan *et al.*, 2012). But behavioural economics has shed light on other, more novel insights on communication-based intervention.

The prospect that human behaviour may depart from standard economic theoretical assumption of informed rational choice, has resulted in increased recognition that the *manner* in which choice is presented may itself be an important part of any policy toolkit (Thaler and Sunstein, 2008), including that for environmental and waste management (Planas, 2013; Croson and Treich, 2014; Ölander and Thøgersen, 2014). Understanding predictable behavioural traits, known as heuristics and biases (Tversky and Kahneman, 1974, 1986), offers considerable scope not only to understand why efforts at stimulating cooperation may not always work, but also on how to design policy which does.

One such bias which has received considerable attention is the role of communication frames and the role of simple cues. Frames relate to the different manner in which equivalent prospects are presented. Given that people have limited time and cognitive capacity to assess all attributes of decision options, framing a prospect one way or the other can influence decision outcomes in several domains (Tversky and Kahneman, 1981; Tversky and Kahneman, 1986). A different presentation of the same prospect can generate weaker or stronger outcomes depending on who is targeted, such as in the field of climate-change, for instance (Nisbet, 2009). This finding also holds true in the field of waste management, where frames have been found to interact with political preferences (McBeth *et al.*, 2013).

Indeed, even subtle and peripheral cues can make a difference to behavioural outcomes. By drawing on recently activated thoughts, primes can trigger different motives to emerge, to the extent that this may stimulate pro-environmental cooperation (Biel and Thøgersen, 2007). Such effects appear to be particularly relevant when the decision is complex and when people are under cognitive load (Tversky and Kahneman, 1981, 1986). Although the effects may be short-lived (Druckman and Leeper, 2012), if a cue induces a decision to *try*, this can lead to long-term habits – a consideration that is particularly relevant to waste management (Viscusi *et al.*, 2011).

3.3.1 *Concerns with Communication as Intervention*

Communication intervention to stimulate household cooperation may, at face value, appear to be more innocuous than price-based intervention. However a number of authors have examined possible unintended consequences of communication in environmental domains, if for no other reasons, because the hefty budgets accorded could be spent more cost-effectively (Burgess, 1990; Cialdini, 2003; Nisbet, 2009; Nolan *et al.*, 2009). Indeed while findings suggest that face-to-face and small group communication improves uptake, yet on the ground several environmental interventions continue to rely on mass media-based communication (Bator and Cialdini, 2000). Leaving aside the possibility that mass media agents may have their own agendas (Davies, 2001), and, that people are hardly ever simply passive receivers of such information (Ajzen, 1992), one realistic concern is that such appeals are simply ignored (Bator and Cialdini, 2000).

In terms of content, one concern that emerges, is that reliance on factual information alone is unlikely to suffice in stimulating environmental cooperation by those who are not interested in environmental issues (Ölander and Thøgersen, 2014). The fairly extensive research on the use of eco-labels provides useful insights here. Studies suggest that it is unlikely that a consumer pays any attention to such labels at all, unless the consumer already values protecting the environment, perceives buying behaviour as an effective means to protect it and perceives the information to be useful for this purpose (Thøgersen, 2000). Trust in the label plays a key role in driving *any* effect (Thøgersen, 2000; Daugbjerg *et al.*, 2014), and can itself be determined by the manner in which the information is presented (Topolansky *et al.*, 2013). By this token, it is a valid question to investigate whether those who are not interested in, say, recycling, may not care about information on the scheme at all - and simply ignore it.

Furthermore, while moral suasion may be a more powerful form of communication, in other environmental domains, caution has been advocated in approaches that induce fear or guilt, for these can be met with avoidance (not paying attention) rather than behavioural change (Rothschild, 1979; Thøgersen, 2005; Brekke *et al.*, 2010). Furthermore, there is a considerable body of work in environmental psychology on the notion that there may be strong interaction effects between value orientations (egoist to altruist, bio-centric to anthropocentric, eco-centric to techno-centric, citizen to consumer, hedonic, gain-framed, normative) and how communication is interpreted (Barr, 2003; Thøgersen, 2004, 2005; Berglund and Matti, 2006; Lindenberg and Steg, 2007; Schultz and Tabanico, 2007; De Groot *et al.*, 2009; Steg and Vlek, 2009). This suggests that predicting the effect of moral suasion on waste management cooperation is also a matter of knowing pre-existing preferences. In one economic study on voluntary recycling, the interaction between government promotion and unfavourable voting preferences actually suppressed cooperation among some of the households exposed to promotion (Briguglio *et al.*, 2015). At the same time, however, framing of content cannot be avoided, making it necessary for policy-makers to decide which frames to activate in communicating with the public (Thaler and Sunstein, 2008; Lakoff, 2010).

Normative communication may well be one of the strongest weapons in the communication toolkit, but it too can backfire if the desired pro-environmental behaviour is presented as regretfully *un*common, thereby promoting a descriptive norm (what people do) that undermines the injunctive norm (what people ought to do) (Cialdini *et al.*, 1991; Cialdini, 2003; Schultz *et al.*, 2007; Goldstein *et al.*, 2008). The *visibility* of a scheme itself (for instance by collecting regularly at the kerb-side) also sends informational signals (Oskamp *et al.*, 1991; Barr, 2003). If the signal given by other people's visible actions is positive then this acts as positive normative communication. But the opposite may well be true if what is visible is a poor effort by others.

Linked to this, is the prospect that the very presence of the attributes of a public-good schemes can themselves be informational, sending a message which can hint at the level of priority that government accords the issue and the role of the individual in it (Sunstein, 1996; Frey and Oberholzer-Gee, 1997; John, 2013). In the absence of communication, incentives can be interpreted as having bought the right to waste (Gsottbauer and van den Bergh, 2011). Even the very level at which the fee is set can send messages about the importance of the issue: very low or very high taxes may be better than intermediate taxes. Low taxes may support morale, high taxes work through price effects, while intermediate taxes may fall short of generating either effect (Gneezy and Rustichini, 2000).

Finally, the behaviour of the policy-making body itself can send communication signals which can complement or undermine the behaviour promoted (Jackson, 2005; Thøgersen,

2005), echoing broader concerns about lack of trust in the communicating body (Collins *et al.*, 2003; Nisbet, 2009; Daugbjerg *et al.*, 2014) and the possibility of communication being seen as green-washing (Glaeser, 2014). Such considerations may not be the most obvious in designing communication of a waste management intervention, but they seem to matter in other public good domains and are worth factoring into the design to avoid the prospect of the medium undermining the message.

3.4 *Synthesis*

In synthesis then, waste management intervention can, and often does involve convenience-based attributes, sometimes complemented with monetary incentives and often with some form of public communication. Such instruments may aim to enhance the (perceived) benefits from cooperation, to reduce the (perceived) costs of cooperation and to increase the (perceived) costs of waste disposal. A marginal tax on household waste disposal seems to incentivize cooperation but political implications, including low rates of substitution into recycling/reduction, the possibility of incentivizing other (polluting) options, and the possibility that taxes suppress the moral benefits, merit consideration. Communication intervention, be it the promotion of scheme attributes (including incentives themselves), awareness-raising on environmental impacts, efficacy, or norms, can also stimulate cooperation. But some considerations merit caution here too, including the prospect that (costly) mass media appeals and promotion can simply be ignored, that communication interacts with motives to create divergent outcomes; and that subtle cues (including scheme attributes themselves) can communicate messages to households.

4. Conclusion

This review started off by presenting waste management as a high-stakes issue and one with considerable private and social costs. The need to divert municipal waste away from end-of-pipe solutions by stimulating household cooperation in waste separation and recycling was presented as an important and widespread policy-objective. A considerable body of research on such cooperation was synthesized in response to two key questions, namely the initial conditions that may be associated with cooperation, and the way intervention can be designed to induce further cooperation. Policy-makers and scheme operators may benefit from the following implications emerging from these findings.

4.1 *Policy Cues*

The insights may be synthesized into three key messages for policy makers. The first is that household cooperation in waste management is stimulated by members' desire to fulfil their moral (environmental, social, political) preferences. Higher cooperation can be expected among households where such favourable preferences exist, all other factors remaining constant. Such households constitute a low-lying fruit and a favourable demographic to start with when rolling out interventions, and it would be useful to identify them, even if this is done through demographic proxies like vote and educational level. The finding that such preferences may be strong enough to see households willing to recycle without incentives is particularly important for municipalities which, for some reason or other, may be unable to institute waste disposal taxes. But even when price-based intervention is envisaged, the presence of moral preferences should still be a factor for consideration to ensure that the manner in which incentives are communicated stimulates rather than crowds-out motivation.

Secondly, the finding that households have limited space and time, and that this constrains cooperation in waste management, suggests that policy makers would do best to avoid neighbourhoods, localities or regions characterized by high constraints. These, in turn, may be proxied by demographic data on poverty, dwelling size, and household size. Additionally, the findings clearly suggest that higher cooperation can be induced by relieving the constraints. Schemes may offer more frequent collection and smaller waste-collection containers to relieve limited space. Simple and clearly communicated waste separation processes can also relieve time constraints. A longer-term consideration is that developments which result in the construction of smaller dwellings could carry with them the added negative prospect of lower participation rates.

Thirdly, this review confirms that intervention may incur unintended consequences. Administrators are therefore called upon to pre-empt side effects (like illegal disposal, regressive impacts) of intervention and to consider not only the attributes of the schemes but also how these are perceived, and how they interact with household members' motives and constraints. One implication of these findings is the need to pay due attention to the subtle cues given by the scheme attributes and sponsors themselves. Earlier commentators have suggested that, in a world where actors are less predictable than rational models would assume, governments need to adjust fiscal and regulatory measures in an iterative process (Shogren and Taylor, 2008). As it becomes increasingly feasible to conduct randomized controlled experiments (Croson and Treich Jackson, 2005, 2014), linking research to policy-development becomes one way to collect evidence and adjust policy (Dolan *et al.*, 2012; Lunn, 2013). This ties in with the potential for future research, discussed next.

4.2 Suggestions for Future Research

Notwithstanding the enormity of the literature on the economics of waste, yet given the diversity in preferences for recycling among municipalities and countries (Kinnaman, 2009), empirical work on household cooperation in waste management continues to be necessary. In cross-country analyses, country-effects tend to be significant, suggesting that institutional and cultural factors play a role (Ferrara and Missios, 2012). And, while the majority of studies to date have focused on the extent to which households separate dry recyclable waste (e.g. paper, plastic, metal and glass), biodegradable waste separation, home-composting and consumption reduction have received far less attention (Thøgersen, 2003; European Environment Agency, 2009; Abbott *et al.*, 2011; Andersen *et al.*, 2012; Ferrara and Missios, 2012).

Under-explored determinants, like political preferences, also merit further study. Political promotion is not uncommon in other public-good domains (Graber and Smith, 2005; John, 2013), and it would seem relevant to examine the interactions between the promotion of waste schemes and political preferences; the impacts of politicizing intervention; and the prospect of emphasizing technocratic expertise as an alternative (Briguglio *et al.*, 2015). More broadly, the waste management field would benefit from studies on communication, including the subtle informational cues that intervention attributes may signal, as witnessed in similar studies in other environmental domains (Graber and Smith, 2005; Nolan *et al.*, 2009; Gsottbauer and van den Bergh, 2011; John, 2013; Glaeser, 2014). As mentioned in the review itself, there seems to be considerable scope to examine interaction effects among the various scheme attributes and between the scheme attributes and the households they target.

For instance, while intervention to stimulate household cooperation has been extensively studied by economists, much of the work has assumed rational self-interest as a response. Behavioural reaction to price is still a young research area (McCaffery and Baron, 2006; Congdon *et al.*, 2009), though fast making its way to the regulatory tool-kits (Dolan *et al.*, 2012; Lunn, 2013). There is potential to consider consequences in the waste management domain (Kinnaman, 2006; Davies and O'Callaghan-Platt, 2008; Fleischer, 2014). The potential to design incentives that combine the power of economics and psychology is one that has been advocated in environmental intervention (Shogren and Taylor, 2008; Venkatachalam, 2008; Gsottbauer and van den Bergh, 2011; Croson and Treich, 2014), and holds promise for improving household waste management too (Croson and Treich, 2014).

Indeed the promise of behavioural intervention more generally is one that is ripe for examination in the waste field. Its potential in stimulating pro-environmental behaviour has been examined elsewhere (Gowdy, 2008; Shogren and Taylor, 2008; van den Bergh, 2008; Venkatachalam, 2008; Croson and Treich, 2014; Ölander and Thøgersen, 2014), and some exponents in the field have singled out waste management as an area ripe for behavioural intervention (Thaler and Sunstein, 2008; Nomura *et al.*, 2011; Planas, 2013). Research on household cooperation could assess behavioural nudges such as whether commitment devises can be employed for waste management; how time preferences influence the decision to store waste; how pro-recycling/composting default options may influence outcomes; how scheme modifications effect habit formation; and how loss-aversion can be used as a frame, among others (see for instance Karp and Gaulding, 1995; Kuo and Perrings, 2010).

Significant and sustained pro-environmental behaviour remains a scarcely documented phenomenon in generally (Shogren and Taylor, 2008; van den Bergh, 2008). Given that the management of waste by households is one area where such behaviour has been observed, often in the absence of any mandatory regime, both with and without financial incentives, the field of waste management offers researchers the opportunity to examine the kind of moral preferences, and policy, that may trigger such cooperation more generally, and beyond the field of waste (Kinnaman, 2009; Kinnaman and Takeuchi, 2014).

Finally, a long standing research question is whether and how recycling spills over to other pro-environmental behaviours, including waste reduction (Thogersen and Grunert-Beckmann, 1997). Recent findings suggest that unless environmental norms are strong, transfers between behavioural categories are few and modest in size (Thøgersen and Ölander, 2003). Of particular concern is the prospect that increased cooperation in waste management is instead off-set, through moral licensing, by negative effects in other domains (Croson and Treich, 2014). This question becomes all the more pertinent to examine as intervention becomes increasingly successful at stimulating household cooperation in waste management.

References

Abbott, A., Nandeibam, S. and O'Shea, L. (2011) Explaining the variation in household recycling rates across the UK. *Ecological Economics* 70(11): 2214–2223.

Abbott, A., Nandeibam, S. and O'Shea, L. (2013) Recycling: Social norms and warm-glow revisited. *Ecological Economics* 90: 10–18.

Adhikari, B.K., Tremier, A., Martinez, J. and Barrington, S. (2010) Home and community composting for on-site treatment of urban organic waste: perspective for Europe and Canada. *Waste Management & Research: The Journal of the International Solid Wastes and Public Cleansing Association, ISWA* 28(11): 1039–1053.

Ahn, T.K., Ostrom, E. and Walker, J. (2010) A common-pool resource experiment with postgraduate subjects from 41 countries. *Ecological Economics* 69(12): 2624–2633.

Ajzen, I. (1992) Persuasive communication theory in social psychology: A historical perspective. in Manfredo M.J. (Ed) *Influencing Human Behavior: Theory and Applications in Recreation and Tourism*, Champaign, IL: Sagamore Publishing, pp. 1–27.

Akers, R.L. (1990) Rational choice, deterrence, and social learning theory in criminology: The path not taken. *Journal of Criminal Law and Criminology* 81: 653.

Andersen, J.K., Boldrin, A., Christensen, T.H. and Scheutz, C. (2012) Home composting as an alternative treatment option for organic household waste in Denmark: An environmental assessment using life cycle assessment-modelling. *Waste Management* 32(1): 31–40.

Ando, A.W. and Gosselin, A.Y. (2005) Recycling in Multifamily Dwellings: Does Convenience Matter? *Economic Inquiry* 43(2): 426–438.

Andreoni, J. (1990) Impure Altruism and Donations to Public Goods: A Theory of Warm-Glow Giving? *Economic Journal* 100(401): 464–477.

Andreoni, J. (1995) Cooperation in Public-Goods Experiments: Kindness or Confusion? *American Economic Review* 85(4): 891–904.

Ashenmiller, B. (2011) The Effect of Bottle Laws on Income: New Empirical Results. *The American Economic Review* 101(3): 60–64.

Barr, S. (2003) Strategies for Sustainability: Citizens and Responsible Environmental Behaviour. *Area* 35(3): 227–240.

Barr, S. (2004) What we buy, what we throw away and how we use our voice. Sustainable household waste management in the UK. *Sustainable Development* 12(1): 32.

Bartelings, H. and Sterner, T. (1999) Household waste management in a Swedish municipality: determinants of waste disposal, recycling and composting. *Environmental and Resource Economics* 13(4): 473–491.

Bator, R.J. and Cialdini, R.B. (2000) The Application of Persuasion Theory to the Development of Effective Proenvironmental Public Service Announcements. *Journal of Social Issues* 56(3): 527–541.

Baumol, W.J. and Oates, W.E. (1988) *The theory of environmental policy*. UK: Cambridge University Press.

Beatty, T.K.M., Berck, P. and Shimshack, J.P. (2007) Curbside recycling in the presence of alternatives. *Economic Inquiry* 45(4): 739–755.

Bel, G., and Gradus, R. (2014). Effects of unit-based pricing on the waste collection demand: a metaregression analysis, *University of Barcelona, Research Institute of Applied Economics* Working paper No. 201420.

Berglund, C. (2006) The assessment of households' recycling costs: The role of personal motives. *Ecological Economics* 56(4): 560–569.

Berglund, C. and Matti, S. (2006) Citizen and consumer: the dual role of individuals in environmental policy. *Environmental Politics* 15(4): 550–571.

Bernheim, B.D. (1994) A Theory of Conformity. *Journal of Political Economy* 102(5): 841–877.

Bernstad, A. (2014) Household food waste separation behavior and the importance of convenience. *Waste Management* 34(7): 1317–1323

Bernstad, A., la Cour Jansen, J. and Aspegren, A. (2013) Door-stepping as a strategy for improved food waste recycling behaviour–Evaluation of a full-scale experiment. *Resources, Conservation and Recycling* 73: 94–103.

Bezzina, F.H. and Dimech, S. (2011) Investigating the determinants of recycling behaviour in Malta. *Management of Environmental Quality: An International Journal* 22(4): 463–485.

Briguglio, M., Delaney, L. and Wood, A. (2015) Voluntary recycling despite disincentives. *Journal of Environmental Planning and Management*: 1–24.

Biel, A. and Thøgersen, J. (2007) Activation of social norms in social dilemmas: A review of the evidence and reflections on the implications for environmental behaviour. *Journal of Economic Psychology* 28(1): 93–112.

Bolsen, T., Ferraro, P.J. and Miranda, J.J. (2014) Are Voters More Likely to Contribute to Other Public Goods? Evidence from a Large-Scale Randomized Policy Experiment. *American Journal of Political Science* 58(1): 17–30.

Bowles, S. (2008) Policies designed for self-interested citizens may undermine "the moral sentiments": Evidence from economic experiments. *Science* 320(5883): 1605–1609.

Bracco, E., Porcelli, F. and Redoano, M. (2013) Political competition, tax salience and accountability: theory and some evidence from Italy. *CESifo Working Paper Series*. Available http://www.econstor.eu/bitstream/10419/71164/1/739962418.pdf. (accessed on August 6, 2014).

Brekke, K.A., Kipperberg, G. and Nyborg, K. (2010) Social Interaction in Responsibility Ascription: The Case of Household Recycling. *Land Economics* 86(4): 766–784.

Brekke, K.A., Kverndokk, S. and Nyborg, K. (2003) An economic model of moral motivation. *Journal of Public Economics* 87; 1967–1983.

Brown, Z.S. and Johnstone, N. (2014) Better the devil you throw: Experience and support for pay-as-you-throw waste charges. *Environmental Science & Policy* 38: 132–142.

Bruvoll, A. and Nyborg, K. (2004) The Cold Shiver of Not Giving Enough: On the Social Cost of Recycling Campaigns. *Land Economics* 80(4): 539–549.

Bruvoll, A., Halvorsen, B. and Nyborg, K. (2002) Households' recycling efforts. *Resources, Conservation and Recycling* 36(4): 337–354.

Bucciol, A., Montinari, N. and Piovesan, M. (2015) Do Not Trash the Incentive! Monetary Incentives and Waste Sorting. *Scandinavian Journal of Economics* 117(4): 1204–1229.

Burgess, J. (1990) The Production and Consumption of Environmental Meanings in the Mass Media: A Research Agenda for the 1990s. *Transactions of the Institute of British Geographers* 15(2): 139–161.

Callan, S.J. and Thomas, J.M. (1997) The impact of state and local policies on the recycling. *Eastern Economic Journal* 23 (4): 411–423.

Callan, S.J. and Thomas, J.M. (2006) Analyzing demand for disposal and recycling services: a systems approach. *Eastern Economic Journal* 32(2): 221–240.

Cárdenas, J. and Ostrom, E. (2004) What do people bring into the game? Experiments in the field about cooperation in the commons. *Agricultural Systems* 82(3): 307–326.

Chetty, R., Looney, A. and Kroft, K. (2009) Salience and Taxation: Theory and Evidence. *The American Economic Review* 99(4): 1145–1177.

Cialdini, R.B. (2003) Crafting normative messages to protect the environment. *Current Directions in Psychological Science (Wiley-Blackwell)* 12(4): 105–109.

Cialdini, R.B., Kallgren, C.A. and Reno, R.R. (1991) A focus theory of normative conduct: A theoretical refinement and reevaluation of the role of norms in human behavior. *Advances in Experimental Social Psychology* 24: 201–234.

Clinch, J.P., Dunne, L. and Dresner, S. (2006) Environmental and wider implications of political impediments to environmental tax reform. *Energy Policy* 34(8): 960–970.

Coffey, D.J. and Joseph, P.H. (2013) A Polarized Environment The Effect of Partisanship and Ideological Values on Individual Recycling and Conservation Behavior. *American Behavioral Scientist* 57(1): 116–139.

Collins, J., Thomas, G., Willis, R., Wilsdon, J. (2003) *Carrots, sticks and sermons: influencing public behaviour for environmental goals*. Demos and Green Alliance.

Congdon, W., Kling, J.R. and Mullainathan, S. (2009) Behavioral Economics and Tax Policy, *National Tax Journal, National Tax Association* 62(3): 375–386.

Convery, F., McDonnell, S. and Ferreira, S. (2007) The most popular tax in Europe? Lessons from the Irish plastic bags levy. *Environmental and Resource Economics* 38(1): 1–11.

Costa, D.L. and Kahn, M.E. (2013) Energy conservation "nudges" and environmentalist ideology: Evidence from a randomized residential electricity field experiment. *Journal of the European Economic Association* 11(3): 680–702.

Croson, R. and Treich, N. (2014) Behavioral Environmental Economics: Promises and Challenges. *Environmental and Resource Economics* 58: 335–351.

Czajkowski, M., Kądziela, T. and Hanley, N. (2014) We want to sort! Assessing households' preferences for sorting waste. *Resource and Energy Economics* 36(1): 290–306.

Dahlén, L. and Lagerkvist, A. (2010) Pay as you throw: Strengths and weaknesses of weight-based billing in household waste collection systems in Sweden. *Waste Management* 30(1): 23–31.

Daugbjerg, C., Smed, S., Andersen, L.M. and Schvartzman, Y. (2014) Improving Eco-labelling as an Environmental Policy Instrument: Knowledge, Trust and Organic Consumption. *Journal of Environmental Policy & Planning* 16(4): 559–575.

Davies, A.R. (2001) Is the media the message? Mass media, environmental information and the public. *Journal of Environmental Policy & Planning* 3(4): 319–323.

Davies, A.R. and O'Callaghan-Platt, A. (2008) Does Money Talk? Waste Charging in the Republic of Ireland: Government, Governance and Performance. *Journal of Environmental Policy & Planning* 10(3): 271–287.

De Groot, J.I.M. and Steg, L. (2009) Mean or green: Which values can promote stable pro-environmental behavior? *Conservation Letters* 2(2): 61–66.

Dijkgraaf, E. and Gradus, R.H.J.M. (2004) Cost savings in unit-based pricing of household waste: The case of The Netherlands. *Resource and Energy Economics* 26(4): 353–371.

Dolan, P., Hallsworth, M., Halpern, D., King, D., Metcalfe, R. and Vlaev, I. (2012) Influencing behaviour: The mindspace way. *Journal of Economic Psychology* 33(1): 264–277.

Druckman, J.N. and Leeper, T.J. (2012) Learning More from Political Communication Experiments: Pretreatment and Its Effects. *American Journal of Political Science* 56(4): 875–896.

Dupont, D.P. (2004) Do children matter? An examination of gender differences in environmental valuation. *Ecological Economics* 49(3): 273–286.

Dupont, D.P. and Bateman, I.J. (2012) Political affiliation and willingness to pay: An examination of the nature of benefits and means of provision. *Ecological Economics* 75: 43–51.

Dupré, M. (2014) The comparative effectiveness of persuasion, commitment and leader block strategies in motivating sorting. *Waste management* 34(4): 730–737.

Edgerton, E., McKechnie, J. and Dunleavy, K. (2009) Behavioral Determinants of Household Participation in a Home Composting Scheme. *Environment and Behavior* 41: 151–169.

European Environment Agency (2009) *Diverting waste from landfill Effectiveness of waste management policies in the European Union.* 7/2009. Denmark Available: http://www.eea.europa.eu/publications/diverting-waste-from-landfill-effectiveness-of-waste-management-policies-in-the-european-union. (accessed on July 1, 2013).

European Environment Agency (2013) *Managing municipal solid waste – a review of achievements in 32 European countries 2/2013.* Denmark Available: http://www.eea.europa.eu/publications/managing-municipal-solid-waste. (accessed on July 1, 2014).

Fehr, E. and Gachter, S. (2000) Cooperation and Punishment in Public Goods Experiments. *American Economic Review* 90(4): 980–994.

Ferrara, I. and Missios, P. (2005) Recycling and waste diversion effectiveness: evidence from Canada. *Environmental and Resource Economics* 30(2): 221–238.

Ferrara, I. and Missios, P. (2012) A Cross-Country Study of Household Waste Prevention and Recycling: Assessing the Effectiveness of Policy Instruments. *Land Economics* 88(4): 710–744.

Fischbacher, U., Gächter, S. and Fehr, E. (2001) Are people conditionally cooperative? Evidence from a public goods experiment. *Economics Letters* 71(3): 397–404.

Fleischer, V. (2014) Curb Your Enthusiasm For Pigouvian Taxes. *SSRN Working Papers* Available at http://papers.ssrn.com/sol3/Papers.cfm?abstract_id=2413066. (accessed on November 25, 2014).

Frey, B. and Stutzer, A. (2006) *Environmental morale and motivation.* Institute for Empirical Research in Economics, University of Zurich.

Frey, B.S. (1997) A constitution for knaves crowds out civic virtues. *The Economic Journal* 107(443): 1043–1053.

Frey, B.S. (1999) Morality and rationality in environmental policy. *Journal of Consumer Policy* 22(4): 395–417.

Frey, B.S. and Jegen, R. (2001) Motivation Crowding Theory. *Journal of Economic Surveys* 15(5): 589–611.

Frey, B.S. and Oberholzer-Gee, F. (1997) The Cost of Price Incentives: An Empirical Analysis of Motivation Crowding-Out. *American Economic Review* 87(4): 746–755.

Fullerton, D. and Kinnaman, T.C. (1996) Household Responses to Pricing Garbage by the Bag. *American Economic Review* 86(4): 971–984.

Fullerton, D., Leicester, A. and Smith, S. (2010) Environmental Taxes. In: Mirrlees, J. ed. *Tax by Design: The Mirrlees Review*. Oxford University Press, Ch 5.

Fuster, A. and Meier, S. (2010) Another hidden cost of incentives: The detrimental effect on norm enforcement. *Management Science* 56(1): 57–70.

Gachter, S. and Thoni, C. (2005) Social Learning and Voluntary Cooperation among Like-Minded People. *Journal of the European Economic Association* 3(2–3): 303–314.

Gamba, R.J. and Oskamp, S. (1994) Factors influencing community residents' participation in commingled curbside recycling programs. *Environment and Behavior* 26(5): 587.

Gerber, A.S. and Huber, G.A. (2010) Partisanship, political control, and economic assessments. *American Journal of Political Science* 54(1): 153–173.

Glaeser, E.L. (2014) The Supply of Environmentalism: Psychological Interventions and Economics. *Review of Environmental Economics and Policy* 8(2): 208–229.

Gneezy, U. and Rustichini, A. (2000) Pay enough or don't pay at all. *The Quarterly Journal of Economics* 115(3): 791–810.

Goldstein, N., Cialdini, R. and Griskevicius, V. (2008) A Room with a Viewpoint: Using Social Norms to Motivate Environmental Conservation in Hotels. *The Journal of Consumer Research* 35(3): 472–482.

Goulder, L.H. and Parry, I.W.H. (2008) Instrument Choice in Environmental Policy. *Review of Environmental Economics and Policy* 2(2): 152–174.

Gowdy, J.M. (2008) Behavioral economics and climate change policy. *Journal of Economic Behavior & Organization* 68(3-4): 632–644.

Graber, D.A. and Smith, J.M. (2005) Political communication faces the 21st century. *Journal of Communication* 55(3): 479–507.

Gsottbauer, E. and van den Bergh, J. (2011) Environmental policy theory given bounded rationality and other-regarding preferences. *Environmental and Resource Economics* 49(2): 263–304.

Guagnano, G.A., Stern, P.C., and Dietz, T. (1995) Influences on Attitude-Behavior Relationships. A Natural Experiment With Curbside Recycling, *Environment and Behavior* 27(4): 699–718.

Hage, O. and Söderholm, P. (2008) An econometric analysis of regional differences in household waste collection: The case of plastic packaging waste in Sweden. *Waste Management* 28(10): 1720–1731.

Hage, O., Söderholm, P. and Berglund, C. (2009) Norms and economic motivation in household recycling: Empirical evidence from Sweden. *Resources, Conservation and Recycling* 53(3): 155–165.

Hahn, R.W. (1989) Economic Prescriptions for Environmental Problems: How the Patient Followed the Doctor's Orders. *The Journal of Economic Perspectives* 3(2): 95–114.

Halvorsen, B. (2008) Effects of Norms and Opportunity Cost of Time on Household Recycling. *Land Economics* 84(3): 501–516.

Hardin, G. (1968) The Tragedy of the Commons. *Science* 162(3859): 1243–1248.

Heyman, J. and Ariely, D. (2004) Effort for Payment a tale of two markets. *Psychological Science* 15(11): 787–793.

Hong, S. and Adams, R.M. (1999) Household responses to price incentives for recycling: some further evidence. *Land Economics* 75(4): 505–514.

Hoornweg, D and Bhada-Tata, P. (2012) *What a waste: a global review of solid waste management*, Urban development series; Knowledge papers no. 15. Washington, DC: World Bank. Available http://documents.worldbank.org/curated/en/2012/03/16537275/waste-global-review-solid-waste-management. (accessed on July 1, 2013).

Hornik, J.A. (1995) Determinants of Recycling Behavior: A Synthesis of Research Results. *Journal of Socio-Economics* 24(1): 105–127.

Ichinose, D. and Yamamoto, M. (2011) On the relationship between the provision of waste management service and illegal dumping. *Resource and Energy Economics* 33(1): 79–93.

Jackson, T. (2005) *Motivating sustainable consumption. A Review of Evidence on Consumer Behaviour and Behavioural Change: A Report to the Sustainable Development Research Network*, Centre for Environmental Strategy, University of Surrey, Guildford.

Jenkins, R. (1993) *The Economics of Solid Waste Reduction: The Impact of User Fees*. Hampshire, England: Edward Elgar Publishers.

Jenkins, R., Maguire, K., and Morgan, C. (2004) Host community compensation and municipal solid waste landfills. *Land Economics* 80(4): 513–528.

Jenkins, R.R., Martinez, S.A., Palmer, K. and Podolsky, M.J. (2003) The determinants of household recycling: a material-specific analysis of recycling program features and unit pricing. *Journal of Environmental Economics and Management* 45(2): 294–318.

Jensen, K.B. (2013) *A handbook of media and communication research: qualitative and quantitative methodologies*. Routledge, USA.

John, P. (2013) All tools are informational now: How information and persuasion define the tools of government. *Policy & Politics* 41(4): 605–620.

Judge, R. and Becker, A. (1993) Motivating recycling: A marginal cost analysis. *Contemporary Policy Issues* 11(3): 58–68.

Kahn, M.E. (2007) Do greens drive Hummers or hybrids? Environmental ideology as a determinant of consumer choice. *Journal of Environmental Economics and Management* 54(2): 129–145.

Kallbekken, S. and Sælen, H. (2011) Public acceptance for environmental taxes: Self-interest, environmental and distributional concerns. *Energy Policy* 39(5): 2966–2973.

Karp, D.R. and Gaulding, C.L. (1995) Motivational underpinnings of command-and-control, market-based, and voluntarist environmental policies. *Human Relations* 48(5): 439–465.

Kinnaman, T.C. (2006) Policy watch: examining the justification for residential recycling. *The Journal of Economic Perspectives* 20(4): 219–232.

Kinnaman, T.C. (2009) The economics of municipal solid waste management. *Waste Management* 29: 2615–2617.

Kinnaman, T.C. and Fullerton, D. (2000) Garbage and Recycling with Endogenous Local Policy. *Journal of Urban Economics* 48(3): 419–442.

Kinnaman, T.C. and Takeuchi, K. (2014) Preface. In Kinnaman, T.C., and Takeuchi, K. eds. *Handbook on Waste Management*. Edward Elgar Publishing, Pages xi–xvi.

Knussen, C. and Yule, F. (2008) I'm Not in the Habit of Recycling. *Environment and Behavior* 40(5): 683–702.

Kollmuss, A. and Agyeman, J. (2002) Mind the gap: why do people act environmentally and what are the barriers to pro-environmental behavior? *Environmental Education Research* 8(3): 239–260.

Kuo, Y. and Perrings, C. (2010) Wasting time? Recycling incentives in urban Taiwan and Japan. *Environmental and Resource Economics* 47(3): 423–437.

Lakoff, G. (2010) Why it matters how we frame the environment. *Environmental Communication* 4(1): 70–81.

Lange, F., Brückner, C., Kröger, B., Beller, J. and Eggert, F. (2014) Wasting ways: Perceived distance to the recycling facilities predicts pro-environmental behavior. *Resources, Conservation and Recycling* 92: 246–254.

Lasswell, H.D. (1948) The structure and function of communication in society. *The Communication of Ideas* 37. Forthcoming.

Ledyard, J. (1995) Public goods: A survey of experimental results. *The Handbook of Experimental Economics*. Princeton, NJ: Princeton University Press.

Lindenberg, S. and Steg, L. (2007) Normative, gain and hedonic goal frames guiding environmental behavior. *Journal of Social Issues* 63(1): 117–137.

Linderhof, V., Kooreman, P., Allers, M. and Wiersma, D. (2001) Weight-based pricing in the collection of household waste: The Oostzaan case. *Resource and Energy Economics* 23(4): 359–371.

Lunn, P.D. (2013) Behavioural economics and policymaking: learning from the early adopters. *The Economic and Social Review* 43(3, Autumn): 423–449.

Manski, C.F. (2000) Economic Analysis of Social Interactions. *Journal of Economic Perspectives* 14(3): 115–136.

McBeth, M.K., Lybecker, D.L. and Kusko, E. (2013) Trash or Treasure: Recycling Narratives and Reducing Political Polarisation. *Environmental Politics* 22(2): 312–332.

McCaffery, E.J. and Baron, J. (2006) Thinking about tax. *Psychology, Public Policy, and Law* 12(1): 106–135.

McKenzie-Mohr, D., Schultz, P.W., Kotler, P. and Lee, N.R. (2011) *Social marketing to protect the environment: What works.* Thousand Oaks, CA: Sage Publications, Inc.

Meier, S. (2007) A survey of economic theories and field evidence on pro-social behavior. *Economics and Psychology: A Promising New Cross-Disciplinary Field* 51–88.

Meneses, G.D. (2010) Refuting fear in heuristics and in recycling promotion. *Journal of Business Research* 63(2): 104–110.

Meneses, G.D. and Palacio, A.B. (2005) Recycling Behavior: A Multidimensional Approach. *Environment and Behavior* 37(6): 24.

Miafodzyeva, S. and Brandt, N. (2012) Recycling Behaviour Among Householders: Synthesizing Determinants Via a Meta-analysis. *Waste and Biomass Valorization* 1–15.

Moore, D.A. and Loewenstein, L. (2004) Self-Interest, Automaticity, and the Psychology of Conflict of Interest. *Social Justice Research* 17(2): 189–202.

Muzafer, S. (1935) A study of some social factors in perception: Bibliography. *Archives of Psychology* 27(187): 53–54.

Nestor, D.V. and Podolsky, M.J. (1998) Assessing incentive-based environmental policies for reducing household waste disposal. *Contemporary Economic Policy* 16(4): 401–411.

Nigbur, D., Lyons, E. and Uzzell, D. (2010) Attitudes, norms, identity and environmental behaviour: Using an expanded theory of planned behaviour to predict participation in a kerbside recycling programme. *British Journal of Social Psychology* 49(2): 259–284.

Nisbet, M.C. (2009) Communicating climate change: Why frames matter for public engagement. *Environment: Science and Policy for Sustainable Development* 51(2): 12–23.

Nixon, H. and Saphores, J.D.M. (2009) Information and the decision to recycle: results from a survey of US households. *Journal of Environmental Planning and Management* 52(2): 257–277.

Nolan, J.M., Schultz, P.W. and Knowles, E.S. (2009) Using Public Service Announcements to Change Behavior: No More Money and Oil Down the Drain. *Journal of Applied Social Psychology* 39(5): 1035–1056.

Nomura, H., John, P.C. and Cotterill, S. (2011) The use of feedback to enhance environmental outcomes: a randomised controlled trial of a food waste scheme. *Local Environment* 16(7): 637–653.

Nyborg, K. and Rege, M. (2003) Does Public Policy Crowd out Private Contributions to Public Goods? *Public Choice* 115(3/4): 397–418.

Nyborg, K., Howarth, R.B. and Brekke, K.A. (2006) Green consumers and public policy: On socially contingent moral motivation. *Resource and Energy Economics* 28(4): 351–366.

Oates, C.J. and McDonald, S. (2006) Recycling and the Domestic Division of Labour. *Sociology* 40(3): 417–433.

OECD (2008) *Household Behaviour and the Environment: Reviewing the Evidence.* Available www.oecd.org/dataoecd/19/22/42183878.pdf. (accessed on July 1, 2013).

Ölander, F. and Thøgersen, J. (2006) The ABC of recycling. *European Advances in Consumer Research* 7: 297–302.

Ölander, F. and Thøgersen, J. (2014) Informing versus nudging in environmental policy. *Journal of Consumer Policy* 37(3): 341–356.

Orbell, J., Dawes, R. and van de Kragt, A. (1990) The Limits of Multilateral Promising. *Ethics* 100(3): 616–627.

Oskamp, S., Harrington, M.J., Edwards, T.C., Sherwood, D.L., Okuda, S.M. and Swanson, D.C. (1991) Factors influencing household recycling behavior. *Environment and Behavior* 23(4): 494–519.

Ostrom, E. (1998) A Behavioral Approach to the Rational Choice Theory of Collective Action: Presidential Address, American Political Science Association, 1997. *The American Political Science Review* 92(1): 1–22.

Ostrom, E. (2000) Collective Action and the Evolution of Social Norms. *Journal of Economic Perspectives* 14(3): 137–158.

Owen, A.L. and Videras, J. (2006) Civic cooperation, pro-environment attitudes, and behavioral intentions. *Ecological Economics* 58(4): 814–829.

Palfrey, T.R. and Prisbrey, J.E. (1997) Anomalous Behavior in Public Goods Experiments: How Much and Why? *American Economic Review* 87(5): 829–846.

Pigou, A.C. (1960) *The economics of welfare*, 4th edn. MacMillan, London.

Palmer, K., Sigman, H., and Walls, M. (1997) The cost of reducing municipal solid waste. *Journal of Environmental Economics and Management* 33(2): 128–150.

Planas, L.C. (2013) Finding a Green Nudge: Moral Motivation and Green Behaviour. *Paris School of Economics Working Papers* Available http://www.parisschoolofeconomics.eu/IMG/pdf/paper_lorenzo_cerda_-_v7.42_2013_11_06.pdf. (accessed on March 29, 2014).

Reschovsky, J.D. and Stone, S.E. (1994) Market incentives to encourage household waste recycling: Paying for what you throw away. *Journal of Policy Analysis and Management* 13(1): 120–139.

Rothschild, M.L. (1979) Marketing Communications in Nonbusiness Situations or Why It's So Hard to Sell Brotherhood Like Soap. *Journal of Marketing* 43(2): 11–20.

Saltzman, C., Duggal, V.G. and Williams, M.L. (1993) Income and the recycling effort: a maximization problem. *Energy Economics* 15(1): 33–38.

Saphores, J.M., Nixon, H., Ogunseitan, O.A. and Shapiro, A.A. (2006) Household Willingness to Recycle Electronic Waste: An Application to California. *Environment and Behavior* 38(2): 183–208.

Schultz, P.W. and Tabanico, J. (2007) Self, Identity, and the Natural Environment: Exploring Implicit Connections With Nature1. *Journal of Applied Social Psychology* 37(6): 1219–1247.

Schultz, P.W., Nolan, J.M., Cialdini, R.B., Goldstein, N.J. and Griskevicius, V. (2007) The Constructive, Destructive, and Reconstructive Power of Social Norms. *Psychological Science* 18(5): 429–434.

Schwartz, S.H. (1977) Normative influences on altruism. In Berkowitz, L. (Ed.) *Advances in experimental social psychology (vol. 10)*, New York, Academic Press, 221–279.

Schwartz, S.H., (1970). Moral decision making and behavior. In: Macaulay, J., Berkowitz, L. eds., *Altruism and Helping Behavior. Social Psychological Studies of Some Antecedents and Consequences*. Academic Press, New York, pp. 127–141.

Shogren, J. and Taylor, L. (2008) On behavioural environmental economics. *Review of Environmental Economics and Policy* 2(1): 26–44.

Sidique, S.F., Joshi, S.V. and Lupi, F. (2010) Factors influencing the rate of recycling: An analysis of Minnesota counties. *Resources, Conservation and Recycling* 54(4): 242–249.

Sidique, S.F., Lupi, F. and Joshi, S.V. (2010) The effects of behavior and attitudes on drop-off recycling activities. *Resources, Conservation and Recycling* 54(3): 163–170.

Steg, L. and Vlek, C. (2009) Encouraging pro-environmental behaviour: An integrative review and research agenda. *Journal of Environmental Psychology* 29(3): 309–317.

Stern, P.C. (2000) Toward a Coherent Theory of Environmentally Significant Behavior. *Journal of Social Issues* 56(3): 407–424.

Sunstein, C. (1996) Social Norms and Social roles. *Columbia Law Review* 96(4): 903–968.

Sussman, A.B. and Olivola, C.Y. (2011) Axe the tax: Taxes are disliked more than equivalent costs. *Journal of Marketing Research* 48 (SPL): S91–S101.

Suwa, T. and Usui, T. (2007) Estimation of Garbage Reduction and Recycling Promotion under the Containers and Packaging Recycling Law and Garbage Pricing. *Environmental Economics and Policy Studies* 8(3): 239–254.

Takahashi, W., Itoh, S. and Tojo, N. (2013) Convenience matters?-A Survey on Waste Sorting Behavior in Swedish Households. *18th Annual Meeting of Society for Environmental Economics and Policy Studies*. Available: https://lup.lub.lu.se/search/publication/4248879. (accessed on November 25, 2014).

Taylor, S. and Todd, P. (1995) An integrated model of waste management behavior A test of household recycling and composting intentions. *Environment and Behavior* 27(5): 603–630.

Thaler, R.H. and Sunstein, C.R. (2008) *Nudge: Improving decisions about health, wealth, and happiness.* Yale University Press.

Thøgersen, J. (1994) A model of recycling behaviour, with evidence from Danish source separation programmes. *International Journal of Research in Marketing* 11(2): 145–163.

Thøgersen, J. (1996) Recycling and morality a critical review of the literature. *Environment and Behavior* 28(4): 536–558.

Thøgersen, J. (2000) Psychological determinants of paying attention to eco-labels in purchase decisions: Model development and multinational validation. *Journal of Consumer Policy* 23(3): 285–313.

Thøgersen, J. (2003) Monetary incentives and recycling: Behavioural and psychological reactions to a performance-dependent garbage fee. *Journal of Consumer Policy* 26(2): 197–228.

Thøgersen, J. (2004) A cognitive dissonance interpretation of consistencies and inconsistencies in environmentally responsible behavior. *Journal of Environmental Psychology* 24(1): 93–103.

Thøgersen, J. (2005) How may consumer policy empower consumers for sustainable lifestyles? *Journal of Consumer Policy* 28(2): 143–177.

Thøgersen, J. (2006) Norms for environmentally responsible behaviour: An extended taxonomy. *Journal of Environmental Psychology* 26(4): 247–261.

Thøgersen, J. and Ölander, F. (2003) Spillover of environment-friendly consumer behaviour. *Journal of Environmental Psychology* 23(3): 225–236.

Thøgersen, J. and Grunert-Beckmann, S. (1997) Values and Attitude Formation Towards Emerging Attitude Objects: From Recycling to General, Waste Minimizing Behavior. *Advances in Consumer Research* 24: 182–189.

Tietenberg, T. (1998) Disclosure Strategies for Pollution Control. *Environmental and Resource Economics* 11(3): 587–602.

Topolansky Barbe, F.G., Gonzalez-Triay, M.M. and Hensel, A. (2013) Eco-labels in Germany. *Journal of Customer Behaviour* 12(4): 341–359.

Torgler, B. and García-Valiñas, M.A. (2007) The determinants of individuals' attitudes towards preventing environmental damage. *Ecological Economics* 63(2–3): 536–552.

Torgler, B., Frey, B.S. and Wilson, C. (2007) Environmental and Pro-Social Norms: Evidence from 30 Countries. *FEEM Working Paper Series* Available http://www.feem.it/NR/rdonlyres/6F19EF93-FBB6-4308-AD6F-48C05D7C84F0/2409/8409.pdf. (accessed on July 1, 2014).

Tversky, A. and Kahneman, D. (1974) Judgment under Uncertainty: Heuristics and Biases. *Science* 185(4157): 1124–1131.

Tversky, A. and Kahneman, D. (1981) The Framing of Decisions and the Psychology of Choice. *Science* 211(4481): 453–458.

Tversky, A. and Kahneman, D. (1986) Rational Choice and the Framing of Decisions. *The Journal of Business*: S251–S278.

Valle, D., Oom, P., Rebelo, E., Reis, E. and Menezes, J. (2005) Combining Behavioral Theories to Predict Recycling Involvement. *Environment and Behavior* 37(3): 364–396.

van den Bergh, J.C.J.M. (2008) Environmental regulation of households: An empirical review of economic and psychological factors. *Ecological Economics* 66(4): 559–574.

Van Houtven, G.L. and Morris, G.E. (1999) Household behavior under alternative pay-as-you-throw systems for solid waste disposal. *Land Economics* 75(4): 515–537.

Venkatachalam, L. (2008) Behavioral economics for environmental policy. *Ecological Economics* 67(4): 640–645.

Vining, J. and Ebreo, A. (1990) What Makes a Recycler? *Environment and Behavior* 22(1): 55–73.

Viscusi, W.K., Huber, J. and Bell, J. (2011) Promoting Recycling: Private Values, Social Norms, and Economic Incentives. *American Economic Review* 101(3): 65–70.

Wakefield, S.E., Elliott, S.J., Eyles, J.D. and Cole, D.C. (2006) Taking environmental action: the role of local composition, context, and collective. *Environmental Management* 37(1): 40–53.

Watkins, E., Hogg, D., Mitsios, A., Mudgai, S., Neubauer, A., Reisinger, H., Troeltzsch, J. and Van Acoleyen, M., 2012. *Use of economic instruments and waste management performances*. European Commission Available http://ec.europa.eu/environment/waste/pdf/final_report_10042012.pdf. (accessed on November 14, 2014).

Wertz, K.L. (1976) Economic factors influencing households' production of refuse. *Journal of Environmental Economics and Management* 2(4): 263–272.

Wright, C., Halstead, J.M. and Huang, J. (2014) 5. Household preferences for alternative trash and recycling services in small towns: is single stream the future of rural recycling? In Kinnaman, T.C. and Takeuchi, K. eds. *Handbook on Waste Management*. Edward Elgar Publishing.

Yau, Y. (2010) Domestic waste recycling, collective action and economic incentive: the case in Hong Kong, *Waste Management* 30(12): 2440–2447.

Zelezny, L.C., Poh-Pheng, C. and Aldrich, C. (2000) Elaborating on Gender Differences in Environmentalism. *Journal of Social Issues* 56(3): 443–457.

7

ONE WITHOUT THE OTHER? BEHAVIOURAL AND INCENTIVE POLICIES FOR HOUSEHOLD WASTE MANAGEMENT

Ankinée Kirakozian

Université Nice Sophia Antipolis and GREDEG/CNRS

1. Introduction

Many studies highlight the evolution of consumption patterns and the increasing power of an ecological conscience as likely to change consumers' behaviours and choice criteria. A growing group of 'pro-environmental' consumers favour environmental and ethical criteria in their consumption choices. At the same time, consumers' requirements have resulted in the creation of products and services that generate significant waste. The increase in their volume is such that waste management currently is a major issue for public authorities. The European Commission estimates that 'Today in the EU, each person consumes 16 tons of materials annually, of which 6 tons are wasted, with half going to landfill'.[1] Generally, law offers a broad definition for the concept of waste, and policy objectives are ambitious. For example, European Directive 75/442/CEE defines waste as 'any substance or object of which the holder disposes or has a duty to dispose of under the national provisions in force', and reducing residual waste to zero by 2020 is a declared aim for the European Commission.

This paper provides a review of the economic literature on household waste management and recycling, which considers unsorted waste (residual waste) as a source of negative externalities, and as wasted resources. This literature is important and diversified for several reasons. These reasons underline the original features of waste as an environmental problem requiring regulation.

First, dealing with an externality requires acknowledgement of a responsible polluter. In the case of waste, there are two entities that can be considered as the polluters: the original producer of the waste, and the ultimate holder of the waste. From an empirical point of view, the evolution of regulation shows that few constraints are placed on producers' behaviour, and suggests that consumers will become strategic actors in the achievement of regulatory objectives. Producers are treated separately with mandatory financial contributions to the organizations responsible for waste management. The system is far from being an environmental policy and will not stem the rise of non-recycled waste. In France, for example, since the implementation of these provisions and until the 2000s, the costs of solid waste management have been increasing at an average of 4.74% a year (Dufeigneux *et al.*, 2003). In this context, there are calls to economists to design economic policies to improve consumers' selective sorting or to achieve the quantitative targets set by regulation.

Secondly, a historical feature is of great importance. The budgetary logic has for long been directed to the regulation of household waste, resulting in a substantial literature on whether household waste management should be delegated.

Thirdly, the regulatory logic is not confined to budgetary logic since ignoring the external cost would result in non-optimal sorting. Were the regulatory focus to be solely on the external costs and their internalization, then, the development of incentive policies would make selective sorting ineffective. Individual sorting requires a public infrastructure which has budgetary consequences which generally are overlooked in conventional environmental policies. It is clear that public policy on waste management should be somewhere between these two extreme positions and should involve a combination of several policy tools (equipment, incentive pricing, etc.).

Fourthly, economic research shows the positive impact of incentives while emphasizing illegal dumping by waste holders. To overcome these externalities, the regulator might need to publish complementary policies, such as subsidies, and provide information on the role of recycling, how to recycle, etc. This reinforces the importance of a policy mix highlighted in research on household waste management (Lehmann, 2012).

Fifthly, participating in recycling can be seen as contributing to a public good. Traditional approaches suggest that decisions respond to rational behaviour, particularly cost savings. However, as highlighted in the behavioural economics literature, households have both intrinsic and extrinsic values in relation to public goods. Deci (1975) considers that intrinsic motivations are defined by the absence of an external reward, as due to 'the person's attitude', and extrinsic motivations as being external to the individual. Thus, personal factors such as emotions, the influence of social interaction, the importance of others' opinions, social approval, etc. need to be taken into account when developing public policies. Therefore, the management of household waste has become an important topic in behavioural economics. The proposition that behavioural tools, such as nudges, could be used to complement incentive pricing, for example, highlights the need for a policy mix.

The paper is organized as follows. Section 2 presents the regulatory and governance framework for waste management. Section 3 introduces the use of economic incentive instruments and their limits. Section 4 describes the incorporation of behavioural instruments into practice. Section 5 concludes.

2. The Waste Management Framework

The economic literature on the general theme of household waste management is diverse and includes several different issues. It is useful first to define a unit of recyclable waste needing a public intervention to ensure its effective recycling in relation to the works reviewed. We consider a unit of waste which yields a Marginal Benefit (*MB*) when reused, and simultaneously implies a reduction in the marginal external cost *MEC* of waste. The justification for regulation depends on three criteria. First, the individual sorting *ex-ante* (i.e. at source) is not profitable for the individual and, therefore, will not be implemented automatically. This situation arises when the marginal cost of individual sorting MC_i is greater than the benefit it yields for the consumer: $MC_i > MB$. Secondly, the *ex post* sorting operated by the local authority (i.e. sorting the mixed detritus collected) should not profitable, even if it leads to the valorization of waste and allows for management of the externality of the residual waste. In the absence of this condition, sorting *ex post* would automatically be implemented by the community, and regulation of individual behaviours would be unnecessary. This situation occurs when the marginal benefit of reusing MB and saving of the external cost of the non-recycled unit, MEC, do not cover the cost of the *ex post* sorting $MC_c : MB + MEC < MC_c$. Finally, *ex ante* individual sorting must be socially beneficial even if this requires an infrastructure whose reported cost per unit of waste considered is α. This situation arises when the marginal benefit of reusing MB and the saving on the marginal external cost of the non-recycled unit, MEC, cover the marginal cost of sorting *ex ante* MC_i plus the cost of the infrastructure α: $MB + MEC > MC_i + \alpha$. Thus, it is rational to introduce regulation to encourage individual sorting for the benefit of the community, if the marginal benefit MB is such that

$$MC_i > MB \text{ and } MC_i + \alpha - MEC < MB < MC_c - MEC \qquad (1)$$

These inequalities define the units of waste that are relevant according to the regulation, that is, those units of waste whose recycling generates an increase in the social surplus and which requires regulation to ensure their recycling. This economic definition of a unit of waste for recycling implies that not all units of waste need to be recycled.[2]

Inequalities (1) implicitly consider an isolated agent looking only at his marginal cost and marginal gain of sorting. An emerging stream of the literature enlarges this picture considering more complex individual motivations for household recycling: peer effect, warm-glow, self-image, reputation effect, etc. (see Section 4). For instance, consider that together with marginal benefit a unit of waste recycled implies a marginal individual reputation: MR_i. The unit is not recycled only if $MC_i > MB + MR_i$. With this decision rule, some units of waste that an agent does not recycled under (1) ($MC_i > MB$), can be recycled when taking into account of marginal reputation ($MC_i < MB + MR_i$). Therefore, the question whether public policies reinforce or weaken the marginal reputation (i.e. whether there is a crowding-in or a crowding-out effect) has to be addressed.

2.1 Regulatory Framework

Environmental regulations such as 'command and control' are aimed at prohibiting and/or limiting the amount of pollution emitted by individuals. Through regulation, public authorities establish a pollution limit they consider socially acceptable and implement appropriate public policies to achieve it. This is the most common tool used by public authorities to curb pollution and can take many forms. It can (i) define environmental quality objectives, (ii) set a maximum acceptable level of pollution (x amount of non-recycled, recycled, incinerated or buried waste) or (iii) impose environmental infrastructure requirements (e.g. prioritizing incinerators with energy recovery), etc. Although this type of regulation helps to achieve environmental objectives (Barde, 1992), it rarely corresponds to an economic optimum in terms of pollution.[3] Also, the social cost of this type of regulation is not minimized, and its effects are limited by its non-incentivizing nature.

For example, the French law no. 92-646 (13 July 1992) recommends a reduction in waste production through the implementation of separated waste collection and recycling schemes. Local regulation sets the rules related to the collection and treatment of waste. It dictates the types of containers for collection, and the collection schedule (day and time, type of waste), etc. These rules constrain the users; for example, if the waste is to be collected twice a week and the container size is set, then the individual is limited in his or her ability to emit waste. The lower the frequency of collection, the more the individual must pay attention to the quantity of waste they produced. Also, if the municipality decides to increase the frequency of kerbside collection of recyclable and residual waste, this should encourage recycling and composting behaviour.

These ideas were examined in Wertz (1976), Gellynck and Verhelst (2007) and Ferrara and Missios (2012), which show that a high frequency of residual waste collection has a positive effect on the quantities of waste produced. Conversely, a low frequency of residual waste collection results in lower amounts of waste produced because of waste storage problems. The result in Yamamota and Yoshida (2014) is ambiguous about the relation between collection frequency and illegal dumping. They show that the frequency of collection of recyclables is significant and negative, that is, that to reduce illegal dumping, recyclable material should be collected less frequently. Stevens (1978) focuses on the density, frequency and proportion of recovered material, and shows that all three have a significant effect on the total cost. The study by Callan and Thomas (2001) confirms this finding. The authors examine spending on waste management (including costs related to the disposal and recycling of waste) by 110 municipalities in Massachusetts. They estimate the cost of the disposal service and the cost of recycling as a function of the quantities of waste recycled or disposed of, the frequency of separated collection, the location of disposal sites, access to infrastructure and state subsidies. They conclude that no economies of scale emerge in the case of waste disposal, which contrasts with what is observed for recycled waste.

From this viewpoint, the problem of waste management can be understood primarily as a public services problem. An important part of the literature focuses on the question of how to secure this service at least cost (see below). Compared to the ideas expressed by the inequalities (1), this literature does not question the value or the form of the regulation, but seeks an organization of waste management that generates the lowest cost (α) to the community.

2.2 Waste Management

2.2.1 Infrastructure

Provision of an appropriate infrastructure is necessary to encourage recycling practices. The availability of services is a determining factor in the participation of residents in sorting (Folz, 1999). Municipalities offer different types of services based on the flows of collected waste (packaging, paper, glass, cardboard, etc.) and types of collection (kerbside or garbage collection station). These vary by municipality and do not have the same effects on the behaviour of individuals.

Sidique et al. (2010) show that kerbside collection systems and garbage collection stations improve recycling rates because they reduce the opportunity costs of recycling. However, they are used by individuals who are already aware of environmental issues and are ready to expend more effort on waste recycling. The idea of effort is well developed in the literature. For example, Oskamp et al. (1991) and Guagnano et al. (1995) show that the simple fact of an available selective sorting container increases the volume of recycled materials. Many studies show that people are likely to participate in an activity if it does not require them to expend too much effort, that is, if it is not too constraining (Vining and Ebreo, 1990; Folz, 1991; De Young, 1993; Guagnano et al., 1995; Knussen et al., 2004; Peretz et al., 2005). Folz (1991) shows that recycling behaviour is greater when the level of effort required is low (shorter distance to a recycling station, no need for sorting by materials, kerbside waste collection). In another study, Folz (2004) shows that what makes recycling services more convenient for individuals is waste collection on the same day as non-recyclable materials collection and collection of mixed rather than sorted recyclable materials.

Abbott *et al.* (2011) analyse the influence of introducing selective recyclable waste collection on household behaviour. They model the recycling rates of English local authorities based on socio-economic and political variables (community's average annual income, household size, population density, frequency of collection by recycling methods, size and type of container). Recycling rates are defined separately for green waste and recyclables. Abbott *et al.* (2011) conclude that the frequency of residual waste collection is inversely proportional to the amount recycled (but is more important for green waste than recyclable waste), meaning that a low frequency of collection increases recycling performance. Extension of kerbside collection, type of container for recycled materials and the lower frequency of residual waste collection play important roles in improving the recycling performance. Abbott *et al.* (2011) show also that the collection method for recyclable materials has an effect on recycling rates (more for recyclables than for green waste). The rate is lower for 50-L containers and higher for non-reusable bags and containers on wheels; for example, 120-L containers show greater increase in recycling rates (+3.4%).

2.2.2 *Private versus Public Management of Waste Collection*

In addition to the choice of waste collection methods, controlling collection costs is a particular objective for local authorities. Direct and delegated (for all or part of the service) management of household waste is often compared. Direct management means that the community bears the infrastructure costs (garbage bins, trucks, containers, garbage collection stations, etc.) and staff costs. Delegated management means that the municipality delegates these responsibilities to one or more companies, either public or private.[4] Delegation is often preferred because operating a waste collection service requires significant specific investments and incurs several costs (of managing the containers, personnel, waste transportation, infrastructure, etc.).

In studies of the costs of solid waste management, many authors show that direct collection is more expensive than delegated collection by service providers. The first study of this type was conducted by Hirsch and Engelberg (1965). They conducted an econometric study of 24 municipalities in the region of St. Louis (Missouri), which showed that there was no difference in the costs of public and private provision. Stevens (1978) examined the cost structure of 340 waste collection companies (both public and private) in the USA, which confirmed of Hirsch and Engelberg (1965)'s results for cities of 50,000 inhabitants or less, but showed also that in larger cities, private providers use more efficient technologies. Whatever the city size, private providers use fewer staff and larger capacity garbage trucks than public monopolies, which enables economies of scale. Hart *et al.* (1996) applied the theory of incomplete contracts and property rights to the choice between public and private provision. Their results suggest that there are greater incentives to reduce costs in the case of private provision. They show that public provision dominates if the decrease in non-compressible costs causes a decrease in the quality of the service. However, as long as the reduction in the quality of the services offered can be controlled by contracts or competition, privatization is more efficient. Dijkgraaf and Gradus (2003) studied the differences in the cost of waste management in the case of public or private provision for 85 Dutch municipalities. They find, in general, that private provision of waste collection is more effective, and achieves a 5% reduction in total costs compared with a public service provider.

Other studies show that differences in the costs of public and private collection are not necessarily significant. For example, Bel and Costas (2006) qualify these results considering the long term: Studying 186 Spanish municipalities, and comparing cities with privatized public provision to cities using a public service, they conclude that there is no significant cost difference. The authors explain this result as due to the benefits of privatization being eroded over time, which is confirmed by Dijkgraaf and Gradus (2007). Finally, Bel *et al.* (2010) conducted a 'meta-analysis' of 27 studies involving very different municipalities, to compare the costs of public and private waste management. The authors assume that competition among private service providers lowers the costs of waste management. However, their study does not reveal a systematic relationship between cost savings and private production.

Focusing on cost minimization of the supply of only the public service, the literature on delegated management ignores the environmental dimension of waste management. Reasoning based on fiscal logic involves comparing two funding opportunities and identical amounts of waste. If we focus more specifically on selective sorting, the efficacy of the alternative providers becomes an issue that has not been tackled in the economic literature. The environmental dimension is crucially important and provides the economic rationale for public policy. A large part of the literature addresses the roots of this issue, that is, the individual Willingness to Pay (WTP) for waste management.

2.3 *Evaluations of the WTP*

WTP evaluates the monetary value that people attribute to environmental goods and services. It can be assessed using a contingent valuation method that involves surveying individuals about their WTP for improvement to environmental quality. This method yields an estimate of the surveyed individuals' WTP for an environmental asset or their willingness to accept an environmental asset (Beaumais and Chiroleu-Assouline, 2001). It is generally used to value a public good to improve the service offered by public authorities. Individuals' WTP has been investigated also in relation to household selective sorting (Lake *et al.*, 1996; Sterner and Bartelings, 1999; Caplan *et al.*, 2002; Aadland and Caplan, 2006; Berglund, 2006; Koford *et al.*, 2012; Beaumais *et al.*, 2014). Common to these studies is the idea of rationalizing public intervention. In inequalities (1), public intervention is socially desirable if the value that individuals attribute to recycling ($MB + MEC$) is high enough compared to its cost ($MC_i + \alpha$).

For example, Lake *et al.* (1996) analyse the WTP for kerbside recycling. In their survey, the majority of respondents are willing to pay for this service. Apart from previous recycling behaviour, the demographic variables do not affect the individuals' WTP for kerbside recycling. Notably, although socio-economic characteristics affect people's decision to pay, they do not determine the effective payment level. Using a mail survey, Sterner and Bartelings (1999) studied the willingness of 450 households in the Swedish municipality of Valberg, to pay for better waste management (which did not involve any additional personal effort or work). Sixty per cent of households considered it unreasonable to pay someone else to sort their waste. However, when conditioning on non-recycling behaviour, 23% of households declared they would prefer to pay in money rather than in time (and effort) for the rational management of waste. Sterner and Bartelings (1999) show also that women, less well-educated people and young people are willing to pay more for waste collection.

A study by Caplan *et al.* (2002), based on a telephone survey of 350 households in the city of Ogden (Utah), estimated the WTP for kerbside recycling. This work focuses on evaluating three options to divert parts of the waste stream away from landfill. The participants were asked to classify the three options in order of preference. The first option corresponds to the traditional system of waste collection, of depositing recyclables and green waste in a container without separating them from other waste at a cost of USD10.65 per month. The second option offered to separate green waste only, for a maximum additional cost of USD2.00 per month. Finally, for a maximum additional cost of USD3.00 per month, the third option allowed for the separation of green waste and recyclables from residual waste. The results of the study show that two-thirds of respondents supported the expansion of kerbside recycling, and that demographic characteristics influence household preferences for alternative waste management systems. More precisely, men, residents aged 45 years, residents who had lived in the city for more than 10 years, and those on low or moderate incomes (less than USD30.000 per annum) prefer the option of 'trash can alone' (option 1); women, residents aged under 45 years, new residents in the community and residents in the medium and high-income categories prefer the option of kerbside garbage and green waste collection (option 3). In a related study, Aadland and Caplan (2006) analysed the costs and benefits of kerbside recycling using a sample of households in 40 cities in the western USA. They were interested in the WTP. Their results show that young people, women, highly educated people, individuals motivated to recycle for ethical reasons, members of environmental organizations, and those who consider their current collection recycling scheme to be satisfactory are willing to pay more.

Berglund (2006) uses a Tobit model to analyse individuals' perception of recycling activities in a municipality in northern Sweden. The system of municipal waste management in this community is fairly representative of Sweden as a whole; households sort their waste at source and take it to a recycling centre. The WTP to leave this activity to someone else is estimated as a linear function of the socio-economic variables (income, gender, age, education, type of housing) and other specific indicators such as the distance to the recycling centre, whether waste recycling collection is a requirement imposed by the authorities, perception of recycling as an enjoyable activity, and, most importantly, the green moral index (GMI). The GMI measures the moral motivation for recycling. The results show that men, younger people, people living in apartments or at a distance from a recycling centre, people who perceive sorting as a requirement imposed by the authorities and people with the lowest GMI tend to have a greater WTP (GMI is a determinant of the individual's WTP to avoid sorting waste at the source). In addition, ethical reasons for recycling result in a lower WTP for another person to take on the recycling activity. The financial cost associated with the recycling effort is lower than the time cost for recycling.

Koford *et al.* (2012) estimate the WTP for kerbside recycling based on a contingent valuation survey of 600 residents of large cities in the south-eastern USA. The results show that people have a mean WTP of USD2.29 per month to participate in a kerbside recycling scheme. High-income households and individuals who consider it an ethical duty to recycle are most likely to exhibit a positive WTP. Koford *et al.* (2012) estimate that an increase of USD1.000 in income leads to an increase in the WTP of 0.0014, and an ethical duty to recycle increases the probability of consenting to pay by 0.24.

Beaumais *et al.* (2014) evaluate the WTP for the case of household waste in Corsica. Their results reveal that house owners and city dwellers have a greater WTP to reduce the externalities associated with waste. They explain this result as due to the fact that owners pay more attention to reducing the externalities of waste because it has a negative effect on the housing

Table 1. Empirical Analyses of Willingness to Pay for Waste Management.

Author/Country	Topics investigated	Major findings
Lake *et al.* (1996)/UK	The willingness to pay for kerbside recycling scheme in the village of Hethersett, South Norfolk.	Socio-economic factors were important in determining the willingness to pay for the scheme, but once people have accepted the payment principle, its magnitude depend mainly upon on the amount of recycling that they were already undertaking before the scheme's implementation.
Bartelings and Sterner (1999)/Varberg, Sweden	The importance of behavioural variables on household waste management decisions.	Economic incentives are not the only driving force behind the observed reduction in municipal waste: Given the proper infrastructure that facilitates recycling, people are willing to invest more time than can be motivated purely by savings on their waste management bill.
Caplan *et al.* (2002)/ Ogden, Utah	Estimation of household's willingness to pay for varied curbside services.	A discrete choice contingent ranking approach is a cost-effective means for municipalities to evaluate waste disposal solution.
Aadland and Caplan (2006)/40 Western US cities	Estimation of social net benefit of curbside recycling over state and local recycling policy.	The estimated mean social net benefit of curbside recycling is almost exactly zero. Several existing curbside recycling programmes in our sample are inefficient use of resources.
Berglund (2006)/Pitea, Sweden	Analyses households' perceptions of recycling activities.	Moral motives significantly lower the costs associated with household recycling efforts.
Koford *et al.* (2012)/ Lexington, Kentucky	Estimation of WTP for curbside recycling.	Monetary incentives had a greatest impact on household recycling, but the monetary incentives interact negatively with communication appeals which by themselves had little impact overall.

market and, therefore, the value of their home. Their results show also that people who understand that they are already paying a fee for waste (16% of respondents) and who respond best to monetary incentives are more likely to accept an increased fee, thus, showing a higher WTP to reduce externalities. Corsicans are aware of the issue of waste management on the island, and the resulting externalities, and want change.

Table 1 summarizes the studies on WTP.

A too low individual WTP indicates that the local authorities cannot expect consumers to properly tackle the problem of selective sorting, and that public policy is required. The problem is related not so much to providing a public waste collection service, but rather to encourage households to recycle. Two broad categories of policy instruments have been studied applied to field: incentive policy, and information provision.

3. The Use of Economic Incentives

The question addressed by the literature discussed in this section is how to encourage or persuade households to recycle using monetary incentives (and to support their cost MC_i as a consequence) when selective sorting is socially beneficial, that is $(MB + MEC > MC_i + \alpha)$. For example, if communities require individuals to pay a tax or a fee for each unit of non-recycled waste, then these individuals will have an incentive to reduce their pollution by increasing selective sorting to avoid paying more. Similarly, if individuals receive a subsidy for each unit of recycled waste, it is in their interests to reduce their residual waste. Hahn and Stavins (1992) show that economic instruments give greater importance to the individual willingness to reduce polluting emissions (households choose their own level and means of waste reduction) than is given by regulatory instruments such as 'command and control' described above.

The public service of household waste disposal comprises its collection and treatment. As already mentioned, local authorities have an obligation to manage waste, which can be financed in three ways. First, it can be financed from the municipality's general budget. Although this is a simple method, it does not provide individuals about the costs generated by the production of waste. Secondly, a garbage collection tax can be imposed to provide the resources to fund the collection and treatment of household waste. This form of tax is relatively simple to implement and enhances users' awareness of the cost attached to managing their waste. However, this flat rate does not send a 'price signal' which might lead individuals to reduce their waste production. The third method is incentive pricing which operates by: (i) identifying the generator of waste, (ii) measuring the quantities of waste generated and (iii) setting a price according to individual effort (Bilitewski, 2008; Reichenbach, 2008). Incentive pricing corresponds to unit pricing, that is, billing based on the quantity of waste generated (which can be measured as weight, volume, per bag or same subscription). This encourages households to change their behaviour by internalizing the negative externalities generated. However, it can induce perverse effects, such as illegal dumping, to avoid paying the tax.

In the following, we discuss the analyses of three major types of incentive instruments (taxes, subsidies and the deposit-refund system) in the economic literature. We show that this literature considers that, to be effective, these incentive instruments need to be coupled with other forms of state intervention.

3.1 *Taxes*

The first articles to focus on incentive pricing are generally empirical. For instance, Wertz (1976) studied the city of San Francisco where incentive pricing was adopted to charge for waste services. Wertz (1976) seeks to explain households' waste production decisions and examines the effect of incentive pricing on the production of waste for different levels of household income. He compares the average production of waste in the city in 1970 to the average amount of garbage produced in other comparable US cities that had not adopted this pricing system. Wertz (1976)'s results suggest that the quantity of waste generated decreases as the waste tax increases (the estimated price elasticity is −0.15, which means that a 1% increase in the incentive pricing causes a decrease of 15% in the amount of waste generated). In contrast, waste generation increases with income.

This work was extended by Jenkins (1993), who modelled residential and commercial demand for waste management, including recycling as an option to reduce waste. Jenkins used data for nine American cities, five of which had an incentive pricing system. The author develops a model in which households utility depends positively on the consumption of goods, and negatively on the quantity of waste recycled. The model of households' utility maximization suggests that the household's income level, the price of consumer goods, the money received for recyclable materials (deposit) and incentive pricing have an effect on the demand for waste services. Jenkins concludes that incentive pricing is more effective for achieving a reduction in waste quantity than a flat-rate tax, in the absence of any possibility of illegal disposal. She estimates that the introduction of a USD0.8 incentive for a 32-gallon container reduced waste by 9.5% without a separate-collection system, and 16% with one.

Several studies (Fullerton and Kinnaman, 1996; Nestor and Podolsky, 1998; Linderhof *et al.*, 2001; Dijkgraaf and Gradus, 2004; Ferrara and Missios, 2012) show that incentive pricing (based on weight, volume, bag or subscription) has a positive impact on waste reduction and increases the quantity of recycled waste, thus, acting as a Pigouvian tax. It also provides individuals with information about the quantity of waste they produce and encourages responsible behaviour and the funding of a waste management service. Non-recycling households pay more, and recyclers pay less. Glachant (2003) and Ferrara and Missios (2005) show that this system of unit pricing not only increases households recycling but also causes a decrease in waste at source. Indeed, the tax encourages individuals to buy products with less packaging, and pushes the industry to change their offers to the provision of 'greener' products.

The study by Fullerton and Kinnaman (1996) is interested in the effect of introducing unit pricing, on the quantity of waste produced, the number and weight of waste containers and the amount of waste recycled. The authors estimate the quantities of waste generated by 75 households[5] in Charlottesville, VA, before and after the introduction of an incentive pricing. In this city, traditional collection is provided by the city and financed by local taxes, and recycling is voluntary (waste is deposited in landfills, and there is no kerbside waste collection). In 1991, the community provided each household with a recycling container and developed a kerbside recycling scheme. In 1992, the city went from a voluntary to an incentive pricing programme based on stickers (unit pricing for weight). The stickers indicate USD0.80 for a 120-L bag collected at the kerbside, and USD0.40 for a 60-L bag; bags with no sticker were not collected. A comparison of the waste stream was made 4 weeks before and 4 weeks after the tax was introduced. The results show a 14% reduction in the weight of waste collected and a 37% increase in the volume and 16% increase in the weight of recyclable materials. However, after estimating illegal waste diversion, the decrease in collected waste weight reduced to 10%.

The consequence of the introduction of illegal waste disposal (illegal dumping, depositing waste in the workplace or in neighbours' bins and burning of waste) is an important topic in this literature. It is considered a negative effect of incentive pricing (Fullerton and Kinnaman, 1996; Linderhof, 2001). Controlling for such anti-social behaviour is costly and difficult to implement, particularly for collective housing, where individual households' practices are difficult to isolate. Fullerton and Kinnaman (1996) propose several arguments against incentive pricing. First, they consider that the administrative and implementation costs are too high. Secondly, they estimate that 28–43% of total waste is diverted away from legal waste flows. However, these results should be interpreted with caution because a study by Linderhof (2001) estimates that illegal disposal represents 4–5% of total flows, that is, 13–17% of total waste reduction. These anti-social behaviours can be explained by differences in individual levels of environmental awareness. However, the negative externalities generated by the tax are difficult to measure and these studies show that, when they occur, anti-social behaviours are insignificant or remain at the margin and diminish over time. According to Fullerton and Kinnaman (1996), the effect of the incentive pricing remains positive and is a source of income which, by encouraging individuals to control the amount of their waste, also reduces waste management costs.

Several empirical studies that compare different pricing systems followed the study by Fullerton and Kinnaman (1996). Using a Tobit model, Nestor and Podolsky (1998) estimate the total waste generated based on the chosen pricing system. In particular, they compare a unit-pricing rule based on bags, to one based on subscription. Individuals who opted for bags were obliged to buy them. Therefore, the costs associated with waste disposal depend on the number of bags used and the waste produced. Individuals who opted for subscription, could choose the number of collections per week, the cost increasing with the frequency. The results in Nestor and Podolsky (1998) show that a system based on unit pricing for bags compared to subscription, leads to a greater reduction in the quantity of waste.

Taking different approach, the study by Linderhof (2001) evaluates the effects of the introduction of the first weight-pricing system in the Dutch municipality of Oostzaan. The authors compare the behaviour of households before and after the introduction of the tax in this municipality. They interviewed 3437 households (accounting for almost the entire population), between 2 and 42 times up to July 1993, that is, before the implementation of the weight-pricing system, and in September 1997 (a total of 42 months). These panel data allow the effects of the new pricing system to be distinguished over the short and the long terms. The authors separately investigate behaviour regarding compostable waste (vegetable, fruit and garden waste) and recyclables (glass, textiles and paper). The weight of waste (alternatively compostable and recyclable) is estimated as a function of the marginal price of waste, household composition, household size and other determinants. Both regressions consider the tax to be effective for reducing waste, and its effect is more significant for compostable waste. In addition, the long-term effects are more important than the short-term effects: Price elasticities are 30% greater over the long term. This suggests that the effects of pricing based on weight are permanent. The results show that 3 years after the introduction of this system, annual collection of all waste had decreased by 42%, and the share of non-recycled waste had decreased by 56%. However, as underlined by the authors, the success of such a scheme can be explained by the fact that the Oostzaan citizens are more environmentally conscious than the average Dutch citizen.

Dijkgraaf and Gradus (2004) also study Dutch municipalities over a 3-year period (between 1998 and 2000). They extend Linderhof (2001)'s study by estimating the effects of four unit pricing systems (based on waste weight, waste volume, bags and collection frequency) on the production of total, unsorted, compostable and recyclable waste. As determinants of the quantity of waste under the different pricing systems, Dijkgraaf and Gradus (2004) consider a range of socio-economic characteristics.[6] They also test whether neighbouring municipalities with no incentive pricing received some of the waste from municipalities with unit pricing. Their results show that with respect to unsorted waste, unit pricing is effective because it reduces the quantity of waste by approximately 50% in the case of pricing based on weight or on bags, by 27% in the case of pricing based on collection frequency, and by 6% if based on waste volume. Similarly, for recyclable waste, the amount increases by 21% in the case of a system based on weight and by 10% in a system based on frequency, while the volume-based system does not yield a significant effect on the quantity of recycled waste. In the case of total waste, all four systems have a significant negative effect on the quantity of waste produced. The systems based on weight and bags are the most effective (they reduce the quantity of waste produced by 38% and 36%, respectively), followed by the frequency system (21% decrease) and the system based on volume (6% decrease only). Concerning illegal dumping in neighbouring municipalities without unit-based pricing systems, the result of the statistical analysis of Dutch citizens does not provide evidence that surrounding municipalities collect part of the waste of municipalities that have unit-based pricing systems. The recent studies by Kinnaman

(2009) and Ferrara and Missios (2012) show weaker results for incentive pricing. However, Ferrara and Missios (2012) emphasize that a volume-based system is more efficient than a weight – and frequency– based system.

Also, in case of monetary incentives, pro–environmental behaviour usually lasts only as long as the incentive is in place, and may even cause motivational crowding–out if it is discontinued (Frey and Jegen, 2001). The authors use the example of children who receive money to mow the lawn and stop doing it if the monetary reward is withdrawn.

3.2 Subsidies versus Deposit-Refund

Subsidies are financial transfers towards individuals, communities and the private sector to encourage waste reduction and the choice of a more sustainable waste treatment (Taylor, 2000). They represent a price signal by increasing the revenue of individuals who perceive them and, therefore, are understood as promoting selective sorting.[7]

Palatnik *et al.* (2005) examine the use of economic incentives in the management of municipal waste to assess the potential benefits of recycling schemes. Their study is based on in two Israeli cities: Tiv'on and Misgav. Forty-eight per cent of Israel's household waste consists of organic material, yard waste and disposable diapers which can be separated from residual waste and recycled. The people of Tiv'on have a choice between a voluntary and a mandatory policy. The voluntary policy enables participants to purchase 500-L concrete containers for USD105 (50% of their real price) in order to separate organic waste from other waste. The mandatory policy involves installation of a 90-L container outside a group of residences, to store non-recyclable waste. Recyclable waste is stored at home, and kerbside collection takes place once a week. The voluntary system is more user-friendly since residents are not required to store any waste at home; they can drop it directly into the concrete containers. The residents of Misgav can buy backyard composters at a subsidized price equal to 50% of their real value. If at least 80% of households opt to buy a home composter, they receive a discount of USD11.5 on the tax for local environmental services. The results show that when the invoice price of waste disposal services increases, the socio-economic characteristics of households have a positive effect on the household decision to buy or not a container for sorting. They show also that if the container prices are not subsidized, people are unwilling to pay the real price. This indicates that the opportunism effect generally attributed to this type of policy is not at work in this example.

The deposit-refund system assumes that when a consumer buys a product, the individual pays an amount that will be refunded on the return of the product or its despatch to a collection centre. The literature review by Lehmann (2012) considers the deposit-refund system as a policy mix, and shows its superiority. Lehmann (2012) considers the deposit-refund system as representing an indirect combination of two public policies: taxes and subsidies. Lehmann (2012) cites Fullerton and Kinnaman (1995) which focuses on waste tax. Fullerton and Kinnaman (1995) show that, to avoid paying more tax, individuals resort to illegal disposal. Policy control is very costly and generates high transaction costs. To reduce these costs, the regulator can subsidize recycling with a deposit-refund system. Lehmann considers this as providing a double advantage. First, the polluter, in order to receive the subsidy, must provide proof of recycling, so it encourages polluters to recycle. Second, it facilitates control because the recycling proofs disclose information about behaviour and, thus, reduce transactions costs.

Several authors (Dinan, 1993; Palmer and Walls, 1997; Palmer *et al.*, 1997; Calcott and Walls, 2000) show the effectiveness of a deposit scheme to decentralize the social optimum in alternative to incentive pricing. Palmer and Walls (1997) present a theoretical partial equilibrium model of the market for a consumer good (consisting of raw and recycled material) that ultimately will be disposed of in a landfill. The model takes account of both individuals decisions about consumption and waste disposal and producers' decisions about inputs. The authors study the consignment and norm of a minimum content of recycled materials (i.e. a product that contains some proportion of recycled material) to achieve a socially efficient outcome. They show that without a tax on production inputs and a subsidy on recycling, the norm is not sufficient to achieve an optimal situation (i.e. an optimal amount of production). They show that this norm encourages use of recycled materials, and discourages use of virgin material. When the marginal productivity of recycled materials is high, the norm increases production, when it is low, it reduces production. In the first case, it should be taxed to reduce waste, and in the second case, it is necessary to subsidize the output to avoid a below optimum result. For the authors, the deposit system is an adequate tool to achieve an optimal situation that equalizes the marginal social cost of disposal by, combining a production tax with a subsidy for recycled products. This means it is unnecessary to combine the deposit with an additional tax. However, the authors specify that subsidizing recycling encourages substitution of raw materials, which might indirectly encourage consumption and waste generation. (The subsidy reduces the real price of a good for consumers even though it is potentially polluting.)

A different partial equilibrium model of waste production and recycling is developed in Palmer *et al.* (1997). This model analyses public policies to reduce quantities of waste, and evaluates the impact of different policies to reduce waste. It models a deposit/refund system, advance disposal fees and recycling subsidies in relation to five recyclable materials (aluminium, glass, paper, plastic and steel). Palmer *et al.* (1997) assume that the price of a product includes a deposit, which is partly or entirely reimbursed when the product is returned (recycled). The deposit acts as a tax on the final material by increasing its price by the amount of the deposit for non-recyclers. The authors then calibrate the model with supply and demand elasticities based on the economic literature; they consider 1990 price and quantity data for each type of material. They then compare the three policies with respect to a 10% reduction in total waste. Palmer *et al.* (1997) show that to achieve such a reduction requires a deposit equal to USD45 per ton. The same reduction in the total amount of waste can be achieved by the application of other policies – advance disposal fees costing USD85, and a subsidy for recycling activity of USD98 per ton. However, these costs are around twice those of the deposit scheme. The deposit has a doubly positive effect because it promotes both source reduction and recycling. A more recent study by Loukil and Rouached (2012) concludes that the deposit system reduces the cost of waste collection, but is not efficient for irregular recyclers.

Fullerton and Wu (1998) develop a general equilibrium model which takes account of households, producers and the influence of production processes decisions[8] on flows of materials. In the same paper, the authors consider the different pricing instruments that act upstream or downstream. They are interested in how these instruments can be used to solve market failures in waste management and achieve the social optimum. Fullerton and Wu (1998) show that a deposit-refund system is not sufficient to achieve the social optimum and should be coupled with a tax on packaging. This is based on the hypothesis the packaging is not recyclable. Fullerton and Wu (1998) examine several other policies, many of which include a subsidy for recyclability and generate the social optimum. Calcott and Walls (2000) show that when taxes and subsidies vary perfectly with recyclability, a tax on products combined with a subsidy of recycling, such as a deposit-refund system, can achieve the social optimum. This is similar to one of the conclusions in Fullerton and Wu (1998). Choe and Fraser (2001) highlight that different combinations of taxes and subsidies can achieve the social optimum and show that flexibility of the instruments occurs only if the individual actions of agents can be targeted by different economic instruments. The authors show that the flexibility of policies depends on the ability of public authorities to introduce appropriate policy instruments to target the specific behaviour of economic agents.

The deposit-refund system is possible for reusable or recyclable products and packaging. Therefore, it assumes that there is a market for recyclable and recycled goods that is more attractive than the market for residual waste. Also, implementation of such a system requires a sufficient number of conveniently accessible sorting centres. It requires the refund to be sufficiently high in relation to the required recycling. Finally, deposit allows people to both report reusable products, but also to return hazardous materials that should not be mixed with other waste and high-value recyclable products (Attar, 2008).

The above studies show that incentives act on extrinsic motivations because they involve monetary or material rewards as defined by Deci (1975).

Table 2 summarizes the studies on incentive instruments.

3.3 *Information Policies*

The origin of waste as an environmental problem arises because a tax (or subsidy), on its own, is not the solution to the environmental issue. Without an efficient infrastructure policy, individual recycling will not be efficient. Similarly, if information on recycling possibilities (where, how, what, etc.) is not made available to consumers, they will under-recycle. Therefore, the literature considers information and infrastructure policies as complementary to economic incentives to promote selective sorting (Aadland *et al.*, 2005).

Information-based instruments are tools that allow for the transmission of knowledge needed by individuals to adopt ecological behaviour. A change in voluntary waste behaviour can reduce the amount of residual waste and increase recycling. This is why information-based instruments are considered voluntary instruments. Grolleau *et al.* (2004) understand individual voluntary commitment as individuals not being forced by the community.

Unlike the instruments discussed so far, information-based instruments can be introduced by local authorities and by organizations, such as public institutions, associations, educators, etc. always with the same purpose of making individuals aware of their duty to adopt more responsible behaviour. Information-based instruments teach individuals to adopt good attitudes, and inform them of the means available. They sensitize people to waste and its characteristics, that is, the materials that constitute waste, and the potentially useful resources that are thrown away. In other words, education and information shape responsible individuals willing responsibly towards the environment, not only to respect nature but also to achieve more rational management of resources. '*Waste Reduction Week*', which was launched in 2009 at the European level, is an example of an information campaign. Alternatively, municipalities could provide interactive information maps showing the location and type of garbage collection stations. The earliest communication campaigns employed ecological arguments to highlight the importance of recycling and communicate good behaviour. However, over time, communities have sought to discipline and educate individuals regarding the norms of good environmental conduct (Rumpala, 1999). Information campaigns might focus on the benefits (or harm) of (not) recycling (Lord and Putrevu, 1998). Waste must be perceived as a reusable resource and a source of income. It is impossible to grab the attention of individuals with different

Table 2. Empirical Analyses of Incentive Instruments in Waste Management.

Author/Country	Topics investigated	Major findings
Jenkins (1993)/USA	The impact of a waste service pricing policy (based on an incentive pricing) on waste generation.	The amount of waste generated is sensitive to the price of waste collection. Incentive pricing is more effective for achieving a reduction in waste quantity than a flat-rate tax, in the absence of any possibility of illegal disposal.
Fullerton and Kinnaman (1995)/Charlottesville, USA	Estimation of the implementation of a unit-pricing programme on the weight of garbage, the number of containers, the weight per can and the amount of recycling.	Households reduced the number of bags, but not necessarily the actual weight of their garbage (households stomped on their garbage to reduce their costs). The weight of recycling increased, and illegal dumping too.
Nestor and Podolsky (1998)/Georgia, USA	Examine the two most common forms of unit pricing (based on bags vs. based on subscription) practiced in the USA.	Households in neither programme engaged in source reduction and households in the can programme increased total waste generation. Compared to the subscription programme, the unit-pricing programme leads to a greater reduction in the quantity of waste.
Linderholf et al. (2001)/ Oostzaan, The Netherlands	Test the effects of weight-based pricing on the collection of household waste.	The weight-based pricing has a strong effect on the amount of waste presented for collection. This pricing appears to be cost-effective, and thus to yield a significant social benefit. Illegal dumping is small.
Dijkgraaf and Gradus (2004)/The Netherlands	Estimate the effects of four unit-based pricing systems (Bag/Weight/ Volume/Frequency) on waste collected in Dutch municipalities.	Unit-based pricing is more effective in reducing unsorted and compostable waste and in increasing recyclable waste. The bag- and weight-based systems perform better than the frequency- and volume-based systems.
Palatnik et al. (2005)/ Israel	Examine the use of economic incentives in municipal waste management.	With low levels of effort needed, households' participation rates in a curbside recycling programme are mainly influenced by economic variables and age. When the required effort level is relatively high, however, households is influenced mainly by their environmental commitment and by economic considerations. In both cases, a subsidy is required in order to achieve an efficient level of recycling.

environmental sensitivities using one means. However, it is possible to identify groups of individuals and to design specific awareness and education campaigns. The advantage of information-based instruments is precisely the flexibility of their design which allows them to reach the greatest number of people.

Some of the work in the literature (Grodzińska-Jurczak, 2003; Aadland *et al.*, 2005; Kinnaman, 2005) examines the influence of information on individual behaviour, other studies focus on the knowledge necessary to overcome environmental problems (Granzin and Olsen, 1991; Oskamp *et al.*, 1991; Pieters, 1991). All of this work confirms the importance of awareness and information in individual recycling or waste reduction behaviour. From a general perspective, to motivate green behaviour, Owens (2000) shows that it is better to inform people about the future environment. Information campaigns that emphasize the catastrophic state of the world motivate people to change their behaviour to become more environmentally friendly, even if it involves personal sacrifices (Griskevicius *et al.*, 2010). Grodzińska-Jurczak (2003)'s study analyses the effect of a good understanding/knowledge of waste on selective sorting. He compares the behaviour of residents in different municipalities, some of whom have been exposed to information through communication campaigns, and some who have not. The author shows that combining an information campaign and a sorting programme has a positive effect on reducing waste. Aadland *et al.* (2005) study a costly kerbside recycling scheme. With the help of a cost/benefit analysis of 4000 US households, the authors propose that individuals should subscribe to a scheme that involves sorting and taking their waste to a landfill. They recommend that communities make the necessary infrastructure available and conduct a parallel communication campaign. Along the same lines, Kinnaman (2005) highlights the need for information campaigns on waste minimization through waste sorting. Individuals exposed to such information acquire a greater knowledge of environmental issues, which has a positive influence on recycling (Granzin and Olsen, 1991; Pieters, 1991). Oskamp *et al.* (1991) show that recyclers are better informed about recyclables and recycling locations compared to non-recyclers.

However, Iyer and Kashyap (2007) show that, although the information can be effective, it is much less effective than economic incentives. However, they add that the effect of an information policy persists, which does not apply to incentives which are withdrawn. Thus, the short-term/long-term distinction is important for policy choice. If communities are aiming at quick results related to behaviour changes, then incentives are the right instrument. If they are seeking outcomes that will endure over time and produce real change in the individual habits, they should develop information-based instruments which will have a more permanent effect on behaviours. Information-based instruments are not alternatives to incentives, rather they are complements. Furthermore, to complement information campaigns, a public infrastructure policy would seem necessary. In the absence of an efficient infrastructure to facilitate sorting behaviour, recycling will not increase (Knussen *et al.*, 2004).

Taxes, subsidies, deposit-refunds, infrastructure policy and information on sorting do not constitute the complete range of public policies to increase individual selective sorting. This is the second original feature of waste management understood as an environmental problem. Recycling is part of broader consumer behaviour. The literature on behavioural economics shows that individuals' decisions respond to factors other than maximizing private interest that can be exploited by other public policies. Social norms, social approval, others' esteem, altruism and others' choices are all important determinants of individual actions. The individual choice of recycling is no exception, as demonstrated by an emerging literature on waste management which is underpinned by behavioural economics.

4. The Incorporation of Behavioural Instruments into Practice

Applying behavioural economics to waste management reveals that in Equation (1) the *MB* an individual obtains from recycling is complex. As explained below, *MB* includes various measures such as the importance given to the environment, the benefit derived from peers' esteem and the value attributed to social norms. We define behavioural instruments as public policies that seek to influence individuals to lead them to adopt behaviours that are aligned to the public interest.

A recent survey by Van den Bergh (2008) highlights studies that show that people are not motivated solely by financial compensation. Van den Bergh (2008) notes that non-monetary instruments can also be used to induce desired behaviour. Therefore, to change individual behaviour, it is important to focus also on social factors such as attitude, social norms and peer pressure. Behavioural incentives are being offered increasingly by public authorities to encourage individuals adopt socially desirable behaviours.

Psychologists and sociologists have conducted extensive studies on the influence of social norms on individual behaviour. These works focus on warm-glow, social pressure and surroundings (Hornik *et al.*, 1995; Courcelle *et al.*, 1998; Cheung *et al.*, 1999) and, more recently, nudges. Economists are incorporating these concepts into analyses of waste management (Brekke *et al.*, 2010; Viscusi *et al.*, 2011; Abbott *et al.*, 2013; Cecere *et al.*, 2014) defined in various ways. For example, Andreoni (1990) defines warm-glow as a feeling of inner welfare that comes from performing a good deed while Brekke *et al.* (2003) translate it as a positive self-image and consider it the threshold to what individuals believe is socially responsible behaviour. Halvorsen (2008) interprets warm-glow as respect for social and moral norms.

4.1 *Understanding More Complex Individual Motivations to Recycle*

Although the study by Bénabou and Tirole (2006) is not focused on waste, it provides guidance to understand this literature. Bénabou and Tirole (2006) distinguish individual actions based on two motivations: the importance of appearing pro-social versus being seen as greedy. The authors model the effect of these arguments on reputation: the individual's perception of others' opinions his or her motivations based on observation of the individual's actions. They stress that this is at the heart of the crowding-out effect.

The decision to recycle can have other motivations. The psychologist De Young (1985), highlights intrinsic motivation (i.e. based on altruism or environmental awareness) and personal satisfaction. He suggests that people may 'do a good deed' for the personal satisfaction they derive from it with no promise of another reward. For Deci (1975), pure altruism and warm-glow are considered intrinsic motivation because the reward is personal and invisible to others. For example, De Young and Kaplan (1985) show that people interested in ecology try to do what they consider to be useful and beneficial and do not seek an economic advantage. McCarty and Shrum (2001) distinguish between people displaying in individualistic behaviour and those displaying collectivist behaviour. Collectivists focus more on the group and on shared objectives compared to individualists. Collectivists attribute a high importance to recycling because they consider the future benefits to society from recycling. Individualists assign low importance to recycling because they focus only on the short-term benefits. Collectivists consider recycling to be important which belief leads to their involvement. D'Amato *et al.* (2014) show that intrinsic motivation for environmental preservation (resulting from the level of knowledge of environmental issues and individual pro-environmental behaviour) positively affects waste reduction. For these authors, there are reciprocal positive and significant links between recycling and waste reduction behaviours. They suggest that recycling and pollution prevention behaviour tend to be self-reinforcing. Ferrara and Missios (2012) consider that intrinsic motivation contributes to moral/social aspects, and show that individuals who show consideration for society tend to engage more extensively in recycling.

We can also distinguish between those who support recycling and those who implement recycling behaviour. This is discussed in the social psychology literature to determine how behavioural and cognitive strategies can change behaviour. Hopper and Nielsen (1991) study both strategies and pay particular attention to the hypothesis that recycling is a form of altruistic behaviour guided by social and personal norms. They point out that recycling is costly to the individual (e.g. in time and effort) and its benefits are neither personal nor immediate, although they are advantageous to the whole society in the long term. Andreoni (1990) develops the concepts of pure and impure altruism. Pure altruism occurs when an individual can improve the lot of his or her friends (e.g. by purchasing a green product); impure altruism refers to a situation where the individual derives no benefit from improving the lot of his or her friends, but, instead, derives a feeling of personal satisfaction from achieving something good.

Peer effects or social approval can act as secondary motivations. Bénabou and Tirole (2006) consider that, although some people are sincerely altruistic, motivations to adopt 'pro-social' behaviour can be explained by the desire to create a positive self-image, but also to establish a certain type of social esteem. The authors assume that the behaviour of some people may not appear rational since individuals adopt pro-social behaviour despite its cost in terms of time, effort and money. The authors emphasize that monetary incentives can crowd out reputation effects. For an individual to gain reputation effect, his or her behaviour must be seen by others as the least greedy. Reputation effects can decrease if individual behaviour is perceived as due to monetary incentives.

In a study of the factors affecting individual recycling and waste reduction behaviour, Cecere *et al.* (2014) assume that agents only respond to government economic incentives, such as taxes and subsidies, and consider motivations that extend beyond economic incentives. In responding to intrinsic motivation, agents may be altruistic and make environmentally friendly choices, maximizing both their individual welfare and the social welfare. Cecere *et al.* (2014) show that in the case of extrinsic motivations, agents are encouraged to engage in pro-environmental behaviour because of external pressures, corresponding to the reputational concerns defined by Bénabou and Tirole (2006). However, note that, as underlined by Deci (1975), social norms and reputation are difficult to classify as intrinsic or extrinsic motivations. For example, if individuals conform to social norm, this may be out of a desire for a good self-image (intrinsic motivation), but may also be to obtain the approval of others (extrinsic motivation).

4.2 *Facing Social Pressure: From Peer Effects to Reputation Effects*

Social norms correspond to the rules of conduct in a particular group. Ajzen and Fishbein (1980) related social norms to social pressure. Social pressure is measured by the individual's beliefs concerning the expectations of others (i.e. family, neighbours, friends) regarding his or her behaviour. Ajzen and Fishbein (1980) assume that an individual will adopt a behaviour if it seems that his or her family, neighbours or friends attach importance to it. In the case of waste, many studies, not always convergent, show a relationship between social norms and recycling (Nyborg *et al.*, 2006; Brekke *et al.*, 2010; Viscusi *et al.*, 2011). For example, Oskamp *et al.* (1991) and Schultz *et al.* (1995) show that participation in kerbside recycling is more prevalent if neighbours and friends also recycle because it creates a social pressure which encourages greater participation in order to avoid negative judgements. Similarly, when social norms are visible to everyone (e.g. using a recycling bin), Vining and Ebreo (1992) show that recycling rates are higher. Berglund (2006) confirms the importance of social pressure for recycling behaviour, especially for children. Nyborg *et al.* (2006) model peer pressure. They assume that a society can be completely 'green' (i.e. everyone makes efforts to preserve the environment) or completely 'grey' (i.e. everyone chooses to pollute). The model equilibrium occurs when everyone acts according to the green or the grey norm. The social norm is based on the hypothesis that moral motivation to act 'green' is important if enough people act in this way; if not, moral motivation is low.

Social pressure can also arise from self-image. Ek and Söderholm (2008) considered whether the consumption of certain goods conveys a self-image of socially responsibility. The utility of this self-image does not result from the consumption of the good as such. It arises instead, from the individual decision to purchase a good based on a selfish desire not to be judged by peers, rather than altruism. For example, a person may decide to use reusable bags for shopping, not out of consideration for the environment, but in order to show this behaviour to others. Brekke *et al.* (2003)'s model assumes that individuals prefer to achieve and maintain a socially responsible self-image. The more that individual's behaviour approaches what he or she considers to be socially responsible, the more his or her self-image improves. The authors conducted a survey to determine the moral motivations for recycling and obtained 1102 responses. Eighty-eight per cent of individuals claimed to recycle because they believed in behaving in the way they would like others to behave. However, 41% recycled in order to be perceived as responsible by their peers. However, declarative surveys have some limitations. For example, individuals may make a particular response in order to be perceived as someone who cares about the environment, but might act quite differently. Czajkowski *et al.* (2014) study individual preferences with respect to households' recycling behaviour. The authors show that behaviours are mainly determined by a feeling of personal moral responsibility to recycle. Fear of social pressure is less important.

Brekke *et al.* (2010) tests social interaction of 'duty-orientation' using the results from a survey on glass recycling behaviour among Norwegian households. A duty-oriented individual is defined by Brekke *et al.* (2003) as someone who prefers a socially responsible self-image and who suffers from loss of self-image if his or her perceived duty to recycle is not fulfilled. Brekke *et al.* (2003) conclude that for a duty-oriented person, responsibility ascription is an inference (i.e. the result of a learning process) and not a choice. Like Nyborg *et al.* (2006), the authors suppose that if there is some doubt over the right thing to do, people infer their individual responsibility by considering others' behaviour.

Concerning responsibility ascription, Brekke *et al.* (2010) suppose that responsibility is accepted if the percentage of others who recycle is greater than a certain individual threshold. Decisions may be motivated by duty-oriented recycling leading to interaction effects from social learning about individual responsibility. A duty-oriented individual will feel loss of self-image if he or she does not fulfil his or her perceived responsibility to recycle. A duty-oriented individual will distinguish the effects of direct social interaction caused by a preference for compliance, and indirect social interaction stemming from responsibility ascription. The direct effect is not affected by the degree of uncertainty of the individual concerning the supposed behaviour of their peers, whereas the indirect effect is completely affected by the supposed behaviour of peers (e.g. the more respondents are confused about the recycling behaviour of their peers, the less they will be willing to accept responsibility). Nyborg *et al.* (2006) show that duty-orientation is a major determinant of declared recycling. They show also that the willingness of respondents to accept recycling is influenced by beliefs about the others' behaviour. This means that their responsibility changes depending on others' behaviour or the certainty on their peers' behaviour. Social learning of responsibility is statistically significant and positive, indicating that the people's propensity to assign responsibility increases with common thinking about how to recycle in their social group. When responsibility is already assigned, a change in perception of the behaviour of others will only affect individual behaviour directly. However, if responsibility is not assigned, an upward revision of the belief that recycling is common practice in the immediate social group of an individual will increase the probability of taking responsibility, which has a positive indirect effect on recycling and increases the probability of direct recycling.

4.3 *Personal Norms versus Social Norms*

Knussen *et al.* (2004) suggest that social pressure does not influence recycling (i.e. there is not a significant correlation). They suggest that social norms may operate at an early point in a recycling scheme, or when a recycling scheme is well-established, after individuals have had time to develop strong attitudes (positive or negative) and are not influenced by external social pressure. The empirical study conducted by Viscusi *et al.* (2011) is important because it investigates the role of 'social norms'[9] on 'pro-environmental' behaviour based on recycling of plastic bottles. The authors evaluate the roles of personal norms (i.e. norms a person imposes on others) and external norms (i.e. norms people perceive as imposed by others). External norms act as a societal reference for appropriate behaviour or pressure to adopt environmentally friendly behaviour. Personal norms can lead to pro-environmental social pressure on others if they are adopted by a part of the population, and can serve as a benchmark for appropriate behaviour that affects the decisions of others. The authors show that, although the variable 'internal private value' is important, 'social norm', reflecting individual guilt, due to the behaviour of neighbours, from not recycling, is not statistically significant.

This results of Viscusi *et al.* (2011) contradicts the findings from the studies discussed earlier, and suggests that social pressure cannot be considered an effective method to change recycling behaviour. Hage and Söderholm (2008), in a Swedish study, qualify these results. The authors show that individual recyclers do not tend to be influenced by friends, family or other important people, but that 'new immigrants' are. They explain this as being due to the fact that, in general, when immigrants arrive in a new country, they are unfamiliar with the laws and regulations, and may not have a good grasp of the local language, which can lead to initially low levels of recycling participation. However, over time, immigrants adjust to the social norms of behaviour and sort (on average, immigrants recycle more than Swedish citizens).

Fornara *et al.* (2011) stress the importance of spatial distance in developing norms. They believe that people living close to each other behave more similarly than people living at a distance. They show that this applies particularly to recycling if it takes place in a specific location. Abbott *et al.* (2013, 2014) study the concept of social norms and adhere to the aspect of visibility. Abbott *et al.* (2013) provide a theoretical and empirical analysis of how social norms and 'warm-glow' affect the relationship between the quality of recycling facilities and recycling efforts. Abbott *et al.* (2014)'s, empirical results confirm the theoretical model's hypotheses of a social norm effect and a slight effect of environmental concern. However, this empirical study fails to establish a significant relationship between warm-glow and recycling.

Abbott *et al.* (2013, 2014) believe that rather than imposing recycling levels on individuals or implementing measures to guide individual behaviour, governments should introduce measures that activate social norms. For example, implementing kerbside collection programmes that make recycling more visible to neighbours might encourage the emergence of a social norm to recycle.

If selective sorting by others and the recycling social norm more generally, are recognized as key determinants of individual choices to recycle, the question for public authorities is how to activate these factors. From this perspective, the use of nudges seems particularly promising.

4.4 *Nudges to the Rescue*

The willingness of individuals to act in a certain way does not necessarily translate into real action. The 2009 study by the European Commission shows that 93% of French citizens believe that climate change is an important problem. However, the same survey shows that only 33% use a transport means with low CO_2 emissions. Similarly, the fact that an individual is informed does not lead necessarily to the right choice. For example, being aware of the fact that failure to recycle increases the cost of household waste disposal does not encourage all individuals to recycle. Several public authorities have experimented with 'nudges', to control the production of waste. Nudges first emerged in the USA. Thaler and Sunstein (2003) consider that a nudge 'guides the choice of individuals to favourable decisions for the community while respecting everyone's freedom to act in his convenience.' The idea is based on work in psychology and behavioural sciences, aimed not at understanding the tools to bring out decision making, but rather to understand those who adopt the reported behaviour. It consists of giving a 'boost' to those individuals who adopt solutions that benefit communities and generally are consistent with the public interest.

Nudges influence decisions and individual actions by acting on the individual's perception of the conduct adopted by a group. They impose an environment-friendly option by making the option seem unique. For example, a ban on the provision of free plastic bags in shops resulted in the default option for individuals to opt for reusable bags. This initiative helped to limit overconsumption and pushed individuals to choose reusable bags. In France, the number of disposable bags distributed in stores decreased from 10.5 billion in 2002 to 1.6 billion in 2008 (Ministry of Ecology, 2010). In Washington DC in 2010, in order to promote the reuse of plastic bag, a tax of 5 cents on plastic bags was introduced. It indirectly caused a 66% decrease in the number of bags retrieved from the Potomac River between 2009 and 2010.

Another effect achieved by nudges consists of encouraging good environmental practices so that they become social norms. For example, Schultz (1999) conducted an experiment on waste recycling in 120 households in the city of Laverne, CA. Every day for a month, households were informed about the number of families (i.e. their neighbours) who participated in recycling household waste, and the quantity of recycled waste. To obtain this information and create proximity, a handwritten note, was glued to their door. The author observed an immediate 19% increase in the volume of recycled waste. Schultz (1999) adds that the effect persisted and the observed increase continued after the end of the experiment. A nudge informs participants about the behaviour of their neighbours by providing information on the social norm of recycling in their neighbourhood.

However, using nudges to disseminate social norms can have adverse effects and social norms can have positive as well as negative effects on individual behaviour. If the social norms of behaviour adopted by the majority of population correspond to behaviour that does not respect the environment, then these social norms will have a negative effect. A study by Schultz *et al.* (2007) focuses on energy consumption in 1000 Californian households and shows that a nudge can have a negative effect. Informing households about their energy consumption compared with the consumption of others in the neighbourhood acts as a nudge diffusing a social norm. However, although their results showed a decrease in energy consumption among high consuming households, they showed also that low-energy households increased their consumption. In addition, nudges do not have the same impact on all individuals. This is confirmed by a study of Schultz and Zelezny (2003) which shows that receptiveness to nudges depends on the individual's level of altruism and the importance given by the individual to environmental issues. Nudges are likely to become important elements in future regulatory systems.

Table 3 summarizes the studies on behavioural instruments.

5. Conclusion

Since the 1970s, many directives and laws have been implemented to regulate waste management to limit its production. New services, such as kerbside recycling, drop-off centres, incinerators and garbage collection stations, have emerged and incentive policies have been implemented. However, the production of household waste countries continues to grow.

The studies presented in this paper show that regulatory solutions alone, although necessary, are failing to reverse the trend of increased waste or to change consumer behaviour. However, economic incentives, which act via a price signal, encourage changes in individual behaviour. Environmental taxation appears particularly effective in the case of household waste. Indeed, empirical studies on the OECD countries show that incentive pricing in the form of progressive taxation based on the weight of garbage, is efficient. This form of taxation encourages and rewards individuals to recycle, and minimizes the amount of residual waste. However, it is difficult to assess and control the negative effects of these policies, as individuals reluctant to comply, may resort to illegal dumping to minimize their tax burden.

Although the effectiveness of economic incentive instruments is not challenged, there are no studies showing whether their withdrawal results in cessation of this behaviour. In addition, tax mechanisms achieve maximum welfare gains only if they are paired with informational and behavioural instruments. These instruments appear to be complementary.

In addition, the studies reviewed show that information-based instruments by increasing consumer awareness of the adverse effects of pollution, encourage the adoption of environmentally friendly behaviour and foster its persistence even if the tax is discontinued. Without information, people cannot understand the consequences of their behaviour. However, knowledge of environmental issues alone does not guarantee adoption of the desired behaviour or eradication of the problem. This is because there is a difference between individuals' intentions and effective actions. The willingness to adopt behaviour and, therefore, to change habits may be limited by the costs involved (e.g. financial, time and convenience costs). Several recent studies highlight the social aspect: awareness of individuals exposed to environmental information depends on the behaviour of their neighbours, social norms or self-image with respect to society, as well as financial incentives. In targeting change in habits and individual practices, informational and behavioural instruments seem to provide the underpinnings of waste management policies.

Although the literature suggests that some policies have stronger effects on the behaviour of individuals, it also suggests that a definitive hierarchization of policies is not possible. Different policies have different effects, some act on the long term and the others on the short term, some

Table 3. Empirical Analyses of Behavioural Instruments in Waste Management.

Author/Country	Topics investigated	Major findings
Hage and Söderholm (2008)/Swedish	The determinants of recycling efforts (in particular, packaging waste) in the case of Swedish households.	Economic and moral motives influence inter-household recycling rates. The property-close collection in multi-family dwelling houses leads to higher collection rates. The strength of moral (self-enforced) norms explains a large part of the variation across households, but the importance of such norms in driving recycling efforts partly diminishes if improved collection infrastructure.
Brekke et al. (2010)/ Norway	Examine if recycling decisions may be motivated by duty-orientation, and if this can lead to interaction effects through social learning of individual responsibility.	Responsibility ascription is influenced by the perception of what others are doing. People are reluctant to accept responsibility based on uncertain information.
Viscusi et al. (2011)/USA	The determinants of recycling behaviour for plastic water bottles.	Private values of the environment are influential in promoting recycling, while the external norm is not. Households' recycling behaviour ts influenced by policies that create economic incentives to promote recycling (recycling laws to reduce the time and inconvenience costs of recycling).
Abbott et al. (2013)/UK	Examine the role of social norms and warm-glow.	The empirical analysis failed to establish a significant relationship between warm-glow and recycling. In the context of household recycling, it may be more attractive to policymakers to rely on social norms rather than other measures to guide behaviour.
Abbott et al. (2014)/UK	Examine the importance of social norms for recycling behaviour.	The study confirms the existence of a social norm effect but fails to establish a significant relationship between warm-glow and recycling.
Cerere et al. (2014)/EU	Examine whether individual waste reduction behaviour is more strongly driven by extrinsic motivations like social norms, or intrinsic motivations like purely altruistic preferences.	In the case of food waste prevention, sustainable behaviour is firmly dependent on intrinsic motivations. Waste reducers tend to exhibit a sort of altruistic motivation, which does not relate to economic incentives or social norm pressures.

affect the volume of waste and some affect behaviour. Most work evaluates the effectiveness of single policies in isolation from other measures. In real life, these instruments coexist, and the complementarities between them need to be taken into account and discussed in depth. In our view, incentive mechanisms that force people to quickly adopt the desired behaviour need to be combined with behavioural instruments that change the preferences of individual agents towards more environmental friendly behaviour.

Finally, public policies on household waste will be effective if producers produce goods for which the 'waste' part of the product is recyclable. Therefore, taxing producers for the non-recyclable part of their product could be considered a useful complementary policy unless changes in households' purchasing behaviour towards products that generate less waste are sufficient to generate a change in the supply of goods.

Acknowledgements

I would like to thank two anonymous referees and Agnes Festre for valuable comments on the earlier version of this paper. It was based on the first chapter of my doctoral dissertation. As such, I would like to thank my thesis supervisor, Christophe Charlier. The usual disclaimer applies.

Notes

1. Communication from the Commission to the European Parliament, the Council, the European Economic and Social Committee and the Committee of the Regions, *Roadmap to a Resource Efficient Europe*, COM(2011) 571 final, Brussels, 20 September 2011.
2. Therefore, the legal definition proposed in the introduction focusing on the 'nature' of waste appears broader. However, note that as *MB* increases because of resources scarcity, residual waste decreases.
3. The economic optimum for pollution is achieved when the marginal cost of reducing the quantity of waste is equal to the marginal cost of the environmental damage associated with the production of waste.
4. Generally, communities employ private companies for the treatment of waste.
5. A total of 97 of 400 households agreed to participate in the study. The final sample included 75 households with complete data.
6. These comprised the municipality's area, average family size in the area, number of non-Western foreigners per inhabitant, percentage of total inhabitants earning a median income, number of houses sold per inhabitant, number of flats sold per inhabitant, an indicator variable for small and large municipalities and percentage of the population aged over 65.
7. Taking a different point of view, De Beir *et al.* (2007) explain that it is necessary to subsidize the recycling sector when there is no competitive waste sector and when the cost of recovery/recycling is high. Conversely, they argue that as soon as recycling activity is profitable, the subsidy becomes unnecessary.
8. The amount of waste generated by the consumption of goods depends on the production process (Producers need to take account of the design of their products and the recyclability of the waste part product).
9. They define social norms as 'normatively appropriate'.

References

Aadland, D., Caplan, A. and Phillips, O. (2005) A Bayesian examination of anchoring bias and cheap talk in contingent valuation studies. Economics Research Institute Study Paper, Vol. 14, pp. 1–1.

Aadland, D. and Caplan, A.J. (2006) Curbside recycling: waste resource or waste of resources? *Journal of Policy Analysis and Management* 25(4): 855–874.

Abbott, A., Nandeibam, S. and O'Shea, L. (2011) Explaining the variation in household recycling rates across the UK. *Ecological Economics* 70(11): 2214–2223.

Abbott, A., Nandeibam, S. and O'Shea, L. (2013) Recycling: social norms and warm-glow revisited. *Ecological Economics* 90: 10–18.

Abbott, A., Nandeibam, S. and O'Shea, L. (2014) Is there a social norm to recycle? In T. C. Kinnaman and K. Takeuchi (eds.), *Handbook on Waste Management* (pp. 53–72). Cheltenham, UK: Edward Elgar Publishing Limited.

Ajzen, I. and Fishbein, M. (1980) *Understanding Attitudes and Predicting Social.* Englewood Cliffs, NJ: Prentice Hall.

Andreoni, J. (1990) Impure altruism and donations to public goods: a theory of warm-glow giving? *Economic Journal* 100(401): 464–477.

Attar, M. (2008) *Les enjeux de la gestion des déchets ménagers et assimilés en france en 2008.* Direction des Journaux Officiels.

Barde, J. (1992) *Économie et politique de l'environnement*, Vol. 2. Paris, France : Presses Universitaires de France, L'économiste.

Beaumais, O., Casabianca, A., Pieri, X. and Dominique, P. (2014) Why not allow individuals to rank freely? A scaled rank-ordered logit approach applied to waste management in Corsica. *Annals of Economics and Statistics* (first round revision).

Beaumais, O. and Chiroleu-Assouline, M. (2001) *Économie de l'environnement.* Bréal.

Bel, G. and Costas, A. (2006) Do public sector reforms get rusty? Local privatization in Spain. *Journal of Policy Reform* 9(1): 1–24.

Bel, G., Fageda, X. and Warner, M.E. (2010) Is private production of public services cheaper than public production? A meta-regression analysis of solid waste and water services. *Journal of Policy Analysis and Management* 29(3): 553–577.

Bénabou, R. and Tirole, J. (2006) Incentives and prosocial behavior. Technical report, National Bureau of Economic Research.

Berglund, C. (2006) The assessment of households' recycling costs: the role of personal motives. *Ecological Economics* 56(4): 560–569.

Bilitewski, B. (2008) From traditional to modern fee systems. *Waste Management* 28(12): 2760–2766.

Brekke, K.A., Kverndokk, S. and Nyborg, K. (2003) An economic model of moral motivation. *Journal of Public Economics* 87(9-10): 1967–1983.

Brekke, K.A., Kipperberg, G. and Nyborg, K. (2010) Social interaction in responsibility ascription: the case of household recycling. *Land Economics* 86(4): 766–784.

Calcott, P. and Walls, M. (2000) Can downstream waste disposal policies encourage upstream 'design for environment'? *American Economic Review* 90(2): 233–237.

Callan, S.J. and Thomas, J.M. (2001) Economies of scale and scope: a cost analysis of municipal solid waste services. *Land Economics* 77(4): 548–560.

Caplan, A.J., Grijalva, T.C. and Jakus, P.M. (2002) Waste not or want not? A contingent ranking analysis of curbside waste disposal options. *Ecological Economics* 43(2–3): 185–197.

Cecere, G., Mancinelli, S. and Mazzanti, M. (2014) Waste prevention and social preferences: the role of intrinsic and extrinsic motivations. *Ecological Economics* 107: 163–176.

Cheung, S.F., Chan, D.K.S. and Wong, Z.S.Y. (1999) Reexamining the theory of planned behavior in understanding wastepaper recycling. *Environment and Behavior* 31(5): 587–612.

Choe, C. and Fraser, I. (2001) On the flexibility of optimal policies for green design. *Environmental and Resource Economics* 18(4): 367–371.

Courcelle, C., Kestemont, M.-P., Tyteca, D. and Installé, M. (1998) Assessing the economic and environmental performance of municipal solid waste collection and sorting programmes. *Waste Management and Research* 16(3): 253–262.

Czajkowski, M., Hanley, N. and Nyborg, K. (2014) Social norms, morals and self-interest as determinants of pro-environment behaviours. Technical report, Memorandum, Department of Economics, University of Oslo.

D'Amato, A., Mancinelli, S. and Zoli, M. (2014) Two shades of (warm) glow: multidimensional intrinsic motivation, waste reduction and recycling. Technical report, SEEDS, Sustainability Environmental Economics and Dynamics Studies.

De Beir, J., Fodha, M. and Girmens, G. (2007) Recyclage et externalités environnementales. *Revue Économique* 58(3): 609–617.

De Young, R. (1985) Encouraging environmentally appropriate behavior: the role of intrinsic motivation. *Journal of Environmental Systems* 15(4): 281–292.

De Young, R. (1993) Changing behavior and making it stick the conceptualization and management of conservation behavior. *Environment and Behavior* 25(3): 485–505.

De Young, R. and Kaplan, S. (1985) Conservation behavior and the structure of satisfactions. *Journal of Environmental Systems* 15(3): 233–242.

Deci, E.L. (1975) *Intrinsic Motivation*. New York: Plenum.

Dijkgraaf, E. and Gradus, R. (2007) Collusion in the Dutch waste collection market. *Local Government Studies* 33(4): 573–588.

Dijkgraaf, E. and Gradus, R.H. (2003) Cost savings of contracting out refuse collection. *Empirica* 30(2): 149–161.

Dijkgraaf, E. and Gradus, R.H.J.M. (2004) Cost savings in unit-based pricing of household waste. *Resource and Energy Economics* 26(4): 353–371.

Dinan, T.M. (1993) Economic efficiency effects of alternative policies for reducing waste disposal. *Journal of Environmental Economics and Management* 25(3): 242–256.

Dufeigneux, J.-L., Tetu, A., Risser, R., Renon-beaufils, M. and Le Lourd, P. (2003) Rapport de l'instance d'évaluation de la politique du service public des déchets ménagers et assimilés.

Ek, K. and Söderholm, P. (2008) Norms and economic motivation in the Swedish green electricity market. *Ecological Economics* 68(1): 169–182.

Ferrara, I. and Missios, P. (2005) Recycling and waste diversion effectiveness: evidence from Canada. *Environmental and Resource Economics* 30(2): 221–238.

Ferrara, I. and Missios, P. (2012) A cross-country study of household waste prevention and recycling: assessing the effectiveness of policy instruments. *Land Economics* 88(4): 710–744.

Folz, D.H. (1991) Recycling program design, management, and participation: a national survey of municipal experience. *Public Administration Review* 51(3): 222–231.

Folz, D.H. (1999) Municipal recycling performance: a public sector environmental success story. *Public Administration Review* 59(4): 336–345.

Folz, D.H. (2004) Service quality and benchmarking the performance of municipal services. *Public Administration Review* 64(2): 209–220.

Fornara, F., Carrus, G., Passafaro, P. and Bonnes, M. (2011) Distinguishing the sources of normative influence on proenvironmental behaviors the role of local norms in household waste recycling. *Group Processes & Intergroup Relations* 14(5): 623–635.

Frey, B.S. and Jegen, R. (2001) Motivational interactions: effects on behaviour. *Annales d'Économie et de Statistique* (63–64): 131–153.

Fullerton, D. and Kinnaman, T.C. (1995). Garbage, recycling, and illicit burning or dumping. *Journal of Environmental Economics and Management* 29(1): 78–91.

Fullerton, D. and Kinnaman, T.C. (1996) Household responses to pricing garbage by the bag. *American Economic Review* 86(4): 971–984.

Fullerton, D. and Wu, W. (1998) Policies for green design. *Journal of Environmental Economics and Management* 36(2), 131–148.

Gellynck, X. and Verhelst, P. (2007) Assessing instruments for mixed household solid waste collection services in the Flemish region of Belgium. *Resources, Conservation and Recycling* 49(4): 372–387.

Glachant, M. (2003) La réduction à la source des déchets ménagers: Pourquoi ne pas essayer la tarification incitative? *Annales des Mines–Responsabilité et Environnement* 29: 58–72.

Granzin, K.L. and Olsen, J.E. (1991) Characterizing participants in activities protecting the environment: a focus on donating, recycling, and conservation behaviors. *Journal of Public Policy & Marketing* 10(2): 1–27.

Griskevicius, V., Tybur, J.M. and Van den Bergh, B. (2010) Going green to be seen: status, reputation, and conspicuous conservation. *Journal of Personality and Social Psychology* 98(3): 392–404.

Grodzińska-Jurczak, M. (2003). The relation between education, knowledge and action for better waste management in Poland. *Waste Management & Research* 21(1): 2–18.

Grolleau, G., Mzoughi, N. and Thiébaut, L. (2004) Les instruments volontaires. *Revue Internationale de Droit Économique* 18(4): 461–481.

Guagnano, G.A., Stern, P.C. and Dietz, T. (1995) Influences on attitude-behavior relationships a natural experiment with curbside recycling. *Environment and Behavior* 27(5): 699–718.

Hage, O. and Söderholm, P. (2008) An econometric analysis of regional differences in household waste collection: the case of plastic packaging waste in Sweden. *Waste Management* 28(10): 1720–1731.

Hahn, R.W. and Stavins, R.N. (1992) Economic incentives for environmental protection: integrating theory and practice. *American Economic Review* 82(2): 464–468.

Halvorsen, B. (2008) Effects of norms and opportunity cost of time on household recycling. *Land Economics* 84(3): 501–516.

Hart, O., Shleifer, A. and Vishny, R.W. (1996). The proper scope of government: theory and an application to prisons. Technical report, National Bureau of Economic Research.

Hirsch, H.R. and Engelberg, J. (1965) Determination of the cell doubling-time distribution from culture growth-rate data. *Journal of Theoretical Biology* 9(2): 297–302.

Hopper, J.R. and Nielsen, J.M. (1991) Recycling as altruistic behavior normative and behavioral strategies to expand participation in a community recycling program. *Environment and Behavior* 23(2): 195–220.

Hornik, J., Cherian, J., Madansky, M. and Narayana, C. (1995) Determinants of recycling behavior: a synthesis of research results. *Journal of Socio-Economics* 24(1): 105–127.

Iyer, E.S. and Kashyap, R.K. (2007) Consumer recycling: role of incentives, information, and social class. *Journal of Consumer Behaviour* 6(1): 32–47.

Jenkins, R.R. (1993). *The Economics of Solid Waste Reduction: The Impact of User Fees*. London, UK: Edward Elgar Publishing Ltd.

Kinnaman, T.C. (2005) Why do municipalities recycle? *Topics in Economic Analysis & Policy* 5(1): 1–25.

Kinnaman, T.C. (2009). The economics of municipal solid waste management. *Waste Management* 29: 2615–2617.

Knussen, C., Yule, F., MacKenzie, J. and Wells, M. (2004) An analysis of intentions to recycle household waste: the roles of past behaviour, perceived habit, and perceived lack of facilities. *Journal of Environmental Psychology* 24(2): 237–246.

Koford, B.C., Blomquist, G.C., Hardesty, D.M. and Troske, K.R. (2012) Estimating consumer willingness to supply and willingness to pay for curbside recycling. *Land Economics* 88(4): 745–763.

Lake, I.R., Bateman, I.J. and Parfitt, J.P. (1996) Assessing a kerbside recycling scheme: a quantitative and willingness to pay case study. *Journal of Environmental Management* 46(3): 239–254.

Lehmann, P. (2012) Justifying a policy mix for pollution control: a review of economic literature. *Journal of Economic Surveys* 26(1): 71–97.

Linderhof, V., Kooreman, P., Allers, M. and Wiersma, D. (2001) Weight-based pricing in the collection of household waste: The Oostzaan case. *Resource and Energy Economics* 23(4): 359–371.

Lord, K.R. and Putrevu, S. (1998) Acceptance of recycling appeals: the moderating role of perceived consumer effectiveness. *Journal of Marketing Management* 14(6): 581–590.

Loukil, F. and Rouached, L. (2012) Modeling packaging waste policy instruments and recycling in the Mena region. *Resources, Conservation and Recycling* 69: 141–152.

McCarty, J.A. and Shrum, L. (2001) The influence of individualism, collectivism, and locus of control on environmental beliefs and behavior. *Journal of Public Policy & Marketing* 20(1): 93–104.

Nestor, D.V. and Podolsky, M.J. (1998) Assessing incentive-based environmental policies for reducing household waste disposal. *Contemporary Economic Policy* 16(4): 401–411.

Nyborg, K., Howarth, R.B. and Brekke, K.A. (2006) Green consumers and public policy: on socially contingent moral motivation. *Resource and Energy Economics* 28(4): 351–366.

Oskamp, S., Harrington, M.J., Edwards, T.C., Sherwood, D.L., Okuda, S.M. and Swanson, D.C. (1991) Factors influencing household recycling behavior. *Environment and Behavior* 23(4): 494–519.

Owens, S. (2000) 'Engaging the public': information and deliberation in environmental policy. *Environment and Planning A* 32(7): 1141–1148.

Palatnik, R., Ayalon, O. and Shechter, M. (2005) Household demand for waste recycling services. *Environmental Management* 35(2): 121–129.

Palmer, K. and Walls, M. (1997) Optimal policies for solid waste disposal taxes, subsidies, and standards. *Journal of Public Economics* 65(2): 193–205.

Palmer, K., Sigman, H. and Walls, M. (1997) The cost of reducing municipal solid waste. *Journal of Environmental Economics and Management* 33(2): 128–150.

Peretz, J.H., Tonn, B.E. and Folz, D.H. (2005) Explaining the performance of mature municipal solid waste recycling programs. *Journal of Environmental Planning and Management* 48(5): 627–650.

Pieters, R.G. (1991) Changing garbage disposal patterns of consumers: motivation, ability, and performance. *Journal of Public Policy & Marketing* 10(2): 59–76.

Reichenbach, J. (2008) Status and prospects of pay-as-you-throw in Europe——a review of pilot research and implementation studies. *Waste Management* 28(12): 2809–2814.

Rumpala, Y. (1999) Le réajustement du rôle des populations dans la gestion des déchets ménagers. du développement des politiques de collecte sélective à l'hétérorégulation de la sphère domestique. *Revue Française de Science Politique* 49(4–5): 601–630.

Schultz, P., Oskamp, S. and Mainieri, T. (1995) Who recycles and when? A review of personal and situational factors. *Journal of Environmental Psychology* 15(2): 105–121.

Schultz, P.W. (1999) Changing behavior with normative feedback interventions: a field experiment on curbside recycling. *Basic and Applied Social Psychology* 21(1): 25–36.

Schultz, P.W. and Zelezny, L. (2003) Reframing environmental messages to be congruent with American values. *Human Ecology Review* 10(2): 126–136.

Schultz, P.W., Nolan, J.M., Cialdini, R.B., Goldstein, N.J. and Griskevicius, V. (2007) The constructive, destructive, and reconstructive power of social norms. *Psychological Science* 18(5): 429–434.

Sidique, S.F., Joshi, S.V. and Lupi, F. (2010) Factors influencing the rate of recycling: an analysis of Minnesota counties. *Resources, Conservation and Recycling* 54(4): 242–249.

Sterner, T. and Bartelings, H. (1999) Household waste management in a Swedish municipality: Determinants of waste disposal, recycling and composting. *Environmental and Resource Economics* 13(4): 473–491.

Stevens, B.J. (1978) Scale, market structure, and the cost of refuse collection. *Review of Economics and Statistics* 60(3): 438–448.

Taylor, D.C. (2000) Policy incentives to minimize generation of municipal solid waste. *Waste Management and Research* 18(5): 406–419.

Thaler, R.H. and Sunstein, C.R. (2003) Libertarian paternalism. *American Economic Review* 93(2): 175–179.

Van den Bergh, J.C.J.M. (2008) Environmental regulation of households: an empirical review of economic and psychological factors. *Ecological Economics* 66(4): 559–574.

Vining, J. and Ebreo, A. (1990) What makes a recycler? A comparison of recyclers and nonrecyclers. *Environment and Behavior* 22(1): 55–73.

Vining, J. and Ebreo, A. (1992) Predicting recycling behavior from global and specific environmental attitudes and changes in recycling opportunities. *Journal of Applied Social Psychology* 22(20): 1580–1607.

Viscusi, W.K., Huber, J. and Bell, J. (2011) Promoting recycling: private values, social norms, and economic incentives. *American Economic Review* 101(3): 65–70.

Wertz, K.L. (1976). Economic factors influencing households' production of refuse. *Journal of Environmental Economics and Management* 2(4): 263–272.

Yamamota, M. and Yoshida, Y. (2014) Does the NIMBY strategy really promote a self-interest?: evidence from England's waste management policy. In *Handbook on Waste Management* (pp. 171–173). Cheltenham, UK: Edward Elgar Publishing.

8

ECONOMIC EVOLUTION IN CHINA'S ECOLOGICALLY FRAGILE REGIONS

Xiangzheng Deng

Chinese Academy of Sciences

Zhan Wang

*Chinese Academy of Sciences
and Beijing Forestry University*

Chunhong Zhao

Texas State University

1. Introduction

The theory of economic evolution has argued that the endogenous innovation drives economic growth whether or not with a consideration of Location Theory (North, 1955; Solow, 1956, 1957; Arrow, 1962). From the perspective of endogenous innovation, philosophical explanations of economic evolution borrow some basic ideas from either Darwin's natural selection or Lamarck's biological evolution (Hodgson and Knudsen, 2006). In the process of economic evolution, it is debatable that innovations are spontaneous free wills or environmental adaptation for survival. Joseph Alois Schumpeter (1934) proposed that firms' behaviours of the investment of the Research & Development (R&D) reflect the capability of innovations and entrepreneurships, indeed, which are endogenous engines to drive economic growth through a non-linear path back to a series of critical points in a dynamic equilibrium (Schumpeter and Opie, 1934; Nelson and Winter, 1982; Winter, 2003). It indicates that R&D can also lead to inefficient investment (Hunt, 2006). Ahmed (1998) addressed that innovation is also a culture because people who are living in different region create various 'innovation cultures and climates'. In those ecological fragile regions, innovation culture does not only have been distorting abstractive innovation climate but also have statistically significant impacts on natural climate and environmental change in the process of economic evolution (Adger, 1999; Adger *et al.*, 2013; Leonard *et al.*, 2013).

Environmental Economics and Sustainability, First Edition. Edited by Brian Chi-ang Lin and Siqi Zheng.
Chapters © 2017 The Authors. Book compilation © 2017 John Wiley & Sons, Ltd. Published 2017 by John Wiley & Sons, Ltd.

From the perspective of Location Theory, climatic conditions, resource endowments, transportation cost and local culture have been always regarded as constraints of maximizing firms' profits and individuals' utilities, thus, interrupting and reshaping the path of economic growth (North, 1955). Both the autonomous factors and the export based markets directly affect the path of regional development, but the debates on which one is more efficiently has no ending yet (Audretsch, 1998). To explain the capital accumulation in a new business circle, neoclassical theory tries to involve viewpoints of public finance, input–output analysis and Nash Equilibrium (Groves and Ledyard, 1977; Duchin, 1992; Fujita and Thisse, 1996; Fujita and Krugman, 2004). These studies have discussed market failures challenging the rational assumptions of theoretical deduction and induction in classical economics about resource allocation, income equality and complete information. Even so, it is very complicated to delineate a path of regional economic growth. In 20th century, the development of intergovernmental activities, complex studies of climate change and experimental studies on individuals' or firms' behaviours have been strikingly propelled to minimize the potential losses of climate change and lower the uncertainties of socioeconomic behaviours. Such that targets of development are to fulfil sustainable development rather than 'creative destruction' (Gowdy, 2008).

Regional specific impacts of climate change drive global concerns when climatic condition and geographic information have been discussed increasingly to become more important to regional development than before. For instance, a challenge to evolutionary economics is to test and assess uncertain shocks and irrational behaviours that affect economic development from the perspective of Location Theory within social dynamics. Academic debates about these nonmainstream points of views have also drawn attentions widely. Stern's paper, *the economics of climate change* (2006), were fiercely criticized by some mainstream of economists (Nordhaus, 2007; Weitzman, 2007; Dasgupta, 2007), and the paper had been under reviewed for two years before finally published on the *American Economic Review* in 2008 (Stern, 2008). These mainstream economists questioned on how large impacts of climate changes on the discounted intergenerational benefits, income inequality and economic efficiency of regional development. Weitzman (2009) even criticized the uncertainty of estimated results on the economic impacts of catastrophic climate change. Despite all that critical comments were strong enough, empirical studies have provided evidence that the spatial distribution of economic activities has been reshaped by these climatic conditions and geographic characteristics. For instance, Zheng and Kahn (2008) have pointed out environmental amenities as key factors having statistically significant impacts on real estate pricing in urban area of China. In addition, due to specific geographic characteristics of a location, the maladaptive climate of industrial production has led to dense pollution in urban area. For example, coastal cities with high moist and less windy days have high possibility of severe air pollution and poor quality of life (Zheng *et al.*, 2014). Especially, arable land suffering from degradation of natural conditions and other unpredictable natural hazards have led to tremendously economic losses of agricultural production (Deschenes and Greenstone, 2007). In contrast to these negative effects of climate changes, warmer weather with more precipitation benefit to agricultural production in relatively higher altitude mountainous region due to earlier germination than before (Mendelsohn *et al.*, 1994). Thus, beyond the risk management of natural hazards, climatic condition and regional characteristics are critical factors of economic evolution needed to be examined from the perspective of Location Theory.

Location accessibility and transportation cost significantly influence on consumers' choices, so that have inevitable impacts on regional agglomeration (Keebleand *et al.*, 1982; Vickerman *et al.*, 1999; Gutiérrez, 2001). High transportation accessibility fosters commercial trade and promotes multi-level communication among various social groups across different regions. Intuitively, knowledge spillover has close relationship with physical distance (Andersson and Karlsson, 2007). It enlightens that studies on regional economic evolution have to take local characteristics into considerations. Hence, Rietveld (1989) has proposed that infrastructure can be a production factor influencing regional private investments and interregional trades; and, government investment on infrastructure can be an endogenous factor to drive regional economic growth (Albalate *et al.*, 2012). Especially, the urban–rural coordinative development has been stimulated by high standard transportation network (Ozbay *et al.*, 2003). Central Place Theory has emphasized that urban expansion with advanced transportation accessibility absorb peri-urban employments moving into cities; and supervene with cheap contracts of land use and other resources utilization at urban fringes to improve the quality of life in urban communities (King, 1985; Adell, 1999). Thereafter, those close connections prosper economic activities, concurrently import and export local resources for political or military purposes. Hence, regional social norms across different cultures are always challenged by some prejudice and discrimination. Cultural elements within economic evolution have uncertain impacts on regional equality. Under this circumstance, the effects of transportation accessibility for improving regional equality are controversial, and needs to be reexamined for different regions, so that Location Theory reinforces that advanced transportation is a critical role to determine the pattern of regional agglomeration.

Relatively scarcity of resource endowments and their uneven distribution reshape social networks in a stochastic process, so that to maximize firms' profits or individuals' utilities is not a divine guide of economic development (Alchian, 1950; Jackson and Watts, 2002; Martin and Sunley, 2006; Glückler, 2007). Studies on evolution of economic theory, thus, is challenged and developed by both natural-science-based empirical analysis and social-science-based experimental results of irrational behaviours tests (Kelm, 1997). Nevertheless, neoclassical economists still stand for laissez-faire and believe economic evolution is from economic system itself (Lo, 2004). Recall evolution of market efficiency, Samuelson (1952, 1954) has addressed that the tendency of economic growth under the linear assumption prone to a stationary time series, and other supplementary theories have tried to explain and fix the uncertainty of market failure. However, the inequality of market power across different polities generates price discrimination, increase transaction cost, lead to inefficient resource allocation, and fundamentally challenge the grounded assumption of unbounded resource utilization over time. Sen (1977) has stated that there are positive and negative freedoms that devote to social inequality. Because resource-based exporting markets distort the assumption of a close economy, interregional and international free trades actually are not free (Isham *et al.*, 2005). Nowadays, it is straightforward that natural resource is one of the most important production factors discussed by energy economists and climatic scientists (Bosello *et al.*, 2007). Research focuses retrospect the hardcore of economics to study efficiency of resource allocation when market failure breaks through the fairy tale of market efficiency, and to review the policy-oriented or private investment of R&D as a critical role to interpose trade-offs for mitigating potential economic losses (Sethi and Somanathan, 1996).

Theoretical studies have examined the path of economic growth in line with endogenous innovation; while empirical analysis have argued that the effects of the initial level of economic base is also a determinate factor (Andrews, 1953). Nelson and Beyers (1998) have examined western rural area of U.S. experienced population growth in 1990s that illustrates that the traditional natural-resource-based economic base is somehow contributing more than other factors to regional economic growth. In those large developing countries, such like China,

India and Brazil, the economic development of ecologically fragile regions is used to lack of well-planned schemes. As personal per capita income increases, rich people require higher standards of clean water, air and blue sky. Industrial production gradually moves out from cities to rural regions, so that rural regions undertake risks of pollution and environmental degradation and having unexpected impacts on the health of future generation, particularly at urban fringes (Homer-Dixon, 1994). Especially, regional economic development in ecologically fragile regions highly depends on natural resource endowments and traditional economic base. Such that leads to the regional and environmental inequality getting worse than before. In recent decades, global warming rises up world attention to ecosystem and natural environment protection. The studies of the regional planning management of the adaptation response to climate change are looking for the thresholds of environmental vulnerability and ecosystem resilience with consideration of both economic base and regional characteristics (Simmie and Martin, 2010). Richardson (1985) has emphasized that there is a long history of documented reviews on economic base model which are developed towards regional case studies for decision-making of economic development with more considerations of local multipliers and cultural elements.

Economic evolution has cultural preference (Bowles, 1998). Neo-institutional theory proposes to minimize transaction cost to remedy market failure and save economic cost of irrational behaviours (Lin, 2007). In a process of learning-by-doing, local culture has itself market of knowledge and itself evolutionary process (Lin, 2008), which creates a unique path of economic growth involving various components of resource endowments, natural environmental conditions, and idiomatical industries in a specific region (Carlsson and Stankiewicz, 1991). Multinational Corporation towards local marketing strategy has suffered from maladaptive regional culture so that had to pay high cost of 'tuition' to learn how to cooperate with local partners (Hennart and Larimo, 1998; Buckley and Casson, 1998; Alden *et al.*, 1999). In those cultural transitions, social norms have been reshaped by global multi-cultural elements, and that further influence on public opinions (Chatman and Flynn, 2001). However, in various social transformations, some local cultures are not influenced by importing cultural elements, while some others do. The consequence of economic evolution, thus, can be determined by cultural transitions critically, or can influence cultural evolution endogenously.

Given the above information, we aim to study the economic evolution in ecologically fragile regions of China. In the rest of this paper, we will first introduce background information of the study regions in underdeveloped western China; then, geographic characteristics of each region are summarized in Section 3; sequentially, the methodology and data statistics from Google Scholar search engine are described in Section 4; based on comparison of research records, research questions are remarked and analysed in Section 5; and finally, this paper ends by discussion of different cultural stages.

2. Background Information

Ecologically fragile regions of China are almost all located in western China, which cover 6.87 million km^2, accounting for 71.54% of the total area of China. According to China Council for International Cooperation on Environment and Development (CCICED) (2012) Annual General Meeting Report, more than 360 million population including 55 minority ethnic groups inhabit there, accounting for 27.04% of the total population of China in 2011. From the perspective of strategic development, other details of ecological vulnerability of western China are shown in Table 1.

Table 1. Overview of Ecological Vulnerability of Western China.

Resource and energy security	• Accounting for 81.1% of exploitable water resources[2] • All of 171 types of mineral resources • 132 types of mineral reserves have been proven • Accounting for 67% of China's fossil energy • Accounting for 65% of China's renewable energy sources[3]
Ecological security	• Owning 85% of China's national nature reserve areas[4] • Owning 70% of the state-level protected ecosystem and species • Accounting for more than 65% of ecological service value of China[5]
Poverty alleviation	• Accounting for 66% of China's poverty population[6] • Poverty rate is almost 17 times that of the eastern area • 95% of absolute poverty population of China are in minority nationality areas, remote areas, border areas and ecologically fragile area, and these areas are mainly in western region • The illiteracy rate among adults (above the age of 15) is 5.41%, 1.33% higher than the national average[7]
Urbanization	• Urbanization rate is as low as 28.70%, which is 7.52% lower than the national average in 2000; after 10 years development, the urbanization rate had increased to 40.48%, which is still 9.20% lower than the national average.
Industry development	• GDP per capita is 25% lower than the national average • Output of energy and mining industry account for 63.41% of the regional output of industry. • Emissions of the 'three wastes' per 10,000 yuan industrial value-added is 1.1 times more than national level
Transformation of economic structure Domestic demand playing larger role	• Western China is a vast area, with an economy below other parts of China. There is huge potential for expanding regional domestic demand.

Notes: Data source from [1]NBSC (National Bureau of Statistics of China). *China Statistical Yearbook* (2011), Beijing; [2](Kong and Hu, 2003); [3]NBSC (2009); [4](Quan *et al.*, 2011); [5]Ecological Environment Protection Research Center (2009); [6]NBSC (2010); [7]NBSC (2011).

In this study, there are five representative geomorphic units selected from ecologically fragile regions of western China, including 10 administrative divisions: Tibet autonomous region (hereinafter abbreviated to Tibet) and Qinghai Province on the Qinghai-Tibet Plateau; Yunnan Province and Guizhou Province on the Yunnan-Guizhou Plateau; Sichuan Province and Chongqing Municipality in the Sichuan Basin; Shaanxi Province, Shanxi Province and Ningxia Hui Autonomous Region (hereinafter abbreviated to Ningxia) on the Loess Plateau; and Xinjiang Uygur Autonomous Region (hereinafter abbreviated to Xinjiang) as the largest province located at the northwestern corner of China (Figure 1). The total area of these study regions accounts for four fifths of the whole western China.

3. Geographical Conditions

The Qinghai-Tibet Plateau (25°–40°N, 74°–104°E) is surrounded by the Kunlun Mountains, the Hengduan Mountains and the Himalayas, which is the largest plateau in China and the

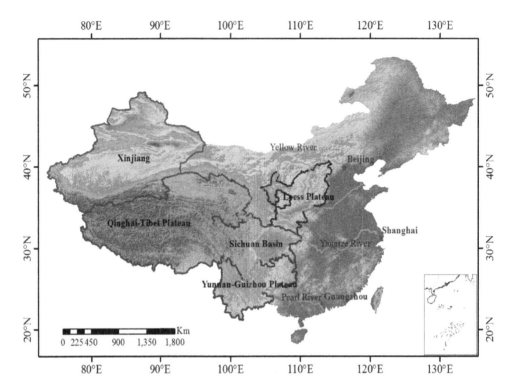

Figure 1. Five Study Regions in a Map of China: The Qinghai-Tibet Plateau, the Yunnan-Guizhou
Plateau, the Loess Plateau, the Sichuan Basin, and the Xinjiang Region.

highest plateau on the Earth. The most part of the Qinghai-Tibet Plateau is located in southwestern China, covering Tibet and Qinghai Province, including a small part of Sichuan
Province, Gansu Province, Yunnan Province and Xinjiang. Due to high altitude, there are less
rainfall and quite dry and thin air solar radiation is relatively strong; and, the temperature is
relatively low with spatial variation mainly because regional climate changes interact with
complex and diverse terrain of microwatersheds. It leads to average temperature in July between 15 and 20 °C which is much lower than other regions' at the same latitude; especially
above 4500 m, the average temperature is below 0 °C, and annually average minimum temperature even around –10 to –15 °C. In general, a maximum of monthly average temperature is still
lower than 10 °C in many regions of the Qinghai-Tibet Plateau (Mo *et al.*, 2004), and the northern Tibet Plateau (the Bayankala Mountain, the Maduo and the Qingshui River and the Qilian
Mountains in Toler) is the centre of frigid highlands with the lowest temperature in China.

   The Sichuan Basin (27–32°N, 101–110°E), the centre of China and the centre of south
Asia, is located in the upstream of the Yangtze River mainly occupied by Sichuan Province
and Chongqing Municipality with a total area of 26 million km^2. The Sichuan Basin are to-
pographically surrounded by connecting mountains at elevation of 2000–3000 m, bordering
on the east of the Qinghai-Tibet Plateau and the Hengduan Mountains; beside the west of the
Mountains of Hubei and Hunan Province; adjacent to the south of the Qinling Mountain across
the Loess Plateau; and, bordering on the north of the Yunnan-Guizhou Plateau. Due to these

topographical characteristics, temperature in Sichuan basin is higher than in other regions at the same latitude. Average temperature in the coldest month is between 5 and 8 °C; and, the minimum temperature is between –6 and –2 °C. The temperature in east side of the basin is higher than the west side, and the south side is higher than the north side. With rare frost and snow, the annual rainfall of the Sichuan Basin is between 1000 and 1300 mm; and, there are abundant precipitations at the edge of the basin where the maximum daily rainfall is between 300 and 500 mm (Li *et al.*, 2015). Moreover, clouds usually stay at relatively low altitude resulting in much foggy and cloudy weather.

The Yunnan-Guizhou Plateau (23°–27°N, 100°–110°E) is the fourth largest plateau with the altitude of 1000–2000 m located in southwestern China. It is adjacent to the Hengduan Mountains on the west side; beside the Sichuan Basin on the north side; next to the Xuefeng Mountain in Hunan Province on the east side; and border on Myanmar, Laos and Vietnam on the southwest corner. Yunnan Province and Guizhou Province are the main part of the Yunnan-Guizhou Plateau. Both regions belong to the humid subtropical zone with the subtropical monsoon climate (except *xishuangbanna* which is the tropical monsoon climate). Climate among micro-watersheds are strikingly different due to the difference of altitude and atmospheric circulation; and the annual temperature is about 12–16 °C varied in terms of the complex terrain (Zhao, 1999), but the difference of annual temperature is moderate because of the relatively warm winters and cool summers.

The Xinjiang Region (35°–50°N, 75°–95°E) is divided into the northern and southern parts by the Tianshan Mountains. The northern Xinjiang has the second largest desert in China – the Gurbantunggut Desert – in the Junggar Basin between the Tianshan Mountains and the Altai Mountains. The southern Xinjiang has the Turpan Depression on the east and the Tarim Basin on the west. The Turpan Depression includes the fourth lowest exposed point on the Earth's surface. The Tarim Basin is between the Tianshan Mountains and the Kunlun Mountains, and inside of which has the largest desert in China – the Taklimakan Desert. Because the Xinjiang is located in deep landlocked region far away from the ocean and surrounded by high mountains, the marine moisture is not easy to enter. Such terrain forms a distinctive temperate continental climate with undulate daytime temperature, long lasting sunshine (annual sunshine time about 2500–3500 hours), less precipitation and dry air. The average annual rainfall in the Xinjiang is about 150 mm with great variation in different areas. The temperature is higher in the south than in the north. In the coldest month (January), the average temperature in Junggar Basin is below –20 °C; and, in the hottest month (July), the average temperature in Turpan is over 33 °C. The Turpan Depression is the hottest and driest area in China, which is so called the 'Fire Island'. The absolute maximum temperature once reached up to 48.9 °C in the city (Gong, 2007), and it was the highest temperature record in Chinese history of meteorological observation.

The Loess Plateau (34°–40°N, 103°–114°E), also known as the Black-Golden Plateau, is covered by the largest number of loess in the world, covering the vast region from the west of the Taihang Mountains to the east of the Riyue Mountain in Qinghai Province, from the south of the Great Wall to the north of the Guanzhong Plain. It is located in China's second-stage ladder of terrain with an area of 620,000 km^2 and the altitude from 800 to 3,000 m, mainly occupied by Shaanxi Province, Shanxi Province, Ningxia Hui Autonomous Region, southeastern Gansu Province, and a small part of northeastern Qinghai Province. The average annual temperature on the Loess Plateau is about 8–14 °C, with a (warm) temperate (continental) monsoon climate. In winter and spring, it is cold, dry and sandy due to the polar air mass; in summer and autumn, it is quite hot and much rainy due to the western Pacific subtropical high pressure and the Indian Ocean low pressure. The average annual rainfall of the Loess Plateau is about 466 mm, and decreasingly spatially distributed from 600 to 700 mm in southeast sub-humid area, to 300 to 400 mm in central semi-arid area, and continually to 100 to 200 mm in northwest arid area. Sixty-five percent of rainfall occurs in summer, and usually 30% of annual precipitation occurs at one-time rainfall, leading to severe soil erosion on the Loess Plateau (Zhang *et al.*, 2012).

4. Method and Data Statistics

A paradigm labelled the 'cluster approach' means that those contrary research results from different research studies are reclassified for pointing out some novel findings or research biases (Light and Smith, 1971). The term of 'meta-analysis' is a comprehensive expansion from the 'cluster approach', which was firstly named to represent the analysis of analyses, as well as to refer to the statistical analysis of a large collection of individual studies' results for the purpose of integrated findings (Glass, 1976, 1984). This method hence has been widely used for natural and social science studies because it emphasizes and summarizes the nuances of previous research findings about a similar or the same research question, objectively examining previous literatures and generally qualifying some conclusions, in order to yield an unbiased conclusion from both quantitative and qualitative summaries of empirical analysis past (Egger *et al.*, 1997). However, the meta-analysis is limited by investigators' preference to the importance of former research studies that result in the new findings still with some subjective judgments or prejudices consequently; not strong enough to be a critical way to draw conclusions that are supposed to be impartial (Bradley *et al.*, 2014). Applications of the meta-analysis in studies of sociology and psychology, hence, call for a restructured and modified approach which is beyond a standard approach because of cultural diversities and cognitive differences across different ethnic groups (Bandura, 2001; Zhao *et al.*, 2007). In this research, thus, we follow a series of steps on reviews and analyses.

(1) To review 'cultural' adaptation to 'climate change' in 'economic evolution' in each case study region, firstly the count number of the searched records on Google Scholar is assumed to represent the degree of innovative knowledge. Hence, we count the number of the combination of these three word groups to present capability of innovation with cultural-oriented adaptation to climate change in economic evolution in each case study region, and then separately compare with the real GDP and the average annual resident consumption (ARC) in available statistical years; thereafter, we question on endogenous innovative knowledge that supposedly has large contribution to economic evolution in ecologically fragile regions of China.

(2) To know relationship between historical climate changes and cultural evolution in each region, each combination including 'climate change', 'cultural transition', and the name of each region is searched on Google Scholar in English separately; and then, records of historical climate change and severe natural hazards are picked up and compared with chronological changes of dynasties in Chinese history.

(3) To understand the critical role of cultural elements in social transformation under the constraints of climate change and geographical conditions, the comprehensive viewpoints of historical literatures are analysed from the perspectives of literature, poem, folk-custom, architecture, art, religion, language, costume, living style, and local cuisine in each case study region.

(4) To further understand cultural trends having impacts on economic evolution, an assumption is discussed that the life-cycle of a culture has itself stages which are involved into the economic evolution. Evidence of indigenous knowledge and regional characteristics that are representatives of different cultural stages responding to climate changes in economic evolution are reviewed and enumerated in this study.

In a short summary of methods, we have modified the 'serious meta-analysis'. Because the Google Scholar is considered as a recommended academic research engine being used by the most of the universities and academic institutes, we adopt counts of records due to the popularity of Google Scholar for collecting papers and articles including patents records and citations at the very first step. It is straightforward to let readers know how few of the relevant research records have been published relevantly to the keywords in those ecological fragile regions of China. In spite of this, these few publications are representing the improvement of civilization apparently presenting the advanced knowledge in human history and published in English at higher ranking journals. We assume the 'documented knowledge' is not always representing human innovation, because cultural transformation and adaptation of natural environment for survival are somehow indeed excluded or being considered as common senses and being accepted that are less important than the innovation of higher advanced technology. We thereby look over the relationship between the performance of economic indicators and the 'culture' elements in the 'documented knowledge' based on the counts of key words (rather than using indicators of education level or other accountable modern cultural indicators proposed by some organizations or programs like UNRISD-UNESCO). If this relationship is statistically significant in 'documented knowledge' according to the analysis, those unobserved cultural changes and adaptive transformation in a long chronological period are inferred more important than we have learnt from the documents (because many western countries have a very short history unlike Ancient China with a long history of various cultural identities from different minorities in the mixed cultural transformation). Furthermore, we test the relationship between 'culture' elements in the 'documented knowledge' and the performance of economic indicators. If it is statistically significant reported by econometric analysis, it will prove that cultural research as a kind of innovation is critical for economic growth, and each region highly possibly has own distinguished culture-labelled adaptation of regional climate change which has different impacts on regional economic growth because of regional culture *per se*.

On Google Scholar, the publications including a word group of 'economic evolution' during past 200 years is about 25,100 records, but merely 10.8% of which are relevant to our study regions, including replicated records across different categories. Table 2 shows the list of the record count of the combinations of these searched word groups; and, the word groups of 'economic evolution' with 'cultural', 'economic evolution' with 'climate change', and 'cultural transition' and 'climate change' account for 60.4% in total.

There are 6,920 records of the combination of the word groups of 'economic evolution' and 'China'; and approximately 3,330 records of the combination of the word groups of 'innovation' and 'economic evolution' and 'China' on Google Scholar; thus, that the total searched word groups about these study regions still occupy about one third of research records of the 'economic evolution' in 'China'. The record count of 'economic evolution' on the Qinghai-Tibet Plateau is the most; of that in the Sichuan Basin is the second most; and sequentially followed in the order are on the Yunnan-Guizhou Plateau, the Xinjiang and the Loess Plateau (See Figure 2).

Table 2. Categorized Record Count of the Searched Word Groups in Study regions on Google Scholar.

Category	Search terms	Records	Percentage
1	'economic evolution' and 'climate change'	205	7.6
1	'economic evolution' and 'cultural'	963	35.5
1	'climate change' and 'cultural transition'	468	17.3
2	'economic evolution' and 'economic base'	47	1.7
3	'economic evolution' and 'location'	906	33.4
4	'economic evolution' and 'natural environment'	87	3.2
4	'economic evolution' and 'resource endowment'	8	0.3
5	'economic evolution' and 'ruggedness'	25	0.9
	Total	2709	100

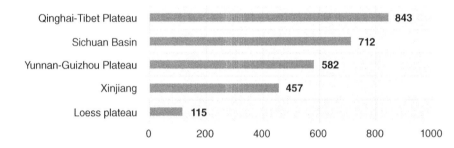

Figure 2. Comparison of the Record Count of the Searched Word Groups in Each Study Regions on Google Scholar.

Comparing the record count of different combinations of word groups in each study region on Google Scholar, we find that regional diversity is quite interesting. With regards to 'economic evolution' the record count of publications including 'climate change' and 'cultural' 'location', or 'ruggedness' on Qinghai-Tibet Plateau are the most, while of that on Loess Plateau are the fewest; the record count of publications including 'economic base' in Sichuan Basin are the most recorded, while of that on Loess Plateau are none; and the record count of publications including 'natural environment' or 'resource endowment' on the Yunnan-Guizhou Plateau are the most recorded, while of that on Loess Plateau are the fewest (See Figure 3).

5. Research Findings

Comparing the ranking order of the record count of the five categories of word groups in each study region on Google scholar to the ranking order of the real GDP in each study region, we find that the Qinghai-Tibet Plateau ranking the highest record count but with the lowest economic production, while it is opposite on the Loess Plateau with the lowest record count but ranking the second highest economic production among the five study regions (See Figures 3 and 4).

The changes of scale and trend of the real GDP in study regions during 1993–2014 are shown on the left-hand side in the Figure 4. The economic performance in the Sichuan Basin is ranking the highest among five regions; which on the Loess Plateau is the second highest; and followed in the order by on the Yunnan-Guizhou Plateau, the Xinjiang and the Qinghai-Tibet Plateau. Whereas, the changes of scale and trend of the average annual resident consumption (ARC)

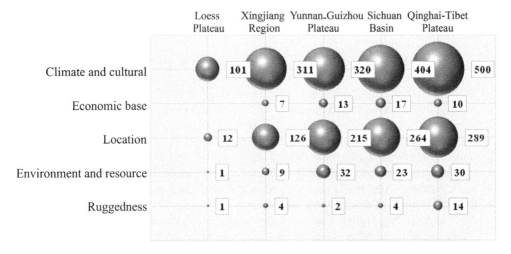

Figure 3. Categorized Comparison of the Record Count of the Searched Word Groups in Study Regions on Google Scholar.

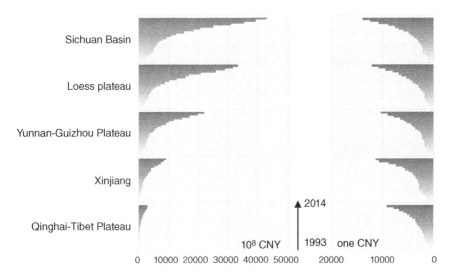

Figure 4. Comparison of the Range of Economic Evolution by Annual GDP (Left) and Average Resident Consumption (Right) in Study Regions, 1993–2014.

(on the right hand side in Figure 4) in all five regions are lower than the national average level respectively. Except on the Qinghai-Tibet Plateau, the changes of scale and trend of ARC in all other four regions are around 10–15 thousands Chinese Yuan. Some remarkable questions are summarized as follows:

i. According to the record count on Google Scholar, the Publications in English including the word group of 'economic evolution' on the Qinghai-Tibet Plateau are the highest number which is much more than that in other ecologically fragile regions of China. However, the actual economic outputs on Qinghai-Tibet Plateau are the lowest in China. If publication records including patents and citations token regional innovation and being highly relevant to economic growth, why 'economic evolution' on Qinghai-Tibet Plateau of China is a contrary case, and other than innovation, what factors determine to regional economic growth;

ii. In the selected ecologically fragile regions, we find that there is a large difference between the highest and the lowest proportion of the regional economic production contributed to the total GDP of China; while it is a relatively small difference from the highest to the lowest of the ARC in each region, and ARC of these regions even tend to be similar. If there is no difference at very beginning of the human history in education among regions individual in each region should have similar social cognitions and economic behaviours. Then, if the average intelligence level of individuals is similar in the study regions, there should be no statistically significant difference of the capability of innovation and creation that contribute to economic growth, and individuals' consumption demands can token their capabilities of that. If these assumptions are correct, it would be reasonable that ARC in other four regions tend to be similar. However, the question is why people in Sichuan Basin have higher level of ARC, and why the record count that to some extent represents the capability of innovation and creation in five regions are different even if they are all in the ecologically fragile regions of China; and

iii. There are the fewest publication records about the Loess Plateau but which has the second highest economic outputs among study regions. Why ARC at there is close to the highest level in the Sichuan Basin and higher than other three regions. If people in study regions have the similar social cognitions and economic behaviours, and endogenous knowledge should be the largest part of contribution to economic evolution, why there are the fewest research records about the Loess Plateau on Google Scholar in English, and what different kind of paths of 'economic evolution' in five study regions happened in documented Chinese history.

5.1 *The Sichuan Basin*

According to the record count of Google Scholar, there are over 56% of records in category 1 including three combinations of key words in Table 3. In the Sichuan Basin, three ancient civilizations in the Baodun ancient city (2500 B.C.), the Sanxingdui ancient city (3000–1000 B.C.), and the Twelve Bridges (or Jinsha culture, 1700–771 B.C.) died out mainly

Table 3. Categorized Record Count of the Searched Word Groups about Sichuan Basin on Google Scholar.

Category	Search terms	Records	Percentage
1	'economic evolution' and 'climate change'		
1	'economic evolution' and 'cultural'	404	56.7
1	'climate change' and 'cultural transition'		
2	'economic evolution' and 'economic base'	17	2.4
3	'economic evolution' and 'location'	264	37.1
4	'economic evolution' and 'natural environment'	23	3.2
4	'economic evolution' and 'resource endowment'		
5	'economic evolution' and 'ruggedness'	4	0.6
	Total	712	100

because regional weather got colder and flood hazards during the first Holocene cold stage (Fu, 2006). Because mountains surround the Sichuan Basin, ancient people in the Sichuan Basin used to migrate back and forth between hillside and the Chengdu Plain. This causes those ancient civilizations dying out from specific location in mountainous regions and move to the places with a relatively lower altitude inside of the Sichuan Basin. For instance, *Bā* ethnic culture started from a branch of Neolithic culture in Ancient China. Until the Spring and Autumn and Warring Stage Period (770–221 B.C.), *Bā* ethnic group was assimilated by *Hàn* ethnic group due to colonization by the Qin Dynasty (770–206 B.C.). A large population growth in the south of the Sichuan Basin started from the Western Han Dynasty (206 B.C. to A.D. 24), and increased twice of population in the Eastern Han Dynasty (A.D. 25–220). This is also supposed to be caused by the weather in the north of Sichuan Basin getting colder during the second Holocene cold stage (Hinsch, 1988). Until the Tang Dynasty (A.D. 618–907), temperature in the Sichuan Basin returned to getting warmer (Ge *et al.*, 2010), but ruggedness of terrestrial surface is still a key constraint of regional economic development. The Poetic Genius in Chinese history, Mr. Bai Li, wrote a poem approximately during A.D. 742–744, *Hard Roads in Shu*, translated into English by an American poet (Bynner and Jiang, 1972), for metaphorizing that 'go into the Sichuan Basin is like to go into the Sky'. Thus, the distinctively geographical conditions form a baronial force having huge impacts on economic evolution in the Sichuan Basin.

Indigenous innovation in the Sichuan Basin made great efforts to economic development. The Dujiangyan Irrigation System was constructed by the Royal Court of the Qin Dynasty during 256–251 B.C., which is the longest still being used irrigation system in Chinese history and the world history, so that has influenced the regional cultivation culture profoundly. Cultivation in the Sichuan Basin can be retrospect back to the Sanxingdui ancient civilization (3000–1000 B.C.). After people moved to the Chengdu Plain gradually, population density inside of the Basin became intense over time, and cultivated land suffering from natural disasters became scare which lead that some of them have to go back to live in some low hill mountainous regions. Minority ethnic group in Chongqing, thus, live on fishing and hunting. Local people were used to wearing simple sackcloth and straw sandals, carrying a bamboo pole balanced on their shoulders to hold necessary provisions for a trip, or to take out local products from the mountains to sell at street market. Because people in Chongqing used to take a bamboo pole or a woody stick, they used to be called *bàng bàng army* that means 'stick army'. Due to the humid weather, local people, like others in many regions of Sichuan, Yunnan, Guizhou, Hubei, and Hunan, prefer to eat spicy and cured food; and, Chongqing is famous for a kind of extreme spicy 'hot pot'. Until 1949, People's Republic of China established, Chongqing was set as a military base and a heavy industry base. Based on this background of strategic development, economic growth in Chongqing was relatively faster than other place in the Sichuan Basin in the past, so that has become a municipality since 1997. In the Sichuan Basin, economic evolution is mainly influenced by population migration and residence shift for struggling with climate changes and geographical conditions. Thus, regional innovation with environmental adaptation in the social transformation is compelled for survival in the Sichuan Basin.

5.2 *The Yunnan-Guizhou Plateau*

According to the record count of Google Scholar, there are over 55% of records in category 1 including three combinations of key words in Table 4. On the Yunnan-Guizhou Plateau, mixed minority culture stimulates regional economic evolution. Yunnan province ranks the number one of the multi-ethnic provinces in China. There are about 25 ethnic groups with a population

Table 4. Categorized Record Count of the Searched Word Groups about *Yunnan-Guizhou Plateau* on Google Scholar.

Category	Search terms	Records	Percentage
1	'economic evolution' and 'climate change'		
1	'economic evolution' and 'cultural'	320	55.0
1	'climate change' and 'cultural transition'		
2	'economic evolution' and 'economic base'	13	2.2
3	'economic evolution' and 'location'	215	36.9
4	'economic evolution' and 'natural environment'	32	5.5
4	'economic evolution' and 'resource endowment'		
5	'economic evolution' and 'ruggedness'	2	0.3
	Total	582	100

of over 4000 people in each group. Guizhou Province is also a multi-ethnic province having 18 ethnic groups. In documented Chinese history, Guizhou Province belongs to China in each dynasty. A few wars happened in Guizhou, and the Sino-Japanese War was the largest in the history. While Yunnan province was conquered by outlanders in each dynasty. Multi-culture in this region facilitates social communication and integration. More interestingly, there were very few inner wars among different tribes among different ethnic groups in the history of Yunnan. The highly possible reason behind that is one of three Ancient Tea Horse Roads passing through Yunnan. This road promotes regional development for selling the Pu'er (or Pu-erh) Tea to Tibet and Beijing. Moreover, each ethnic culture has its own strict disciplines and regulations to precaution moral hazards when facing conflicts of economic benefits. For instance, each ethnic group has its own settlements, specific style of clothes and hair accessories. When public resource needs to be shared, the patriarch of the tribe makes decisions or negotiates with the patriarch of another tribe.

Mountainous and semi-mountainous terrain conditions with climate changes in micro-watersheds foster natural habitats and diverse cultures on the Yunnan-Guizhou Plateau. Yunnan Province is across the north tropic, the south subtropical, the mid-subtropical, the northern subtropical, the south temperate, the mid-temperate, and the north temperate (plateau climate), in total seven climate zones. There are also eight large lakes and over 600 rivers with uneven precipitation severely that causes high geo-risk of debris flow. Local people learn ecological knowledge from their ancestors and believe their faiths can survive their lives, as well as protect their settlements (Zhang, 2011). For example, traditions of the ethnic groups, *Yí*, *Wǎ* and *Dé'áng*, set logging ban in the Longshan forestry where is beside their settlements because they believe deities are living there (Guan and Liu, 2014). These kinds of religions highly influence regional environmental conservation and climate adaptation. In Guizhou Province, there are a plenty of mineral resources in mountainous regions including mercury, barite, sandstone, diabase, phosphorus, bauxite, rare earth, magnesium, manganese, gallium, coal, antimony, gold and pyrite, so that Guizhou is so-called 'Coal-sea in South of China'. Climate also varies in micro-watersheds. There is a local old saying, 'four seasons in a Mountain, different weather in ten miles', to illustrate climatic diversity. In addition, the area of rocky desertification and dry river valley are still expanding, which increases natural hazards and endangers agricultural production (Wang *et al.*, 2004). Ancient *Tǔ* ethnic people in Guizhou, thus, construct houses with stilted fir as feet of the houses on semi-mountain to avoid flooding or mud-rock flows. The

Table 5. Categorized Record Count of the Searched Word Groups about *Xinjiang Region* on *Google Scholar.*

Category	Search terms	Records	Percentage
1	'economic evolution' and 'climate change'		
1	'economic evolution' and 'cultural'	311	68.1
1	'climate change' and 'cultural transition'		
2	'economic evolution' and 'economic base'	7	1.5
3	'economic evolution' and 'location'	126	27.6
4	'economic evolution' and 'natural environment'	9	2.0
4	'economic evolution' and 'resource endowment'		
5	'economic evolution' and 'ruggedness'	4	0.9
	Total	457	100

most of them believe a successful family will bring flourish and prosperity; thus, mixed marriage among minority and *Hàn* ethnic group in mountainous and semi-mountainous regions boost cultural transition (Ran, 2010). This lights up economic evolution through seasonally trading natural resources and absorbing outlanders to settle down in history continually.

5.3 *The Xinjiang Region*

According to the record count of Google Scholar, there are over 68% of records in category 1 including three combinations of key words in Table 5. In documented Chinese history of the Xinjiang Region, human activities occurred in the Neolithic Age. In the Western Han Dynasty (202 B.C. to A.D. 8), it was called Serindia (*Xīyù* in Chinese means the Western Regions). In 138 B.C., the Emperor Wu (156–87 B.C.) of the Western Han Dynasty dispatched envoy Mr. Qian Zhang (164–114 B.C.) to establish diplomatic relation to the countries or tribes in the Western Regions, and to build up the Silk Road. Since the Tang Dynasty (A.D. 618–907), the Xinjiang and its surrounded regions have been governed by Ancient China. Until the Qing Dynasty (A.D. 1636–1912), it was renamed as 'Xinjiang', and then population significantly increased in the Ili City due to military garrison during the Qianlong Emperor (A.D. 1711–1799). In history of the Xinjiang, the pillar industry is animal husbandry. After the People's Republic of China established, the Xinjiang Production and Construction Corps settled down to support local agricultural production. This oasis economic evolution does not only stimulate regional prosperity (Qiao *et al.*, 2009), but also generate social frictions between minority ethnic groups and the Chinese Central Plain Culture (or *Hàn* culture). First, local language is totally different from Chinese mandarin. Public schools of K-12 level teach in Uygur, Han, Kazakh, Kyrgyz, Mongol, Xibe and Russian. Second, over 95% of population is not *Hàn* ethnic group people, and most of them believe some religions including Islam, Buddhism, Lamaism (Tibetan Buddhism), Christianism, Catholicism, Orthodox and Shamanism. There are over 24 thousand temples, and over 98% of them are Moslem temples. Third, their etiquettes and customs are quite different from *Hàn* ethnic group.

Climatic factors have critical impacts on changes of people's mood and behaviours (Kasper *et al.*, 1989). Dry and hot weather with large daytime temperature difference and many windy days foster plenty of luscious fruits and local people's ebullient characters. The weather also impels local preference to wear waistcoats, and women to wear a hood. In ancient time, transportation accessibility is quite low in many regions of the Xinjiang. Horses and camels are the main transportation tools, so that local people prefer to wear boots. This makes identify different ethnic groups easily. Due to dry climate, food is easily to be stored and dried which let the Xinjiang be famous for various dry fruits, such like raisin and dried cantaloupe. Because of lacks of diversity of grains, traditional local food is a kind of very dry pancake, named *náng* in Chinese. After 1949, the Xinjiang Production and Construction Corps enter and garrison the Xinjiang. Their highly productive agricultural productions prosper regional economy, but also lead to income inequality that significantly influence on the social frictions and living style of local people. Urbanization breaks the traditions of 'temple life' and leads to diverse ethos serving to various interest groups, so that reshape the path of regional development. Considering the debates about the positive or negative impacts of local Moslem religion on economic evolution (Abuduli, 2010), we cannot make a conclusion about which culture is superior. However, we can conclude that the unique economic evolution in the Xinjiang follows the traditional inheritance and has been influenced by their own cultural force.

5.4 *The Qinghai-Tibet Plateau*

According to the record count of Google Scholar, there are nearly to 60% of records in category 1 including three combinations of key words in Table 6. On the Qinghai-Tibet Plateau, population is much less than other regions in China due to atrocious weather and physical geographic conditions. In the Tang (A.D. 618–907) and the Song (A.D. 960–1279) Dynasties, Qinghai and Tibet was named *TŭFān* in Chinese which was the first regime on the Qinghai-Tibet Plateau; and they were governed by Ancient China from the Yuan Dynasty (A.D. 1271–1368). From the Qing Dynasty (A.D. 1636–1912) to present, the territory of Qinghai and Tibet almost were not changed in Chinese history. Local Tibetans had been divided into multi-tribes obeying serf system culture from the Tang Dynasty (A.D. 618–907) to A.D. 1951. Local patriarchal culture is mixed with religion of the Tibetan Buddhism, so that the patrician of each tribe held absolute power of institutions in the past. Conflicts between theocracy and democracy had influenced regional political stability all the time. Under this Polity of Caesaropapism, the historical population in Tibet was 0.8 million in total, while Qinghai was near to 1.5 million. After 1949, Qinghai Province has been governed by the P.R. of China; until 1951, the Chinese

Table 6. Categorized Record Count of the Searched Word Groups about *Qinghai-Tibet Plateau* on Google Scholar.

Category	Search terms	Records	Percentage
1	'economic evolution' and 'climate change'		
1	'economic evolution' and 'cultural'	500	59.3
1	'climate change' and 'cultural transition'		
2	'economic evolution' and 'economic base'	10	1.2
3	'economic evolution' and 'location'	289	34.3
4	'economic evolution' and 'natural environment'	30	3.6
4	'economic evolution' and 'resource endowment'		
5	'economic evolution' and 'ruggedness'	14	1.7
	Total	843	100

People's Liberation Army entered in Tibet; until 1965, the present Tibet was established. In recent 50 years, the quality of life represented by the value of the average annual resident consumption (ARC) of Qinghai and Tibet has been improved significantly. According to the statistics of ACR during 1993–2014, local ACR has been close to the level of other regions in ecologically fragile regions of China. Until 2014, population in Tibet reached 3.18 million, and in Qinghai reached 5.83 million.

Mountainous condition and harsh climate limit local people's choices of migration into the Qinghai-Tibet Plateau. Climate change in this region experienced a similar changing process as other regions in documented Chinese history, but with a relatively larger range of changes in temperature and precipitation (Song et al., 2012). The frigid highlands determine cold weather and limit regional economic activities; and we guess there are some relationships between harsh climate and local religious inclination. As similar as in the Xinjiang, the religion in Qinghai and Tibet has both positive and negative impacts on economic evolution and environmental protection. Because of the limitation of cultivation in this region, economic development is highly depending on natural grassland and mineral resources. Animal husbandry hence is the pillar industry until now. Worse than in the Xinjiang, climatic hazards on the Qinghai-Tibet Plateau lead to over 25% of livestock dead before being sold or eaten (Yin et al., 2014). Regional industrialization even did not occur due to immigrations mainly for religious purposes, so that development of advanced technology was deterred. Emigration moved to the relatively low altitude fringes of the Qinghai-Tibet Plateau, and also took their religion and culture to the border regions of Sichuan and Yunnan Provinces. Moreover, Tibetan believe the Buddha and some unknown the Holy Spirit living at the snow covered peak of mountain, so they have never climbed up to the top, even never try to climb, and even to think about that is prohibited in their faiths. These thoughts from some mysterious religions form local esteem to natural resource and environment that to some extent protect ecosystems in many mountainous regions on the Qinghai-Tibet Plateau and the border regions of Sichuan and Yunnan; but also to some extent hinder innovative spirits of scientific exploration, and make outlanders are very hard to be allowed to invest business there. Interestingly, research studies about this region are much more than any other ecologically fragile regions of China, however, we did not find convictive evidence to prove positive relationship between research records and economic growth on the Qinghai-Tibet Plateau.

Local indigenous knowledge is distinctive and obvious. For instance, traditional housing structure has been inherited almost everywhere at Tibetan settlements. The architectural explanation of Tibetan housing has proved that their housing structures are climate adaptation (Zhang, 2008). The flat roof is for absorbing solar energy and keeping warm during night time; and, the edge of eaves and windows are piled with coloured wood for sheltering from rains, and these white or red coloured wood on the wall for striking people from the outside view. Because of the low production of agriculture, the most of Tibetan people eat mutton, beef, buttered tea and zanba; but local people do not eat the meet that was just slaughtered in a day, named nyin sha, because they believe every life has its soul which will leave in a day after it dead, so that they will eat them after a day past. Some of Tibetan living at the east of the Qinghai-Tibet Plateau do not eat fish, snake and frog also because they believe these animals are the embodiments of sacred dragons. Actually, that somehow protects biodiversity in the upstream Yangzi River. In addition, the convention of Tibetan funeral is celestial burial. In their folk custom, people only in upper class can be executed by celestial burial. After they died, their bodies will be cut into several pieces and transported to a specific 'holy' place to wait for wild vultures to eat them all. Specialist Tibetan monks take in charge of this ceremony in every day. We think these folk customs let Tibetan is a part of natural food chain to provision local biodiversity.

To respect of local religions and folk customs, exploration of natural resource on the Qinghai-Tibet Plateau is also restricted by some strategic development policies of the current Chinese government. This shapes the region prone to developing tourist economy, but facing a slow urban growth and an increase of inequality of the quality of life between urban and rural residents. In those far rural regions on the Qinghai-Tibet Plateau, people still rely on pastoral and agricultural production with a low economic efficiency. Comparing to Tibet, Qinghai Province is trying to develop manufacture and absorbing investments in the Golmud City, we will remain concerns about this trend. To short summarize, economic evolution on the Qinghai-Tibet Plateau in documented Chinese history is somehow hindered by local religion and folk customs mainly due to geographic limitation and atrocious climate but obviously preserving regional environment and ecosystem.

5.5 *The Loess Plateau*

According to the record count of Google Scholar, there are near to 88% of records in category 1 including three combinations of key words in Table 7. The Loess Plateau suffers from climate changes in history severely, but is a typical region which has developed in western China successfully. The upstream and midstream Yellow River lie on the Loess Plateau. The upstream Yellow River after flowing down from the Qinghai-Tibet Plateau passes through the south of Gansu Province firstly. There were three times of large deforestation for reclamation in the Qin Dynasty (221–207 B.C.), the Ming Dynasty (A.D. 1368–1644) and the Qing Dynasty (A.D. 1636–1912). This leads to environmental degradation severely, having great impacts on water loss and soil erosion in south of Gansu and north of Shannxi, and also results in local people suffering from extreme poverty in modern history.

Economic evolution in this region has been influenced by mixed effects of cultural evolution in which local culture experienced three stages of development: culture-hindered, culture-mixed and culture-impelled. During the Wei-Jin Period and the Southern and Northern Dynasties (A.D. 220–589), regional climate was cold. There were social chaos with melees among vassal states. After the Tang Dynasty (A.D. 618–907) unified the all vassal states, Ancient China achieved the most prosperous period; interestingly, weather got warmer during

Table 7. Categorized Record Count of the Searched Word Groups about Loess Plateau on Google Scholar.

Category	Search terms	Records	Percentage
1	'economic evolution' and 'climate change'		
1	'economic evolution' and 'cultural'	101	87.8
1	'climate change' and 'cultural transition'		
2	'economic evolution' and 'economic base'	0	0.0
3	'economic evolution' and 'location'	12	10.4
4	'economic evolution' and 'natural environment'	1	0.9
4	'economic evolution' and 'resource endowment'		
5	'economic evolution' and 'ruggedness'	1	0.9
	Total	115	100

that time period. Then, during the Five Dynasties and Ten Kingdoms (A.D. 907–960), climate in Ancient China became cold again, wars among vassal states occurred again (Ge *et al.*, 2014). We cannot reject that continuous wars occurred during cold periods that brought negative impacts on economic growth in history, and that also broke through cultural parclose among different ethnic groups. Typical provinces like the Ningxia was subordinate to Shannxi and Gansu Province in the Qing Dynasty (A.D. 1636–1912), and it became a province until 1957 since many *Huí* ethnic groups have settled down there. Because the Silk Road has been across Ningxia from the Eastern Han Dynasty, regional transportation has been developed which promotes commercial trade and cultural communication, so that mixed-culture has positive impacts on economic development. Skills of agriculture production and engineering of environmental management also push economic growth with technical innovation, such as making glass and planting some imported seeds including pepper, grape, pomegranate and carrot, etc.

Another case study region is Shanxi Province, which has been an important military prefecture since every dynasty of Chinese history, and even so-called the cradle of Chinese civilization. Cultivation culture was documented from ancient Yao time (2447–2307 B.C). According to the latest archaeological findings, researchers infer that the centre of the Yao time was in the south of Shanxi where was also the location of the centre of the Western Zhou Dynasty (1046–771 B.C.) in documented Chinese history. During the Spring and Autumn and Warring Stage Period (770–221 B.C.), Shanxi was occupied by the Jin State (632–349 B.C.), so that its abbreviation in Chinese is *Jìn*. As a rich region in history, population has increased there in two millenniums continually. Agricultural activities hence have huge impacts on regional environment. Soil degradation becomes to impede traditional cultivation. Droughts and plagues of pests even induced chaos and rebellion that consequently led to changes of dynasties (Dai *et al.*, 2009; Fan, 2010). Local people have to live on other business. Until the late of the Qing Dynasty (A.D. 1636–1912), there were many famous merchants holding a large business and formed a new trend of social ethos in mercantilism. They opened *Piào Hào* in large cities, which are similar to those present private banks to support small business, so that boomed national economy at that time.

This kind of pro-business culture actually restrains from environment degradation getting worse and drives economic growth efficiently. After those rich merchants went back to hometown, they built up large houses; thus, Shanxi is the province with the most ancient buildings in China. Even so, those rich people kept a simple living due to their traditional living style with the harsh weather in the past. People in the north of Shanxi eat processed *Avena chinensis*, potato and maize as their staple food because where mainly grow these kinds of plants due to the cold weather; while people in the south usually eat processed wheat, millet and maize. Miscegenation in history has not been limited that somehow facilitates cultural exchanges. Thus, economic evolution on Loess Plateau experienced three stages of cultural transition: culture-hindered, culture-mixed and culture-impelled. Even if the documented innovation records are less than about the Qinghai-Tibet Plateau, economic performance on the Loess Plateau is still higher than other regions in ecologically fragile regions of China because of those undocumented indigenous knowledge throughout cultural evolution.

6. Discussions and Conclusions

In ecologically fragile regions of China, climatic factors and natural geographical characteristics are constraints of economic evolution. In a process of social transformation, local culture adapts and shapes regional environment interactively and dynamically. Innovation throughout cultural transition has involved tremendous indigenous knowledge unpublished on journals or books. This forms traditions of local culture being inherited generation by generation. Genetic facts also illustrated climate adaptation within cultural transition in many species and human ourselves (Smith, 1987; Boyd and Richerson, 1988; Rehfeldt *et al.*, 1999; Rogoff and Ebrary, 2003; Klein, 2009; Boyd and Richerson, 2009; Richerson *et al.*, 2010; Ammerman and Cavalli-Sforza, 2014).

From the record counts in recent 200 years on Google Scholar, we search eight combinations of key word groups to examine economic evolution in each selected part of ecologically fragile regions of China. We find that the climate and culture are the main concerns; then the location ranking at the second place; the environment and resource are placed at the third place; the economic base is at fourth place; and the ruggedness is the lowest. These results match our assumptions that culture and climate are the most important to economic evolution in ecologically fragile regions in modern Chinese history. More interestingly, the number of research records in English which are supposed to symbolize endogenous innovation is not as much as the numbers of real economic performance in modern Chinese history. For instance, higher economic outputs on the Loess Plateau with lower research records in English on Google Scholar, while, the Qinghai-Tibet Plateau has the lowest economic outputs with the most concerns from English world.

To further understand relationships between research records and economic development generally, we also analyse variants of dictators in study regions. By constructing panels, we test whether five categories of innovative knowledge have impacts on real GDP and the average resident consumption (ARC) during 1993–2014, and find some interesting results. See Table 8. In the base model (a), we assume final demand of individuals' consumption determines economic outputs over time; then in the model (b), historical endogenous knowledge of 'economic base' are assumed to be highly relevant to economic growth which drives economic outputs over time; and in the model (c), adaptive 'cultural' response to 'climate change' is assumed to be the dictator for economic growth of regional development. To analyse three models with the fewest bias and the least heteroscedasticity (Shonkwiler and Yen, 1999), three dictators are tested by two instrumental variables: first lag of real GDP and first lag of ARC. Estimations of three models by employing two-stage least square (2SLS) report that the adaptive 'cultural' response to 'climate change' determines real GDP as an engine of 'economic evolution' in the study regions. Therefore, it further addresses that a comprehensive understanding of the adaptive 'cultural' response to 'climate change' is determinate in ecologically fragile regions of China.

By elaborating previous research about study regions, we find that there are three stages of cultural transition in economic evolution in ecologically fragile regions of China. The Qinghai-Tibet Plateau and the Xinjiang region are culture-hindered adaptation in economic evolution to climate change in social transformation mainly due to traditional religions and distinctive folk customs. The Yunnan-Guizhou Plateau is culture-mixed adaptation in economic evolution mainly because multi-ethnic groups coexist under diverse climates in micro-watersheds. The Sichuan Basin is cultural-impelled adaptation in economic evolution to regional environmental change. There people migrate back and forth between mountainous and plain regions mainly for survival under variance of regional climate changes and the ruggedness of geographical conditions. The Loess Plateau has experienced culture-hindered and culture-mixed adaptation due to its important military location and long history of economic base. This forms a distinctive local culture which can self-impel technological innovation through advanced transportation induced multi-cultural communication. The cultural elements are the most important

Table 8. Estimations of Innovative Knowledge in Five Categories on Real GDP in Ecologically Fragile Regions of China, 1993–2014.

	Variable	Code	Model (a) Coef.	Model (a) SE	Model (a) P > t	Model (b) Coef.	Model (b) SE	Model (b) P > t	Model (c) Coef.	Model (c) SE	Model (c) P > t
Dependent variable	real GDP	lngdp									
Independent variable	ARC	lnarc	−0.135	0.1021	0.189	0.207***	0.0639	0.001	0.207***	0.0639	0.001
	cultural and climate change	lncc	−0.512	0.4987	0.306	1.087***	0.3240	0.001	1.087***	0.3240	0.001
	economic base	lneb	−0.681	0.5782	0.240	1.206***	0.3703	0.001	1.206***	0.3703	0.001
	location	lnlc	1.094	0.9788	0.265	−2.072***	0.6314	0.001	−2.072***	0.6314	0.001
	environment and resource	lner	−0.226	0.2095	0.282	0.439***	0.1371	0.002	0.439***	0.1371	0.002
	ruggedness	lnrg	−0.041	0.0467	0.384	0.085**	0.0338	0.013	0.085**	0.0338	0.013
	first lag of real GDP	L1.lngdp	1.102***	0.0792	0.000	0.838***	0.0498	0.000	0.838***	0.0498	0.000
Dependent variable	ARC	lnarc									
Independent variable	first lag of ARC	L1.lnarc	0.984***	0.0141	0.000	0.291	0.2195	0.187	0.411***	0.1057	0.000
	first lag of real GDP	L1.lngdp	0.012	0.0071	0.106	−0.211*	0.1110	0.059	−0.311***	0.0535	0.000
	intercept	_cons	0.158*	0.0851	0.064	1.280	1.3232	0.334	4.849***	0.6374	0.000

Summary statistics:

Model	Equation	R^2	RMSE	F-stat	P
(a)	lngdp	0.998	0.0630	246295	0.000
(a)	lnarc	0.990	0.0647	4806.7	0.000
(b)	lngdp	0.998	0.0550	323031	0.000
(b)	lnarc	0.036	1.0052	1.81	0.167
(c)	lngdp	0.998	0.0550	323031	0.000
(c)	lnarc	0.259	0.4842	16.92	0.000

Variable specification:

Model	Endogenous variables	Exogenous variables
Model (a)	lngdp, lnarc	lncc, lneb, lnlc, lner, lnrg
Model (b)	lngdp, lnarc	L1.lngdp, L1.lnarc
Model (c)	lngdp, lnarc	L1.lngdp, L1.lnarc

Notes: * $0.05 < P \leq 0.1$; ** $0.01 < P \leq 0.05$; *** $P \leq 0.01$.

factor to the economic evolution on the Loess Plateau, which experiences all three stages of cultural transition under the limitations of climate changes and regional characteristics in social transformation. Thus, the real economic performance on the Loess Plateau is higher than the most of ecologically fragile regions in China even if research records in English are less than other regions on Google Scholar.

The implication of this study is that the English world has different preferences from Chinese native researchers which lead to lower research records of the Loess Plateau on Google Scholar. Another explanation is that indigenous knowledge throughout cultural evolution have already solved some real problems and have been applied in daily living before those are documented and published. This argument needs to be figured out in reviews of historical documents of a specific region.

Acknowledgements

Thanks Xi Chu from Hubei University of China for collecting historical documents. This research was financially supported by China National Natural Science Funds for Distinguished Young Scholar (Grant no.71225005), the National Key Programme for Developing Basic Science in China (Grant no. 2012CB955700), and the Key Projects in the National Science & Technology Pillar Program (Grant no. 2013BAC03B03). We sincerely thank the editorial assists from Professor Donald George and Professor Siqi Zheng for finalizing this paper being published.

References

Abuduli, A. (2010). Uighur islamic culture life from the economic perspective. *Social Sciences in Xinjiang* (5): 74–78. (in Chinese)

Adell, G. (1999) Theories and models of the peri-urban interface: A changing conceptual landscape. Available on-line at http://discovery.ucl.ac.uk/43/1/DPU_PUI_Adell_THEORIES_MODELS.pdf

Adger, W.N. (1999) Evolution of economy and environment: An application to land use in lowland Vietnam. *Ecological Economics* 31(3): 365–379.

Adger, W.N., Barnett, J., Brown, K., Marshall, N. and O'Brien, K. (2013) Cultural dimensions of climate change impacts and adaptation. *Nature Climate Change* 3(2): 112–117.

Ahmed, P. K. (1998) Culture and climate for innovation. *European journal of innovation management* 1(1): 30–43.

Albalate, D., Bel, G. and Fageda, X. (2012) Beyond the efficiency-equity dilemma: Centralization as a determinant of government investment in infrastructure. *Papers in Regional Science* 91(3): 599–615.

Alchian, A.A. (1950) Uncertainty, evolution, and economic theory. *The Journal of Political Economy* 58(3): 211–221.

Alden, D.L., and Batra, R. (1999) Brand positioning through advertising in Asia, North America, and Europe: The role of global consumer culture. *The Journal of Marketing* 63(1): 75–87.

Ammerman, A.J. and Cavalli-Sforza, L.L. (2014) *The Neolithic Transition and the Genetics of Populations in Europe.* Princeton University Press.

Andersson, M., Karlsson, C., IHH, N., IHH, Centre for Innovation Systems, Entrepreneurship and Growth, Internationella Handelshögskolan, & Högskolan i Jönköping. (2007) Knowledge in regional economic growth-the role of knowledge accessibility. *Industry and Innovation* 14(2): 129–149.

Andrews, R.B. (1953) Mechanics of the urban economic base: Historical development of the base concept. *Land Economics* 29(2): 161–167.

Arrow, K.J. (1962) The economic implications of learning by doing. *The Review of Economic Studies* 29(3): 155–173.

Audretsch, B. (1998) Agglomeration and the location of innovative activity. *Oxford Review of Economic Policy* 14(2): 18–29.

Bandura, A. (2001) Social cognitive theory: An agentic perspective. *Annual Review of Psychology* 52(1): 1–26.

Bosello, F., Roson, R. and Tol, R.S. (2007) Economy-wide estimates of the implications of climate change: Sea level rise. *Environmental and Resource Economics* 37(3): 549–571.

Bowles, S. (1998) Endogenous preferences: The cultural consequences of markets and other economic institutions. *Journal of Economic Literature* 36(1): 75–111.

Boyd, R., and Richerson, P. J. (2009) Culture and the evolution of human cooperation. *Philosophical Transactions of the Royal Society B: Biological Sciences* 364(1533): 3281–3288.

Bradley, R., Greene, J., Russ, E., Dutra, L., and Westen, D. (2014) A multidimensional meta-analysis of psychotherapy for PTSD. *American Journal of Psychiatry* 162: 214–227.

Buckley, P.J. and Casson, M.C. (1998) Models of the multinational enterprise. *Journal of International Business Studies* 29(1): 21–44.

Bynner, W., and Jiang, K. (1972) The Jade Mountain: A Chinese Anthology, Being Three Hundred Poems of the T'ang Dynasty 841: 618–906. Vintage Books USA.

Carlsson, B. and Stankiewicz, R. (1991) On the nature, function and composition of technological systems. *Journal of Evolutionary Economics* 1(2): 93–118.

CCICED Task Force Report. (2012) *Strategy and Policies on Environment and Development in Western China*, China Council for International Cooperation on Environment and Development (CCICED), CCICED 2012 Annual General Meeting, December 12–14, 2012.

Chatman, J.A. and Flynn, F.J. (2001) The influence of demographic heterogeneity on the emergence and consequences of cooperative norms in work teams. *Academy of Management Journal* 44(5): 956–974.

Dai, J., Ge, Q., Xiao, S., Wang, M., Wu, W. and Cui, H. (2009) Wet-dry changes in the borderland of Shaanxi, Gansu and Ningxia from 1208 to 1369 based on historical records. *Journal of Geographical Sciences* 19(6): 750–764.

Dasgupta, P. (2007) The Stern Review's economics of climate change. *National Institute Economic Review* (199): 4–7.

Deschenes, O. and Greenstone, M. (2007) The economic impacts of climate change: Evidence from agricultural output and random fluctuations in weather. *The American Economic Review* 97(1): 354–385.

Duchin, F. (1992) Industrial input-output analysis: Implications for industrial ecology. *Proceedings of the National Academy of Sciences* 89(3): 851–855.

Ecological Environment Protection Research Center. (2009) *Current status and adaptive strategy of ecological environment in the western region* (in Chinese). China Development Observation, Tsinghua University, 5: 29–33.

Egger, M., Smith, G. D., Schneider, M. and Minder, C. (1997) Bias in meta-analysis detected by a simple, graphical test. *BMJ* 315(7109): 629–634.

Fan, K.W. (2010) Climatic change and dynastic cycles in Chinese history: A review essay. *Climatic Change* 101(3–4): 565–573.

Fu, S. (2006) The ancient shu regional environmental evolution and the study on the relationship between the ancient shu culture (*Doctoral dissertation*, Chengdu University of Technology). (In Chinese)

Fujita, M. and Krugman, P. (2004) The new economic geography: Past, present and the future. In *Fifty Years of Regional Science* (pp. 139–164). Berlin Heidelberg: Springer.

Fujita, M. and Thisse, J.F. (1996). Economics of agglomeration. *Journal of the Japanese and International Economies* 10(4): 339–378.

Gardiner, B., Martin, R. and Tyler, P. (2010) Does spatial agglomeration increase national growth? some evidence from Europe. *Journal of Economic Geography* 11(6): 979–1006.

Ge, Q.S., Zheng, J.Y., Hao, Z.X., Shao, X.M., Wang, W.C. and Luterbacher, J. (2010) Temperature varia-
    tion through 2000 years in China: An uncertainty analysis of reconstruction and regional difference.
    Geophysical Research Letters 37(3).

Ge, Q., Fang, X. and Zheng, J. (2014) Learning from the historical impacts of climatic change in China.
    Advances in Earth Science 29(1): 23–29.

Glass, G.V. (1976) Primary, secondary, and meta-analysis of research. *Educational Researcher* 5(10):
    3–8.

Glass, G.V., MacGaw, B. and Smith, M.L. (1984) *Meta-Analysis in Social Research*. Beverly Hills, CA:
    Sage.

Glückler, J. (2007) Economic geography and the evolution of networks. *Journal of Economic Geography*
    7(5): 619–634.

Gong, X. (2007) Spatial-temporal analysis on variation characteristics and driving factors of desertifica-
    tion in Xinjiang, Urumchi, Xinjiang University. (in Chinese)

Gowdy, J.M. (2008) Behavioral economics and climate change policy. *Journal of Economic Behavior &
    Organization* 68(3): 632–644.

Groves, T. and Ledyard, J. (1977) Optimal allocation of public goods: A solution to the "free rider"
    problem. *Econometrica* 45(4): 783–809.

Guan, C. and Liu, S. (2014) Review of traditional ecological culture of Yunnan ethnic research. *China
    Economist* 7: 60–62. (in Chinese)

Gutiérrez, J. (2001) Location, economic potential and daily accessibility: An analysis of the accessibility
    impact of the high-speed line Madrid–Barcelona–French border. *Journal of Transport Geography*
    9(4): 229–242.

Hennart, J.F. and Larimo, J. (1998) The impact of culture on the strategy of multinational enterprises:
    Does national origin affect ownership decisions? *Journal of International Business Studies* 29(3):
    515–538.

Hinsch, B. (1988) Climatic change and history in China. *Journal of Asian History* 22(2): 131–159.

Hodgson, G.M. and Knudsen, T. (2006) Dismantling Lamarckism: Why descriptions of socio-economic
    evolution as Lamarckian are misleading. *Journal of Evolutionary Economics* 16(4): 343–366.

Homer-Dixon, T.F. (1994) Environmental scarcities and violent conflict: Evidence from cases. *Interna-
    tional security* 19(1): 5–40.

Hunt, R.M. (2006) When do more patents reduce R&D? *American Economic Review* 96(2): 87–91.

Isham, J., Woolcock, M., Pritchett, L. and Busby, G. (2005) The varieties of resource experience: Natural
    resource export structures and the political economy of economic growth. *The World Bank Economic
    Review* 19(2): 141–174.

Jackson, M.O. and Watts, A. (2002) The evolution of social and economic networks. *Journal of Economic
    Theory* 106(2): 265–295.

Kant, S. (2003) Extending the boundaries of forest economics. *Forest Policy and Economics* 5(1): 39–56.

Kasper, S., Wehr, T.A., Bartko, J.J., Gaist, P.A. and Rosenthal, N.E. (1989) Epidemiological findings of
    seasonal changes in mood and behavior: A telephone survey of Montgomery County, Maryland.
    Archives of General Psychiatry 46(9): 823–833.

Keeble, D., Owens, P.L. and Thompson, C. (1982) Regional accessibility and economic potential in the
    European Community. *Regional Studies* 16(6): 419–432.

Kelm, M. (1997) Schumpeter's theory of economic evolution: A Darwinian interpretation. *Journal of
    Evolutionary Economics* 7(2): 97–130.

King, L.J. (1985) Central place theory. *Regional Research Institute, West Virginia University Book
    Chapters*.

Klein, R.G. (2009) Darwin and the recent african origin of modern humans. *Proceedings of the National
    Academy of Sciences of the United States of America* 106(38): 16007–16009.

Kong, X. and Hu, Y. (2003) Superiorities, emphases and countermeasures on development of energy
    industry in China's western region. *Resources & Industries* 4: 49–52.

Leonard, S., Parsons, M., Olawsky, K. and Kofod, F. (2013) The role of culture and traditional knowledge in climate change adaptation: Insights from East Kimberley, Australia. *Global Environmental Change* 23(3): 623–632.

Li, S., Yang, S. and Liu, X. (2015) Spatiotemporal variability of extreme precipitation in north and south of the Qinling-Huaihe region and influencing factors during 1960–2013. *Progress in Geography* 34(3): 354–363.

Light, R.J. and Smith, P.V. (1971) Accumulating evidence: Procedures for resolving contradictions among different research studies. *Harvard Educational Review* 41(4): 429–471.

Lin, B.C.A. (2008) More Government or Less Government? Further Thoughts for Promoting the Government. *Journal of Economic Issues* 42(3): 803–821.

Lin, C.A. (2007) A new vision of the knowledge economy. *Journal of Economic Surveys* 21(3): 553–584.

Lo, A.W. (2004) The adaptive markets hypothesis: Market efficiency from an evolutionary perspective. *Journal of Portfolio Management* 30: 15–29.

Martin, R. and Sunley, P. (2006) Path dependence and regional economic evolution. *Journal of Economic Geography* 6(4): 395–437.

Mendelsohn, R., Nordhaus, W. D. and Shaw, D. (1994) The impact of global warming on agriculture: A Ricardian analysis. *The American Economic Review* 84(4): 753–771.

Mo, S., Zhang, B. and Cheng, W. (2004) The main environmental effect of the Qinghai-Tibet plateau. *Progress in Geography* 23(2): 88–96. (in Chinese)

Nelson, P.B. and Beyers, W.B. (1998) Using economic base models to explain new trends in rural income. *Growth and Change* 29(3): 295–318.

Nelson, R.R. and Winter, S.G. (1982) The Schumpeterian tradeoff revisited. *The American Economic Review* 72(1): 114–132.

Nelson, R.R. and Winter, S.G. (2002) Evolutionary theorizing in economics. *Journal of Economic Perspectives* 16(2): 23–46.

Nordhaus, W.D. (2007) A review of the stern review on the economics of climate change. *Journal of Economic Literature* 45(3): 1.

North, D.C. (1955) Location theory and regional economic growth. *The Journal of Political Economy* 63(3): 243–258.

Oxley, L. (1994) Cointegration, causality and Wagner's Law: A test for Britain 1870–1913. *Scottish Journal of Political Economy* 41(3): 286–298.

Ozbay, K., Ozmen-Ertekin, D. and Berechman, J. (2003) Empirical analysis of relationship between accessibility and economic development. *Journal of Urban Planning and Development* 129(2): 97–119.

Qiao, X., Yang, D. and Zhang, X. (2009) Evolution stages of oasis economy and its dependence on natural resources in Tarim River Basin. *Chinese Geographical Science* 19(2): 135–143.

Quan, J., Ouyang, Z., Xu, W. and Miao, H. (2011) Assessment of the effectiveness of nature reserve management in China. *Biodiversity and Conservation* 20(4): 779–792.

Ran, G. (2010) Guizhou history of immigration and family ethics in the Ming dynasty research. Doctoral dissertation, Fudan University. (in Chinese)

Rehfeldt, G.E., Ying, C.C., Spittlehouse, D.L. and Hamilton, D.A. Jr (1999) Genetic responses to climate in Pinus contorta: Niche breadth, climate change, and reforestation. *Ecological Monographs* 69(3): 375–407.

Richardson, H.W. (1985) Input-output and economic base multipliers: Looking backward and forward. *Journal of Regional Science* 25(4): 607–661.

Richerson, P.J., Boyd, R. and Henrich, J. (2010) Gene-culture coevolution in the age of genomics. *Proceedings of the National Academy of Sciences* 107(Supplement 2): 8985–8992.

Rietveld, P. (1989) Infrastructure and regional development. *The Annals of Regional Science* 23(4): 255–274.

Rindos, D., Carneiro, R.L., Cooper, E., Drechsel, P., Dunnell, R.C., Ellen, R.F. and Boyd, R. (1985) Darwinian selection, symbolic variation, and the evolution of culture [and Comments and Reply]. *Current Anthropology* 26(1): 65–88.

Robson, A.J. (1995) The evolution of strategic behaviour. *Canadian Journal of Economics* 28(1): 17–41.

Rogoff, B. and Ebrary, I. (2003) *The cultural nature of human development*. Oxford, New York: Oxford University Press.

Roos, M.W. (2005) How important is geography for agglomeration? *Journal of Economic Geography* 5(5): 605–620.

Samuelson, P.A. (1952) Spatial price equilibrium and linear programming. *The American Economic Review* 42(3): 283–303.

Samuelson, P.A. (1954) The pure theory of public expenditure. *The Review of Economics and Statistics* 36(4): 387–389.

Schumpeter, J.A., and Opie, R. (1934) *The Theory of Economic Development: An Inquiry into Profits, Capital, Credit, Interest, and the Business Cycle*, Cambridge, Mass: Harvard University Press.

Sen, A.K. (1977) Rational fools: A critique of the behavioral foundations of economic theory. *Philosophy & Public Affairs* 6(4): 317–344.

Sethi, R. and Somanathan, E. (1996) The evolution of social norms in common property resource use. *The American Economic Review* 86(4): 766–788.

Shonkwiler, J.S. and Yen, S.T. (1999) Two-step estimation of a censored system of equations. *American Journal of Agricultural Economics* 81(4): 972–982.

Simmie, J. and Martin, R. (2010) The economic resilience of regions: Towards an evolutionary approach. *Cambridge Journal of Regions, Economy and Society* 3(1): 27–43.

Smith, E.A. (1987) Culture and the evolutionary process. robert boyd, peter J. richerson. *American Anthropologist* 89(1): 203–205.

Solow, R.M. (1956) A contribution to the theory of economic growth. *The Quarterly Journal of Economics* 70(1): 65–94.

Solow, R.M. (1957) Technical change and the aggregate production function. *The Review of Economics and Statistics* 39(3): 312–320.

Song, C., Pei, T. and Zhou, C. (2012) Review of the Qinghai-Tibet Plateau temperature changes Since 1960. *Progress in Geography* 31(11): 1503–1509. (In Chinese)

Stern, N. (2008) The economics of climate change. *The American Economic Review* 98(2): 1–37.

Stern, N.H. (2006) *Stern Review: The Economics of Climate Change*, Vol. 30. London: HM Treasury.

Vickerman, R., Spiekermann, K. and Wegener, M. (1999) Accessibility and economic development in Europe. *Regional Studies* 33(1): 1–15.

Wang, S.J., Liu, Q.M. and Zhang, D.F. (2004) Karst rocky desertification in southwestern China: Geomorphology, landuse, impact and rehabilitation. *Land Degradation & Development* 15(2): 115–121.

Weitzman, M.L. (2007) A review of the Stern Review on the economics of climate change. *Journal of Economic Literature* 45(3): 703–724.

Weitzman, M.L. (2009) On modeling and interpreting the economics of catastrophic climate change. *The Review of Economics and Statistics* 91(1): 1–19.

Winter, S.G. (2003) Understanding dynamic capabilities. *Strategic Management Journal* 24(10): 991–995.

Yin, F., Deng, X., Jin, Q., Yuan, Y. and Zhao, C. (2014) The impacts of climate change and human activities on grassland productivity in Qinghai Province, China. *Frontiers of Earth Science* 8(1): 93–103.

Zhang, C., Ren, Z. and Li, X. (2012) The loess plateau vegetation response to temperature and rainfall. *Scientia Agricultura Sinica* 45(20): 4205–4215. (in Chinese)

Zhang, W. (2011) Yunnan ethnic customs and habits of environmental protection. *Legal System and Society* 6: 200. (in Chinese)

Zhang, Y. (2008) Tibetan traditional residential building climate suitability study. Doctoral dissertation, Xi'an University of Architecture and Technology.

Zhao, H.A.O., Wayne, S.J., Glibkowski, B.C. and Bravo, J. (2007) The impact of psychological contract breach on work-related outcomes: A meta-analysis. *Personnel Psychology* 60(3): 647–680.

Zhao, J. (1999) *Geography of Mainland China* (581 pp). Beijing: Higher Education Press. (In Chinese)

Zheng, S. and Kahn, M.E. (2008) Land and residential property markets in a booming economy: New evidence from Beijing. *Journal of Urban Economics* 63(2): 743–757.

Zheng, S., Sun, C., Qi, Y. and Kahn, M.E. (2014) The evolving geography of China's industrial production: Implications for pollution dynamics and urban quality of life. *Journal of Economic Surveys* 28(4): 709–724.

9

GLOBALIZATION AND CLIMATE CHANGE: NEW EMPIRICAL PANEL DATA EVIDENCE

Maoliang Bu

Nanjing University
School of Business & Hopkins-Nanjing Center

Chin-Te Lin

Université Paris 1 Panthéon Sorbonne
Graduate School of Mathematics

Bing Zhang

State Key Laboratory of Pollution Control and Resource Reuse
School of the Environment
Nanjing University & School of Government
Nanjing University

1. Introduction

In recent years, globalization and its effects on the environment have garnered enormous attention in connection with the heated debate over the so-called 'pollution haven hypothesis (PHH)', which argues that pollution-intensive industries will move from developed countries with stringent environmental regulations to developing countries with lax environmental regulations (Eskeland and Harrison, 2003; Copeland and Taylor, 2004; Bu *et al.*, 2011; Cole *et al.*, 2011). As a phenomenon, globalization has thus far proven to be too complicated to be examined through the lens of any single of its facets (such as its economic, cultural and political facets), thus indicating that a multi-angle spatial vision must be constructed (Held, 1999; Held and McGrew, 2003).

Previous studies of this subject in the economics literature have generally suffered from two main constraints. First, most studies rarely consider a sufficiently large number of countries, with most samples consisting of one or a few countries that do not provide a general global picture. Second, regarding the dimension of globalization, nearly all the studies take the form

Environmental Economics and Sustainability, First Edition. Edited by Brian Chi-ang Lin and Siqi Zheng.
Chapters © 2017 The Authors. Book compilation © 2017 John Wiley & Sons, Ltd. Published 2017 by John Wiley & Sons, Ltd.

of either trade or foreign direct investment (FDI), and dimensions of globalization other than economic globalization have been largely ignored (Frankel, 2003).

FDI has been in the spotlight with regard to economic globalization because of the importance attributed to greenhouse gas (GHG) emissions and global warming. Held (1999) describes globalization as a historical process that transforms the spatial organization of social relations and transactions by developing transcontinental or interregional networks of interactions through which power is exercised. However, Albrow (1996) sees globalization in the spillovers of various actions, values, technology and products, which implies that – beyond economic globalization – the international political and organizational struggle and cross-cultural broadcasting are imperceptibly transforming our environment on a certain level through political and social globalization.

Pollution issues cannot be assessed from a single perspective. Since the mid-1980s, globalization has been associated with a remarkable growth in the level of popular concerns for political, economic and sociocultural issues – including pollution – on a global basis due to accelerated economic growth, intimate regional cooperation and widespread cultural broadcasting. Among the concerns, Rodrik and Wacziarg (2005) indicate that political institutions play a key role in global negotiations and have been recognized to exert an important influence on world economic growth. This recognition has attracted more attention to the link between political pluralism and economic liberalization and development, which may have led to increased pollution levels based on all the linkages. At approximately the same time, environmental reforms (mainly in OECD countries) also began to detach economic growth from intensifying environmental or ecological disruptions, which served to enable economic growth in some cases despite an absolute decline in resource consumption and pollution. In transition economies (mainly non-OECD countries), only an improving democracy has a significant effect on political and economic conditions (Rodrik and Wacziarg, 2005), which may lead to better environmental quality.

Generally, globalization not only eliminates border barriers around the world through its own pluralism but also liberalizes the circulation of investment and sociopolitical flows. However, while higher levels of globalization can mean the advancement of our society, it can also lead to environmental degradation. Because climate change is considered a challenge to our future development, an increasing amount of research has focused on untangling the relationship between the environment and how the multiple aspects of globalization affect different types of FDI and firms' relocation choices – how technological and knowledge spillovers work in more than just an economic sense. However, it has thus far been difficult to understand the extent to which environmental quality is influenced by the current wave of social and political globalization.

Some research has intended to include political concerns – at least partially. For example, Barrett and Graddy (2000) find that increases in civil and political freedoms significantly improve environmental quality, and Fredriksson and Mani (2004) find that the combination of trade integration and political stability enhances the stringency of environmental regulation. Nonetheless, few researchers have explored globalization using a comprehensive analysis.

This paper aims to rectify this deficiency in the literature by integrating the theoretical principles developed by Grossman and Krueger (1991) with empirical panel data evidence and the new KOF globalization index. Adopting a panel data sample of 166 countries from 1990 to 2009, our results suggest that, on average, increased carbon emissions move in tandem with higher levels of economic, social and political globalization and that this effect varies by OECD and non-OECD country group. Further evidence reveals this coordinated relationship after we decompose the major contributors of carbon emissions to identify emissions from the manufacturing and construction sector. We therefore provides consistent evidence and further discussion of pollution haven effects in terms of climate change.

The remainder of this paper is organized as follows. Section 2 presents a literature review of pollution haven studies and the analysis framework. Section 3 presents our basic empirical strategy, including the model, the data and our instrumental variable (IV) method. Section 4 explains and discusses the estimation results. The conclusions are presented in Section 5.

2. Literature Review and Analytical Framework

2.1 *Literature Review*

Sanna-Randaccio (2012) summarizes the conclusions of several papers and indicates that the importance of low-carbon FDI from developed countries and emission-saving technology from multinational enterprises (MNEs) may improve the environmental quality in non-OECD countries by easing the degradation related to climate change. Thus far, empirical research (e.g., Frankel, 2009) based on cross-country data finds no support for pernicious effects of trade with certain measures of environmental degradation. In another summary of empirical studies, Erdogan (2014) indicates that empirical studies have not found widespread support for pollution haven effects that are triggered by FDI flows from developed to developing countries. The empirical evidence does suggest that trade and growth will lead to degradation of some environmental measures, but carbon emissions may be an exception. A number of pioneering papers by John List and a series of researchers have explored the time series properties of many types of pollutants to test the convergence of pollution levels across states and countries. Thus, Strazicich and List (2003) examine the convergence properties of carbon emissions over a panel dataset of 21 industrial countries from 1960 to 1997 and find evidence that carbon emissions patterns have converged. Brock and Taylor (2010) reinvestigate the Environmental Kuznets Curve (EKC) with a modified approach and connect the EKC to the Solow model. Using carbon emission data from 173 countries over the pre-Kyoto period, that is, 1960–1998, the evidence developed by Brock and Taylor (2010) also provides an answer for current disputes regarding the EKC and carbon emissions, as well as other pollutants. Some researchers believe that differences in carbon emissions evidence emerge because carbon emissions are an externality that can be addressed only at the global level (and not at the national level) because of free rider problems. Thus, institutions of governance are necessary at the multinational level, and these have not been in place until the recent wave of globalization.

As a result, globalization, economic growth and the environment may not necessarily be in conflict. Air pollution problems require both an adequate level of income and an effective mechanism of supervision and governance. Thus, externalities such as GHG emissions and other air pollutants are likely the consequence of global interactions. National governments cannot address these types of externalities on an individual basis but only with a global mechanism. Our research contributes mainly by attempting to provide a general overview to elucidate these problems and to show how globalization is linked to environmental problems and the heated debates involving carbon emissions.

2.2 *Analysis Framework*

The pioneering work by Grossman and Krueger (1991) is central to this paper. It not only led to a subsequent burgeoning literature on the EKC but also developed a convention of decomposing trade's influence on the environment into three categories of effects: technological, scale

Table 1. Theoretically Predicted Effects of Globalization on the Environment.

	Economic globalization	Social globalization	Political globalization
Technology effect	+	+	?
Scale effect	–	?	?
Composition effect	+/–	?	?
Overall	?	?	?

Note: +/–/? stand for positive/negative/unknown effect, respectively. The table integrates the author's work with Grossman and Krueger (1991).

and compositional. These three categories are assumed to have positive, negative and unknown effects on the environment, respectively. Within this framework, beyond economic globalization, we integrate other dimensions of globalization, including social globalization and political globalization as we move toward an analysis of globalization's effects on the environment. The theoretical predictions of the effects of globalization on the environment are summarized in Table 1. First, with economic globalization, the effects are straightforward and are similar to those addressed in Grossman and Krueger (1991). Second, social globalization, as defined in the KOF index, indicates increasing linkages among international news, books, McDonalds, and the Internet. It is a process through which more international social integration might generate more environmental technology spillovers that lead to better environmental quality. Meanwhile, this process also brings changes in lifestyle and consumption from developed to developing countries that are not necessarily environment or carbon friendly. Third, political globalization, which is often ignored by economists, directly impacts how international institutions work and bring about change (e.g., the international conferences on climate change).

Given that the mechanisms for why and how social and political globalization affect carbon emissions are less straightforward than those for economic globalization, further explanations based on previous studies must be explored. With regard to social globalization, there are at least three alternative but non-exclusive theoretical explanations, namely, transportation, lifestyle changes and technology spillovers. First, as critical drivers of globalization, transport systems (as one important component of social globalization) have contributed greatly to carbon emissions. Taking the example of air transport, between 1990 and 2004, GHG emissions from aviation increased by 86%. In the case of India, between 2005 and 2007, domestic airline companies ordered a total of 500 new airplanes from aircraft manufacturers Airbus and Boeing to cover new travel needs. Second, given limited natural resources, environmentalists have long warned developing and transition countries about trying to emulate Western lifestyles. However, due to the wave of social globalization, the South has actually been catching up to the North in terms of lifestyle, even though the income gap between the South and the North has not significantly decreased. These lifestyle changes are often associated with deforestation, which makes carbon emissions even worse. Third, unlike the previous two mechanisms, social globalization can also be positively related to reductions in carbon emissions, such as through technology spillovers. That is, more personal contacts and information flows stimulate more spillovers of environmental friendly technologies. In addition, such changes also bring more environmental awareness to developing countries. For example, since Beijing Olympic Games (a good example of social globalization), the Chinese authorities introduced a partial ban on car traffic in the city.

With regard to the mechanisms for political globalization's effects on carbon emissions, political scientists have gradually included climate politics in mainstream political science research (Bernauer, 2013). Spilker (2012a, 2012b) suggests three mechanisms for how membership in intergovernmental organizations (IGOs) impacts the environmental performance of developing countries. First, at least in principle, IGOs can compel member states to obey their rules by raising the reputational stakes for reneging on agreements. Second, IGOs create norms that define good behaviour – and what constitutes bad conduct. Third, although countries become members of an IGO for specific reasons, for example, financial assistance, they are also exposed to the other purposes of the organization, such as environmental protection. For example, by joining the Association of Southeast Asian Nations (ASEAN) in 1997, Laos was required to implement a number of agreements pertaining to making agri-economic development more sustainable, which as a side effect positively affected Laos's environment. When applying the above three mechanisms to the specific issue of carbon emissions, however, we must remember the differences between developed and developing countries. Taking the Kyoto Protocol as an example, the Annex I Parties with carbon reduction targets are generally developed countries, while developing countries generally do not have carbon reduction targets. Given this difference, it is not diffucult to understand the recent report by the International Energy Agency (IEA) stating that the carbon dioxide (CO_2) emissions of developing countries "increased at a much faster rate" than the CO_2 emissions of industrialized countries.

To summarize, the influence of social and political globalization on climate change deserves at least equal attention as economic globalization. To some extent, economic integration can actually be regarded as the result of political arrangements and social/cultural proximity. Balli and Pierucci (2015) highlight the role of political and social globalization in the following question: if political and social globalizations are taken into account, does economic integration still play a role? Although our paper investigates the three aspects of globalization separately, it will be interesting to compare the extent of each. We will return to this point later when we discuss the empirical results.

Therefore, using the globalization index (KOF), we hope to present a fresh perspectives on how developed and developing countries compete and interact with one another under the framework of globalization. We intend to discuss the heated debates on pollution havens in combination with the multi-faceted aspects of globalization and other hypotheses addressed by economists, sociologists and political scientists.

3. Empirical Strategy

3.1 Model

Following Grossman and Krueger (1991), we begin by estimating the following reduced-form equation for the time variation with countries to identify the effects of globalization on the environment. We predict outwards to see whether income will converge by controlling income per capita and its square term. The panel data model is a time-variant model that explains pollutant emissions in country i and period t by:

$$Epc_{it} = \gamma_i + \theta_t + \beta_1 Y_{it} + \beta_2 Y_{it}^2 + \beta_3 Gindex_{it} + \beta_4 Economic\ structure_{it} + \varepsilon_{it} \qquad (1)$$

where Epc is per capita pollutant emissions denoting the pollutant emission variable, γ represents country-specific intercepts, θ represents time-specific intercepts, and economic structure

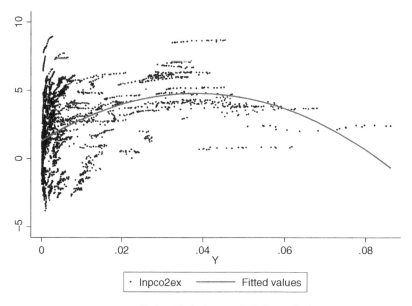

Figure 1. Carbon Emissions and GDP per Capita.

Note: The figure shows the relationship between carbon emissions and GDP per capita with full sample. The left axis indicates the emissions level of CO_2 in logarithm.

represents the manufacturing value added to the GDP to capture the structural change over time and Y represents per capita GDP in logarithms of constant year US \$. The square term of Y is also included in the model following the classic setting of the Environmental Kuznets Curve which is an inverted U shape. The scatterplot for carbon emissions and GDP per capita is presented in Figure 1, which intuitively supports the inverted U shape instead of a N or S shape.[1]

Gindex refers to the level of globalization using the KOF index, which is based on 23 variables that relate to the different dimensions of overall globalization in 207 countries (we consider the overall globalization index for 161 countries, the economic globalization sub-index for 135 countries, the social globalization sub-index for 163 countries and the political globalization sub-index for 166 countries). The overall index and the sub-indices assume values scaled from 1 (minimum globalization) to 100 (maximum globalization). The 2015 KOF globalization index is available for the 1970–2011 period. These 23 variables are consolidated into six groups, and the groups are further combined into three sub-indices and one overall index of globalization in reasonable percentages derived using an objective statistical method (Dreher 2006; Dreher and Gaston, 2008; Dreher *et al.*, 2008b). In this research, we adopt the 1990–2009 data to examine globalization's effect on pollutant emissions. The three sub-indices of globalization lead us to the following equation:

$$Epc_{it} = \gamma_i + \theta_j + B_1 Y_{it} + B_2 Y_{it}^2 + B_3 Sub\text{-}index_{it} + \beta_4 Economic\ structure_{it} + \varepsilon_{it} \quad (2)$$

where *Sub-index* refers to the level of economic globalization, social globalization or political globalization, respectively and separately.

According to the KOF index, these types of globalization are defined as follows:

- *Economic globalization* is characterized as two main group variables: (i) actual flows (trade, foreign direct investment, portfolio investment, and income payment to foreign nationals) and (ii) restrictions (hidden import barriers, mean tariff rate taxes on international trade, and capital restrictions).
- *Social globalization* includes three groups of variables: (i) data on personal contacts (telephone traffic, transfers, international tourism, foreign population, international letters), (ii) data on information flows (internet users, television, trade in newspapers) and (iii) data on cultural proximity (number of McDonald's restaurants, number of IKEA stores, trade in books).
- *Political globalization* is characterized by four different variables: embassies in foreign countries, national membership in international organizations, participation in U.N. Security Council Missions, and international treaties.

3.2 *Data Resource and Descriptive Statistics*

The data source for *Epc* is from Climate Data Explorer (World Resources Institute, 2015), which provides comprehensive data on greenhouse gas emissions.[2] Given the accessibility of data we adopt three different measurements for the dependent variable (*Epc*): overall GHGs, overall CO_2 and CO_2 from the manufacturing and construction sector. The relationship between these three measures can be described as follow. According to the database, CO_2 emissions is the major component of overall GHG emissions, which consists of four different types of emissions, with total CO_2 at 73% on the average and the rest at 27% (overall totals of CH_4, N_2O and F-gas). Moreover, as for CO_2 emissions itself, three sectors produce the majority, of emissions, namely, transportation (22%), electricity and heat (42%), manufacturing and construction (19%). Because the manufacturing and construction sector is more associated with the pollution haven effect, we therefore focus on this sector to test the effect.

Table 2 reports the data sources and the descriptive statistics for two country subgroups. We use two country subgroups for the 1990–2009 period (see the Appendix Table A1 for countries includ in this research) for two reasons: first, this research tries to examine how long the period of globalization after the 1980s affected the environment; second, previous research mainly addressed the carbon emissions problem in the pre-Kyoto period (before 1998). Frankel (2009) suggests that since the common view of a series of international environmental protocols settled down, we might observe the influence among all countries by considering an extended time period after 2000. In Figure 2, we show the relationship between GHG emissions and the overall globalization index in a subsample. In most cases, our findings indicate that comparatively lower globalization levels with higher pollutant emissions characterize the majority of non-OECD countries, with a correlation coefficient of 0.41.

3.3 *Instrumental Variable Method*

Since the globalization index may be endogenous in the FE estimation, the instrumental variable method is adopted to tackle this issue. Following Felbermayr and Gröschl (2013) and Eppinger and Potrafke (2016), we use the exogenous component of trade openness predicted by geography and natural disasters as an IV for globalization variables in our model.

Table 2. Variable Definitions and Descriptive Statistics.

Variable	Definitions & source	OECD countries (n = 24)					Non-OECD countries (n = 142)			
		Mean	Std. Dev.	Min	Max	Obs.	Std. Dev.	Min	Max	Obs.
Overall globalization (1990–2009)	Dreher (2006) and Dreher et al. (2008b)	75.32	14.78	29.67	92.50	480	15.21	11.47	92.38	2948
Economic globalization (1990–2009)	Dreher (2006) and Dreher et al. (2008b)	72.96	14.19	19.59	95.62	460	17.43	9.94	99.16	2413
Social globalization (1990–2009)	Dreher (2006) and Dreher et al. (2008b)	71.79	19.07	8.38	93.68	480	19.29	6.95	93.16	2988
Political globalization (1990–2009)	Dreher (2006) and Dreher et al. (2008b)	85.79	13.52	14.19	98.26	480	22.34	1	98.43	3048
Ln(GDP per capita)	(Million constant (2005) US$), WDI 2015	10.37	0.48	8.51	11.36	480	1.34	3.91	10.96	2952
Ln(GDP square per capita)	(Million constant (2005) US$),	107.79	9.65	72.42	129.13	480	20.71	15.30	120.326	2952
	WDI 2015									
Ln(Greenhouse gas)	MtCo2e, CIAT	5.16	1.58	1.01	8.83	460	2.12	-3.33	9.13	3027
Ln(CO_2 emission)	MtCo2, CIAT	4.83	1.63	0.64	8.67	480	2.42	-3.81	8.93	3075
Ln(Manufacturing & construction)	MtCo2, CIAT	3.09	1.57	-0.77	6.55	480	2.10	-4.61	7.71	2095
Economic structure	Manufacturing, value added (% of GDP) WDI 2015	17.28	4.45	5.25	30.23	442	7.81	0	43.54	2559
Predicted trade openness (1990–2008)	Eppinger and Potrafke (2016) based on data by Felbermayr and Gröschl (2013)	47.76	25.39	10.72	144.06	449	42.72	1.39	541.12	2555

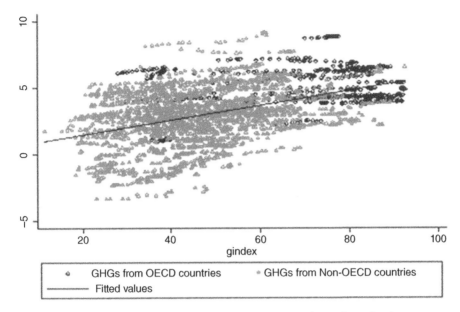

Figure 2. GHG Emissions and Overall Globalization in the Cross-Section.

Note: The figure shows GHG emissions (from 1990 to 2009) and overall globalization index (from 1990 to 2009) by country type. The left axis indicates the emissions level of GHGs in logs. The correlation coefficient is 0.43.

Frankel and Rose (2005) have attempted to isolate the effects that trade has independent of income by means of a gravity model[3] by first considering the relationship between pollution and income. They find consistent support for the EKC in much of the literature for all three air pollution types (SO2, NO_x and PM). However, the results regarding CO_2 emissions are not consistent with our findings. Felbermayr and Gröschl (2013) show that natural disasters in one country influence the trade of its trading partners and develop a concept that is best illustrated with the following example: An earthquake affecting country A will increase the trade volumes of other countries to country A. Moreover, the trade increases will be larger when a trading country is located closer to country A. Eppinger and Potrafke (2016) elaborate upon this notion and address the causality problems by proposing that the geographic component of trade openness from the original model proposed by Frankel and Romer (1999) should be an IV for globalization. Felbermayr and Gröschl (2013) further suggest the importance of considering the exogenous component of geography and natural disasters in predicting trade openness as an IV for globalization. Therefore, the difference between Frankel and Romer (1999) and Eppinger and Potrafke (2016) is that their identification strategy is designed explicitly for the income-growth-nexus but not for examining the influence of globalization. Therefore, Frankel and Romer's (1999) results are not robust to the inclusion of geographic controls in the second stage of the model. Eppinger and Potrafke (2016) mainly address this problem by controlling for any observed or unobserved country-specific effects in their panel approaches which allows the use of IVs in a panel data model and for the control of the bias.

Eppinger and Potrafke (2016) build their IV model by improving upon the Frankel and Romer (1999) model and their IV is generally constructed in two steps: Eppinger and Potrafke

(2016) estimate a reduced gravity model on a large sample of country pairs that explains the bilateral trade openness of country i to trade with country j in year t by natural disasters in country j. They further apply Poisson Pseudo Maximum Likelihood (PPML) to predict their instrumental variables. The modified gravity equation proposed by Frankel and Romer (1999) is grounded in their methodology, which explains the bilateral trade openness (the sum of imports and exports as a share of GDP) of the trade between country i and country j in year t with respect to country j following natural disasters in country j and the disaster variables that are exogenous to country i are shown as

$$
\begin{aligned}
Trade\ openess_{ijt} = {} & \gamma_0 + \gamma_1 \ln(Population)_{it} + \gamma_2 \ln(Population)_{jt} + \gamma_3 \ln(Distance)_{ij} \\
& + \gamma_4 \ln(Border)_{ij} + \gamma_5 Disaster_{jt} + \gamma_6 Disaster_{jt} \times Border_{ij} \\
& + \gamma_7 Disaster_{jt} \times \ln(Population)_{jt} + \gamma_8 Disaster_{jt} \times \ln(Area)_{jt} \\
& + \gamma_9 Disaster_{jt} \times \ln(Dist.fin.center)_{jt} + \delta_i + \delta_j + \delta_t + \varepsilon_{ijt}
\end{aligned}
\tag{3}
$$

From Equation (3), Eppinger and Potrafke (2016) generally obtain a predicted value for yearly bilateral trade openness – the IV adopted in this paper. The identifying assumption in the model of this research is that natural disasters in third countries have no effect on the pollutant emissions of a country other than through trade. In any event, similar omitted variables that influence growth, such as geographic and cultural characteristics, would also bias the estimates of trade openness. As a variable in the second stage, the model includes a large sample of country pairs that explains *bilateral* trade openness (the sum of imports and exports as a share of GDP) of country i to trade with country j in year t following natural disasters in country j, population, bilateral geographic variables (the logarithm of bilateral distance and a border dummy), and several interactions of the disaster variable. Following Frankel and Romer (1999), the model also includes a border dummy (equal to one for neighbouring countries) and the interaction terms assume that disasters in large countries, neighbouring countries, and countries that are closer to financial centres have stronger effects on bilateral openness measures. To best determine the effectiveness of the IV, we include our first stage regression results in all of our estimation result tables in the following form, where ∂_{it-1}^{FG} denotes the one-year lag in predicted trade openness as suggested by Eppinger and Potrafke (2016)[4].

$$
Gindex_{it} = \theta_j + B_1 \partial_{it-1}^{FG} \gamma_i + B_2 Y_{it} + B_3 Y_{it}^2 + \beta_4 Economic\ structure_{it} + \varepsilon_{it}
\tag{4}
$$

4. Empirical Results

4.1 *Results using the Overall Globalization Index*

We start by reporting the results using the overall globalization index; we report the results using the sub-globalization index in later sub-sections. Table 3 presents the results for all three dependent variables (GHG, CO_2 and CO_2 from the manufacturing and construction sector). For every three columns in Table 3 (also in Tables 4–6), the first is based on the full sample and, the second and third are based on the OECD and non-OECD subsamples, respectively, in order to ease comparisons among them. Columns 1–9 of Table 3 show the initial results using the overall globalization index with the fixed effect estimation, and the 2SLS estimation results follow in columns 10–18. The results are robust to standard errors corrected for heteroskedasticity and are clustered at the country level. As shown in Table 3 columns 1, 4 and 7, the coefficient of the overall globalization index is positive and reaches the 1%

Table 3. Regression Results with Overall Globalization Index (All Pollutants).

| | Panel fixed effects estimates | | | | | | | | | 2SLS Panel fixed effects estimates | | | | | | | | |
| | (1) | (2) GHGs | (3) | (4) | (5) CO_2 | (6) | (7) | (8) CO_2 from M/C sector | (9) | (10) | (11) GHGs | (12) | (13) | (14) CO_2 | (15) | (16) | (17) CO_2 from M/C Sector | (18) |
Dependent Variable	All	OECD	Non-OECD	All	OECD	Non-OECD	All	OECD	Non-OECD	All	OECD	Non-OECD	All	OECD	Non-OECD	All	OECD	Non-OECD
Gindex	0.0104***	0.0013	0.0110***	0.0167***	0.0026	0.0176***	0.0141***	−0.0081*	0.0165***	0.0200***	−0.0544	0.0203***	0.0288***	−0.0698	0.0296***	0.0565***	−0.1270	0.0563***
	(6.265)	(0.650)	(6.148)	(5.965)	(0.950)	(5.911)	(3.068)	(−1.994)	(3.324)	(4.874)	(−0.746)	(5.061)	(4.122)	(−0.502)	(4.265)	(2.615)	(−0.746)	(2.872)
Y	0.705***	6.211***	0.363	2.229***	6.090***	2.287***	1.571**	7.835***	1.008	0.770***	14.28	0.510	2.115***	16.52*	2.291***	0.217	22.53	−0.547
	(2.816)	(6.591)	(1.134)	(5.298)	(3.412)	(4.423)	(2.192)	(3.290)	(1.026)	(2.962)	(1.283)	(1.451)	(4.361)	(1.809)	(3.739)	(0.194)	(0.948)	(−0.353)
Y^2	−0.020	−0.288***	0.004	−0.101***	−0.272***	−0.106***	−0.069	−0.366***	−0.032	−0.039**	−0.611*	−0.021	−0.116***	−0.689	−0.130***	−0.0437	−0.930**	0.010
	(−1.157)	(−6.145)	(0.179)	(−3.867)	(−3.141)	(−3.097)	(−1.465)	(−3.103)	(−0.484)	(−2.239)	(−1.648)	(−0.848)	(−4.011)	(−0.839)	(−3.259)	(−0.768)	(−2.083)	(0.112)
Economic structure	0.009***	0.005	0.009***	0.020***	0.003	0.022***	0.045***	0.019*	0.048***	0.008***	0.002	0.007***	0.015***	−0.001	0.016***	0.045***	0.013	0.046***
	(3.290)	(1.214)	(3.086)	(3.683)	(0.715)	(3.735)	(4.501)	(2.368)	(4.545)	(2.809)	(0.098)	(2.547)	(2.663)	(−0.036)	(2.728)	(4.345)	(0.396)	(4.355)
Constant	−1.728*	−28.29***	−0.698	−9.961***	−29.13***	−10.34***	−8.027***	−38.30***	−6.187*	−1.120	−72.86	−0.407	−8.234***	−86.71	−9.107***	−0.947	−120.7	1.249
	(−1.846)	(−5.959)	(−0.611)	(−5.817)	(−3.190)	(−5.246)	(−3.016)	(−3.185)	(−1.744)	(−1.126)	(−1.193)	(−0.322)	(−4.059)	(−0.770)	(−3.847)	(−0.206)	(−0.918)	(0.210)
R^2	0.439	0.379	0.456	0.440	0.470	0.445	0.226	0.203	0.240	0.208	0.055	0.103	0.420	0.059	0.333	0.049	0.074	0.057
Observations	2834	432	2402	2853	442	2411	2069	442	1627	2444	416	2028	2453	423	2030	1911	423	1488
First stage										FE	FE	FE	FE	FE	FE	FE	FE	FE
Lag predicted trade openness										0.1822***	0.0596**	0.1949***	0.1806***	0.0430*	0.1951***	0.1770***	0.0430*	0.1985***
										(5.33)	(2.06)	(5.48)	(5.37)	(1.66)	(5.49)	(3.91)	(1.66)	(3.97)
F-test on excl. instrument										28.43	4.26	30.06	28.85	2.77	30.11	15.32	2.77	15.74
F-test, p value										(0.000)	(0.044)	(0.000)	(0.000)	(0.101)	(0.000)	(0.000)	(0.101)	(0.000)

Note: Asterisks indicate significance levels: *$p < 0.1$, **$p < 0.05$, ***$p < 0.01$.

Robust *t*-statistics for FE estimates and *z*-statistic for 2SLS estimates reported in parenthesis (standard errors clustered by country).

Instrumental Variable: Lag predicted trade openness (Felbermayr and Gröschl, 2013) and (Eppinger and Potrafde, 2016).

Table 4. Regression Results with Globalization Index (Overall Green House Gas Emission).

	Panel fixed effects estimates									2SLS Panel fixed effects estimates								
	(1)	(2)	(3)	(4)	(5)	(6)	(7)	(8)	(9)	(10)	(11)	(12)	(13)	(14)	(15)	(16)	(17)	(18)
	All	OECD	Non-OECD	All	OECD	Non-OECD	All	OECD	Non-OECD	All	OECD	Non-OECD	All	OECD	Non-OECD	All	OECD	Non-OECD
E-glob	0.0065*** (5.481)	0.0020 (1.274)								0.0213*** (3.528)	0.0574 (0.426)							
S-glob			0.0068*** (5.287)	0.0074*** (4.257)	-0.0004 (-0.266)							0.0215*** (3.710)	0.0238*** (3.931)	-0.0613 (-0.658)				
P-glob						0.0086*** (4.351)	0.0055*** (6.524)	0.0018 (0.720)	0.0055*** (6.354)						0.0233*** (4.172)	0.0129*** (4.169)	-0.0163 (-1.032)	0.0136*** (4.227)
Y	1.121*** (4.567)	6.342*** (6.535)	0.963*** (2.986)	0.750*** (2.906)	6.531*** (6.777)	0.336 (1.048)	0.601** (2.458)	6.273*** (6.833)	0.350 (1.120)	1.198*** (4.089)	1.970* (1.750)	1.092*** (2.588)	0.896*** (3.011)	21.60 (0.945)	0.396 (1.026)	0.539** (2.030)	7.488*** (4.002)	0.438 (1.288)
y^2	-0.044*** (-2.746)	-0.296*** (-5.918)	-0.033 (-1.467)	-0.018 (-1.026)	-0.301*** (-6.352)	0.010 (0.449)	-0.008 (-0.478)	-0.290*** (-6.282)	0.010 (0.466)	-0.070*** (-3.346)	-0.163 (-0.426)	-0.063** (-2.034)	-0.049** (-2.247)	-0.929** (-2.179)	-0.013 (-0.467)	-0.016 (-0.993)	-0.343*** (-3.911)	-0.010 (-0.441)
Economic structure	0.007*** (2.645)	0.005 (1.166)	0.008** (2.579)	0.009*** (3.314)	0.004 (1.186)	0.009*** (3.123)	0.009*** (3.408)	0.005 (1.394)	0.0086*** (3.214)	0.006** (1.970)	-0.006 (-0.194)	0.006* (1.944)	0.010*** (3.067)	-0.002 (-0.076)	0.009*** (2.722)	0.009*** (3.242)	-0.001 (-0.156)	0.009*** (3.040)
Constant	-2.805*** (-2.943)	-28.75*** (-6.043)	-2.414*** (-2.086)	-1.984*** (-2.070)	-30.08*** (-6.115)	-0.677 (-0.594)	-1.417 (-1.538)	-28.77*** (-6.361)	-0.679 (-0.607)	-2.405*** (-2.150)	-1.670 (-0.024)	-2.316 (-1.554)	-1.547 (-1.446)	-114.1 (-0.897)	-0.031 (-0.022)	-0.501 (-0.472)	-33.99*** (-3.879)	-0.250 (-0.198)
R^2	0.436	0.389	0.447	0.407	0.377	0.428	0.427	0.382	0.439	0.090	0.019	0.046	0.144	0.089	0.281	0.232	0.034	0.136
Observations	2383	419	1964	2871	432	2439	2929	432	2497	2179	403	1776	2480	416	2064	2534	416	2118
First stage										FE	FE	FE	FE	FE	FE	FE	FE	FE
Lag predicted trade openness										0.1607*** (3.49)	0.1116** (3.22)	0.1759*** (3.54)	0.1380*** (4.36)	0.0404* (1.81)	0.1532*** (4.87)	0.2463*** (5.91)	0.1052* (1.89)	0.2254*** (5.65)
F-test on excl. instrument										26.45	10.35	27.01	35.46	4.71	36.25	32.94	25.36	32.36
F-test, p value										(0.000)	(0.001)	(0.000)	(0.000)	(0.001)	(0.000)	(0.000)	(0.008)	(0.000)

Note. Asterisks indicate significance levels: $*p < 0.1$, $**p < 0.05$, $***p < 0.01$.
Robust t-statistics for FE estimates and z-statistic for 2SLS estimates reported in parenthesis (standard errors clustered by country).
Instrumental Variable: Lag predicted trade openness (Felbermayr and Gröschl, 2013) and (Eppinger and Potrafke, 2016).

Table 5. Regression Results with Globalization Index (Overall Carbon Emission).

	Panel fixed effects estimates									2SLS Panel fixed effects estimates								
	(1)	(2)	(3)	(4)	(5)	(6)	(7)	(8)	(9)	(10)	(11)	(12)	(13)	(14)	(15)	(16)	(17)	(18)
	All	OECD	Non-OECD	All	OECD	Non-OECD	All	OECD	Non-OECD	All	OECD	Non-OECD	All	OECD	Non-OECD	All	OECD	Non-OECD
E-glob	0.0118*** (5.814)	0.0028 (1.348)	0.0126*** (5.885)							0.0321*** (3.201)	0.0615 (0.518)	0.0330*** (3.308)						
S-glob				0.0122*** (4.717)	-0.0007 (-0.421)	0.0135*** (4.661)							0.0353*** (3.614)	-0.0979 (-0.432)	0.0351*** (3.804)			
P-glob							0.0084*** (4.979)	0.0043 (1.295)	0.0086*** (4.951)							0.0192*** (3.636)	-0.0186 (-0.760)	0.0207*** (3.754)
Y	2.705*** (6.273)	6.205*** (3.465)	3.107*** (5.863)	2.298*** (5.287)	6.590*** (3.718)	2.245*** (4.293)	2.073*** (5.341)	6.294*** (4.242)	2.230*** (4.681)	2.688*** (5.095)	2.634*** (2.270)	3.132*** (4.448)	2.311*** (4.326)	31.31* (1.756)	2.130*** (3.101)	1.772*** (3.716)	7.846*** (2.593)	2.147*** (3.792)
Y^2	-0.129*** (-5.002)	-0.278*** (-3.140)	-0.159*** (-4.577)	-0.099*** (-3.640)	-0.292*** (-3.362)	-0.096*** (-2.780)	-0.082*** (-3.465)	-0.281*** (-3.835)	-0.094*** (-2.974)	-0.160*** (-4.532)	-0.190 (-0.559)	-0.193*** (-3.891)	-0.133*** (-3.895)	-1.328 (-0.570)	-0.119*** (-2.685)	-0.084*** (-3.107)	-0.349** (-2.462)	-0.113*** (-3.112)
Economic structure	0.019*** (3.146)	0.003 (0.567)	0.021*** (3.291)	0.020*** (3.693)	0.003 (0.650)	0.021*** (3.723)	0.019*** (3.698)	0.005 (1.211)	0.020*** (3.724)	0.012* (1.922)	-0.009 (-0.285)	0.014** (2.084)	0.018*** (2.983)	-0.007 (-0.152)	0.019*** (2.927)	0.016*** (3.204)	-0.004 (-0.370)	0.017*** (3.327)
Constant	-11.21*** (-6.262)	-29.52*** (-3.260)	-12.78*** (-6.304)	-10.34*** (-5.823)	-31.96*** (-3.529)	-10.30*** (-5.134)	-9.489*** (-5.999)	-30.51*** (-4.123)	-10.15*** (-5.608)	-9.976*** (-4.668)	-6.144 (-0.104)	-11.91*** (-4.550)	-8.892*** (-4.065)	-169.4 (-0.544)	-8.566*** (-3.233)	-7.293*** (-3.660)	-37.14*** (-2.601)	-8.703*** (-3.962)
R^2	0.432	0.476	0.441	0.417	0.465	0.422	0.429	0.485	0.432	0.276	0.022	0.274	0.342	0.092	0.247	0.431	0.043	0.335
Observations	2402	429	1973	2890	442	2448	2950	442	2508	2188	410	1778	2489	423	2066	2543	423	2120
First stage										FE	FE	FE	FE	FE	FE	FE	FE	FE
Lag predicted trade openness										0.1582*** (3.50)	0.0577*** (2.18)	0.1758*** (3.54)	0.1368*** (4.39)	0.0416** (2.49)	0.1532*** (4.87)	0.2447*** (5.94)	0.0945*** (3.25)	0.2530*** (5.67)
F-test on excl. instrument										20.25	14.10	12.50	19.26	6.22	23.68	35.34	10.58	32.10
F-test, p value										(0.000)	(0.000)	(0.001)	(0.000)	(0.013)	(0.000)	(0.000)	(0.001)	(0.000)

Note: Asterisks indicate significance levels: *$p < 0.1$, **$p < 0.05$, ***$p < 0.01$.

Robust *t*-statistics for FE estimates and *z*-statistic for 2SLS estimates reported in parenthesis (standard errors clustered by country).

Instrumental Variable: Lag predicted trade openness (Felbermayr and Gröschl, 2013) and (Eppinger and Potrafke, 2016).

Table 6. Regression Results with Globalization Index (Carbon Emissions from Manufacturing and Construction Sector).

	Panel fixed effects estimates									2SLS Panel fixed effects estimates								
	(1)	(2)	(3)	(4)	(5)	(6)	(7)	(8)	(9)	(10)	(11)	(12)	(13)	(14)	(15)	(16)	(17)	(18)
	All	OECD	Non-OECD	All	OECD	Non-OECD	All	OECD	Non-OECD	All	OECD	Non-OECD	All	OECD	Non-OECD	All	OECD	Non-OECD
E-glob	0.0086*** (2.898)	-0.0020* (-1.759)								0.0607** (2.245)	0.0919 (0.421)							
S-glob			0.0098*** (3.039)	0.0116** (2.088)	-0.0073** (-2.154)	0.0150* (2.415)						0.0586** (2.428)	0.0767** (2.381)	-0.178 (-0.498)	0.0725*** (2.838)			
P-glob							0.0068*** (2.997)	-0.0069* (-1.957)	0.0074*** (3.047)							0.0455*** (2.679)	-0.0339 (-1.384)	0.0486*** (2.720)
Y	1.638** (2.080)	7.257*** (2.915)	1.012 (0.909)	1.670*** (2.288)	8.511*** (3.016)	0.946 (0.957)	1.679** (2.474)	7.000*** (2.853)	1.325 (1.427)	1.054 (0.967)	-1.104 (-0.061)	0.504 (0.308)	0.424 (0.345)	49.44 (0.568)	-1.345 (-0.748)	-0.005 (-0.004)	6.762** (2.140)	0.073 (0.047)
y^2	-0.065 (-1.268)	-0.346** (-2.745)	-0.023 (-0.301)	-0.071 (-1.493)	-0.397*** (-2.878)	-0.024 (-0.363)	-0.067 (-1.506)	-0.333** (-2.732)	-0.043 (-0.671)	-0.104* (-1.661)	-0.073 (-0.115)	-0.063 (-0.619)	-0.074 (-1.064)	-2.091 (-0.578)	0.055 (0.524)	-0.015 (-0.222)	-0.311** (-2.040)	-0.025 (-0.277)
Economic structure	0.046*** (4.361)	0.022** (2.495)	0.046*** (4.387)	0.045*** (4.437)	0.019* (2.497)	0.047*** (4.536)	0.041*** (4.403)	0.017* (1.868)	0.043*** (4.337)	0.045*** (4.530)	0.004 (0.074)	0.048 (4.597)	0.052*** (4.490)	0.002 (0.022)	0.050*** (4.781)	0.044*** (3.501)	0.007 (0.539)	0.046*** (3.380)
Constant	-8.578*** (-2.931)	-34.90** (-2.812)	-6.569 (-1.637)	-8.481*** (-3.103)	-42.06** (-2.935)	-6.032* (-1.677)	-8.628*** (-3.440)	-33.21** (-2.677)	-7.496** (-2.261)	-3.946 (-0.874)	15.72 (0.144)	-2.872 (-0.465)	-1.274 (-0.252)	-271.0 (-0.558)	4.294 (0.617)	-0.948 (-0.188)	-30.55* (-1.931)	-1.424 (-0.243)
R^2	0.221	0.195	0.232	0.227	0.212	0.244	0.223	0.202	0.231	0.010	0.001	0.019	0.031	0.110	0.033	0.099	0.059	0.047
First stage										FE	FE	FE	FE	FE	FE	FE	FE	FE
Observations	1908	429	1479	2106	442	1664	2166	442	1724	1771	410	1361	1947	423	1524	2001	423	1578
Lag predicted trade openness										0.1763*** (2.91)	0.0577** (2.18)	0.2042*** (2.93)	0.0704*** (4.02)	0.0416** (2.49)	0.1485*** (8.35)	0.2152*** (4.61)	0.094*** (3.25)	0.2246*** (10.22)
F-test on excl. instrument										8.46	4.75	8.61	16.19	6.22	23.68	21.24	10.58	17.75
F-test, p value										(0.004)	(0.030)	(0.004)	(0.000)	(0.013)	(0.000)	(0.000)	(0.001)	(0.000)

Note: Asterisks indicate significance levels: *$p < 0.1$, **$p < 0.05$, ***$p < 0.01$.

Robust *t*-statistics for FE estimates and *z*-statistic for 2SLS estimates reported in parenthesis (standard errors clustered by country).

Instrumental Variable: Lag predicted trade openness (Feibermayr and Gröschl, 2013) and (Eppinger and Potrafde, 2016).

significant level. This result suggests that an increased globalization level is associated with higher environmental pollution. We further compare the differences in the results for OECD and non-OECD countries. The initial results support the pollution haven effect for different performances with increased globalization in terms of climate change. The only negative and significant result in column 8 at the 10% level suggests a necessary discussion on carbon emissions from the industrial subsector, although the inference is not necessary true for OECD countries.

Our results also suggest that the higher the proportion of GDP derived from manufacturing is, the worse the environmental quality will be. In addition, the results are clearer for OECD countries, which we can attribute to the advantages of cleaner technologies, cleaner production procedures and effective environmental regulations in improving environmental quality, even with a higher contribution to GDP from manufacturing. Otherwise, this finding may be consistent with the pollution haven hypothesis, such that developed countries move their heavy polluting industries to non-OECD countries.

The 2SLS estimation results are presented on the right side of Table 3 (columns 10–18), which take the one-period lag of the predicted trade openness as an instrumental variable following Eppinger and Potrafke (2016). In the first stage, the IV has a significant effect on globalization across our panel with an F-statistic above Stock and Yogo's (2005) 20% critical value. These findings suggest that the partial correlation described in the OLS model slightly rejects a causal effect of globalization on pollutant emissions. We report 2SLS estimates based on the full panel set for the period from 1990–2009, although the entire one-year lag predicted trade share might not have a strong effect on the KOF globalization index in full periods of our data, indicating a potential problem of a weak IV. In general, the results of 2SLS estimations in Table 3 consistently support by the prior results. Further detailed discussion, including sub-indicator effects of globalization on pollution, is provided in the following section.

4.2 Greenhouse Gas and Carbon Emissions

After investigating the effect of overall globalization on climate change, we now decompose the overall globalization index into three sub-indexes and report the individual effects of each. Tables 4 and 5 present the results using as dependent variable of GHGs and CO_2 respectively, considering the separate effects of three sub-globalization indexes economic, social and political.

As discussed earlier, we are more interested in the comparisons between different country groups. As shown in columns 2, 5 and 8 for the OECD countries and columns 3, 6 and 9 for the non-OECD countries in both Tables 4 and 5, the coefficient of the economic, social and political index is still positive and significant in columns 3, 6 and 9. However, it is not significant in columns 2 and 5 and 8 in both Tables 4 and 5. Therefore, it can be inferred that an increased level of economic, social and political globalization is associated with higher pollutant emissions for non-OECD countries. In addition, the results for the sub-globalization index for GHGs and carbon emissions show that increased globalization – whether economic, social or political globalization – leads to higher environmental degradation for non-OECD countries. However, a significant effect cannot be found for OECD countries. Based on these results, we cannot prove that the significant increase in the volume of emissions in non-OECD countries is associated with the transfer of pollution from OECD countries. Conversely,

MNEs may demonstrate some positive effects from technology spillovers through a variety of globalization channels or greener FDI. Therefore, increasing emissions in non-OECD countries may be regarded as a reflection of long-run progress and economic transition. Thus far, this initial finding for greenhouse gas and carbon emissions might not sufficiently clarify the debate regarding whether a higher level of globalization will result in the transfer of polluters from home countries to developing countries using aggregate indicators. Therefore, we take one step further to analyse the major concern of pollution haven effects – carbon emissions from the manufacturing and construction sector.

4.3 CO_2 emissions from the Manufacturing and Construction Sector

The results for carbon emissions from the manufacturing and construction sectors are reported in Table 6. In Section 4.1, we reported that overall globalization has a negative coefficient at a 10% significant level in column 8 (OECD country) of Table 3. This finding indicates that increased globalization positively affects the contribution of the manufacturing and construction sector in improving the environmental quality in OECD countries. However, the mechanism under globalization is not clear from these initial results. Our evidence from the estimation of the sub-dimensions of globalization in Table 6 further supports the pollution haven effects, demonstrating that higher economic, social and political globalization leads to a cleaner environment in OECD countries and to almost continuous environmental degradation in non-OECD countries.

The evidence from the manufacturing and construction sector directly supports the existence of pollution haven effects between OECD and non-OECD countries. There are two main causes for these pollution haven effects in the manufacturing and construction sector. First, theoretical research (Sanna-Randaccio and Sestini, 2012) suggests that the fear of moving all production abroad by means of FDI between two countries (with and without more stringent climate measures) is mainly due to high transport costs. However, Reinaud (2008) analyses job losses in the home country and direct carbon emissions increases in less environmentally stringent countries and finds that characteristics such as low income, high labour intensity, and comparatively lower environmental standards characterize non-OECD countries but that the actual transfers from the polluting manufacturing and construction industries occur not only by means of FDI but also through regional integration and cultural unifications.

Second, it is not only economic globalization that enables OECD countries to shift those high-carbon industries to developing countries, but also political and social globalization. More interestingly, our findings support the view of Balli and Pierucci (2015) who argue that the role of political and social globalization can be even larger than that of economic globalization. Indeed, in columns of 2, 5 and 8 of Table 6, the absolute value of the coefficient of political globalization (0.0069) and social globalization (0.0072) are greater than that of economic globalization (0.0020). This finding again highlights that globalization should not be simplified to only economic globalization.

Potential endogeneity problems associated with globalization may bias the estimation results. In general, the results of the IV models (as shown on the right side of Table 6) are consistent with the results of the previous FE models. The coefficient of economic social and political globalization on emissions from the manufacturing and construction subsector in the OECD country sub-sample were not significant. In the first stage, the IV has a positive and significant effect on globalization and the three sub-globalization indicators with an *F*-statistic above the Stock and Yogo's (2005) 15% critical value. We further do the Hausman test for the comparison between the favour of FE and 2SLS models. The test results generally favor the FE models, regarding the inference of non-OECD counties remains unchanged.

5. Conclusion

This paper investigates the relationship between globalization and climate change by adopting the new KOF globalization index and carbon emissions data. Our results suggest that, on average, increased carbon emissions move in tandem with higher levels of economic, social and political globalization and this effect varies by OECD and non-OECD country group. Further evidence adopting data from the manufacturing and construction sector suggest that globalization is negatively related to emissions from OECD countries but positively related to emissions from non-OECD country group. These findings jointly support the pollution haven effects in terms of climate change. Our estimation results are robust to different model settings, alternative dependent variable measurements and the adoption of IV methods.

To the best of our knowledge, this analysis is the first that links climate change and globalization in a broad sense (previous studies mainly focus on either trade or FDI) based on large scale sample data. We believe that such analysis can shed some light on the field on globalization and the environment, and contribute to the global policy making on climate change issues.

Acknowledgements

The authors thank two anonymous referees and editor Siqi Zheng for very helpful comments. They are also thankful for valuable comments from Donald A. R. George, Kenichi Imai, Chi-ang Lin, Leslie Oxley and other participants at the Journal of Economic Surveys 2016 Special Issue and International Conference: The Economics of Climate Change in August 2015 in Taipei, Taiwan. The first author is grateful for the support of the Alexander von Humboldt Foundation. This paper is supported by the National Science Foundation of China (Grant No. 71273004, 71322303 & 71403117), the Science Foundation of Jiangsu Province (No. BK20130572) and the fund from China's Ministry of Education (No. 14JHQ017).

Notes

1. To rule out the possibility of other forms of EKC, we also applied the Likelihood Ratio Test (LRT) for the robustness check. The results are available upon request.
2. For the detailed data see http://www.wri.org/resources/data-sets/cait-us-states-greenhouse-gas-emissions.
3. The gravity model specifies the exogenous determinants of a country's level of trade distance from major trading partners, including common borders or languages, landlockedness, size, income per capita and others.
4. We acknowledge Peter Eppinger and Niklas Portafke for sharing data and Gabriel Felbermayr and Jasmin Gröschl for providing their data and codes to compute the initial predicted trade openness values.

References

Albrow, M. (1996) *Global Age*. Oxford: Blackwell Publishing Ltd.
Balli, F. and Pierucci, E. (2015) *Globalization and international risk-sharing: do political and social factors matter more than economic integration?* No.2015-04. Centre for Applied Macroeconomic Analysis, Crawford School of Public Policy, The Australian National University.

Barrett, S. and Graddy, K. (2000) Freedom, growth, and the environment. *Environment and Development Economics* 5: 433–456.

Bernauer, T. (2013) Climate change politics. *Annual Review of Political Science* 16: 421–448.

Brock, W.A. and Taylor, M.S. (2010) The green Solow model. *Journal of Economic Growth* 15: 127–153.

Bu, M., Liu, Z. and Gao, Y. (2011) Influence of international openness on corporate environmental performance in China. *China & World Economy* 19: 77–92.

Cole, M.A., Elliott, R.J.R. and Okubo, T. (2011) *Environmental outsourcing.* Discussion Paper Series DP2011-12. Research Institute for Economics & Business Administration, Kobe University.

Copeland, B.R. and Taylor, S. (2004) Trade, growth, and the environment. *Journal of Economic Literature* 42: 7–71.

Dreher, A. (2006) Does globalization affect growth? Evidence from a new index of globalization. *Applied Economics* 38: 1091–1110.

Dreher, A. and Gaston, N. (2008) Has globalization increased inequality? *Review of International Economics* 16: 516–536.

Dreher, A., Gaston, N. and Martens, P. (2008b) *Measuring Globalisation – Gauging Its Consequences.* New York: Springer.

Eppinger, P. and Potrafke, N. (2016) Did globalization influence credit market deregulation? *The World Economy* 39(3): 426–443.

Erdogan, A.M. (2014) Foreign direct investment and environmental regulations: a survey. *Journal of Economic Surveys* 28: 943–955.

Eskeland, G.S. and Harrison, A.E. (2003) Moving to greener pastures? Multinationals and the pollution haven hypothesis. *Journal of Development Economics* 70: 1–23.

Felbermayr, G. and Gröschl, J. (2013) Natural disasters and the effect of trade on income: a new panel IV approach. *European Economic Review* 58: 18–30.

Frankel, J.A. and Romer, D. (1999) Does trade cause growth? *American Economic Review* 89: 379–399.

Frankel, J.A. (2003) *The environment and globalization.* Working Paper No. 10090. Cambridge, MA: National Bureau of Economic Research.

Frankel, J.A. and Rose, A.K. (2005) Is trade good or bad for the environment? Sorting out the causality. *Review of Economics and Statistics* 87: 85–91.

Frankel, J.A. (2009) *Environmental effects of international trade.* Harvard Kennedy School Faculty Research Working Paper RWP 09-006.

Fredriksson, P.G. and Mani, M. (2004) Trade integration and political turbulence: environmental policy consequences. *Advances in Economic Analysis & Policy* 4(2), Article 3.

Grossman, G.M. and Krueger, A.B. (1991) *Environmental impacts of a North American Free Trade Agreement.* Working Paper No. 3914. Cambridge, MA: National Bureau of Economic Research.

Held, D. (1999) *Global Transformations: Politics, Economics and Culture.* Stanford, CA: Stanford University Press.

Held, D. and McGrew, A. (2003) Political globalization: trends and choices. In I. Kaul, P. Conceicao, K. Le Gouven, and R.U. Mendoza (eds.), *Providing Global Public Goods: Managing Globalization* (pp. 185–224). Oxford: Oxford University Press.

Reinaud, J. (2008) *Issues Behind Competitiveness and Carbon Leakage. Focus on Heavy Industry.* IEA Information Paper 2. Paris: IEA.

Rodrik, D. and Wacziarg, R. (2005) Do democratic transitions produce bad economic outcomes? *American Economic Review* 95: 50–55.

Sanna-Randaccio, F. (2012) *Foreign Direct Investment, Multinational Entreprises and Climate Change.* Milan: Fondazione Eni Enrico Mattei (FEEM).

Sanna-Randaccio, F. and Sestini, R. (2012) The impact of unilateral climate policy with endogenous plant location and market size asymmetry. *Review of International Economics* 20: 580–599.

Spilker, G. (2012a) Helpful organizations: membership in inter-governmental organizations and en-
   vironmental quality in developing countries. *British Journal of Political Science* 42(02): 345–
   370.
Spilker, G. (2012b) *Globalization, Political Institutions and the Environment in Developing Countries.*
   New York and London: Routledge
Stock, J. H. and Yogo, M. (2005) Testing for weak instruments in linear IV regression. Chapter 5 in
   Identification and Inference in Econometric Models: Essays in Honor of Thomas J. Rothenberg,
   edited by DWK Andrews and JH Stock.
Strazicich, M.C. and List, J.A. (2003) Are CO_2 emission levels converging among industrial countries?
   Environmental and Resource Economics 24: 263–271.
World Resources Institute. (2015) *CAIT Climate Data Explorer.* Washington, DC: World Resources
   Institute. Available at: http://cait.wri.org (accessed on March 5, 2015)

Appendix

Table A1. *List of Countries Considered in this Research*

Sample of OECD countries, n = 24			
Australia (1971)	Austria	Belgium	Canada
Denmark	Finland (1969)	France	Germany
Greece	Iceland	Ireland	Italy
Japan (1964)	Luxembourg	Netherlands	New Zealand (1973)
Norway	Portugal	Spain	Sweden
Switzerland	Turkey	United Kingdom	United States

Sample of Non-OECD Countries, n = 142			
Afghanistan	Albania	Algeria	Angola
Antigua & Barbuda	Argentina	Armenia	Azerbaijan
Bahamas	Bahrain	Bangladesh	Barbados
Belarus	Belize	Benin	Bhutan
Bolivia	Bosnia & Herzegovina	Botswana	Brazil
Brunei	Burkina Faso	Burundi	Cambodia
Cameroon	Cape Verde	Central African Republic	Chad
Chile	China	Colombia	Comoros
Congo, Dem. Rep.	Congo, Rep.	Cote d'Ivoire	Czech Republic (1995)
Croatia	Cuba	Cyprus	Djibouti
Dominica	Dominican Republic	Ecuador	Egypt
El Salvador	Eritrea	Estonia	Ethiopia
Fiji	Gabon	Georgia	Ghana
Grenada	Guatemala	Guinea	Guinea-Bissau
Guyana	Hungary (1996)	Honduras	India
Indonesia	Iran	Jamaica	Jordan
Kazakhstan	Kenya	Kiribati	Kyrgyzstan
Laos	Latvia	Lebanon	Lesotho
Lithuania	Macedonia, FYR	Madagascar	Malawi
Malaysia	Maldives	Mauritania	Mauritius

Sample of Non-OECD Countries, n = 142			
Mexico (1994)	Moldova	Mongolia	Morocco
Mozambique	Myanmar	Namibia	Nepal
Nicaragua	Niger	Nigeria	Oman
Pakistan	Palau	Panama	Papua New Guinea
Paraguay	Peru	Philippines	Poland (1996)
Qatar	Romania	Russian Federation	Rwanda
Sao Tome & Principe	Saudi Arabia	Senegal	Seychelles
Sierra Leone	Singapore	Slovenia	South Korea (1996)
Solomon Islands	Slovakia (2000)	South Africa	Sri Lanka
St. Kitts and Nevis	St. Lucia	St. Vincent and the Grenadines	Sudan
Suriname	Swaziland	Syria	Tajikistan
Tanzania	Thailand	Togo	Tonga
Trinidad & Tobago	Tunisia	Turkmenistan	Uganda
Ukraine	United Arab Emirates	Uruguay	Uzbekistan
Vanuatu	Venezuela	Vietnam	Yemen
Zambia	Zimbabwe		

Note: Many countries participate in OECD after 1961 (the beginning of OECD). Therefore, following the previous empirical researches' design on sub-sample regression, once a country participates in OECD group after 1990, we will regard that country as non-OECD country across our time period from 1990 to 2009. The join time of those non-original members are reported in parenthesis.

10

A SURVEY OF THE LITERATURE ON ENVIRONMENTAL INNOVATION BASED ON MAIN PATH ANALYSIS

Nicolò Barbieri, Claudia Ghisetti and Marianna Gilli

University of Ferrara and SEEDS
Ferrara

Giovanni Marin

IRCrES-CNR, Milano, SEEDS
Ferrara and
OFCE-SciencesPo
Sophia Antipolis France

Francesco Nicolli

IRCrES-CNR, Milano, SEEDS
Ferrara and University of Ferrara

1. Introduction

The achievement of strong decoupling between economic growth and environmental degradation crucially depends on technological improvements which reduce environmental pressure from production and consumption (Popp *et al.*, 2010). Differently from other complementary forces which contribute to improved environmental quality – such as structural changes in production and consumption patterns towards cleaner sectors and products or a reduction in the scale of the economy –, technological change aimed at improving environmental quality and at decreasing environmental pressure also reduces the cost of meeting environmental targets for society as a whole. Therefore, environmental technological change may potentially lead to win-win situations in which improvements in environmental quality and economic growth coexist. This potential for win-win outcomes has attracted the attention of policy makers, who have devoted an increasingly larger share of government budget to stimulating the generation and diffusion of environmentally beneficial technologies (EEA, 2014).

Environmental Economics and Sustainability, First Edition. Edited by Brian Chi-ang Lin and Siqi Zheng.

Environmental technological change also plays a relevant role in actual policy debate, especially after the launch of the Circular Economy package in December 2015, which seeks to boost European (EU) competitiveness through new business opportunities and innovative and 'circular' means of production and consumption. More specifically, higher resource efficiency in economic processes can be achieved by reducing the use of resources along the various production chain phases, their initial extraction and the disposal into the environment. An important role in this transition is played by economic composition and innovation intensity of the economy, as well as by the environmental and industrial policy settings, all elements addressed in this paper. In this view, environmental innovation (EI) can be seen both as a potential factor that intermediates policy effects on resource efficiency, and a channel to increase overall environmental efficiency of the entire production process. In simpler terms, moving towards a circular economy involves a rethinking of production cycles, production technologies, consumer behaviour and environmental policies, which are all factors that hinge heavily on the concept of EI. Even more interestingly, the intersection between EI and the EU environmental agenda does not limit to these considerations, as technological change can play a relevant role also in the strategies for decarbonising Europe. The roadmap towards a low-carbon economy by the European Commission, in fact, sets out ambitious targets in terms of emission reduction to be reached by 2050. In this context, technology, as well as socioeconomic and policy issues, can play a relevant role in reaching these stringent policy goals (EEA, 2014), as shown in some recent contribution like EEA (2015) for the transport sector and Schmidt *et al.* (2012) for the energy sector. Some more insights on this topic can be found in Section 5 of this paper.

So far, a consistent research effort has been made to analyse EI, interpreted according to one of the widely accepted definitions of the Measuring Ecoinnovation project as '*the production, assimilation or exploitation of a product, production process, service or management or business methods that is novel to the firm [or organization] and which results, throughout its life cycle, in a reduction of environmental risk, pollution and other negative impacts of resources use (including energy use) compared to relevant alternatives*' (Kemp & Pearson, 2007, p. 7). Whereas the focus has mostly been on EI, the term ecoinnovation can be defined as a subclass of EI, which happens when innovations improve not only environmental but also economic performance (Ekins, 2010). Given the broad spectrum of contributions in this field, our paper is aimed at systematizing them by providing an original methodology to identify the main paths of development within this strand of the literature and to derive implications in terms of main findings and possible extensions of key emerging themes.

Ours is not the first paper which attempts to offer a detailed review of the literature on EI. One of the most comprehensive reviews of this literature is a paper by Popp *et al.* (2010), in which a thorough analysis of the economics of environmental technological change is proposed. After defining the concept of environmental technological change and the mechanisms behind its functioning, the authors move on to describe the policy implications emerging from a better understanding of said technological change. The literature review by Ambec *et al.* (2013) also focuses on how environmental regulation affects innovation, but it differs from the work by Popp *et al.* (2010) since it centres around the argument that well-designed regulation can enhance competitiveness by stimulating the search for new, profitable opportunities through EI. This argument, known as the 'Porter Hypothesis' (Porter & Van der Linde, 1995), is explored in Ambec *et al.* (2013) in both its theoretical foundations and empirical evidence. The review of Dechezlepretre and Sato (2014) looks at the impact of EI on competitiveness, showing that recent empirical analysis has found very small effects of environmental regulation on productivity, employment and competitiveness. On the other hand, the authors highlight the role played by environmental regulations as drivers for the development of green technologies which are likely to have economy-wide benefits. Besides potentially positive impacts of EI on business performance (also see UNEP, 2014), it contributes substantially to reducing environmental pressures from production and consumption activities. These benefits for the society as a whole are often neglected in the literature that evaluates the impact of EI. However, depending on the type of environmental pressure at stake and the type of innovation that is considered, the relative and absolute magnitude of benefits linked to EI for business (private) and society (public) may differ substantially. This heterogeneity in the distribution of benefits from EI is indeed crucial to understand whether innovation is driven by business opportunities or public policies. A discussion and review of the literature on the determinants of environmental technological change is presented by Del Río (2009). This work combines qualitative and quantitative approaches and it concludes by providing suggestions for future research, to complement different theoretical perspectives and to account for *'the interplay between the variables influencing environmental technological change and the interaction between the different stages of this process, including the invention stage'* (Del Río, 2009, p. 871). An attempt in this direction is the paper by Cecere *et al.* (2014), in which the literature on EI is reviewed by using an evolutionary approach and by stressing the role of technological lock-ins and path dependence in order to better understand which barriers challenge the development and uptake of EI. The presence of initial advantages in relation to existing technological trajectories – which are often pollution-intensive – can create lock-ins which come at the expense of EI uptake. These lock-ins prevent the uptake of radical innovations like, for instance, those represented by alternative engine technologies, such as electric or fuel cell vehicle technology (Oltra & Saint Jean, 2009). Still focusing on technological EI, the review by Allan *et al.* (2014) analyses the last stage of the Schumpeterian innovation process connecting the 'invention', 'innovation' and 'diffusion' phases (Schumpeter, 1942), since it is *'through the process of diffusion that the (environmental) benefits of a new technology come to be widely enjoyed'* (Allan *et al.*, 2014, p. 2).

Starting from these premises, this contribution has several interrelated purposes, that is: i) presenting a broad and up-to-date review which includes academic contributions on the topic of EI; ii) developing and adopting a rigorous methodology in order to identify the main knowledge patterns in EI studies; iii) identifying the main macrothemes in this specific field by means of the proposed methodology and iv) proposing a research agenda based on future extensions and macrothemes saturation.

Coherently with Rennings (2000), this paper adopts multidisciplinary lens to positively benefit from both neoclassical and evolutionary approaches to the innovation studies, as the study and understanding of EI is complex and thus in need for methodological pluralism. Whereas neoclassical approaches can better contribute to the understanding of EI as characterized by a 'double externality' and thus in need for a regulatory push and pull stimulus and a proper incentivizing system, evolutionary approaches are better equipped in explaining the relevance of the context in which EI emerge and evolve (or do not emerge nor evolve), EI's knowledge trajectories as well as the importance of social and institutional innovations required for their diffusion (Rennings, 2000).

The methodology used in this paper builds on the empirical analysis of a citation network for scientific articles. In this network, scientific articles and books are the nodes, whereas citations are the links connecting them.[1] Thanks to the methods proposed by Hummon and Doreian (1989, 1990), it is possible to weight the network based on the importance of its nodes and to identify the most representative subnetworks. This technique, called Main Path Analysis, helps us to define streams of knowledge of particular significance for the development of the EI literature. Indeed, differently from other surveys, this methodology allows us to select papers regarding main knowledge advances in the field of EI, exploring their distinctive features. However, although this rigorously determines our initial set of articles, we have added other papers which cite those already included, in order to present a valuable and complete survey of knowledge trends in this field.

The structure of the paper is as follows. Section 2 explores how the citation network is built and the methodology used to identify the most relevant papers contributing to the development of the literature on EI. Sections 3–6 analyse the topics deriving from the main path analysis. Section 7 concludes by summarizing the main findings and discussing either the need and potential for future contributions or the presence of possible saturation in a field where limited future extensions are envisaged.

2. Knowledge Advances Related to EI

In order to reduce the arbitrariness which often affects review exercises, we identify the knowledge codified in scientific articles and books, upon which our discussion is built, through a combined process based on keyword searches and network analysis. This allows us, on the one hand, to outline a selection of scientific outputs related to EI and, on the other hand, to single out the main knowledge advances characterizing the literature.

Firstly, we conduct a keyword search in the ISI Web of Science (Thomson Reuters: http://thomsonreuters.com/en.html, last accessed: November 2014). This database is used in other studies that carry out network analysis of scientific papers (Mina *et al.*, 2007; Consoli & Ramlogan, 2008; Lu & Liu, 2014) and provides up-to-date information on research outputs often used in bibliometric analyses. We then identify relevant documents for our survey by searching the main unstructured items (i.e. title and abstract) for keywords such as 'environmental innovation', 'environmental technologies', 'environmentally friendly technologies', etc. using different combinations. The result of the search process is a collection of 2033 articles and books, to which related citing documents are also added. Furthermore, in order to reduce the number of irrelevant items and to exclude those which do not cite any documents within the above sample, we focus on 'internal' citations among the documents. That is, following Martinelli and Nomaler (2014), we only include articles and books citing the initial sample of 2033 items. After cleaning for missing information (some articles do not report the names of the authors, the title, etc.), the final sample comprises 833 items. We then collect the relevant articles and books and build the citation network. Figure 1 shows the resulting map in which the documents are the nodes and the citations are the arcs connecting them. The result is a directed acyclic network with temporal dimension, made of 833 nodes and 2055 citations among them. This means that the network does not present loops (i.e. if scientific paper A cites B, B cannot cite A) and it is directed, that is, its edges have an orientation (e.g. A cites B). From Figure 1, we can identify three main groups of nodes. The first is a highly connected group of nodes with a high number of backward and forward citations. These nodes are located in the dense core of nodes in the centre of the network. The second type refers to nodes that are connected to the network through few links and are placed in the peripheral area of the network. Finally, there are nodes not connected to the main network. These are the isolated nodes in the boarder of the figure and they can be defined as subnetworks. Since the seminal works by Garfield (1955), Garfield *et al.* (1964) and De Solla Price (1965), citations have been used to detect main scientific advances within a network of scientific papers. Articles in academic

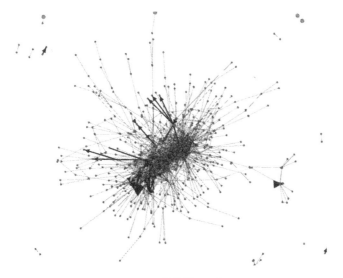

Figure 1. Full Network.
Source: Own elaboration.

journals provide a wealth of information. Among other things, citations play a pivotal role in tracing 'prior art' upon which new knowledge is built. In addition, citations highlight the fact that connected articles share common content (Hummon & Doreian, 1989, 1990). Following this approach, citation graphs can be used to analyse scientific and technological knowledge advances both synchronically and diachronically (among others: Mina *et al.*, 2007; Consoli & Ramlogan, 2008; Barberá-Tomás & Consoli, 2012; Epicoco, 2013; Lu & Liu, 2014; Martinelli & Nomaler, 2014). However, since networks are usually characterized by a complex structure of nodes and links, Hummon and Doreian (1989, 1990) propose three indices to identify main streams of knowledge within directed networks, that is, the Main Path Analysis.

In order to trace the main advances in the literature on EI and to single out the most relevant documents, our survey uses the Critical Path Method (CPM) algorithm implemented in Pajek, a software program for the analysis and visualization of large networks, adopted here to extrapolate the main directions along which knowledge trajectories evolve. While the technicalities of this method are detailed elsewhere (Batagelj *et al.*, 2014), here we focus on describing the output generated using this technique. CPM identifies essential subnetworks by computing all the source-sink paths linking each *startpoint* to each *endpoint*. The former indicates nodes which do not cite any previous nodes but which are cited by following ones. The latter indicates nodes which are not cited by any following nodes but which are linked to previous ones. Then, CPM selects the source-sink path with the largest total sum of weights. The weights are used as a proxy for the importance of the unit/arc within the network. In relation to this, we calculate traversal weights using the Search Path Count (SPC) method (Batagelj, 1991, 2003), which measures the importance of the arcs linking the nodes, following Hummon and Doreian's main path analysis. This is done by counting the number of times a source-sink path passes through an arc, divided by the total number of source-sink paths in the network. That is, the higher the number of times an arc is included in source-sink paths, the greater its weight, and therefore, its importance. The output of this process is a set of articles representing the most important part of the network.

Figure 2. Longest Source-Sink Path Detected Using the CMP Method. In Dark-Grey, the Most Important Path within the Whole Network, Identified by the CMP Path with SPC Weights.

Source: Own elaboration.

In addition, we propose a second application of the CPM algorithm assuming all nodes/arcs to be equally important, instead of calculating them by means of the SPC algorithm. In this way, we trace the longest source-sink path characterizing the literature on EI, which identifies the backbone structure of the network.

As shown in Figure 2, the most important subnetwork detected via the first algorithm, which uses SPC weights to calculate arc importance (red nodes), is also included in the longest path outlined by the second application, which is based on equally weighted arcs (light-grey nodes).

By collecting the documents identified using these two algorithms, we obtain a subset of 32 scientific articles which we adopt as a starting point to investigate how the literature on EI has developed over the last few decades. These articles are listed in Table 1 in which the papers retrieved through the methodology described in this section are identified.

Interestingly, it is possible to detect four subtopics or branches among these contributions. The first one refers to the drivers of EI, paying particular attention to Environmental Management Systems (EMS). The second stream of articles discusses the economic implications of EI production and adoption. The third topic relates to the effects of innovation on environmental performance, a rather unexplored line of investigation which has been growing in recent

Table 1. Articles Surveyed.

Article	Journal	Main path	Subtopic	Type of analysis	Geographical coverage
Alpay et al. (2002)	American Journal of Agricultural Economics	No	Policy inducement mechanism	Meso	Mexico
Ambec et al. (2013)	Review of Environmental Economics and Policy	No	Policy inducement mechanism	Theoretical	N.A.
Antonioli et al. (2013)	Research Policy	Yes	Determinants of EI; Policy inducement mechanism	Micro	Italy
Antonioli et al. (2016)	Economics of Innovation and New Technologies	No	Environmental effects of EI	Micro	Italy
Barbieri (2015)	Ecological Economics	No	Policy inducement mechanism	Micro	All Countries
Beise & Rennings (2005)	Ecological Economics	Yes	Policy inducement mechanism	Theoretical	N.A.
Berman & Bui (2001)	Review of Economics and Statistics	No	Policy inducement mechanism	Meso	Los Angeles (USA)
Brunnermeier & Cohen (2003)	Journal of Environmental Economics and Management	No	Policy inducement mechanism	Meso	USA
Cainelli & Mazzanti (2013)	Research Policy	Yes	Determinants of EI	Meso	Italy
Cainelli & Mazzanti (2013)	Research Policy	Yes	Environmental effects of EI	Micro	Italy
Cainelli et al. (2012)	Industry and Innovation	Yes	Determinants of EI	Micro	Italy
Carrión-Flores & Innes (2010)	Journal of Environmental Economics and Management	No	Environmental effects of EI	Micro	USA
Cheng et al. (2014)	Journal of Cleaner Production	No	Economic effects of EI	Micro	Taiwan
Corradini et al. (2014)	Ecological Economics	Yes	Determinants of EI; Environmental effects of EI	Meso	14 EU countries
Costantini & Crespi (2008)	Ecological Economics	Yes	Policy inducement mechanism	Macro	OECD countries
Costantini & Crespi (2013)	Journal of Evolutionary Economics	Yes	Policy inducement mechanism	Macro	OECD countries
Costantini & Mazzanti (2012)	Research Policy	Yes	Policy inducement mechanism	Macro	EU
Costantini et al. (2013)	Ecological Economics	Yes	Environmental effects of EI	Meso	Italy
Cuerva et al. (2014)	Journal of Cleaner Production	No	Determinants of EI - EMS	Micro	Spain
De Marchi & Grandinetti (2013)	Journal of Knowledge Management	No	Determinants of EI	Micro	Italy
De Marchi (2012)	Research Policy	No	Determinants of EI	Micro	Spain
De Vries & Withagen (2005)	Working Paper	No	Policy inducement mechanism	Macro	OECD countries
Dechezlepretre and Sato (2014)	Policy Report	No	Economic effects of EI	Survey	N.A.
Demirel & Kesidou (2011)	Ecological Economics	Yes	Determinants of EI	Micro	UK

(continued)

Table 1. (*Continued*)

Article	Journal	Main path	Subtopic	Type of analysis	Geographical coverage
Demirel & Kesidou (2011)	Ecological Economics	Yes	Determinants of EI - EMS	Micro	UK
Duchin *et al.* (1995)	Ecological Economics	Yes	Economic effects of EI	Theoretical	N.A.
Faucheux & Nicolaï (1998)	Ecological Economics	Yes	Economic effects of EI	Theoretical	N.A.
Ghisetti & Quatraro (2013)	Ecological Economics	Yes	Policy inducement mechanism	Meso	Italy
Ghisetti & Quatraro (2013)	Ecological Economics	Yes	Determinants of EI	Meso	Italy
Ghisetti & Rennings (2014)	Journal of Cleaner Production	Yes	Economic effects of EI	Micro	Germany
Ghisetti and Pontoni (2015)	Ecological Economics	No	Determinants of EI	Survey	N.A.
Ghisetti *et al.* (2015)	Research Policy	No	Determinants of EI	Micro	11 EU countries
Gilli *et al.* (2013)	The Journal of Socio-Economics	No	Environmental effects of EI	Meso	5 EU countries
Gilli *et al.* (2014)	Ecological Economics	No	Environmental effects of EI	Meso	10 EU countries
Horbach & Rennings (2013)	Journal of Cleaner Production	No	Economic effects of EI	Micro	Germany
Horbach (2008)	Research Policy	Yes	Determinants of EI; Determinants of EI - EMS	Micro	Germany
Horbach (2010)	Journal of Economics and Statistics	No	Economic effects of EI	Micro	Germany
Horbach *et al.* (2012)	Ecological Economics	No	Determinants of EI	Micro	Germany
Jaffe & Palmer (1997)	Review of Economics and Statistics	Yes	Policy inducement mechanism	Meso	USA
Jaffe & Stavins (1995)	Journal of Environmental Economics and Management	No	Policy inducement mechanism	Theoretical	N.A.
Jaffe *et al.* (2002)	Environmental and Resource Economics	No	Environmental effects of EI; Policy inducement mechanism	Theoretical	N.A.
Johnstone *et al.* (2010)	Environmental and Resource Economics	No	Policy inducement mechanism	Macro	OECD countries
Kesidou & Demirel (2012)	Research Policy	Yes	Determinants of EI	Micro	UK
Lanoie *et al.* (2008)	Journal of Productivity Analysis	No	Policy inducement mechanism	Meso	Quebec (Canada)
Lanoie *et al.* (2011)	Journal of Economics & Management Strategy	No	Economic effects of EI	Micro	USA, Germany, Hungary, Japan, France, Norway
Marin & Mazzanti (2013)	Journal of Evolutionary Economics	Yes	Environmental effects of EI	Meso	Italy

Table 1. (*Continued*)

Article	Journal	Main path	Subtopic	Type of analysis	Geographical coverage
Marin (2014)	Research Policy	No	Economic effects of EI	Micro	Italy
Mazzanti & Montini (2010)	Ecological Economics	Yes	Environmental effects of EI	Meso	Italy
Mazzanti & Zoboli (2006)	Ecological Economics	Yes	Policy inducement mechanism	Theoretical	N.A.
Mazzanti & Zoboli (2009)	Ecological Economics	Yes	Economic effects of EI	Meso	Italy
Mazzanti & Zoboli (2009)	Ecological Economics	Yes	Environmental effects of EI	Meso	Italy
Mazzanti *et al.* (2015)	Empirica	No	Policy inducement mechanism	Meso	EU
McGuire (1982)	Journal of Public Economics	No	Policy inducement mechanism	Theoretical	N.A.
Nesta *et al.* (2014)	Journal of Environmental Economics and Management	No	Policy inducement mechanism	Macro	OECD countries
Parry (1995)	Resource and Energy Economics	Yes	Policy inducement mechanism	Theoretical	N.A.
Pethig (1976)	Journal of Environmental Economics and Management	No	Policy inducement mechanism	Theoretical	N.A.
Popp (2002)	American Economic Review	Yes	Policy inducement mechanism	Meso	USA
Popp (2003)	Journal of Policy Analysis and Management	No	Policy inducement mechanism	Micro	USA
Popp (2005)	Ecological Economics	Yes	Determinants of EI	Survey	N.A.
Porter & Van der Linde (1995)	Journal of Economic Perspectives	No	Economic effects of EI; Policy inducement mechanism	Theoretical	N.A.
Porter (1991)	Scientific American	No	Policy inducement mechanism	Theoretical	N.A.
Rehfeld *et al.* (2007)	Ecological Economics	Yes	Determinants of EI; Determinants of EI - EMS	Micro	Germany
Rennings (2000)	Ecological Economics	Yes	Determinants of EI	Theoretical	N.A.
Rennings *et al.* (2006)	Ecological Economics	Yes	Determinants of EI - EMS	Micro	Germany
Requate (2005)	Ecological Economics	Yes	Policy inducement mechanism	Theoretical	N.A.
Wagner (2007)	Research Policy	Yes	Determinants of EI - EMS	Micro	Germany
Wagner (2008)	Ecological Economics	Yes	Determinants of EI - EMS	Micro	9 EU countries
Wang *et al.* (2012)	Energy Policy	No	Environmental effects of EI	Meso	China
Weina *et al.* (2016)	Environmental Economics and Policy Studies	No	Environmental effects of EI	Meso	Italy
Ziegler & Nogareda (2009)	Research Policy	Yes	Determinants of EI - EMS	Micro	Germany

Note: Type of analysis: micro, meso (sectoral and/or regional), macro, theoretical and survey.
The column Main Path specifies if the paper has been detected through the Main Path algorithm or not.

Table 2. Summary Statistics of the Articles Surveyed.

Year	<2000	2000–2005	2006–2010	>2010		Tot
No. of articles	10	12	18	37		77
Subtopics	Determinants of EI	Determinants of EI - EMS	Economic effects of EI	Environmental effects of EI	Policy inducement mechanism	Tot
No. of articles	16	9	11	13	28	77
Geographical level	All countries	EU countries	N.A.	OECD countries	Single country	Tot
No. of articles	1	8	19	6	43	77
Level of analysis	Macro	Meso	Micro	Survey	Theoretical	Tot
No. of articles	6	21	31	3	16	77
Top 5 Journals	Ecological Economics	Research Policy	Journal of Environmental Economics and Management	Journal of Cleaner Production	Environmental and Resource Economics	Tot
% of articles	35.1	16.9	6.5	5.2	3.9	67.5

years. Finally, the last branch focuses on the inducement effect of environmental policies on EI, exploring the theoretical framework outlined by the Porter Hypothesis.

The majority of those articles present original empirical analysis, which exploit mainly two typologies of data sources to measure EI: either survey or patent data.[2] In the following sections of this paper, we develop our analysis starting from this subclassification and, in order to provide a more exhaustive discussion of these themes, we also consider some of the citing articles connected to the subset identified through our methodology. By doing so, we expand our sample to include the first set of citations, thus enhancing the value of our analysis, but without impacting on its reliability. Indeed, citations represent knowledge links among articles and, thanks to this feature, they can be used to identify documents which share at least some common pieces of knowledge. Finally, for the sake of completeness, certain relevant related papers are included in the analysis of the main topics. The following sections discuss these main topics related to EI, focusing on the articles found using this combined process. The whole set of papers surveyed are presented in Table 1, whereas Table 2 reports the number of articles by year, subtopic, geographical level, level of analysis and journal.

3. Determinants of EI

EI are characterized by a so-called 'double externality' (Rennings, 2000), since firstly they reduce the production of negative environmental externalities and secondly they might produce positive knowledge externalities. Indeed, the knowledge featured in these innovations might spill over the boundaries of the firms developing and/or adopting them and be beneficial to other firms. This special nature is the reason why a recent strand of literature has emerged with the purpose of investigating the determinants of EI adoption, that is, the elements triggering success in EI uptake. Such strand of literature, represented by several contributions along the main path shown in Table 1 above, acknowledges that EI are not only technologi-cal, but also organizational, social and institutional innovations (Horbach, 2008). Moreover, their understanding greatly benefits from merging multiple disciplines *'including evolution-ary economics and technological change theories, industrial economics, systems analysis and operations research, sociology and political sciences, actor-network and communication the-ories, organizational change, and knowledge management'* (Del Río *et al.*, 2010, p. 542).

Consensus has emerged on the relevance of a set of elements which jointly stimulate EI adoption by firms. These can be grouped into four clusters of determinants labelled, respec-tively, 'Market-pull', 'Technology-push', 'Firm-specific factors' and 'Regulation' (Horbach, 2008; Horbach *et al.*, 2012; for a review Ghisetti & Pontoni, 2015). Market conditions, such as expectations of future turnover, previous economic performance, demand for new ecoproducts or consumer preferences, have been confirmed to frame the 'green' choices of firms. Techno-logical conditions have been found to be as important as market conditions to stimulate EI adoption. They depend mostly on the knowledge-capital endowment of firms – which can be increased through R&D investments or activities – but also on organizational capabilities and organizational innovations. A subfield of this literature, which proves to be a relevant research sector also in our paper sample, focuses on analysing environmental management schemes (EMS) and their bidirectional effects on EI, as outlined in Section 3.1 below. The group of drivers defined as 'Firm-specific factors' includes all those firm characteristic, such as size, location, sector and age, which generally influence – together with other more relevant de-terminants – a firm's innovativeness. More so than standard innovations, EI are characterized by the so-called 'regulatory (policy) push/pull effect' (Rennings, 2000), since they are mainly regulation-driven, and regulation acts bilaterally on both the supply side (push) and the demand side (pull). By changing the relative prices of production factors or by setting new (environ-mental) standards, existing as well as forthcoming policies induce (environmental) innovations in each of the phases of the Schumpeterian innovation process, from invention to adoption and diffusion (Popp, 2005). Besides this standard inducement mechanism, Ghisetti and Quatraro (2013) detect the presence of corporate socially responsible behaviours by firms, consisting in innovation reactions to worse environmental performance when policy stimulus is weaker. The literature on the so-called 'Porter Hypothesis', discussed in Section 6, assesses the role and effects of such policy stimulus. Kesidou and Demirel (2012) extend the investigation on the determinants of EI by analysing the different roles which these clusters of determinants play in the various phases of the innovation process. Market conditions, and in particular demand factors, are found to be key determinants for the initial phase of the (eco-)innovation process, as they significantly affect firm decisions concerning EI uptake. However, they do not affect the (eco-)investment phase. In other words, market conditions encourage firms to enter the 'en-vironmental realm', but the magnitude of their environmental investments depends on other determinants, specifically cost savings, organizational capabilities and stricter regulations. The existing literature on the determinants of EI has centred around some or all of these clusters of determinants, with 'Firm-specific factors' usually acting as indispensable control variables in most studies to date. Nevertheless, these works widely differ not only for what concerns the core determinants under scrutiny, but also in the nature and coverage of their research as well as in the broadness of the concept of EI.

The papers included in our main path investigate the determinants of EI either in empiri-cal terms (e.g. Horbach, 2008; Demirel & Kesidou, 2011; Cainelli *et al.*, 2012; Kesidou & Demirel, 2012; Cainelli & Mazzanti, 2013) or from a theoretical point of view (e.g. Rennings, 2000; Popp, 2005). The analysis is carried out at multiple levels: not only the firm (micro) level (e.g. Horbach, 2008) but also different countries (macro) as well as sectors (meso; e.g. Corradini *et al.*, 2014). Furthermore, the focus is not only on the manufacturing sector but also on the service sector and its interplay with the former, although no evidence is found of an environmental policy transmission effect from manufacturing to services (Cainelli & Mazzanti, 2013). Another feature which is worth stressing is that the literature on the determinants of EI may examine either a single country, such as Germany (Horbach, 2008), the United Kingdom (Demirel & Kesidou, 2011; Kesidou & Demirel, 2012) and Italy (Cainelli *et al.*, 2012; Cainelli & Mazzanti, 2013; Ghisetti & Quatraro, 2013) or multiple countries, such as the EU 15 (Corradini *et al.*, 2014).

Lastly, broader definitions of EI encompassing all kinds of innovations leading to environmental improvements are found alongside studies which adopt more stringent criteria to define innovations. For instance, Demirel and Kesidou (2011) focus on the drivers of different typologies of EI: End-of-Pipe Pollution Control Technologies, Integrated Cleaner Production Technologies and Environmental R&D. They find confirmation that different types of EI are indeed influenced by different determinants. Horbach *et al.* (2012) differentiate among 12 innovations depending on their environmental impacts (such as material, energy, air pollution, CO_2, water, soil, waste and other dangerous substances). They then assess the effects of the four clusters of determinants on different types of EI and come to a similar conclusion, that is, different types of EI are affected by different determinants. More recently, this literature has broadened its scope by investigating the role of determinants which are interactive in nature, such as those stemming from knowledge acquired through cooperation in R&D or interaction with external information partners, suppliers or knowledge sources, like research centres or universities. Cainelli *et al.* (2012) analyse the likelihood of EI adoption by firms operating within a local production system, in order to shed light on the role of interfirm network relationships, agglomeration economies and internationalization strategies in stimulating EI uptake. Their main findings confirm that cooperating in R&D is a relevant determinant of EI, but the actors with which a firm cooperates do matter as a stimulus for EI. As an extension of this concept, De Marchi and Grandinetti (2013) and De Marchi (2012) show that the knowledge required for EI adoption is far greater than the firms' traditional knowledge base, so that acquiring it from outside the boundaries of the firm – specifically by cooperating in R&D activities – becomes a core determinant of EI. Coherently, not only formalized cooperation in R&D but also strong reliance on external sources of information are relevant determinants of EI (Ghisetti *et al.*, 2015).

A further strand of literature – which is closely related to the one outlined above, since it analyses EI determinants and cites those included in the main path – focuses on testing the existence of complementarities among environmental and non-EI activities. Antonioli *et al.* (2013) study the presence of complementarities between organizational innovation and training and their joint effect on EI, in both non-ETS and ETS sectors (where the effect is stronger). Not surprisingly, such complementarities are not widespread, due to the still limited diffusion of ecofirms in Italy, the country analysed in their research.

3.1 *Environmental Management Systems*

Organizational capabilities and practices concerning the environment which may favour the adoption of EI are found at the intersection between the 'Technology push' cluster and the one called 'Firm-specific factors'. Organizational capabilities and practices of the 'green' type are usually developed contextually with the implementation of an EMS. An EMS represents a for-malized change in the organization of a firm that is defined as '*a collection of internal efforts at formally articulating environmental goals, making choices that integrate the environment into production decisions, identifying opportunities for pollution (waste) reduction and imple-menting plans to make continuous improvements in production methods and environmental performance*' (Khanna & Anton, 2002, p. 541).

As the papers in our main path are EU-centric, it is worth noting that two main EMS frame-works are widely diffused across EU countries: the European Commission's Eco Management and Audit Scheme (EMAS) and the International Organization for Standardization's ISO14001 standard.

As mentioned in Section 2, a group of papers in our main path revolves around analysing the linkages existing between organizational innovation, mainly EMS and EI adoption. Most empirical studies find that the implementation of an EMS favours the adoption of EI (Wagner, 2007, 2008). Rehfeld *et al.* (2007) test the effects of environmental organizational measures on environmental product innovations in German firms. They conclude that having introduced either an EMAS or an ISO14001 certification positively influences the adoption of environ-mental product innovations. Similarly, Wagner (2007) investigates the role played by EMS in inducing EI and identifies a positive and significant effect on process EI, while no effect is found for product EI. This points to the conclusion that the implementation of an EMS stim-ulates EI, but only when innovations leading to environmental improvements alter production processes rather than firm products. As complementary evidence, Wagner (2008) shows that environmental product innovations are more heavily influenced by other elements than by EMS certifications. In particular, environmental product innovations are affected by market research on green products and ecolabelling instruments which inform consumers about the 'green' content of products. Demirel and Kesidou (2011) introduce, among the determinants of EI, a variable which measures organizational capabilities in terms of the presence of any EMS. The authors find that an EMS can affect end-of-pipe technologies adoption and investment choices in environmental R&D, while no effect is detected on pollution abatement innovations. Lastly, Horbach (2008) controls for the role of an EMS in determining EI and finds a significant and positive effect not only on EI but also on general innovations.

A peculiarity of this literature is the ways in which an EMS is measured empirically. The more general framework including any organizational changes related to the environment (as in Horbach, 2008 or Rehfeld *et al.*, 2007) is challenged by more detailed approaches in measur-ing EMS. For instance, Wagner (2007, 2008) constructs an index based on 10 EMS elements: written environmental policy, procedure for identification and evaluation of legal requirements, initial environmental review, definition of measurable environmental goals, programme to at-tain measurable environmental goals, clearly defined responsibilities, environmental training programme, environmental goals are part of a continuous improvement process, separate envi-ronmental/health/safety report or environmental statement and audit system to check environ-mental programme. Instead, Rennings *et al.* (2006) choose to focus only on EMAS-certified firms and analyse how different characteristics of the environmental management scheme – mainly, its maturity, its strategic importance and its learning processes – affect EI adoption. The maturity of the EMS is assessed according to: the age of the EMAS, the existence of double revalidations of the EMAS, prior experience in the organization of environmental pro-tection and previous ISO 14001 certification. In confirming that an EMS is a key determinant of process EI, the authors also find that environmental process innovations depend in particular on the maturity of the EMS, pointing to the main conclusion that the careful designing of an EMS is crucial in order to stimulate EI.

An extension of this strand of literature is found in Ziegler and Nogareda (2009). They explore the potential reverse causality between EMS and EI to determine whether EMS adoption is a consequence of prior EI adoption. Despite some caveats due to the cross-sectional data set which does not allow them to control for unobserved firm heterogeneity, the authors find evidence of a bidirectional link between EMS and EI. Overall, we might conclude that EI are stimulated by the existence of organizational capabilities within the firm, signalled by the presence of EMS certifications. Yet, also the opposite holds true: prior EI makes it easier for firms to decide to obtain an EMS certification. A further relevant extension is developed by Inoue *et al.* (2013) who, like Rennings *et al.* (2006), consider not only the mere presence of a certification but also its maturity: the longer a firm has been certified, the more it innovates. Their paper differs from the study by Rennings *et al.* (2006) in that its focus is on ISO14001 rather than on EMAS, but, similar to previous studies, the main conclusion is that firms with greater certification experience, that is, ISO 14001-certified for a long time, do innovate more, as environmental R&D expenditure significantly increases. The crucial role of an EMS is also confirmed by evidence on small and medium enterprises (Cuerva *et al.*, 2014).

4. Economic Effects of EI

Assessing the economic consequences of EI development and adoption is particularly relevant for policy makers. Firstly, it constitutes a crucial component of ex post evaluation of policies directly or indirectly aimed at stimulating EI. These effects should be considered among the net benefits of policies stimulating EI together with the benefits for the society as a whole of reduced environmental externalities. Secondly, understanding the extent to which EI influence economic performance has important implications linked to the potential use of environmental and more specific EI-inducing policies as tools for industrial policy (e.g. EC, 2014; Dechezlepretre & Sato, 2014). EI may influence in an asymmetric way short-term measures of profitability (e.g. stock market returns, profits) and long-term performance (e.g. productivity, international competitiveness, survival, firm growth). According to the seminal paper by Porter and Van der Linde (1995), regulation-induced EI are more likely to have positive impacts on long-term performance rather than short-term measures.

Four papers included in the main path deal with the role played by EI in influencing economic performance. The theoretical work by Facheux and Nicolaï (1998) shows that the firms' strategies for the endogenization of technological change (e.g. EI) can give rise to 'win-win' situations. Their examination concludes that new forms of governance are needed in order to pursue ecological-economic sustainability through environmental technological change. In their study on international trade, Duchin *et al.* (1995) confirm that EI can have positive effects on trade, opening up new markets, even though this does not fully offset the costs of environmental regulation in terms of foregone profits. The paper by Mazzanti and Zoboli (2009) does not specifically refer to EI in its empirical analysis. It explores the connection between economic efficiency (labour productivity) and environmental performance (emission intensity) in several Italian sectors, finding a generally negative relationship between the two measures for a variety of air emissions. However, the section discussing the implications of the results is particularly interesting, as it provides an original conceptual framework which links EI to their potential for enhancing both economic and environmental performance. The authors point out that environmental technologies and innovations play a crucial role in the joint dynamics of environmental and economic performance. Finally, the article by Ghisetti and Rennings (2014) can be seen as a typical direct empirical assessment of the economic returns deriving from EI. The authors look at the extent to which EI adoption by German firms influences their financial performance, measured in terms of returns on sales (operating revenues from sales). Their econometric analysis, based on two waves of the Mannheim Innovation Panel, determines that, while EI aimed at improving resource and energy efficiency have a positive influence on financial performance, those aimed at reducing externalities tend to worsen the financial performance of adopting firms.

Besides the articles in the main path, the empirical literature linking EI to differences in economic performance has been growing rapidly in recent years. We group some relevant contributions according to the dimension of economic performance which they consider. The existing literature mostly tries to assess the effects of EI on some financial performance indicators (including measures of firm productivity). Among the citing papers, Lanoie *et al.* (2011) investigate the full chain of causality from environmental regulatory stringency to environmental and financial performance, identifying EI as the most relevant mediator in this relationship. Evidence based on a sample of about 4200 facilities from seven OECD countries shows that environmental R&D has a positive effect on a binary indicator of business performance, even though this does not fully offset the costs of environmental regulation in terms of foregone profits. Marin (2014) examines the effects of EI (measured in terms of environmental patents) on productivity by analysing a panel of Italian manufacturing firms. The results based on a CDM model accounting for simultaneity and endogeneity in the innovation variable, show that the return of environmental patents in terms of productivity is substantially smaller than the return of nonenvironmental patents. Finally, Cheng *et al.* (2014) detect a positive relationship between EI (process, product and organizational EI) and business performance in a sample of Taiwanese firms. They find that the effect of organizational EI is mediated by process and product EI, while the effect of process EI is in turn mediated by product EI.

Some recent contributions also focus on the job creation potential of EI. Horbach (2010) looks at the net employment effect caused by the introduction of new environmental products or services in a sample of German firms belonging to the environmental sector. His findings point to a job creation effect of EI greater in magnitude than the one found for other kinds of innovations. In the same vein, Horbach and Rennings (2013) show that employment growth in German innovative firms is slightly stronger if these firms also introduce material and energy-saving innovations, while environmental product innovations and end-of-pipe innovations play no role.

The evidence reviewed so far which looks at international competitiveness, employment, financial performance and productivity and concerning the potential of EI for stimulating economic performance improvements yields mixed conclusions, also due to the variety of performance measures and empirical approaches adopted.

5. Environmental Effects of EI

Research papers about the effects of innovation on environmental performance are still rather scant, both along the main path described in Section 2 and in the literature in general.

According to Jaffe *et al.* (2002), technological change is considered pivotal in the achievement of environmental sustainability. However, two considerations can be drawn from the analysis of the papers found along the main path: first, there is no single and common mechanism through which innovation exerts its effect on environmental performance; second, innovation alone is not sufficient to ensure a reduced environmental impact.

Green technological change can affect environmental as well as economic performance by intensifying the effects of other key variables. In relation to this, Mazzanti and Zoboli (2009) look at data for 29 sectors in Italy and six pollutants over the 1991—2001 period. Innovation effects are not observed directly but as elements contributing to increased labour productivity (i.e., labour productivity increases thanks to the introduction of new products or processes). In the study by Marin and Mazzanti (2013), which analyses the relation between the environment and labour productivity in Italy in the years 1990–2007, innovation efforts are proxied including data on R&D. The results show the weak economic relevance of innovation efforts, indicating that it is not yet possible to regard them as drivers of improved environmental performance.

A second channel through which innovation can influence environmental performance is linked to administrative and geographical features. Local governments and regulations as well as local industrial specialization and innovative capabilities act by influencing the decisions of firms in neighbouring territories. Mazzanti and Montini (2010) analyse environmental performance in relation to a set of 10 pollutants in Rome and in the region of Lazio, then compare it to the average Italian performance. They find that the regional environmental performance of Lazio tends to be better than the national one. This result is due to structural and economic conditions which make Lazio a less emission- and energy-intensive region in comparison to the national average. However, other factors too play a significant role in promoting emission reduction, like private and public expenditure in R&D and their interaction and, more importantly, technological change. Innovation, in particular, appears to be the predominant factor, assuming even greater importance than environmental policies. Costantini *et al.* (2013) consider the role of innovation, regional environmental spillovers and environmental policies and look at the determinants of sectorial environmental performance in Italy. Their results show that innovation spillovers and environmental spillovers can drive regional and sector-specific environmental outcomes. According to the authors, this may indicate the presence of sector agglomerations in restricted areas as well as common innovation patterns within regions (i.e. common choices in the adoption of cleaner or dirtier technologies within certain geographical areas). They conclude that spillovers may play an even greater role than innovation itself in defining environmental performance. Neglecting such spatial dimension could thus lead to biased interpretations, but how to capture such spillovers in practice is crucial and incorrect choices may influence results as well. Within the literature on EI, Antonioli *et al.* (2016) suggest alternative ways to account for innovation spillovers, spanning from a broader one constructed as the share of EI in contiguous municipalities independently on the sector in which the firm operates, to a stricter one built with respect to EI adopted in the same sector and within the same administrative border.

The third and final channel through which innovation affects environmental sustainability is linked to the presence of cross-sectorial spillovers. As underlined by Dopfer (2012), it is at the mesolevel that innovations spread more significantly. Therefore, cross-sectorial spillovers may allow innovations to be more widely adopted and, consequently, contribute to increasing potential environmental benefits. Corradini *et al.* (2014), who investigate the link between environmental protection and innovation, analyse 23 manufacturing branches in the EU15 from 1995 to 2006. They find a positive relation between investment decisions concerning innovation by one sector and pollution abatement efforts by other sectors. R&D investments in one sector positively react to pollution abatement choices in other sectors. Moreover, environmental spillovers prove to be more important than knowledge spillovers in determining environmental performance.

The review of the papers found along the main path reveals the existence of three main mechanisms through which innovation can affect environmental performance: first, by intensifying the effect of other variables which are relevant to achieve improved environmental outcomes; second, by influencing decisions by agents in neighbouring areas and regions (spatial spillovers); third, by affecting environmental and investment decisions by agents (sectorial spillovers).

As a corollary, we wish to underline that the citing papers provide a limited contribution to the existing literature, tackling the topic only partially. Gilli *et al.* (2013) describe the joint environmental, economic and innovation performance of five main EU countries, namely Germany, France, Italy, the Netherlands and Sweden, which display different economic and institutional characteristics. The resulting picture highlights two main issues: firstly, there exists a discrepancy among northern and southern EU countries in terms of both innovation and environmental performance; secondly, a link between worse environmental performance and more limited adoption of innovation is systematically found, suggesting that innovation can be crucial in the achievement of improved environmental outcomes.

Another area of research explores the interactions or complementarities between different factors at the firm level and their joint effect on environmental performance. Gilli *et al.* (2014) use a sample of EU countries to investigate the existence of integration between the adoption of EI and other innovation practices (i.e., organizational, product and process innovation) at the sectorial level. Their results show that complementarities are not always a prevalent factor supporting improved environmental performance, except in the case of the manufacturing sector, which has the ability to best integrate EI with product innovation.

The analysis of complementary effects triggered by several factors also looks at the integration between the manufacturing and service sectors, based on the idea that innovation adoption in the manufacturing sector induces the introduction of cleaner practices in several branches of the service industry connected to manufacturing. Using a sample of 8161 Italian firms in the service sector, Cainelli and Mazzanti (2013) find that policies targeting the manufacturing sector are likely to induce innovation adoption in the service sector, especially when considering innovation practices aimed at abating CO_2 emissions and improving energy efficiency.

It is worth considering a few relevant studies which do not emerge directly or indirectly from the main path analysis but primarily focus on investigating the effects of innovation on air pollution. These papers share the idea that the diffusion of innovations makes the adoption of new technologies less expensive for firms, improving overall environmental performance. Wang *et al.* (2012) analyse the impact of both fossil fuel and carbon-free technological advancements on CO_2 emissions across 30 Chinese provinces between 1997 and 2008. They find that, while dirty technologies do not appear to affect CO_2 levels, green technologies have a significant influence on pollution abatement, particularly in western China. Carrión-Flores and Innes (2010) study the bidirectional link between EI and air pollution in 127 American manufacturing industries over the 1989–2004 period. Their findings confirm that there is a negative and significant relation in both directions: innovation reduces the cost of meeting pollution targets, while more stringent pollution targets increase the potential cost-saving benefits of environmental R&D, leading to more innovation.

Finally, a recent paper by Weina *et al.* (2015) analyses the relation between CO_2 emissions and green technologies in 95 Italian provinces over the 1990–2010 period. The authors conclude that, although green technologies do not play a significant role in improving environmental outcomes, innovation can improve overall environmental efficiency, measured as the ratio between polluting emissions and value added. Finally, they show that this evidence is consistent across different areas of the country.

6. Policy Inducement Mechanism

Policy inducement is one of the most consolidated mechanisms described in the literature on EI, which, starting from the original idea by Porter (1991) and Porter and Van der Linde (1995), postulates that a properly designed policy framework may provide firms with the right incentives to develop new innovations and promote technological change (a recent detailed survey of the Porter Hypothesis can be found in Ambec *et al.*, 2013). This theory is in contrast with conventional wisdom, dominated by the idea that environmental regulations necessarily increase internal costs for compliant firms and, as a consequence, negatively influence a country's ability to compete on the international markets (see, among others: Pethig, 1976; McGuire, 1982). Porter and Van der Linde (1995) criticize this idea starting from the basic assumption of static technology, typical of traditional studies on environmental regulation and competitiveness. They show that, when shifting to a dynamic context, the loss of competitiveness ascribable to increased compliance costs is partially offset by an increase in innovation performance induced by the regulation. In particular, their 1995 article describes several channels through which this mechanism can act. Firstly, well-designed policies advise companies about possible inefficiencies or better technological options; secondly, they reduce uncertainty regarding innovative abatement activities and thirdly, they put pressure on firms' cost functions, thus stimulating cost-saving innovations.

Among the papers in our main path, the seminal contribution by Jaffe and Palmer (1997) further develops this idea, proposing a taxonomy of the different versions of the original Porter Hypothesis which can be adopted in empirical research. The first perspective, known as the 'Narrow Porter Hypothesis', states that only certain types of environmental policies are actually able to stimulate both innovation and overall competitiveness, following the idea that instrument design does matter. A second perspective, also known as 'Weak', postulates that environmental regulatory systems do not have a predetermined effect on competitiveness but always stimulate certain kinds of innovation (which partially offset the loss of competitiveness due to compliance costs). Finally, the last version of the Porter hypothesis, that is, the 'Strong' one, says that efficiency gains due to induced innovation effects are able to completely offset the loss of competitiveness caused by increased marginal costs related to compliance with environmental regulations. In other words, this approach suggests that stringent environmental regulations promote competitiveness across firms and countries.

Two articles included in our main path concentrate specifically on the 'Narrow' version. Requate (2005), in particular, presents a review of the existing literature on the effects of different policy designs on innovation performance. The main conclusion is that, under competitive conditions, instruments which provide incentives through the price mechanism usually perform better than command and control policies, since they give firms more freedom to find the best technological solutions to minimize compliance costs and they also provide continuous innovation stimulus. On the contrary, in the case of imperfect market conditions, policy conclusions are less clear-cut. Moreover, the survey presents a ranking of different policy options based on the existing literature, showing, for instance, that under competitive conditions there is no difference between auctioning permits and grandfathering. Finally, the main literature surveyed in Requate (2005) confirms that, in case of myopic environmental policies or long-term commitment to the level of policy instruments, emission taxes are more effective than allowances in inducing innovation, because permit prices fall after the diffusion of a new technology, providing a weak incentive for firms to invest in further abatement technologies. These results are in line with the original predictions by Porter and Van der Linde, who argue that command and control instruments are able to induce innovation only if they have some particular characteristics: 1) they must not force firms to adopt a specific (best) technology; 2) the stringency of the instruments must increase continuously and 3) the regulatory process must be certain and consistent over time. A more recent paper by Costantini and Crespi (2013) tackles the 'Narrow' hypothesis from a broader perspective, showing that, also in the case of the energy policy mix, efficient design does indeed matter and an incoherent policy portfolio may actually have negative effects on the development and diffusion of environmentally friendly technologies. On the contrary, when environmental policies are efficiently supported by technology policies, which help firms to respond to changes in external constraints, environmental regulation may positively affect international competitiveness in the export of energy technologies, providing evidence of the relevance of a narrow Porter-like effect.

The 'Weak' hypothesis is probably the version that has been more thoroughly investigated by the academic literature – a tendency confirmed by the presence of three papers in our main path. These works study the phenomenon from different perspectives: two of them focus on the mesolevel and the third one on the microlevel. The citing papers also include several empirical macroanalyses. The above-mentioned contribution by Jaffe and Palmer (1997), for instance, is based on a panel of U.S. manufacturing industries over the 1973–1991 period. Their analysis finds evidence supporting the weak Porter hypothesis when using R&D expenditure as a proxy for innovation activities, while no effect is found when considering total patents (the choice of using total patents rather than green patents is the most criticized aspect of this work and is supposed to be the cause of the nonsignificant effect). The second article in our sample adopting a mesoapproach, Popp (2002), studies the standard inducement mechanism using data on the U.S. energy market from 1970 to 1994. It confirms that both energy prices and the quality of the stock of knowledge exert a significant and positive effect on patenting. Among the citing papers, for instance, Brunnermeier and Cohen (2003) detect a significant impact of pollution abatement expenditure and a nonsignificant effect of the number of air and water pollution inspections on the number of green patent applications in a data set covering 146 U.S. manufacturing industries at the three-digit SIC level from 1983 to 1992. In a more recent work, Mazzanti et al. (2015) study EU sectors in 2006–2008 and find that, on the one hand, more regulated sectors are more likely to adopt CO_2-reducing innovations and, on the other hand, intersector integration and knowledge sources matter, meaning that sectors with more emission-intensive upstream 'partners' innovate more to reduce their CO_2 footprint. Moving on to the microperspective, Popp (2003) finds a positive effect of the tradable permit scheme for Sulphur Dioxide on EI in a sample of 186 U.S. plants over the years 1972–1997. Moreover, focusing on the automotive sector, Barbieri (2015) provides evidence into the inducement effect of different EU environmental policies, such as post-tax fuel prices, environmental vehicle taxes, CO2 standards and EU emission standards, on green patenting activities of assignees. In addition, Mazzanti and Zoboli (2006) analyse the innovation inducement mechanism of the EU End-of-Life Vehicles (ELVs) Directive and show that the effects of economic instruments '*in systemic and dynamic settings critically depend on where, along the 'production chain', and how, in terms of net cost allocation, the incentive is introduced*' (Mazzanti & Zoboli, 2006, p. 334). The authors highlight that the effectiveness of economic instruments (in this case, free take-back of ELVs) in achieving policy objectives, and therefore in creating innovation and innovation paths in complex industrial system, depends on interindustry incentive transmission. In other words, incentives provided by the economic instrument may be transmitted from an industry which has received them to upstream or downstream industries along the production chain. The final effectiveness of the instrument builds upon the ability of innovations to create self-sustaining markets.

Finally, two of the most commonly cited cross-country studies are by De Vries and Withagen (2005) and Johnstone *et al.* (2010). The former finds some evidence of the weak version of the Porter hypothesis by studying the effects of SO_2 environmental regulation on national patent counts in related technological classes. The latter finds generally strong evidence of a policy inducement mechanism in the renewable energy sector. Interestingly, the paper by Johnstone *et al.* (2010) concludes that different instruments have heterogeneous inducement effects on different renewable energy technologies, depending on their degree of technological maturity, a result which is strictly linked to the narrow version of the Porter Hypothesis. In a more recent paper, Nesta *et al.* (2014) extend the work by Johnstone *et al.* (2010) by accounting for the possible simultaneity bias of the innovation-policy relationship, an issue often overlooked in previous empirical studies. They also show that the inducement effect of renewable energy policies is stronger when applied to competitive markets.

Finally, the 'Strong' version of the Porter Hypothesis tests whether there is a link between environmental regulation and firm competitiveness. This research question has been the starting point of the entire inducement debate, and a good survey of early contributions can be found in Jaffe and Stavins (1995), in which most of the papers considered point to a negative effect of environmental regulation on productivity. The research articles in our main path, however, reject this early evidence, confirming the presence of a Porter-like mechanism. Furthermore, they all focus on the macrolevel. Costantini and Mazzanti (2012) apply a gravity model to the EU 15, considering the years 1996–2007. They find that environmental policies do not seem detrimental to export competitiveness and, specifically, some energy tax policies positively influence trade patterns. Expanding on standard lead market models, Beise and Rennings (2005) show that, under certain conditions (increasing global demand and regulatory support), environmental regulation can incentivize the development of market opportunities in foreign countries, due to a first mover advantage linked to the development of policy-induced ecoefficient innovations. Similarly, Costantini and Crespi (2008) adopt a gravity model for trade and conclude that environmental regulation represents a significant source of comparative advantages, due to its positive effect on innovation. Moving on to the citing papers, some complementary evidence can be found at the mesolevel. Berman and Bui (2001) and Alpay *et al.* (2002) study refineries in the Los Angeles area and food processing industries in Mexico, respectively, and find evidence of the strong version of the Porter hypothesis. In their study on 17 Quebec manufacturing sectors, Lanoie *et al.* (2008) detect a modest but significant effect of regulation on competitiveness once the dynamics of the process (i.e. lag of regulation) is taken into account.

Summing up, the core of this literature is in line with mainstream theory of environmental policies, which leads to the conclusion that economic instruments are generally better suited at promoting technical change than regulatory mechanisms (Jaffe *et al.*, 2003). Innovation and technical change allow firms to reduce compliance costs, while emission standards and other command and control regulations do not push firms to go beyond the obligatory standard. In the case of energy, for instance, this effect is even more evident, as instruments like feed-in tariffs, increasing the energy producer surplus, stimulate sectorial demand for innovation. On the contrary, quantity-based regulations like renewable energy certificates do not produce surplus for producers, hindering innovation activities. Some recent contribution, however, questioned this approach. Fischer *et al.* (2003), for instance, shows as policy inducement effects are more driven by industry-specific factors than by policy design, while Bauman *et al.* (2008) studied the circumstances under which command and control instruments have a stronger inducement effect with respect to economic instruments. Nevertheless, an evolutionary approach to environmental policies has enriched such literature as well. The latter is characterized by its focus on the need for properly designed policies to avoid technological lock-ins of incremental (suboptimal) EI at the expenses of radical and systemic ones (Del Río *et al.*, 2010) and by the recognition that policy instruments should differently fit each phase of the innovation process, from invention to diffusion (Jänicke & Lindemann, 2010). Despite these recent contributions, an organic theory on environmental policy has not emerged yet in the evolutionary literature, leaving room for future development of this fast growing discipline.

7. Discussion, Further Developments and Conclusions

Drawing a single conclusion for such a vast research field is certainly no easy task. If we keep to our division of contributions among subtasks, several different remarks can be made. Firstly, the 'determinants of EI' and 'inducement mechanism' subfields have a long tradition in academic research, which is reflected by the large number of available contributions and by coherent and robust evidence in the literature. On the other hand, the 'environmental effects' field is still in the early stages of development, with several open lines of research. Similarly, the literature on 'economic effects' can be expanded in numerous ways. Future directions of research can thus be highlighted.

For what concerns environmental effects, if the contributions summarized in Section 5 are considered, it is evident that they mostly focus on the regional level, with the majority being based on a single-country case study. Although these works highlight some interesting mechanisms through which EI can influence environmental quality, similar studies at the cross-country level (i.e. EU or OECD) are potentially of far greater interest, in view of the heterogeneous economic and institutional conditions as well as varying degrees of environmental responsibility awareness which can be analysed using longitudinal data. In addition, papers studying non-OECD countries are also extremely limited in number. A possible reason for the lack of broader investigations might be the scarcity of adequate and relevant data. A second point emerging from our research is the absence of a framework of reference, probably because of the relative novelty of this research strand in the literature. The majority of the articles presented in this section uses a number of hybrid environmental-economic indicators to describe environmental performances. This allows to account for the effect of economic growth on the environment, since often polluting emissions do not have market values by themselves.

Among the surveyed papers, the most widely used are environmental productivity and its reciprocal, emission intensity. Environmental productivity is introduced in Repetto (1990) and is computed as the ratio of value added to polluting emissions (e.g. GDP/CO_2); the indicator improves if its value increases. A positive change in the indicator might, however, not reflect an improvement of the environmental performance (the denominator) but solely an improvement in the economic performance (value added), which is the numerator. Thus, environmental productivity can reveal an increased environmental efficiency of economic activities but not an improvement of the environment conditions in absolute terms. From a mere environmental perspective, it might be more relevant to study the total emissions variation. Emission intensity, computed as the ratio of polluting emissions to value added (e.g. CO_2/GDP), carries a more straightforward information, since it can be interpreted as the emissions created by producing each unit of output. Similarly, holding emissions constant, an increase in value added reduces the emission intensity indicators' value (which is a positive result in this case) but it can only highlight that a firm or a sector has improved its environmental efficiency, not that there has been a reduction in polluting emissions.

To sum up, both environmental productivity and emission intensity are very useful indicator to assess the gains in environmental efficiency at the sectorial or at the firm level but not reliable to assess the achievement of a reduced level of emissions, which is, ultimately, the target set by most of the policy strategies. Future research might therefore focus more on the analysis of EI as a driver of an improved environmental performance. A third and final remark is that papers in this field often consider only the sectorial level of analysis. This is certainly the most appropriate dimension for these studies because of its importance in the diffusion of innovation. Nevertheless, efforts should be directed, on the one hand, at firm-level analyses to better understand the microeconomic dynamics leading to the achievement of better environmental outcomes and, on the other hand, at country-level investigations, which would shed light on the macroeconomic dynamics driving aggregate environmental performance.

A second strand of literature with potentially interesting extensions is the one regarding economic effects, in which many theoretical and empirical issues remain open to further investigation. The first issue concerns the dimensions of economic performance to be analysed. While many papers deal with measures of financial performance and productivity, little evidence is currently available about the job creation potential of EI and, to the best of our knowledge, no evidence is available about international competitiveness investigated at the microlevel. Moreover, these different measures of economic performance are generally analysed in isolation. For this reason, empirical analysis fails to account for possible asymmetries (and trade-offs) between short-term measures of performance and long-term measures. Therefore, the joint assessment of different measures is a promising line of research with the aim of accounting explicitly for heterogeneous effects of EI on different measures. Other open lines of research regard methodological advances which may improve the understanding of the link between EI and economic performance. One of the most promising lines of research tries to provide a joint assessment of the full link of causality among environmental regulation, EI and economic performance (e.g. Lanoie *et al.*, 2011; Van Leeuwen & Mohnen, 2013). The combination of these three dimensions allows scholars to draw on the theoretical and methodological advances achieved by two parallel strands of literature, that is, the one looking at the drivers of EI and the one looking at the effects of EI. It should be noted, however, that these approaches require fairly complex modelling efforts and detailed data on regulatory stringency, innovation and performance. Finally, while firm-level empirical analyses are crucial to identify causal links between EI and economic performance, little effort has been made to evaluate how EI affects players (e.g. firms, workers, etc.) not developing or adopting EI and, more generally, the general equilibrium effects of EI. This kind of evidence is important to identify winners and losers in EI development and adoption as well as the distributional impact of EI. When looking at aggregate effects, it is also important to account for interactions across different sectors in the development and diffusion of EI. Even though this issue was already investigated in few recent contributions reviewed earlier in this paper (e.g. Cainelli & Mazzanti, 2013; Mazzanti *et al.*, 2015), further research is needed to evaluate the relevance of cross-sectoral diffusion of knowledge related to EI as well as to quantify the role played by environmental regulation in manufacturing sector as a driver of EI in the service sector. As the service sector is increasing its share in EU economies (despite the nonbinding target set by the European Commission of increasing the share of manufacturing to 20% of value added by 2020),[3] the assessment of how EI is adopted and developed within the service sector as well as its impact on the (economic and environmental) performance of the service sector itself is particularly important.

Regarding employment, a growing stream of literature follows Horbach (2010) and Horbach and Rennings (2013) in looking at the net job creation of EI (Licht & Peters, 2013, 2014; Gagliardi *et al.*, 2016). Yet, evidence is absent on gross job creation and job destruction – particularly relevant due to the asymmetry between the social costs of destroying existing jobs and the social benefits of creating new jobs – and on the types of jobs created and destroyed by EI. The recent discussion on green jobs (ILO, 2013; OECD, 2014) shows that jobs created by environmental technologies are not necessarily high-wage and highly skilled jobs. Moreover, besides differentials in work conditions and earnings in jobs induced by EI, differences in required skills need to be assessed, with the aim of identifying potential skill gaps to be filled through education and training. Further theoretical and empirical analysis is needed in this regard to provide policy makers with appropriate guidance. For what concerns international competitiveness and trade, the increasingly popular analyses at the macro and sectorial level (e.g. Costantini & Mazzanti, 2012) have not yet been complemented by firm-level investigations. Microlevel analyses are especially significant to obtain more robust evidence on the causal links between EI and competitiveness – which may be influenced by various confusing factors in more aggregate studies – and, more importantly, to understand the mechanisms through which EI affect competitiveness. To name a few, we may think of the distinction between intensive and extensive margins of exporting firms or the assessment of the relationship between EI and distribution of partner countries and competitors, which can assist policy makers in the fields of trade regulation and industrial policy.

As for the remaining subfields, that is, policy inducement mechanism and determinants of EI, there is much less room for further research, since the debate has reached a certain level of maturity, at least in the empirical analysis. Nevertheless, as already underlined by Jaffe *et al.* (2002), the complex mechanisms linking technological change, EI, environmental policies and climate change '*cannot be resolved at a purely theoretical level or on the basis of aggregate empirical analysis alone*', but require detailed investigation in order to truly understand sectorial differences and circumstances which can influence the scale of these effects and not only lead to their potential presence. According to Jaffe *et al.* (2002), this is feasible only by increasing research efforts from multiple, extended points of view. In conclusion, we believe that the literature can indeed be expanded in this direction, enriching the existing debate with more qualitative evidence from case study research or other approaches.

Box 1 - Summary of the suggestions for further research

Environmental effects

- Cross-country-level studies (i.e. European Union or OECD and non-OECD countries) are needed to analyse the heterogeneous economic and institutional conditions as well as varying degrees of environmental responsibility awareness.
- Need to include pure environmental performances variables, such as the absolute level of polluting emissions beside hybrid economic-environmental indicator, to assess the impact of EI in the environment and the achievement of international environmental policy goals.
- Firm-level analyses are required to better understand the microeconomic dynamics leading to the achievement of better environmental outcomes.
- Country-level investigations would shed light on the macroeconomic dynamics driving aggregate environmental performance.

Economic effects

- More focus is needed on job creation potential of EI.
- The assessment of the effects of EI on international competitiveness at the macrolevel would provide further evidence on leaders and laggards countries in EI development adoption. Further investigation is required in understanding the full link of causality between regulation, EI and economic performance.
- Assessment of the differential between actors who adopt EI and those who do not adopt EI to identify winners and losers in EI development and adoption as well as the valuation of its distributional impacts.

Employment

- Need to shed light on the effects of EI on gross job creation and job destruction, which is relevant to the asymmetry between the social cost of job destruction and the social benefit of job creation.
- Description of the types of job which are created (and/or destructed) by EI.
- Description of the differences in skills required for the green jobs versus nongreen jobs and of their implication on education and training.

International competitiveness and trade

- Microlevel studies are needed to complement the firm-level investigation and to obtain robust evidence on the causal link between EI and competitiveness.

Policy inducement mechanism and determinants of EI

- Further investigation can be directed to truly understand sectorial differences and circumstances which can influence the scale of these effects and not only lead to their presence.

Acknowledgements

The authors acknowledge financial support through the PRIN-MIUR 2010–11 Italian National Research Project 'Climate changes in the Mediterranean area: scenarios, mitigation policies and technological innovation' (2010S2LHSE_002). The authors thank two anonymous referees for useful insights and comments. Usual disclaimers apply.

Notes

1. As it is explained in details in the next section, the network is built using scientific articles and books retrieved through keyword search. The network employs citations as arcs connecting the documents.
2. The meta-analysis on the literature on EI determinants proposed by Ghisetti and Pontoni (2015) shows that this trade-off between using survey versus patent data lead 30% of the scrutinized articles to choose patent data and 70% innovation survey data. Both measures face advantages and drawbacks which have been deeply discussed by previous literature (e.g. Pavitt, 1985; Griliches, 1990; Acs *et al.*, 2002). Using patent statistics to proxy EI has limitations related to patents' sector- and time- specificity, to the existence of nonpatentable innovations or (contrarily) of strategic patents, to the presence of alternative protection tools, to the fact that only a fraction of innovations are technological (thus patentable) and that associated costs make large firms more likely to patent than small ones. Alternatively, the use of direct EI counts is possible thanks to the existence of broad data sets (such as the Community Innovation Survey in Europe) that overcome the drawbacks of patent data but have the limitations of allowing mainly cross-sectional analysis (due to data availability) and of losing the richness of information on the specificity of the domain of the innovation and its relation to the existing knowledge base that are available (instead) in patent data.
3. Communication from the Commission to the European Parliament, the Council, the European Economic and Social Committee and the Committee of the Regions 'For a European Industrial Renaissance', 21 January 2014, COM(2014) 14 final.

References

Acs, Z.J., Anselin, L. and Varga, A. (2002) Patents and innovation counts as measures of regional production of new knowledge. *Research Policy* 31: 1069–1085.

Allan, C., Jaffe, A. B. and Sin, I. (2014) Diffusion of green technology: a survey. Motu Economic and Public Policy Research Working Paper 14-04.

Alpay, E., Kerkvliet, J. and Buccola, S. (2002) Productivity growth and environmental regulation in Mexican and US food manufacturing. *American Journal of Agricultural Economics* 84(4): 887–901.

Ambec, S., Cohen, M. A., Elgie, S. and Lanoie, P. (2013) The Porter hypothesis at 20: can environmental regulation enhance innovation and competitiveness?. *Review of Environmental Economics and Policy* 7(1): pp. 2–22.

Antonioli, D., Mancinelli, S. and Mazzanti, M. (2013) Is environmental innovation embedded within high-performance organisational changes? The role of human resource management and complementarity in green business strategies. *Research Policy* 42(4): 975–988.

Antonioli, D., Borghesi, S. and Mazzanti, M. (2016) Are regional systems greening the economy? Local spillovers, green innovations and firms' economic performances. *Economics of Innovation and New Technology, forthcoming.* http://dx.doi.org/10.1080/10438599.2015.1127557.

Barberá-Tomás, D. and Consoli, D. (2012) Whatever works: uncertainty and technological hybrids in medical innovation. *Technological Forecasting and Social Change* 79(5): 932–948.

Barbieri, N. (2015) Investigating the impacts of technological position and European environmental regulation on green automotive patent activity. *Ecological Economics* 117: 140–152.

Batagelj, V. (1991) *Some mathematics of network analysis.* Network Seminar, Pittsburgh, PA: Department of Sociology, University of Pittsburgh.

Batagelj, V. (2003) Efficient algorithms for citation network analysis. arXiv preprint cs/0309023.

Batagelj, V., Doreian, P., Ferligoj, A. and Kejzar, N. (2014) *Understanding Large Temporal Networks and Spatial Networks: Exploration, Pattern Searching, Visualization and Network Evolution.* West Sussex, UK: Wiley.

Bauman, Y., Lee, M. and Seeley, K. (2008) Does technological innovation really reduce marginal abatement costs? Some theory, algebraic evidence, and policy implications. *Environmental & Resource Economics* 40: 507–527.

Beise, M. and Rennings, K. (2005) Lead markets and regulation: a framework for analyzing the international diffusion of environmental innovations. *Ecological Economics* 52(1): 5–17.

Berman, E. and Bui, L. T. (2001) Environmental regulation and productivity: evidence from oil refineries. *Review of Economics and Statistics* 83(3): 498–510.

Brunnermeier, S. B. and Cohen, M. A. (2003) Determinants of environmental innovation in US manufacturing industries. *Journal of Environmental Economics and Management* 45(2): 278–293.

Cainelli, G. and Mazzanti, M. (2013) Environmental innovations in services: manufacturing–services integration and policy transmissions. *Research Policy* 42(9): 1595–1604.

Cainelli, G., Mazzanti, M. and Montresor, S. (2012) Environmental innovations, local networks and internationalization. *Industry and Innovation* 19(8): 697–734.

Carrión-Flores, C. E. and Innes, R. (2010) Environmental innovation and environmental performance. *Journal of Environmental Economics and Management* 59(1): 27–42.

Cecere, G., Corrocher, N., Gossart, C. and Ozman, M. (2014) Lock-in and path dependence: an evolutionary approach to eco-innovations. *Journal of Evolutionary Economics* 24(5): 1037–1065.

Cheng, C. C., Yang, C. L. and Sheu, C. (2014) The link between eco-innovation and business performance: a Taiwanese industry context. *Journal of Cleaner Production* 64: 81–90.

Consoli, D. and Ramlogan, R. (2008) Out of sight: problem sequences and epistemic boundaries of medical know-how on glaucoma. *Journal of Evolutionary Economics* 18(1): 31–56.

Corradini, M., Costantini, V., Mancinelli, S. and Mazzanti, M. (2014) Unveiling the dynamic relation between R&D and emission abatement: national and sectoral innovation perspectives from the EU. *Ecological Economics* 102: 48–59.

Costantini, V. and Crespi, F. (2008) Environmental regulation and the export dynamics of energy technologies. *Ecological Economics* 66(2): 447–460.

Costantini, V. and Crespi, F. (2013) Public policies for a sustainable energy sector: regulation, diversity and fostering of innovation. *Journal of Evolutionary Economics* 23(2): 401–429.

Costantini, V. and Mazzanti, M. (2012) On the green and innovative side of trade competitiveness? The impact of environmental policies and innovation on EU exports. *Research Policy* 41(1): 132–153.

Costantini, V., Mazzanti, M. and Montini, A. (2013) Environmental performance, innovation and spillovers. Evidence from a regional NAMEA. *Ecological Economics* 89: 101–114.

Cuerva, M. C., Triguero-Cano, Á. and Córcoles, D. (2014) Drivers of green and non-green innovation: empirical evidence in low-tech SMEs. *Journal of Cleaner Production* 68: 104–113.

De Marchi, V. (2012) Environmental innovation and R&D cooperation: empirical evidence from Spanish manufacturing firms. *Research Policy* 41(3): 614–623.

De Marchi, V. and Grandinetti, R. (2013) Knowledge strategies for environmental innovations: the case of Italian manufacturing firms. *Journal of Knowledge Management* 17(4): 569–582.

De Solla Price, D.J. (1965) Networks of scientific papers. *Science* 149: 510–515.

De Vries, F. P. and Withagen, C. (2005) Innovation and environmental stringency: the case of sulfur dioxide abatement. CentER Discussion Paper Series No. 2005–18.

Dechezlepretre, A. and Sato, M. (2014) The impacts of environmental regulations on competitiveness. Policy brief November 2014, Grantham Research Institute on Climate Change and the Environment, Global Green Growth Institute.

Del Río, P. (2009) The empirical analysis of the determinants for environmental technological change: a research agenda. *Ecological Economics* 68(3): 861–878.

Del Río, P., Carrillo-Hermosilla, J. and Könnölä, T. (2010) Policy strategies to promote eco-innovation. *Journal of Industrial Ecology* 14(4): 541–557.

Demirel, P. and Kesidou, E. (2011) Stimulating different types of eco-innovation in the UK: government policies and firm motivations. *Ecological Economics* 70(8): 1546–1557.

Dopfer, K. (2012) The origins of meso economics. *Journal of Evolutionary Economics* 22(1): 133–160.

Duchin, F., Lange, G. M. and Kell, G. (1995) Technological change, trade and the environment. *Ecological Economics* 14(3): 185–193.

EC (2014) For a European industrial renaissance, communication of the European Commission COM 014/2014.

EEA (2014) Resource-efficient green economy and EU policies. EEA Report No 2/2014. European Environment Agency, Copenhagen.

EEA (2015) *Technological Solutions and Behavioural Change Needed to Decarbonise Transport*. Copenhagen: EEA.

Ekins, P. (2010) Eco-innovation for environmental sustainability: concepts, progress and policies. *International Economics and Economic Policy* 7(2-3): 267–290.

Epicoco, M. (2013) Knowledge patterns and sources of leadership: mapping the semiconductor miniaturization trajectory. *Research Policy* 42(1): 180–195.

Faucheux, S. and Nicolaı, I. (1998) Environmental technological change and governance in sustainable development policy. *Ecological Economics* 27(3): 243–256.

Fischer, C., Parry, I.W.H. and Pizer, W.A. (2003) Instrument choice for environmental protection when technological innovation is endogenous. *Journal of Environmental Economics and Management* 45: 523–545.

Gagliardi, L., Marin, G. and Miriello, C. (2016) The greener the better? Job creation and environmentally friendly technological change. *Industrial and Corporate Change* online first.

Garfield, E. (1955) Citation indexes for sciences. *Science* 122: 108–111.

Garfield, E., Sher, I. H. and Torpie, R. J. (1964) *The Use of Citation Data in Writing the History of Science*. Philadelphia: Institute for Scientific Information.

Ghisetti, C. and Pontoni, F. (2015) Investigating policy and R&D effects on environmental innovation: a meta-analysis. *Ecological Economics* 118: 57–66.

Ghisetti, C. and Quatraro, F. (2013) Beyond inducement in climate change: does environmental performance spur environmental technologies? A regional analysis of cross-sectoral differences. *Ecological Economics* 96: 99–113.

Ghisetti, C. and Rennings, K. (2014) Environmental innovations and profitability: how does it pay to be green? An empirical analysis on the German innovation survey. *Journal of Cleaner Production* 75: 106–117.

Ghisetti, C., Marzucchi, A. and Montresor, S. (2015) The open eco-innovation mode. An empirical investigation of eleven European countries. *Research Policy* 44(5): 1080–1093.

Gilli, M., Mazzanti, M. and Nicolli, F. (2013) Sustainability and competitiveness in evolutionary perspectives: environmental innovations, structural change and economic dynamics in the EU. *Journal of Socio-Economics* 45: 204–215.

Gilli, M., Mancinelli, S. and Mazzanti, M. (2014) Innovation complementarity and environmental productivity effects: reality or delusion? Evidence from the EU. *Ecological Economics* 103: 56–67.

Griliches, Z. (1990) Patent statistics as economic indicators: a survey. *Journal of Economic Literature* 28: 1661–1707.

Horbach, J. (2008) Determinants of environmental innovation—new evidence from German panel data sources. *Research Policy* 37(1): 163–173.

Horbach, J. (2010) The impact of innovation activities on employment in the environmental sector-empirical results for Germany at the firm level. *Journal of Economics and Statistics* 230(4): 403–419.

Horbach, J. and Rennings, K. (2013) Environmental innovation and employment dynamics in different technology fields–an analysis based on the German Community Innovation Survey 2009. *Journal of Cleaner Production* 57: 158–165.

Horbach, J., Rammer, C. and Rennings, K. (2012) Determinants of eco-innovations by type of environmental impact—the role of regulatory push/pull, technology push and market pull. *Ecological Economics* 78: 112–122.

Hummon, N. P. and Doreian, P. (1989) Connectivity in a citation network: the development of DNA theory. *Social Networks* 11(1): 39–63.

Hummon, N. P. and Doreian, P. (1990) Computational methods for social network analysis. *Social Networks* 12(4): 273–288.

ILO (2013) Methodologies for assessing green jobs. International Labour Organization, Policy Brief.

Inoue, E., Arimura, T. H. and Nakano, M. (2013) A new insight into environmental innovation: does the maturity of environmental management systems matter?. *Ecological Economics* 94: 156–163.

Jaffe, A. B. and Palmer, K. (1997) Environmental regulation and innovation: a panel data study. *Review of Economics and Statistics* 79(4): 610–619.

Jaffe, A. B. and Stavins, R. N. (1995) Dynamic incentives of environmental regulations: the effects of alternative policy instruments on technology diffusion. *Journal of Environmental Economics and Management* 29(3): S43–S63.

Jaffe, A. B., Newell, R. G. and Stavins, R. N. (2002) Environmental policy and technological change. *Environmental and Resource Economics* 22(1-2): 41–70.

Jaffe, A. B., Newell, R. G. and Stavins, R. N. (2003) Technological change and the environment. In: K.-G. Mäler, J.R. Vincent, (eds.), *Handbook of Environmental Economics*, pp. 461–516. Amsterdam, The Netherlands: Elsevier.

Jänicke, M. and Lindemann, S. (2010) Governing environmental innovations. *Environmental Politics* 19(1): 127–141.

Johnstone, N., Haščič, I. and Popp, D. (2010) Renewable energy policies and technological innovation: evidence based on patent counts. *Environmental and Resource Economics* 45(1): 133–155.

Kemp, R. and Pearson, P. (2007) Final report MEI project about measuring eco- innovation. European Environment.

Kesidou, E. and Demirel, P. (2012) On the drivers of eco-innovations: empirical evidence from the UK. *Research Policy* 41(5): 862–870.

Khanna, M. and Anton, W. R. Q. (2002) Corporate environmental management: regulatory and market-based incentives. *Land Economics* 78(4): 539–558.

Lanoie, P., Patry, M. and Lajeunesse, R. (2008) Environmental regulation and productivity: new findings on the Porter hypothesis. *Journal of Productivity Analysis* 30(2): 121–128.

Lanoie, P., Laurent-Lucchetti, J., Johnstone, N. and Ambec, S. (2011) Environmental policy, innovation and performance: new insights on the Porter hypothesis. *Journal of Economics & Management Strategy* 20(3): 803–842.

Licht, G. and Peters, B. (2013) The impact of green innovation on employment growth in Europe. WWWforEurope Working Paper 50.

Licht, G. and Peters, B. (2014) Do green innovations stimulate employment?–firm-level evidence from Germany. WWWforEurope Working Paper 53.

Lu, L. Y. and Liu, J. S. (2014) A survey of intellectual property rights literature from 1971 to 2012: the main path analysis. Management of Engineering & Technology (PICMET), 2014 Portland International Conference on (pp. 1274–1280) IEEE.

Marin, G. (2014) Do eco-innovations harm productivity growth through crowding out? Results of an extended CDM model for Italy. *Research Policy* 43(2): 301–317.

Marin, G. and Mazzanti, M. (2013) The evolution of environmental and labor productivity dynamics. *Journal of Evolutionary Economics* 23(2): 357–399.

Martinelli, A. and Nomaler, Ö. (2014) Measuring knowledge persistence: a genetic approach to patent citation networks. *Journal of Evolutionary Economics* 24(3): 623–652.

Mazzanti, M. and Montini, A. (2010) Embedding the drivers of emission efficiency at regional level—analyses of NAMEA data. *Ecological Economics* 69(12): 2457–2467.

Mazzanti, M. and Zoboli, R. (2006) Economic instruments and induced innovation: the European policies on end-of-life vehicles. *Ecological Economics* 58(2): 318–337.

Mazzanti, M. and Zoboli, R. (2009) Environmental efficiency and labour productivity: trade-off or joint dynamics? A theoretical investigation and empirical evidence from Italy using NAMEA. *Ecological Economics* 68(4): 1182–1194.

Mazzanti, M., Marin, G., Mancinelli, S. and Nicolli, F. (2015) Carbon dioxide reducing environmental innovations, sector upstream/downstream integration and policy: evidence from the EU. *Empirica* 42(4): 709–735.

McGuire, M. C. (1982) Regulation, factor rewards, and international trade. *Journal of Public Economics* 17(3): 335–354.

Mina, A., Ramlogan, R., Tampubolon, G. and Metcalfe, J. S. (2007) Mapping evolutionary trajectories: applications to the growth and transformation of medical knowledge. *Research Policy* 36(5): 789–806.

Nesta, L., Vona, F. and Nicolli, F. (2014) Environmental policies, competition and innovation in renewable energy. *Journal of Environmental Economics and Management* 67(3): 396–411.

OECD (2014) Issue note addressing social implications of green growth: inclusive labour markets for green growth. Green Growth and Sustainable Development Forum, 13–14 November 2014.

Oltra, V. and Saint Jean, M. (2009) Sectoral systems of environmental innovation: an application to the French automotive industry. *Technological Forecasting and Social Change* 76(4): 567–583.

Parry, I. W. (1995) Optimal pollution taxes and endogenous technological progress. *Resource and Energy Economics* 17(1): 69–85.

Pavitt, K. (1985) Patent statistics as indicators of innovative activities: possibilities and problems. *Scientometrics* 7(1): 77–99.

Pethig, R. (1976) Pollution, welfare, and environmental policy in the theory of comparative advantage. *Journal of Environmental Economics and Management* 2(3): 160–169.

Popp, D. (2002) Induced innovation and energy prices. *American Economic Review* 92(1): 160–180.

Popp, D. (2003) Pollution control innovations and the Clean Air Act of 1990. *Journal of Policy Analysis and Management* 22(4): 641–660.

Popp, D. (2005) Lessons from patents: using patents to measure technological change in environmental models. *Ecological Economics* 54(2): 209–226.

Popp, D., Newell, R. G. and Jaffe, A. B. (2010) Energy, the environment, and technological change. *Handbook of the Economics of Innovation* 2: 873–937.

Porter, M.E. (1991) America's green strategy. *Scientific American* 264(4).

Porter, M. E. a¹ d van der Linde, C. (1995) Toward a new conception of the environment-competitiveness relationship. *Journal of Economic Perspectives* 97–118.

Rehfeld, K. M., Rennings, K. and Ziegler, A. (2007) Integrated product policy and environmental product innovations: an empirical analysis. *Ecological Economics* 61(1): 91–100.

Rennings, K. (2000) Redefining innovation—eco-innovation research and the contribution from ecological economics. *Ecological Economics* 32(2): 319–332.

Rennings, K., Ziegler, A., Ankele, K. and Hoffmann, E. (2006) The influence of different characteristics of the EU environmental management and auditing scheme on technical environmental innovations and economic performance. *Ecological Economics* 57(1): 45–59.

Repetto, R. (1990) Environmental productivity and why it is so important. *Challenge* 33–38.

Requate, T. (2005) Dynamic incentives by environmental policy instruments—a survey. *Ecological Economics* 54(2): 175–195.

Schmidt, T. S., Schneider, M. and Hoffmann, V. H. (2012) Decarbonising the power sector via technological change – differing contributions from heterogeneous firms. *Energy Policy* 43: 466–479.

Schumpeter, J. (1942) *Capitalism, Socialism and Democracy. Harper & Brothers*, New York, United States.

UNEP (2014) The Business Case for Eco-Innovation. ISBN: 978-92-807-3334-1.

Van Leeuwen, G. and Mohnen, P. A. (2013) Revisiting the Porter hypothesis: an empirical analysis of green innovation for the Netherlands. UNU-MERIT Working Paper Series 2.

Wagner, M. (2007) On the relationship between environmental management, environmental innovation and patenting: evidence from German manufacturing firms. *Research Policy* 36(10): 1587–1602.

Wagner, M. (2008) Empirical influence of environmental management on innovation: evidence from Europe. *Ecological Economics* 66(2): 392–402.

Wang, Z., Yang, Z., Zhang, Y. and Yin, J. (2012) Energy technology patents–CO_2 emissions nexus: an empirical analysis from China. *Energy Policy* 42: 248–260.

Weina, D., Gilli, M., Mazzanti, M. and Nicolli, F. (2016) Green inventions and greenhouse gas emission dynamics: A close examination of provincial Italian data. *Environmental Economics and Policy Studies* (e-published ahead of print).

Ziegler, A. and Nogareda, J. S. (2009) Environmental management systems and technological environmental innovations: exploring the causal relationship. *Research Policy* 38(5): 885–893.

11

ECONOMIC TARGETS AND LOSS-AVERSION IN INTERNATIONAL ENVIRONMENTAL COOPERATION

Doruk İriş

Sogang University

Politics is too serious a matter to be left to the politicians.—Charles de Gaulle

1. Introduction

In many economic models, we assume that governments make optimal choices for their country by taking into account the benefits and the costs to the country. However, in reality, governments' objectives often differ from that of their countries, since they have additional incentives to be reelected. In this paper, we argue that similar situation also exists when governments decide on their emission cuts. It is widely known that political parties consider economic benefits to be of greater importance since these benefits are more visible and certain to voters than the results of environmental policies.[1] As a result, they would have additional incentives to introduce some populist policies in order to achieve some economic targets. Political parties could perceive these targets as critical levels and believe economic benefits below these targets would displease voters. Furthermore, political parties would be averse to perform poorly in these economic aspects, since it might cost them the next election. For example, an increase in gasoline tax could be better for the country but not eventually implemented due to such distortionary incentives of the ruling party. In this paper, we aim to understand the implications of such possibly relevant incentives on international environmental cooperation.

To model this, we assume that political parties perceive economic benefits from emission not only in absolute levels but also as gains or losses relative to their economic targets. Furthermore, the political parties are averse to insufficient economic performances. More specifically, economic targets are reference levels such that, if a country's economic benefit from emissions is higher than its economic target, then its leaders find the economic performance sufficient

Environmental Economics and Sustainability, First Edition. Edited by Brian Chi-ang Lin and Siqi Zheng.

(i.e., a gain). However, if the benefit is less than its economic target, then its leaders find the economic performance insufficient (i.e., a loss). Thus, this paper introduces the widely used phenomena of reference-dependent preferences and loss-aversion into the international environmental cooperation.

Kahneman and Tversky (1979) argue that people perceive outcomes as gains and losses relative to a reference level, which may be current assets, the *status quo*, or expectations, rather than final wealth or a welfare level. Furthermore, people exhibit loss-aversion, which is the tendency to strongly prefer avoiding losses to acquiring gains. Reference-dependence and loss-aversion have been employed to provide insight into various phenomena both at the individual and government level by economists, political scientists, and psychologists.[2]

The motivation and the behavior of the model described above can be observed in two possible scenarios. First, political parties are rational; they take actions to maximize not only the net benefit to the country, but also their own private interests to increase the prospects of winning elections (Persson and Tabellini, 2000; Besley, 2006). They can seek these interests because voters may be incapable of making optimal choices due to their biases, limited knowledge, and limited cognitive abilities. For instance, rational political parties may be reluctant to change to greener policies if voters are averse to economic losses (Alesina and Passarelli, 2015), or if they are influenced by special interest groups (Grossman and Helpman, 1994). In the latter case, parties may strive to reach an economic target because of strong business lobbyists expecting some economic targets to be achieved (Dietz *et al.*, 2012). Oates and Portney (2003) provide an extensive review of lobby groups on environmental policies.

Second, political parties may share such limitations of rationality themselves and be unable to make optimal choices. Simon (1985) argues that political parties exhibit bounded rationality, especially when decisions are complex. Caplan (2008) argues that voters keep electing politicians who either share their biases or else pretend to, resulting in bad policies winning again and again by popular demand. Congleton (1992) argues that politicians tend to be myopic. They are often driven by electoral cycles and short-term interests. Thus, they neglect long-term costs of climate change for the short-term economic benefits, even though it is against societal interests. Gsottbauer and van den Bergh (2013) study the impact of voters' and politicians' bounded rationality and social preferences on bargaining in international climate negotiations. They illustrate how different deviations from rationality change the incentives to cooperate. Conrad and Kohn (1996) provide empirical evidence that SO_2 permit markets does not respond to public policies as policymakers expected.

Bendor *et al.* (2011), in their recent book on behavioral theories of elections, show that political parties and/or voters' aspiration (reference) levels influence party competition, turnout, and voters' choices of candidates. Schumacher *et al.* (2015) explain why governments change their election platform more often than opposition parties. They argue with empirical evidence that parties with low aspiration change more when they are in government than in opposition due to loss-aversion. For example, when the German Green Party moved into office first time as the coalition partner of Social Democratic Party in 1998, they changed their platform significantly. In short, the economic issues became more important, while environmental issues became less important. Even though it costed the party some activists and many loyal voters, it was able to remain as an attractive coalition partner and achieved the highest nationwide votes ever.[3,4]

Reference points are argued to be *status quo* or endowment (Tversky and Kahneman, 1991), formed based on social comparisons (Shafir *et al.*, 1997), or based on goals and aspirations (Heath *et al.*, 1999). In our model, a country's economic target could be determined by its past performance and targets (*status quo*), current and expected future performances (expectations), performances of other countries (social comparison), and political parties' declarations, among others (ideally backed by empirical evidence.) For instance, overly optimistic declarations might cause ambitiously high economic targets. Miler (2009), using personal interviews with political elites and a quasi-experimental design, finds that politicians often use decision heuristics and suffer from overoptimistic forecasts. Similarly, Frankel (2011) studies the forecasts of real growth rates made by official government agencies in 33 countries. He finds that forecasts have a positive average bias and that this bias is even stronger in economic booms. In addition, while economic busts lower the voters' expectations, it also raises attention in economic issues relative to environmental ones and, thus, can increase the economic targets.[5]

Since economic targets may depend on numerous variables, we follow the mainstream loss-aversion literature and assume countries' economic targets to be exogenous. Moreover, we allow economic targets and economic target concerns (i.e., how much targets are valued comparing to the benefit and the cost of emissions and, how averse political parties are to insufficient economic performances) to differ between the countries. We also allow countries to differ in their development levels, particularly in their technological efficiencies. In this context, a technologically efficient (developed) country needs to emit less than a (developing) country that is not as technologically efficient in order to generate the same economic surplus.

To address the consequences for international environmental agreements (IEAs) of economic targets and loss-aversion, we develop a dynamic game in which countries face a free-riding public goods problem and attempt to maintain cooperation in their national emission strategies. Here, emitted pollution is assumed to be transboundary. We restrict our attention to IEAs that are self-enforcing, as in Ferrara *et al.* (2009) and Hadjiyiannis *et al.* (2012), since there is no supranational authority to enforce environmental policy mechanisms. In this context, a country prefers to sustain cooperation on agreed-upon emission policies, as long as the discounted future welfare losses from a breakdown in international environmental cooperation outweigh the one-time gain of a unilateral deviation from the cooperative path.

We abstract from any participation considerations, which have been at the center of IEA literature (D'Aspremont *et al.*, 1983; Hoel, 1992; Carraro and Siniscalco, 1993; Barrett, 1994). Barrett (2005) and Finus (2008) provide excellent reviews of the literature. Instead, we look for the sustainability of a cooperative emission level, particularly the most cooperative emission level, by countries aiming to achieve their economic targets and that are averse to economic losses within the context of a self-enforcing IEA involving full participation. We compare the sustainability of a cooperative emission level by studying different sets of countries that vary in terms of their economic targets, economic target concerns, and technological efficiencies. We examine sets of countries that are both symmetric and asymmetric in terms of these characteristics. Note that much of the literature on IEAs examines the case of symmetric countries. However, only a few studies provide a theoretical examination of countries that are asymmetric in terms of their size and marginal damage from pollution (Kolstad, 2010), marginal costs and benefits of abatement (McGinty, 2007; Pavlova and de Zeeuw, 2013), and technologies (Mendez and Trelles, 2000).

Furthermore, we separate from the electoral process for the tractability of the model and focus on their potential effects on political parties. Based on empirical evidence, Cazals and Sauquet (2015) show that political leaders' levels of commitment to IEAs differ based on the timing of elections. Buchholz *et al.* (2005) provide a theoretical examination of the implications of the electoral process for IEAs, and find significant adverse effects. In their model, two countries bargain on a treaty that binds once it is reached. On the other hand, in our model, the agreement is self-enforcing, the game is infinitely repeated, and played among n countries.

Our analysis on economic targets provide the following findings. First, we show that if a country has stronger economic target concerns, that is, it values its economic targets more and/or becomes more averse to economic losses, then this country finds it more difficult to sustain cooperation. However, higher economic target concern in one country facilitates sustainability of an agreed cooperative emissions in other countries owing to strategic substitutability of emission levels. Second, in the case that all countries have stronger economic target concerns, sustaining an agreed-upon cooperative emission level might become easier for some sufficiently developed countries but harder for some developing countries. So, an agreed cooperative emission level could not be sustained after all countries having stronger economic target concerns if a transfer mechanism is absent.

Third, we show that a decrease in a country's ability to sustain cooperation means the most (lowest) cooperative emission level this country can sustain increases. Thus, the most cooperative emissions countries can sustain can be ordered from the lowest to highest as follows: no country cares about economic targets, all countries reach their targets, and no country reaches its targets.

Finally, our analysis on asymmetry in technological efficiencies provides the following findings. Consistent with Mendez and Trelles (2000), the more asymmetric the countries are in their technological efficiencies, the more difficult it is for them to sustain a cooperation emission level. Furthermore, we show that the impact of further asymmetry in economic target concerns is ambiguous. Asymmetry in economic target concerns may correct the negative impact of asymmetry in technological efficiencies on sustaining cooperation if economic target concerns are lower for developing countries and higher for developed countries. Otherwise, it becomes another obstacle for countries to support a greater degree of international environmental cooperation. These results provide another perspective on why leaders have to be further motivated for greener policies by citizens when they are to negotiate in the international arena.

The remainder of this paper is organized as follows: Section 2 reviews the literature. Section 3 presents the basics of the model. Section 4 characterizes the static Nash equilibrium of our model. Section 5 analyzes the dynamic game. Section 6 provides two numerical analysis: the first subsection studies the impact of economic target concerns on the most cooperative emissions. The second subsection analyzes the model for technologically asymmetric countries and gives insights of North–South model. Finally, Section 7 offers concluding remarks and relates the predictions of our model to the ongoing U.N. Climate Summits. The Appendix contains supporting calculations not included in the primary paper as well as the proofs of propositions and Lemma 1.

2. Literature Review

2.1 *Rationality of Individuals and Political Entities*

During the last decades, ample evidence from psychology and lab experiments, and more recently, also from field data, field experiments, and brain scans show that people are not fully rational and self-interested, despite its central role in standard economic analysis in the 20th century. Behavioral economics builds new models with the aim of increasing psychological realism of economic analyses and, thus, improve the field of economics by developing new theoretical understandings, making better predictions, and advise better policies. There have been already several surveys and books comprehensively reviewing the field. A recent example, DellaVigna (2009) provides an excellent survey on the empirical evidence of nonstandard preferences (self-control problems, reference-dependent preferences, and social preferences), nonstandard beliefs (overconfidence, law of small numbers, and projection bias), nonstandard decision making (framing, limited attention, menu effects, persuasion and social pressure, and emotions), and their impacts on market behavior. Camerer *et al.* (2003) and Kahneman and Tversky (2000) contain many of the early pioneering works, both theoretical concepts and applications. Camerer and Loewenstein (2003) and Fudenberg (2006) discuss the past, present, and future of behavioral economics. In addition, Kagel and Roth (1995) and Camerer (2003) are the two important sources for the methods and findings of the experimental economics.

Simon argued that politicians are also boundedly rational. More specifically, politicians have selective attention especially when they are under stress and have time constraints. Moreover, they often make decisions based on imperfect information. As a result of such constraints, they make mistakes, often decide some options that are good enough rather than the optimal one maximizing the social welfare (satisficing heuristic) (Simon, 1985). Conlisk (1996) and Mc-Fadden (1999) argue that bounded rationality is also important explanatory variable in large organizations, including national governments. In his review of bounded rationality in political science, Jones (1999) observes that both individuals and groups do not respond perfectly in complicated environments. Tetlock (2005) provides empirical evidence of many policy experts' inaccuracies in forecasting and concludes that experts are inclined to the same biases as nonexperts. Similarly, Fischhoff *et al.* (1982) show that experts often make mistakes owing to their misinterpretation of risks. Johnson and Tierney (2003) and Kahneman and Renshon (2009) applied Prospect Theory (a theory heavily based on loss-aversion and reference levels; Section 2.2 discusses in detail) to international relations and show that decision biases and heuristics can elevate international conflicts rather than cooperation. Gsottbauer and van den Bergh (2013) discuss the role of various actors' (from citizens to politicians) bounded rationality and other-regarding preferences on climate change negotiations.

Modern neoclassical economics models have been criticized for treating households, firms, countries, and other organizations as fully rational individuals. Behavioral and experimental economists clearly show the limitations of rationality for the individuals. Many have also argued (and some provide evidence) that politicians, experts, and organizations also share some of the decision biases and, thus, have some limitations in rationality, as discussed in the previous paragraph. Still, the agents at certain levels seem to be more rational than individuals.

In the last 15 years, experiments study whether groups behave differently than individuals. They almost uniformly show that groups act more rational than individuals. Charness and Sutter (2012) review the literature comparing group behavior with individual behavior and provide three lessons. First, they take studies of investment or portfolio decisions, tournaments, and tasks requiring the ability to reason and conclude that groups are more cognitively sophisticated. Second, they benefit from various real-effort and productivity field experiments and conclude that groups can help with self-control and productivity problems. Third, they review studies focusing on trust, social dilemma, and coordination games and conclude that groups may decrease welfare because of stronger self-interested preferences. While in the first two lessons group decision-making help individuals containing their behavioral biases, third lesson show that group decision-making can have a detrimental effect on social welfare. Nevertheless, group behavior, while still not the same, is closer to the standard economic model's prediction.

On the other hand, İriş *et al.* (2015) study the role of delegation and public pressure in a climate change experiment. In their experiment, four elected delegates, representing their sub-groups, play a one-shot threshold public goods game in which the aim is to avoid losses that can ensue if the sum of their contributions falls short of a threshold. So, this is a disaster scenario and avoiding it requires collective action while individually each delegate has free-riding incentives. They show that delegation leads to a small decrease in the group contributions. Public pressure is defined as a form of teammates' messages to their delegate and design to be payoff-inconsequential. Nevertheless, public pressure has a significant negative effect on contributions. The reason for the latter finding is that delegates tend to follow the lowest of the public good contributions suggestions by their teammates. Interestingly, the standard model predicts no difference between individual and delegate behavior with or without public pressure. Delegate behavior with public pressure could shed further lights on why groups behave more self-interestedly in such coordination and social dilemma games.

2.2 *Loss-Aversion and Reference-Dependent Preferences*

Kahneman and Tversky's Prospect Theory explain most of the experimental evidence on decision making under risk, unlike the standard model.[6] The model is characterized by four components: loss-aversion, reference-dependence, diminishing sensitivity (people are more sensitive to changes around reference level than changes far from it), and probability weighting (people subjectively overweight low probabilities and underweight high probabilities). Tversky and Kahneman (1992) develop a new model by allowing decision weights to be cumulative rather than separable, incorporating rank-dependent utility (Quiggin, 1982). Tversky and Kahneman (1991) also apply the reference-dependent preferences to riskless choice settings, such as to incorporate the initial entitlements (*status quo*) into consumer theory.

Most of the follow-up literature, including this paper, employ a simplified version of the Prospect Theory by adopting only loss-aversion and reference-dependence (DellaVigna, 2009). Reference-dependent preferences help explain ubiquitous phenomena such as excessive aversion to small risks in the laboratory (Kahneman and Tversky, 1979), endowment effect for inexperienced traders (Kahneman *et al.*, 1991), resistance of lowering consumption in response to bad news about future income (Bowman *et al.*, 1999), the reluctance to sell houses at a loss (Genesove and Mayer, 2001), equity premium puzzle in asset returns (Benartzi and Thaler, 1995; Barberis *et al.*, 2001), the disposition effect, that is, the tendency to sell winners rather than losers in financial markets (Odean, 1998), eliminating paradoxical effects of monetary variance in macroeconomic policy (Ciccarone and Marchetti, 2013), inefficient task allocation in contract theory (Daido *et al.*, 2013), the energy paradox (Greene, 2011), target earnings in labor supply decisions (Camerer *et al.*, 1997; Fehr and Goette, 2007), the tendency to insure against small risks (Sydnor, 2010), and effort in the employment relationship (Mas, 2006), among many others.

While reference-dependence and loss-aversion help explain ubiquitous phenomena, how the reference points are determined remains an open question. The reference points are generally assumed to be exogenous. Recently, Kőszegi and Rabin (2006) develop a new model of reference-dependence in which the reference points are determined endogenously by the economic environment. They assume that a person's reference point is the person's rational expectations about the outcomes, which are determined in a personal equilibrium. Their model requires the expectations to be consistent with the optimal behavior given expectations. Their paper has received have attention by many researchers.

Several field experiments have employed subjects with trading experience and find no evidence of loss-aversion (List, 2003, 2004). Thus, they conclude that experience mitigates loss-aversion. Kőszegi and Rabin (2006) provide another explanation. They argue that experience does not affect experienced subjects' loss-aversion, but it influences the reference point formation. Thus, if experienced subjects expect to sell their objects, then selling the object is not regarded as a loss.

Several studies examine how behavioral economics can advance the science of environmental and resource economics. Shogren *et al.* (2010) argue that loss-aversion could be crucial for nonmarket valuations. Gsottbauer and van den Bergh (2013) argue that political leaders frame the climate change problem as a loss or a gain to alter behavior to promote greener policies (e.g., Al Gore) or to favor inaction (e.g., the Bush administration.) To the best of our knowledge, İriş and Tavoni (2015) is the only other study, which employs loss-aversion to examine international environmental agreements. They investigate the impact of loss-aversion with respect to a threshold amount of environmental damage, which is viewed as indicative of an approaching catastrophe. Our study differs significantly from that of İriş and Tavoni (2015), because the latter focuses on coalition formation, and particularly the sizes of coalitions and the types of countries that form a coalition in the case of asymmetry in their beliefs on environmental safe operating limits (references) and in their perceived vulnerability when a threshold is exceeded (loss-aversion). This paper contributes to this literature by bringing issues from the political economy into the international environmental cooperation.

There are several excellent reviews of reference-dependent preferences. As mentioned before, DellaVigna (2009) surveys the empirical evidence of reference-dependent preferences and their impacts on market behavior. Barberis and Thaler (2003) provide another excellent review of reference-dependent preferences on finance, and Mercer (2005) on political science and international relations. Two other interesting papers worth mentioning are Wang *et al.* (2016) and Chen *et al.* (2006). Wang *et al.* (2016) conduct an international survey and collect measurements of the loss-aversion parameter in 53 countries. Their study analyzes the systematic difference of loss-aversion across cultures and regions. On the other hand, Chen *et al.* (2006) show that not only humans but also capuchin monkeys exhibit reference-dependence and loss-aversion.

Most of the ideas of behavioral economics, as well as loss-aversion, date significantly back in time. As noted by Camerer and Loewenstein (2003), Adam Smith's relatively less well-known book "*The Theory of Moral Sentiments*" profoundly discusses the psychological principles of individual behavior. Many behavioral economists have influenced by the ideas of this book. In fact, Smith also comments on the idea of loss-aversion (Smith, 1892, p. 311): "we suffer more ... when we fall from a better to a worse situation, than we ever enjoy when we rise from a worse to a better."

3. The Model

We assume the world consists of n countries.[7] The countries have perfect information about the world, and decide simultaneously on an emission level of a pollutant substance, $x_i \in (0, 1)$. Emissions have a negative environmental effect and give rise to negative externalities owing to transboundary effects. In other words, emissions in country i pollute the environment in country i, as well as in other countries. However, emissions are unavoidable for production, which creates surpluses for producers and consumers. Our model builds on the work of Mendez and Trelles (2000) and incorporates countries' economic targets into the problem. The net-benefit function for country i, which also aims to reach its *economic target*, is as follows:

$$B_i(x_1, \ldots, x_n) = b_i(x_i) - p_i(x_1, \ldots, x_n) + \gamma_i t_i \left(x_i, b_i^R\right) \tag{1}$$

where country i's economic benefit $b_i(x_i)$ depends only on its emissions, the cost of pollution $p_i(x_1, \ldots, x_n)$ depends on all countries' emission levels, and the target utility $t_i(x_i, b_i^R)$ depends on the country's emissions and economic target b_i^R. The scaling factor $\gamma_i > 0$ measures how much country i cares about its target utility relative to the benefits and costs of emissions. We assume the following functional forms:

$$b_i(x_i) = x_i^{\alpha_i} \tag{2}$$

$$p_i(x_1, \ldots, x_n) = x_i^{\alpha_i} \left(x_i + \sum_{j \neq i} x_j \right) \tag{3}$$

$$t_i \left(x_i, b_i^R\right) = \begin{cases} \left(b_i(x_i) - b_i^R\right), & \text{if} \quad b_i(.) \geq b_i^R \\ \lambda_i \left(b_i(x_i) - b_i^R\right), & \text{otherwise} \end{cases} \tag{4}$$

A higher value of the country i's exogenously determined technological inefficiency $\alpha_i \in (0, 1)$ requires higher emissions to reach a given economic benefit.[8] We call country i "developing" if it is technologically inefficient (relatively high α_i), and "developed" if it is technologically efficient (relatively low α_i). We use $\alpha \equiv (\alpha_1, \ldots, \alpha_n)$ to denote the vector of countries' technological inefficiency parameters and normalize them, $\sum_{j=1}^{n} \alpha_j = 1$.

Note that the economic benefit function $b_i(x_i)$ is strictly increasing, concave, and $b_i(0) = 0$. The cost of pollution $p_i(x_1, \ldots, x_n)$ is strictly increasing in all terms, $p_i(0, \ldots, 0) = 0$, and has the following two properties: (i) $\frac{\partial p_i}{\partial x_j} < \frac{\partial p_i}{\partial x_i}$ for $j \neq i$, and (ii) $p_i(x_1, \ldots, x_n) > p_j(x_1, \ldots, x_n)$ if $\alpha_i < \alpha_j$. Property (i) implies that a marginal increase in domestic emissions is more damaging than the same marginal increase in another country. This means that either the emission has additional local effects separate from the global effects, or in addition to the real effects, it has psychological effects, such as people feeling guilty about their own country's emissions. Property (ii) implies that, regardless of sources, people in developed countries are more environmentally aware and perceive more of environmental damage than people do in developing countries.[9]

The target utility $t_i(x_i, b_i^R)$ captures a country being averse to losing its economic benefits relative to its economic target b_i^R. We can consider this to be country i's economic reference level. In other words, if the economic benefit reaches this *level*, $b_i(.) \geq b_i^R$, then the country is satisfied by the positive difference, which it perceives as a gain. On the other hand, if the economic benefit does not reach the target, $b_i(.) < b_i^R$, then the country is disappointed by this negative difference, which it perceives it as a loss. Moreover, countries tend to strongly prefer avoiding economic losses to acquiring gains, relative to the economic target. The loss-aversion parameter $\lambda_i > 1$ measures how country i values losses versus gains. The function $t_i(.)$ is increasing in its emission level, decreasing in its economic target, and independent of how much other countries emit.

The net-benefit function of country i with an economic target simplifies to the following:

$$
B_i\left(x_1, \ldots, x_n, \Lambda_i, b_i^R\right) = \begin{cases} x_i^{\alpha_i}\left(1 + \gamma_i - x_i - \sum_{j \neq i} x_j\right) - \gamma_i b_i^R, & \text{if} \quad b_i^G(.) \geq b_i^R \\ x_i^{\alpha_i}\left(1 + \Lambda_i - x_i - \sum_{j \neq i} x_j\right) - \Lambda_i b_i^R, & \text{otherwise} \end{cases}
\tag{5}
$$

where $\Lambda_i = \gamma_i \lambda_i < 1$ captures the economic target concerns of country i in the loss domain. Country i, with an economic target, initially maximizes the objective function in the first row, $B_i^G(.)$. If the economic benefit reaches the target, $b_i^G(.) \geq b_i^R$, then country i is in the gain domain and its net benefit is determined. However, if the economic benefit does not reach its target, $b_i^G(.) \leq b_i^R$, then country i is in the loss domain and maximizes the objective function in the second row, $B_i^L(.)$.[10] For a *standard* country i, there is no target utility in (1).

Any country i belongs one of the three types $\theta_i \in \{L, G, S\}$: that fails to reach its economic target (L); that reaches its economic target (G); and with no economic target (S). We use $\theta \equiv (\theta_1, \ldots, \theta_n)$ to denote the vector of countries' types. In order to study the impact of different types of countries, we solve the model for the case in which all countries fail to reach their economic targets. The results for the other types of countries can be found by simply applying $\Lambda_i = \gamma_i$ for any country i reaching its economic target (G), and $\Lambda_i = 0$ for any standard country i (S). Comparing the types (L) and (G) gives us the implication of the kink caused by the loss-aversion parameter. Note also that Λ_i increases as a country's type changes in the direction of $S \to G \to L$.

4. Static Game

The aim of this section is to characterize the noncooperative Nash equilibrium of n technologically asymmetric countries with economic targets. The Nash equilibrium serves as a credible punishment or threat to support international environmental cooperation in the repeated setting examined in the following section.[11]

In the noncooperative Nash solution, each country sets its emission level where the marginal benefit is equal to the marginal cost. We find the best response function BR_i and Nash emission for country i x_i^N using the standard first-order condition $\partial B_i^L(.)/\partial x_i = 0$, as well as some additional algebra

$$
\frac{\partial B_i^L(.)}{\partial x_i} = \alpha_i x_i^{\alpha_i - 1}\left(1 + \Lambda_i - x_i - \sum_{j \neq i} x_j\right) - x_i^{\alpha_i} = 0
\tag{6}
$$

The first-order condition shows that economic target concerns Λ_i increases the marginal benefit of emissions. Multiplying the first-order condition by $x_i^{1 - \alpha_i} > 0$ gives

$$
\alpha_i\left(1 + \Lambda_i - \sum_{j=1}^n x_j\right) - x_i = 0 \quad \text{for} \quad i = 1, 2, \ldots, n
\tag{7}
$$

and determines the best response function for country i

$$
BR_i(x_{-i}) = \frac{\alpha_i\left(1 + \Lambda_i - \sum_{j \neq i} x_j\right)}{1 + \alpha_i}
\tag{8}
$$

where $x_{-i} \equiv (x_1, \ldots, x_{i-1}, x_{i+1}, \ldots, x_n)$. Note that country i's emission level when it best responds to other countries' emissions increases in its economic target concerns, that os, higher Λ_i, and as it becomes technological less efficient, that is, higher α_i. Summing n equations in (7) and solving for the total emission level gives

$$\sum_{j=1}^{n} x_j^N = \frac{\sum\limits_{j=1}^{n} \alpha_j + \sum\limits_{j=1}^{n} \alpha_j \Lambda_j}{1 + \sum\limits_{j=1}^{n} \alpha_j} \tag{9}$$

where x_j^N is country j's Nash emission level. Substituting (9) into (7) and using $\sum_{j=1}^{n} \alpha_j = 1$ gives the Nash emission level below

$$x_i^N = \frac{\alpha_i}{2}\left(1 + \Lambda_i(2 - \alpha_i) - \sum_{j \neq i} \alpha_j \Lambda_j\right) \tag{10}$$

Equation (10) shows that stronger country i's economic target concern, that is, an increase in Λ_i, imply a higher Nash emission level for country i. In other words, Nash emission level of a country with an economic target places more value on the economic benefits than a standard type country does, and even more so if it is a type L than G. On the other hand, a higher Λ_j for any other country j implies a lower Nash emission level for country i. This is due to the environmental concern of country i about the higher environmental pollution caused by country j. Note also that country i's Nash emission level increases as the country becomes technologically less efficient, that is, higher α_i, and as the other countries become technologically more efficient, that is, lower α_js.[12]

For any given types θ, the Nash emission levels are inefficiently high (i.e., $x_i^O < x_i^N$ for all i), where the optimum level of emissions $x^O \equiv (x_1^O, \ldots, x_n^O)$ maximizes the countries' joint net benefits $\sum_{i=1}^{n} B_i$. This is because emissions are transboundary and the negative spillover effects are not internalized when the countries act noncooperatively.[13]

5. Dynamic Game

In this section, we study the repeated interaction between countries. More precisely, the static game analyzed in the previous section is repeated infinitely many times in the dynamic game, and countries discount the future period by a discount factor $\delta \in (0, 1)$. We focus on self-enforcing IEAs. Thus, countries cannot make binding commitments. In such a setting, countries can sustain international environmental cooperation, the degree of which depends on how severely they can credibly punish a deviator. Our aim in this section is to examine the consequences of economic targets and loss-aversion for the sustainability of a cooperative emission equilibrium in the framework of an IEA with full participation. Thus, our framework is in line with the U.N. Climate Summits, in which participation has been almost universal.

Countries employ infinite Nash reversion strategies to enforce environmental cooperation.[14] We focus on cooperative subgame-perfect equilibria in which the following hold: (i) along the equilibrium path, the countries implement cooperative emission levels in each period; and (ii) if at any point in the game a defection occurs, all countries revert to noncooperative Nash emission levels from the following period onward. Each country i will prefer to emit at the cooperative emission levels if its net benefit from cooperating is no less than its payoff from defection. The latter payoff consists of a one-period gain from deviation and the discounted net benefit of playing Nash reversion forever; that is

$$\frac{1}{1-\delta}B_i\left(x^C, \Lambda, \alpha, b_i^R\right) \geq B_i\left(BR_i\left(x_{-i}^C\right), x_{-i}^C, \Lambda, \alpha, b_i^R\right) + \frac{\delta}{1-\delta}B_i\left(x^N, \Lambda, \alpha, b_i^R\right) \quad (11)$$

where $\Lambda \equiv (\Lambda_1, \ldots, \Lambda_n)$ is the vector of economic target concerns, indicating also the country types θ, $x^C \equiv (x_1^C, \ldots, x_n^C)$ is the vector of cooperative emission levels, and $BR_i(x_{-i}^C)$ is the best response function of country i when other countries emit at the agreed cooperative emission levels. From Friedman (1971), we know that for a sufficiently high discount factor δ and any given economic target concerns Λ, there is a subgame-perfect Nash equilibrium at a vector of cooperative emission levels x^C, such that $x_i^C \in [\overline{x}_i^C, x_i^N)$, where $\overline{x}_i^C$ is the most cooperative emission level country i can sustain.

Substituting cooperative emissions x^C, the best response function in (8), and Nash emission in (10) into $B_i^L(.)$ give the net-benefit functions when all countries cooperate, when country i unilaterally deviates while others continue to cooperate, and at the Nash emissions, respectively:[15]

$$B_i^L\left(x^C, \Lambda, \alpha, b_i^R\right) = \left(x_i^C\right)^{\alpha_i}\left(1 + \Lambda_i - x_i^C - \sum_{j \neq i} x_j^C\right) - \Lambda_i b_i^R \quad (12)$$

$$B_i^L\left(BR_i\left(x_{-i}^C\right), x_{-i}^C, \Lambda, \alpha, b_i^R\right) = \frac{1}{\alpha_i}\left(\frac{\alpha_i}{1+\alpha_i}\left(1 + \Lambda_i - \sum_{j \neq i} x_j^C\right)\right)^{1+\alpha_i} - \Lambda_i b_i^R \quad (13)$$

$$B_i^L\left(x_1^{NL}, \ldots, x_n^{NL}, \Lambda, \alpha, b_i^R\right) = \alpha_i^{\alpha_i}\left(\frac{1 + \Lambda_i(2 - \alpha_i) - \sum_{j \neq i}\alpha_j\Lambda_j}{2}\right)^{1+\alpha_i} - \Lambda_i b_i^R \quad (14)$$

Similar to public goods game, we have $B_i(BR_i(x_{-i}^C), x_{-i}^C, \Lambda, \alpha, b_i^R) > B_i(x^C, \Lambda, \alpha, b_i^R) > B_i(x^N, \Lambda, \alpha, b_i^R)$. We take the terms on the RHS over to the LHS in (11) and call this country i's sustainability function $S_i(x^C, \Lambda, \alpha, \delta)$. Substituting (12), (13), and (14) into (11) give the sustainability function, $S_i(.) =$

$$\frac{\left(x_i^C\right)^{\alpha_i}}{1-\delta}\left(1 + \Lambda_i - x_i^C - \sum_{j \neq i}x_j^C\right) - \frac{\left(\frac{\alpha_i\left(1+\Lambda_i - \sum_{j \neq i}x_j^C\right)}{1+\alpha_i}\right)^{1+\alpha_i}}{\alpha_i}$$

$$- \frac{\delta\alpha_i^{\alpha_i}}{1-\delta}\left(\frac{1 + \Lambda_i(2-\alpha_i) - \sum_{j \neq i}\alpha_j\Lambda_j}{2}\right)^{1+\alpha_i} \quad (15)$$

Given the parameters of the model, the sustainability function gives nonnegative values for sustainable cooperative emission levels, and gives negative values for unsustainable cooperative emission levels. In this paper, our main concern is how the economic target concerns affect the sustainability of an agreed cooperative emissions. An increase in country i's economics target concerns Λ_i does only increase the impact of the target utility. It means that the impact of this increase depends on the levels of the economic benefit $b_i(.)$ and the economic target b_i^R. Note that the economic target parameters in $S_i(.)$ cancel each other out $(\Lambda_i b_i^R(\frac{1}{1-\delta} - 1 - \frac{\delta}{1-\delta}) = 0)$. Thus, the country's economic target only determines its type, but has no other effect on sustainability. Therefore, given the types, the impact of an increase in economic target concerns on sustainability depends on the economic benefit levels when country i cooperates $b_i^C = b_i(x_i^C)$, when it unilaterally deviates while others continue to cooperate $b_i^D \equiv b_i(BR_i(x_{-i}^C))$, and at the Nash emissions $b_i^N \equiv b_i(x_i^N)$.

Our first proposition describes the impact on sustaining a cooperative emission level if country i is more concerned about its economic target. This increase in economic target concerns can be due country i's type changing in the direction of $S \rightarrow G \rightarrow L$.

Proposition 1. *Given any cooperative emission levels x^C, technological inefficiencies with $\sum_{j=1}^{n} \alpha_j = 1$, economic target concerns Λ, and a common discount factor δ, if country i is more concerned about its economic target, that is, higher Λ_i, then*

(i) *it is more difficult to sustain cooperation at the agreed cooperative emission x^C for country i, that is, $\partial S_i / \partial \Lambda_i < 0$, and*

(ii) *it is easier for any country j to sustain cooperation at x^C, that is, $\partial S_j / \partial \Lambda_i > 0$.*

An increase in country i's economic target concerns increases its marginal benefit from emission. Since $x_i^C < x_i^N < BR_i(x_{-i}^C)$ for any θ, the economic benefits at these emission levels are ordered as follows: $b_i^C < b_i^N < b_i^D$. Furthermore, while country i's cooperative emission level does not change, its Nash emission level and emission level when it unilaterally deviates from the cooperative emission level increases in Λ_i. These imply a stronger incentive to deviate and, thus, a decrease in $S_i(.)$. Sustaining cooperation at x^C becomes more difficult for country i. On the other hand, an increase in Λ_i for any other country j only decreases country j's Nash emission level because of the strategic substitutability of countries' emission levels, thus lowering its incentive to deviate from the agreed cooperative emissions. Therefore, sustaining cooperation at x^C becomes easier for country j.

Next, we discuss the impact on sustaining a cooperative emission level if all countries are more concerned about their economic targets. To this end, we increase the economic target concerns uniformly, while still allowing these concerns to be different from each other.

Proposition 2. *Given any cooperative emission levels x^C, technological inefficiencies with $\sum_{j=1}^{n} \alpha_j = 1$, economic target concerns Λ, and a common discount factor δ, an equal increase in all countries economic target concerns, $d\Lambda_i = d\Lambda_j \ \forall ij$, impedes country i sustaining cooperation at x^C if $dS_i = \frac{\partial S_i}{\partial \Lambda_i} d\Lambda_i + \sum_{j \neq i} \frac{\partial S_i}{\partial \Lambda_j} d\Lambda_j < 0 \Leftrightarrow*

$$b_i^C - (1 - \delta)b_i^D + \frac{1}{2}(1 + \alpha_i)\delta(n - 3 - \alpha_i(n - 2))b_i^N < 0 \qquad (16)$$

(i) *If $\alpha_i \leq \frac{n-3}{n-2}$, which requires $n \geq 4$, then b_i^N enters nonnegatively and the inequality (16) does not hold for sufficiently large δ. Otherwise, b_i^N enters negatively and the inequality (16) or the opposite can hold.*

(ii) *It is easier for the inequality (16) to hold for a lower x_i^C and higher x_j^Cs.*

While Proposition 1 examines the impact of one country being more concerned about its economic targets, Proposition 2 examines the impact of all countries having stronger concerns about their economic targets. Thus, for each of n countries, there are two effects, as discussed in Proposition 1: (i) an increase in Λ_i hinders sustaining cooperation for country i, but

(ii) facilitates cooperation for any other country j. If the inequality (16) holds, Proposition 1(i) dominates (ii) when all countries have stronger economic target concerns. If the opposite of inequality (16) holds strictly, then (ii) dominates (i).

The first point in Proposition 2 states that if there are sufficiently many and patient countries, (ii) dominates (i) for a technologically not very inefficient country i. If any of these conditions fail to hold, then depending on the specific parameter values (i) or (ii) dominates the other. To gain more insight into this, first note that the number of countries and countries' technological inefficiencies are linked due to the normalization, $\sum_{j=1}^{n} \alpha_j = 1$. An increase in the number of countries requires at least some countries to become technologically more efficient. For any given number of countries, a country i being sufficiently technologically efficient and, thus, sufficiently environmentally aware, imply the other countries to be sufficiently technologically inefficient and environmentally unaware. For such a developed country i, the effect (ii) would become stronger since increase in Nash emission levels owing to the increase in economic target concerns would be smaller; and, the effect (i) would be weaker, since increase in Nash emission levels and emission levels when country i unilaterally deviates from the cooperative emission level owing to the increase in economic target concerns would be smaller. Note that if (i) dominates (ii) for some countries and they cannot sustain cooperation at x^C anymore, then IEA would break down.

The second point in Proposition 2 states that if country i agrees on a more cooperative emission level $\bar{x}_i^C$ or some other countries js agree on a less cooperative emission levels $\bar{x}_j^C$s, then it is easier for the inequality (16) to hold. The intuition is straightforward: a more cooperative (lower) emission level $\bar{x}_i^C$ would reduce country i's economic benefit at cooperative emission level and a less cooperative emission levels $\bar{x}_j^C$s would increase country i's economic benefit when it unilaterally deviates from the cooperative emissions.

5.1 Sustainability, The Critical Discount Factor, and The Most Cooperative Emissions

In all the propositions, we study how changes in economic target concerns, either country i's or any other country j's or all countries, affect the sustainability a cooperative emission level, given the agreed-upon cooperative emission levels x^C and a common discount factor δ. Alternatively, we could study the impact of economic target concerns on the critical discount factor above which x^C can be sustained by country i or on the most cooperative (minimum) cooperative emission levels $\bar{x}^C$ for a given δ. To this end, first we solve the no-defection condition (11) for δ and obtain the critical discount factor above which x^C can be sustained by country i[16]

$$\delta \geq \underline{\delta}_i(x^C, \Lambda, \alpha) = \frac{B_i^D - B_i^C}{B_i^D - B_i^N} \tag{17}$$

where B_i^C, B_i^D, and B_i^N are abbreviations of the net-benefit function when all countries cooperate, when country i unilaterally deviates while others continue to cooperate, and at the Nash emissions, respectively. At its critical discount factor $\underline{\delta}_i(x^C, \Lambda, \alpha)$, country i can just sustain the agreed cooperative emissions x^C, thus, its sustainability function equals to zero, $S_i(x^C, \Lambda, \alpha, \underline{\delta}_i) = 0$.

So far, we have studied how changes in economic target concerns affect countries sustaining cooperation at a x^C. Next, we study the relationship between country i's ability to sustain cooperation at a x^C and its critical discount factor. This allows us to interpret our previous results from the perspective of countries' patience levels.

Lemma 1. *Given any cooperative emission levels x^C, technological inefficiencies with $\sum_{j=1}^{n} \alpha_j = 1$, economic target concerns Λ, if country i's ability to sustain cooperation at x^C increases (decreases) for some reason other than discount factor δ and cooperative emission levels x^C, $S_i'(x^C, \delta_i) > (<)S_i(x^C, \delta_i)$, then the critical (minimum) discount factor above which x^C can be sustained by country i decreases (increases), $\underline{\delta}'_{i}(x^C) < (>)\underline{\delta}_{i}(x^C)$.*

If country i's ability to sustain cooperation at x^C has increased for whatever reason other than δ_i and x^C, then the critical discount factor before the increase does not bind for sustaining cooperation at x^C. This means that country i can sustain agreed cooperative emission x^C with some discount factors lower than the critical discount factor before the increase. Thus, the critical discount factor decreases after the increase in country i's ability to sustain cooperation at x^C. A decrease in critical discount factor $\underline{\delta}_i(x^C)$ means even some other relatively impatient country is can start sustaining cooperation at x^C. Similarly, a decrease in country i's ability to sustain cooperation at x^C requires $\underline{\delta}_i(.)$ to increase and, thus, only sufficiently patient country is can continue sustaining cooperation at x^C.

Next, we study the relationship between country i's ability to sustain cooperation at x^C and the most cooperative emission level it can sustain. This allows us to interpret our previous results from the perspective of lowest emissions countries can sustain.

Proposition 3. *Given any technological inefficiencies with $\sum_{j=1}^{n} \alpha_j = 1$, economic target concerns Λ, and a sufficiently high discount factor δ_i of country i,*

 (i) *If country i's ability to sustain cooperation at x^C increases (decreases) for some reason other than discount factor δ_i and cooperative emission levels x^C, that is, $S_i'(x^C, \delta_i) > (<)S_i(x^C, \delta_i)$, then country i's most cooperative emission decreases (increases), $\overline{x}_i'^C < (>)\overline{x}_i^C$.*
 (ii) *If all countries' abilities to sustain cooperation at x^C increase (decrease) for some reason other than discount factor δ_i and cooperative emission levels, x^C, that is, $S_i'(x^C, \delta_i) > (<)S_i(x^C, \delta_i)$ for all i, then the most cooperative emission levels countries can sustain decrease (increase), $\overline{x}'^C < (>)\overline{x}^C$ in all dimensions.*

The intuition behind the Proposition 3 is similar to the one underlying Lemma 1. Basically, after any country's ability to sustain cooperation at x^C increases for whatever reason other than its discount factor and cooperative emission, the critical discount factor before the increase does not bind for sustaining cooperation at x^C. This means that countries with higher ability to sustain cooperation at x^C can support a greater degree of international environmental cooperation.

An interesting point is that a country j's ability to sustain cooperation at x^C increases as x_i^C decreases if $b_j^C > b_j^D(1 - \delta)$.[17] This means that country i becoming more cooperative in its emission level allows some sufficiently patient countries to also emit more cooperatively.

6. Extensions

6.1 Symmetric Countries

In this subsection, we assume countries to be symmetric. More specifically, we assume countries to be identical in their technological inefficiencies, $\alpha_i = 1/n$ for any i, economic target concerns, $\Lambda_i = \Lambda_j$, and agreed cooperative emission levels, $x_i^C = x_j^C \ \forall \ ij$. As in Proposition 2, we study the impact of all countries being more concerned about their economic targets.

Proposition 4. *Given technological inefficiencies* $\alpha_i = 1/n$ *for any i, a common discount factor* δ, *and identical economic target concerns* $\Lambda_i = \Lambda_j \ \forall ij$, *the most cooperative emission level country i can sustain* $\overline{x}_i^C$ *increases in economic target concerns if, that is,* $\partial S_i / \partial \Lambda_i < 0 \Leftrightarrow$

$$b_i^C < (1 - \delta) b_i^D + \frac{\delta}{2} \left(\frac{n+1}{n} \right) b_i^N \qquad (18)$$

Basically, the condition (16) simplifies to the condition (18) under symmetry. To investigate further this scenario, we also resort to a numerical analysis. We assume that there are two countries i and j, identical in their technological inefficiencies $\alpha_i = \alpha_j = 1/2$, in their types $\theta_i = \theta_j$, in their discount factor $\delta_i = \delta_j = 0.99$, and agree to cooperate by emitting the same amount $x_i^C = x_j^C$. Moreover, we assume that economic target concerns are $\Lambda_i^L = \Lambda_j^L = 0.3$ for loss, $\Lambda_i^G = \Lambda_j^G = 0.15$ for gain, and $\Lambda_i^S = \Lambda_j^S = 0$ for standard types. We summarize the findings in Figure 1. It shows how sustainability functions change against emissions with any country i's type $\theta_i \in \{L, G, S\}$. The dotted, dashed, and continuous curves represent countries being loss (L), gain (G), and standard (S) types, respectively. Each curve intersect the zero value line twice: the smaller emission level is the most cooperative emission level countries can sustain and the higher emission level is the Nash emission level.

For sufficiently high δ, we find that for some relatively high (less) cooperative emission levels the condition (18) does not hold, meaning that a joint increase in economic target concerns can increase the sustainability for such relatively high (less) cooperative emissions. On the other hand, if the countries agree on a low (more) cooperative emission level, then a joint increase in economic target concerns decreases the sustainability functions and, thus, the most cooperative emission levels of loss, gain, and standard types of countries are ordered as follows: $\overline{x}_i^{CL} > \overline{x}_i^{CG} > \overline{x}_i^{CS}$, for any i. Therefore, economic target concerns could be another reason preventing countries to support a greater degree of international environmental agreements.

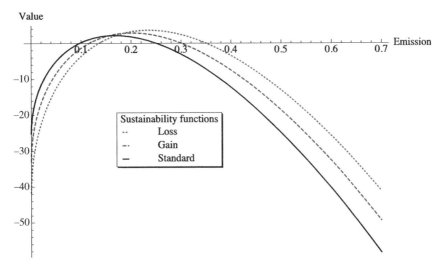

Figure 1. The Most Cooperative Emissions.

6.2 *Asymmetry in Technology*

Next, we examine the impact of countries becoming more or less asymmetric in their technologies, in addition to their possibly asymmetric economic target concerns. This analysis allows us to study a North–South relations model as well as a North–North model. To this end, we employ a numerical analysis with two countries to incorporate how technological inefficiencies α_i and α_j, with $\alpha_i + \alpha_j = 1$, and different types $\theta = (\theta_i, \theta_j)$ affect countries' ability to sustain cooperation. Figure 2 contains two subfigures. Each shows how the sustainability of a symmetric cooperative emission, set to $x^C = (0.22, 0.22)$ here, against country i's technological inefficiency α_i changes with country i's type $\theta_i \in \{L, G, S\}$. The two subfigures differ by the other country j's type $\theta_j \in \{L, S\}$. Bold sustainability functions belong to country i and light sustainability functions belong country j. The dotted, dashed, and continuous curves represent country i being in a loss (L), gain (G), and standard (S) domain, respectively.

In both subfigures, the symmetry in technologies helps to sustain cooperation. The developing country fails to sustain cooperation if countries are sufficiently asymmetric in their technologies. For instance, in Subfigure 2 a, where $\theta_j = L$, cooperation can be sustained by both countries at approximately $\alpha_i \in (0.52; 0.62)$, $\alpha_i \in (0.46; 0.58)$, and $\alpha_i \in (0.44; 0.56)$ for $\theta_i = S$, G, and L, respectively. Country i can sustain cooperation for values of α_i below the upper limit and country j can do so for values of α_i above the lower limit. As Λ_i increases, in other words, as the country i's type changes in the direction of $S \rightarrow G \rightarrow L$, the upper limit decreases, and sustaining cooperation becomes more difficult for country i. At the same time, the lower limit increases, making it easier for country j to sustain cooperation, as shown in Proposition 1.

In the case of technological asymmetries, an increase in economic target concerns might help or hinder sustaining a cooperative emission. Figure 2 shows that a more developed country can sustain cooperation at the agreed-upon emission level regardless of the economic target concerns. However, economic target concerns do matter for the sustainability of the less developed country. if country i is less developed (i.e., $\alpha_i s > 0.5$), regardless of economic target concerns of the other country j, having stronger economic target concerns hinders its ability to sustain cooperation at the agreed-upon emission level. On the other hand, the more developed county j having stronger economic target concerns facilitate sustaining cooperation for the less developed country i. Thus, the best scenario for the countries to sustain cooperation is the developing country i has weaker and the developed country j has stronger economic target concerns. However, if one considers that developed countries have more established political and economic institutions and would have weaker economic target concerns than developing countries, then economic target concerns enter as another difficulty for supporting substantial international environmental cooperation.

6.3 *Comparative Statics Analysis with Economic Targets*

In all our propositions, we focus on the impact of countries being more concerned about their economic targets Λ. Alternatively, we could examine the impact of countries having more ambitious economic targets b^R. This may lead to two possible scenarios. First, if a country continues to be in a gain or loss after an increase in its economic target b_i^R, then its objective function does not change. In this case, its emission level and sustainability functions remain the same. Second, if a country starts failing to reach its economic benefit after an increase in its economic target, then it will start maximizing $B_i^L(.)$. In this case, it will have stronger

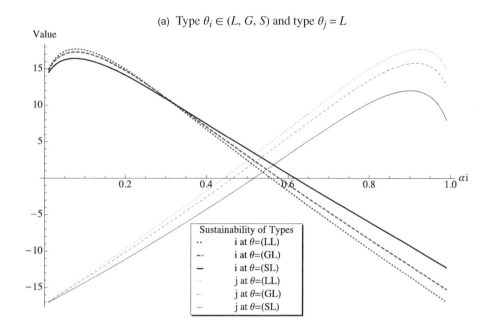

(a) Type $\theta_i \in (L, G, S)$ and type $\theta_j = L$

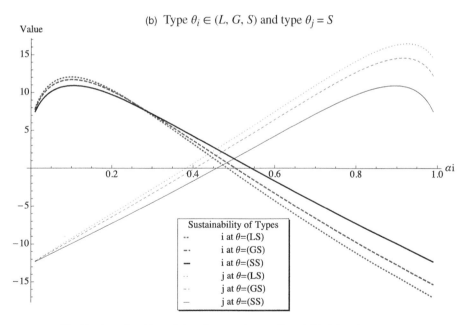

(b) Type $\theta_i \in (L, G, S)$ and type $\theta_j = S$

Figure 2. The Net Benefit of Sustaining Cooperation at $x^C = (0.22, 0.22)$ for Country-Type Pair $\theta = (\theta_i, \theta_j)$, when the Loss-Aversion Parameter $\lambda_i = 1.5$ and the Scaling Factor $\gamma_i = 0.1$, for All i, and Technological Inefficiency α_i, When $\alpha_i + \alpha_j = 1$, at Discount Factor $\delta = 0.99$.

Note: Countries sustain cooperation for nonnegative values. Bold sustainability functions represent country i and light sustainability functions represent country j. The dotted, dashed, and continuous lines represent country i's type being L, G, and S, respectively.

concerns about its economic targets. Therefore, the second scenario leads to identical implications discussed in the propositions.

7. Conclusion

Motivated by the fact that many policy decisions are often influenced by political parties' incentives to be elected, we examine the implications for IEAs on transboundary emissions on a country's motivation to reach their economic targets and being averse to failing to achieve their economic targets. More specifically, we examine whether countries having stronger economic target concerns help or hinder the sustainability of agreed-upon cooperative emissions in the context of self-enforcing IEAs, which require full participation.

We find that the stronger a country's concern about its economic targets, the more difficult it is for the country to sustain cooperation, but the easier it is for other countries to do so. If all countries have stronger economic target concerns and are sufficiently patient, then such concerns can facilitate sustaining cooperation for sufficiently developed countries in the presence of developing countries, but the effect is ambiguous for a developing country. If the countries are symmetric in all dimensions, then those with stronger economic target concerns hinder sustaining cooperation. This means that countries need to be much more patient to continue sustaining the agreed cooperative emission levels or the most cooperative emission levels countries can sustain increase and, thus, these emission levels cannot be sustained for the same patience level.

The real IEAs, such as climate change, are much more complex than the simple model utilized here. They require international coordination to agree on the cooperative emission levels, in which countries often fail to keep their promises. We show that even in a world in which sustaining the most cooperative emissions is effortless, ambitious economic targets owing to an incentive to be elected lead to IEAs with less cooperative emission levels than could be achieved without such concerns.

Thaler and Sunstein (2008), in their highly influential book, suggest nudges. It is a design of a choice environment using frames and defaults, among others, that alters people's behavior in a predictable way, without mandating a particular action or changing economic incentives, in order to overcome behavioral failures. However, the impact of nudges is limited if policymakers suffer from such behavioral failures, either directly or through voters, as discussed in the introduction.

It appears that correcting the incentives leading to ambitious economic targets and an aversion to economic losses require a strong call for action at the subnational level. As citizens of the earth, we should talk more about the environmental problems and raise public awareness to incentivize political parties to pursue greener policies.[18]

Acknowledgement

I gratefully acknowledge the financial support by the Sogang University Research Grant 2013 and helpful comments and suggestions of the editor and two referees that helped improve the paper.

Notes

1. For instance, United States. http://www.pollingreport.com/prioriti.htm
2. We review this literature in Section 2.2.

3. See the supporting information provided in Schumacher *et al.* (2015) for more detailed political history of the German Green Party.
4. We further review the literature on rationality of voters and politicians in Section 2.1.
5. For instance, public polls show that voters prioritize economic issues and neglect environmental ones more during 2008 crisis. http://www.people-press.org/2015/01/15/publics-policy-priorities-reflect-changing-conditions-at-home-and-abroad/.
6. Kahneman and Tversky (1979) is the second most cited article in economics in the period 1970–2006 (Kim *et al.*, 2006).
7. For convenience, we use the word "country" to refer to both a country and its political leader.
8. Note that country i's economic benefit is increasing in its own emissions $\frac{\partial b_i}{\partial x_i} = \alpha_i x_i^{\alpha_i - 1} > 0$, but decreasing in its technological inefficiency $\frac{\partial b_i}{\partial \alpha_i} = x_i^{\alpha_i} \ln x_i < 0$.
9. Neumayer (2002) shows that democracies exhibit stronger international environmental commitment than nondemocracies. This supports property (ii) if one accepts that democracies are also more developed.
10. For some parameter values, countries can fail to reach their economic target when maximizing $B_i^G(.)$ and then reach their economic target when maximizing $B_i^L(.)$. This maximization procedure is to eliminate potential loops.
11. The static Nash equilibrium would be the unique equilibrium for the dynamic game as well if an IEA was not feasible (e.g., owing to exogenous, political reasons, or because countries are impatient and do not value the future).
12. See the Appendix for calculations.
13. Using the first-order conditions, $\partial \sum_{i=1}^{n} B_i^L / \partial x_i = 0$, the optimum level of emissions under full symmetry becomes: $x_i^O = \frac{\alpha_i (1+\Lambda_i)}{n(1+\alpha_i)}$. There are no closed-form solutions for optimum emissions in the case of asymmetry. Nevertheless, they are not needed for the sustainability of IEAs.
14. We employ infinite Nash reversion strategies for simplicity, but they have well-known credibility issues. Instead, we could consider other strategies, such allowing renegotiation (Barrett, 1994; Asheim and Holtsmark, 2009). In these cases, the degree of cooperation that any type of countries could sustain would be quantitatively different. Nevertheless, all the forces leading to the qualitative results would remain the same.
15. More detailed calculations are provided in the Appendix.
16. See the Appendix for more detailed calculations.
17. See the Appendix for detailed calculations.
18. Communication and raising public awareness is one of the four strategic priorities of the U.N. Environmental Program's climate change program. http://www.unep.org/pdf/UNEP_CC_STRATEGY_web.pdf.

References

Alesina, A. and Passarelli, F. (2015) Loss aversion in politics. Working Paper 21077, National Bureau of Economic Research.
Asheim, G. and Holtsmark, B. (2009) Renegotiation-proof climate agreements with full participation: conditions for pareto-efficiency. *Environmental and Resource Economics* 43(4): 519–533.
Barberis, N. and Thaler, R. (2003) A survey of behavioral finance. In G. Constantinides, R.M. Stulz, M. Harris, (eds), *Handbook of the Economics of Finance*, Vol. 1B: Financial Markets and Asset Pricing, chapter 18 (pp. 1053–1128). Amsterdam, The Netherlands: Elsevier.

Barberis, N., Huang, M. and Santos, T. (2001) Prospect theory and asset prices. *Quarterly Journal of Economics* 116(1): 1–53.

Barrett, S. (1994) Self-enforcing international environmental agreements. *Oxford Economic Papers* 46: 878–894.

Barrett, S. (2005) The theory of international environmental agreements. In K.G. Mäler, and J.R. Vincent (eds), *Handbook of Environmental Economics*, Vol. 3, Chap. 28 (pp. 1457–1516). Amsterdam, The Netherlands: Elsevier.

Benartzi, S. and Thaler, R.H. (1995) Myopic loss aversion and the equity premium puzzle. *Quarterly Journal of Economics* 110(1): 73–92.

Bendor, J., Diermeier, D., Siegel, D.A. and Ting, M.M. (2011) *A Behavioral Theory of Elections*: Princeton, NJ: Princeton University Press.

Besley, T. (2006) *Principled Agents?: The Political Economy of Good Government (Lindahl Lectures on Monetary and Fiscal Policy)*. Oxford: Oxford University Press.

Bowman, D., Minehart, D. and Rabin, M. (1999) Loss aversion in a consumption-savings model. *Journal of Economic Behavior & Organization* 38(2): 155–178.

Buchholz, W., Haupt, A. and Peters, W. (2005) International environmental agreements and strategic voting. *Scandinavian Journal of Economics* 107(1): 175–195.

Camerer, C., Babcock, L., Loewenstein, G. and Thaler, R. (1997) Labor supply of New York city cab-drivers: one day at a time. *Quarterly Journal of Economics* 112(2): 407–441.

Camerer, C.F. (2003) *Behavioral Game Theory: Experiments in Strategic Interaction*. Princeton, NJ: Princeton University Press.

Camerer, C.F. and Loewenstein, G. (2003) Behavioral economics: past, present, and future. In C.F. Camerer, G. Loewenstein and M. Rabin (eds), *Advances in Behavioral Economics*, Chap. 1 (pp. 3–51). Princeton, NJ: Princeton University Press.

Camerer, C.F., Loewenstein, G. and Rabin, M. (eds) (2003) *Advances in Behavioral Economics*. Princeton, NJ: Princeton University Press.

Caplan, B. (2008) *The Myth of the Rational Voter: Why Democracies Choose Bad Policies*. Princeton, NJ: Princeton University Press.

Carraro, C. and Siniscalco, D. (1993) Strategies for the international protection of the environment. *Journal of Public Economics* 52(3): 309–328.

Cazals, A. and Sauquet, A. (2015) How do elections affect international cooperation? Evidence from environmental treaty participation. *Public Choice* 162(3–4): 263–285.

Charness, G. and Sutter, M. (2012) Groups make better self-interested decisions. *Journal of Economic Perspectives* 26(3): 157–176.

Chen, M.K., Lakshminarayanan, V. and Santos, L.R. (2006) How basic are behavioral biases? Evidence from capuchin monkey trading behavior. *Journal of Political Economy* 114(3): 517–537.

Ciccarone, G. and Marchetti, E. (2013) Rational expectations and loss aversion: potential output and welfare implications. *Journal of Economic Behavior & Organization* 86(C): 24–36.

Congleton, R.D. (1992) Political institutions and pollution control. *Review of Economics and Statistics* 74(3): 412–421.

Conlisk, J. (1996) Why bounded rationality? *Journal of Economic Literature* 34(2): 669–700.

Conrad, K. and Kohn, R.E. (1996) The US market for SO_2 permits: policy implications of the low price and trading volume. *Energy Policy* 24(12): 1051–1059.

Daido, K., Morita, K., Murooka, T. and Ogawa, H. (2013) Task assignment under agent loss aversion. *Economics Letters* 121(1): 35–38.

D'Aspremont, C., Jacquemin, A., Gabszewicz, J.J. and Weymark, J.A. (1983) On the stability of collusive price leadership. *Canadian Journal of Economics/Revue canadienne d'Economique* 16(1): 17–25.

DellaVigna, S. (2009) Psychology and economics: evidence from the field. *Journal of Economic Literature* 47(2): 315–372.

Dietz, S., Marchiori, C. and Tavoni, A. (2012) Domestic politics and the formation of international environmental agreements. Working Paper 87, Grantham Research Institute on Climate Change and the Environment.

Fehr, E. and Goette, L. (2007) Do workers work more if wages are high? Evidence from a randomized field experiment. *American Economic Review* 97(1): 298–317.

Ferrara, I., Missios, P. and Yildiz, H.M. (2009) Trading rules and the environment: does equal treatment lead to a cleaner world? *Journal of Environmental Economics and Management* 58(2): 206–225.

Finus, M. (2008) Game theoretic research on the design of international environmental agreements: insights, critical remarks, and future challenges. *International Review of Environmental and Resource Economics* 2(1): 29–67.

Fischhoff, B., Slovic, P. and Lichtenstein, S. (1982) Lay foibles and expert fables in judgments about risk. *American Statistician* 36(3): 240–255.

Frankel, J. (2011) Over-optimism in forecasts by official budget agencies and its implications. *Oxford Review of Economic Policy* 27(4): 536–562.

Fudenberg, D. (2006) Advancing beyond "advances in behavioral economics." *Journal of Economic Literature* 44(3): 694–711.

Genesove, D. and Mayer, C. (2001) Loss aversion and seller behavior: evidence from the housing market. *Quarterly Journal of Economics* 116(4): 1233–1260.

Greene, D.L. (2011) Uncertainty, loss aversion, and markets for energy efficiency. *Energy Economics* 33(4): 608–616.

Grossman, G.M. and Helpman, E. (1994) Protection for sale. *American Economic Review* 84(4): 833–850.

Gsottbauer, E. and van den Bergh, J.C. (2013) Bounded rationality and social interaction in negotiating a climate agreement. *International Environmental Agreements: Politics, Law and Economics* 13(3): 225–249.

Hadjiyiannis, C., İriş, D. and Tabakis, C. (2012) International environmental cooperation under fairness and reciprocity. *B.E. Journal of Economic Analysis & Policy* 12(1): 1–30.

Heath, C., Larrick, R., and Wu, G. (1999) Goals as reference points. *Cognitive Psychology* 38(1): 79–109.

Hoel, M. (1992) International environment conventions: the case of uniform reductions of emissions. *Environmental and Resource Economics* 2(2): 141–159.

İriş, D. and Tavoni, A. (2015) Tipping points and loss aversion in international environmental agreements. Working Paper.

İriş, D., Lee, J. and Tavoni, A. (2015) Delegation and public pressure in a threshold public good game: theory and experimental evidence. FEEM Working Paper No. 26.2016.

Johnson, D.D.P. and Tierney, D. (2003) Essence of victory: winning and lowing international crises. *Security Sciences* 13(2): 350–381.

Jones, B.D. (1999) Bounded rationality. *Annual Review of Political Science* 2: 297–321.

Kagel, J.H. and Roth, A.E. (eds) (1995) *The Handbook of Experimental Economics*. Princeton, NJ: Princeton University Press.

Kahneman, D. and Renshon, J. (2009) Why hawks win. *Foreign Policy* 158: 34–38.

Kahneman, D. and Tversky, A. (1979) Prospect theory: an analysis of decision under risk. *Econometrica* 47(2): 263–291.

Kahneman, D. and Tversky, A. (eds) (2000) *Choices, Values, and Frames*. New York: Cambridge University Press.

Kahneman, D., Knetsch, J.L. and Thaler, R.H. (1991) Anomalies: the endowment effect, loss aversion, and status quo bias. *Journal of Economic Perspectives* 5(1): 193–206.

Kim, E.H., Morse, A. and Zingales, L. (2006) What has mattered to economics since 1970. *Journal of Economic Perspectives* 20(4): 189–202.

Kolstad, C.D. (2010) Equity, heterogeneity and international environmental agreements. *B.E. Journal of Economic Analysis & Policy* 10(2): 1–17.

Kőszegi, B. and Rabin, M. (2006) A model of reference-dependent preferences. *Quarterly Journal of Economics* 121(4): 1133–1165.

List, J.A. (2003) Does market experience eliminate market anomalies? *Quarterly Journal of Economics* 118(1): 41–71.

List, J.A. (2004) Neoclassical theory versus prospect theory: evidence from the marketplace. *Econometrica* 72(2): 615–625.

Mas, A. (2006) Pay, reference points, and police performance. *Quarterly Journal of Economics* 121(3): 783–821.

McFadden, D. (1999) Rationality for economists? *Journal of Risk and Uncertainty* 19(1): 73–105.

McGinty, M. (2007) International environmental agreements among asymmetric nations. *Oxford Economic Papers* 59(1): 45–62.

Mendez, L. and Trelles, R. (2000) The abatement market a proposal for environmental cooperation among asymmetric countries. *Environmental and Resource Economics* 16(1): 15–30.

Mercer, J. (2005) Prospect theory and political science. *Annual Review of Political Science* 8: 1–21.

Miler, K.C. (2009) The limitations of heuristics for political elites. *Political Psychology* 30(6): 863–894.

Neumayer, E. (2002) Do democracies exhibit stronger international environmental commitment? A cross-country analysis. *Journal of Peace Research* 39(2): 139–164.

Oates, W.E. and Portney, P.R. (2003) The political economy of environmental policy. In K.-G. Mäler and J.R. Vincent (eds), *Environmental Degradation and Institutional Responses*, Vol. 1: Handbook of Environmental Economics, Chap. 8 (pp. 325–354). Amsterdam, The Netherlands: Elsevier.

Odean, T. (1998) Are investors reluctant to realize their losses? *Journal of Finance* 53(5): 1775–1798.

Pavlova, Y. and de Zeeuw, A. (2013) Asymmetries in international environmental agreements. *Environment and Development Economics* 18: 51–68.

Persson, T. and Tabellini, G. (2000) *Political Economics: Explaining Economic Policy*. Cambridge, MA: MIT Press.

Quiggin, J. (1982). A theory of anticipated utility. *Journal of Economic Behavior & Organization* 3(4): 323–343.

Schumacher, G., van de Wardt, M., Vis, B. and Klitgaard, M.B. (2015) How aspiration to office conditions the impact of government participation on party platform change. *American Journal of Political Science* 59(4): 1040–1054.

Shafir, E., Diamond, P. and Tversky, A. (1997) Money illusion. *Quarterly Journal of Economics* 112(2): 341–374.

Shogren, J.F., Parkhurst, G.M. and Banerjee, P. (2010) Two cheers and a qualm for behavioral environmental economics. *Environmental and Resource Economics* 46(2): 235–247.

Simon, H.A. (1985) Human nature in politics: the dialogue of psychology with political science. *American Political Science Review* 79: 293–304.

Smith, A. (1759/1892) *The Theory of Moral Sentiments*. New York: Prometheus.

Sydnor, J. (2010) (Over)insuring modest risks. *American Economic Journal: Applied Economics* 2(4): 177–199.

Tetlock, P.E. (2005) *Expert Political Judgment: How Good It Is? How Can We Know?* Princeton, NJ: Princeton University Press.

Thaler, R.H. and Sunstein, C.R. (2008) *Nudge: Improving Decisions about Health, Wealth, and Happiness*. New Haven, CT: Yale University Press.

Tversky, A. and Kahneman, D. (1991) Loss aversion in riskless choice: a reference-dependent model. *Quarterly Journal of Economics* 106(4): 1039–1061.

Tversky, A. and Kahneman, D. (1992) Advances in prospect theory: cumulative representation of uncertainty. *Journal of Risk and Uncertainty* 5(4): 297–323.

Wang, M., Rieger, M.O. and Hens, T. (2016) The impact of culture on loss aversion. *Journal of Behavioral Decision Making*, forthcoming.

Appendix: Calculations and Proofs

A.1 Calculations

A.1.1 Technological Inefficiency and Nash Emissions

$$
\frac{\partial x_i^N}{\partial \alpha_i} = \frac{1}{2}\left(1 + \Lambda_i(2 - \alpha_i) - \sum_{j \neq i} \alpha_j \Lambda_j\right) - \frac{\alpha_i}{2}\Lambda_i
$$

$$
= \frac{1}{2}\left(1 + 2\Lambda_i(1 - \alpha_i) - \sum_{j \neq i} \alpha_j \Lambda_j\right) > 0 \tag{A1}
$$

It is straightforward to see $\partial x_i^N / \partial \alpha_j < 0$.

A.1.2 Net-Benefit Functions

It is straightforward to see that substituting cooperative emissions into $B_i^L(.)$ gives (12). Let us substitute the best response function in (8) into $B_i^L(.)$ to find the net-benefit function when country i unilaterally deviates while others continue to cooperate, $B_i^L(BR_i(x_j^C), x_j^C, b_i^R) =$

$$
= \left(\frac{\alpha_i}{1 + \alpha_i}\left(1 + \Lambda_i - \sum_{j \neq i} x_j^C\right)\right)^{\alpha_i}\left(1 + \Lambda_i - \sum_{j \neq i} x_j^C - \frac{\alpha_i}{1 + \alpha_i}\left(1 + \Lambda_i - \sum_{j \neq i} x_j^C\right)\right) - \Lambda_i b_i^R
$$

$$
= \left(\frac{\alpha_i}{1 + \alpha_i}\left(1 + \Lambda_i - \sum_{j \neq i} x_j^C\right)\right)^{\alpha_i}\left(\frac{1}{1 + \alpha_i}\left(1 + \Lambda_i - \sum_{j \neq i} x_j^C\right)\right) - \Lambda_i b_i^R \tag{A2}
$$

$$
= \frac{1}{\alpha_i}\left(\frac{\alpha_i}{1 + \alpha_i}\left(1 + \Lambda_i - \sum_{j \neq i} x_j^C\right)\right)^{1 + \alpha_i} - \Lambda_i b_i^R
$$

We substitute Nash emission in (10) into $B_i^L(.)$. Using (9) and some algebra gives the net benefit at the Nash emissions, $B_i^L(x_1^{NL}, \ldots, x_n^{NL}, b_i^R) =$

$$
= (x_i^{NL})^{\alpha_i}\left(1 + \Lambda_i - \sum_{i=1}^{n} x_i^{NL}\right) - \Lambda_i b_i^R
$$

$$
= \left(\frac{\alpha_i}{2}\left(1 + \Lambda_i(2 - \alpha_i) - \sum_{j \neq i} \alpha_j \Lambda_j\right)\right)^{\alpha_i}\left[1 + \Lambda_i - \frac{1 + \sum_{j=1}^{n} \alpha_j \Lambda_j}{2}\right] - \Lambda_i b_i^R
$$

$$
= \alpha_i^{\alpha_i}\left(\frac{1}{2}\left(1 + \Lambda_i(2 - \alpha_i) - \sum_{j \neq i} \alpha_j \Lambda_j\right)\right)^{\alpha_i}\frac{1}{2}\left(1 + 2\Lambda_i - \sum_{j=1}^{n} \alpha_j \Lambda_j\right) - \Lambda_i b_i^R \tag{A3}
$$

$$= \alpha_i^{\alpha_i} \left(\frac{1}{2} \left(1 + \Lambda_i(2 - \alpha_i) - \sum_{j \neq i} \alpha_j \Lambda_j \right) \right)^{\alpha_i} \frac{1}{2} \left(1 + \Lambda_i(2 - \alpha_i) - \sum_{j \neq i} \alpha_j \Lambda_j \right) - \Lambda_i b_i^R$$

$$= \alpha_i^{\alpha_i} \left(\frac{1 + \Lambda_i(2 - \alpha_i) - \sum_{j \neq i} \alpha_j \Lambda_j}{2} \right)^{1 + \alpha_i} - \Lambda_i b_i^R$$

A.1.3 *Critical Discount Factor*

The conditions (11) and (17) are equivalent. For notational simplicity, let us use B_i^C, B_i^{BR}, and B_i^N for net-benefit functions when all countries cooperate, when country i unilaterally deviates while others continue to cooperate, and at the Nash emissions, respectively.

$$\frac{1}{1 - \delta} B_i^C \geq B_i^{BR} + \frac{\delta}{1 - \delta} B_i^N \Leftrightarrow$$

$$B_i^C \geq (1 - \delta) B_i^{BR} + \delta B_i^N \Leftrightarrow$$

$$\delta \left(B_i^{BR} - B_i^N \right) \geq B_i^{BR} - B_i^C \Leftrightarrow \tag{A4}$$

$$\delta \geq \frac{B_i^{BR} - B_i^C}{B_i^{BR} - B_i^N}$$

A.1.4 *Interdependence of Countries' Most Cooperative Emissions*

$$\frac{\partial S_j}{\partial x_i^C} = -\frac{(x_j^C)^{\alpha_j}}{1 - \delta} + \left(\frac{\alpha_j}{1 + \alpha_j} \left(1 + \Lambda_j - \sum_{i \neq j} x_i^C \right) \right)^{\alpha_j} \Leftrightarrow \tag{A5}$$

$$= -\frac{b_j^C}{1 - \delta} + b_j^D$$

For $\frac{\partial S_j}{\partial x_i^C} < 0$, we should have: $b_j^C > b_j^D(1 - \delta)$.

A.2 *Proofs*

Proof of Proposition 1. We take the derivative with respect to (i) $\Lambda_i = \gamma_i \lambda_i$:

$$\frac{\partial S_i}{\partial \Lambda_i} = \frac{1}{1 - \delta} \underbrace{(x_i^C)^{\alpha_i}}_{b_i^C} - \underbrace{\left(\frac{1 + \Lambda_i - \sum_{j \neq i} x_j^C}{1 + \alpha_i} \right)^{\alpha_i}}_{b_i^{BR}}$$

$$- (2 - \alpha_i)(1 + \alpha_i) \frac{\delta}{2(1 - \delta)} \underbrace{\alpha_i^{\alpha_i} \left(\frac{1 + (2 - \alpha_i)\Lambda_i - \sum_{j \neq i} \alpha_j \Lambda_j}{2} \right)^{\alpha_i}}_{b_i^{NL}}. \tag{A6}$$

For country i's sustainability to decrease in its economic target concerns, $\frac{\partial S_i}{\partial \Lambda_i} < 0 \Leftrightarrow$

$$b_i^C < \delta \underbrace{\frac{1}{2}(2 - \alpha_i)(1 + \alpha_i)}_{>1} b_i^{NL} + (1 - \delta)b_i^{BR} \tag{A7}$$

Since $x_i^{NL} > x_i^C$ and $BR_i(x_{-i}^C) > x_i^C$, we have $b_i^{NL} > b_i^C$ and $b_i^{BR} > b_i^C$. Then, any point in convex combination of b_i^{NL} and b_i^{BR} is also higher than b_i^C, which completes part (i) of the proof.

Let us now take the derivative of S_j with respect to (ii) $\Lambda_i = \gamma_i \lambda_i$:

$$\frac{\partial S_j}{\partial \Lambda_i} = (1 + \alpha_j)\frac{\delta}{1 - \delta} \underbrace{\alpha_j^{\alpha_j} \left(\frac{1 + (2 - \alpha_j)\Lambda_j - \sum_{i \neq j}\alpha_i \Lambda_i}{2} \right)^{\alpha_j} \frac{\sum_{i \neq j}\alpha_i}{2}}_{b_j^{NL}} > 0 \tag{A8}$$

This condition always holds because it is the same condition required for the Nash emissions to be positive in (10), completing the proof of part (ii). $\qquad\square$

Proof of Proposition 2. Total derivation of the sustainability function with respect to countries economic target concerns, $d S_i = \frac{\partial S_i}{\partial \Lambda_i} d\Lambda_i + \sum_{j \neq i} \frac{\partial S_i}{\partial \Lambda_j} d\Lambda_j$:

$$d S_i = \left(\frac{b_i^C}{1 - \delta} - b_i^{BR} - \frac{(2 - \alpha_i)(1 + \alpha_i)\delta}{2(1 - \delta)}b_i^{NL} \right) d\Lambda_i + \sum_{j \neq i} \frac{(1 + \alpha_i)\delta \sum_{j \neq i}\alpha_j}{2(1 - \delta)}b_i^{NL}d\Lambda_j \tag{A9}$$

Note that $\sum_{j \neq i}\alpha_j = 1 - \alpha_i$. The sustainability of country i increases by an equal increase in all countries economic target concerns ($d\Lambda_i = d\Lambda \;\forall i$) if $d S_i > 0 \Leftrightarrow$

$$b_i^C - (1 - \delta)b_i^{BR} - \frac{(2 - \alpha_i)(1 + \alpha_i)\delta}{2}b_i^{NL} + (n - 1)\frac{(1 + \alpha_i)\delta(1 - \alpha_i)}{2}b_i^{NL} > 0 \Leftrightarrow$$

$$b_i^C - (1 - \delta)b_i^{BR} + \frac{(1 + \alpha_i)\delta}{2}b_i^{NL}((n - 1)(1 - \alpha_i) - 2 + \alpha_i) > 0 \Leftrightarrow \tag{A10}$$

$$b_i^C - (1 - \delta)b_i^{BR} + \frac{(1 + \alpha_i)\delta}{2}b_i^{NL}(n - 3 - \alpha_i(n - 2)) > 0$$

(i) The last parenthesis becomes positive if $\alpha_i \leq \frac{n-3}{n-2}$, which also requires $n \geq 4$. In this case, the condition (16) does not hold for sufficiently large δ. Otherwise, we need to know specific parameter values in order to determine whether the condition (16) holds or not.

(ii) It is easier for the condition (16) to hold for a lower x_i^C, since the only term that depends on it in the condition (16) is b_i^C, which decreases for a lower x_i^C. On the other hand, It is easier for the condition (16) to hold for higher x_j^Cs, since the only term that depends on them in the condition (16) is b_i^D, which increases for higher x_j^Cs.

Proof of Lemma 1. Given the parameters of the model, let $\underline{\delta}_i(x^C)$ be the critical discount factor so that $S_i(x^C, \underline{\delta}_i) = 0$. Suppose, for some reason other than discount factor δ_i and cooperative emissions x^C, country i's sustainability increases, $S_i'(x^C, \underline{\delta}_i) > S_i(x^C, \underline{\delta}_i) = 0$. Therefore, there exists another $\underline{\delta}_i'$ such that $S_i'(x^C, \underline{\delta}_i') = 0$ and $\underline{\delta}_i'(.) < \underline{\delta}_i(.)$. $\qquad\square$

Proof of Proposition 3.

(i) Suppose country i's sustainability increases for some reason other than its discount factor δ_i and cooperative emissions x^C. We know by Lemma 1 that if $S_i'(x^C, \delta_i) > S_i(x^C, \delta_i)$ for any cooperative emissions x^C, then $\underline{\delta}'_{-i}(x^C) < \underline{\delta}_i(x^C)$. Furthermore, from (17), we have

$$B_i^D - B_i^C = \underline{\delta}_i(\overline{x}^C)\left(B_i^D - B_i^N\right)$$
$$B_i'^D - B_i'^C = \underline{\delta}'_{-i}(\overline{x}^C)\left(B_i'^D - B_i'^N\right) \tag{A11}$$

Since $\underline{\delta}'_{-i}(\overline{x}^C) < \underline{\delta}_i(\overline{x}^C)$:

$$B_i'^D - B_i'^C < \underline{\delta}_i(\overline{x}^C)\left(B_i'^D - B_i'^N\right) \Leftrightarrow$$
$$\left(1 - \underline{\delta}_i(\overline{x}^C)\right)B_i'^D < B_i'^C - \underline{\delta}_i(\overline{x}^C)B_i'^N \tag{A12}$$

meaning that the no-defection condition (17) does not bind for country i at the $(\overline{x}^C, \underline{\delta}_i(\overline{x}^C))$ pair. Note that B_i^N does not depend on the cooperative emissions. Moreover, B_i^D does not depend on country i's cooperative emissions. Thus, country i can sustain cooperation at $\hat{x}^C$ such that $\hat{x}_i^C < \overline{x}_i^C$ and $\hat{x}_j^C = \overline{x}_j^C$ for any j. Since these arguments apply to any $(\overline{x}_i^C, \underline{\delta}_i(\overline{x}^C))$ pair for any $\underline{\delta}_i(\overline{x}^C)$ that countries can maintain some cooperation, we have that for any such δ, $\overline{x}_i'^C < \overline{x}_i^C$.

(ii) Let all countries' sustainability functions increases for some reason other than its discount factors and cooperative emissions. For any country i, the condition (A12) does hold. For any cooperative emissions x^C lower than $\overline{x}^C$ in all dimensions, net benefit under defection is higher at x^C than at $\overline{x}^C$

$$B_i\left(BR_i\left(x_{-i}^C\right), x_{-i}^C, \Lambda, b_i^R\right) > B_i\left(BR_i\left(\overline{x}_{-i}^C\right), \overline{x}_{-i}^C, \Lambda, b_i^R\right) \tag{A13}$$

Furthermore, for such a $x^C < \overline{x}^C$, net benefit under cooperation is also higher at x^C than at $\overline{x}^C$

$$B_i\left(x^C, \Lambda, \alpha, b_i^R\right) > B_i\left(\overline{x}^C, \Lambda, \alpha, b_i^R\right) \tag{A14}$$

By the continuity of $B_i(.)$, there exist a cooperative emissions vector $\tilde{x}^C < \overline{x}^C$ such that for any country i the condition (1.2) still holds. Since these arguments apply to any $(\overline{x}_i^C, \underline{\delta}_i(\overline{x}^C))$ pair for any $\underline{\delta}_i(\overline{x}^C)$ that countries can maintain some cooperation, we have that for any such δ, $\overline{x}'^C < \overline{x}^C$. $\qquad \square$

Proof of Proposition 4. Country i's sustainability function under symmetry

$$S_i^= = \frac{\left(x^C\right)^{1/n}}{1-\delta}\left(1 + \Lambda_i - nx_i^C\right) - n\left(\frac{1}{n+1}\left(1 + \Lambda_i - (n-1)x_i^C\right)\right)^{\frac{n+1}{n}}$$
$$-\frac{\delta(1/n)^{1/n}}{1-\delta}\left(\frac{1+\Lambda_i}{2}\right)^{\frac{n+1}{n}} \tag{A15}$$

We take the derivative with respect to Λ_i in order to capture the impact of having different degrees of economic target concerns Λ_i or types changing in the direction of $S \to G \to L$:

$$\frac{\partial S_i^=}{\partial \Lambda_i} = \frac{\left(x_i^C\right)^{1/n}}{1-\delta} - \left(\frac{1}{n+1}\left(1+\Lambda_i - (n-1)x_i^C\right)\right)^{1/n}$$

$$- \left(\frac{n+1}{n}\right)\frac{\delta}{2(1-\delta)}(1/n)^{1/n}\left(\frac{1+\Lambda_i}{2}\right)^{1/n} \tag{A16}$$

Any country's sustainability decreases as its economic target concerns increase, $\frac{\partial S_i^=}{\partial \Lambda_i} < 0 \Leftrightarrow$

$$\underbrace{\left(x_i^C\right)^{1/n}}_{b_i^C} < (1-\delta)\underbrace{\left(\frac{1}{n+1}\left(1+\Lambda_i - (n-1)x_i^C\right)\right)^{1/n}}_{b_i^D} + \underbrace{\frac{\delta}{2}\left(\frac{n+1}{n}\right)\left(\frac{(1+\Lambda_i)}{2n}\right)^{1/n}}_{b_i^N} \tag{A17}$$

By Proposition 2, we know that if all countries sustainability functions decrease, then the most cooperative emissions countries can sustain increases, completing the proof. $\qquad\square$

12

COOPERATIVE GAME THEORY APPLIED TO IEAS: A COMPARISON OF SOLUTION CONCEPTS

Marco Rogna

University of Trento

1. Introduction

Game theory (GT) is the study of mathematical modelling of rational players interacting with each other and it has been extensively applied in the environmental context, ranging from fisheries management to natural resources extraction and waste treatment (Zara *et al.*, 2006a, 2006b). A subtopic that has received special attention is environmental pollution. As soon as the potential negative impact of anthropogenic emissions on the earth's ecosystem was widely recognized by the scientific and international community, different models have been envisaged in order to represent the possible interactions of countries to coordinate their efforts in abating emissions. Based on earlier models of transboundary pollution, a full class of new models has born to depict the 'global warming game' (Maler, 1989).

Although the solution concepts that have been adopted are usually already present in the game theoretical literature, it is still important to note that the 'global warming game' has its own specificities; indeed it is now possible to speak, without the risk of adding unjustified emphasis, of a new strand in that literature. Three elements, and their specific combination, can be considered the distinctive features of this particular game: the character of the players, the strategies at their disposal and the effects produced by their cooperative behaviour. Starting with the first, countries are the common unit of analysis (players, for game theory) and the game consists of constituting an international environmental treaty (IEA). Although this may appear quite natural, it is not trivial if examined more carefully. Countries, in fact, are neither the direct producers of emissions and pollution nor the direct recipients of their negative consequences. They act, therefore, as mediators between polluters (firms, consumers) and pollutees (people in general, for an anthropocentric perspective). According to the Coase Theorem (Coase, 1960), the problem can be solved by the market alone, through the law of demand and supply, but this would imply that pollution – or its complement, environmental quality – is a normal, 'priceable' good. Given that pollution is an externality and environmental quality a public, rather than a private, good, polluters and pollutees cannot use the market as an exchange platform unless a superior authority has previously defined appropriate property rights.

This leads to the second specificity, that is the strategy space defining this environmental game. It is possible to differentiate at least two distinct, although interconnected, classes of choices faced by countries. First of all, an IEA is a treaty and therefore a country has a di-chotomous choice between being or not a signatory. This decision can be additionally divided into two steps, that of signing and then ratifying the treaty, as recognized, for example, in the model of Köke and Lange (2013). In general, however, this possibility is simply disregarded and the simplifying assumption of perfect coincidence between the two steps is adopted.[1] The second strategic choice regards the optimal level of emissions or abatement to adopt. From a modelling perspective, speaking of emissions or abatement is equivalent since one is the complement of the other, so their use depends simply on author's preferences.[2] Three further clarifications are required. First, since countries bargain as representatives of their popula-tion, a model presenting a country's unique utility function implicitly relies on the assumption that the intra-state bargaining processes have already been solved. This constitutes a parallel with the role played by the representative agent in several models, where this role is here taken by the state itself. The second point regards the enforceability of state decisions. Countries are supposed to 'play' as rational actors. Therefore, besides having a single utility function, they are also supposed to possess full enforceability of their decisions. If this happens through a tax or a marketable quota mechanism (in the dedicated literature it has been largely demonstrated that the two mechanisms, under certain assumptions, are equivalent (Perman et al., 2003)) or through other instruments, is not important, but the central point to stress is that a country has a mechanism to perfectly implement the decision\strategy chosen. The third specificity concerns the outcome of cooperation which always generates positive externalities given that it reduces pollution.[3]

To sum up, in this paper IEAs are conceived to be games in which players are countries, sup-posed to be rational, utility maximizing agents. They have a double, interconnected, strategy space constituted by the choice of cooperate (being part of the agreement) or not cooperate (remaining outside) and a continuous choice on the level of emissions\abatement to adopt. The constitution of an IEA always generates positive externalities. Bearing these distinguish-ing characteristics in mind, this paper analyses the cooperative approach, describing the main solution concepts adopted in the literature, applied to the 'global warming game'.

2. Cooperative versus Non-Cooperative Approach

Since this paper deals with cooperative GT (CGT), it is opportune to give its definition and to stress the difference with the non-cooperative approach (NCGT). First of all, however, it is useful to recall a general definition of GT. This discipline can be described as the mathematical modelling of situations of conflict and cooperation that, starting from assumptions about the strategic behavioural patterns of players, provides their resulting pay-offs according to the adopted solution concepts (Zara et al., 2006). Bearing this definition in mind, the words of Osborne and Rubinstein (1994) clearly explain the difference between the two approaches:

A coalitional model (a cooperative model, ndr) is distinguished from a non-cooperative model primarily by its focus on what groups of players can achieve rather than on what individual players can do and by the fact that it does not consider the details of how groups of players function internally.

Another way to explain this difference refers to the enforceability of agreements. NCGT models situations where this enforceability is absent, so that players are free to strategically pursue their own objectives, whereas CGT mainly considers the allocation of cooperative gains resulting from binding agreements (Zara *et al.*, 2006a). Adopting this last view and considering the structure of the international community, based on the principle of state sovereignty, it could seem more appropriate to adopt an NCGT approach to model the 'global warming game'. However, two arguments can be used to contradict this thesis.

The first stems from the words of Osborne and Rubinstein (1994). The authors point that the two approaches differ on their focus. It is therefore a matter of perspective, a matter of what the researcher wants to investigate and which questions she wants to answer. The problem of agreement enforceability is simply disregarded. Criticizing a coalitional model on the ground that it assumes enforceability in a situation where it does not exist, although usually rewarding, could actually cause a simple deviation from the focal point. In choosing this approach, in fact, the researcher already knows its limits and this criticism becomes a mere pleonasm. The second point should be limited to the case of IEAs and derives from a peculiar development of the literature in this field. NCGT aims at investigating the constitutional process of a coalition (an IEA) under a positive perspective (Chander and Tulkens, 2006). For positive perspective, it is meant the logical (rational) outcome of a given situation. In other words, the formation of the coalition must be in the self-interest of the constituting parties that act under the typical assumption of rationality. Consequently, the most important property that the coalition must hold is stability. This concept is operationally translated into the conditions that, once a coalition has been formed, no one of the non-signatories should find rewarding to enter the agreement and no one of the signatories has an incentive to leave (d'Aspremont *et al.*, 1983). Mathematically, this is expressed as

$$\forall i, \quad \Pi_{i \in S}(S) \geq \Pi_{i \notin S}(S - i) \quad \text{and} \quad \Pi_{i \notin S}(S) \geq \Pi_{i \in S}(S + i)$$

where $\Pi_{i \in S}$ and $\Pi_{i \notin S}$ indicate, respectively, the utility a country i enjoys being, and not being, part of coalition S. When the two inequalities are satisfied, the coalition S is stable. Two things worth to be mentioned. The first is that the focus on stability clearly amounts to consider primarily the number of coalition participants or, equivalently, the number of IEA's signatories. This, in fact, seems to be the primary objective of NCGT applied to this field (Zara *et al.*, 2006b). The second aspect relates to the fact that the stability concept used here is reminiscent of the stability set proposed in Von Neuman and Morgenstern (1947), a typical cooperative solution, although they are not coincident (Chander and Tulkens, 2006). In performing this analysis, however, a vast part of the non-cooperative literature, namely, the one adopting Reduced-Stage Game (RSG) models, considers only a particular type of free riding: external free- riding (Finus, 2008). With this expression, it is meant a country that stays outside the agreement but enjoys the positive externalities generated by it. The internal dimension of free riding, where a country joins the agreement but does not comply with it, instead, is rarely taken into consideration as recognized[4] by McEvoy and Stranlund (2009) and Finus (2008). Disregarding this dimension implies to assume agreement enforceability. It then follows that this concept cannot be used any more as a discriminant between CGT and NCGT.

Although the border line between the two approaches is more blurred than in other fields, nonetheless they remain deeply separated in a crucial point: results. NCGT generally predicts the formation of a small stable coalition (SSC) (Carraro and Siniscalco, 1993; Barrett, 1994; Diamantoudi and Sartzetakis, 2006), whereas the cooperative one asserts that the grand coalition (GSC) can be formed (Chander and Tulkens, 1995; Tulkens and Chander, 1997; Germain *et al.*, 2010). Tulkens (1997) has dedicated a whole paper to explain in detail what causes this gap. The most important point is the fact that, in the cooperative approach, countries are given the Core solution (the comprehensive coalition) in the first step, and then are asked if they want to leave it, whereas the NCGT starts from the bottom, meaning the situation in which countries are singletons and have to agree to some form of cooperation (Tulkens, 1997). The other main difference, whose examination is postponed, is the fact that the cooperative approach assumes a strong reaction from the side of the coalition to the potential defection of one of its members. Such defection, in fact, causes a complete breaking up of the whole coalition. Apart from this last critical aspect, it is possible to note that the main difference is a matter of perspective, as the definition of Osborne and Rubinstein (1994) underlines.

At this point, however, one might wonder which is the utility of the cooperative approach if this disregards a crucial aspect such as the one of the IEA's formation process. The answer needs a premise. Full cooperation is globally optimal. This derives from well-known public goods theory (Samuelson, 1954) according to which a Pareto efficient solution in presence of a public good can be achieved only if all the interested parties are involved in the process of its allocation. From this, it follows that cooperation is desirable in itself. CGT, in fact, is said to adopt a normative perspective (Chander and Tulkens, 2006), rather than a positive one, meaning that it pursues cooperation as a goal, not a simple rational consequence. The aim becomes then to define the allocation that renders cooperation feasible and more acceptable. It can be said that it is an allocation, rather than a constitution, game. Its first goal, rendering cooperation feasible, is then subject to the constraint of satisfying individual rationality, whereas the second, related to acceptability, is bounded by the concepts of equity and fairness (Young, 1994). These can be given a general, normative meaning, or a narrower, practical one. In the first case, they have to be intended as a principle of justice, a moral attitude, whereas in the second they provide indications to shape concrete behaviours. This last interpretation presupposes a synthesis and, generally, a compromise, between the abstract principle and the material conditions of the case at hand (power considerations). The satisfaction of individual rationality constitutes this last element. The solution concepts adopted by CGT can be considered as different forms of compromise between these two requirements.

3. Solution Concepts

This section introduces and describes the most used solution concepts of CGT applied to the IEAs' field. It therefore considers only a subset of the many solution concepts adopted by CGT. Prevalence is given to single point rather than set solutions. The distinction between these two categories is self-contained in their names. Set solutions, in fact, define the whole space in which cooperation (GSC) can be sustained, whereas a single-point solution indicates a precise allocation able to perform the same task. The choice of focusing on the second category is due to this last consideration. A set solution, in fact, still leaves unsolved the problem of defining which equilibrium will emerge in the particular game at hand, providing just a space identification inside which multiple equilibria are possible (actually, every point in this space is an equilibrium). Another way to interpret the difference between the two categories recalls the distinction between feasibility and acceptability mentioned before. A set solution can be said to consider only the first element, providing an indication of all the possible allocations that are feasible, whereas a single-point solution is reached by adopting a specific equity concept, according to which there will be a unique allocation.

A further consideration needs to be done regarding the nature of the games under consideration. Cooperative games are usually divided in two categories: games with (TU) and without transferable utility (NTU) (Osborne and Rubinstein, 1994; Zara *et al.*, 2006a). The difference is easy to figure out. TU games assume that players' utility can be transferred among them (e.g. lump-sum payments in money or goods), whereas NTU games do not allow for this. Therefore, the TU assumption implies that the worth of a coalition, calculated as the sum of the utilities of its members, can be divided among them in any possible way (Zara *et al.*, 2006a). Conversely, in the NTU case, coalition members are constrained to enjoy the utility that they self-generate. Obviously, in this second class of games, it will be generally more difficult to obtain cooperation since transfers cannot be used as an instrument to induce it. Given that countries are the players in the considered game and that their utility is generally proxied by GDP, there seems to be no ground to refuse the TU assumption.

3.1 A Standard Coalitional Game and the Characteristic Function

Given a game $\Gamma(N, v)$ with a number n of players (countries, in the present case, where $n > 2$), define as N the set of all players: $N = 1, 2, ..., n$. Furthermore, denote a *coalition S* as a strict subset of $N : S \subset N$. The set N is also a coalition, namely, the *grand coalition*, including all players. Finally, define as Σ the set that collects all the possible coalitions – among which the empty set $\emptyset$ – which will necessarily have 2^n elements. It has to be noted that the n players, called *singletons*, are also treated as single member coalitions. The following necessary step to characterize a coalitional game is to define a characteristic function v, intended as a real-valued function that assigns a value to each one of the coalitions included in the set Σ. The value $v(S)$, since we are considering a TU game, can be interpreted as the total pay-off available for distribution among the members of coalition S (Osborne and Rubinstein, 1994). By assumption, $v(\emptyset) = 0$, meaning that the empty coalition has a zero value.

Definition. A TU coalitional game $\Gamma(N, v)$ in characteristic function form consists of a finite set of players N and a function v that assigns to each non-empty subset S of N a real number $v(S)$, representing the utility of S available for distribution among its members.

In the large set of games in characteristic function form, particular classes have been individuated according to the properties of the same characteristic function: *convex (supermodular)*, and *superadditive* games. The first class is a subset of the second. In order for a game to be defined convex, the characteristic function must satisfy the following inequality:

$$v(S) + v(T) \leq v(S + T) + v(S \cap T), \quad \forall\, S, T \subseteq N$$

Driessen (2013) shows the equivalence between convexity and supermodularity of v. A characteristic function is supermodular if:

$$v(S \cup i) - v(S) \leq v(T \cup i) - v(T), \quad \forall\, S \subseteq T \subseteq N \setminus \{i\} \text{ and } \forall\, i \in N$$

From this last condition, it can be said that a cooperative convex game is one in which, starting from a given coalition, the marginal contribution a player brings to it increases monotonically by increasing the size of the same coalition. Superadditivity, instead, can be considered as a weaker version of convexity, requiring that the characteristic function satisfies the following property:[5]

$$v(S) + v(T) \leq v(S + T), \text{ where } S \text{ and } T \text{ are disjoint coalitions: } S \cap T = \emptyset$$

It will be seen later on why these two properties are really important in a coalitional game. For the moment, it is sufficient to note that, when superadditivity holds, the characteristic value of every coalition $S \neq N$ cannot be higher than the value of the grand coalition. Obviously, this is true for convexity as well.

At this point, it is necessary to define the characteristic function itself

$$v(S) = \sum_{i \in S} \Pi_i(\phi_1, ..., \phi_n)$$

This is simply the sum of the utilities (indicated by $\Pi_i(.)$) of all coalition's members, given the strategies (ϕ_i) adopted by all the players in the game. It is then possible to link a coalitional form of a game with its strategic form. From standard GT, it is known that an n-players game is composed by the $2n$-tuple $(\Phi_1, ..., \Phi_n, \Pi_1, ..., \Pi_n)$ where Φ_i is the set of pure strategies of player i and $\Pi_i(\phi_1...\phi_n)$ is the pay-off of player i if player 1 uses the strategy $\phi_1 \in \Phi_1$ and player 2 uses $\phi_2 \in \Phi_2,...$, and player n $\phi_n \in \Phi_n$ (Ferguson, 2005). Therefore, from a standard game in strategic form, the passage to a coalitional form game entails to give a value to each possible coalition taking into consideration the strategies adopted by its members and the ones of the non-members. In the IEA game, the set of strategies Φ_i is the level of emissions or abatement that each country will undertake. Coalition members are supposed to coordinate their strategies in order to maximize their global welfare that, as just shown, coincides with the characteristic value of the same coalition (Zara *et al.*, 2006b). The strategies chosen by the players outside the coalition depend on the model assumptions. This topic will be discussed in the following section together with the first solution concept: *the Core*. Resuming what said in this section, an n-players game in coalitional form is a game defined by the pair (N, v) that focuses on the coalitions' outcome (characteristic value) rather than on the outcome achieved by single players.

3.2 *The Core and Its Various Declinations:* α, β *and* γ

In partial contradiction with what said before, the first solution concept that will be examined, the Core, is a set rather than a point solution. This deviation is due to the fact that the Core is a fundamental notion in CGT, it is useful to compute other point solutions and it is helpful in explaining the assumption regarding the non-members' behaviour in the IEA game. Assuming that $v(N)$ is higher than every other $v(S)$, it seems rational for the players of the game to form the grand coalition. The problem, in presence of transferable utility, becomes then to agree upon the amount that each player should receive (how to split the pie) (Ferguson, 2005). An *imputation* $\mathbf{x} = (x_1, ..., x_n)$ is a pay-off vector that defines the sum – the amount of utility – that each player should receive, if that imputation will be accepted. The Core (N,v) is defined as the set of all imputations that satisfies the following conditions:

(1) $\sum_{i \in N} x_i = v(N)$

(2) $\sum_{i \in S} x_i \geq v(S), \quad \forall S \subset N$

The first condition is a simple consequence of rationality and states that the entire value of the grand coalition should be distributed among players (efficiency condition), whereas the second one is what really defines the Core. Basically, each player should get an amount at least equal to what she could get in any of the subcoalitions that she could form. In this way, no one has an incentive to leave the grand coalition. This second condition can be further divided into two parts. The first, quite obvious, says that every player must get more than what she could achieve playing alone: $x_i \geq v(\{i\})\ \forall i \in N$. The second part, instead, includes also the other subcoalitions with two or more players and defines, through the condition $\sum_{i\in S} x_i \geq v(S)$, the stability of an imputation. In words, it can be said that the Core collects all the efficient imputations that satisfy stability (Ferguson, 2005). As anticipated, neither it considers any principle of equity or fairness nor it provides a clear indication on which imputation to prefer but still it discriminates between games that can support, on the ground of stability, the grand coalition and the ones that cannot. This last case happens when the Core is an empty set.

Recalling the definition of the characteristic value of a coalition S as $v(S) = \sum_{i\in S} \Pi_i(\phi_1...\phi_n)$, it is clear that its definition depends from the strategies adopted by its members as well as the ones undertaken by the players 'outside'. Coalition members are supposed to act in order to maximize $v(S)$ itself. It is then required to assume which is the behavioural pattern followed by the 'outsiders'. Three such assumptions have emerged in the CGT literature. The first is the most pessimistic one, supposing that non-members will adopt the most detrimental strategy at their disposal in order to contrast S. Once this assumption is adopted, we will speak of α-characteristic function and α-Core. Therefore, $v(S)$ will be defined by a *maxmin* principle, as to say, it is the maximum pay-off that a coalition can guarantee to itself knowing that non-members will act in order to minimize it:

$$v_\alpha(S) = \max_{\phi_S \in \Phi_S} \min_{\phi_{N\backslash S} \in \Phi_{N\backslash S}} \Pi_S(\phi_S, \phi_{N\backslash S})$$

The α-Core is simply the Core under this particular assumption. The β-characteristic function (and β-Core), instead, is obtained by adopting a *minmax* principle. In words, by assuming that the coalition can achieve the minimum among the maximum pay-offs that it is able to guarantee to itself after that the strategies of the players have been fixed (Zara *et al.*, 2006a):

$$v_\beta(S) = \min_{\phi_{N\backslash S} \in \Phi_{N\backslash S}} \max_{\phi_S \in \Phi_S} \Pi_S(\phi_S, \phi_{N\backslash S})$$

The last Core concept, the γ-Core, has been developed by Tulkens and Chander (1997) specifically to deal with IEAs and other environmental games. The γ-characteristic function implies two main assumptions: first, that players remaining outside coalition S do not form any other coalition, so they act as singletons, and secondly that they do not take any particular action, neither to contrast nor to favour, the formed coalition. They behave neutrally, following self-interest in a rational way:

$$v_\gamma(S) = \max_{\phi_S \in \Phi_S} \Pi_S(\phi_S, \phi_{N\backslash S}) \quad \text{where } \phi_{N\backslash S} \text{ results from}$$

$$\max_{\phi_{i|i\in N\backslash S} \in \Phi_{i|i\in N\backslash S}} \Pi_{i|i\in N\backslash S}(\phi_{i|i\in N\backslash S}, \phi_{N\backslash S,\{i\}}, \phi_S), \quad \forall\, i \in N \backslash S$$

Outsiders ($is \in N \backslash S$), therefore, act in a competitive way both among each other and towards the formed coalition S, with the only aim of maximizing private utility.

3.2.1 *Which Core is Appropriate for an IEA Game?*

The α- and β-Cores, theorized by Aumann (1959), have been discussed in the early stage of development of the environmental CGT literature, but have been almost completely abandoned after the introduction of the γ-Core. Laffont (1977) has shown that, in a game characterized by an economy with detrimental externalities (such as environmental games), the α and β assumptions coincide. Maler (1989) has been the first to discuss the problem of these assumptions when applied to the environmental field. In its 'Acid Rain' game, he has hypothesized that there is no upper bound to the level of pollution that countries can produce. Since, as stated in the introduction, the strategy space of a country is given by the amount of pollution it will generate, this means that, under α and β assumptions, all the non-members will produce an infinite level of pollution. Even placing some kind of 'technical' upper bound to the level of pollution feasibly deliverable, this does not solve the conceptual problem of why non-members should actually adopt this strategy. Generating positive externalities, a coalition favours also outsiders, therefore it should be in their interest not to contrast its formation. Secondly, such a high level of pollution is detrimental, therefore irrational, also for themselves.

Tulkens and Chander (1997) have then envisaged a new type of Core concept, whose main assumption is the simple rationality of players. Instead of using their production economy, it is simpler to explain the idea behind it making use of the emissions' benefit and damage functions. Under this setting, the monetary utility $[\Pi_i]$ obtained by a country i is given by a benefit function $[B_i(\cdot)]$ having as argument own emissions $[e_i]$ – recall that emissions generate a benefit being a proxy for production and, consequently, consumption – minus a function $[D_i(\cdot)]$ describing the environmental damage caused by pollution that, in presence of a global pollutant, will have as argument the sum of the emissions produced by all countries $[\sum_i e_i]$:

$$\Pi_i = B_i(e_i) - D_i\left(\sum_i e_i \right)$$

From basic optimality conditions, it is known that the pay-off of i is maximized when $B_i' = D_i'$. From what said till now, it becomes clear that the strategy space of i, under the sole assumption of rationality, becomes narrowly bounded till being a single value. It is possible to define the strategic choice of a country as a deterministic choice obtained by simply equating the first derivative of two known (by assumption) functions. Given that the damage function has the sum of all countries' emissions as its argument, this implicitly creates a strategic game that, in absence of any further assumption, takes the form of a Cournot game if the damage function is convex. The alternative would be a Stackelberg game in case a first move advantage is given to some players. In the dedicated literature, this assumption has been often used, guaranteeing the advantage to the coalition (Barrett, 1994; Diamantoudi and Sartzetakis, 2006; Sartzetakis and Strantza, 2013). However, it has been criticized as theoretically ungrounded by Finus (2008). It has to be noticed a strong convergence between the cooperative and the non-cooperative literature in representing the pay-off function of players. Generally, it is assumed a concave benefit and a convex damage function. The first complies with the non-satiety, but marginal declining satisfaction of consumption, that is standard in economic theory, whereas the second derives from environmental science according to which ecosystem resilience and absorption capacity suffer from saturation. The game so depicted has a single Nash equilibrium found as the solution of the maximization problem just described. Chander and Tulkens (1995) call it the *disagreement point* and it gives the characteristic value of the singletons' coalitions, $v(\{i\})$, also called the reservation utility of players. Till here, CGT and NCGT do not show any difference.

Once players are allowed to form (or discuss the formation of) coalitions, they will act in the interest of the same coalition, if they are members, or in their private interest if non-members.

Acting in the interest of the coalition translates in maximizing the sum of the pay-off functions of all its members:

$$\max_{e_{i}|i\in S} \sum_{i\in S} \Pi_i \quad \rightarrow \quad \max_{e_{i}|i\in S} \sum_{i\in S} \left(B_i(e_i) - D_i\left(\sum_i e_i \right) \right)$$

The coalition will therefore act as a single entity and, in this role, will play the same game just described with all the other players, that, according to the γ assumption, will keep their rational, self-interested behaviour and will act as singletons. It must be noted that the γ assumption can be decomposed into two distinct assumptions, each related to one of the two (inter-connected) strategic spaces composing the IEA game. The first relates to the amount of pollution, the choice of the level of emissions, outsiders will undertake. The second regards their possibility to form one, or potentially more, competing coalitions other than the one currently existing. As said, this possibility is basically excluded. Whereas the first assumption is decisively justified, from a conceptual point of view, by rationality, the second, instead, appears more as a simplifying device.[6] In fact, several papers, among which Eyckmans and Finus (2004), Buchner and Carraro (2005), Eyckmans *et al.* (2012) have dropped it, allowing for the coexistence of more than one coalition with several players. This would imply to switch from a characteristic to a partition function form game. This paper, however, will align with the vast majority of the literature on IEAs, both cooperative and non-cooperative, assuming that only a non-singleton coalition can be formed. A further point must be made. Recalling that a coalition always generate positive externalities, the γ assumption means that non-members, by standing as singletons, actually adopt the worst strategy at their disposal from the coalition point of view. As for the basic non-cooperative case, a unique Nash equilibrium will form (this has been called in Chander and Tulkens (1995) *partial agreement Nash equilibrium – PANE*). Another important property that follows from the structure of the game and from the γ assumption is that every change in the emissions level of one player will cause a partially offsetting reaction (best reply function) from the others (Finus, 2000). A way to avoid this is to use a quadratic benefit in combination with linear damage functions, for which there is no reply to a variation in the level of emissions of other players. However, this formulation misses to capture an important feature of the pollution problem: its increasing harmful effect.

Finally, it is possible to arrive at the distinctive feature between CGT and NCGT in their application to IEAs. Given that the γ assumption basically reproduces exactly the same behavioural pattern adopted by NCGT for non-members and considering that the way a coalition acts is also identical, the difference must be searched somewhere else. Tulkens and Chander (1997) have first tested two non-cooperative solution concepts: the *strong Nash equilibrium* and *the coalition-proof Nash equilibrium*. The first has been disregarded since it does not exist for this type of games, whereas the second, introduced by Bernheim *et al.* (1987), is actually the solution adopted by NCGT. Tulkens and Chander (1997) declared to be unsatisfied with this solution since it is suboptimal (not Pareto efficient) and since it implies that a deviation of a coalition (a set of members leaving a coalition) does not cause any reaction from the remaining members. As stated in the introduction, the main difference of the two approaches can be described as a matter of perspective. NCGT starts from the bottom, the disagreement point, and look at which coalition can be built, whereas CGT assumes the existence of the grand coalition and examines if there are incentives for leaving it. Anyway, this is not the end of the story. The reaction of the remaining members to a deviation of a coalition (as usual, in the CGT jargon, this means also a single player, a singleton) is also central in order to theoretically justify the feasibility of the cooperative approach. In fact, when they examine the incentive to leave the grand coalition, CGT adopters consider only the pay-offs that players can achieve forming sub-coalitions and the singletons' pay-offs are the ones obtained in the disagreement state. This means that the pay-offs achievable by being non-members (free riders, in the NCGT jargon) are simply disregarded. The justification of this strong limitation stays on the reaction of members to deviations that implies to break the coalition and to play the disagreement strategy (Tulkens and Chander, 1997). Much of the controversy between the two approaches has been focused on this assumption, with NCGT supporters claiming that this threat is not credible.

3.3 *The Solution of Chander and Tulkens*

The point solution proposed by Chander and Tulkens (1995) has two interesting and appealing properties. The first is that it lies in the Core, so that it preserves the individual rationality of cooperating. The second is that it uses the same elements of the countries' pay-off function (namely, the benefit and damage functions and their parameters) to define the imputation vector to be adopted. Each of its ith elements is composed by two parts: country i's pay-off obtained in the full cooperative case ($S = N$) plus a transfer: $x_i = \Pi_i(e_i^*) + T_i$, with e_i^* being the equilibrium level of emissions of country i participating to the grand coalition. The important part is constituted by the transfer T_i and the rule defining it:

$$T_i^* = \left[B_i(\bar{e}_i) - B_i(e_i^*) \right] + \frac{D_i'}{\sum_i D_i'} \left[\sum_i B_i(e_i^*) - \sum_i B_i(\bar{e}_i) \right]$$

$$\sum_i T_i = 0$$

where $\bar{e}$ is the equilibrium level of emissions at the disagreement point. Since the sum of T_i over the is is equal to zero, it is easy to check that $\sum_i x_i = \sum_i \Pi_i^* = v(N)$, so that the group rationality and efficiency condition is met. Explicitly writing the pay-off of a country when the grand coalition is implemented, $B_i(e_i^*) - D_i(\sum_i e_i^*)$, helps to easily understand what will be the final imputation received and the ratio behind this transfer scheme:

$$x_i = B_i(\bar{e}_i) - D_i \left(\sum_i e_i^* \right) + \frac{D_i'}{\sum_i D_i'} \left[\sum_i B_i(e_i^*) - \sum_i B_i(\bar{e}_i) \right]$$

A country will then receive an amount equal to its benefit function valued at the disagreement point, so when its emissions and, consequently, the value of the same function, is maximum. To this, it is subtracted the value of the damage function with emissions as in the full cooperative case, so when it is the lowest. From what just said, it is clear that the term inside the square brackets is always negative. This term will then be subtracted proportionally to the magnitude of the parameter describing the importance of the environmental damage for a country compared to (divided by) the sum of the same parameter over all countries. In other words, the first, always positive, term is diminished in a way that is proportional to the vulnerability of a country to pollution. This is justified since pollutees need to pay polluters in order to induce them to cooperate by compensating them for their forgone benefits obtained by emitting. However, as explained in Chander and Tulkens (2006), this solution is actually favourable to pollutees. In fact, they will pay polluters just up to the point that will induce them to cooperate, but the actual surplus of cooperation is retained by the same pollutees.

3.4 *The Shapley Value*

The Shapley value (Shapley, 1953) is a point solution concept that has found some applications in the context of pollution problems, for example, in Botteon and Carraro (1997) and Petrosjan and Zaccour (2003). It can be considered part of a broad family of (both set and point) solution concepts that rely on the mechanism of objections and counter-objections well described in Osborne and Rubinstein (1994). This class of solutions, differently from the Core that poses only an 'immediate' feasibility constraint, considers the chain of events that the deviation of a coalition may trigger. Also in this case feasibility is the central aspect, but it is evaluated only on the ultimate outcome produced by a deviation (Osborne and Rubinstein, 1994). Parts of this category are: the Stable set, the Bargaining set, the Kernel, the Nucleolus and the Shapley value. The first, introduced by Von Neuman and Morgenstern (1947), will not be considered since it has never been applied to environmental problems. Furthermore, it is a superset of the Core (Osborne and Rubinstein, 1994) and not only, being a set solution, allows for multiple equilibria but, for a single game, there can be more Stable sets. The following three solutions are strongly interconnected being the first a superset of the second and this of the latter (Driessen, 2013). Only the Nucleolus, the sole point solution among the three, will be described specifically in the next section.

The mechanism of objections and counter-objections allows to define a stable state, obtained when they reciprocally nullify. At its base there is a mix of considerations about power relations and fairness. Different weights attributed to these elements give rise to the multiplicity of solution concepts mentioned. The Shapely value focuses primarily on the marginal contribution that a player brings to a coalition. The objections that a coalition member can claim to another player for a certain imputation are twofold. She can claim that, leaving the coalition, will cause a loss to that player greater, for this last, than accepting the alternative imputation she is proposing. Alternatively, she can object that there is the possibility for her and the other members to make a coalition without the accused player that will leave her better off and the remaining players at least as good as before. Basically, she can induce the others to exclude the contested player. A counter-objection is simply the same argumentation put forth by the accused player. An important consideration to be made is that the Shapley value considers at one time all the subgames present in a game. In other words, it requires that the objection\counter-objection nullification holds for all the subgames. This last sentence expresses the *balanced contributions property*. In order for this property to hold, it is required to assign to each player a value ψ such that:

$$\psi_i(N, v) - \psi_i\left(N \setminus \{j\}, v^{N \setminus \{j\}}\right) = \psi_j(N, v) - \psi_j\left(N \setminus \{i\}, v^{N \setminus \{i\}}\right)$$

where $(N \setminus \{j\}, v^{N \setminus \{j\}})$ and $(N \setminus \{i\}, v^{N \setminus \{i\}})$ indicate the subgames of $\Gamma(N, v)$ where players j and i are, respectively, excluded. The only value ψ that satisfies this condition is the Shapley value that, therefore, will be the imputation chosen ($\psi = x$) (Osborne and Rubinstein, 1994). The formula for calculating it is given by

$$\psi_i(v) = \sum_{S \in N \setminus \{i\}} \frac{(|S| - 1)!(n - |S|)!}{n!} [v(S \cup \{i\}) - v(S)]$$

where $|S|$ indicates the cardinality of the coalition S. The term in the square brackets describes the contribution player i brings to the coalition S. The sum is used to consider the (marginal) contribution that a player provides to all the possible coalitions of a game (all the subgames). Finally, the expression preceding the square brackets is used to give a weight to each such contribution considering the probability a player has to actually 'produce' it. The denominator, in fact, is the number of all permutations of the n players, whereas the numerator expresses the number of these permutations in which the $|S|$ members of S come first than player i $((|S| - 1)!$ ways), and then the remaining $n - |S|$ players $((n - |S|)!$ ways). ψ_i is the average contribution brought by player i to the grand coalition if the players sequentially form this coalition in a random order (Ferguson, 2005). A possible extension of the Shapley value is to consider different probabilities in which coalitions can form. The random order just mentioned, in fact, implies to assume equal probabilities. In this case, we would speak of *Weighted Shapley value*. A literature review describing the various weighting schemes and computation devices adopted can be found in Kalai and Samet (1987).

Regarding the properties shown by the Shapley value, it has to be pointed that it is the only solution concept contemporaneously satisfying *efficiency*, *symmetry*, *dummy axiom* and *additivity*. According to Hoàng (2012), the satisfaction of all these properties is compensated by an important drawback since the Shapley value does not always fall into the Core. However, it does in convex games (Zara *et al.*, 2006). Applying this concept to IEA games leads to reward that countries having a high level of pollution. In fact, these are the ones whose inclusion in an agreement is most profitable from the global point of view. From another perspective, it could be said that the agreement would obtain scarce results without their presence. The solution of Chander and Tulkens takes into consideration this fact, but grants them only the sufficient benefits in order to make their participation rational. The surplus obtained from cooperation is given to polluted countries. With an imputation obtained through the Shapley value, instead, they have to give part of this surplus up to polluters.

3.5 *The Nucleolus*

The Nucleolus, introduced by Schmeidler (1969), is a point solution that, as anticipated, is contained both in the bargaining set and in the Kernel. Furthermore, when the Core is non-empty, it is also a subset of this last. In order to understand the mechanism of objections and counter-objections at its base, it is required to introduce the notion of the *excess* of S: $e(S, x) = v(S) - x(S)$; where $x(S) = \sum_{i \in S} x_i$ (Osborne and Rubinstein, 1994). When $e(S, x)$ is positive, it represents the amount that the coalition will loose if that imputation will be implemented. On the contrary, when negative, it constitutes the surplus that the coalition receives from that imputation. It is then possible to define an objection having as argument an imputation $\mathbf{x}$ and a coalition S with related *excess* $e(S, x)$ to another imputation $\mathbf{y}$ if $e(S, y) > e(S, x)$ (e.g. $x(S) > y(S)$). A counter-objection is consistent if it does exist another coalition T for which $e(T, x) > e(T, y)$ and $e(T, x) \geq e(S, y)$. Compared to the Shapley value, it is possible to see that the Nucleolus uses coalitions as the main argument to make objections and counter-objections. Also in this case, the Nucleolus is defined as the equilibrium point where the two balance each other.

The other – actually the standard – way to define the Nucleolus is by saying that it individuates the imputations vector $\mathbf{x}$ for which the vector $E(x)$ is *lexicographically* minimum (Osborne and Rubinstein, 1994). In order to understand this characterization, it is necessary to define the vector $E(x)$ and the word 'lexicographically'. Starting with an imputation vector $\mathbf{x}$, it is possible to arrange the $2^n - 2$ coalitions' excesses in a non-increasing order. $E(x)$ will then be the vector collecting this excesses: $E(x) = e_l(S, x)$, $l = 1, ..., 2^n - 2$. Now, consider an alternative imputation, $\mathbf{y}$, and repeat the same operation creating $E(y)$. It is then required to compare the first element (the one with the highest value, since they are ordered decreasingly) of the two vectors. The one having a lower value will be preferred. Once it is not possible to further minimize it, switch to the second element and continue till the last. The lower bound for minimizing the first element is actually given by the second one. In fact, when the first reaches this level, further minimizing it will cause it to move on the second place given that the $E(x)$ vector must be ordered decreasingly. Therefore, as stated by Serrano (1999), the nucleolus maximizes recursively the pay-off of the worst-treated coalitions. The same author underlines that it can be interpreted as an application of the Rawlsian *maximin* principle (Rawls, 1971) applied to coalitions interpreted as independent subjects. The Nucleolus satisfies several properties that will be just mentioned. The first two are individual and group rationality. The third, being in the Core when this is not an empty set, is actually a proof in itself of the previous ones. The Nucleolus is unique (a point solution) and never empty. Finally, it satisfies consistency, covariance, anonymity and efficiency.

3.5.1 Computing the Nucleolus

The calculation of the Nucleolus requires a computational burdensome procedure even in presence of relatively simple 'games'. In their presentation of an analytic procedure to compute it, Leng and Parlar (2010) provide a review of the various algorithms present in the literature to efficiently solve the linear programming (LP) system necessary to find it. Here, it will be simply presented the standard procedure without taking into consideration the problem of computational steps.

Recall the definition of the excess, $e(S, x) = v(S) - \sum_{i \in S} x_i$, and remember that, excluding the empty and the grand coalition, there will be $l = 2^n - 2$ excesses so that it is possible to write $e_l(S_l, x)$. The Nucleolus is found by solving $\min_x \max[e_1(S_1, x), ...e_l(S_l, x)]$. A simple example, with three players, can help to further clarify the procedure. The coalitions' set will be $\Sigma \setminus \emptyset, N = (S_1 = 1; S_2 = 2; S_3 = 3; S_4 = 1, 2; S_5 = 1, 3; S_6 = 2, 3)$. The minimization problem will then be

$$\min_{x_1, x_2, x_3} \max[e_1, e_2, e_3, e_4, e_5, e_6]$$

s.t.

$$e_1 = v(S_1) - x_1$$

$$e_2 = v(S_2) - x_2$$

$$e_3 = v(S_3) - x_3$$

$$e_4 = v(S_4) - x_1 - x_2$$

$$e_5 = v(S_5) - x_1 - x_3$$

$$e_6 = v(S_6) - x_2 - x_3$$

$$x_1 + x_2 + x_3 = v(N)$$

This problem amounts to distribute the value $v(N)$ among x_1, x_2 and x_3 respecting the given conditions.

4. A Rawlsian Solution Concept Bounded by Individual Rationality

The aim of this section is to introduce an alternative solution concept that, although lying in the Core, fosters the redistribution of utility. In order to introduce it, two additional solution concepts will be shortly described.

4.1 *The Strong ϵ-Core and the Least Core*

The Strong ϵ-Core has been introduced by Shapley and Shubik (1966) as a way to find the Core even when this set is actually empty. They have shown that, for an appropriate value of $\epsilon \in \Re$ there will always be an imputation lying in the Core. The Strong ϵ-Core can be defined as:

$$C_\epsilon(N, v) = \left\{ x \in \Re^N : \sum_{i \in N} x_i = v(N); \sum_{i \in S} x_i \geq v(S) - \epsilon, \ \forall S \subseteq N \right\}$$

It can be seen that, when ϵ is positive and large enough, even a game with an empty Core will admit at least one element in this set. The value of ϵ can be interpreted as a penalty that members should pay in order to leave the grand coalition. Instead of thinking at ϵ as a value exogenously given, it is possible to interpret it as a variable to be minimized (Bilbao, 2000). This amounts to solve the following system of equations:

$$\min_\epsilon z = \epsilon$$

$$\text{s.t.}$$

$$\sum_{i \in N} x_i = v(N)$$

$$\sum_{i \in S} x_i \geq v(S) - \epsilon, \qquad \forall S \subset N$$

Its solution, that requires to find both the imputation vector and ϵ, being both variables, gives the Least Core. This is a point solution with redistributive properties similar to the Nucleolus. In order to understand why, let us hypothesize to have a game with non-empty Core. Furthermore, consider two coalitions with an equal number of members. One is 'weak', meaning that it has a low characteristic value, whereas the other is 'strong'. In the minimization process, as said, both ϵ and the imputation vector will be defined. This means that, in order to have the lowest possible ϵ, the imputations of the members of the 'weak' coalition will be prioritized. Therefore, although the procedure to find (and the idea behind) the two solution concepts are quite different, the Least Core and the Nucleolus will give an imputation vector with similar characteristics.

4.2 *The Minimum Feasible Core (MF Core)*

The system of equations that is used to find the Least Core can be slightly changed to find another useful concept: the MF Core. This is not an interesting solution in itself, since it is not efficient, but can be used to define the pure surplus generated by cooperation once the individual rationality constraint has been satisfied. Consider the following system of equations:

$$\max_\eta z = \eta$$

$$\text{s.t.}$$

$$\sum_{i \in N} x_i = v(N) - \eta$$

$$\sum_{i \in S} x_i \geq v(S) \qquad \forall S \subset N$$

Although very similar to the program defining the Least Core, two crucial modifications have been applied: the position of the variable and its maximization rather than minimization. Basically, this solution tells which is the minimum characteristic value that the grand coalition must have in order to sustain full cooperation or, in order for the Core to be non-empty. This value is simply found as $v(N) - \eta$. The value of η can therefore be interpreted as the pure surplus (if positive) of cooperation, whereas the associated imputation vector as the minimum amount that each player should receive in order not to leave the grand coalition. A negative η, such as a positive ϵ in the previous case, indicates that the game has an empty Core.

A final example can help to understand this mechanism. Let us think that each coalition $S \neq N$ is represented by an empty bottle. The bottles can have different dimensions and their volume is given by $v(S)$. The owners of a bottle are the players member of that coalition. The grand coalition, instead, is a barrel having an amount of liquid equal to $v(N)$. Now, under the assumption that one unit of liquid corresponds to a unit of volume, we need to give a certain amount of it to each player (defining an imputation) in order to fill up all the bottles. When a player is given a unit of liquid, this will contribute to fill in one unit of volume of all the bottles owned by her. Therefore, three conditions are possible. One is that there is not enough liquid to fill up all the bottles, one is that the liquid is exactly enough to do it and, finally, the last corresponds to have some spear liquid. Finding the MF Core tells us which would be the imputation in the middle case (how much liquid each player should receive), and, through the value of η, how much liquid we lack to reach this point (negative η) or how much there is in excess (positive η).

4.3 A 'Revisited' Nash Bargaining Solution and the Rawlsian Nucleolus

Remembering what said about the Nucleolus, this solution concept can be considered as a way to implement the Rawlsian *maximin* principle. This is actually true, but the potential flaw of this method in representing this principle is to consider coalitions as subjects. In reality, it does not really make sense to speak of the welfare of a coalition with two or more players. Welfare is an attribute of players alone. A redistributive principle should have them, and only them, as the main target. Before presenting a modified version of the Nucleolus that takes into consideration this aspect, it is opportune to further discuss the MF Core.

Remembering what said in the introduction, a solution concept is made of two parts. From one side, it has to satisfy power relations assuring individual (and group) rationality. From the other, it has to provide a fair and equitable division, therefore, it is required to possess such a criterion of fairness and equity imbued on it. The MF Core, however, allows to completely separate the two aspects given that it provides the minimum sufficient condition to satisfy the first requirement. Basically, after that the MF Core imputation vector has been established (since now on it will be identified as $\mathbf{x}^\eta$), a new game can be thought regarding the way of dividing the surplus η. A first obvious solution would be to divide it in equal parts so that the final imputation would be $\mathbf{x} = \mathbf{x}^\eta + \frac{\eta}{n}$. This allocation sounds very appealing specially considering, as suggested, the splitting of the cooperative surplus as a cooperative bargaining problem whose starting condition is the imputation vector $\mathbf{x}^\eta$. This assumption would mean that the reservation utility of each country is: $r(\{i\}) = \mathbf{x}_i^\eta$. Therefore, it is easy to check that $\frac{\eta}{n}$ is the allocation that maximizes the Nash Bargaining solution: $\arg \max_{\lambda_i} \prod_i ((x_i^\eta + \lambda_i \eta) - x_i^\eta) = \prod_i (\lambda_i \eta) = \frac{1}{n}$. Compared to the 'classical' Nash Bargaining solution, the difference stays in the alternative reservation utilized: the utility obtained in the disagreement point has been substituted by the MF Core imputation. Therefore, this solution is named 'revisited' Nash Bargaining solution.

The fairness of this allocation, however, can be questioned. Splitting equally the surplus of cooperation, in fact, is surely equitable only if the 'power game' determining the MF Core imputation vector is taken for granted. In other words, the power asymmetries at its root are considered natural and are fully justified on a moral base. Redistribution, therefore, does not find any valid reason for being implemented.

In the 'global warming game', however, this point of view can hardly be sustained. Indeed, it would imply to accept and to morally justify the fact that countries are affected differently from climate change on the simple base of their geographical position and that the most affected ones have to pay by themselves for this disadvantage. Furthermore, it also means to justify GDP inequalities and to wipe away the historical dimension of the pollution problem. Given the strong association between GDP level and the world share of cumulative emissions, measured in terms of CO_2 ppm, this last element is the most difficult to accept (Shukla, 1999). A redistributive policy, in the IEA context, appears therefore an appropriate choice. However, unless introducing an altruistic attitude of countries that modifies their pay-off function, as done, for example, in Lange and Vogt (2003) and Grüning and Peters (2010), the postulate of self-interest imposes a strong lower bound on the amount that can be feasibly redistributed. This bound, as stated, is simply the MF Core imputation vector. The surplus, however, can be freely – meaning, without affecting the cooperative outcome – allocated in order to, at least partially, the starting asymmetries. The problem to be solved will then be:

$$\max_{\lambda_i} \min_i \left(x_i^\eta + \lambda_i \eta \right)$$

$$\text{s.t.}$$

$$\sum_i \lambda_i = 1$$

where $\min(x_i^\eta + \lambda_i\eta) = \min(x_1^\eta + \lambda_1\eta, ..., x_n^\eta + \lambda_n\eta)$. Regarding the relation with the Nucleolus, the present solution can be considered as a modification of that concept in order to base its redistributive properties only on the singletons coalitions. Once solved for λ_i the given maximization problem, the final imputation vector will be: $\mathbf{x}^{RN} = x_i^\eta + \lambda_i\eta$, where the superscript 'RN' stays for *Rawlsian Nucleolus*, the chosen name for this solution concept.

5. A Numerical Comparison of Solution Concepts

The aim of this section is to provide a comparison of the countries' utility achieved in a standard IEA cooperative game applying the different solution concepts previously discussed: the Chander and Tulkens solution, the Shapley value, the Nucleolus, the Least Core, the revisited Nash Bargaining solution and the Rawlsian Nucleolus. The model used to perform this comparison is a standard economic–environmental model with a quadratic concave emissions benefit and a quadratic convex damage functions: $B_i(e_i) = a_i(e_i - \frac{1}{2}b_ie_i^2)$; $D_i(E) = \frac{1}{2}d_i(E)^2$, with $E = \sum_i e_i$; $i = 1, ..., n$. As in Chander and Tulkens (1995), it will be adopted a γ-characteristic function, therefore, when a coalition form, the other members are supposed to pursue, as singletons, their self-interest. A country welfare function is given by

$$\Pi_i = a_i \left(e_i - \frac{1}{2}b_ie_i^2 \right) - \frac{1}{2}d_i(E)^2$$

The model, under the assumption of symmetric countries (identical parameters), can be easily solved analytically. For convenience, three cases are treated separately: the Nash equilibrium (all countries act as singletons), the partial Nash equilibrium (PANE) and the full cooperation case (grand coalition). Solving for emissions in the three cases gives

Nash Equilibrium

$$e_i = \frac{a}{ab + |N|d} \qquad\qquad E = \frac{|N|a}{ab + |N|d}$$

PANE

$$e_i^s = \frac{ab + (|N| - |S|)d(1 - |S|)}{b(ab + (|N| + |S^2| - |S|)d)} \qquad e_i^{ns} = \frac{ab + d(|S|^2 - |S|)}{b(ab + (|N| + |S|^2 - |S|)d)}$$

$$E = \frac{|N|a}{ab + (|N| + |S|^2 - |S|)d}$$

Grand Coalition

$$e_i = \frac{a}{ab + |N|^2d} \qquad\qquad E = \frac{|N|a}{ab + |N|^2d}$$

In the PANE case e_i^s and e_i^{ns} stay, respectively, for the emissions of a signatory and a non-signatory, $|S|$ indicates the number of coalition members and $|N|$ the total number of players.[7] By plugging these values in the pay-off functions, it is possible to find the welfare of each country and, consequently, the characteristic value of the coalitions.

At the beginning of the previous chapter, two properties of characteristic functions have been mentioned: convexity and superadditivity. The importance of the first stems from the Bondareva–Shapley theorem, that establishes a sufficient and necessary condition for a game to have a non-empty Core: *balancedness*. A game is balanced when:

$$\sum_{S \in \Sigma} \rho_S v(S) \leq v(N) \quad \text{for every balanced collection of weights } \rho_S$$

The collection of weights $(\rho_S)_{S \in \Sigma}$ is a vector of scalars in [0,1] with dimension 2^n and it is balanced if, for every player i, the sum of it over all the coalitions that include $i - 2^{n-1}$ coalitions – is equal to one: $\sum_{S \in \Sigma, S \ni i} \rho_S = 1$ (Osborne and Rubinstein, 1994). Convex games are known to be always balanced, therefore they have a non-empty core (Dubey and Shapley, 1984). Superadditivity, instead, only guarantees that the characteristic value of the grand coalition is not lower than the characteristic value of any other subcoalition: $v(N) \geq v(S)$, $\forall S \subset N$. Recalling what said regarding the efficiency of an allocation referred to a public good, that is maximized when all the interested parties are included in its definition (Samuelson, 1954), it follows that a coalition should always get a benefit by expanding its membership. Superadditivity captures this, but it is not a sufficient condition to proof balancedness, therefore the Core might be empty.

Dubey and Shapley (1984) have proved balancedness for certain classes of not convex games, among which the production market game, the pure exchange market game and the transshipment game. Upon the introduction of certain mild restrictions – all the parameters (a, b and d) have positive values and no player generates a negative utility in any possible coalition – the present model, although not necessarily convex, always has a non-empty Core. The last claim has been proved by Helm (2001), whereas a simple numerical example, with identical players, is provided in Appendix A.1 in order to show that convexity is not a necessary property of the game. Superadditivity, instead, it is (proof is given in Appendix A.2).

A final remark is related to the restrictions on parameter values. Their strict positivity does not really need a justification since it is a necessary condition for the concavity of the benefit function and the convexity of the damage function to hold. Setting their values in order that no player in any coalition obtains a negative utility could appear more arbitrary. However, it seems quite natural that, even in the disagreement point, countries still enjoy a positive utility. Once this condition is assured – for the case of identical players it requires that $\frac{ab}{d} >$ $|N|(|N| - 2) = \frac{B''}{D'} > |N|(|N| - 2)$ – superadditivity implies that no player can be worst off in any coalition S ($|S| \geq 2$) than in the disagreement point. Furthermore, since a coalition generates positive externalities, also non-members cannot experience a reduction in their level of utility. Therefore, setting appropriate values for non-negative utilities in the disagreement point is sufficient to guarantee strictly positive utilities in all other cases. An analytic proof of this claim, for identical players, is given in Appendix A.3.

5.1 Characteristic Values with Asymmetric Countries

The scenario with symmetric countries is not really interesting given the purpose of comparing the mentioned solution concepts. It can be checked, in fact, that, in this case, the imputation vector obtained and, therefore, countries' welfare, would be identical for all the solutions adopted. In order to give a touch of realism to the model while keeping its interpretation as simple as possible, only five countries will be considered and the parameters to vary are b and d. The first, that describes the magnitude of the marginal decrease of emissions benefits, is fundamental to determine the optimal level of the same emissions. For a given level of emissions, in fact, its magnitude is inversely correlated with the final utility achieved. It is therefore used to simulate the wealth, or the technological level, of a country. Three values will be used: High Wealth (HW) = 0.01, Medium Wealth (MW) = 0.02 and Low Wealth (LW) = 0.028. The parameter a, instead, will be kept equal for all countries and will be equal to 8. The other parameter to vary, d, represents the degree a country is affected by pollution. A higher value implies that a country is more vulnerable to the detrimental effects of climate change. Also in this case three levels will be adopted: high (HD = 0.0024), medium (MD = 0.00225) and low (LD = 0.002) vulnerability. Combining them, five types of countries are simulated. They are shown in decreasing order of 'power endowment':

1. High Wealth – Low Damage HWLD: $a = 8$; $b = 0.01$; $d = 0.002$;
2. High Wealth – High Damage HWHD: $a = 8$; $b = 0.01$; $d = 0.0024$;
3. Medium Wealth – Medium Damage MWMD: $a = 8$; $b = 0.02$; $d = 0.00225$;
4. Low Wealth – Low Damage LWLD: $a = 8$; $b = 0.028$; $d = 0.002$;
5. Low Wealth – High Damage LWHD: $a = 8$; $b = 0.028$; $d = 0.0024$

5.2 A Comparison of Distributive Properties

In Table 1, it is possible to see the imputation vectors obtained with the different solution concepts. As said, each imputation corresponds to the final utility obtained by a country. The first two columns, in reality, show how pay-offs will be distributed in the Nash equilibrium (disagreement point) and in the grand coalition without any transfer scheme. The row displaying the summation of utilities testifies the benefit provided by cooperation. For a comparison between the characteristic value of the grand coalition and all the other partial coalitions, see Table B.1 in Appendix. It should also be noticed that the distribution obtained without transfer

Table 1. Imputation Vectors from Different Solution Concepts.

Countries	Nash Equilibrium	No Redistribution	Shapley Value
HWLD	310.7	312.6	331.5
HWHD	292.3	302.7	314.2
MWMD	100.6	125.3	118.7
LWLD	54.9	79.8	70.8
LWHD	37.1	69.9	55.1
Utility Sum.	795.5	890.4	890.4
Utility Prod.	1.86E+010	6.62E+010	4.83E+010

Countries	Least Core	CT solution	Nucleolus
HWLD	329.6	327.8	329.6
HWHD	311.2	312.9	311.2
MWMD	119.5	119.9	119.6
LWLD	73.9	72.1	73.9
LWHD	56.1	57.7	56.1
Utility Sum.	890.4	890.4	890.4
Utility Prod.	5.08E+010	5.12E+010	5.08E+010

Countries	MF Core	Rawlsian Nucleolus	'R' Nash Barg.
HWLD	326.8	326.8	334.3
HWHD	311.2	311.2	318.6
MWMD	110.1	110.1	117.5
LWLD	58.9	71.2	66.4
LWHD	46.2	71.2	53.6
Utility Sum.	853.2	890.4	890.4
Utility Prod.	3.05E+010	5.67E+010	4.46E+010

is actually the most egalitarian: the product of utilities is the highest compared with the one obtained from any other solution concept. However, this imputation does not satisfy the boundaries imposed by the MF Core, with the first two countries obtaining a lower value.

Comparing the various solution concepts, it can be first noticed that they are all efficient since the summation over all imputations is equal to the characteristic value of the grand coalition. The only one failing is the MF Core, but it has already been explained that this solution is not useful in itself. Furthermore, they all lie in the Core. The similarity between the Least Core and the Nucleolus is confirmed till the point that, with only one decimal number displayed, they appear identical. Regarding their (re)distributive properties, the Rawlsian Nucleolus is the one that advantages the most the 'weakest' countries and maximizes the product of utilities. The imputation having the opposite effect is not the one obtained with the Shapley value, as could have been expected, but the one realized through the revisited Nash Bargaining solution. Dividing the cooperative surplus in equal parts advantages strong players beyond the value of their marginal contribution over all coalitions.

An interesting comparison can be done between the CT solution and the Rawlsian Nucleolus. Chander and Tulkens (2006) affirm that their solution is the most favourable possible for pollutees. However, its redistributive properties are lower than the ones of the Rawlsian Nucleolus. One can suspect that the difference stays in the fact that this numerical example portrays differences both in the environmental damage parameter and in the emissions benefit one. This aspect, however, is not fundamental. Even allowing for symmetric benefit functions, the obtained imputation vector is different.[8] This is due to the fact that in the CT solution pollutees are required to compensate polluters for their forgone emissions benefit. This is the lower bound, whereas the Rawlsian Nucleolus uses the MF Core as lower bound. The due compensation is reduced by the increase in the utility that also polluters enjoy thanks to a better environmental quality. However, what Chander and Tulkens claim is actually true. Furthermore, it is also appropriate their claim that this solution concept correspond to the polluters pay rule. However, another principle discussed during the Kyoto negotiation for dividing the burden of contrasting climate change refers to the concept of capacity, strictly related to the one of vulnerability (Heyward, 2007). The damage caused by pollution differs not only according to some physical properties such as the geographical position of a country, but also given its ability to take counteractive measures (resilience). This is likely to be positively correlated with the economic condition of a country. Unless the damage parameter already takes this into consideration, the Rawlsian Nucleolus appears to better address the vulnerability problem.

5.3 A Comparison of Incentives to, and Potential Losses from, Free Riding

This section will continue the comparison of solution concepts adopting a more non-cooperative perspective. In particular, they will be evaluated in light of their ability to prevent the damages from internal free riding. This last concept is different from the usual meaning that takes in the non-cooperative literature, where it is considered as the practice of non-participating to an environmental agreement benefiting from the positive externalities generated by a coalition. In this case, instead, the participation to the grand coalition is taken as granted. However, a country can decide to cheat and to re-optimize its emissions' level taking the optimal level (from the collective point of view) adopted by the other countries as given. In choosing how much to emit, an internal free rider will face the following maximization problem:

$$\max_{e_{fr}} \Pi_{fr}^+ = B_{fr}(e_{fr}) - D_{fr}(E^* - e_{fr}^* + e_{fr})$$

The subscript fr indicates the free rider and Π_{fr}^+ is the pay-off obtained through the re-optimization. From the sum of all optimal emissions E^*, it is subtracted the share produced by the same free rider, e_{fr}^*, that will now substitute it with the result obtained from the re-optimization problem, e_{fr}. Obviously, this level will be higher and will be found through the usual optimality condition: $B_{fr}' = D_{fr}'(E^* - e_{fr}^*)$. In order to free ride, instead of simply leaving the grand coalition, a free rider must still obey to the transfer scheme adopted. Although it has not been provided any formula defining a transfer for the solutions other than the one suggested by Chander and Tulkens, this is easily found: $T_i = x_i - \Pi i^*$. This holds for all solution concepts and it is trivial to show that the final utility obtained by a country is equal to the imputation itself: $\Pi_i = \Pi i^* + T_i = \Pi i^* + (x_i - \Pi i^*) = x_i$. In presence of free riding, however, this pay-off is modified in the following way:

$$\Pi_{fr} = \Pi_{fr}^+ + (x_{fr} - \Pi_{fr}^*) \qquad \text{(free rider)}$$
$$\Pi_{i/fr} = \Pi_{i/fr}^- + (x_{i/fr} - \Pi_{i/fr}^*) \qquad \text{(coalition members other than free rider)}$$

Table 2. Gains and Losses from Free Riding.

Free Rider	HWLD	HWHD	MWMD	LWLD	LWHD
HWLD	**24.75**	−13.85	−12.98	−11.54	−13.85
HWHD	−10.95	**22.50**	−12.32	−10.95	−13.14
MWMD	−5.52	−6.62	**11.83**	−5.52	−6.62
LWLD	−4.05	−4.86	−4.55	**8.98**	−4.86
LWHD	−3.86	−4.63	−4.34	−3.86	**8.19**

Note: Numbers in bold individuate the values relative to the player that is free riding.

The re-optimization problem faced by a free rider and its solution are independent from the imputation adopted. Moreover, the utility gain obtained by free riding is also independent from the solution concept adopted. In order to see this, just recall the definition of the final free rider pay-off given above: $\Pi_{fr}^+ + (x_{fr} - \Pi_{fr}^*)$. Its positive deviation from the utility that she would receive by respecting the rules, equal, as shown, to the same imputation, is given by: $\Pi_{fr}^+ + (x_{fr} - \Pi_{fr}^*) - x_{fr} = \Pi_{fr}^+ - \Pi_{fr}^*$. The imputations cancel out and what is left is a constant. The same holds for the loss suffered when it is another country to free ride. Table B.2 in Appendix displays all the countries' pay-offs for the different solution concepts in presence of free riding. Table 2, instead, shows the gains – on the main diagonal – and the losses – on all the other cells, obtained and suffered when the country displayed on the left column free ride. As said, this table is the same for every solution concept adopted. What changes, instead, is the ratio of the gains and losses over the utility achieved in complying with the coalition rules. In order to obtain this, it is simply necessary to divide each row of the previous table by the same imputation vector (through a cell by cell, not a matrix division). Table B.3 in Appendix displays all the coefficients so found. The values on the main diagonal can be interpreted as an index of the incentive a country has to free ride. In fact, if utility is measured in terms of GDP, this would translate in the percentage (after having been multiplied by 100) of GDP a country could obtain from a cheating behaviour. Obviously, the more favourable an imputation is to this country, the less significant the potential gain will be. Furthermore, this index, being built as a ratio of potential gains to a reference utility level, is not affected, in its representation of incentives, from the magnitude of the sole gains or from the starting conditions of a country. Proportionality should assure a balanced picture. On the other side, there are the remaining values of the described matrix. These represent the percentage loss a country would face in case another free ride. It is then a measure of risk in participating to a coalition with a given imputation vector. The more favourable is an imputation to this country, the lower will be the suffered damage (again, in terms of GDP percentage). It can be noticed that imputation vectors that favour wealthy nations reduce the risk that they will free ride. However, they also increase the damages suffered by other countries in case they will free ride. The opposite hold for imputations favouring weak countries. These last will be less tempted to free ride, but the avoided risk, at global level, will be less significant since the damage that they can inflict is lower. Finally, they will be less affected from deviations from wealthy notions that, however, will be more likely.

The problem with such a matrix is that it does not give a clear and immediate touchstone for comparing solution concepts. What is required is a single index able to measure the overall risk caused by free riding when a given imputation is implemented. This single index can be

Table 3. Overall Free Riding Potential Loss Index.

Shapley value	−0.140809
Chander and Tulkens solution	−0.136577
Least Core	−0.137407
Nucleolus	−0.137424
Rawlsian Nucleolus	−0.127944
'R' Nash Barg.	−0.146289

built in the following way. In order to show the necessary steps, the index coefficients table related to the Shapley value (Table B.3) will be taken as an example. Let us write the transpose of it in matrix form:

$$A = \begin{bmatrix} 0.0746 & -0.0330 & -0.0167 & -0.0122 & -0.0116 \\ -0.0441 & 0.0716 & -0.0211 & -0.0155 & -0.0147 \\ -0.1094 & -0.1038 & 0.0996 & -0.0384 & -0.0366 \\ -0.1629 & -0.1546 & -0.0779 & 0.1268 & -0.0545 \\ -0.2514 & -0.2385 & -0.1202 & -0.0882 & 0.1486 \end{bmatrix}$$

The element in the main diagonal, the incentive indexes, are extracted in order to form a vector h, keeping the same vertical order:

$$h = \begin{bmatrix} 0.07464 \\ 0.07160 \\ 0.09961 \\ 0.12676 \\ 0.14862 \end{bmatrix}$$

Multiplying A, with the diagonal elements substituted by zeros, with h gives the vector q representing the overall risk faced by each country. In fact, each row of A displays the potential loss suffered by a country when each of the others free ride. The matrix multiplication with vector h weights the potential loss caused by a country deviation with the incentive that this country has to actually deviate. It can be contested that the vector h is used here as a measure of probability although it is actually far from being so. This critics is effectively reasonable. However, such a probability measure would be impossible to build, specially in this simple model setting. The magnitude of potential gains from free riding is therefore chosen as a second best, although with consciousness about its limitations. Once obtained the vector q, the final synthetic index is given by the summation of all its elements: $q \times i'$ (where i' is a vector of ones having same length as q). Basically, the overall potential loss caused by free riding in a given coalition for a given imputation vector is given by the sum of the same potential losses faced by each country. Table 3 reports the built indexes for each solution concept.

From Table 3, it can be seen that, although the more redistributive solution concepts foster the incentive to free ride of wealthy nations, whose deviation is the most detrimental, this is more than compensated by the higher imputations attributed to the other countries. The final index of free riding potential losses is the lowest for the Rawlsian Nucleolus, followed by the Chander and Tulkens solution. This last is closely followed by the Nucleolus and the Least Core, again almost identical. Finally, the Shapley value and the revisited Nash Bargaining.

This classification mirrors exactly the one representing the distributive properties of solution concepts. The fact that redistribution minimizes potential free riding losses can appear counter-intuitive. On this regard it has to be noticed that it is not the absolute value of the losses to be minimized (as seen, this is constant), but the proportion each country will loose compared to its starting pay-off. If it was the absolute value of the losses to be weighted by the pseudo measure of probability of free riding, the result would have been different. However, this index appears to be justified since it can be seen as a representation of the potential losses in terms of GDP percentages. The focus is on each country and on its relative wealth, rather than in the overall value of the loss. The potential contrast with the cooperative perspective, more focused on global wealth, is settled by the fact that, when examining the risk of free riding, each country evaluates it on the base of its own potential losses.

6. Conclusions

This paper has offered an overview of the most popular solution concepts derived from CGT that have found an application in the environmental field. In particular, the focus has been placed on a specific sub-topic, namely, the constitution of an IEA to control the emissions of pollutants. After having briefly revised some fundamental concepts of CGT and having characterized the specificities of the game theoretical framework underpinning an IEA, the differences between the cooperative and the NCGT approach have been examined concluding that the perspective from which they look at the problem is the main point of departure. The other important element differentiating them is the way in which coalition members reply to a deviation from a cooperative behaviour of one of them.

   The solution concepts taken into consideration have been the Core, together with its refinements: the Strong ϵ-Core and the Least Core. Moreover, solution concepts based on the idea of objections and counter-objections have been discussed: the Shapley value and the Nucleolus. An important solution in the game theoretical field of environmental economics, namely, the Chander and Tulkens solution, has also been examined. Finally, two alternative concepts have been proposed: the Rawlsian Nucleolus and a revisited Nash Bargaining solution, both based on the idea of the MF Core. The Rawlsian Nucleolus has been named in this way for its redistributive properties that favour the most disadvantaged, whereas the latter solution split the cooperative gain in equal shares among the cooperating parts. The difference between the solution proposed originally by Nash is that the reservation utilities applied here are the ones obtained through the MF Core.

   The last part of the paper has been dedicated to a numerical exercise based on a standard game of emissions optimization in order to compare the properties of the mentioned solution concepts in terms of welfare distribution and ability to minimize the potential damages of internal free riding. The conclusion of the first analysis has shown that the Rawlsian Nucleolus is actually the most beneficial solution for poor countries largely affected by the detrimental consequences of climate change. The redistribution obtained through this method goes beyond the one achieved by the CT solution since the surplus is assigned on the base of final utility – prioritizing countries with the lowest – and it has the MF Core imputation as lower bound rather than emissions benefit in the disagreement point. Whereas the latter concept can be identified with the principle of polluters pay, the first further includes the criterion of vulnerability. However, it has to be underlined that such concept, if applied in a real context, could over-represent the entitlements of poor countries simply given their low economic level. This would cause a detachment from the pure environmental field and could undermine the acceptability of this solution. The proposed revisited Nash Bargaining solution, instead, rewards wealthy nations, therefore high polluters, even more than the Shapley value.

The last part tries to introduce an element of non-cooperative game theory in the cooperative perspective underpinning the paper: free riding. The link between the two approaches has been a theme largely debated, specially in the environmental context. After more than 20 years a satisfactory solution has yet to come. This paper, therefore, does not pretend to achieve such goal. However, it offers an index, based on potential losses measured in terms of utility (GDP) proportions, that can be used as a preliminary instrument to evaluate the intrinsic free riding risk of losses present in a coalition for a given imputation vector. The ranking of the examined solution concepts under this regard mirrors exactly what emerged for the redistributive properties. The more a solution concept redistributes wealth, the lower will be the overall risk of losses due to free riding.

Notes

1. Under this assumption, therefore, a signatory is automatically a ratifier. Some examples of this approach are: Carraro and Siniscalco (1993); Barrett (1994); Chander and Tulkens (1995); Tulkens and Chander (1997); Botteon and Carraro (1997).
2. Emissions have been used by: Carraro and Siniscalco (1993); Chander and Tulkens (1995); Botteon and Carraro (1997); whereas abatement has been used in Barrett (1994). There are also examples that allow contemporaneously for both the possibilities (Diamantoudi and Sartzetakis, 2006; Sartzetakis and Strantza, 2013). This case could still be reduced to a single choice, over net emissions, achievable through two options.
3. An exception to this statement is represented by games based on a Stackelberg form of competition between the coalition and the countries remaining outside it, where the first move advantage is assumed to be held by the coalition itself. See, for example, Barrett (1994) and Sartzetakis and Strantza (2013).
4. This dimension is explicitly addressed by Dynamic Game (DG) models such as the ones presented by McEvoy and Stranlund (2009) and Finus (2000) However, they are only a subgroup of the non-cooperative literature about IEAs.
5. Recalling the definition of convexity - $v(S) + v(T) \leq v(S + T) + v(S \cap T), \quad \forall S, T \subseteq N$ - it is clear that, since it must hold for all coalitions S and T, meaning also disjoint coalitions, it encompasses the superadditivity condition. In fact, when S and T are disjoint, $v(S \cap T) = v(\emptyset) = 0$, and therefore the inequality defining convexity collapses into the one defining superadditivity.
6. Diamantoudi and Sartzetakis (2002) justify this assumption on an empirical ground noticing that "IEAs are usually unique and fostered by the United Nations".
7. The subscript i on the parameters' letters has been dropped due to the assumption of symmetric countries.
8. This has been tested adopting a single parameter b for all countries whose value has been set equal to 0.02. Results, however, are not reported here.

References

Aumann, R.J. (1959) Acceptable points in general cooperative n-person games. *Contributions to the Theory of Games* 4: 287–324.

Barrett, S. (1994) Self-enforcing international environmental agreements. *Oxford Economic Papers* 46: 878–894. Available at: http://www.jstor.org/stable/2663505 (Last accessed 15 April 2016).

Bernheim, B.D., Peleg, B. and Whinston, M.D. (1987) Coalition-proof Nash equilibria I. Concepts. *Journal of Economic Theory* 42(1): 1–12.

Bilbao, J.M. (2000) *Cooperative Games on Combinatorial Structures*. Dordrecht, The Netherlands: Kluwer Academic.

Botteon, M. and Carraro, C. (1997) Environmental coalitions with heterogeneous countries: burden-sharing and carbon leakage. Fondazione Eni Enrico Mattei Working Paper (24.98). Available at: http://www.ekf.vsb.cz/export/sites/ekf/projekty/cs/weby/esf-0116/databaze-prispevku/1998/NDL1998-024_CC_coalition.pdf (Last accessed 15 April 2016).

Buchner, B.K. and Carraro, C. (2005) Regional and sub-global climate blocs. *A game-theoretic perspective on bottom-up climate regimes*. Available at: http://papers.ssrn.com/sol3/papers.cfm?abstract_id=774144.

Carraro, C. and Siniscalco, D. (1993) Strategies for the international protection of the environment. *Journal of Public Economics* 52(3): 309–328.

Chander, P. and Tulkens, H. (1995) A core-theoretic solution for the design of cooperative agreements on transfrontier pollution. *International Tax and Public Finance* 2(2): 279–293.

Chander, P. and Tulkens, H. (2006) Cooperation, stability and self-enforcement in international environmental agreements: a conceptual discussion. SCAPE Policy Research Working Paper Series 0609, National University of Singapore, Department of Economics, SCAPE. Available at: http://ideas.repec.org/p/sca/scaewp/0609.html (Last accessed 15 April 2016).

Coase, R.H. (1960) The problem of social cost. *Journal of Law and Economics* 3: 1.

d'Aspremont, C., Jacquemin, A., Gabszewicz, J.J. and Weymark, J.A. (1983) On the stability of collusive price leadership. *Canadian Journal of Economics* 14(1): 17–25.

Diamantoudi, E. and Sartzetakis, E.S. (2002) International environmental agreements—the role of foresight. Technical Report. Available at: https://ideas.repec.org/p/aah/aarhec/2002-10.html (Last accessed 15 April 2016).

Diamantoudi, E. and Sartzetakis, E.S. (2006) Stable international environmental agreements: an analytical approach. *Journal of Public Economic Theory* 8(2): 247–263.

Driessen, T.S.H. (2013) *Cooperative Games, Solutions and Applications*, Vol. 3. Springer Science and Business Media, Berlin.

Dubey, P. and Shapley, L.S. (1984) Totally balanced games arising from controlled programming problems. *Mathematical Programming* 29(3): 245–267.

Eyckmans, J. and Finus, M. (2004) An almost ideal sharing scheme for coalition games with externalities. Available at: http://papers.ssrn.com/sol3/papers.cfm?abstract_id=643641 (Last accessed 15 April 2016).

Eyckmans, J., Finus, M. and Mallozzi, L. (2012) A new class of welfare maximizing sharing rules for partition function games with externalities. Bath Economics Research Paper 6. Available at: http://opus.bath.ac.uk/32513/1/06_12.pdf (Last accessed 15 April 2016).

Ferguson, T. (2005) Game theory: games in coalitional form. Available at: Game theory: Games in coalitional form.

Finus, M. (2000). *Game Theory and International Environmental Co-Operation: A Survey with an Application to the Kyoto-Protocol*. Fondazione Eni Enrico Mattei. Available at: http://users.uom.gr/esartz/teaching/genvecon/IEAsurvey(Finus).pdf (Last accessed 15 April 2016).

Finus, M. (2008) Game theoretic research on the design of international environmental agreements: insights, critical remarks, and future challenges. Available at: http://dspace.stir.ac.uk/bitstream/1893/1099/1/finus08,%20International%20Review.pdf (Last accessed 15 April 2016).

Germain, M., Tulkens, H. and Magnus, A. (2010) Dynamic core-theoretic cooperation in a two-dimensional international environmental model. *Mathematical Social Sciences* 59(2): 208–226.

Grüning, C. and Peters, W. (2010) Can justice and fairness enlarge international environmental agreements? *Games* 1(2): 137–158.

Helm, C. (2001) On the existence of a cooperative solution for a coalitional game with externalities. *International Journal of Game Theory* 30(1): 141–146.

Heyward, M. (2007) Equity and international climate change negotiations: a matter of perspective. *Climate Policy* 7(6): 518–534.

Hoàng, N.-D. (2012) Part of the series Operations Research Proceedings. *Algorithmic Cost Allocation Games: Theory and Applications* (pp 599-604). Berlin: Springer Berlin Heidelberg.

Kalai, E. and Samet, D. (1987) On weighted Shapley values. *International Journal of Game Theory* 16(3): 205–222.

Köke, S. and Lange, A. (2013) Negotiating environmental agreements under ratification uncertainty. Beiträge zur Jahrestagung des Vereins für Socialpolitik 2013: Wettbewerbspolitik und Regulierung in einer globalen Wirtschaftsordnung Session: Climate Policy III, No. E04-V2. Available at: http://www.econstor.eu/handle/10419/79952 (Last accessed 15 April 2016).

Laffont, J.-J. (1977) *Effets Externes et Théorie économique*, Vol. 13. Éditions du Centre national de la recherche scientifique.

Lange, A. and Vogt, C. (2003) Cooperation in international environmental negotiations due to a preference for equity. *Journal of Public Economics* 87(9): 2049–2067.

Leng, M. and Parlar, M. (2010) Analytic solution for the nucleolus of a three-player cooperative game. *Naval Research Logistics* 57(7): 667–672.

Maler, K.-G. (1989) The acid rain game. *Studies in Environmental Science* 36: 231–252.

McEvoy, D.M. and Stranlund, J.K. (2009) Self-enforcing international environmental agreements with costly monitoring for compliance. *Environmental and Resource Economics* 42(4): 491–508.

Osborne, M.J. and Rubinstein, A. (1994) *A Course in Game Theory*. Cambridge: MIT Press.

Perman, R., Ma, Y., McGilvray, J. and Common, M. (2003) *Natural Resource and Environmental Economics*, 3rd edn. Harlow: Pearson Education.

Petrosjan, L. and Zaccour, G. (2003) Time-consistent Shapley value allocation of pollution cost reduction. *Journal of Economic Dynamics and Control* 27(3): 381–398.

Rawls, J. (1971) *A Theory of Justice*. Cambridge, MA: Harvard University.

Samuelson, P.A. (1954) The pure theory of public expenditure. *Review of Economics and Statistics* 36(4): 387–389.

Sartzetakis, E.S. and Strantza, S. (2013) International environmental agreements: an emission choice model with abatement technology. Technical Report 5/2013, University of Macedonia. Available at: http://maecon.uom.gr/wp-content/uploads/2013/09/dp052013.pdf (Last accessed 15 April 2016).

Schmeidler, D. (1969) The nucleolus of a characteristic function game. *SIAM Journal on Applied Mathematics* 17(6): 1163–1170. Available at: http://epubs.siam.org/doi/abs/10.1137/0117107 (Last accessed 15 April 2016).

Serrano, R. (1999) Four lectures on the nucleolus and the kernel delivered at the Hebrew University of Jerusalem 10th summer school in economic theory. *Department of Economics*, Brown University, pp. 1–2. Available at: http://www.econ.brown.edu/faculty/Serrano/pdfs/nuclkern.pdf (Last accessed 15 April 2016).

Shapley, L.S. (1953) A value for n-person games. In *Classics in Game Theory*. Princeton: Princeton University Press.

Shapley, L.S. and Shubik, M. (1966) Quasi-cores in a monetary economy with nonconvex preferences. *Econometrica: Journal of the Econometric Society* 34(4): 805–827.

Shukla, P.R. (1999) Justice, equity and efficiency in climate change: a developing country perspective. *Fairness Concerns in Climate Change,* Chapter 9, London: Earthscan Publications. Available at: http://www.decisioncraft.com/energy/papers/ecc/sidc/Equity/ecc.pdf (Last accessed 15 April 2016).

Tulkens, H. (1997) Cooperation vs. free riding in international environmental affairs: two approaches. CORE Discussion Papers 1997052, Université catholique de Louvain, Center for Operations Research and Econometrics (CORE). Available at: http://ideas.repec.org/p/cor/louvco/1997052.html (Last accessed 15 April 2016).

Tulkens, H. and Chander, P. (1997) The core of an economy with multilateral environmental externalities. *International Journal of Game Theory* 26(3): 379–401.

Von Neuman, J. and Morgenstern, O. (1947) *Theory of Games and Economic Behavior*. Princeton: Princeton University Press.

Young, H.P. (1994) Cost allocation. In *Handbook of Game Theory with Economic Applications* (chapter 2, pp. 1193–1235). Amsterdam: Elsevier. Available at: http://www.sciencedirect.com/science/article/pii/S15740-00505800669 (Last accessed 15 April 2016).

Zara, S., Dinar, A. and Patrone, F. (2006a) Cooperative game theory and its application to natural, environmental, and water resource issues: 1. Basic theory. World Bank Policy Research Working Paper (November 2006), (4072). Available at: https://openknowledge.worldbank.org/handle/10986/8852 (Last accessed 15 April 2016).

Zara, S., Dinar, A. and Patrone, F. (2006b) Cooperative game theory and its application to natural, environmental, and water resource issues: 2. Application to natural and environmental resources. World Bank Policy Research Working Paper (November 2006) (4073). Available at: http://dx.doi.org/10.1596/1813-9450-4073 (Last accessed 15 April 2016).

Appendix

A.1 Examples of convex and non-convex games

As a starting point, recall the supermodularity condition, remembering that proving supermodularity is equivalent to proof convexity:

$$v(S \cup i) - v(S) \leq v(T \cup i) - v(T), \quad \forall\, S \subseteq T \subseteq N \setminus \{i\} \text{ and } \forall\, i \in N$$

Consider a standard environmental game where counties' pay-offs have the same form as described in Section 5. For simplicity, consider identical countries with the following parameters' values: $a = 15$, $b = 0.02$ and $d = 0.00225$. Since countries are identical, it is irrelevant which player i is chosen to check the supermodularity condition. Furthermore, the only relevant difference between coalitions is their cardinality. Therefore, by considering the cardinality of a coalition as a variable, named s, and considering the function $f(s) = v(s) - v(s - 1)$, supermodularity, in this case, requires that $\frac{\partial f}{\partial s} > 0$. In Tables A.1 and A.2, it is possible to observe the normalized results of the mentioned environmental game for, respectively, 6 and 12 players (the parameters are kept constant in both cases). By comparing the last columns of the two tables, it is possible to observe that the 6 players game is actually convex since the values of the column monotonically increase in the number of coalition members (first column), whereas the game with 12 players is not. In fact, the last column of Table A.2 reaches the maximum value for the coalition with cardinality equal to eight.

Table A.1. Game with Six Players.

Cardinality of S	$\Pi_i(S)$	$v(S) = |S|\Pi_i(S)$	$v(S) - v(S - 1)$
1	0.0	0.0	0.0
2	9.5	19.1	19.1
3	29.9	89.6	70.6
4	56.0	223.8	134.2
5	83.2	416.0	192.2
6	108.4	650.2	234.2

Table A.2. Game with 12 Players.

Cardinality of S	$\Pi_i(S)$	$v(S) = |S|\Pi_i(S)$	$v(S) - v(S-1)$
1	0.0	0.0	0.0
2	5.9	11.9	11.9
3	21.8	65.5	53.6
4	43.3	173.0	107.6
5	66.2	331.2	158.2
6	87.8	527.1	195.9
7	106.4	745.1	218.0
8	121.4	971.2	226.2
9	132.8	1195.1	223.9
10	140.9	1409.2	214.1
11	146.2	1607.7	198.5
12	148.7	1784.7	177.1

A.2 Proof of superadditivity

Consider a standard environmental game as described in Section 5, having n players. For convenience, consider again the case where countries are identical. With $\bar{e}_i^*$ identify the optimal level of emissions of player i at the disagreement point. Clearly, when forming a coalition, players cannot improve their utility by increasing the amount of emissions compared to the current one. This stems from the fact that, by maximizing the coalition utility, each member of the same coalition must take into consideration the damage caused to the others. For each player $i \in S$, therefore, optimal emissions shift from $\bar{e}_i^* : B_i' = D_i'$ in the disagreement point to $e_i^*(S) : B_i' = \sum_{i \in S} D_i'$, when coalition S is formed. However, since being part of a coalition translates into maximizing the joint utility of its members, given by the sum of their private utilities, and given the fact that the level of emissions is a free variable, simply bounded to be non-negative, nothing prevent coalition members to adopt the same amount of emissions they had when they were not coalesced. Therefore, it cannot be that $\sum_{i \in S} \Pi_i(e_i^*(S)) < \sum_{i \in S} \Pi_i(\bar{e}_i^*)$, otherwise players in S would choose the level of emission $\bar{e}_i^*$. This assures that $v(S)$ is at least equal to the sum of $v(\{i\})$ of all the members of S. By analogy, it is possible to extend the same reasoning to any union of disjoint coalitions. This proofs that $v(S+T) \geq v(S) + v(T)$ $\forall$ $S \cap T = \emptyset$.

A.3 Proof of non-negativity of players pay-offs for all coalition sizes when all pay-offs in the disagreement point are positive

In Section 5 can be found the optimal level of emissions expressed in analytic form for the disagreement point, the PANE case and the grand coalition. By plugging in these expressions into the pay-off functions of a country, it is possible to derive the conditions assuring its non-negativity. By substituting, for ease of notation, the lower case s to $|S|$ and n to $|N|$ and starting with the disagreement point, we have

$$\Pi_i > 0 \quad \text{if} \quad a\left(\left(\frac{a}{ab+nd}\right) - \frac{b}{2}\left(\frac{a}{ab+nd}\right)^2\right) - \frac{d}{2}\left(\frac{na}{ab+nd}\right)^2 > 0$$

Table B.1. Characteristic Values for All Coalitions.

Characteristic Value		Coalition Members	Characteristic Value		Coalition Members
v({HWLD})	310.65	1	v(16)	724.61	1,2,3
v({HWHD})	292.26	2	v(17)	479.93	1,3,4
v({MWMD})	100.56	3	v(18)	416.26	1,4,5
v({LWLD})	54.91	4	v(19)	462.86	2,3,4
v({LWHD})	37.14	5	v(20)	399.00	2,4,5
v(6)	607.12	1,2	v(21)	202.67	3,4,5
v(7)	414.14	1,3	v(22)	661.11	1,2,5
v(8)	367.78	1,4	v(23)	464.37	1,3,5
v(9)	350.76	1,5	v(24)	675.94	1,2,4
v(10)	396.14	2,3	v(25)	447.37	2,3,5
v(11)	349.66	2,4	v(26)	807.00	1,2,3,4
v(12)	332.64	2,5	v(27)	794.27	1,2,3,5
v(13)	156.97	3,4	v(28)	743.10	1,2,4,5
v(14)	139.56	3,5	v(29)	542.03	1,3,4,5
v(15)	93.42	4,5	v(30)	526.37	2,3,4,5
Grand Coalition v(N)				890.40	

Solving it and eliminating the denominator (necessarily positive), it is possible to find that

$$\Pi_i > 0 \quad \text{if} \quad \frac{ab}{d} > n(n-2).$$

For the grand coalition, instead, we have

$$\Pi_i > 0 \quad \text{if} \quad a\left(\left(\frac{a}{ab+n^2d}\right) - \frac{b}{2}\left(\frac{a}{ab+n^2d}\right)^2\right) - \frac{d}{2}\left(\frac{na}{ab+n^2d}\right)^2 > 0$$

This is always true for positive values of parameters since:

$$\Pi_i > 0 \quad \text{if} \quad \frac{ab+n^2d}{2} > 0$$

Finally, in the PANE case, for $i \in S$, we have

$$\Pi_i > 0, \quad \text{if} \quad a\left(\left(\frac{ab+(n-s)d(1-s)}{b(ab+(n+s^2-s)d)}\right) - \frac{b}{2}\left(\frac{ab+(n-s)d(1-s)}{b(ab+(n+s^2-s)d)}\right)^2\right) +$$

$$-\frac{d}{2}\left(\frac{na}{b(ab+(n+s^2-s)d)}\right)^2 > 0$$

Simplifying and deleting the denominator leads to

$$a^2b^2 + 2abd(n+s^2-s) + d^2(n+s^2-s)^2 - abdn^2 - d^2n^2s^2 > 0$$

By separating the components of the expression, it is possible to see that $d^2(n+s^2-s)^2 - d^2n^2s^2 > 0$ since $s < 1+s-\frac{s}{n}$ being $s < n$. It then remains

$$a^2b^2 + 2abd(n+s^2-s) - abdn^2 > 0$$

Table B.2. Pay-offs under Free Riding.

Free Rider	Shapley Value				
HWLD	**356.28**	300.38	105.73	59.29	41.24
HWHD	320.59	**336.72**	106.39	59.88	41.95
MWMD	326.02	307.60	**130.54**	65.31	48.47
LWLD	327.49	309.37	114.16	**79.81**	50.24
LWHD	327.68	309.60	114.37	66.97	**63.28**
	Chander and Tulkens solution				
HWLD	**352.57**	299.02	106.89	60.54	43.89
HWHD	316.88	**335.37**	107.56	61.14	44.60
MWMD	322.31	306.24	**131.70**	66.56	51.12
LWLD	323.78	308.01	115.32	**81.06**	52.89
LWHD	323.97	308.24	115.54	68.23	**65.93**
	Least Core				
HWLD	**354.38**	297.39	106.55	62.35	42.26
HWHD	318.68	**333.73**	107.22	62.94	42.97
MWMD	324.11	304.61	**131.36**	68.37	49.49
LWLD	325.58	306.38	114.98	**82.87**	51.25
LWHD	325.77	306.61	115.19	70.03	**64.30**
	Nucleolus				
HWLD	**354.35**	297.37	106.63	62.33	42.24
HWHD	318.66	**333.72**	107.30	62.92	42.95
MWMD	324.09	304.60	**131.44**	68.35	49.47
LWLD	325.56	306.36	115.06	**82.85**	51.23
LWHD	325.75	306.59	115.27	70.01	**64.28**
	Rawlsian Nucleolus				
HWLD	**351.57**	297.31	97.10	59.62	57.31
HWHD	315.87	**333.66**	97.77	60.21	58.02
MWMD	321.30	304.54	**121.91**	65.64	64.54
LWLD	322.77	306.31	105.53	**80.14**	66.31
LWHD	322.96	306.53	105.75	67.31	**79.35**
	'R' Nash Barg.				
HWLD	**359.01**	304.76	104.54	54.83	39.79
HWHD	323.32	**341.10**	105.21	55.42	40.50
MWMD	328.74	311.98	**129.35**	60.85	47.01
LWLD	330.22	313.75	112.97	**75.35**	48.78
LWHD	330.41	313.97	113.19	62.51	**61.82**
	HWLD	**HWHD**	**MWMD**	**LWLD**	**LWHD**

Note: Numbers in bold individuate the values relative to the player that is free riding.

Table B.3. Index Coefficients of Free Riding Incentives and Risk.

Free Rider	Shapley Value				
HWLD	**0.07464**	−0.04407	−0.10937	−0.16293	−0.25137
HWHD	−0.03303	**0.07160**	−0.10376	−0.15458	−0.23849
MWMD	−0.01665	−0.02108	**0.09961**	−0.07794	−0.12025
LWLD	−0.01221	−0.01546	−0.03836	**0.12676**	−0.08817
LWHD	−0.01164	−0.01474	−0.03657	−0.05448	**0.14862**
	Chander and Tulkens solution				
HWLD	**0.0755**	−0.0443	−0.1083	−0.1601	−0.2398
HWHD	−0.0334	**0.0719**	−0.1028	−0.1519	−0.2275
MWMD	−0.0168	−0.0212	**0.0986**	−0.0766	−0.1147
LWLD	−0.0123	−0.0155	−0.0380	**0.1246**	−0.0841
LWHD	−0.0118	−0.0148	−0.0362	−0.0535	**0.1418**
	Least Core				
HWLD	**0.07507**	−0.04450	−0.10862	−0.15620	−0.24681
HWHD	−0.03322	**0.07228**	−0.10305	−0.14819	−0.23416
MWMD	−0.01675	−0.02129	**0.09893**	−0.07472	−0.11807
LWLD	−0.01228	−0.01561	−0.03810	**0.12152**	−0.08657
LWHD	−0.01171	−0.01488	−0.03632	−0.05222	**0.14592**
	Nucleolus				
HWLD	**0.0751**	−0.0445	−0.1085	−0.1562	−0.2469
HWHD	−0.0332	**0.0723**	−0.1030	−0.1482	−0.2342
MWMD	−0.0167	−0.0213	**0.0989**	−0.0747	−0.1181
LWLD	−0.0123	−0.0156	−0.0381	**0.1216**	−0.0866
LWHD	−0.0117	−0.0149	−0.0363	−0.0522	**0.1460**
	Rawlsian Nucleolus				
HWLD	**0.0757**	−0.0445	−0.1179	−0.1622	−0.1946
HWHD	−0.0335	**0.0723**	−0.1119	−0.1539	−0.1846
MWMD	−0.0169	−0.0213	**0.1074**	−0.0776	−0.0931
LWLD	−0.0124	−0.0156	−0.0414	**0.1262**	−0.0683
LWHD	−0.0118	−0.0149	−0.0394	−0.0542	**0.1151**
	'R' Nash Barg.				
HWLD	**0.0740**	−0.0435	−0.1105	−0.1739	−0.2582
HWHD	−0.0328	**0.0706**	−0.1048	−0.1650	−0.2450
MWMD	−0.0165	−0.0208	**0.1006**	−0.0832	−0.1235
LWLD	−0.0121	−0.0152	−0.0387	**0.1353**	−0.0906
LWHD	−0.0115	−0.0145	−0.0369	−0.0581	**0.1527**
	HWLD	**HWHD**	**MWMD**	**LWLD**	**LWHD**

Note: Numbers in bold individuate the values relative to the player that is free riding.

that is true for $\frac{ab}{d} > n^2 - 2(n + s^2 - s)$. Let us consider the case when S includes all players but one: $s = n - 1$. We then have

$$\frac{ab}{d} > n(4 - n) - 4$$

that is always true for positive a, b and d and $n \geq 2$. For $s = 2$, instead, we have

$$\frac{ab}{d} > n(n - 2) - 4$$

Compared to the parameters' restriction necessary to assure non-negativity in the disagreement point ($\frac{ab}{d} > n(n - 2)$), this is clearly milder and it actually becomes milder by increasing the size of S. For $s = 3$, for example: $\frac{ab}{d} > n(n - 2) - 6$. This proofs that, for avoiding negative pay-offs, it is just necessary to settle appropriate parameters' values for the disagreement case.

INDEX

Printed and bound by CPI Group (UK) Ltd, Croydon, CR0 4YY

13/04/2025

14656568-0003